THE LAST MILES

Open the Door: The Life and Music of Betty Carter
By William R. Bauer

Jazz Journeys to Japan: The Heart Within
By William Minor

Four Jazz Lives
By A. B. Spellman

Lester Young
By Lewis Porter

The Last Miles
By George Cole

THE LAST MILES

THE MUSIC OF MILES DAVIS, 1980–1991

GEORGE COLE

THE UNIVERSITY OF MICHIGAN PRESS
ANN ARBOR

Published in the United States of America by the University of Michigan Press 2005
First published by Equinox Publishing Ltd. 2005

Manufactured in Great Britain

Library of Congress Cataloging-in-Publication Data applied for

ISBN 0-472-11501-4

To the memory of my parents, Johnny and Esther

contents

acknowledgements

A book like this would not have been possible without the tremendous help and support of so many people. First, I'd like to thank everybody who agreed to be interviewed for this book (in many cases, more than once). I am acutely aware that for anyone who has ever worked with Miles, there is a danger of suffering from "Miles fatigue" due to the number of people who want to ask you questions about Miles and nothing else.

Fortunately, many people have the same attitude of Dave Holland, who, when asked whether he ever got tired of talking about Miles, replied: "I'm appreciative of the opportunity I had to be around him and play and I feel that the least I can do is to share those experiences. I understand completely why the interest is there and the fascination. He was a great musician and a great artist."

The following people kindly agreed to be interviewed:

Kei Akagi, Don Alias, Anthony Barboza, Matthew Barley, Tom Barney, John Beasley, Easy Mo Bee, the late Bob Berg, John Bigham, Jean-Paul Bourelly, Bobby Broom, Chuck Brown, Paul Buckmaster, Hiram Bullock, Glenn Burris, Alan Burroughs, Dr. George Butler, Ndugu Chancler, Mino Cinelu, Lucky Cordell, Pete Cosey, Felton Crews, Paulinho DaCosta, Cheryl Davis, Joey DeFrancesco, Thomas Dolby, Reggie Dozier, George Duke, Bill Evans, Sammy Figueroa, Barry Finnerty, Robben Ford, Sayydah Garrett, Zane Giles, Bibi Green, Randy Hall, Michael Henderson, Dave Holland, Adam Holzman, Robert Irving III, Munyungo Jackson, Annabel Jankel, D'Anthony Johnson, Deron Johnson, Darryl Jones, Chaka Khan, Katia Labèque, Gilles Larrain, Dave Liebman, Wayne Linsey, Tommy LiPuma, Ron Lorman, Eric Lynch, Teo Macero, Rick Margitza, Branford Marsalis, Marilyn Mazur, Joseph "Foley" McCreary, Dewayne "Blackbyrd" McKnight, Gordon Meltzer, Jay Messina, Palle Mikkelborg, Jason Miles, Bruce Miller, Marcus Miller, Cornelius Mims, Patrick Murray, Joanne Nerlino, Richard Patterson, Steve Porcaro, Don Puluse, Steve Reid, Sid Reynolds, Jeff Richman, Benny Rietveld, Wallace Roney, Mark Rothbaum, Paolo Rustichelli, David Sanborn, John Scofield, David Scott, Milan Simich, Otha Smith, Francesca Spero, Mike Stern, Clive Stevens, Steven Strassman, Angus Thomas, Steve Thornton, Allan Titmuss,

Stanley Tonkel, Michal Urbaniak, Garth Webber, Ricky Wellman, Vince Wilburn Jr, Mike Zwerin.

I'd also like to acknowledge the help of the following in providing information, helping to arrange interviews and opening doors:

Albey Balgochian of Abasses.com, Ron Barboza, Dal Booth, Stephanie Brown, Andree Buchler, Paul Buckmaster, David Burrell, Anders Chan-Tidemann, Marjolaine Cinelu, Jilly Clarke, Beth Comstock, Collelane Cosey, Felton Crews, Arice DaCosta, Kevin Davis, Wendy Day from the Rap Coalition, Mike Dibb, Nick Fielding, Joe Fields, Mike Florio, Tom Goldfogle, Sophie Graham, Bibi Green, Arlo Hennings, Louise Holland, Andrew Holmes, Jørgen H. Jangmark, Chaz Jankel, Sharon Kelly of Sony Music UK, Ramsey Lewis, Alison Loerke, Ron Lorman, Don Lucoff, Tammy McCrary, Gordon Meltzer, Patrick Murray, Melanie Nichols, Dana Pennington, Ruth Rosenberg, Genowefa Sadkiewicz, Susan Scofield, Francesca Spero, Robyn Toledo, Linner S. Vasoll, Edi Weitz, manager of Marcus Miller's website, and Judie Worrell. If I have forgotten anyone, please forgive me and be assured that your help was greatly appreciated. I'd like to thank Vince Wilburn Jr for his help and support and Robert Irving III, who provided a vast amount of information over a long period.

Paul Buckmaster, Randy Hall, Robert Irving III, Jack Kenny, Gordon Meltzer, Palle Mikkelborg, Francesca Spero and Vince Wilburn Jr. read draft sections or chapters and made valuable comments and corrections. It goes without saying that any errors are my sole responsibility.

I've been very fortunate to have Ian Carr, author of *Miles Davis: The Definitive Biography* (and in my view, the best all-round book on Miles) and Jan Lohmann (whose book, *The Sound of Miles Davis*, is a bible for anyone doing research on the music of Miles) as friends. Both have generously provided much help and information over the years.

I'd also like to thank my brother John and friends Tom Callaghan, Merlin John and Hugh John who have provided many interesting discussions about Miles and his music over the years. Thanks to Peter Dracup for introducing me to the music of Miles. Jack Kenny and David Murphy have provided lots of support and encouragement as I worked on this project.

Anyone writing about Miles is invariably following in the footsteps of others and I'd like to acknowledge the work of Ian Carr, Jan Lohmann, Peter Losin, Enrico Merlin and Paul Tingen. Thomas Hoenisch set up a wonderful website (now sadly gone) that contained hard-to-find articles on Miles. The Miles Davis Discussion Forum, a vibrant online community devoted to Miles and his music, has provided much information and many insights over the years.

A thank you also to Anthony Barboza, Philippe Dutoit, Jak Kilby, Katia Labèque, Ron Lorman, Sid Reynolds, Peter Schandorf, Milan Simich, Peter Symes and Allan Titmuss for providing the photographs for this book.

I'd also like to thank my series editor Alyn Shipton for his support and belief in my project, my copy-editor Sarah Norman for all her hard work and patience, Chris Allen, Mark Lee, plus Janet Joyce, Valerie Hall and everybody else at Equinox Publishing.

A special thanks to my family, Rita, Tom and Rob for all their support.

Finally, a thank you to Miles for all the wonderful music.

1 prelude

August 25, 1991, Hollywood Bowl, California. The concert was short – about half the length of a normal gig – but it was special, because it was the last time Miles Davis would appear live on stage. In barely a month's time, Miles would be dead, ending a remarkable musical career that spanned six decades. In that time, Miles had changed the face of jazz at least four times but his spirit, attitude and music resonated beyond the realms of jazz.

When Miles died he left behind an amazing body of work, but he also left much controversy about the nature and the value of the music he produced in the last decade of his life. Argument has raged over whether Miles was merely coasting or whether he was still producing music that was of equal stature to that played in other periods in his life. But that night in Hollywood, these arguments seemed light years away as Miles stood on the stage with his band, seemingly so full of life.

The Hollywood Bowl concert was the last of a tour that had taken in Europe and the U.S. Sitting amongst the audience were celebrities such as the saxophonist Wayne Shorter, who had played with Miles in the great 1960s quintet, the singer Joni Mitchell and the comedian Bill Cosby, an old friend of Miles. Miles's band had been pared down to a sextet and was smoking. The group members – Kenny Garrett on saxophone, Foley on lead bass, Deron Johnson on keyboards, Richard Patterson on bass and Ricky Wellman on drums – were laying down powerful grooves and rich aural textures. The concert began with a funky workout of the pop song "Perfect Way" before segueing into the slow blues of "Star People" (also known as "New Blues"). Miles's spirits were high and he even played a short rendition of "Happy Birthday" during his solo (presumably to Wayne Shorter, who was celebrating his birthday).

But looking back, there were signs that all was not well. The tune "Hannibal" lasted for almost eighteen minutes, but Miles was barely heard until the last five minutes, as if he had been conserving his energy for the finale. The Cyndi Lauper tune "Time After Time" – normally a tour-de-force performance – lasted just four and a half minutes and Miles's playing seemed to run out of steam towards the end. During the concert, the band members were given lots of space to stretch out and solo, and for much of the time Miles's horn was silent.

This partly reflected the fact that Miles's musical direction now gave his pared-down band more freedom, more flexibility and more scope for improvisation. But it was also because Miles's energy levels were ebbing away. "I remember the concert was short," says Deron Johnson. "Sometimes we'd play for three hours, but this was much shorter. It all depended on whether Miles was in the mood and that night he didn't want to stretch out. It was short, but the people loved it." After performing for less than ninety minutes, Miles left the stage, with the audience's cheering and hollering ringing in his ears for the last time.

2 introduction

"Don't play something unless you mean it." *Miles talking to musician Robert Irving III*

Miles Davis entered my life at a relatively late age – when I was in my mid-twenties – but it's no exaggeration to say that from that moment on, things would never quite be the same again. There is hardly a day when I don't listen to the music of Miles Davis and there is hardly a time when his sound fails to move me. For anyone else who loves the music of Miles, this will not come as much of a surprise.

But what many people may find surprising is that the music I play the most is not from Miles's '50s period (when he recorded albums such as *Porgy and Bess* and *Kind Of Blue*) or the '60s (with the second great quintet of Wayne Shorter, Herbie Hancock, Ron Carter and Tony Williams). It isn't even from the '70s, when Miles fused jazz with rock to produce masterpieces such as *Jack Johnson* and *Bitches Brew*. In fact, the music I play is mainly from Miles's last decade, from 1981 to 1991.

I say surprising because a number of people I talk to (including some who are Miles's fans) tend to dismiss this period, suggesting that at best Miles was coasting, and at worst he had sold out and was more interested in being hip or making money. It is the contention of this book that this view is wrong and that Miles continued to make music that was fresh, challenging and engaging right up to his death. That isn't to say that everything Miles played or recorded in this period was good, but in my view (and the view of many of the people interviewed for this book), much of the music Miles made and played in his last decade has much value.

It was the fact that Miles refused to stand still and wanted to remain contemporary that enabled him to dominate the jazz world for so long. In the process of changing, Miles lost many old fans, but each reincarnation would see him attract a younger, fresher audience. That is exactly what happened in my case. I was brought up on a diet of soul and funk music – Motown, Atlantic, the Philly Sound, Sly Stone, James Brown, Kool and the Gang, Earth ,Wind & Fire to name but a few. I even listened to rock and pop, but I never listened to jazz because it sounded "old" to me.

It was in 1981, when a friend brought over the Miles Davis album *The Man With The Horn*. He put it on my turntable and we listened to it. The first two tracks sounded "heavy," and I was just about to suggest that we play something else when the track "Shout" boomed through the speakers. I liked it immediately. It was funky and it made my feet tap. We turned the LP over. The first track "Aida" had a catchy bass line but it was the next tune, the title track, that again caught my attention. It sounded almost like a soul ballad and included something that sounded like a wah-wah guitar but wasn't quite that. My friend told me it was Miles Davis playing his trumpet through a wah-wah pedal.

I went out and bought *The Man With The Horn* for myself and soon I was beginning to appreciate the rest of the music. From that moment on, I was hooked. I bought every new Miles Davis album and saw him play in London every time he visited the UK between 1983 and 1991. I also started to work backwards through his immense catalogue and was amazed at the way his music had radically transformed throughout the years. Through this I learned to appreciate the genius of Miles – and the talents of many of the gifted musicians who played with him, such as pianist Bill Evans and saxophonists John Coltrane and Wayne Shorter. But as much as I can appreciate the timeless beauty of *Kind Of Blue*, the amazing virtuosity of the second great quintet or the power and energy of *Agharta*, I still find myself listening to Miles's later works.

The genesis for this book came in 1998, when I interviewed George Duke. During the course of our talk, Duke told me about how he had got involved with the making of the *Tutu* album. He also told me some fascinating tales about Miles. It occurred to me that very little had been written about Miles's last years, the period that interested and inspired me the most. For a variety of reasons, my idea for a book which covered this period was put on hold until 2001. In that time, several books have been published that also cover Miles's final decade. I will now explain why none of these is the same as this book.

In 1998, Ian Carr published an updated edition of his biography, *Miles Davis: The Definitive Biography* (formerly called *Miles Davis: A Critical Biography*). The new edition added around 250 new pages, most of which covered Miles's last years. Carr fills in many gaps and introduces much new information. And, refreshingly, he is enthusiastic about this period.

By contrast, in the same year, writer Jack Chambers published an updated edition of his book *Milestones*, which combined two previous books (*Milestones* 1 and 2) into a single volume and included a new introduction. The new edition of *Milestones* is 762 pages long. *Milestones* 2 was published in 1985 and ended with a brief look at the album *Decoy*, released the previous year. But in the updated version, Chambers devotes almost no space to Miles's post-1984 period.

Instead, his new introduction devotes much space to rubbishing this period – and the fans of the music. According to Chambers, fans of Miles's 1980s music "made few demands. For them, just showing up was enough. So Davis gave them freak music."[1] Chambers added for good measure that Miles's played "kid's music"[2] that was "dominated by three-chord riff tunes."[3] It is attitudes such as this that prompted me to write this book. The last decade of Miles's life was highly productive, despite his various physical ailments and declining health. He released eleven albums under his own name (on two sharing credits with Marcus Miller and Michel Legrand). He played on a handful of soundtrack albums and was guest artist on around a dozen albums. He played many live concerts and was in the process of completing another album (*Doo-Bop*) when he died. During this period, Miles played jazz, funk, rock, pop, big-band, go-go and hip-hop (and orchestral if you want to include the concert Miles recorded in July 1991 which saw him playing the classic arrangements of Gil Evans). It was also a period that began with Miles working with some old friends and associates such as Gil Evans, Teo Macero and Stanley Tonkel, and ending with a collaboration with a young and unknown hip-hop artist.

Two further books which also look at Miles's last decade have since been published. Paul Tingen's *Miles Beyond: The Electric Explorations of Miles Davis 1967–91* is superbly researched and unveiled many new facts about Miles's music. But Tingen's book covers a much wider period than this book and, what is more, Tingen approaches Miles's music from a rock music perspective, when funk was a much stronger influence on the music of Miles's final decade.[4] John Szwed's *So What: The Life of Miles Davis* was published in 2002. The 488-page book is well researched and Szwed uncovers a lot of new information about Miles's early life. But the last ten years of Miles's life and music are skipped over in about fifty pages.

The books by Carr and Tingen are highly recommended to anyone interested in Miles's final decade, but they still leave many gaps, such as how did Miles work with the group of young Chicagoan musicians who pulled him out of retirement? What was the story behind the *Rubberband* sessions of 1985/86 that resulted in Miles abandoning three months' work in the studio? How did Miles get into hip-hop? How did Miles work on-stage and in the studio? How were musicians hired and fired? What is more, I wanted to hear about Miles's music from the people who understand it best – the musicians who played with him and recorded with him and the producers he worked with.

When I began this book, I set out to interview as many of the band members Miles had from 1981–1991. The task took almost three years, but by the end thirty-one of the thirty-six band members of Miles's final decade had kindly agreed to share their memories of Miles with me (only one member could not be traced, despite my best efforts). It means that every guitarist, bassist and keyboardist Miles had in his last bands gives their story. As do many producers, session musicians and engineers. Unless otherwise stated, all quotes in this book are from interviews given to the author.

Members of Miles's road crew provided valuable insights into how Miles liked to sound when playing live. I also spoke to photographers and video directors who worked with Miles in this period, and they provide a fuller picture of the man. Insights from members who played with Miles before the 1980s also help us to understand a little more about Miles and his music. I also spoke to Miles's nephew, Vince Willburn Jr., and his only daughter Cheryl, who talks about growing up with Miles.

This book is not a biography, although key events in Miles's life are covered. Anyone wanting to know more about the life of Miles should read his autobiography or Ian Carr's book. Swzed's book provides a good picture of Miles's early life. I decided to tell the story of Miles's music in his last decade through the albums he made and so each album has at least one chapter devoted to it. I also wanted to know the story behind each track Miles recorded – what was the motivation or the inspiration behind the music? How was it recorded and where did the title come from? The structure means readers can either read this book from cover to cover to gain a picture of how Miles's music evolved, or they can simply dip in and out of chapters as they wish.

No book about the music of Miles would be complete without a look at the music he played live on-stage, and the biggest chapter is devoted to Miles's live performances. This chapter also includes interviews with many musicians who never recorded with Miles and some who don't even appear on the various live recordings released after Miles's death.

Through their testaments, we hear how Miles recruited band members, how they learned the music, how he directed them on-stage and why they left. Many also talk about Miles as a man, a musician and a band leader and reflect on their time with him. My hope is that, after reading this book, you will have a much clearer idea about the music of Miles's final decade and hopefully conclude that the music Miles made in this period cannot simply be dismissed.

3 miles – the man

"When you listen to Miles play, that's who he was, whatever social armour that he put on." *David Sanborn, saxophonist*

What made Miles Davis so special? Why was he such a colossus not just in jazz but in the wider world? The answer is that Miles had a unique set of qualities that enabled him to see the world, music and people in different ways. "How many people have been on this planet since the human race?" asks Mark Rothbaum, Miles's former manager. "Billions and billions and billions, and there are similarities between them all. And there was no similarity between Miles and anybody else. He was so unique I can't imagine anybody coming close to what he was about."

Miles also seemed to be ahead of almost everyone – including his fans and his critics. The British composer and arranger Paul Buckmaster, who worked with Miles several times, describes how music that Miles made more than thirty years ago still sounds fresh, exciting and innovative to him. "Miles's recordings are a timeless expression of human creativity at their best," he says. "When I listen to the recordings he made in the 1970s, they sound as if they were recorded tomorrow or in ten years' time. To me, they come from the future, from some future star."

Some people describe Miles as being "technically limited" as a trumpeter and give the example of how Miles struggled to fill the shoes of Dizzy Gillespie in Charlie Parker's band. But there is more to being a great musician than being technically proficient. What also matters is being able to project your emotions via your instrument and touch people. Miles had this gift. Miles had sound that was so joyful that it could make your heart dance in rhythm. But he also had a sound that could be so mournful that it could make you feel like the whole world is sitting on your shoulders. Bassist Darryl Jones describes being at Miles's home one day, when Miles picked up his trumpet. "I remember Miles played these three notes. The first one hit me, the second one knocked me off my feet, and the third put me back on my feet. I just said 'Oh Miles!'"

But Miles could also touch people who knew little about music. The British critic Kenneth Tynan reported how one day he was playing *Kind Of Blue* in his study when his nine-year-old daughter came in to be kissed. "She listened for a moment and then said 'That's Miles Davis,'" recalled Tynan. "I asked her how she could tell. 'Because,' she replied, 'he sounds like a little boy who's been locked out and wants to get in.'"[1] Almost thirty years later, the writer Paul Tingen would recall an almost identical incident, only this time it was a five-year-old girl listening to *Tutu*. "He sounds like a little boy who's looking for his mum," she said when she heard Miles's sound.[2] The trumpeter Wallace Roney recalls hearing the sound of Miles's horn when he was aged around three. "My father was a great jazz fan, and when he played Miles Davis something just clicked. I knew then that I wanted to play the trumpet."

"The trumpet really went out in the '50s. Then Bird [Charlie Parker] brought the sax in," notes record producer and music promoter Milan Simich. "By the '60s, the trumpet wasn't really a hip instrument anymore and when rock came in with guitar, forget it. But the sax has always been there. Look at The Rolling Stones, Bruce Springsteen, these guys use sax players. [But] Miles still had that mystique with the trumpet to the very end. The way he'd hold it and flick his tongue out, like a snake. When he was playing the wah-wah, [it] was beyond hip."

Miles also had an attitude to music that meant that he was always pushing himself and his musicians. Saxophonist Branford Marsalis, who recorded with Miles in 1983, notes, "There are very few conceptualists in music, so Miles could always hear shit that the other guys couldn't hear. The worst thing in the world for me is a musician that's in a comfort zone. One old New Orleans showbusiness guy once said to me, 'Find a couple of good ideas and stick to them and everybody will know it's you.' That's not why I play jazz. Miles really knew how to put musicians in situations that forced them to be better. That forced them to improve, whether they wanted to or not and I always enjoyed that. That's why he was Miles Davis and we're not."

Miles always liked musicians to put themselves on the line musically. He would rather you tried and failed than stayed in a safe groove. "I remember we were listening to a tape of one of the performances at Gil's house and Miles was there, and I was petrified because I was playing this solo and Miles was listening to it," recalls saxophonist David Sanborn. "At one point I did something that sounded a little outré and I remember thinking 'Oh man, I wish I hadn't played that.' And I remember Miles saying 'You should have played it twice.' I wasn't quite sure what he meant but I assumed it was 'If you're going to fuck up, make it right or turn it into something.'"

Miles always embraced change and was always looking ahead. Darryl Jones wonders whether this attitude was the result of Miles playing with Charlie Parker when he was a teenager. "Al Foster once told me that Miles was in awe of Charlie Parker and a lot of his behaviour was influenced by Bird. I read the book *Bird Lives!* [written by Ross Russell] and there's a part in it where the author describes how Bird is wearing a white suit in the Birdland club and the young guys are looking at him like he's old. It occurred to me that was where maybe Miles got the attitude 'I refuse to stand still. I'm not gonna be a guy wearing a white suit ten years into my career and have the young guys looking at me in the way that they looked at Bird, as if I was old.'"

Another of Miles's great strengths was his ability to assemble a cast of musicians who would gel together. Miles looked for certain qualities in musicians, as Robert Irving III, Miles's musical director for five years, notes. "What Miles looked for in a musician was confidence without egotism, enthusiasm about the music, a sense of humour and a willingness to work hard to perfect the music," he says. Irving adds that Miles also liked musicians who showed a willingness to accept criticism and had an open-minded disposition regarding change, with regards to new approaches to one's instrument and the music.

Almost everyone who has ever played with Miles talks about his great strength as a band leader. "Miles is one of the greatest teachers that ever lived. It wasn't teaching in the form of 'A + B = C,'" notes Don Alias, who played in Miles's band in the early 1970s, "it was through observing him that you learned about Miles and about music. If your mind and your ears were open, you'd learn so much. Ninety-five per cent of the time his observations were right on the money. Just being around him and observing the things that he did and the decisions that he made." Michael Henderson, who was recruited to Miles's band while still a teenager, recalls, "Miles was a director. With his hands, with a look, with trumpet, with his facial expression – every way and any way. No one was like him. He was an incredible man. He was a beautiful man. He was a gem to me. He always took care of me."

Miles was also renowned for letting his band members shine. "I never heard Miles play anything that was to prove a point," says bassist Dave Holland, who played with Miles in the late '60s and early '70s. "He always played things that were musical necessities. Some musicians will get up on stage and try and show you how great they are, or prove that they're the band leader and do a lot of callisthenics and gymnastics over the instruments. I never felt that was what was happening with Miles. Miles would play his part and back off and let everyone else have a chance. He gave everybody in the band at least if not more room to play than he took himself, and that was a long tradition. Coltrane used to take fifteen-minute solos and Miles would take two choruses. There was a certain modesty, honesty and a generosity to him."

Even musicians who failed to meet Miles's expectations and only stayed in the band for a short period have positive things to say about the experience, as is the case with drummer Ndugu Chancler, who left the band after a European tour in 1971. "Miles didn't like the way Ndugu had his drums tuned on the tour," recalls Alias, "and he'd come to my room and say 'Don, go and show Ndugu how to tune his drums.' Then he'd ask someone else. Ndugu was a bit stubborn because he had tuned up his drums in a certain way and that was his only jazz set. He didn't do it until the last day of the tour but Miles came down and fired him. If Miles wanted you to do something, it wasn't a question of not doing it – you just did it."

"I was young. I was nineteen years old and I'm on the greatest jazz gig of my life," says Chancler. "I don't regret it because it changed my direction and it set me up to be who I am now. I learned so much and it did so much for me. Miles taught me how to grow up. Forget I lost the gig: I learned more than I could have possibly learned on the gig. In the long run I learned more about Miles. Things worked out in the long run in that I went to Miles Davis school. Funnily enough, Miles and I became better friends later."

No examination of Miles's music can avoid looking at Miles's character and personality, although the man and the music are inseparable. As Sanborn notes, "When you listen to Miles play, that's who he was, whatever social armour that he put on." Humans are complex beings and Miles was more complex than most. As bassist Benny Rietveld puts it: "We are never really privy to most people's inner worlds. With someone like Miles, I think the case becomes even more clouded. There are layers and layers of mystery there: public persona, lore passed down by contemporaries, our own imaginings and even the subject's own considerable amount of personal change (especially one who has 'reinvented' himself so many times). Now he's gone of course, those puzzles will never be solved."

"Some things are just family traits, like I do what I wanna do most of the time, regardless of what everybody says, because I'm the one that has to live with it," says Miles's daughter Cheryl. "I liked father because a lot of the time I think change is good. He had a different ear for things. He was right on target with humour. He was a good cook. I think he was a double Gemini, which almost gives him the ability to be four different personalities, along with being creative. I like the fact that he elevated his lifestyle. He had pretty houses and everything."

Many people recall Miles's powerful persona, such as art curator Joanne Nerlino, who held Miles's first art exhibition at her New York gallery in 1989. She remembers when Miles entered the gallery. "I walked up to the door to greet him and I realized that I had never encountered his kind of energy before," she says, "and as I walked towards him, I felt as though I was in slow motion and not in control of my legs. I shook his hand, and realized mine was trembling. I was hoping he didn't notice. Later he told me that he had noticed, but thought it was his hand that was trembling."

Miles knew he exerted a powerful influence over people and sometimes he would abuse this power. "He was a bully," asserts Branford Marsalis. "I remember when I was a kid and there was a *Down Beat* article where he said 'Freddie Hubbard ain't shit.' I had the records and Freddie Hubbard was a bad motherfucker [that is, a fine player]. So, you read this. Our parents raised us to be independent thinkers and not just follow a trend, so when I read this it wasn't like I was reading the words of Jesus. For a lot of people when Miles spoke it was like the words of the Messiah. But I thought 'what the fuck is this about? Freddie Hubbard is a bad cat – what the hell is he doing?'"

Years later, Marsalis met Hubbard and discovered that he had been upset about what Miles had said and still hung on to some of the pain. "I thought 'why is Freddie upset about that?'" adds Marsalis. "Then I started to understand the strength of Miles and that he was a genius. He had the inner strength to suffer the indignities of being bludgeoned every night by Charlie Parker and his band because he had his eye on the larger picture. With his own intelligence and his own perseverance he forced himself into a formidable jazz conceptualist. Jazz history has tons of great jazz players, but there are very few conceptualists and Miles was one of them. But at the same time, he would use that strength to bully and manipulate the musicians and manipulate people. At the end of the day, they bank on the fact that they have enough cachet that people will stand there and take their shit because they're a genius."

"He didn't have many social graces. He was very intelligent, but at the same time he had this streak that was very infantile," recalls Simich. "You'd ask him for an autograph and he'd belt you in the face. It was very classless. How much that had to do with his voice or other insecurities, I didn't give a shit. It doesn't really matter because he is jazz. I don't think it matters what he was because what he did was so immense. To take this popular form which became an art form and then transcend it and become Miles. He was always being compared with Picasso and everybody knows he's about art. Same with Miles. Mention Miles Davis and people know it's jazz."

Chaka Khan, a good friend of Miles in his later years, says: "A lot of people didn't understand him or were afraid of him because of his brutal honesty. He was like a five-year-old child who had not learned etiquette yet. He said exactly what he felt and a lot of people were frightened by that, but I loved it. I learned to stay honest and not to be afraid of anything. You shouldn't try and hide from telling the truth. That's my philosophy and I got that from Miles."

Miles lays much of himself bare in his autobiography, where he chronicles his brutal treatment of women – beating them up, pimping off them or being unfaithful. It is a catalogue of behaviour that outraged many who read it.[3]

But behind the brutal persona was another side to Miles. Ndugu Chancler notes: "I was intimidated by Miles, because I thought he was this real strong figure. It took me years to realize that Miles was a very shy and somewhat introverted person that liked people but didn't know how to express and show that he liked them overtly. But once you cracked that inner wall, you were in."

"All this stuff about him being 'The Prince of Darkness.' He was one of the funniest guys. His one-liners beat anything I've ever heard. I hardly ever saw him serious and he was a regular guy," says Rothbaum. "He was a great cook. He'd sit on his bed and point to you and direct you to making a bouil-labaisse or a scampi and you'd make this incredible dish never knowing what you did. And he did it by just pointing that bony forefinger. I felt a lot of love from him."

"Miles loved being a part of a band and I always thought that was really more important to him than anything," says Simich. This observation helps explain why so many of Miles's associates talk so warmly about him and especially recall his sense of humour. Richard Patterson, bassist in Miles's last band, recalls: "To me Miles was one of the funniest comedians I have met – he was just so witty. I think Miles was very shy. He liked his family and the band was his family. That was when he would open up, crack jokes and tell stories. When it came to the media, he shied away, which is why I think a lot of peo-ple thought he was arrogant. But once you were inside that family circle, you saw the real Miles."

"If I think about Miles fifty times, one of those times I'll think about him and want to cry. But for the other forty-nine times I think about him, I'll laugh or I'll see some beautiful woman somewhere and I'll hear him talking in my ear 'look at that bitch,'" says Darryl Jones. "Working with Miles was the most incredible experience of my life," says Patrick Murray, Miles's concert sound engineer in the late '80s. "He was an amazing person. He was a true musical genius. One of a kind. He could be really nice, really mean and really funny. He loved to grab your nose as he walked by you while you were sleeping on the plane."

Miles was human, and like all humans he was flawed. He could be kind, he could be cruel, he could be selfish and he could be generous. But none of this should detract from achievements. One of Miles's greatest gifts was his belief that, musically, almost anything is possible and permissible. Rules were made to be broken, conventions there to be challenged. This gave many artists the confidence and the courage to extend themselves and the music, through which countless people have benefited. As Buckmaster puts it: "Miles opened so many doors for so many people."

4 miles – his life and music before 1975

"I don't know what jazz people are going to do without father around to change things or mix it up a little bit. They always waited for him to do something." *Cheryl Davis, Miles's daughter*

"Miles IS Jazz." *Milan Simich, producer and promoter*

The story of Miles Davis is not a rags-to-riches tale. It is not about the poor boy who managed to escape from the ghetto to become one of the most influential artists of the twentieth century. But it is about a man whose talent, courage, instinct, intuition and determination enabled him to change the face of jazz at least four times.

Miles Dewey Davis III was born in Alton, Illinois on May 26, 1926, but his family soon moved about twenty-five miles north to East St. Louis, Missouri. Miles had a comfortable, middle-class upbringing. His grandfather had been a landowner and his father was a successful dentist. His mother, Cleota Henry Davis, was well regarded in the community. The home had a maid and, later, Miles's father would buy a 300-acre farm, with horses, cows and pigs. Miles's daughter Cheryl recalls the visits to her grandparents' home. "My grandfather had a farm. He had a big Coca-Cola bin with ice and Cokes in it. I thought that was just it! It was just like a store! To me it was like 'Does everybody have this?' I don't think so."

Miles said that he got his looks, love of clothes and sense of style from his mother and his attitude, confidence, identity and racial pride from his father. He also thought that he had inherited his father's bad temper. Miles also had an older sister, Dorothy, and a younger brother, Vernon, and the three siblings were close. However, Miles had a difficult relationship with his mother and his parents did not get on well and would often argue and even throw things at each other. Later on, they would separate.

From a materialistic point of view, Miles had a comfortable upbringing, but the reality was that the Davis's were a black family growing up in a racist society, where schools were segregated and discrimination was more often the norm than the exception. Those early experiences of racism left an indelible mark on Miles's psyche. Miles soon became interested in music and would listen to the radio. When he was about nine or ten, he acquired his first trumpet. When Miles was thirteen, his father gave him a new trumpet and he began taking lessons from one of his father's patients and drinking companion, Elwood Buchanan. Miles also met trumpeter Clark Terry, who became his friend and mentor.

When Miles was sixteen, he met Irene Cawthon at their local high school and they became romantically attached. Irene would later bear three of his children, Cheryl (born in 1944), Gregory (1946) and Miles IV (1950). In 1943, when Miles was seventeen, Irene encouraged him to apply for a job with a local band, Eddie Randle's Blue Devils. Miles got the gig and stayed with the band for around a year. In 1944, Miles had what can only be described as a life-changing experience when the Billy Eckstine Band played at the Plantation Club in St. Louis, Missouri. Eckstine's band included trumpeter Dizzy Gillespie and saxophonist Charlie "Yardbird" Parker, two of the pioneers of bebop, a hot, energetic style of playing that developed in New York in the early 1940s. Miles described the event as "the greatest feeling I ever had in my life – with my clothes on ... The way that band was playing music – that was *all* I wanted to hear," he said.[1] And there was more, because Dizzy Gillespie would later ask Miles to bring his trumpet and sit in with the band for two weeks. Miles was just eighteen, and after meeting Parker and Gillespie he knew he wanted to leave home and go to New York, the jazz capital of the world. Miles's father paid for him to attend the world-renowned Juilliard music school in New York, but Miles's primary purpose for moving to New York was to find Bird.

Branford Marsalis says Miles's determination to find Parker says a lot about his attitude to jazz. "When you talked to Miles about jazz – and he said it in his book – he would say that he came to New York to play with Charlie Parker. Now that's a very interesting statement to make, because Charlie Parker was one of the great geniuses of jazz. But so was Duke Ellington, so was Billie Holiday, so was Louis Armstrong, so was Coleman Hawkins and they were all there. But Bird was like the *enfant terrible*, the bad boy of the scene. He showed up late in crumpled suits and he was the one black guy who stood up to the system of social oppression. And Miles wanted to be around him, the controversial, bad figure of jazz. He wanted to be on the cutting edge of the hip shit and Bird was the hippest shit there was. Now the amazing thing about Miles was that if he had to become a seriously bad-ass trumpet player to do that, he was willing to do that. But the original reason to do that had nothing to do with his profound love of jazz, but more to be on the scene with the baddest dude."

Marsalis says Miles's attitude is in stark contrast to other musicians of that era. "When you hear other people talk about those times, for instance, someone like Dizzy would say, 'Man, when you go to New York all these baddest motherfuckers are there. I played with this one and that one and in this band.'

But Miles's shit was 'I came here to play with Bird and none of these other motherfuckers mattered to me.' So when I look at a statement like that, he certainly doesn't mean the music. When jazz ceased being popular in pop culture, when rock 'n' roll supplanted jazz as the bohemian music of American culture, Miles said 'fuck jazz' and put on some high heels and a wig. He didn't hesitate, and I find that funny that in all these scholarly interpretations of Miles, nobody ever brings this shit up and there's plenty of anecdotal evidence – there's plenty of evidence from Miles's own mouth. But it goes against the opinion that Miles was always the cutting-edge genius of the music."

But this point of view overlooks the fact that at the time Miles was an impressionable teenager, so it's not surprising that Parker's hipness and attitude would appeal to him. And there's plenty of contrary evidence that Miles did care about jazz. "I think the schools should teach kids about jazz or black music," he said. "Kids should know that America's only original cultural contribution is the music that our black forefathers brought from Africa, which was changed and developed here."[2] But at the same time, Miles didn't want jazz to become a dead language or a museum piece. He knew that jazz would only thrive and develop through a process of evolution and by assimilating elements from other musical genres, such as rock, pop and funk.

Milan Simich has no doubts about Miles's place in jazz: "Miles IS Jazz," he says. "Everyone else, even people like [John] Coltrane and Duke [Ellington] all belong to a certain era, a certain genre of jazz and as wonderful as they are, they'll always be known for that. But Miles is jazz. He represents the totality of jazz. And when he came back, he was still able to go into something else."

Miles finally caught up with Parker and Gillespie and the three of them would spend a lot of time in the jazz clubs on New York's 52nd Street. Miles soon decided to drop out of Juilliard, and his first recording session took place in the spring of 1945 on a date with the Herbie Fields Band. When Miles was just nineteen, he joined Parker's band and was part of the quintet that recorded "Now's The Time." Miles idolized Parker, but the latter was not averse to treating his young sideman badly, such as telling his drug dealers that Miles would pay off any debts owed to them. Parker would sometimes leave young Miles on-stage while he went downstairs for a fix. Some believe that Miles's experiences with Parker profoundly influenced the way he would later treat many of his band members.

In August 1947, Miles entered his first sessions as leader and recorded several tunes including "Milestones" and "Half Nelson," with a band that included Parker and Max Roach on drums. Miles left Parker's band in late 1948 and formed his own groups. One of these was a nonet that included saxophonists Lee Konitz and Gerry Mulligan. It was during this period that Miles would form a life-long friendship and working partnership with the arranger Gil Evans, a quietly-spoken Canadian, who was fourteen years older than Miles and whose basement apartment became a magnet for many young jazz musicians. "He was a beautiful person," said Miles, "and we loved being around him because he taught us so much, caring for people and about music."[3] Miles would later describe Evans as "probably my best and oldest friend."[4]

At first sight, the close relationship between Miles and Evans might seem incongruous. Evans was white, soft-spoken and modest about his achievements – the antithesis of Miles. But David Sanborn, who knew both men, says: "I always felt they were much more similar than different. Jazz musicians have a way of putting up an image and sometimes it's a matter of keeping other people at bay. In a way it's a form of protection. I think that Miles was more sensitive, insecure, questioning. He was a very complex person and certainly the image that he projected was an aspect of his personality but I think there was a lot more going on at a lot deeper level which he had very much in common with Gil. On the surface, Gil was a little more laid back, but Gil could be incredibly stubborn about things. There was a level of communication between the two and a real love."

The recordings the nonet made at the time were later released as an album, *The Birth Of The Cool*, so called because Miles and Evans turned their backs on the fast, frenzied, frenetic bebop style of playing and adopted a "cooler" approach to the music, which used more space and fewer notes. In 1949, Miles travelled to France with the Tadd Dameron Band to play at the Paris Jazz Festival. It seemed that Miles's career was on the up, but on his return to New York Miles grew depressed.

This was mainly as a result of his experiences in France, where he discovered that jazz musicians were revered and where he had felt like he was being treated like a human being. He was also missing a woman he had fallen in love with while in Paris, Juliette Greco. Miles said she was probably the first woman he had had loved as an equal human being. Miles's depression led him to taking heroin and soon he was a junkie. The next four years would be barren from a musical point of view, with Miles playing fewer dates in the clubs and the recording studio. At this point, Miles was supporting his drug habit by borrowing money, pimping and even stealing from his friends, including Clark Terry.

It was during this period that Miles signed to a small jazz label, Prestige Records, owned by Bob Weinstock. In 1951, Miles made his first recordings for Prestige, including several sessions with Sonny Rollins. But Miles was on a downward spiral and knew he had to do something about it. So he went to his father's farm and kicked his habit by withdrawing completely from heroin – cold turkey. However, Miles's life would rarely be free of drugs. But in 1954 Miles was on his way back up and the year marked a time when there was a significant rise in both Miles's creativity and his reputation. In March and April, he recorded with bands that included Horace Silver on piano, Percy Heath on bass and Art Blakey or Kenny Clarke on drums. One of these sessions (which also included trombonist J. J. Johnson and saxophonist Lucky Thompson) produced the classic tune "Walkin'." In December, Miles recorded "Bags' Groove," with pianist Thelonious Monk.

In 1955, Miles assembled what became known as the first great quintet, with John Coltrane on saxophone, Red Garland on piano, Paul Chambers on bass and Philly Joe Jones on drums. The band Miles assembled illustrated one of his great strengths: his ability to not only spot talent but also to know when the chemistry was right between musicians. "Look at his track record and the people he hired. Who had more phenomenal bands like him?" says Branford Marsalis. "It's like 'they leave, he gets another one.' He was always trying to find the right guys. He was always trying to find the right combinations of guys. Most musicians don't really hear music that way – who works well with what and what direction is the music supposed to be going? They spend a lot of time thinking about their own solos, so that it ruins any possibility for them to see the music in the larger context, which Miles always saw."

In 1955, Miles played at the Newport Jazz Festival and went down a storm. The performance resulted in producer George Avakian signing Miles to Columbia Records. However, Miles still had more than a year to run on his Prestige contract, but he came up with a deal with Weinstock that resulted in a phenomenal level of productivity over a twelve-month period, when the quintet recorded a string of classic jazz albums – *Workin'*, *Steamin'*, *Relaxin'* and *Cookin'*. The quintet also recorded *'Round About Midnight*, Miles's first album for Columbia.

In 1957, Miles was in Paris recording the soundtrack to the film *Ascenseur pour l'échafaud*, which the director Louis Malle had asked him to compose. In the same year, he recorded the first of several orchestra masterpieces with Gil Evans, *Miles Ahead* (the others were *Porgy and Bess* recorded in 1958 and *Sketches Of Spain*, recorded in 1959 and 1960). In December 1957, the quintet became a sextet with the addition of Julian "Cannonball" Adderley on alto saxophone. Over the next twelve months, the sextet's line-up would change as Bill Evans replaced Red Garland on piano and Jimmy Cobb took over the drummer's chair. In 1958, a new woman came into Miles's life. Frances Taylor was a classical dancer who Miles had seen perform many times. She moved in with him and they were soon joined by Miles's three children and Taylor's son, Jean-Pierre, from her first marriage. Miles and Taylor married in 1960.

Cheryl Davis describes what it was like growing up at the time. "People think my father's kids had monumental experiences, but we just had an ordinary life. We were just children. Those were the times when children were children. They didn't have 'bring your child to work day.' If my father called you and you said 'what?' or 'uh? uh?' that was unacceptable. You had to be where he was when he called your name within minutes. And he'd be saying,

'I need something from the store' or 'you do this.' My father never hit me but it was understood that if he wanted us we went to him."

Miles kept his children away from the music scene. "My father went on tour in the summer and I either went to summer school or I had a job – no tours for me! And my father wasn't the kind of artist who had kids at his feet when he was doing something. For instance, I went to see [cousin] Vince [Wilburn Jr] at a recording studio and the engineer did not believe it was the first time I had ever been to a studio. I was nearly fifty-eight at the time."

The environment we grow up in represents normality and our parents are simply part of that normality – even when others see them as something extraordinary. "I don't know when I realized that my father was special. I just knew that I had different parents," says Cheryl Davis. "You have to be in everybody else's household to know what the norm is. We didn't go in other people's households. You just came home from school and did your homework. People who came over to my house probably thought my household was different, but I didn't know that. I knew that my mother was real pretty and my father was really handsome and my grandmother was really pretty. And they used to wear nice clothes and we used to have nice things around us. And I didn't know that most musicians weren't like him. I didn't know they didn't drive cars like father drove or lived in houses like we did. When he used to come home from Europe, he used to smell different and his pockets would have strange money in them and he'd have these beautiful scarves around his neck."

In 1958, Miles started working with another musical collaborator; it heralded the beginning of a working partnership that would last for a quarter of a century. Teo Macero was a saxophonist and a composer, and had played with Charles Mingus and Thelonious Monk. Macero joined Columbia Records as a music editor in the mid-1950s and began working with Miles and Gil Evans on the editing of *Porgy and Bess*. "I've got some things that are incredible that we put together later and have never seen the light of day," says Macero. "I took all the out-takes of *Porgy and Bess* and made it into a suite and it's a wonderful suite. It's probably some of the best stuff that Miles ever did and it's not on the record. I was working on that with Gil – I was doing the editing with him. He made his decision and I guess Miles accepted it, but the best stuff was still left on the tape! When I went back and took a look at it, I said 'Holy shit, this is really much better than the original.'"

Macero says there was a strong trust between him and Miles from the start: "I think it was right from the very beginning because he knew I had played with Charles Mingus and Monk and a lot of other people. I was a composer and doing this and that. So I think the trust was there right from the very start because he knew I wasn't going to screw him up and if anything try to figure some of these things out and make them better." Another reason was that Macero had a personal quality that appealed to Miles. Macero was not afraid to say what he thought, whether it was to a musician, an engineer, a record executive – or Miles.

In March and April 1959, the sextet (with Wynton Kelly playing piano on one number) attended two recording sessions that would result in *Kind Of Blue*, the most celebrated album in jazz history and whose opening track, "So What," is one of the most famous tunes in jazz. *Kind Of Blue* saw Miles changing direction yet again, moving from hard bop to "modal jazz," where the music was based around scales rather than chords.

But while *Kind Of Blue* was undoubtedly a high point in Miles's musical career, it also marked the beginning of the end of the sextet, with both saxophonists leaving within twelve months of the recording sessions. Miles would spend the next three years experimenting with new players, evaluating the results and continuing to search for the right mix of talent.

By the summer of 1964, he had found it with what became known as Miles's second great quintet – Miles, pianist Herbie Hancock, saxophonist Wayne Shorter, bassist Ron Carter and seventeen-year-old drummer Tony Williams. All were virtuosos, but as far as Miles was concerned Williams was the creative spark. "I was learning something new every night with that group. One reason was that Tony Williams was such a progressive drummer," said Miles.[5] Williams's explosive polyrhythmic drumming would drive the band to new heights and in new directions and the band pushed at the boundaries of jazz and took improvisation to a new level. The band recorded a string of albums, including *ESP*, *Miles Smiles*, *Sorcerer* and *Nefertiti*. Sadly, it was also around this time that Miles's marriage to Frances Taylor collapsed, although they would not divorce until 1968.

In 1967, rock was the dominant music of western culture, and while jazz was not dead it certainly was not as healthy as it had been a decade earlier. Jazz clubs were closing down, record sales were falling and it was getting harder to earn a living on the road. Once again, Miles's keen sense for what was the music of today saw him changing his musical direction. Miles was a musical chameleon who would readily adapt to new musical environments and he started working with electric instruments.

The first public results of his experiments to fuse elements of rock and jazz were to be found on the 1968 album *Miles In The Sky*. The first track, "Stuff," saw Herbie Hancock play electric piano and Ron Carter electric bass over a funky shuffling beat that signalled the start of a radical change in the direction of Miles's music. On the second track, "Paraphernalia," George Benson played electric guitar.

At the time, no one – perhaps not even Miles – knew just how radical his next musical direction would be. But after recording these two tracks, Miles seemed to step back from electric instruments, because the rest of the album and its follow-up, *Filles De Kilimanjaro*, were dominated by acoustic instruments. However, for Macero, those first steps into electric sound were a revelation: "When Miles got to the Fender Rhodes and electronic instruments you could create sounds that you couldn't do with a regular keyboard," he says. "You had the guitars and the Fender Bass. There was some shit you couldn't do with a regular set-up. That was interesting for me because I always wanted to be part of the electronic age. I like the acoustic instruments but there comes a time when you need that driving force and the electronics can come through."

In the same way that Bob Dylan's move to electric guitar would horrify many of his fans, so Miles alienated a sizeable number of his existing fan base by switching to electric. But others were excited, including Simich: "When he went electric I thought it was incredible that this guy who had all this other shit would go with this. It was just mind-boggling," he said. Electric instruments allowed Miles to explore new musical directions and express himself in different ways.

Filles De Kilimanjaro marked the beginning of yet another change to the line-up of Miles's band, with Englishman Dave Holland replacing Carter on bass and keyboardist Chick Corea replacing Herbie Hancock on two tracks, "Mademoiselle Mabry" and "Frelon Brun." "Mademoiselle Mabry" was named after singer and model Betty Mabry, who became the second Mrs Miles Davis in 1968. She also immersed Miles even deeper into rock culture, changing his style of clothing and introducing him to Jimi Hendrix.

The following year, Miles recorded *In A Silent Way*, with three keyboardists – Joe Zawinul, Chick Corea and Herbie Hancock, the English guitarist John McLaughlin, bassist Dave Holland and drummer Tony Williams. The resulting music was a revelation and further fused jazz and rock. Miles's music had been edited since the 1950s, but now producer Teo Macero's editing role became more adventurous and inventive.

If Miles's association with electric sounds was conceived with *Miles In The Sky*, it crystallized with the release of *Bitches Brew* in 1970, which saw Miles combine rock and jazz elements to create fusion. Miles did not invent fusion, but his move into the genre encouraged many jazz musicians to follow in his footsteps. For *Bitches Brew*, Miles used a vast ensemble of musicians to produce multi-layered, multi-textured soundscapes that were essentially created live in the studio and during the post-production stage.

The players on *Bitches Brew* included Wayne Shorter on soprano saxophone, Bennie Maupin on bass clarinet, Joe Zawinul and Chick Corea on keyboards, Dave Holland and Harvey Brooks on bass, Lenny White and Jack DeJohnette on drums, Don Alias on percussion (he also played drums on the track "Miles Runs The Voodoo Down") and John McLaughlin on guitar. Many of these musicians would go on to form fusion bands of their own such as Return to Forever (Corea and White), Weather Report (Shorter and Zawinul) and The Mahavishnu Orchestra (McLaughlin).

Don Alias describes what it was like going into the session and working with Miles. "I walked into that session and I knew that something was going to happen. Wayne was there, McLaughlin – all of these great musicians were there. We didn't really realize how innovative and new the music was going to be or the impact you were going to have. It wasn't a finished product, but we were all sitting there and thinking 'Wow, this is new.'"

Alias adds that the direction the musicians received from Miles was minimal. "He had very little to say to you in the studio. Miles always had this great ability to pick out the musicians apropos for the music that he intended to play. He was always very good at choosing the right people for what he wanted to do. Most of the time, it was as simple as 'go' and 'stop.' We seldom did any more than one or two takes for the *Bitches Brew* set. He'd always had little sketches, little jottings of melodies that he wanted you to play. Very simple, and he always left it up to the musicians to contribute to the music."

Teo Macero also used the studio as an extra instrument – cutting and splicing tapes, adding effects such as echo and reverb, and creating loops and edit points that brought a new dimension to the sound. Today's recording studios are full of technology that makes it quick and easy to edit and manipulate sound, but back then the tools of the trade were much cruder, as Macero explains: "We had to do it with a razor blade. It wasn't with these ProTools [editing software] where you could put it through a computer and make a nice splice there. You did it with a 16/30 [tape reel]. We would work hours to find the right splice and to find the right beat and to find the right accent. You had to find the right incoming sound, the right outgoing sound. It was very difficult. You'd have to copy it, cut it, try it and then abandon the whole thing until the next day and try it again. It was tough."

Macero used a process called a three-machine splice. "You make the cut, you put the good part on one of the machines. You take the next part that you're going to cut into. You want to be able to echo that. So you put that on to another machine and the third machine is the final master. So when the first one goes through you kick in the second machine to make a bridge. That was one of the tricks that we had. Or I would put a cymbal smash over it. I did that even with a Johnny Mathis record. There was something wrong so I went into the echo chamber with a cymbal and went shum! You had to be inventive! I would do anything to make it right," he says.

Macero adds that in order to be a good editor "You just have to use your imagination and your mind. If you go in there with blinders on, forget it – you're gonna come out with nothing. You gotta go in there with a positive attitude and that's how I approach all the artists the same way. To try and enhance it if I could and if I couldn't to make it the best way we could do it. To me it was badge of honour to do it right." Macero's role in the making of

Bitches Brew has been the source of much discussion over the years – just how big a role did he play in the final product?

Macero has no doubts about the part he played on *Bitches Brew*. "I'm a composer. I was a co-composer rather than a producer. He'd just finish a piece and I was let loose. I'd ask Miles 'Can you do it again?' and he'd say no. So I'd make loops and bridges and when he heard it, he'd say 'I knew you were going to do that.'" Macero believes that his role was similar to that of producer George Martin working with The Beatles. "I was like George Martin. I had a similar role with Miles. If he [Martin] hadn't been there, there wouldn't have been any Beatles. I was in London once and I got access to the recording room. I saw the four of them and they were really not players. It was the weakest kind of playing. I don't think The Beatles gave him credit. They should get down on their knees and thank George Martin. They don't give producers the credit."

Engineer Stanley Tonkel, who worked with Macero on most of Miles's albums in the 1960s and '70s, adds: "When Miles joined Columbia he had done some recording for other companies, but he was primarily a musician and didn't know about technology and recording. He left a lot of work for Teo. He would do listening sessions with Teo. They would discuss what they wanted to use and then Miles went on his way. If Miles was alive today, he'd tell you he did it all himself. It was all him. He didn't have any technical assistance. You hear little of the engineers and what they did." The engineers at Columbia also developed equipment that enabled Macero to add effects such as echo and to shift the sound stage.

Tonkel adds: "Teo was very instrumental in those early albums of Miles. He was as much a part of the manufacturing and recording as Miles was. Teo was involved in the organization and the editing, and the remixing and the balances. Later on, around the period of *Bitches Brew*, Miles got more involved in the editing process, but in the beginning he was content to tell Teo what he liked and didn't like. Teo was doing it together with Miles."

The arranger and composer Paul Buckmaster agrees that Macero played a major role on *Bitches Brew*: "On *Bitches Brew*, he did this incredible, beautiful editing, in effect contributing to the compositional structure. There is nothing to compare with what Teo Macero did on *Bitches Brew*. There are edits on *In A Silent Way* and they are more like the standard type of editing. For example, on 'It's About That Time' there are a couple of edits which are structural and which perhaps pre-echo what he was then to do on *Bitches Brew*. I'm making an assumption that Teo thought 'this is interesting.' Did he go into the studio on *Bitches Brew* with the intention of doing what he did, or when the recordings unfolded, he began to see the possibilities? I would say the composers on *Bitches Brew* are Miles Davis and Joe Zawinul. But the third composer should be Teo Macero. In fact, Miles Davis and Teo Macero made those albums."

Macero adds: "I had been doing [that type of editing] for a long time on my own music back in the 1950s. Things just got a bit more complicated [on *Bitches Brew*]." Macero also claims that "Some things we had to manufacture with Miles. When he got a wah-wah pedal, he didn't know what to do with it, so I would do it in the editing room."

But the extent of Macero's role is disputed by many musicians who played in sessions where Miles and Macero worked together. "Nobody produced Miles's records really. Teo used to produce Miles's records because Miles would go in and record fragments of shit and Teo would put them together. But when it comes to what musicians will play and what musicians you'll use and how they will sound, no one takes a peep except Miles Davis. Miles's records used to say on the cover 'Directions in music by Miles Davis', because he was exactly right," says Branford Marsalis.

Bassist Michael Henderson – who played with Miles from 1970 until the mid-1970s, says: "Teo had a lot of influence, but I remember that nobody edited my playing. There was no edit and no sampling of my bass line but he did sample a lot of other things." Don Alias adds: "Miles was in control of the whole business, in terms of anyone else contributing to the structure or where the music's going to go. There was much talk about how much Teo had contributed to the music in the past. On the records that I did with Miles, Teo was not an occurrent force; maybe in the background he was, but I wasn't privy to that. As far as I was concerned, Miles was in complete control of the whole business."

Dave Holland says: "I know that in the studio Miles was very firm in telling Teo to keep out of it. Teo would come into the studio to make some suggestions and Miles would be quite rude to him and say something like 'Go back in your box' or probably something more explicit! But what I heard was that the final edits were done by Teo with Miles's approval. If you listen to the music, you can see there was quite a bit of editing. There was definitely some compositional editing but how much of that was Teo and how much was Miles ... I have no idea what the balance of the decision was."

Another area of controversy was the role other musicians played in compositions that were credited solely to Miles. Bill Evans, for example, claims to have composed "Blue In Green" on *Kind Of Blue*[6] and during the making of the 1983 album *Star People* several tunes were produced by Gil Evans transcribing solos by Mike Stern and John Scofield. But, as Dave Holland explains, the process of composition in jazz is not easily defined. "That's the case with a lot of jazz composers, because what you're doing is continuing to adapt the compositional ideas you have to the individual players that you have to play it. And, as they come up with ideas and interpretations of what they're playing, you incorporate those things into it. When we were in the studio with Miles, he would have some definite ideas and starting points but then he'd ask you to try different things to see what you might come up with in terms of interpreting them. He liked the collaborative aspect of the music. He liked to evolve the music in a collaborative way."

Holland recalls an occasion when Miles thought his name should be added to something Holland had composed. "I went to Miles's house fairly frequently when I was with the band. He had a piano in his living room and he encouraged me to get to the keyboard. There was a certain type of chord thing he was working on and I went home and wrote something for myself which explored some of those ideas. It didn't steal them but it was within those concepts and I remember Miles calling up and saying 'Did you finish that tune? My name should be on it!'"

But John McLaughlin has no doubts that Miles deserved all the credit. "Let's make it perfectly clear," he told writer Bill Milkowski, who suggested that McLaughlin should share co-composer credit on some parts of the *Jack Johnson* album, "what happened with all the musicians who played with Miles in the studio was strictly Miles's doing... Miles's records were always quite carefully directed by him, orchestrated in a way that was not quite obvious... it was absolutely Miles's vision – the way the concepts would go. I think we have to put the credit on Miles. We all had ideas. Everybody would come up with things – a riff or a motif. But they were all really in the function of Miles and his music."[7]

Bitches Brew and the follow-up album, *Jack Johnson*, saw Miles forge jazz and rock, but now he was about to add another element to his music – funk. In April 1970, Miles had hired a nineteen-year-old bass player Michael Henderson to play on the *Jack Johnson* sessions. That autumn, Henderson joined Miles's band and would remain until Miles dropped out of the music scene five years later.

Until then, Miles's bassists had come from the jazz world and their first instrument was the double-bass. But Henderson was primarily a funk bassist, who had played with Marvin Gaye, Aretha Franklin and Stevie Wonder and on various sessions at Motown Records in Detroit. His mentor was the Motown bassist James Jamerson. However, it would be wrong to describe Henderson as purely a funk bassist. Henderson may have only played funk bass with Miles's band but: "We played everything in Detroit. It wasn't just R&B. It was jazz too. All the players who were on Motown played as much jazz as R&B. You had to be able to play it all or you didn't exist. He just caught me playing R&B with Stevie Wonder. If it had been with The Spinners, we would have been doing things like 'Fascinating Rhythm' and all that uptempo jazz," says Henderson.

Henderson stayed at Miles's home in New York, where they worked out his role in the band. "I'd spend a lot of time talking with Miles about how to do things. He'd come up with most of the ideas. He'd play the parts and say 'Let's try this, let's go there, let's do this,' and I could change up every now and then. He wanted to definitely keep it in a certain vein," says Henderson. Under Miles's tuition, Henderson became "the master of ostinato," playing circular, repetitive riffs for long stretches at a time – sometimes he would play three notes for twenty minutes or more.

The role never got boring, says Henderson. "It was more of a feeling, an attitude and an arousal. If you stay there you're gonna reach what you're going for. It was all variation. If you listen closely, it was never the same – I never played the notes the same. You may say it's just three notes, but there are ten million variations of those three notes and that's what I played."

Despite his growing interest in funk, Miles would continue to add jazz players to his band's line-up, with musicians such as drummer Jack DeJohnette, keyboardists Keith Jarrett and Lonnie Liston Smith and saxophonist Gary Bartz. In April 1971, Miles's lover Marguerite Eskridge gave birth to Miles's fourth child and third son, Erin. When Miles came to record a new album the following year, *On The Corner*, it was the music of James Brown and Sly Stone that were uppermost in his mind. Miles was keen to reach a black audience with *On The Corner*, but Miles being Miles didn't plan to collaborate with someone from the world of funk; instead he chose a young, white Englishman with a background in classical and pop music called Paul Buckmaster.

Buckmaster had first met Miles in 1969, and in 1972 he got a call from Miles to help him with his work on *On The Corner*. "I don't know if Miles was looking for what he got on *On The Corner*. In fact, I'm convinced he didn't know what he was looking for," says Buckmaster. It was through Buckmaster that Miles became interested in the music of the avant-garde composer Karlheinz Stockhausen. "I related to Miles some of the thoughts and ideas of Stockhausen I had read in articles like 'play something next to what you hear,' and 'think of what comes before what you're playing and what comes after it.' We live in this 'now' moment and there's this flow of continuity from the future to the past or from the past to the future – which way does it go? Perhaps this is why music is the most sublime of the arts is because it has this dynamic, living, temporal moment-to moment thing. Music connects us to the simultaneity of eternity," says Buckmaster.

But the resulting music on *On The Corner* is not "Stockhausen meets Sly Stone," says Buckmaster. "I don't think it sounds like that for a minute. I had brought a couple of Stockhausen albums with me when I visited Miles and the reason I brought them is that on one of them was a trumpet statement like a little motif that reminded me so much of what Miles might have played that I thought 'I've got to let Miles hear this.' I never had any intention of writing music that was Stockhausen-like." Miles and Buckmaster worked with an ensemble of musicians that included Chick Corea, John McLaughlin, Herbie Hancock, Michael Henderson, Don Alias, Bennie Maupin and Badal Roy on tabla. With its multi-layered, repetitive rhythms, circular grooves, looped drum rhythms, swirling sitars, saxophones and percussive effects weaving in and out of the music, *On The Corner* was a challenge to the ears, and it alienated many fans and critics. Writer Bill Cole described it as "an insult to the intellect of the people."[8]

Even Buckmaster was dissatisfied with the results, which he blames mainly on a lack of time and preparation. "In retrospect, I would have taken more time to properly compose some complete pieces, not just the fragmentary sketches that turned out to be the basis for the pieces that make up the album *On The Corner*, the tracks 'Ife' [on the *Big Fun* album], and the hitherto unreleased 'Jabali'. As it was, there was no time to execute that, and what we have is the result of a series of rather basic jams, using the sketches as a general guide. Perhaps the thematic materials were just not enough to move the level of performance to an advanced step on from *Bitches Brew*, which is what I was looking for. But there should have been more compositional organisation – that's my regret," he says.

Buckmaster describes the daunting experience of giving the musicians the parts to play. "So there I was, at twenty-six, a musician with experience as a pop arranger, and some experience as a composer and improvisational musician with a classical background. But with nothing to really prepare me for this: a Miles Davis recording session with some of the most prominent and brilliant instrumentalist-composers waiting for well-worked-out parts for, at least sections (as in *Bitches Brew*), of the thematic/improvisational elements that would be assembled and edited into complete pieces. But instead, what I had was these sketch–fragment–motifs, based on some ideas from Miles and from me."

However, Michael Henderson says the sessions felt good to both Miles and the musicians. "We played that stuff straight down. We didn't stop. When Miles counted if off, we were rolling. The only overdubbing they did was some bells and some handclaps. Miles was as happy as a schoolkid when we finished that session. That music was just great. When I first heard that on some big old speakers in Miles's house after we did the session, it was incredible. It was like all the food in the world on one table." Don Alias says: "Miles was a great innovator and always constantly changing his music. It turned people's heads. This [today's] generation is crazy about that music; they sample it. It was very innovative."

Even Buckmaster has reassessed the album after more than thirty years. "*On The Corner* turned out to be influential to a lot of other musicians, and a new generation of recording artists. Listening to it now, I can dig certain passages, and really appreciate and enjoy them. I just listened to tracks five to eight, and I think they're great. I can now clearly hear my compositional elements [both] in the keyboard parts, as well as the wind instruments. I must say, it's much more interesting and multi-layered than I originally thought.

'One And One,' for instance, opens with this beautiful, long exposition-improvisation by Bennie Maupin on bass clarinet, playing harmonics in the high register."

Miles's output during 1967–75 was phenomenal. He released a string of studio albums (*Filles De Kilimanjaro, In A Silent Way, Bitches Brew, A Tribute To Jack Johnson, On The Corner* and *Get Up With It*), a double album that mixed live and studio tracks (*Live Evil*) and a handful of live double albums climaxing with *Agharta* and *Pangaea*.

The last two albums were recorded in two concerts on February 1, 1975 at the Osaka Festival Hall in Japan. By the time Miles recorded these concerts, his music was dense, challenging and dominated by powerful rhythms. It was music that seemed to have no beginning or end, where tunes would merge into each other, creating a seamless tapestry of sound. Miles's music was elastic, constantly changing shape and form. There was also much drive and energy to the music, with constant twists and turns; for both player and listener, it was like riding a rollercoaster.

In 1975, Miles's band comprised guitarists Pete Cosey and Reggie Lucas (Cosey also played a primitive synthesizer, the EMS Synthi A, plus hand percussion), Michael Henderson on bass, Mtume on percussion, Al Foster on drums and Sonny Fortune on saxophone and flute. Miles described his music as having: "settled down into a deep African thing, a deep African-American groove, with lots of emphasis on drums and rhythm."[9]

But in the process, Miles left many older fans behind, who could not understand or appreciate his use of electronics or the more abstract elements of the music. "He was like the general looking at the fort and they had a moat and we were going to get in that fort. That was the attitude of the band. We didn't give a shit what the critics said," said Henderson. "People are gonna like what they like, but if you don't like it, respect it. Respect that I have the right to do what I do. Because with or without you, we're going do it anyway. Jazz is funk; funk is jazz. At any moment in jazz, the beat can go to funk. What are you going to do? Keep it down to four bars so I won't disturb the patrons while they're eating their steaks?"

Henderson recalls the Osaka concerts: "The Japanese people were very beautiful and they came in with their suit and ties on and we proceeded to blow the roof off the suckers with a million amplifiers. I had no idea what the Japanese people were going to do, and at the end of the day they gave us a standing ovation that was almost as long as the concert."

The music, recorded that afternoon, begins with Miles playing a simple riff on the organ, followed by some *Superfly/Shaft*-style wah-wah guitar from Cosey and Lucas, and the rhythm section of Foster, Henderson and Mtume kicking into life and laying down a powerful funk groove. On the opening track, "Prelude," Miles plays wah-wah trumpet and organ, and the tune also features some nimble saxophone playing from Fortune, and some scorching guitar work from Cosey. The evening concert became the album *Pangaea*, Miles's last official album release before his long break from public performance, and it is a recording that provides some clues about Miles's physical and emotional state. Writing about Miles's playing on *Pangaea*, Miles's biographer Ian Carr says: "Although he is in good lip, and often creates strong rhythms, his sound is intensely mournful – almost weary. It is characterised by sadness which seems all-pervasive, and even the bursts of energy have a certain desperation."[10] Indeed, there are times on *Pangaea* when Miles sounds as if he is sobbing into his trumpet.

Henderson felt that the band was set for even bigger things. "By 1975, the band was really opening up; we were really getting ready to turn in something else. I even recorded my song 'You Are My Starship' [later a hit single with Norman Connors] in the studio with Miles. Keith Jarrett was on the piano and Al Foster on drums. I had a feeling the music was probably going to get even more funkier. I think we could have rolled on a couple more years and done some other stuff."

But apart from a few more concerts later that year and several studio sessions the following year, this was as far as the band would go. Soon, Miles would drop out of the music world for five years. A combination of ill-health, physical exhaustion and creative burn-out had taken its toll on Miles. "I quit primarily because of health reasons, but also because I was spiritually tired of all the bullshit I had been going through for all those long years," said Miles. "I felt artistically drained, tired. I didn't have anything else to say musically."[11]

Miles was in a lot of physical pain. He suffered from sickle-cell anaemia, an inherited condition that mainly affects black people, and which produces abnormal red blood cells. Sickle-cell anaemia creates circulation problems, which cause pain, especially in the joints. Miles also had osteoarthritis in his left hip, which was causing him to limp on stage and, during the next few years, Miles's afflictions would include pneumonia, a hernia, a bleeding ulcer, bursitis (inflammation of the joints), throat nodules and diabetes. "Sometimes he'd get sick. He had a lot of pain and he did concerts when he was in pain. It was sad at that point," says Henderson.

Mark Rothbaum, who started working for Miles in 1972 and became his manager six years later, traces many of Miles's health problems back to a car crash he had in October 1972, when Miles broke both ankles. "If you look at photos of 1971–72, you see a featherweight boxer, he was just ripped and was in wonderful condition and he was at the top of his game; *Bitches Brew*, *Jack Johnson* and all the music that he was making in that time had the vitality of a professional athlete," he notes. "The car wreck decimated Miles. He was taking painkillers, he was taking cocaine, basically trying to numb out the pain he was in." In December 1975, Miles would receive one of the first artificial hip joints, but his health problems would not be over. "The first versions of the artificial hip were heavy. If Miles had had the operation a few years later, he would have been better off, but then, if this had happened a few years earlier, he would have been in a wheelchair," says Rothbaum.

Saxophonist Dave Liebman, who played with Miles in 1973–74, notes that: "When your leg hurts and you can't walk it's really a drag, especially for a guy who liked to box and be as active as he was … I think it got him down and was part of the depression that got to him in the '70s." Drugs played a part, too. Adds Liebman: "There were lots of drugs around, pills and cocaine and this affected everything: it affected his relationships, the way everyone reacted to each other – it made everyone not sane."[12]

Mark Rothbaum says it was hard for Miles to avoid drugs. "The West Side of Manhattan where Miles lived was referred to then as 'The Kibbutz', because all these people lived there: Sly Stone, actors, jazz musicians – every street had a famous person living in it, and those kinds of artists attract all sorts of people and drugs were very easy to get. At the time, the marketing and promotion of cocaine was enormous, with movies like *Superfly*, the Clyde Barrow [gangster] look. It was an awful time. Artists get wealthy but they're also subject to unscrupulous people who separate them from their money and there were tons of people to separate Miles from his money. He was a sitting duck with his pain and his appetite for drugs."

In April 1975, Sam Morrison replaced Fortune on saxophone, and Miles's band spent the rest of the year either in the recording studio or touring the U.S. Miles's last concert before his retirement was in New York Central Park on September 5, 1975. Another concert, due to be held in Miami, was cancelled because Miles was sick and exhausted. "He couldn't contemplate anything; he couldn't go back, he couldn't go forward, he was just stifled by trying to negotiate the pain," says Rothbaum. Miles Davis may have been a giant of jazz, a musical legend, but he was still a human being, and not even he could combat the accumulating physical stresses on his body – or the demons beginning to take hold in his head.

5 into the shadows

"Before jumping on the thing that Miles was merely indulging himself and drugging up, one has to remember that the guy was in a lot of pain." *Paul Buckmaster, composer, arranger*

"A lesser person would have just died. It was an incredible comeback – one of the great moments of all time." *Mark Rothbaum, Miles's ex-manager*

The years 1976 to 1980 are often described as Miles's "lost years," "silent years" or "missing years;" but whatever you call them they were certainly the most chaotic years of his life. And for anyone who cared about Miles, they were also the most worrying. Miles had had major physical and emotional problems before in his life – during the 1950s, for example, he acquired a heroin habit which became so bad that he had to drop out of the music scene for a time. And bouts of sickness seemed to be a common theme throughout Miles's life. But none of those dark periods could match the journey of self-destruction that Miles seemingly embarked upon in the mid-1970s.

Miles's own description of this period describes a life that revolved around drink, drugs and debauchery. It was a time when he retreated from public view, closed the door on the world and retired to his New York brownstone house in West 77th Street. It was a period when he entered a dark world of depression and paranoia. "I became a hermit, hardly ever going outside. My only connection with the outside world was mostly through watching television – which was on around the clock – and the newspapers and magazines I was reading."[1]

Miles described his living conditions: "The house was a wreck, clothes everywhere, dirty dishes in the sink, newspapers and magazines all over the floor, beer bottles and garbage and trash everywhere. The roaches had a field day."[2] Miles adds that he was addicted to painkillers such as Percoden and Secondal, as well as drinking a lot of lager and cognac. He was also snorting coke and injecting speedballs – a powerful cocktail of heroin and cocaine. He was into kinky sex and claimed to have slept with numerous women during this period – sometimes having more than one woman in his bed at a time.[3] He also suffered episodes of drug-induced paranoia, once confusing snow falling on his Ferrari with cocaine. On another occasion, he attacked a woman in an elevator thinking she had climbed into his car.[4]

All in all, it is a deeply disturbing portrait of a man whose life was spiralling out of control. But how accurate is it? Mark Rothbaum, who had looked after the running of Miles's day-to-day life during this period and who became his manager in 1978, does not recognize the portrait of Miles described in the autobiography and which has subsequently gained wider currency. "Someone described the years I had managed Miles [as a time when] he was living in filth and was perverted. I have to say that the time I represented Miles, he was very sick. I know what pain he was in. I don't think the greater world knows how hard it was for him just to live," says Rothbaum. "To read about the squalor and deprivation he lived in and that there were cockroaches and rats – it's bullshit. This was a guy that was eating his hamburgers and watching football. On a June day in New York, when you become aware it's going to be summer soon, he'd be sitting out front of his house in 77th Street in the little patio area and just talking with the neighbours and bullshitting around. There's the story of some old black guy who walks by and says 'Miles Davis, I love that music of yours, but I don't like this new shit that you're into,' and so Miles says 'Should I wait for you, motherfucker?'"

There is no doubt that Miles exaggerated some of his descriptions of this period. For example, he told writer Cheryl McCall: "I was nuts... [I got] so bored that you can't realize what boredom is. I didn't come out of my house for about four years."[5] Miles did have long periods were he stayed indoors, but he also went out and about and even left New York at one stage. Miles also claimed: "From 1975 until early 1980 I didn't pick up my horn; for over four years, didn't pick it up once."[6] Yet a number of people recall him playing trumpet during this period and on at least one occasion Miles's performance was taped.

Miles's description of this time also suggests that he had lost the need, drive and the motivation to play music, but in 1976 he was in the recording studio several times; in 1977, he rehearsed with a new band, and at one point even considered going on tour. In 1978 he was in the recording studio again recording music, and in 1979 there were several (albeit aborted) attempts at recording.

Yet there is also no doubt from the description of many of those who saw Miles during this period that there was a worrying decline in his health and well-being. Lydia DeJohnette and her husband Jack, who had been a drummer in Miles's band in 1969–71, recalled visiting Miles: "He used to have this enormous television screen with a horrible picture and very bad reception. It was on 24 hours a day and he'd just sit there watching it with the blinds drawn. He was also doing a lot of bad drugs too," she said. She also noted that Miles would not bother getting dressed and would eat leftovers.[7]

Eric Nisenson, a writer who became friendly with Miles during this time, described Miles's home as being like "a Playboy pad gone to seed." "There was a large projection television but a couple of the bulbs were burnt out...there were boxes all around the house."[8] Nisenson also described going on errands for Miles, which often involved picking up packages from drug dealers.[9]

Teo Macero also visited Miles at this time and found the experience somewhat unsettling: "You had to go to his place and stand up because you were afraid of the rats and the roaches that were going to get in your coat. Dishes were piled up and in the sink, dirty, filthy... He was ill from his hip operation and other physical problems, and I think he had a lot of mental problems too."[10] And there were times when things looked so grim that some wondered whether Miles would live or die. John McLaughlin visited Miles during the dark period and was gravely concerned: "I was very worried about him, very worried about whether he would live or die."[11]

Miles's behaviour towards his friends could at times be bizarre, worrying and unpredictable, as jazz guitarist George Benson noted. Benson had known Miles since the early 1960s. Benson recalls him and Miles being at a garage together getting their cars repaired when Miles spotted him: "I was a little afraid...I saw him running across the street towards me shouting 'Hey George! Hey George!' I said 'Uh uh.' I had just recorded a version of his song 'So What' and I had done some crazy things to the song, so I said to myself 'Well, maybe he's dissatisfied – I guess I'd better get my guards up.' So he was shouting at me and running towards me and when he got over to me he said 'Man, you tore that song up. I sure like what you did with my song, man!' I was thoroughly relieved, I can tell you that!"[12] Miles's relationship with his oldest sons, Gregory and Miles IV, also deteriorated during this period.

Miles might have spent a lot of time cooped up at home but, in the early years of his retreat at least, he did not lack visitors. Many old friends and musical colleagues made the trip to Miles's home, including Max Roach, ex-partner Jackie Battle, Al Foster, Gil Evans, Dizzy Gillespie, Herbie Hancock, Ron Carter, Tony Williams, road manager Jim Rose and Philly Joe Jones. There were also many visitors from the entertainment world including the black comedian Richard Pryor, actress and long-time friend Cicely Tyson, Clint Eastwood, John Lennon, Sly Stone and Mick Jagger.[13]

But as Miles's condition worsened, the number of visitors dropped off. "After a while many of my old musician friends stopped coming by, because a lot of the time I wouldn't let them in. They got sick and tired of that shit so they just stopped coming," said Miles.[14] Miles began to feel lonely. "None of my old friends were coming around, except Max [Roach] and Dizzy [Gillespie]," said Miles. "Then I started to miss them guys, the old guys, the old days, the music we used to play. One day I put up all these pictures all over the house of Bird, Trane [Coltrane], Dizzy, Max, my old friends."[15] Lydia

DeJohnette described this poignant scene to Ian Carr: "I compared it to seeing a bad B-movie of a has-been movie star. That sort of lost star living in their dreams and memories."[16]

But between the periods of drugs and self-imposed isolation, Miles continued to think about music, although some of the motivation may have also been about making money. In 1976, Miles's record contract came up for renewal and Columbia created a special fund, which provided him with a regular payment. This was only the second time Columbia had set up such a fund – the concert pianist Vladamir Horowitz had received similar treatment. At one stage, Miles was using around $500-worth of cocaine a day and he claimed that a combination of smart investments and "a few rich white ladies" helped keep him solvent.[17] But he played down the role of Teo Macero and the generosity of his record label Columbia in also keeping him solvent during this period.

Miles's huge catalogue of unreleased material was another source of funds for Miles, says Macero. "He needs thirty thousand dollars, he needs forty thousand dollars. I would say [to Columbia Records] 'Okay, write him out a cheque, and I kept feeding Miles this money all the time ... I said 'You don't have to worry, Miles. I'm gonna feed the furnace and put the stuff out.'"[18] A double album, *Circle In The Round*, was released by Columbia Records in 1979, featuring unreleased tracks from recording sessions from the 1950s to 1970. In 1981, Columbia followed this up with another double album, *Directions*, with most tracks taken from sessions from the late 1960s.

Although Columbia Records had hundreds of hours of unreleased material in its vaults, the company wanted some fresh product from Miles. It is also likely that the record company was looking for material that was more commercial than that which was held in its archives. Various record company executives would make their way to Miles's brownstone house in an attempt to get him to record again, including Columbia's president Bruce Lundvall, but to no avail.[19]

It is worth noting that Miles had not planned such an extensive break from music and that his band members at the time were also in the dark about Miles's intentions. "When Miles stopped in 1975 I had no inkling that he would be away for so long. The reason he stopped was to have the hip operation. There was no indication it would be a long or short time. It almost seemed timeless because we were still in the process of recording," says guitarist Pete Cosey. Bassist Michael Henderson adds that he also had no idea how long Miles would be out of action. Miles had his hip replacement operation in December 1975 and spent the first part of 1976 convalescing.

In 1976, there was talk of Miles collaborating again with Gil Evans on a recording of *Tosca*, but nothing ever came of this. But in March 1976, Miles was back in the studio with most of his current band members, including drummer

Al Foster, Michael Henderson, Pete Cosey, Sam Morrison and guest keyboardist Mark Johnson, who was a friend of Henderson. On the aural evidence available, Miles played little, if any, trumpet on these sessions, preferring to direct operations and play the organ. Teo Macero was also in the studio.

"Throughout the time that we didn't play [live]; we recorded at different times in the studio. Normally we'd record in a small studio in 51st Street, but those sessions took place in a larger studio," says Cosey. Several tunes were recorded: an unknown slow-funk number and a rocking uptempo tune, "Back Seat Betty," dominated by clavinet and splashing cymbals. This tune is a showcase for Johnson's keyboard skills, who plays fast, fluent lines.[20]

The band also recorded a gentle tune by Sam Morrison, "Song Of Landa," and an atmospheric guitar piece featuring whistling and bird sound effects, "Mother Dearest Mother," composed by Cosey. "I wrote it in honour of my mother and even recorded it in my studio with a child singing some lyrics. I also did a version with me singing on it. I once gave George Benson a tape of the song to see if he might record it," says Cosey. An alternative version of "Song Of Landa" appeared on Morrision's 1976 album *Dune* on EastWind Records, but so far the rest of this music has not been officially released.

On the aural evidence alone, it is hard to determine the direction of Miles's music at this stage, but there are some tantalizing glimpses of a subtle move into new areas. However, as most of the music seems to be work in progress, we can never be fully certain about the direction Miles's music might have taken if he had not gone into such a prolonged retirement. It would be more than six months before Miles recorded again, and by that time Miles had reached his fiftieth birthday in May.

Miles's discographer Jan Lohmann records in his book *The Sound of Miles Davis* that Miles was in the studio again on November 30, 1976, along with Al Foster, guitarist Larry Coryell and at least two unknown musicians. There were two more sessions on 27 and 29 December with Miles, Cosey, Henderson, Foster, Mtume and possibly second guitarist Reggie Lucas. The music produced from this session seems to be a combination of old and new music, and excerpts of it were used for a commercial for TDK tape.[21]

As far as is known, these sessions were the last time Miles's last pre-retirement band ever recorded together, and soon after his band had began drifting away to pursue other projects. "When we stopped playing, Roberta Flack tried to get the whole band to play for her," says Cosey. "She used to watch us play with Miles a lot. Michael, Mtume and Reggie Lucas played with her for a time." Michael Henderson later teamed up with drummer Norman Connors, who recorded the hit "You Are My Starship," written and sung by Henderson. Later on, Henderson would pursue a solo career. Lucas and Mtume moved into writing and production, working with artists such as Roberta Flack, Donny Hathaway and Stephanie Mills. Lucas went on to write and produce the bulk of Madonna's debut album, while Mtume would front a band bearing his name. Foster began doing session work around New York and would later record a solo album, *Mr. Foster*.

But during this period, Cosey still held out the hope that the band might re-form. "Miles told me that when we start back [i.e. reform the band], everything would be right and everyone would make a good amount of money and things would be on a proper level as far as touring. I chose to wait and stay, because I always enjoyed that band – that was one of my favourite bands of all time."

Cosey would visit Miles regularly. "I used to stay with him from time to time and we would cook for one another and we always enjoyed each other's company. I was one of the few people to whom he would give his [house] keys, because he didn't trust other people. I was offered an apartment where his son used to live but I had my family and it wouldn't have been large enough. In retrospect it was a call for help, because he didn't have the need for the drugs when certain people were around, like Mtume, Michael Henderson or myself. He always seemed inspired by the feeling that the musicians gave to him. That would feed him and so there wasn't a need to escape with chemicals."

Miles seems to have avoided the recording studio in 1977, but he was not totally inactive from a musical point of view. In that year, Pete Cosey put together a band that included Miles, Al Foster, Sam Morrison on flute and sax and a young bass player called Caprice. "Miles liked him and said 'He's strong,'" recalls Cosey. Cosey thinks percussionist Azzedin Weston, son of pianist Randy Weston, may also have played in the band. "That session was beautiful – it was smoking. That was done in his living room. At the end, we had silence; everyone was so elated by what had taken place and Miles said 'I haven't played in two years!' and everybody laughed. I have a tape of that session," says Cosey. The guitarist hoped that the rehearsal might lead to more work with Miles, but no further progress was made. Cosey now believes he knows why. "I didn't understand at the time how besieged he was by people who were pushing chemicals on him. That was the main problem."

In 1977 Gil Evans helped Miles put together a band featuring Masabumi Kikuchi on keyboards, Pete Cosey on guitar, Sly Stone on bass and drummer Jack DeJohnette. Kikuchi told writer Stephanie Stein Crease: "Miles had a tour job lined up and he really wanted to go. We waited for two days at Miles's house, Pete, Jack and me, and Sly never showed up. Then Miles got an infection in his knees and had to go to the hospital for special surgery. The tour never happened... what we were doing was jazz-rock, very dark. I wish it had happened – the music was great."[22]

In early 1978, Miles was persuaded to leave New York and head for Connecticut, thanks to an invitation by Julie Coryell, who was married to jazz guitarist Larry Coryell. She invited Miles to stay at the home of her friend

Elena Steinberg, where the two women looked after Miles. While staying in Connecticut Miles was introduced to a New York-based guitarist Barry Finnerty, and the two men even composed a tune together, although it was never recorded (see next chapter). Miles also asked Larry Coryell to help him work on a piece, which Coryell described as "Basically a shuffle with two ninth chords a half-step apart [played] over a rolling bass figure in F, with a couple of 'jungle' fragments as melody to be played by myself."[23] When Miles returned to New York, he contacted producer Teo Macero to arrange a recording session.

The session took place on March 2, 1978 and the musicians taking part were Miles (on organ), Larry Coryell, Masabumi Kikuchi and George Paulis on keyboards, bassist T. M. Stevens and Al Foster on drums. Bobby Scott arranged the horn charts. Several takes were recorded and although Coryell says Miles was pleased with the results, the music has yet to see light of day.[24] Later that year, Miles found himself in jail for failing to pay maintenance to his former lover Marguerite Eskridge, mother to their son Erin. It cost Miles $10,000 to get out of jail.

Columbia Records was still trying to get Miles back into the recording studio and still sending executives around to see him. One of them was Columbia's new vice-president Dr. George Butler, who joined the company from Blue Note Records and whose responsibilities covered jazz, blues, gospel and some classical music. "When I joined Columbia, I had lost track of Miles and discovered he was still on Columbia. I decided to call him and introduce myself and just let him know that he had a friend," says Butler. "I knew that a number of people from Columbia had tried getting Miles to record again and failed. I thought I would visit him and talk about three things that interested him most – cars, boxing and clothes. I didn't have a great deal of knowledge about these subjects, but I pretended I knew more than I did. I knew I was not going to talk to Miles about music."

Miles invited Butler over to his home. When Butler arrived, he found it was dark, with all the blinds pulled down. As Butler walked up the stairs to Miles's living room, he couldn't see where he was going and had to feel his way. The only source of illumination in the apartment was the television Miles kept on twenty-four hours a day. One thing Butler had learned from other executives who had visited Miles was that he had a habit of putting on a boxing glove and then whacking them with it. On one visit, Miles began reaching for a glove, so Butler informed him that he was trained in martial arts and Miles put down the glove. Butler would end up visiting Miles every morning, five days a week for nine months, either talking to him about the three main topics of discussion, or watching television with him.

Meanwhile, Miles was being visited by his nephew Vince Wilburn Jr., who would occasionally fly from Chicago to New York to see his uncle. On one trip, he brought along a friend, the saxophonist Glenn Burris. "Miles had two personalities and lifestyles. When he lived in Manhattan he was a hardcore, heartless type of guy. He was definitely cold to Vince and called him all kinds of names. I was shocked. So the visit wasn't warm at all," recalls Burris. After the visit, Wilburn flew back to Chicago, but Burris stayed on in New York to catch up with some old friends. "When I couldn't stay any longer, I called Miles and said 'It was very nice meeting you, but I have to go now, I've run out of money.' He invited me to stay with him and I stayed the summer. I was in a constant state of paranoia. He had no set time to do anything. When he woke up, he woke up and when he slept he slept. I didn't want to be asleep when he was awake – he was very bizarre. But there were times when he talked about the past and I learned so much – it was the greatest experience any musician could have."

Miles and Burris would hang out together in New York. "We would go to a restaurant called The Only Child, which I think he owned. We'd also go to Sweet Basil [a jazz club] and sometimes we'd play together impromptu. He'd play lines and have me copy them. There'd be other musicians around, like [saxophonists] Gary Bartz and George Coleman and he'd make references to them to me, saying 'They can't play shit,' and I'd say, 'But Miles, they played with you!' You never really knew what to take literally. You never really knew what he meant. Miles entertained regularly; people were in and out there regularly – Chaka Khan, Willie Nelson, a violinist from some orchestra. I couldn't believe it: the people he was reaching transcended jazz." Burris eventually flew back to Chicago, but would see Miles again the following year when work began on the comeback album *The Man With The Horn*.

Meanwhile, Butler was still visiting Miles, hoping to make a breakthrough. For the first five months of Butler's visits, he and Miles talked about everything but music. By now, Butler was starting to feel that he was wasting his time, as he recalled: "I was beginning to feel that I would not succeed and was getting a little bored. Miles had made up his mind. He had this little piano that only had about one or two keys that worked, then one day he said 'Listen George, this is something I'm just thinking about.' But because only a couple of keys worked, I could not make out what sound he was trying to play, so I just said 'Miles, that sounds very interesting.'"

Butler decided it would be nice to buy Miles a new piano for his birthday. "I chose one and it cost over $100,000. I went to Bruce Lundvall and said 'Bruce, Miles doesn't have a piano and I've chosen one for him, but it costs over $100,000,' and Bruce just said 'Get it.' It blew my mind." Butler arranged for the piano to be delivered to Miles's home, but Miles wouldn't let the delivery men in, so they called Butler.

Butler called a mutual friend of him and Miles, the DJ Ed Williams, who lived close to Miles. Williams managed to persuade Miles to open the door.

"Ed told me that when Miles saw the piano, there were tears in his eyes," says Butler. Butler called Miles. "Miles was not one for saying hello or goodbye on the phone, so when I called he just said 'What do you want?' Then he muttered something and hung up the phone," recalls Butler. But Miles would ring Butler to thank him in his own inimitable style. "Miles called and said 'Thanks George,' and slammed the phone down before I could say 'You're welcome,'" recalled Butler.[25]

Butler visited Miles the next day. "The piano was set up and it looked fantastic, but we continued to talk about our usual subjects. I thought 'This guy just isn't going to get excited. This went on for a while and then one day he said 'George, listen. I got some ideas.' I thought that I'd better not get excited, but when he started playing some chords, it sounded fantastic. Then he started talking about the people he wanted to work with, like Pete Cosey and Al Foster."

Another person Miles wanted to work with again was Paul Buckmaster, the English arranger/composer who had worked with Miles on *On The Corner*. "George Butler called me and said 'Miles, would like you to come to New York and work with him on some recordings?'" recalls Buckmaster, who remembers that in New York that year "It was ninety degrees Fahrenheit and ninety per cent humidity and there was a garbage strike."[26]

Buckmaster found a different Miles from the person he had last worked with in 1972. "Miles had let things go and let himself go. There were drug dealers and he was taking medication for his physical condition," notes Buckmaster. "He was in considerable discomfort if not outright pain. He didn't make a song and dance about his pain, but I remember him sitting at the piano and wincing. His elbows, wrists and knuckles were in a lot of pain. He'd wince when he was getting up or sitting down or when climbing the stairs, so that hip must have given him a lot of trouble. So before jumping on the thing that Miles was merely indulging himself and drugging up, one has to remember that the guy was in a lot of pain."

Miles had asked Buckmaster to work on one piece, "Love Don't Live Here Anymore," a melancholy ballad from the soul group Rose Royce. He also wanted the Englishman to write some new material. "I was over at his place almost everyday and some days I stayed away in order to write. [Music contractor] Gene Bianco gave me the keys to his apartment and let me use a piano to write some music. I didn't want to work at Miles's because his piano was falling to bits," recalls Buckmaster. For some reason, Miles seems to have kept Buckmaster away from his brand new piano.

Buckmaster also met Gil Evans and for a time it looked as if Evans might also be involved in the project. Buckmaster spent a lot of time at Evans's apartment and both of them would listen to a lot of music together. "We were both fans of [composer] Olivier Messaien's music and we were very aware of its congruence with Miles's tonal and harmonic palette," says Buckmaster. "Had the situation with Miles and ourselves been less disordered, this would certainly have been one avenue of exploration for the recordings that never happened." Sadly, Miles's condition meant that little progress was being made and Evans abandoned any idea of working with Miles again at this stage. "Gil lost interest towards the end," says Buckmaster.[27]

When Buckmaster had prepared some material, he asked Bianco to put together a group of session musicians to record the music. The musicians Bianco assembled for the session were drummer Buddy Williams, keyboardist Onaje Allen Gumbs, percussionist George Devens, guitarist Lou Volpe and a young bassist who was a rising star on the New York session scene, Marcus Miller. Buckmaster played organ. "We never recorded 'Love Don't Live Here Anymore,' but we recorded fragments of some pieces I had scribbled down at Miles's," recalls Buckmaster. "I had written down some of the chords he had played on the piano and some of the melodies. At one point I asked 'Miles, are you playing trumpet?' and he said he wasn't; then I asked him about his embouchure and he said it was okay. There was a trumpet on the side and he picked it up and played some phrases which were just brilliant. I wrote them down and used them with the other pieces and wrote up several short sections. I was expecting Miles to turn up at the sessions and direct them. We recorded the small sections as repetitious loops. I just said 'Jam on it, guys.'"

But Miles never appeared. "When I took the cassette to Miles I said 'What happened?' and he said that I hadn't told him about the session. I played him the cassette and he said he quite liked what he heard. Obviously had he been there it would have been something else, because what was missing was Miles's melodic sense, his harmonic sense, his sense of time – his groove," says Buckmaster.

However, Miles had no intention of completing the sessions that Buckmaster had directed. But Mark Rothbaum says a meeting with Frank Sinatra would spur Miles on to make more music. "He called me and said he wanted to go and see Sinatra at Carnegie Hall. After the concert, a beautiful woman took him backstage and afterwards he called me and said 'Get the boys together – Al Foster, Pete [Cosey] and a few others,'" says Rothbaum.

But before those sessions would take place, Miles would face yet another crisis and one that would put him at the crossroads between life and death. "I phoned Miles every day to check he was ready before I went over to his place," says Buckmaster. "One time, he didn't answer the phone all day and so I decided to walk over there." By the time Buckmaster arrived at Miles's it was dusk, and Miles's house was in darkness. Buckmaster knocked on the door. A curtain twitched on the first floor and then Miles appeared at the front door. Miles invited Buckmaster inside and he discovered that the electricity had been turned off because Miles had forgotten to pay the bill. Some

Jewish funeral candles were rustled up and used to illuminate the gloomy living room.

"He was in a bad way when I arrived," says Buckmaster, "and he dozed off on the couch and I just sat there looking at him. When Miles woke up, he said 'What are you doing?' and I said that I thought he ought to go to bed." Miles went off to his bedroom, while Buckmaster sat in the darkness – by now all the candles had gone out. Buckmaster dozed off occasionally, but it wasn't easy to sleep, as there were roaches crawling around the room. It was in the small hours of the morning that Buckmaster made a fateful decision to call Miles's sister Dorothy in Chicago. Buckmaster told her he was concerned about Miles's health and suggested she come over to New York. "Dorothy said she had to go to a cousin's funeral, so I said to Dorothy 'The dead can take care of themselves, come and take care of the living,'" says Buckmaster.

Dorothy agreed to fly to New York the next day, and when she arrived she took control of the situation. She arranged for the power to be restored and for the house to be cleaned and also called up people for help. One of these was the actress Cicely Tyson, who had been in a relationship with Miles back in the 1960s. Although the romance ended, she and Miles remained good friends. "When Cicely arrived, she glared at me as if to say 'And who are you?'" recalls Buckmaster. Meanwhile, Miles was perplexed. "He asked me 'What the fuck are you doing?'" says Buckmaster, "and I told him that I thought he needed some help."

Singer Chaka Khan also arrived to lend a hand and took Miles away from the apartment. Not long after, Buckmaster left. "I think after the time I made that call it was the last time I saw Miles [in this period]," says Buckmaster. "Cicely Tyson kept everybody away." Buckmaster would next see Miles again in 1989, when Miles was playing in London.

But although the situation had seemingly reached a crisis point, Butler apparently decided to make one last effort to get Miles recording again. Buckmaster recalls that after Dorothy had arrived in New York, he was asked by Butler to stay on and work with Pete Cosey on some new music for Miles. The musicians on the new sessions were Cosey, Buckmaster (who played keyboards), drummer Doni Hagen (who would go on to play on Marvin Gaye's *Midnight Love* album), Ron Johnson (former bassist with Buddy Miles, and Ike and Tina Turner) and John Stubblefield on saxophone. Stubblefield had played on the track "Calypso Frelimo" on Miles's 1974 album, *Get Up With It*. He had simply been in the studio as a guest of Cosey's. "John was in the control room with his horn. Miles saw him, pointed to his horn and told him to join the session," says Cosey.

The music Pete Cosey's band played was very different from that played by the band that recorded *Pangaea* and *Agharta*. "The music had different time signatures," says Cosey. "One was a James Brown-type piece that has a unique time stop between the bass and the drums. It would have been fantastic. We were rehearsing some of my music and some of Paul's and Miles's music. Those would have been some fantastic sessions had they taken place." "One track, 'Electric Circle,' was brilliant," recalls Buckmaster. "It was an extended blusey-sounding melody that goes round in a long extended circle and maybe that's why he gave it that title. It was on my brain so much that I transcribed it and called Pete in the mid-'80s and asked him if I could make a recording of it, but he said no."

During this period, Buckmaster asked a friend, the composer and musician, J. Peter Robinson, to come to New York and help with a Miles recording. "He stayed for about a week, but nothing happened," says Buckmaster. What is more, the Pete Cosey sessions were also abandoned after Miles failed to turn up. "Miles got into an altercation with a pharmacist," says Cosey. "I spoke to both Miles and the pharmacist about the incident and apparently Miles requested something and the guy got smart and so Miles took his arm and swept the merchandise off the counter. The guy hit him with a telephone on the collarbone and so Miles missed the sessions."

The band was waiting for Miles in the studio and when Butler heard that Miles would be absent, he cancelled the sessions. "We were in the studio ready to record and George Butler said Miles had cancelled sessions before and he didn't want to take another chance with him," says Cosey. "We conversed with Miles by phone from the studio and he told George that he wanted us to record and that he would definitely come and play on it. Miles was very pleased with what had taken place, because we had been rehearsing at his home and he heard everything and was quite elated. But I guess George's head was in another place."

Buckmaster recalls a conversation with Butler. "I said to him 'I don't think this is working,' and he said, 'I don't think so too.'" Buckmaster packed his bags and left New York, flying off to San Francisco to record an album with the pianist Rodney Franklin. Although Buckmaster is disappointed that he never got to record again with Miles, he says: "We have to put the 1979 experience down to an abortive attempt with regard to making a recording but not in terms of me phoning Dorothy. That was the turning point for Miles's recovery from self-exile. Cicely Tyson took him away and cleaned him up."

Miles was still not making any music, but he was cleaning himself up and acknowledged his debt to Tyson: "She helped run all those people out of my house; she kind of protected me and started seeing that I ate the right things and didn't drink too much. She helped get me off cocaine. She would feed me health foods, a lot of vegetables, and a whole lot of juices. She turned me on to acupuncture to help get my hip back in shape. All of sudden I started thinking clearer and that's when I really started thinking about music again," said Miles.[28]

Tyson undoubtedly played a significant role in nursing Miles back to health (although even Miles admitted that he still continued to snort cocaine), but Rothbaum says: "Credit is given to Cicely Tyson, but the credit is all Miles's. A lesser person would have just died. It was an incredible comeback: one of the great moments of all time." After several false starts, Miles was at last ready to make music again. And the motivation for doing so would come from a city that would have a great impact on the music Miles played in the last ten years of his life – Chicago.

6 *the man with the horn* (52:47)

Columbia CK 36790

Recorded	May 1980 – March 1981
Released	Autumn 1981
Producer	Teo Macero
Executive producer	George Butler
Engineers	Stanley Tonkel, Don Puluse ("Fat Time" only)
Tracks	"Fat Time," "Back Seat Betty," "Shout," "Aida," "The Man With The Horn," "Ursula"

"I really believe Miles wanted to be a pop star." *Randy Hall, musician*

"If Miles had wanted a jazz band he would never have chosen our band." *Glenn Burris, musician*

Background to the album

The Chicago Group

Chicago, Illinois has a special place in the history of jazz and blues, and so it's fitting that the Windy City would play a pivotal role in the last decade of Miles's musical history. Chicago is a city steeped in sound. It pours out of bars and clubs. It floats out of open windows, while behind closed doors countless musicians practise and rehearse. Music is alive on the streets, in school talent shows and in a thousand and one venues around Chicago. Music is the heartbeat that drives the pulse of the city.

Jazz may have been born in New Orleans, but it would scramble to its feet in Chicago. Chicago's vibrancy and energy would soon attract jazz musicians from all over the USA including Louis Armstrong and Joe King Oliver. In the 1920s, Chicago Jazz, a variant of New Orleans Jazz, was being spearheaded by a group of young white musicians that included Benny Goodman and Gene Krupa. The list of jazz musicians born or raised in Chicago or who have strong musical connections with the city reads like a Who's Who of Jazz: Lester Bowie, Anthony Braxton, Steve Coleman, Richard Davis, Chico

Freeman, Bunky Green, Lionel Hampton, Eddie Harris, Earl Hines, Ramsey Lewis and Phil Upchurch. Some, such as Jack DeJohnette, Herbie Hancock and Lee Konitz, would play with Miles

For many people Chicago is the home of the blues, and in 1950 two Polish brothers Leonard and Phil Chess formed Chess Records, a label that would take the Chicago blues sound around the world. Blues giants such as Muddy Waters and Howlin' Wolf would travel from the South to Chicago and record with the Chess brothers.

Other artists associated with Chess included Chuck Berry, Bo Diddley and John Lee Hooker (who would record *The Hot Spot* soundtrack with Miles in 1990). Miles was born up on the Mississippi River near East St. Louis and so the blues were in his blood. "That kind of music stayed with me," said Miles, "that blues, church, back-road funk kind of thing, that southern, midwestern, rural sound and rhythm. I think it started getting in my blood on them spook-filled Arkansas back-roads after dark when the owls came out hooting."[1]

Miles also had a blood connection with Chicago. It was here where his sister Dorothy and his nephew Vince Wilburn Jr. lived. And so it was from this remarkable city that Miles would find his first studio group of the 1980s, as well as many members of his last working bands, including four bass players, two guitarists, one drummer and a keyboardist/musical director. What is even more extraordinary is that all these musicians were young (mostly in their early twenties) and all of them had either played together in local bands and talent shows around Chicago or had known each other through the city's thriving network of musicians. The common link between them all was Vince Wilburn Jr.

When Wilburn was around six years old, Miles persuaded his parents to buy his little nephew a drum kit. "I had always been fascinated by the drums," recalls Wilburn. "I remember going to New York with my cousin Gregory [Miles's second child from his relationship with Irene Cawthon] and seeing Uncle Miles play. I don't know why, but I always thought that at the end of the gig I would take the drums home with me."

Wilburn and most of his musical contemporaries grew up in and around Chatam, a district on the South Side of the city, located between 87th and 79th Streets. Chatam had once been a white neighbourhood but was now predominantly black. It was a pleasant, middle-class neighbourhood with neat bungalows, manicured lawns and no crime. Those who knew Dorothy Wilburn describe her as a kind woman with a big heart. She also loved music, especially the piano, and Wilburn says that his mother had turned Miles onto the pianist Ahmad Jamal. So it was no surprise that Dorothy actively encouraged Vince and his friends to develop their musical talents, allowing the basement of the family home to be used as a rehearsal room, complete with piano.

The Chicago music scene has always been vibrant, but in the 1970s it was especially so. Around the corner from Wilburn lived the soul group The

Impressions. Local bands such as Earth, Wind & Fire, The Staples Singers and The Dells were having hits in the soul and pop charts. Soul singer Curtis Mayfield, whose *Superfly* soundtrack was one of the biggest-selling black albums of the '70s, had his Curtom studio based in the north side of Chicago.

There was also PS Studios, which was used by many jazz artists such as Ramsey Lewis, Noel Pointer and Phil Upchurch. The trumpeter Paul Serrano, a friend of Miles, owned the studio. Every major record company had a distributor based in Chicago, and an area around 22nd Street and Michigan Avenue was known as "Record Alley," because so many record labels – including Vee-Jay, Chess-Checker and MGM – had offices there.

The Chicago music scene was so active that Motown session musicians would even travel from Detroit to find work there. "Man, there was a lot of music and so many cats were playing. We were just keen to play some music. It was so beautiful," recalls Wilburn. Wilburn's home was close to the Regal Theatre on 47th Street, where his mother would often take him to see live music. And of course, whenever Miles was in town, his family would go and watch him perform and then he'd stay over at the Wilburns' house.

When Wilburn was at kindergarten, he met Randy Hall and they became life-long friends. Hall's first musical instrument was the piano, but at thirteen he switched to the guitar, studying in Chicago with an English jazz guitarist called Peter Budd. Despite Budd's best efforts, Hall developed the technique of using his thumb as a pick, which combined fluency with a hard percussive edge to create an explosive sound.

Wilburn remembers: "A friend of mine said 'You know Randy's playing guitar just like Jimi Hendrix?' so I went to see Randy and he just floored me. We started to play together when we were around thirteen." The teenagers took their music seriously, and later on Hall would go on to study music at Berklee College of Music in Boston and also the American Conservatory of Music in Chicago. Wilburn would also attend the American Conservatory of Music.

In 1974, when the two young musicians were aged sixteen, they joined a local band called Time, Space & Distance (like many bands around this time, the name – and the music – was inspired by the success of Earth, Wind & Fire). David Scott, a guitarist who would later play with Wilburn and Hall in a couple of local bands, recalls that it was a good time to be growing up as a young musician: "When I was a kid, music wasn't a business – you just played for fun." When Time, Space & Distance went off to play in LA, Wilburn and Hall were too young to go with them, but the youngsters were fast gaining a reputation around the Chicago music scene and would play on recording sessions for local bands such as The Dells.

When Hall and Wilburn were both aged around seventeen, they came under the wing of Pete Cosey, the guitarist who had played with Miles's band in 1973–75 and who would work with Miles in 1979 on some material for a possible comeback album. Asked what he did with Hall and Wilburn, Cosey recalls: "I sort of prepared them to a certain degree and I would teach them whatever they asked me." "We were doing gigs with Pete, festivals and things like that. I would play guitar and Pete would play bass," says Hall. "Pete was great and would show us all kinds of things. He'd go out and get us Kentucky Fried Chicken and we'd play together," adds Wilburn.

Randy Hall also knew another guitarist in high school called Alan Burroughs. "Randy was one year younger than me and we were like the guitar darlings of the school. We were kinda rivals but we had a lot of respect for each other. We sometimes played on the same talent shows. I also knew Vince although we didn't hang out together," recalls Burroughs. Burroughs also met another guitarist from New York called Bobby Broom. The two became close friends and would often jam together. Later on, Broom would move to Chicago, where he would get to know many of the musicians who went on to play with Miles. Both Broom and Burroughs would themselves play in Miles's band in early 1987.

In 1975, Hall went off to study at the Berklee College of Music and Wilburn joined a local band, Chicago City Limits. The band would recruit guitarist Otha Smith and bassist Richard Patterson, both then aged around seventeen. Smith and Patterson had grown up on the far South Side of Chicago, less than ten miles from the state border.

Smith remembers that the strong musical influences at this time around Chicago were Earth, Wind & Fire, Rufus (with Chaka Khan), The Jazz Crusaders and Stevie Wonder. "But for jazz we grew up in the advent of fusion," says Smith. "Richard and I started playing music at the same time and mimicking the Brothers Johnson! Because we started learning a variety of music, such as Billy Cobham, Tower of Power, Stanley Clarke, Santana, we stood out from the other pop/soul/R&B musicians."

"Everywhere you turned, there was a musician. In the area where Richard and I lived, there were at least three bands within a quarter-mile radius. When bands rehearsed in the garage in the summers, we'd open the big doors to see who would get the biggest crowd. This would be fun until someone complained or the cops came around," says Smith.

It was in the summer of 1975 when Patterson's and Smith's orbits coincided with Wilburn's. Patterson was away at college studying engineering when a friend told him that his cousin played in a Chicago band called Chicago City Limits, which was looking for a bass player. "When I got back to Chicago I went to Vince's house and joined the band," says Patterson. Smith also passed an audition.

But Chicago City Limits performed only a few gigs as the band focused on writing and recording. "It never took off, but as Vince knew Randy, another band was growing in the background," says Smith. Chicago City Limits disbanded in 1976 and most of the members went on to form a fusion group called

Data. The new group now included Hall – back from his year at Berklee – and three other new members, David Scott on guitar, Steve LeFlora on keyboards and Glenn Burris, a saxophonist, whose playing was inspired by Bunky Green and Steve Coleman. "I met Randy, Vince and Richard at a summer music programme," recalls Burris. LeFlora didn't stay with Data for long and was replaced by Robert (Bobby) Irving III, a native Chicagoan who had spent the past eight years living in North Carolina and was just relocating back to Chicago.

Irving had studied music composition and arranging at the University of North Carolina. "At the time, my exposure to jazz was limited to artists like The Crusaders, Ramsey Lewis and Herbie Hancock," he recalls. Data worked with the musical arranger Tom Tom 84,[2] who also had connections with other local acts such as Ramsey Lewis and Earth, Wind & Fire.

Meanwhile, Wilburn was also hanging out with two other local bassists, Darryl Jones and Angus Thomas, both of whom would join Miles's band in the 1980s. "You would play with people around the city and meet other musicians on the circuit," recalls Jones. "I lived a few doors down from Angus and I was introduced to Vince, who was going out with Angus's sister. It was through Vince that I met people like Randy Hall and [bassist] Felton [Crews] and Bobby. I was pretty close to the band when they started recording with Miles."

Angus Thomas was six years older than Jones and used to hang out with Jones's older brother Leslie. "Angus was someone I used to look up to," says Jones. When Thomas was in the eighth grade he played bass at a talent show which Jones attended. "Darryl came up to me – he must have been around nine or ten – and said 'I want to play guitar like you,'" says Thomas. I said 'I don't play guitar, I play bass.' Anyway, Darryl got himself an acoustic guitar and we took two strings off it and started practising on that. Later on, Darryl's mother bought him a bass guitar and he started taking bass lessons – he was my first student," says Thomas.

Jones remembers the rich musical environment he grew up in. "There used to be these jams where different musicians would just get up and play – there was a lot of improvisation. But I'd also play in high school talent shows as well as gigs outside of school. If there were an election, we'd play for the politicians, so I was getting the kind of experience that professional musicians would get. When I got to college I realized that my experience was different from the other students. Their school curriculum was different. They had been drawing screws and stuff, and I had just played for four years."

One of the places where Jones would jam would be in the basement at the home of guitarist Jean-Paul Bourelly, who recalls: "Darryl was sixteen at the time and I was seventeen. Bobby Irving, Vince Wilburn, Randy Hall – I knew all those guys and we'd all play together." Bourelly left Chicago and settled in New York when he was nineteen. He would go on to carve out a successful solo career as well as play with various artists including McCoy Tyner, Elvin Jones and Miles – he would appear on Miles's 1989 album *Amandla*. Chicago's mix of urban and rural populations influenced the city's art and culture, says Jones: "You've got this Mississippi River influence meeting this urban energy and the musicians carry that feeling with them. [We were] slick like the city but soulful like the country all at once."[3]

Data performed in clubs and venues all around Chicago, with names like The Happy Medium, Ding Bats and High Chaparral. Sometimes they would open for major acts such as Kool and the Gang, although some gigs were memorable for other reasons. "I remember we were playing at one place and the audience were silent. They didn't clap, they didn't say anything," recalls Hall. "It wasn't until we started packing away our instruments that they suddenly started applauding us, which we thought was a bit strange. When we mentioned this to the venue's manager, he said 'Oh, didn't I tell you? They're all deaf children!'"

Data signed up with a management team that was also linked to the funk band The Ohio Players. Data's management got the band to record a demo album and booked them on a big showcase performance held at McCormick Place, one of Chicago's largest conference centres located on South Lake Shore Drive. The aim of the showcase was to bring local bands to the attention of record labels and the group attracted the attention of Atlantic Records. Data's management started negotiations with them.

Atlantic had been impressed enough to offer Data a recording advance, but in the words of Hall: "Our management made a fatal mistake. Atlantic made us a good offer but instead of taking it, one of our managers decided to see if he could get even more money from someone he knew at Columbia Records. What he didn't know was that this guy was also a good friend of the person who had offered us the contract at Atlantic. When the two of them discovered what was happening, both labels dropped us."

Data sacked their management and hired a new manager, Lucky Cordell, a well-known DJ in Chicago, known to his radio listeners as "The Baron of Bounce." "I started radio in the 1950s and at the time every DJ had a nickname. I gave myself that name because I liked to play uptempo numbers and get people bouncing," recalls Cordell. Cordell managed to get Data a recording contract with ABC Dunhill, but it was one of the shortest record deals in history: "We got a deal with ABC Dunhill, who I think were going to cut some test records to see what potential we had, but we never even got that far, because we were dropped after just a day or two," says Scott.

Cordell explains why the deal was so short-lived: "It was very good music, but at the time the competition was very intense when it came to getting a deal. There were many independent producers who would record an artist with their own money and then try and get a major interested. The record labels had so much material coming in that if something didn't bowl them over instantly or if something else came along, they would pass on it. They were a fine group of young people and I wished them well." Scott says: "I remember Vince telling his Uncle Miles what had happened and Miles was upset. He told Vince to sack our manager and said he would get the band a deal with his record company, but I don't think Vince took him seriously at the time."

The aborted record deals meant that morale dropped sharply amongst the band members and Data began to self-destruct. Smith decided to leave the band and focus on session work, while Patterson went off to pursue a teaching degree. Patterson may have left the band, but the Miles connection was not totally severed because in 1990 he would join Miles's band, becoming the last bass player in a Miles Davis band.

But in 1979 another band rose from the ashes of Data, and one that would have a wider musical palette than Data's. The new band was called AL7, a play on the word "All." In many societies, the number seven has a symbolic meaning and the choice reflected the band's growing interest in mysticism and metaphysics. AL7 saw the arrival of a new bass player, Julius Bradley, but he was in turn replaced by Felton Crews, whose background included rock, funk and fusion – his first professional gig came while he was still in high school, when he was asked to back up singer Minnie Riperton. Crews had met Wilburn at a rehearsal through a mutual music associate: "Our pocket was tight from the start and Vince recommended me to the group," remembers Crews.

AL7 comprised Hall, Irving, Wilburn, Scott, Crews, Burris, Joel McGhee on second saxophone and Will Singleton on percussion. There were also two female background singers, Sand Hall (short for Saundra – she is Randy Hall's sister) and Joan Walton-Collaso. Irving describes AL7's music as "progressive, alternative pop with a few fusion tunes."

David Scott elaborates: "Funk was the music of our time but we were also studying jazz and listening to rock 'n' roll, and progressive stuff like Billy Cobham, Chick Corea, John McLaughlin, George Duke and Frank Zappa – anything that was not normal. We were trying to stretch out and play things that had not been played before. At the time, Chicago bands prided themselves on being original and coming up with something that was unique to the band."

AL7 played some local gigs at clubs, private parties and high-school events, but much of the time was spent rehearsing and writing material, says Scott: "Music consumed a lot of our time but for us it was fun and I considered all the guys as friends and family. We were very serious for teenagers and I don't see that kind of dedication or fun today because music is a business."

AL7's musical prowess had attracted the attention of Tom Tom 84. "Tom Tom became interested in the group and booked studio time for us to go in and demo some music for Maurice White [leader of Earth, Wind & Fire] to check out," remembers Irving. During these sessions, AL7 recorded several tracks including "Space", "I Am"[4] and "Life Ain't Nothing But A Party."

It was the Tom Tom 84 session and a phone call from Miles to his sister Dorothy that would result in some members of AL7 working with Miles and motivating Miles to return to music. Miles had always been close to Dorothy and would call her almost every day, even when on tour. He also took a keen interest in his nephew's musical development and whenever Wilburn was rehearsing with his band at home in the basement, Miles would ask Dorothy to put Vince on the phone.

There was always a *frisson* of excitement whenever Miles spoke to Wilburn and sometimes the phone would be passed around to other band members. Not everyone found it easy talking to Miles. "I would freeze and Miles would say 'What's happening? Put Vince back on the phone,'" says Patterson. Scott adds: "We were just excited we were talking to Miles, but of course Vince wasn't star-struck like the rest of us."

Miles would also listen to the band playing over the phone and occasionally offer the young musicians advice or encouragement: "He'd ask to speak to me and say things like 'That was a good solo and that kind of stuff," recalls Hall. Smith remembers that "Some of the comments he gave at the time seemed very cold and harsh. But when we started to understand what he meant, we looked for this guidance all the time. Miles told me once, after listening to a song where I had a solo, 'Learn how to play a one-note solo, then your shit will come together.' I didn't have a clue what he was talking about. Over a few weeks it started to sink in, when I heard a Larry Carlton solo. This changed my approach to guitar playing forever. I didn't want to mimic Carlton, but it changed who I listened to and how."

It was during one of these calls in early 1980 that Miles heard the demo track "Space" and was gripped by the music. "Space" was a funky number with an open hi-hat sound, supported by a clavinet, moog synthesizer and bass. The song had been written by Irving, who remembers Miles raving about the moog sound. It was this tune that would result in a radical change in Miles's musical direction and see four of the young Chicago musicians becoming Miles's first studio band for almost five years.

Around the same time that Miles heard "Space," he had been working again with Pete Cosey. Cosey had assembled a band and even recorded some backing tracks, although Miles had yet to make an appearance in the recording studio with him. The music produced by Cosey for Miles was a world away from the pop/funk of AL7, so why did Miles change his mind?

Miles admits that, at the time, he wasn't clear about where he wanted to go musically: "I knew I had to go someplace different from where I had been the last time I had played, but I also knew I couldn't go back to the real old music either. I still didn't know who to get in the band because while I was off I hadn't listened to music and didn't know who was around or who could play. That was all a mystery to me, but I wasn't worried because things like that just work themselves out."[5]

Pete Cosey says health problems, coupled with the fact that Miles was being "besieged by people pushing chemicals at him," meant that Miles's head was not clear. Family pressure also played a part. During Miles's retirement, Wilburn would often visit his uncle in New York. "We would sit up and talk about music and he'd show me these chords and voicings," says Wilburn. "Sometimes I would ask him about playing again and I would cry and he would say 'Get out of here now.'"

Scott believes the timing was right for both Miles and Wilburn: "We were practising hard but not getting many gigs and not making a record deal. I think Vince talked Miles into coming out of his shell. Vince talked to Miles over a long time and I think eventually Miles just gave in." Felton Crews agrees that the timing was right: "The band didn't seem to be going anywhere and I was close to leaving when I got the call that Miles wanted us to play with him."

Family pressure also came from Miles's sister Dorothy. "Dorothy once explained to me that she had read the riot act to Miles," recalls Cosey. "She told him he was wasting so many of his resources and opportunities. She said to him 'Why are doing this? If you're not going to do something you should give little Vincent a chance.' I'm sure she worked on his conscience. The family were there and Vince had a group of guys to play with and that's what went down."

Dave Liebman, the saxophonist who had played with Miles in 1973–74, also believes that the family connection dictated Miles's musical path at this stage: "Miles wanted what was most convenient and Vince was there and I guess he had these guys together as a unit. It was easy for Miles – he didn't have to start going out to find guys."

Miles's shaky chops, lack of musical direction and low confidence are also likely to have motivated him to work with a group of young and relatively unknown musicians rather than going into the studio with an all-star band. The family connection through Wilburn Jr. must have also provided him with some comfort and security. All these factors certainly played a part in coaxing Miles back to the music scene, but it mustn't be forgotten that it was the music played by The Chicago Group that was the main source of inspiration for Miles's return. AL7 played the music of the day – funk – and this was the route Miles would take in the next phase of his musical career.

But what isn't so clear is the motive behind Miles's decision to work with AL7 – did he want to record his new album with the band or was he simply planning to work with AL7 on one track ("Space") in an effort to help them secure a record deal, possibly with Columbia Records? Hall and Irving believe it was the latter. "I guess he was doing it to help Vince and was going to try and get us a record deal. But once he heard our music he decided he wanted to record with us. We were going up to do one song but then Miles said 'Just keep cutting!'" says Hall. Irving is also adamant that "'Space' was the only tune that we were to record with Miles."

Hall recalls his reaction when Wilburn told him that they were going to record with Miles. "It was like a dream. I wasn't afraid – I don't think any of us were. We had been working hard on our music for so many years and by the time we were twenty Vince and me were like old pros." Miles's decision to work with AL7 was a great opportunity for the young musicians, but a bitter blow for Cosey. The decision by Miles to record with his nephew and friends ended what had been a long and productive musical partnership between him and Cosey. The two men lost touch after that.

Miles decided to bring four members of AL7 to New York: Wilburn, Hall, Irving and Crews; and in April 1980 the four of them flew from Chicago to New York. Glenn Burris arrived later and Scott says the original plan was for him – and possibly some other group members – to follow at a later date. Although the group of young musicians were going to New York ostensibly to cut one track with Miles, they decided to bring along a package of songs they had written. It was a wise decision, because they would end up spending more than sixty hours in the studio recording many tracks.

Whatever Miles's intentions, Columbia Records were obviously pleased that, after several false starts, Miles seemed to be serious about making music again. George Butler, vice-president of Columbia's jazz division and the man who had been trying to coax Miles back into the music scene for months, was in overall charge of the project. Miles's long-time producer Teo Macero was drafted in. But when Miles had initially planned returning to the music scene, he wasn't keen to work with Macero again: "I was through with Teo Macero. I said I would only work with George [Butler] and everyone agreed with that."[6]

For some reason, which Miles does not explain in his autobiography, he later relented and agreed to work again with Macero. It's reasonable to assume that Miles realized at the time that he was going to need someone to support him in the studio and that the best man to have around was Macero. Columbia pulled out all the stops to help ease Miles back into the music scene. Wilburn and his friends were booked into a high-class hotel and limousines would take them from their hotel to the studio (the limousine company even got a name check in the album credits).

Irving was the first of the Chicago musicians that Miles called and he was invited to go round to Miles's home for lunch. When Irving arrived, Miles – who was wearing a black and red three-quarter satin lounge jacket and black trousers – greeted him with a godfather-style kiss on both cheeks and invited him in. Irving noticed that Miles was also limping and using a cane. "Miles was surprised that I was as short as him because he said I sounded taller on the phone. He was a great host and made me feel very relaxed. He said I reminded him of himself when he was my age (I was twenty-five)," says Irving.

Later on, Miles asked Irving to play something for him on the piano, and while Irving was playing Miles reached over Irving's shoulders and played

some chords. "He opened up my awareness to the vast harmonic possibilities that existed," says Irving. "He warned me about the tendency to play too
much and he told me to listen to what was going on around me musically
and respond to it only if I had something important to say. He said 'Don't
play something unless you mean it.' He told me about having to ask Herbie
[Hancock] not to play too much and said that Bill Evans was his favourite
pianist when it came to this kind of approach." Crews also recalls that "Miles's
direction was usually cleaning up individual bad habits, but for the most part
we had the freedom of creative expression."

Hall also remembers the first time he met Miles. "I walked in and I was
clean. I had a double-breasted blue suit and Miles said 'Goddamn – man, you
are a pretty nigger.' So we sat and talked and he just played the tapes of our
music." The period was especially exciting for Hall, who had never been to
New York before. "Miles took us to a Cuban restaurant called Victor's and I
had never had Cuban food before. One day I was riding around New York in
a limousine and we went past Carnegie Hall and through Central Park. The
flowers were blooming and the trees were budding – I felt like Jed Clampett
of the Beverly Hillbillies! It was like going from chitlins to caviar! I was in New
York, playing with Miles Davis and getting paid for it. It was like 'Does it get
any better than this?'" David Scott remembers Hall calling him regularly from
New York. "He'd say things like 'Check this out. I ordered room service this
morning and the orange juice cost eighteen dollars.' Then he'd tell me the
price of everything else on the menu."

Although Miles had the option of recording with the saxophonist Glenn
Burris, for some reason he decided to look for another one and, in doing so,
chose a young, unknown saxophonist called Bill Evans. According to Wilburn,
"Glenn was a bad motherfucker but Miles already had Bill when he flew to
us to New York." Bill Evans had got the gig through his association with Dave
Liebman.

In 1978, Liebman was holding a saxophone workshop in Illinois, as part of
a jazz summer school run by the saxophonist Jamey Aebersold. Sitting in the
audience were Bill Evans and a few of his friends. "It was the first time I had
done any teaching and it seems that Bill and his friends had requested me as
a teacher. That's where I met Bill," says Liebman. Evans, who was twenty-two
at the time, had grown up in Hillsdale, just outside Chicago and had begun
playing piano at the age of six (he performed classical piano concerts when
he was a teenager). He later switched to the clarinet and saxophone and
studied music at North Texas State University. His early saxophone influences
included Bunky Green, Joe Daley, Charlie Parker and Sonny Stitt.

In 1979, Evans moved to New York to be at the heart of the city's vibrant
live jazz scene and to study at the William Patterson College in New Jersey. By
coincidence, Evans and a group of friends ended up living in a loft in the next

street to Liebman's home. "We started hanging out together and I would also teach Bill," says Liebman. Then in April 1980, Miles called Liebman out of the blue: "Miles said 'Who you got?' – he didn't even say hello. So I said 'Are you going to start up again?' and Miles said something like 'I want to.' So I said 'There's a kid who lives down the street who's good,' and Miles asks 'Who does he sound like?' and I said 'He sounds like me and Steve [Grossman, who played with Miles in 1970].' Then he says 'Give me his number.'"

When Liebman told Bill Evans that he had recommended him to Miles, Evans was flattered but he didn't expect much to come of it, not least because Miles had been out of the music scene for years. But he was in for a surprise. When one of his friends handed Evans the phone and said it was Miles, his hands were already sweating: "He said 'Are you Bill Evans?' Then he goes 'Are you better than John Coltrane and Cannonball Adderley and Charlie Parker?' and he's naming all these guys."[7] Evans, whose experience up to that point was limited to playing in college bands and sitting in on a few gigs around New York and Boston, knew the next answer could determine his future. "Now the telephone is practically slipping out of my hand and I'm thinking 'It all comes down to this, doesn't it?' So I said 'Miles, I just play the best I can,' and he starts laughing and says 'Why don't you come on down?'"[8]

When Evans arrived at Miles's home, Irving was present and Evans's audition consisted of him playing over a vamp with Irving on piano. Evans recalls Miles saying to him, "You know, if I played saxophone, I'd want to play it like you. I love that style."[9] Irving says that Evans's attitude also helped him get the gig with Miles. "Bill was cool and confident without being cocky and Miles observed this. Miles asked us all how we liked him and the vote was unanimous." Irving also has a theory as to why Miles chose Evans over Burris: "Glenn was coming mostly from a post-bop direction while Bill utilized more European nuances in his solo style." Although Burris would not play on *The Man With The Horn*, he was present at the workshops and recording sessions, contributing ideas and even co-writing one of the tunes that made it on the album.

It is difficult to overstate the impact and influence Evans would have on Miles's life over the next few years, with Evans playing the role of a friend, confidant, minder, chaperon, musical collaborator, talent spotter and road manager. It was a surprising development because the contrast between the two men could not have been starker, as Evans notes: "He's coming from a period where he's doing drugs, drinking beer and getting drunk and I didn't do any of that. He's got this white kid coming from college, who plays sax, who works out and doesn't do drugs and I'm going to watch out for him."[10]

In one of those strange acts of symmetry, Bill Evans the saxophonist found himself in the same position as Bill Evans the piano player, who had played with Miles in 1959. Both men were the only white members in a Miles Davis sextet. "Bill's this white kid from Illinois and he's working with these black guys, but we loved Bill. Bill and I became good friends. You have to remember that what was happening to us was also happening to him too," says Hall.

Miles set up a collaborative composition workshop at his home, hiring sound equipment from a local audio company. The Chicago Group would meet at Miles's home and begin working on the tunes they had brought with them. The workshops were intensive and typically lasted for around twelve hours. During the workshops, Miles would sit at a Farfisa organ directing operations, but did not play any horn.

Soon, what began as a project to record one tune grew into a full-blown album project. Irving believes this happened because "Miles had not had any interaction with young musicians for many years and the process by which we were creating music fascinated him." Hall adds: "Miles liked it so much and Columbia liked that Miles liked it, so we just kept working."[11] The workshops were the greatest music school anyone could have, says Hall: "Miles was so open about teaching you anything. I remember him going to the piano and showing me some substitution chords which you could use instead of a regular triad or chord to make the music more colourful."

Irving says that Miles's presence had subtly helped to bend and shape the music into other areas: "Without this, we were for the most part imposing AL7's concept and structure on Miles. Nevertheless, Miles loved what we were doing." The developmental workshops were productive but Irving has two big regrets over them: "I wish the jam sessions had been recorded because we explored areas beyond the songs we brought from Chicago. And if Miles had been playing trumpet with us, that magical sound of his horn would have led us like the Pied Piper into the direction we needed to be musically and, of course, he would have placed his signature on more of our music. As a composer, I have found that melody and tone are the driving forces behind great composition and we didn't have Miles's melodic voice to lead us."

But Miles was in no shape to play the trumpet – physically, mentally or emotionally – and ill-health coupled with a heavy intake of cocaine and alcohol meant he was in no position to provide The Chicago Group with the direction they wanted. It was only later, when his confidence began to return, that Miles had a clearer idea about the musical direction that he wished to take. This helps to explain why there would be yet another major shift in Miles's music during the making of *The Man With The Horn*.

"I think Miles was just as excited as we were. He'd be asking us 'What time are you going to be here tomorrow? Be here at ten o'clock,'" says Hall. "He'd send out for food from a local restaurant and there'd be beer all day. He even cooked for us. I remember Miles making us some catfish that he marinated in Jack Daniel's!" The group would also hang out with Miles after the workshops and often go out with him in the evening to clubs. "Miles would also give the young musicians plenty of guidance and advice. "Miles was like a father to us," says Irving.

By the time The Chicago Group got to Columbia Studios, the music had been structured into a basic song form. The music Miles created with The Chicago Group was very different from the music he had played before his retirement and which was captured on albums such as *Agharta* and *Pangaea*. Gone were the vast musical soundscapes, with tunes or themes merging into each other and where the music was like a liquid, with no fixed shape and capable of flowing in many directions. Now, the songs were back to the standard theme-solo-theme structure and Miles's dark, dense, electric sound of the 1970s, with its African, rock and funk influences, was replaced by one that was contemporary, commercial – even catchy.

Only The Chicago Group would be involved in the recordings of the basic tracks – Miles would overdub his parts much later. According to a report filed by Howard Mandel in *Down Beat*,[12] Angela Bofill added backing vocals to some of the tracks, but in fact she was not present at any of the sessions, even though Miles repeats the same error in his autobiography.[13]

Waiting for the band at the studio were Teo Macero and engineer Stan Tonkel, who had worked with Miles and Macero on many of Miles's albums such as *In Concert*, *Big Fun*, *Live Evil* and *Get Up With It*. According to Irving, Macero's creative input during the sessions was almost non-existent: "Teo was a technician who captured the sound onto 24-track analogue tape. That was his gig and he did it well without dictating any creative ideas. If he did have any opinions he kept them to himself. Maybe that was something he had acquired from working with Miles."

Burris adds: "From a musical standpoint, I didn't see Teo do anything. He was more of an engineer." Hall found Macero's mode of operation a little unsettling: "I really respect Teo but his thing is that he's a great editor. Miles would play maybe twenty or thirty solos and Teo would edit it. I don't remember Teo being meticulous about anything. When we played, we just did it and moved on and there was none of that 'Do it again' or 'That was better.' I'm not saying Teo isn't a meticulous producer, but maybe that was a style of what Miles's music was about."

Hall suspects that Macero's seemingly casual production methods were partly as a result of Macero's low opinion of the music. "I don't think Teo respected it," he says. Macero says that the music produced by The Chicago Group "wasn't bad, but it wasn't great. It wasn't up there with what Miles was doing. Miles at that time was very sick. He was really in a bad way and I don't think he really knew what the hell was happening there. It was all right, but it wasn't really Miles. If we had put Miles on it, it probably would have been a helluva lot better." Wilburn's response is blunt: "I don't think Teo was into it but Miles was, so we didn't give a fuck what others thought of it."

George Butler, who had taken on the role of executive producer, was rarely present at the sessions and his main job seemed to be sending Miles the weekly cheques and keeping an eye on the recording budget. "George was just happy that Miles was recording, although he did lament the amount of money we were spending at the hotel," says Irving.

In May, just when the recording sessions had begun, Miles was hospitalized with a serious leg infection and Evans's job was to keep him informed about progress of the recording sessions. "When Miles was in hospital he would call me at the studio and ask me how things were going. I would play some of the tracks over the phone to him," says Evans. It's not entirely clear how many tracks The Chicago Group recorded during these sessions. Hall recalls the group bringing "thirteen or fourteen" tunes to New York. Mandel's report suggests fourteen tracks,[14] while Irving told writers Dery and Doerschuk the number was "about fifteen"[15] and author Paul Tingen "nineteen."[16]

The tracks included "The Man With The Horn," "Shout," "Space," "Burn," "Solar Energy," "Spider's Web," "Mrs. Slurpey," "Thanksgiving," "1980s," "Tradition 106," "I'm Walking On A Cloud," "I Am," "Life Ain't Nothing But A Party" and "I'm Blue." According to Macero's notes on the sessions, other tunes recorded included "Wake Up," "Unconditional Love" and "So Good."[17] Irving cannot recall "So Good" but says: "'Wake Up' was a vocal tune composed by Randy Hall and me. It was a very progressive/melodic rock-funk tune. It was written prior to 'Shout' and in retrospect I think 'Shout' may have been derived from 'Wake Up,' which was more harmonically sophisticated. 'Shout,' however, had a more primal quality to it. 'Unconditional Love' was a Randy Hall vocal ballad."

The group also recorded several untitled tracks. The music recorded by The Chicago Group reflected the diverse musical experiences they got from playing in Chicago, as Hall explained to Mandel: "There's something for everybody. Vocals, electronics to appeal to young people. It's commercial enough that people who never heard Miles before will get it. Older fans of his will dig it too. Some tunes are like pop. It's into a wide spectrum. The music is mostly ballads, but there's uptempo funk, fusion, an open hi-hat sound with lots of drive that Miles taught Vince to play, hip melodies on the top, lots of melodic changes."[18]

At the time of writing, only three of the tunes recorded during these sessions have been commercially released. "Shout" and "The Man With The Horn" are on *The Man With The Horn* album, and a live version of the rock-funk number "Burn" (played by a different band) appeared on *The Complete Miles Davis At Montreux* boxed set. But what about the rest of the music? Irving says tracks such as "Space" and "Solar Energy" were in a similar vein to "Shout." "Mrs. Slurpey" and "Life Ain't Nothing But A Party" had vocals. "Tradition 106" was a Brazilian bossa-nova tune written by Evans and Irving.

"I'm Walking On A Cloud" was a Felton Crews composition he describes as "smooth funk."

Glenn Burris had composed a tune, "He She Love," which Miles apparently liked a lot. "It was about the duality of men and women and was in a similar vein to Madonna's 'Justify My Love,'" he says. "Miles loved the song and when he was at the studio he told Teo to record it. So after Miles leaves, Teo says 'Let's start,' but for some reason Vince didn't want to do it. I remember lying on top of the recording console and sulking." Wilburn says: "I liked the tune, [but] I just felt it was too controversial for Miles."

"I'm Blue" is of particular interest because Scott says it was originally planned as the title track of Miles's new album. The tune, about the end of a relationship and featuring lyrics, was written by Scott and Hall and, in the words of Scott, is: "A funk ballad with a side of jazz. It's a soulful ballad but not in the traditional sense of R&B. The verse is modern minor blues and most of the chords have some suspension. The chorus has a minor basis with what I would call a floating augmented chord around A minor."

"Miles loved it and played it over and over again, but he didn't want to have two ballads on the album," says Hall. Scott believes that "I'm Blue" was the inspiration for *The Man With The Horn*'s title track: "I think that music was born out of 'I'm Blue.' They have similar changes and melodies," graciously adding, "I think 'The Man With The Horn' was the better choice."

The planned single recording became more an album's worth of material because Miles had liked the music, says Hall: "I know a lot of people think the only reason we got in with Miles was because of Vince but, believe me, if the music wasn't happening Miles would never have done it. At the time, everyone was sending him tapes and songs, but it was not happening. We were the first to go into the studio and work with him. We were the catalyst that got him back and playing, but I don't think we've had the recognition for that."

Miles, however, did acknowledge his debt to the young band: "Playing with this group got me back in touch with music. When I was retired, I wasn't hearing any melodies in my head because I wouldn't let myself think about music. But after being in the studio with those guys, I started hearing melodies again, and that made me feel good."[19]

Hall believes that Miles didn't want to go back and do the music he had done before the five-year break. He also wanted wider recognition: "Miles wanted to be accepted by the kids. Miles wanted to be contemporary. He wanted to be new and fresh." Burris believes that "Miles believed that you had to go beyond yourself and push the envelope and not be safe, and that's why he sought out R&B. Miles told me he was really bored with traditional jazz. If you listen to the music we made with Miles, Bobby doesn't get to solo, and in the jazz tradition the pianist plays solo. But that wasn't what Miles got the band for. Our band was designed for commercial appeal and it was not about jazz and that's what the critics didn't understand. If Miles had wanted a jazz band he would never have chosen our band."

Miles may have liked the music, but during the initial stages of recording he stayed at home when The Chicago Group went into the studio. Hall says that although Miles was not physically present during the early sessions, he had a presence in the studio: "As we were recording he was on the phone, listening to the music and directing us. It was like he was there." Hall also recalls that it was hard getting Miles into the studio: "I think for the first few times we went in, he was motivating himself. I guess it was a big step for him to go back in."

When Miles finally did return to the studio, it was a major event and Butler was excited by the prospect. But his excitement soon gave way to concern: "The first thing I noticed was that there was no horn. I was looking at the fellows I had brought in and the sums of money I was paying them and the hotel. Many of them were ordering room service sufficient for ten people and all I could think was dollars and Miles Davis with no horn."[20] Butler adds that he later realized that Miles had been orchestrating things.

Irving recalls a conversation with Macero that finally resulted in Miles going into the studio to play trumpet: "Teo said to me 'The music's great, but it's nothing without Miles." It took a bit of persuasion to get Miles to go into the studio with his horn and Irving remembers Miles sheepishly agreeing to do so. When Miles finally did return to the studio and play some horn, it soon became clear why he had been so reluctant to do so. Butler recalls: "Miles came into the studio with his horn and I'm excited and thought 'Miles is going to play the horn.' Then he put the horn up to his mouth and without the embouchure all you got was wind and that frightened me because I'm thinking I've paid out a fortune to get these fellows in town and Miles can't produce a tune."[21]

Irving remembers Miles apologizing and saying, "Man, I got to get my chops back." Irving, who used to play trombone and so knew all about the importance of keeping your lip in shape, told Miles not to worry and that it would just take time. But Miles was clearly concerned. When Hall and Miles shared a limousine on the journey back from the studio, Miles was unusually quiet. "He was looking really worried about his chops – he was very depressed. He didn't say nothing, which just wasn't Miles," says Hall. "Miles was like a big kid and loved playing around, but he just sat there with his glasses on. I'll never forget the scene and I just felt for him. He was one of the greatest trumpet players of all time, a legend, and he couldn't play."

Miles would not attempt to play over The Chicago Group's material until months after the group had finished their work and headed back to Chicago. The Chicago Group sessions finished in June and, as they packed up their things, the young musicians were excited about being on Miles's new album. Irving told Mandel: "We're going to turn some heads around. People will be imitating songs; they'll be imitating Vince's drumming."[22] There was also talk of Miles touring with the group in Europe and Japan. But when it came to completing his comeback album, Miles would yet again switch his musical direction.

The period between the summer of 1980 and January 1981 was one of rest, recuperation and revival for Miles and he spent much of the time in the company of Bill Evans. "We'd hang out every day. He'd call me up. It was like my new best friend was Miles Davis. I was as close as you could get to being a real good friend," says Evans.[23] The two men would spend hours talking about sport or music, walking the streets of New York together or visiting jazz clubs. Later on, they would play music together at Miles's house. Evans's role included looking after large rolls of money for Miles, which he sometimes secreted in his sock.

Evans's friendship with Miles would occasionally put him in some tricky situations. "My whole role in the beginning ... was just to keep him out of trouble," says Evans. "Sometimes I'd go to these after-hours places with him just making sure he wouldn't get into trouble – I didn't want anybody to shoot him. So sometimes if I thought it was a little crazy I'd just grab him and pick him up and carry him outside. He'd be kicking and screaming and he'd get into a boxing position and say 'Okay, it's just you and me' and I'd say 'What are you going to do? You're five foot four.' Then he'd smile and say 'Alright, let's go home.'"[24]

On another occasion, Miles took Evans to Harlem, leaving the young musician standing on the street corner for more than an hour and a half while he went off to score some drugs. Evans, the only white man in the area for miles, would be alone, sometimes with thousands of dollars of Miles's money in his pocket. Evans didn't know it at the time, but Miles was telling people that Evans was his bodyguard. "He's telling some of these guys 'If you mess with him, he'll flip out and kill everybody.' Some of them would say [to me] 'What sort of martial arts do you excel in?' and I'd say 'I don't know what you're talking about, I'm a musician!'" says Evans.[25]

One evening, Miles and Evans went to see Dave Liebman playing at a club in New York called Seventh Avenue South. Liebman's band included drummer Adam Nussbaum and a guitarist who was making a name for himself on the jazz scene called John Scofield. After the gig, Liebman hung out with Miles. "I asked Miles 'Do you like my guitar player?' and Miles said 'No,' so I said: 'I think he's going to be your guitar player, man.'"

Liebman's uncanny ability to spot musicians who would be right for Miles would prove to be spot-on yet again, because Scofield would later play with Miles for three years, and inspire Miles to play more of the blues in his live act. Liebman also had a hand in the recruitment of another guitarist for Miles's band. "I was playing at a club in Boston and I introduced Bill to Mike Stern. I said to Bill 'You guys ought to get together.'" Evans and Stern would play together with Miles for more than two years.

On September 15, 1980, Bill Evans, the pianist who had played with Miles in the late 1950s, died. Evans had played on the *Kind Of Blue* album and his sparse, delicate playing style had had a great influence on the album's music. Evans was just fifty-one when he died and had suffered from drug addiction. Evans's demise deeply affected Miles: "His death made me real sad, because he had turned into a junkie and I think he died from complications of that. The year before Bill died, Charlie Mingus had died, so a lot of my friends were going."[26] Evans's death was a stark reminder to Miles about his own mortality. Miles says he cut down on his drug usage in 1980, although he was still getting high on beer, cognac, champagne and cocaine.[27]

Evans's death may have been a factor in motivating Miles to start to practise playing the horn again and, by the end of the year, he was beginning to get his chops together, although it would be a long time before he fully regained range, stamina and control. In late 1980, one of the first things Miles did was to let some of The Chicago Group members know he was back in business. "When I was back home in Chicago, I got a call about 8 am in the morning from Miles. He said 'Hey man, I want you to hear something' and he started playing. He was just playing scales and runs and riffs and he was really happy," says Hall. Irving also got a call from Miles: "He said 'Check this out,' and then started playing over a tape recording of 'Shout.' He was back and proud and he told me he was going back into the studio to record on some of the tracks." These incidents show that, behind his seemingly invincible Prince of Darkness image, Miles was a person with his own insecurities and who cared about how others saw him, particularly if they were musicians he respected.

Miles began overdubbing The Chicago Group's tracks in January 1981 and decided to bring in some other musicians as well. He picked two New York session players, guitarist Barry Finnerty and percussionist Sammy Figueroa. Finnerty was born in San Francisco and migrated from the piano to the electric guitar when he was thirteen. After playing in gigs around San Francisco, he moved to New York in 1973 aged twenty-one. Soon he was playing with a number of jazz artists including Chico Hamilton, Flora Purim and Airto Moreira, Hubert Laws, Joe Farrell and the Brecker Brothers. In 1979, he started playing with The Crusaders and appeared on the international smash hit album *Street Life*.

In his autobiography Miles says: "I didn't know anything about either of them [Finnerty and Figueroa],"[28] which is odd, because Miles had met Finnerty more than two years earlier at the home of Elena Steinberg in Connecticut, where he had been joined by Julie and Larry Coryell. "I met Miles when he was in retirement – Julie had invited me up to her house for a few days," says Finnerty. Finnerty showed Miles his Guitarorganizer, a custom-built Les Paul that could be made to sound like an organ and which also interfaced with an

Arp Odyssey synthesizer. "It made quite a racket!" says Finnerty – it can be heard on the Brecker Brothers' *Heavy Metal Bebop* album.

During their stay in Connecticut, Miles and Finnerty composed a tune together, called "Try This," with Miles playing keyboards and Finnerty on guitar. "I gave Miles a ride back to New York and we went to a friend's of his where we listened to the cassette [featuring 'Try This'] over and over, and snorted long lines [of cocaine] into the night," says Finnerty. It seems that, even then, Miles was thinking about returning to the music scene, as Finnerty recalls a conversation with Miles: "He said he would call me when he got a band together and he asked who he should get on saxophone. I suggested Alex Foster,[29] but it was Bill Evans who called me up."

Miles had been in a bad shape the last time Finnerty had seen him (he was recovering from a car accident). "But in 1981 he was feeling a lot better, although he was doing quite a lot of cocaine," says Finnerty, adding: "Miles could be the nicest guy in the world; he was funny and he was a great cook. But he also had a mean side, a side that he used to see how much shit people would take from him because he was Miles. And he would respect you more if you didn't take any shit from him because, as you can well imagine, most people would eat a heaping helping of his horseshit just to be in his illustrious presence."

Figueroa was a seasoned pro on the session scene, working a lot with the Atlantic Records producer Arif Mardin. Figueroa got the Miles gig through his participation on Chaka Khan's first solo album *Chaka*, released in 1978. "Teo told me that Miles loved that album and played it non-stop. He asked Teo who the percussionist was, and Teo told him it was me," remembers Figueroa. In fact, Figueroa only plays on one track, "A Woman In A Man's World," and his performance is subtle and restrained. However, Wilburn says he also recommended Figueroa to Miles on the strength of his playing with Ashford and Simpson.

All this was enough to convince Miles that Figueroa was the man for him. Miles may have liked Figueroa's playing, but that wouldn't stop him giving the percussionist a hard time in the studio. "I remember when Sammy first got to the studio, he came and spoke to me. I just told him 'Play, don't talk.' He said he had to tune his drums up. I told him again just to play. He said 'But Miles, my drums sound horrible when they're not tuned properly, so I'm not gonna play them like that.' So I told him 'Motherfucker, you'd better play!' So he did and I hired him."[30]

Figueroa confirms that this incident took place (Figueroa would also discreetly tune his drums once Miles had left the studio), but he says that their initial meeting was even more dramatic than this. "When Miles heard it was me playing on Chaka's album he asked Teo to call me, but Teo says 'Why don't you call him?' So Miles calls and it's like 2 am in the morning and I'm fast asleep. I pick up the phone and I hear this voice and I didn't know who it was. Then I thought it was my friend [trumpeter] Lew Soloff who likes playing practical jokes. So I say 'Come on Lew, it's 2 am in the morning.' And the voice says 'Motherfucker, it's me. It's Miles Davis!' So I put the phone down on him.

"Five minutes later the phone rings again and the voice says 'I'm gonna kick your ass, you little spic!' So I say 'Lew, come on,' and Miles says 'This is not Lew! When I see you I'm gonna punch you in the stomach!'" It was only when Macero grabbed the phone and explained the situation that Figueroa realized he had made a giant *faux pas*. "I started apologizing to Teo and he said 'Don't worry. Can you get down to the studio now?' I didn't realize they were recording so late. So I got dressed and went to Columbia Studios."

When Figueroa arrived in the studio he saw Miles and, before he could introduce himself, Miles hit him hard in the stomach. "It was so hard that I almost fell down and I couldn't breathe. I got so pissed I lost it and hit him in the mouth and he fell on to a piano. Teo comes running in asking what's going on and Miles gets up rubbing his mouth and says 'Damn, that was good.' I say 'What do you mean?' and he says 'That was a good right hook.' He then takes me to a bar around the corner from the studio and after that we became real good friends."

With Finnerty and Figueroa on board, Miles began overdubbing. Even though Miles had been working hard on his chops, he was still struggling to get his lip back. The British saxophonist Clive Stevens, a friend of Figueroa, was present at one of the recording sessions. "Miles was in the studio with Teo Macero, George Butler and Stanley Tonkel and he was really suffering and playing out of tune. But they were all telling Miles that he sounded fine – they weren't being honest with him. Then I discovered that Miles was playing dry – without any echo or reverb added in the mix. I find that it helps to have some reverb when you're recording. I wanted to say to these people 'Why don't you help him?' but I didn't feel it was my place to comment."

Macero confirms that Miles was in a bad way during the overdubbing sessions and that a few technical tricks were sometimes required to obtain the desired performance: "He was on drugs. We had to slow the [tape] machines down, make bridges and all kinds of things. He'd get out there to play and go [blows a raspberry]. He couldn't play." Sometimes Macero would look for fragments of performances and patch them together. "If I could [I'd] find another little piece and another little piece and lay it in," he says.

Miles's playing may have been weak at this stage, but Butler recalls the reaction of Columbia's president Bruce Lundvall when he played him the demos from the sessions. "I didn't tell him it was Miles but when I put the demo on, I could tell he was getting excited when he realized who it was," recalls Butler. "He then called all the top executives and told them to get down to the conference room straight away. So the executives turn up wondering what's going on and then Bruce plays them the demos and the guys go 'That sounds like Miles!' They all jumped up and were excited. Everyone wanted to tell the world, but Bruce swore them to secrecy and said that the record wasn't done yet."

Bill Evans helped Miles pick the songs from The Chicago Group sessions, but after overdubbing on just two or three tracks Miles decided that he had to take yet another musical direction. "After I listened to what we had done, I realized that we needed something else, some other kind of music to make a whole album," he said. "Despite all that time in the studio we used only two songs from those sessions on the album. It wasn't that they weren't good musicians – they were. It's just that I needed something else to satisfy what *I* wanted to do."[31] Macero confirms that Miles played on only a few of The Chicago Group tunes: "I think we just did one or two and the other ones we couldn't do because he couldn't play. I've got the tracks here [at home] and there's no trumpet on there."

Miles's biographer Ian Carr believes that the diverse range of musical styles recorded by The Chicago Group "must have set alarm bells ringing in Miles's head,"[32] while the writer Paul Tingen offers a more direct assessment: "The music simply wasn't good enough."[33] The music recorded by The Chicago Group was certainly closer to pop than jazz; more funk than swing. Finnerty describes the music as "Collegiate and not up to the calibre of a Miles recording. The Chicago Group sounds okay on the tunes that made it onto the record. I mean them no disrespect but they really weren't of the same level of musicianship as the top New York cats. I mean, at any given time, few are." But Irving disputes this assessment and says the problem was more to do with a lack of direction: "I think that our level of musicianship would have allowed us to easily move into the same direction as the new group had Miles been playing trumpet."

After recording a few of The Chicago Group tunes, Miles played the results to a number of friends and musicians including Al Foster, Cicely Tyson and Dave Liebman. The reaction of some musicians, such as Liebman and Foster, was negative. "It didn't work out," says Liebman. "I think it was too commercial even for Miles! I just don't think he wanted to do that. I couldn't see him with a singer anyway."

Irving says that Foster told Miles: "'These guys are taking you too fast musically,' so they shifted into a different direction." But Hall recalls Foster's criticism being even more forceful: "I remember Al Foster being in the studio and telling Miles that the music was beneath him. During that time, a lot of people were telling Miles that. Miles really respected Al and I remember him saying 'I just had the greatest drummer in the world tell me that this music was beneath me.' It hurt Miles; it hurt all of us. Al worked on Miles and that's one of the reasons that the band that did all that recording didn't go out and tour with him."

Bill Evans also spent time with Miles discussing the musical direction he should take. Both felt that Miles needed to bring in fresh players. "Miles and me were really good friends by that time and we both discussed forming a 'real' playing band with great players," says Evans. "The Chicago Group were primarily funk/R&B musicians who would not have had the versatility in a live concert-setting to play jazz, funk or whatever." Whether the young musicians were capable of providing this type of support for Miles at the time is debatable, especially when one considers the wealth of experience they had gained from their playing days in Chicago.

Wilburn has no doubts about The Chicago Group's ability and versatility: "Fuck Bill Evans. Fuck Dave Liebman. Fuck Barry Finnerty. We could have played anything. Miles directed everything we did: even when he wasn't in the studio, he was on the phone and I took all the tapes to him every day. We took our direction from Miles. I get fed up when I hear people describing our music as bubblegum music. We were just young musicians trying to play music. The music was what Miles heard. It was all about Miles; this is what he wanted to record. Miles didn't have to record our music and he didn't have to release it."

Although Irving is disappointed that Miles did not use more of The Chicago Group's material, he now believes it was the right step for Miles to take. It was Irving's cousin William Cohen – who had played bass with Etta James and others while stationed in Germany during a stint in the US Army – that made him understand why Miles had decided to abandon most of The Chicago Group's material and record new music with a new band.

"My cousin was proud that I had reached such a high plateau in the jazz world," says Irving. "He also knew who Miles was and where he had come from. However, when he heard *The Man With The Horn* he shocked me by saying 'Oh no, you guys went in the wrong direction … you should not have gone there with Miles.' He was visibly disturbed. He then pulled out some vintage Miles Davis and played me examples that displayed the continuum we had broken by [taking] such a wide leap ahead, particularly the title track. This experience helped me accept the harsh media criticism with better understanding."

Hall says the first time he knew that Miles was recording some other music was when Miles played him a track over the phone featuring The New York Band. Scott discovered things had changed when he tried contacting an attorney who had been handling the royalty negotiations during the period when it looked as if Miles would be using "I'm Blue" on his new album. Up to that point, Miles or Columbia Records had been paying the bills. "I had been talking to the attorney for some time, but then one day when I called her she told me that it would cost me so much to speak with her. I figured then that Miles must have decided to pass on the song," he says.

For the new band, Finnerty suggested that Miles recruit one of the New York session scene's top drummers, either Buddy Williams or Steve Gadd, but Miles wanted to work with Al Foster again. He also decided that his new band would consist of Foster, Evans, Finnerty and Figueroa. But he now needed a new bassist and Evans pointed Miles in the direction of Marcus Miller, a bass player who at the age of just twenty-one had already gained a solid reputation around the session scene. Miller had got his first recording session at the age of sixteen, on Lenny White's *Big City* album. Although Miller was primarily a funk player, his talent and versatility had resulted in him playing on a diverse range of recording sessions: by the time he started playing with Miles, Miller's recording credits included Lee Ritenour, David Sanborn, Roberta Flack and Elton John.

Miller was on a country-and-western session when Miles called the studio. "Miles left a message for me to call him. I read the message, 'Call Miles.' I figured it was a joke, but I couldn't afford not to find out. Miles answered and told me to be at CBS recording studio in two hours."[34] Miller had been present at an aborted 1979 session that was supposed to involve Miles, so it's perhaps not surprising that he asked Miles, "Are you gonna be there?" to which Miles answered, "I'll be there if you'll be there."[35] Miller went to the studio and recalls that "Two hours later I was recording with him, along with Bill Evans, Barry Finnerty, Al Foster and Sammy Figueroa. Those sessions eventually became part of the *The Man With The Horn* album."[36]

The New York Band

Miles now had a core group of New York-based musicians – Foster, Miller, Evans, Finnerty and Figueroa – and he began working on new tunes. Miles's working arrangements were very loose and his rehearsals were more like workshops, with lots of exploration and experimentation. Rehearsals would take place at Miles's house or at the studio. When asked about how the band prepared for *The Man With The Horn* recordings, Finnerty recalls: "Prepare? You just showed up. Miles was pretty unpredictable. He might have planned to do something but if that didn't go right he'd try something off the cuff." Figueroa adds: "It was a challenge because you might do something one day and the next it would be different and so I'd say to Miles 'We didn't do this yesterday,' and Miles would say 'Fuck you, this is not yesterday, this is today."

Miller told Tingen that "For most of the tracks he had a few notes, just enough for everybody to unify. When we were playing, no matter how far out we got, those three or four notes would focus everybody and then we could go again. It was a cool concept."[37] By providing just the basic framework for tunes, recording sessions were essentially jams, with the musicians having to listen carefully to what everybody else was doing and react to whatever happened in the studio.

Sammy Figueroa remembers how Miles worked. "He didn't really have a form. He had an idea of how it would evolve but there wasn't much of a structure. He would hear something in his head and he would come into the studio and play a couple of notes on a piano. Then he'd say 'Let's play through this,' and we would start playing. He would point at people and say things like 'Don't play on this, play later.' He would go through the band, 'Okay, you play,' and he would orchestrate it. When he had finished he would say to you 'Remember what you did?' and I'd say 'Yes,' and he'd reply 'That's what I want you to do, no more, no less,' and he'd do that for every musician."

Tonkel notes that "Miles would come to the studio and work in the way his spirit moved him." But Macero recalls that Miles's working methods often left him with a lot of post-production work in the editing studio. "It was a big job trying to piece some of the stuff together and to figure out what the hell he was trying to do, and to make it coherent and consistent. He never had a score. He never had parts. There was nothing. He'd leave at the end of the day and all you had was what was on the tape – nothing to go by. You'd have a cue sheet and then he'd object to my making the numbers like 'take one, take two,' and so I said 'Fuck it, just keep on playing.' The tape machines were going constantly in the studio, so I had to get what I could get. Sometimes a little of that was very good and we'd use that and make a loop on that. I took bits and pieces and put them all together. To me it was a normal day in the editing room."

During the initial sessions, Miles relied heavily on a wah-wah pedal. In the 1970s, Miles had used the wah-wah as a means of extending the range and function of the trumpet. This was because Miles heard sounds in his head that were beyond the range of an acoustic instrument. He also wanted the trumpet to sound more like an electric guitar than a horn. But during *The Man With The Horn* sessions, the wah-wah was being used as a prop, a crutch to support Miles's weak lip and fragile confidence.

But soon, the wah-wah would go and Miles would revert to using a horn without any electronics. Miles says: "One day somebody hid my wah-wah – I think it was Sammy because he was always trying to get me to play without it. At first that fucked me up, but after I started playing without it for a while I was all right."[38] Figueroa confirms that it was indeed him who hid the wah-wah: "Miles was playing a wah-wah pedal and he sounded like shit. I said 'Miles, why are you using the wah-wah? Man, why don't you play straight?' He said 'Fuck you.'" When Miles went to the bathroom Figueroa hid the wah-wah behind a baffle (sound screen).

Figueroa takes up the story again. "So Miles returns and he says to me 'Where's my wah-wah?' and I say I don't know. He accuses me of hiding it so I say 'Miles, you do so much blow [drugs], you probably swallowed it,' and he goes, 'Yeah, right,' and all the time he's looking around for the wah-wah pedal. So I said 'Miles, why don't you just play?' and he did. He didn't sound that great, but started getting into it again and he started hitting the notes."

Once again, Macero's main role during the recording sessions appears to have been more on a technical level than a creative one. While Miles orchestrated the band, Macero worked with the engineer to record the music. Finnerty recalls one of the rare moments when Macero would make a suggestion. "At one point I was trying to work out a guitar part and Teo came into the room and said to Miles 'That was hip what Barry was doing – you should have him play that.' Miles looked at him incredulously and said 'YOU thought that was hip?' Then he looks at me and says 'DON'T play it!'"

In January and possibly February 1981, Miles recorded three tunes with The New York Band, "Aida," "Ursula" and "Back Seat Betty," all composed by Miles and named after women he knew. But before the recording sessions for *The Man With The Horn* were completed, Miles made yet another change to his band personnel. Mike Stern replaced Barry Finnerty, who had played guitar on all three tunes plus "Shout" from The Chicago Group sessions. The third band line-up on the album, The Fat Time Band, would see a marked improvement in Miles's performance and also inspire him to go back on the road, taking most of the band members with him.

The *Man With The Horn* sessions

The Chicago Group sessions: May–June 1980 / January 1981

"Shout" (5:53)

Composers	Randy Hall, Robert Irving III, Glenn Burris
Musicians	Miles, trumpet; Randy Hall, mini moog synthesizer; Robert Irving II, Yamaha CP30; Felton Crews, bass; Vince Wilburn Jr., drums; Bill Evans, soprano saxophone; Barry Finnerty, guitar; Sammy Figueroa, percussion
Producer	Teo Macero
Arrangers	Randy Hall, Robert Irving III, Glenn Burris
Engineer	Stanley Tonkel
Recorded	Backing track, probably May or June 1980; overdub session with Miles, Finnerty and Figueroa, January 1981, Columbia Studios, New York
Live performances	None

"Shout" is a disco-soul track clearly designed to get your feet tapping, and it is no accident that it is the most commercial track on the album – Miles wanted a wider exposure beyond the jazz world. With "Shout" he certainly got it. "Shout" was written by three members of The Chicago Group: Randy Hall, Robert Irving III and Glenn Burris. Hall and Irving had written much of the tune but Hall felt that something was missing. "Glenn had written a song with a little bridge that I liked and I said to Bobby 'Why don't we use it?'" says Hall. Burris was initially unhappy about his song being cannibalized in this manner, although the royalties and co-writer's credit probably helped to overcome any initial reservations that he might have had.

The original plan was to play the song's bass line on a mini moog synthesizer, but bassist Felton Crews had other ideas: "Being the bass player in the band I felt like I should have played on every tune, so as Randy and Bobby and Glenn were finishing the arrangement, I wrote out a bass line to fit the mini moog line. In the finished version the mini moog was gone and the bass guitar had prevailed again," says Crews.

The backing track was recorded with Irving on keyboards, Hall on mini moog, Crews on bass, Evans on soprano saxophone and Wilburn on drums. When Miles came to overdub the track in January 1981, he decided he wanted to use some other musicians to fatten the sound, so he brought in Barry Finnerty on guitar and Sammy Figueroa on percussion.

"Shout" starts with a funky jangling guitar lick played by Finnerty, with Figueroa copying the lick on his conga drums. Finnerty recalls the problems he had getting the guitar part that Miles wanted. "I remember Miles playing the track for me and saying 'Play dadaladaladalada!'" says Finnerty. "After determining the chord to be played, I asked 'Where do you want me to play it?' He just got more exasperated and demanded 'Just play dadaladaladalada!!' This went on for about fifteen minutes with me trying it in many different places in the measure and him saying 'NO, PLAY DADALADALADALADA!' before I finally got it where he wanted it: 1, 2, 3, 4, dadaladaladalada!" [Miles wanted Finnerty to play at the end of the bar, on the first sixteenth note after the fourth beat].

Miles plays open horn on the track, playing a repeated four-note motif followed by a sharp stab that sounds as if he's playing "Shout!" Hall thinks they called the tune "Shout" because "We wanted to shout to the world that Miles was back." Vince Wilburn Jr. plays in a straight-ahead style, occasionally using a syn drum. Crews's bass line – consisting of three slurred notes followed by some nimble fingerwork – is excellent and really drives the tune along. "Felton added a great bass whip," says Irving.

Bill Evans plays a soprano saxophone solo that lasts around a minute and half, but it is clearly an uncomfortable experience. The tenor sax was Evans's first-choice instrument and it shows, because on "Shout" he sounds shrill and at times struggles to reach some of the high notes. Evans is philosophical about Miles wanting him to play soprano sax: "I played tenor on his recordings later on. He just liked to hear my soprano at the time. After all, it was his band." At the end of Evans's solo, Miles enters again, playing the four-note motif until the fadeout. Listening to "Shout," it's easy to see what motivated Miles to record on it. Not only is the track highly commercial, but from a technical point of view it makes few demands on a trumpet player.

"Shout" was also remixed for a 12-inch single with remixes by DJ Jimmy Simpson. There are two remixes, one lasting 4:43 and the other 7:15. Although Miles plays the same horn on both remixes, Simpson made some changes to the bass and saxophone, as well as adding an electric piano. The remixes are funkier than the original, with Crews's bass line now augmented by some popped strings. Crews says that it isn't him playing on the remix. "It hurt me when I first heard it, but at least they kept my bass line in." Evans's solo is also longer, although it's not clear whether Simpson used a session player to extend it, or if he simply took it from an unedited take.

"Shout" is sequenced as the third track on *The Man With The Horn* and, after the opening two tracks featuring the New York-based musicians ("Fat Time" and "Back Seat Betty"), it comes as something of a surprise. Its inclusion on *The Man With The Horn* certainly raised the hackles of fans and critics alike. Many of them picked up on a comment made by Miles to writer Cheryl McCall: "Randy, my young nephew and Bobby, they all write great music for me. [When] I need a bubblegum song, I just call up Randy and say 'Randy send me a bubblegum song like "Shout".'"[39]

Hall laughs when he recalls this comment: "Miles was right, but that was what he wanted. We could have done stuff that was more in the vein of what he went on to do, but he wanted that crossover between something that could be played on regular radio and what he was. I really believe Miles wanted to be a pop star. I remember Miles calling me and thanking me because "Shout" had got to number one on one of the charts."

Miles had always had an ear for contemporary music, and around 1979–80 the airwaves were filled with the sound of disco music from acts such as Chic ("Le Freak," "Good Times"), Rick James ("Super Freak"), Sister Sledge ("We Are Family," "He's The Greatest Dancer") and Kool and the Gang ("Ladies' Night," "Celebration"). Even artists from the rock and pop worlds jumped aboard the disco bandwagon including Blondie ("Heart Of Glass"), Abba ("Dancing Queen") and Rod Stewart ("Do Ya Think I'm Sexy?"). So if Miles wanted to reach a wider audience and especially a black audience, then disco/funk music offered the best route.

Miles himself said: "As a musician and as an artist, I have always wanted to reach as many people as I could through my music. And I have never been ashamed of that. Because I never thought that the music called 'jazz' was ever meant to reach just a small group of people... I always thought it should reach as many people as it could, like so-called popular music, and why not? I never was one of those people who thought that less was better; the fewer who hear you, the better you are."[40]

It's easy to see why "Shout" left so many of Miles's fans feeling somewhat perplexed. The track is pure disco, contains no jazz elements and bears no relationship to the preceding music on the album. And while Miles's playing is surprisingly strong, it's also anonymous and could easily be mistaken for dozens of other players (and here Herb Albert's playing on the tune "Rise" comes to mind). But when one considers the music Miles played in the mid-1980s, with pop songs such as "Time After Time" and "Human Nature" becoming a core part of his repertoire, then recording "Shout" doesn't seem so incongruous. Irving was right, though: "Shout" was a leap too far, too soon, but it was a direction Miles would take just a few years down the road.

There's some confusion over when this track was recorded. Noted Miles discographers Jan Lohmann[41] and Enrico Merlin[42] put the recording date as May 1981, and even the Sony Master Series CD and the SACD versions of *The Man With The Horn* give the same date. Teo Macero's notes on the recording sessions add further confusion. Macero claims that the first sessions took place on August 2, 1980, but that this was followed up by new sessions with a new band on May 6, 1981 – three mixes were produced from the sessions.[43]

But there are several good reasons to suspect that "Shout" was recorded in May or June 1980. First, Irving recalls Miles calling him in late 1980 and playing over the backing track of "Shout." Second, Finnerty and Figueroa were brought in to overdub on "Shout" in January 1981. Finnerty would leave Miles's band around late February (see "Fat Time") so he could not have played on "Shout" if it had been recorded in May 1981.

What's more, in January 1981, Miles decided he wanted to change direction and move away from The Chicago Group sound, so why would he and Columbia Records then go to all the bother and expense of bringing the young musicians back from Chicago to record just one track – especially as Miles already had lots of similar-sounding material in the can? Macero's notes have to be treated with caution because, by August 1980, the group had left New York and returned to Chicago. What is more likely is that Macero's notes refer to editing or mixing sessions.

"The Man With The Horn" (6:36)

Composers	Randy Hall, Robert Irving III
Musicians	Miles, trumpet; Randy Hall, lead and background vocals, guitar, celsete, mini moog synthesizer; Robert Irving III, acoustic piano, Yamaha CP30; Felton Crews, bass; Vince Wilburn Jr., drums

Producer	Teo Macero
Arrangers	Randy Hall, Robert Irving III
Engineer	Stanley Tonkel
Recorded	Backing track, probably June 1980; Miles overdub, January 1981, Columbia Studios, New York
Live performances	None

If the presence of "Shout" was a surprise, then "The Man With The Horn" was something of a shock. Miles often liked to surprise his listeners and he certainly succeeded with the inclusion of this pop-soul ballad that even includes a vocalist. In fact, Miles had pulled a similar stunt on his 1967 album *Sorcerer* (which, incidentally, featured a photograph of Miles's future third wife Cicely Tyson on the cover). The album, which features six tracks from Miles's great 1960s quintet of Ron Carter, Herbie Hancock, Wayne Shorter and Tony Williams, ends with a tune whose presence on the album has perplexed Miles's fans to this day.

The track, "Nothing Like You," was recorded in 1962 and includes Miles, saxophonist Wayne Shorter, drummer Jimmy Cobb, bassist Paul Chambers and Bob Dorough on piano and vocals. The track was arranged by Gil Evans. "Nothing Like You" is a swinging number that includes a saccharine vocal from Dorough and lyrics straight out of the "moon in June" school of songwriting ("Never were lips so kissable, never were eyes so bright"), which make one wonder what Miles was doing recording it let alone putting it onto one of his albums. Some critics have made similar comments about "The Man With The Horn."

"The Man With The Horn" was the last track to be recorded by The Chicago Group and the idea for it came from Randy Hall, recalls Irving: "Randy initiated the idea one evening after our workshop session at Miles's home. We were nearing the end of our stay in New York and Randy felt that we needed to make a final contribution that would be special to Miles. He told me he had a great idea and sang the melody for the first line, 'Smooth, suave, debonair, describes a man so rare.' I found the chords on the keyboard and added the words, 'like fine wine he gets mellower with age ...' The song continued to write itself. After the song was written, we deliberated over the intro. We recorded it the next morning."

Hall picks up the story: "Miles really liked my voice, but I didn't think I would actually be singing on a Miles Davis record. Bobby and I wanted to compose a homage to Miles, so we sat down and wrote 'The Man With The Horn.'" Hall sings both lead and background vocals: "Angela Bofill was supposed to join us but for some reason it didn't happen, so I sang all the parts," says Hall.

"The Man With The Horn" has an atmospheric opening, with a sweeping synthesizer, piano, bass and swirling cymbals courtesy of Wilburn. A mention here should be made of Crews's fine understated bass playing on this track. Hall plays a lovely synthesizer patch, before starting to sing the first line.

As Hall sings, Miles can be heard playing beneath him, using a trumpet connected to a wah-wah pedal. Miles was using the wah-wah in a effort to hide the difficulties he was having in recovering his embouchure, but ironically, rather than masking his problems, the wah-wah seems to emphasize them.

The song's chorus simply consists of two repeated lines, "He's the man, he's the man with the horn, blow on, blow on," doubled-tracked by Hall. When Miles plays his solo (again using the wah-wah pedal), it is obvious that his chops are down. The solo is painful to listen to because Miles is clearly struggling to play many of the notes, occasionally battling to maintain pitch. What is more, the wah-wah makes Miles sound mournful. Yet, despite these technical flaws, Miles still manages to squeeze a lot of raw emotion out of his trumpet.

The song follows a basic verse–chorus–verse structure, with later lyrics talking about Miles "crying melodies for tears," and "masters never having to race." The final verse is different from the rest, with lyrics that directly address Miles and the chorus sung at the end of each line. During this section, Wilburn's bass drum becomes noticeably more prominent. The track then fades out.

Hall's vocal performance shows that indeed he does have a fine voice (just listen to how he sustains the note when he sings the word "tears") but he wasn't totally happy with his performance. "I wanted to do more vocals and when I sang the song I did it as a guide vocal. But Miles liked what he heard and that's what went down. Miles had a thing about doing something the first time. He would say 'When you do it the first time you should really try and do it because that might be it.'"

Marvin Gaye did a similar thing when recording the title track of his album *What's Going On*. Eli Fontaine is a saxophonist session player who had been booked by Gaye to play the opening section. As Fontaine was warming up to record, the studio tape machine was running. Fontaine played a few phrases to prepare himself and was then surprised to find that Gaye had decided that this was exactly what he wanted. Gaye thanked Fontaine for his efforts and then sent him home.[44]

Hall says Miles loved the tune and the fact that Miles made it the title track would seem to confirm this assessment. Irving adds: "It was a tribute to a living legend. Miles accepted it like he would have accepted a birthday card. I remember one critic who said that the lyrics were like an epithet. Miles was flattered that we thought of him in that way. It was not very often that he would receive accolades of this nature from anyone."

But although Miles, Irving and Hall liked the tune, most critics were not so generous in their assessment. Indeed, the title track probably received more critical flak than any other tune Miles played in his comeback years, with the possible exception of some of the music that appears on Miles's posthumous album *Doo-Bop*. Paul Tingen describes the title track as a "mediocre ballad played without much distinction and featuring embarrassing lyrics paying homage to Miles."[45]

Ian Carr adds: "The lyrics... are mediocre and the whole thing seems soft-centred except for Miles's contribution."[46] Others raised their eyebrows at Miles playing on what was effectively his own eulogy.[47] Don Puluse says that, while he likes *The Man With The Horn* album, "I was not sure how the title track fit with previous Miles albums." Some of these comments are rather harsh, because "The Man With The Horn" is a fine track, but there is no escaping the fact that it sounds wrong in the context of the rest of the album and Miles's musical progression.

Even so, Hall says Miles wanted to make this type of music in order to reach an audience beyond jazz. "I remember helping my father work on a house he owned in the Chicago ghetto and I went along to the store to buy something for him. On my way to the store I could hear 'The Man With The Horn' playing over a radio and I'm thinking, 'Wow, they're playing Miles in the ghetto.' That's what Miles wanted to do: he wanted to reach out to the black audience."

Hall and Irving were planning to perform "Shout" and "The Man With The Horn" with Miles at a concert in Chicago, but for some reason it never happened. However, Hall has performed the tune live, most notably with ESP2, a band formed by Irving, which included many members who played with Miles (namely Hall, Irving, drummer Ricky Wellman, percussionist Mino Cinelu and keyboardist Adam Holzman). The song was performed in Stuttgart, Germany, in July 1994 and released on DVD seven years later.[48] "That was the first time I performed the song live," recalls Hall. "I would have loved to have sung it live with Miles."

The New York Band sessions (January–March 1981)

"Aida" (8:13)

Composer	Miles Davis
Musicians	Miles, trumpet; Barry Finnerty, guitar; Bill Evans, soprano saxophone; Marcus Miller, bass; Al Foster, drums; Sammy Figueroa, percussion
Producer	Teo Macero
Arranger	Miles Davis
Engineer	Stanley Tonkel
Recorded	Probably January 1981, Columbia Studios, New York
Live performances	June 1981 – September 1982

"Aida" was the first track to be recorded by The New York Band and, for Marcus Miller, it was a baptism of fire. When Miller first arrived at the studio and saw Miles, he said: "I'm Marcus Miller." Miles replied, "I'm Miles" – and then walked out of the studio.[49] When Miles returned, Miller mentioned that he was Wynton Kelly's cousin, the pianist who played with Miles in 1959–63 – he's on the track "Freddie Freeloader" on the *Kind Of Blue* album. Miles didn't respond. "So I thought 'First wrong thing I said,'" says Miller. After playing for a short while, Miles then asked Miller if he had ever played with Kelly. When Miller told him that he was young when Kelly had died (Miller had been just eleven years old), Miles said "He was a genius. His touch, his touch."[50]

But Miles hadn't finished playing mind games with Miller, as the young bassist discovered when Miles demonstrated the part he wanted him to play on a tune. "He showed me a couple of notes on the piano," recalls Miller. "He said 'This is what we're going to play: F-sharp, G.' I'm going 'That's it?' and he says 'That's it. You got it?' I say 'I've got it: F-sharp, G – no problem.'"[51] When the band started playing, Miller stuck resolutely to his instructions, but then Miles stopped the band in the middle of the take and said to Miller, "Are you just going to play F-sharp and G and that's it?" Miller replied, "Oh, I'm sorry. I'm just doing what you told me; now I understand – it's loose."[52] The band then started to record another take. "So we play again," says Miller, "and this time I play F-sharp, G, E, A-flat, G-flat, E, Z! [laughs] I play every note I've got on my bass! And Miles stops the band again and says 'Man, what the hell are you doing? Just play F-sharp and G and then shut up.'"[53]

Miller didn't let himself get flustered by Miles's irrational behaviour, deciding that "He's just messing with me. It's cool, so let me just ignore him and make this music sound right to me. So I play and this time he lets the take go by." Miller also recalls that at the end of the take, when the band was waiting to hear his reaction, Miles said, "You're all playing like a bunch of faggots." "But on his way out he looks at me and gives me a wink and I think 'Okay, I made it through phase one!'"[54] The next day Miller went around to Miles's house to hang out and it was here that Miles asked him to join the band.

"Aida," named after Aida Chapman, a friend of Miles (she even gets a name check on the album sleeve), is a high-energy funk workout which starts with a rapid-fire bass intro by Miller, joined by Foster who plays a power-house combination of hard snare, bass drum and splashing cymbals. When you listen to the bass line on "Aida," it's soon clear that Miller decided to ignore Miles's instruction to stick rigidly to the F-sharp and G vamp and, in the opening minute alone, Miller is already popping strings, slurring notes and adding extra notes to the original two-note vamp.

Finnerty's playing consists of a series of subtle chords and voicings which increase the tension in the music. Miles enters playing a ten-note motif on open horn, which he repeats throughout the track, although occasionally switching to a higher key when doing so. Miles hadn't found his lip yet, but his trumpet playing sounds strong, and at times he even slides into the upper register. Evans gets to solo on soprano saxophone, but he sounds shrill and unfocused and, by the time the solo ends, Evans has run out of ideas.

Miles repeatedly plays the ten-note motif until the end of the track, although just as "Aida" is about to fade out, it becomes an eight-note motif. There is nothing particularly subtle about "Aida" but of all the tracks on *The Man With The Horn*, it is the one with the most power and energy – characteristics that were used to good effect when it was played live.

"Back Seat Betty" (11:17)

Composer	Miles Davis
Musicians	Miles, trumpet; Barry Finnerty, guitar; Marcus Miller, bass; Bill Evans, saxophone; Al Foster, drums; Sammy Figueroa, percussion
Producer	Teo Macero
Arranger	Miles Davis
Engineer	Stanley Tonkel
Recorded	Probably January 1981, Columbia Studios, New York
Live performances	October 1981 – March 1983

"Back Seat Betty" was named after Miles's second wife, the former model and singer Betty Mabry. The couple had met in early 1968, when Mabry was aged twenty-three and Miles was in his early forties. They married in September of that year. Betty was a strong, independent woman who wore a giant afro, hot pants and boots. As Miles observed: "Betty was a free spirit ... who was a rocker and a street woman...she was raunchy and all that kind of shit."[55] Miles was clearly beguiled by Mabry, putting her photograph on the cover of his new album *Filles De Kilimanjaro* and naming one of the tracks – "Mademoiselle Mabry" – after her.

Mabry is credited with introducing Miles to Jimi Hendrix and switching Miles from his sharp Italian-cut suits to way-out fashions of the 1960s. Miles said, "Betty was a big influence on my personal life...she was just ahead of her time."[56] Mabry also knew Sly Stone, whose sound would influence Miles's musical direction in the 1970s. Miles said, "The marriage only lasted about a year, but that year was full of new things and surprises and helped point the way to go, both in my music and, in some ways, my lifestyle."[57] Miles and Gil Evans arranged the track "You And I" (credited to Betty Davis and Miles) on her 1975 album *Nasty Girl*. Miles discographer Jan Lohmann says an unidentified trumpet player on the track could be Miles.[58]

It's rumoured that Betty Mabry had written her own song about Miles on her 1974 album *They Say I'm Different* (her name was Betty Davis on the album cover). The track "He Was A Big Freak" is about a lover who liked being beaten with a lavender whip and includes lyrics about tying up her lover and beating him as he begged for more. Miles always insisted that the song was about Hendrix rather than him. Whether this had influenced Miles's decision to give a rather unflattering title to the new track dedicated to Betty Mabry is unclear.

"Back Seat Betty" was in fact the third tune Miles named after his former wife and the second time he had used the same title. In 1976, Miles went into the studio several times and recorded with some of his regular band members, including drummer Al Foster, bassist Michael Henderson and guitarist Pete Cosey. Cosey recalls Miles recording a tune called "Back Seat Betty." "When *The Man With The Horn* came out, some of my friends told me that Miles had a track on the album called 'Back Seat Betty.' But when I heard the music I realized it wasn't the same tune as the one we had cut," recalls Cosey.

The 1976 track has appeared on the bootleg *Unknown Sessions Vol. 1*, where it's known as "Untitled Tune."[59] Cosey is certainly correct in his assessment: the two tunes are very different. While the first version of "Back Seat Betty" is an uptempo number, complete with a long funky clavinet solo, the tune on *The Man With The Horn* is a dark, mid-tempo rock-funk number with no keyboards.

"Back Seat Betty" starts with Finnerty playing a couple of power chords that are played through an effects unit that coarsens the sound. "That intro was made up on the spot," says Finnerty. "Miles just looked at me and said 'Play something.'" Miller and Foster then lock together in a slow-funk groove that hardly changes throughout the track. Thirty seconds into the track, Miles enters playing the theme on muted horn. When Finnerty plays the power chords again, Foster's swirling cymbals float underneath them.

"Occasionally Miles would point at me to play the part again. I believe there was no editing," says Finnerty, adding that "I often thought I should have asked for co-writer's credit on that one since the rest of the tune was basically a jam. The intro seemed to be the most significant thematic material in the tune." What is not in dispute is Finnerty's highly creative playing, which adds a rich variety of colours and textures to the sound.

Miles later switches to open horn, playing a series of high notes and sounding much stronger than on The Chicago Group recordings. Bill Evans solos adequately for several minutes and the slow-funk groove continues until the track begins to wind down (where one of the band members can be heard shouting "whoo!"). Ian Carr has pointed out that "Back Seat Betty" has a similar feel to "Miles Runs The Voodoo Down" on the album *Bitches Brew*[60] and, around the ten-minute mark, Miles comes close to playing the same theme before ending with a flurry of notes, just before the track fades out.

The unedited version of this take reveals that Macero edited out almost four minutes of music, most of it being removed from the section featuring Evans's solo. An alternate take of "Back Seat Betty" lasts for more than eighteen and a half minutes and there are some interesting differences between it and the released version. The alternate take is rockier and Finnerty's opening power chords are even more distorted, producing a dirtier, nastier sound. Foster plays a lot of open hi-hat, and during one of his power chord intervals Finnerty almost gets to solo, finishing off the chords with a fast run of notes that sound closer to Eddie van Halen than Wes Montgomery.

"Back Seat Betty" has a dark, cold, slightly menacing air about it and, while Macero made a good job in editing the material he had to hand, the track would have benefited by being shortened by several minutes. There just isn't enough going on to sustain the interest (it is the longest track on the album) and once the musicians have set up the groove there's little change in mood or tempo. Miles's music would often take listeners on a journey of highs and lows, twist and turns, and changing moods and colours, but when you listen to "Back Seat Betty" it's like travelling through a dark, flat, monochrome landscape.

"Ursula" (10:40)

Composer	Miles Davis
Musicians	Miles, trumpet; Barry Finnerty, guitar; Marcus Miller, bass; Bill Evans, saxophone; Al Foster, drums; Sammy Figueroa, percussion
Producer	Teo Macero
Arranger	Miles Davis
Engineer	Stanley Tonkel
Recorded	Probably January 1981, Columbia Studios, New York
Live performances	October 4, 1981?

If listeners were already feeling somewhat bemused by the eclectic mix of music found on *The Man With The Horn*, then they were about to be even more surprised by the final track. "Ursula," with its jazz-swing rhythm, takes Miles's music back to the early '60s. Marcus Miller plays a walking bass line and Foster plays in a straight-ahead bebop style, with the right hand setting up a pulse on the ride cymbal and the left hand playing a variety of patterns and accents on the snare and tom-toms. Miles had stopped playing this type of music more than twenty years earlier and quite why he decided to go back to it is not clear. Miles was better known for moving forward musically and his decision to look backwards for inspiration was a shock for many, although no doubt it was a pleasant surprise for fans of his older music.

"Ursula" is basically a jam and the kind of music Miles could play with his eyes shut. The track starts with Miller's bass line, and Miles enters almost immediately on muted horn, sounding strong. Foster and Miller really swing together. Foster's drumming sounds deceptively simple, but listen carefully and you can hear him playing a whole series of inventive patterns. Figueroa provides tasteful support on conga, but it's not until two and a half minutes into the track that we get to hear Finnerty.

Finnerty explains the reason for his late entry: "We had just gotten to the studio and I was putting new strings on my guitar. I was midway through tuning them up when I looked up and to my shock the red light was on! Miles was soloing! I put my ear to my guitar and tuned it up as best I could (they didn't have silent in-line tuners in those days) and kind of wormed my way in tentatively with some chords." At one point, there's a sharp switch in key and tempo and the track really swings, with Miller switching out of the walking bass line and Foster providing some tasteful rimshots.

Bill Evans solos on soprano saxophone and it's one of his best on the album, building up to an explosive pitch. But Evans wasn't finished yet, as Finnerty discovered. "Bill Evans soloed for quite a while, I thought, and then started to taper off his solo. Now, if you listen really closely to the track you can hear this. He had basically finished his solo, and you can hear me start to play what I thought was going to be mine [at 6:35]. But then, in what I still consider to be an unprecedented display of musical rudeness, he decided he wanted to play some more and started soloing again, effectively cutting me off. I was not pleased, but being the sensitive musician I am I didn't get into a war of notes with him."

At the conclusion of Evans's solo, Miles re-enters with Figueroa playing along with him, repeating Miles's phrases on his conga drums. The track continues to swing along until Miles starts repeatedly playing a phrase which signals that the track is starting to wind down. Finally, "Ursula" comes to a complete stop, although right after this Miles can be heard saying, "Yeah, play that Teo."

Two mysteries surround "Ursula." The first is whether Miles ever played this track live. In Japan, an album called *Miles! Miles! Miles!*[61] features a concert Miles played at Shinjuru Nishiguti-Hiroba on October 4, 1981, during his summer tour of the country. The album's second track, which lasts for just two minutes, is called "Ursula," yet sounds very different from the track on the album. First, Miller plays a funk-bass riff rather than a walking bass line and Foster's drumming has lost all its jazz characteristics, basically consisting of a simple bass drum/hi-hat drum pattern. Cinelu accompanies them on conga and bells, and Stern gently plays some sparse chords in the background. Miles's playing is also in a different style from that played on the album.

Miles's discographer Jan Lohmann says it doesn't sound like "Ursula" to him, and what's more, the track seems to be a one-off as Lohmann has no other record of it in any of the hundreds of Miles's concerts he has chronicled during the 1980s. The track title begs the question: who was "Ursula"?

According to Finnerty she was "A very fine German chick, a friend of Miles." Finnerty and Figueroa recall seeing her around the studio and Finnery remembers one incident that demonstrates Miles's dry sense of humour. "After the ['Ursula'] take, Teo came out into the room and asked 'What do you want to do now, Miles?' Miles looked at him, looked over at her, paused a moment for effect, and, in that trademark hoarse whisper of his, said 'Fuck.' And that was the end of the session!"

The Fat Time Band session (probably March 1981)

"Fat Time" (9:57)

Composer	Miles Davis
Musicians	Miles, trumpet; Mike Stern, guitar; Marcus Miller, bass; Bill Evans, saxophone; Al Foster, drums; Sammy Figueroa, percussion
Producer	Teo Macero
Arranger	Miles Davis
Engineer	Don Puluse
Recorded	March 1981,[62] Columbia Studios, New York
Live performances	August 1981 – March 1983

There was some drama behind "Fat Time," the last track that was planned to be recorded by The New York Band. As usual, Miles assembled the musicians at his home for a rehearsal, but on one particular day things were not going smoothly, as Miles explained: "The rehearsals went real good and everybody was playing what I wanted, except for Barry Finnerty when we were rehearsing the last track on the album … Barry is playing this shit I don't like on his guitar so I tell him not to play it, but he keeps playing it the way he wants."[63]

Miles told Finnerty to leave the room, play what he wanted to play and then return to play what Miles wanted. But when Finnerty returned, things had not improved, said Miles, mainly because Finnerty was "a very opinionated guy and doesn't like it when somebody tells him what to play. He comes back in after a while and we start all over again and he played the same thing, so I told him not to play anymore. I went into the kitchen and got a bottle of Heineken and poured the beer on his head."[64]

Finnerty sprang up from his chair, complaining that Miles could have electrocuted him. Miles replied, "Fuck that shit; I told you not to play that chord, motherfucker, and I mean *don't* play it and if you *got* to play it, then play it across the street like I told you."[65] But Finnerty insists that he was not being stubborn, and explains that the day had not started well for him. "I was in another studio recording a demo for my would-be new-wave rock-singer girlfriend when I got a call that Miles wanted to rehearse that day. I was feeling a bit pressured by my girlfriend and having to leave on short notice but of course I couldn't say no to Miles, so I went over to his house. The guys were there and Miles wanted to work on a groove he had in mind."

Miles demonstrated some chords to Finnerty, who recalls: "He tried to show me what to do by playing it on the piano and, despite what he says in his book, I tried to play it to the best of my ability. But it was unclear; he was not the best piano player, and it seemed to me every time I would try to duplicate what he was doing he would say 'No!' and play something completely different. I may have gotten a bit flustered, plus in the back of my mind was my girlfriend waiting at the other studio. Miles had a bottle of Heineken and he came and poured some of it on my head, and some went all over my prized '59 Les Paul. I got pissed off and went back to the other studio. But I didn't think the damage was irreparable (to our relationship, I mean; my axe was okay)."

Finnerty left, not knowing he would never play with Miles again. Bill Evans says the problem was down to personalities: "It's just human nature that some people get along and some people don't. Miles and Barry never really hit it off. No big argument or anything like that." But Finnerty says he and Miles did get on well together: "Me and Miles had got on fine except for that Heineken incident. We hung out on several occasions and laughed a lot as we put bad things up our nostrils. I believe he was hurt too over what happened, but since he was Miles he couldn't say anything to me."

Finnerty goes on to allude that the problem was more about him and Evans, describing one of several moments of friction between the two of them. "At one of the earlier sessions Miles had decided to try to record the tune that we had done years earlier at Julie Coryell's house ['Try This']. I found the tape and wrote out a cool melody; we rented an Arp Odyssey synth so we could jam off the same sample and hold sequencer groove (the synth would keep time and we would play to its beat).

"We were in CBS Studios and we were just starting to get it together when Bill Evans suddenly stood up and said 'This sounds like shit; I don't want to play this.' I was dumbfounded. 'What do you mean?' I said. 'Miles wants to do it.' 'Well, it sounds like shit; I don't want to do it.' I didn't know what to do; I couldn't think straight. I looked at Miles, who just shrugged his shoulders and said 'Well, let's play something else then.' If I had done anything else like if I had said 'So go home Bill,' Miles would have probably respected me more, and the tune would have been recorded."

Finnerty also recalls telling Evans about a possible conflict of interest between Miles and The Crusaders: "I had... made the mistake of telling Bill Evans that I didn't know what I was going to do about the gigs I had already committed to with The Crusaders that year, and I found out later that he had told Miles that I was going with them...effectively ensuring that I would be off the gig."[66]

With Finnerty now gone, Miles needed a new guitarist and once again he turned to Bill Evans for advice: "He trusted my judgement when it came to recommending musicians. I was his liaison with the outside jazz world at the time. I never recommended anyone he didn't like. I was on a roll, I was young and somewhat in tune with what was going on in the New York jazz scene at the time," recalls Evans. The guitarist Evans recommended was Mike Stern, who was born in 1953, studied at Berklee College of Music and had played with Blood, Sweat and Tears – he appeared on the album *Brand New Day*.

At the time, Stern was playing with the Billy Cobham band. "Bill [Evans] and I had played a couple of gigs together in Boston and I remember Bill telling me he was playing with Miles – I didn't believe him at that point!" says Stern. "One day Bill tells me that Miles is getting ready to go on the road and that if it didn't work out with Barry Finnerty – who's an excellent guitar player – he would recommend me to Miles. Bill said he felt like there was something between Barry and Miles. Anyway, I'm playing with Billy and Bill calls me up and says 'Guess who I'm bringing along!' I went 'Oh shit.'"

Miles and Evans turned up for the band's second set and Miles was so taken by Stern's playing that he called Cobham off the bandstand. "We're in the middle of a tune and suddenly there's no drummer," says Stern. "Miles had told Billy 'Tell your guitarist to show up at Studio B Columbia at six o'clock in a couple of days' time.'" Evans says that when you recommend a guitar player to Miles "You've got to think about what Miles wants to hear. He likes Jimi Hendrix and hot lines. A straight bebop guitarist wouldn't do it. Mike is a real good guy. He looks different, he thinks different and he plays different; he has a real good technique and can handle the bebop bridges where Miles swings. What else could you want?"[67]

With Stern, Miles got a new guitar sound, as jazz guitarist Jeff Richman notes: "Barry Finnerty did not have any solos on *The Man With The Horn*, so it's very hard to compare him with Stern in that regard. But Barry was playing a Les Paul guitar, which has a thicker, darker and smoother sound – his rhythms and voicings were especially rich and creative on 'Back Seat Betty.' Mike's [Fender] Telecaster was much brighter, thinner and more explosive. He played on only one tune, which happened to be the first track, and he produced a gloriously innovative guitar solo. It was also Miles's first album in five years, so Mike was in the right place at the right time for sure."

When Stern arrived at Columbia Studios, Miles asked him to play on top of a track that had already been recorded. Stern recalls: "I was kinda messing around but I didn't think the tune really needed it. I thought the tune was done and told Miles, who said 'Okay, that's cool.'" Stern also spent some time hanging at Miles's house with Evans and remembers how well Miles and Evans got along together: "They were just hysterical together. I remember Miles and Bill were discussing something and Miles says 'You're talking shit; I gotta change your channel,' and he pointed a TV remote control at Bill! It was nice hang, the vibe was good and everything was loose."

Stern recalls that the band didn't really rehearse "Fat Time." "He banged out a couple of chords on the piano and when we got to the studio he said to me 'Like Spanish, like Spanish.'" On another occasion Miles was trying to explain something to Stern: "He said 'We'll do this, we'll do that,' then he just said 'Fuck it, just play.' Bill came up to me and said 'Just play your ass off; don't even listen to Miles. He doesn't care as long as it comes out good.'"

Stern adds: 'We didn't really know what he was talking about. When we started playing in the studio, we just listened to each other." He says this wasn't too challenging for the band because the forms were simple and everyone followed Miles: "He had a way of playing that made it easy to follow. The melodies were so strong and sometimes he would show you what the next section was going to be. He wanted that looseness and that's what he got, but at the same time it was also clear."

The engineer on "Fat Time" was Don Puluse, who had joined Columbia Records in 1965 and had recorded many artists including Sly Stone, Chicago, The Mahavishnu Orchestra, Woody Shaw and Dexter Gordon. Puluse was originally brought in to mix the album, but found himself engineering the last track to be recorded for the album. "I felt uncomfortable doing this session because, as I recall, Stan had a session scheduled for [concert pianist] Glen Gould and expected Miles to be finished the day before. I actually used the set-up Stan had been using, so was literally sitting in for the recording. We used a large speaker as a monitor instead of headphones, which was placed in front of Miles." The arrangement caused lots of sound to leak from the mix Miles was listening to, an arrangement Puluse notes was not "The best for sound, but whatever makes the artist happy has to work."

"Fat Time" starts with Miller playing a bouncing bass line and Al Foster laying down a skipping drum pattern to create a groove that was apparently based on a New Orleans beat Miles had taught Foster. Miles enters on muted horn about a minute into the track and Stern begins to play sparse, delicate lines, sounding as if he's feeling his way into the tune. Soon after, Stern starts copying Miles's phrases.

Also around the one-minute mark, there's a shift in key and Foster begins playing a military-style drum pattern on the snare. The Spanish vibe Miles was looking for can also be clearly heard in his playing during this section. There is another switch in modulation and Miller's playing becomes funkier, with lots of popping and thumping on the strings of his Fender bass.

Bill Evans solos on soprano saxophone and it's his best one on the album. On The Chicago Group recordings, Evans's playing often sounds shrill and strained, but on "Fat Time" he plays excellently. As soon as Evans finishes his solo Stern immediately begins his, suggesting that either Miles pointed at

Stern to indicate he should start playing, or there is some sharp editing by Macero. Stern plays the only guitar solo on the album and it is a superb one, with lots of fast runs and explosive notes. Richman, who transcribed the solo for *Down Beat* magazine,[68] says: "[What] is especially interesting [is] Stern's use of bent notes that change the pitch." Richman also notes that at times Stern plays four-note descending-pattern triplets that are slightly delayed over the bar line, but still end up perfectly in time.

What is also worthy of note is the stirring support provided by the rhythm section of Foster and Miller – at times it's hard to believe that such a fat sound is being created by just guitar, drums and bass (if Figueroa is also playing at this point, his contribution is buried in the mix). Jimi Hendrix, of course, often played with the same line-up. "The thing I felt that was really cool was that Marcus and Al are just a phenomenal talent. Marcus is more of a funk player who can play all kinds of music and although Al played in Miles's [1970s] electric band, he's really more of a bebop player. The two of them playing together was beautiful," says Stern.

Stern's guitar playing sounds rough and raw and that is definitely what Miles wanted, Stern says. Even so, Stern was not entirely pleased with his performance: "I thought the track we cut was an out-take. I didn't have my amp set right and I was real depressed by the solo, but Miles really dug it."[69] Stern adds, "I said to Miles 'Miles, are we going to do another take? That was a little rough around the edges,' but Miles said somebody had once told him that 'When you're at a party, you've gotta know when to leave.' I love that line. Miles had a sense for that."

After Stern's solo, Miles re-enters and immediately brings everything down. In fact, at one point, the sound level is so low you can even hear Miller's fingers scratching the strings on the fret board. It's at this point that the tune seems to be heading towards its conclusion, but Miles isn't finished yet and Stern starts playing a riff that increases the tension.

Miller begins thumping his bass and then there follows the most dramatic moment in the whole recording when Miles enters on open trumpet and Foster immediately switches to open hi-hat. The music shifts again, with Stern repeating the riff he played earlier and Miller's thumping bass line again building up the tension (Macero had looped this section to extend the ending). Finally, there is a loud blast of trumpet and the track ends. Well not quite, because listen carefully and you can hear Miles's raspy voice saying, "Try that."

Of all the music Miles produced during *The Man With The Horn* sessions, "Fat Time" is the most successful piece. Although it is still essentially a jam, "Fat Time" sounds more focused and more coherent than the rest of the music on the album. For the first time, you get a true feeling of a band playing together and there is clearly a strong chemistry between the musicians.

Miles was so pleased with Stern's contribution that he named the track after him. At the time, Stern weighed around sixty pounds more than he does today and Miles would often greet him with the expression "S'happenin' Fat Time?" Stern recalls, "Bill Evans called me and said 'He's gonna call that tune "Fat Time" – you got a tune named after you.' I was thrilled."[70] Stern returned the compliment on his 1989 album *Jigsaw* on a track called "Chief" – the name many band members called Miles.

But if "Fat Time" was a happy experience for Stern, it was a crushing blow for Finnerty, who recalls: "Bill Evans was in charge of calling the guys and telling them about what was happening with sessions, rehearsals and so on. After the Heineken rehearsal, I called him quite a few times and he kept telling me 'I haven't heard anything yet. I don't know what's happening.' Then, about six to eight weeks later, he called me up. 'Hey man, I got a copy of the record. Come over and hear it; you sound great on it.' I went over and to my surprise Mike Stern was also there. That was when I found out that he had done the other tune ['Fat Time'], and that he had gotten the only guitar solo on the record." After recording "Fat Time," Miles knew he had the nucleus of an excellent touring band and everyone involved in the recording (with the exception of Figueroa) would go on the road with Miles for the next two years. The word was out: Miles was coming back. The world was eagerly awaiting the return of Miles and the release of his first album of new material for more than five years. When *The Man With The Horn* finally arrived, the reaction of both fans and critics would show, yet again, that wherever Miles went musically, controversy was not far behind.

The Man With The Horn: the verdict

The Man With The Horn album was released in autumn 1981, with a curious cover featuring a metallic dummy's head placed next to a mirror. It is a mysterious and slightly menacing image. *The Man With The Horn* may have been eagerly awaited by fans and critics (not to mention Columbia Records' executives), but its reception was somewhat lukewarm. Typical was the reaction of *Down Beat* magazine, which buried its review in the middle of its new releases section. Reviewer W. A. Bower awarded Miles's new album three stars – a 'good' rating. Bower said, "Let's get this out of the way. This record gets three stars because it's Miles Davis."[71]

Bower added that, while most artists would be happy to be rated as good, it wasn't sufficient for an artist such as Miles Davis. "Whether he likes it or not," Bower declared, "Miles Davis carries the weight – burden if he chooses to see it that way – of his past achievements." Bower's verdict was that "This record – parts of it – are pleasant. That's all. No more."[72] Miles noted that "Although the record sold well, the critics universally didn't like the music. They said my playing sounded weak and that I was 'only a shadow of my former self,' but I knew it was going to take a while to get my chops together."[73]

With Miles emerging after such a long play-off, his confidence low, his technique shattered by lack of practice and his mind affected by drugs, it's not surprising *The Man With The Horn* is one of the most perplexing albums of his comeback years. Perplexing because it's an album where the parts are greater than the sum. Individually, some of the music works well, but collectively the album is a confusing (and confounding) mixture of musical styles that often conflict with each other. The fact that the album has three different bands also adds to the lack of coherence and consistency in the music.

However, "Fat Time" shows that, even with half a musical idea, Miles could still produce music that sounds fresh and engaging. For all its simplicity, "Aida" has an energy and a vitality all of its own, and while "Back Seat Betty" is over-long, it has its moments of interest. These tracks were a product of Miles's creative talents and inspiration, his band's ability to create music from so little structure and direction, and Macero's post-production skills in the editing suite.

It is the tunes from The Chicago Group that cause the biggest difficulties and that is simply because they are the right tunes on the wrong album. "Shout" is a catchy disco number and "The Man With The Horn" has a strong melody and Hall is an excellent singer. One has to concur with Hall's observation that "Miles should have made two albums – one with our band and the other with his second band."

It is worth remembering that barely three years after the release of *The Man With The Horn*, Miles would record and perform pop tunes by artists such as Michael Jackson, Tina Turner, Toto and Cyndi Lauper, some of which would be played live right up to his final concert. By including the two Chicago Group tunes, it could be argued that (yet again) Miles was simply ahead of both his fans and critics.

Some critics have suggested that Miles included the two Chicago Group selections as an act of gratitude or generosity to the young musicians,[74] but this is only part of the story. There's no doubt that Miles was grateful to The Chicago Group for awakening his interest in music, but if that was merely the case, why not simply use just one of their tracks on the album? Miles also wanted to showcase the talents of the four young Chicago players and in this respect he was successful, because all of them benefited enormously by their association with Miles (see below). Last but not least, Miles also loved the music he made with the young musicians.

As Wilburn puts it: "Miles didn't have to put 'The Man With The Horn' and 'Shout' on his album – nobody put a shotgun to his head. Miles heard what he heard. It wasn't about nepotism – it was about the music. Miles could have said to George Butler at any time 'Fuck it' if he wanted to do something else. Miles believed in us and we believed in ourselves." Glenn Burris says: "*The Man With The Horn* could have been a classic if they had marketed it right. If they had pushed the title track it could have reached the masses. I don't see that as bubblegum at all; I think it's a great song."

Those who criticize Miles should remember that he also wanted to sound contemporary, garner airplay and reach a wider audience and, once again, this strategy worked. But the price Miles paid for this was an album that as individual tracks works well, but which collectively is too diverse, too diffuse and – for some listeners – too pop-oriented.

Those who participated in the album project have fond memories, even the young Chicagoan musicians who had expected Miles to release an album's worth of their material. "I was a little disappointed," admits Crews, "but the album turned out to a good mix after all. I just wished we could have done some of our free-form jam tunes also. I didn't hear much criticism and I didn't mind because I felt that at least I was in the larger arena and was being judged by the masses as opposed to have never being heard at all. *The Man With The Horn* was a great introduction to the music industry for all of us and it was a proud moment knowing that we were helping to launch a new era for one of the greatest talents in the music world."

Irving says: "I remember being fascinated by the raw energy of the performance and the subtleties of the arrangement in the way Miles cued and changed with one note. 'Aida' was my favourite. The experience with Miles was like a high and that was starting to wear off. The exposure was life-changing, but it was over for now." Irving adds that the fact that Miles did not use a keyboard player for the remaining tracks nor take one on the road gave him hope that Miles might be leaving the chair free for him. Irving went back to Chicago and worked with Ramsey Lewis, playing on several of his albums. Later on, Irving would focus on production work. Hall was headhunted by the soul/funk/R&B group Pleasure, and became the band's lead singer: "They had a deal with RCA and later on I would get my own solo deal with the label. I had so many opportunities as a result of working with Miles," he says.

Miles may have decided to switch musical direction, but all of The Chicago Group would play with Miles again at a future date. Irving joined Miles's band in 1983, staying for five years and becoming Miles's musical director. Irving also helped produce two later albums, *Decoy* and *You're Under Arrest*. Wilburn was just happy to see his uncle making music again. After playing with Miles, Wilburn went on to play with the soul/funk group Cameo and, later on, would spend time on the road working as Miles's assistant. He also helped produce *Decoy* and *You're Under Arrest*, and joined Miles's band in 1985, staying in the drummer's chair for two years.

Crews joined Miles's band in 1986, staying for nine months, and worked with Miles on the movie soundtrack *Street Smart*. Crews also co-wrote a song with Miles for a project for Mick Jagger. The song, "I'm Coming Back To You," had a similar groove to The Rolling Stones' song "Miss You," although business issues meant that the song was never recorded. Hall would co-produce a new Miles album in 1985, although at the time of writing this is still unreleased. Burris played on the sessions.

Barry Finnerty has bitter-sweet memories of the making of *The Man With The Horn*: "At least I'm on it. But it would have been nice to have had a solo and recorded the tune Miles and I wrote." Sammy Figueroa returned to the New York session scene and remained an in-demand player. He kept in touch with Miles and recalls sitting in on some live performances.

Bill Evans, Mike Stern, Marcus Miller and Al Foster would go on to tour with Miles, staying together as a band for more than two years. Miller says: "On *The Man With The Horn* I like 'Aida' and 'Fat Time.' I really like the way those things came out because you can hear everybody introducing themselves to each other with their instruments and I like that."

When asked about his thoughts on *The Man With The Horn*, Evans says, "In general I like the record. I have a lot of great memories from this time in my life." His message to the critics is simple: "This was Miles's comeback. The world was lucky he was playing."

7 *we want miles* (76:43)

Columbia 469402 2

Recorded	June–October 1981
Producer	Teo Macero
Executive producer	George Butler
Engineers	Bud Graham, Don Puluse, Hank Altman, Ted Brosnan
Released	Summer 1982
Tracks	"Jean-Pierre," "Back Seat Betty," "Fast Track," "Jean-Pierre," "My Man's Gone Now," "Kix"

"Within each breath, each note, it was magical." *Mino Cinelu, percussionist*

Background to the album

In spring 1981, Miles felt ready to go back on the road. It was six years since Miles's last appearance on a stage with his own band and, while his chops were down, his spirits were up because he knew he had the basis of a superb touring band. He told his manager Mark Rothbaum to contact Boston-based promoter Freddie Taylor, who booked four nights (June 26-29 inclusive) at a small club in Boston called Kix. Rothbaum also contacted George Wein, who had been promoting jazz acts at the Newport Jazz Festival since 1964. Wein booked Miles for two shows at the Kool Jazz Festival, taking place at Avery Fisher Hall in New York's Lincoln Centre on July 5. Later that year, Miles went on a seven-concert tour to Japan, playing concerts in Tokyo, Osaka, Nagoya and Fukuoka from 2-10 October.[1] Recordings taken from these engagements would be used to produce *We Want Miles*. The gigs would also do much to boost Miles's bank balance. Miles said he got $60,000 for the Kix gigs ($15,000 per night), "around $90,000" for the Avery Fisher Hall concerts and $700,000 plus travel and accommodation expenses for the Japan tour.[2]

But before Miles embarked on his comeback tour he needed to find a new band member. "I liked the way we were playing together, but I felt I needed another kind of percussionist," said Miles,[3] without elaborating. Sammy Figueroa, who had played percussion on *The Man With The Horn* album, says the problem was that he had too many session commitments and so couldn't go on tour. Whatever the reason, Miles found the percussionist he needed by sheer chance.

Mino Cinelu was born in Martinique, but raised in Paris. Cinelu grew up influenced by the sound of Jimi Hendrix and Miles, and learned to play guitar, drums and percussion. "I heard *Kind Of Blue* and *On The Corner. Bitches Brew* was a memorable album for me," he says. In the late 1970s, Cinelu moved to New York with the ambition of making a living as a professional musician. He also had a premonition: "I always felt that if Miles saw me we would play together. I don't know why and at the time I didn't know how to contact Miles. I didn't have his address or anything."

In 1981 Cinelu was playing in an R&B combo called The Frank and Cindy Jordan Band. The band – which played music in the style of Ashford and Simpson – had been playing gigs around Queens and New Jersey, with Cinelu on drums. But just before they were due to play at Mikell's, a club located close to Harlem, Cinelu asked if he could switch to percussion: "I wanted to get back to playing percussion, so it was just by luck that when Miles saw me he wanted a percussionist," says Cinelu.

Mikell's was owned by two friends of Miles, Mike and Pat Mikell, and, on the night Cinelu played, Miles was sitting in the front row of the audience. "I didn't recognize him. At the time his health was not great," recalls Cinelu. Miles was watching Cinelu intently. "He was staring, not at me but through me, but I felt very relaxed and I guess that's what appealed to him. Our eyes met a couple of times and I wonder how I would have reacted if I had known it was him," he adds. Even so, Cinelu had a feeling that this was no ordinary night because "The musicians were all playing for longer than usual."

When the set was over, Cinelu stepped off the stage and walked past Miles who grabbed his arm and said "You're a motherfucker." Cinelu thanked Miles for the compliment and then pulled Miles's hand off his arm before walking away. Then Mike Mikell said to Cinelu: "Do you know who that was?" When Cinelu shook his head, Mikell told him the identity of the mystery admirer. "I said 'Oh shit' and I went back and told Miles it was a pleasure to meet him, but Miles ignored the small talk and asked me for my number."

A short while later Miles called Cinelu at home: "He said 'Come to the studio, you motherfucker' and then hung up," recalls Cinelu. "I was living in New Jersey at the time and I didn't have his address so I had no idea where to go or how to contact Miles." A short while later, the phone rang again. "This time a guy says 'Hello, I'm Bill Evans.'" Cinelu immediately thought it was Bill Evans, the pianist who had played with Miles on *Kind Of Blue*, and so began saying how much he admired his work. "Then he said, 'No, no. I'm a saxophone player,' and I thought 'That's the second time I've goofed!'" laughs Cinelu.

Evans gave Cinelu Miles's address and he set off to meet him. When Cinelu arrived at Miles's home, the door was answered by Mike Stern. Cinelu, who at this stage was simply expecting to talk things over with Miles, was surprised when Miles suggested that they play something together. "I didn't have any equipment, so I looked around his house and found a cymbal, a drum and some sticks – that was enough for me." Cinelu then joined in a jam session with Miles and Stern. Miles was impressed. "He told me I could swing on a cup," recalls Cinelu.

It was during this time that Miles was reunited with two of his old road crew, Jim Rose and Chris Murphy. During Miles's layoff, the two men had been doing various jobs and, at the time Miles contacted them again, both were driving taxis – Rose first heard about Miles's comeback plans from a chance remark by a passenger. Miles was very happy to see the return of Rose and Murphy. "When I saw those guys – both with long hair – I just hugged them. I was so glad they had come back," he said.[4] Murphy also recalls how pleased Miles was to see them again. When he and Rose first went to see Miles at his home, Miles stood between them, put his arms over their shoulders and then lifted his feet off the floor so that they were carrying him in mid-air. At the same time, Miles laughed out loud, telling the assembled band members "Now I'm ready! Now I'm ready!"[5]

Rose and Murphy then set about buying new horns for Miles, recruiting new sound and lighting specialists and developing a wireless amplification system for Miles to use on-stage. This latter development would transform the way Miles played live. Now he was no longer constrained by having to stand in front of a microphone, but could wander around the stage (and even off-stage) without losing contact with the PA system.

But while the preparations for the technical aspects of the shows were painstakingly thorough, the band rehearsals were a much looser affair. The rehearsals took place at Miles's home on West 77th Street and Miles's attitude and approach to the concert preparations were both surprising – and somewhat disconcerting – for his young band members. "It was very informal. We didn't know what the hell was going on and I don't think Miles did and that was part of the thing that I really dug about him. When he was starting a new band he was searching and he had a vague idea of where he wanted to go," says Stern.

The rehearsals, which were more like jam sessions, were used more for exploration and experimentation than for the crafting of a concert set. "A lot of the time he would just sit for a while and let us play stuff and try a couple of different things. It didn't have it completely together when we started playing. Some of us were like 'What the fuck! He's got a couple of power chords here and then what?' He wanted that looseness and he had a kind of idea about the attitude he wanted the music to sound like and a few structural things. It certainly wasn't all written out. There were no notes on paper so he kept it really open," adds Stern.

This lack of preparation made the band increasingly anxious. Bill Evans told writer Ian Carr that "We never really went over tunes from beginning to end. We were just having a barbecue and hanging out ... there was no real rehearsal and he says 'Okay, well that's good enough ... we'll go to the gig.' We were petrified. We were all on the phone saying 'It's all over. His career's over. Our career's are over. It's never going to work.'"[6]

Stern felt especially anxious when he heard about Miles's plans for the band line-up. "I was nervous enough about Miles. Miles said 'Let's go on the road,' and I said 'Great. Who's going to play keyboards?' And he said 'No keyboards, just you.' I said 'Miles, are you sure?' and he said 'Don't worry about it, I'll hear it.'" Stern knew that Miles wanted an open sound and in fact Stern had worked in line-ups with saxophonist Jerry Bergonzi and trumpeter Tiger Okoshi that played without a keyboard player. But as Stern explains: "It wasn't like brand new, but with Miles it was a whole different ball game. But it worked out great."

Miles's return to the music world was a major event that received headline news coverage around the world. The Avery Fisher Hall concerts, which were part of the Kool Jazz Festival, received unprecedented levels of publicity in the press, radio and television. "I knew things were cooking when I heard Bill Cosby one night on *The Johnny Carson Show* talking about the buzz in New York over Miles's comeback," says Murphy. "This air of anticipation put an awful lot of pressure on the young guys – especially Mike Stern, who was insecure to begin with. No one wanted to let Miles down. It was wonderful to see how Miles responded to this, praising the players, acting fatherly and reassuring them that he was happy to have them with him."[7]

"The whole thing was overwhelming because it was Miles Davis and you couldn't help but think 'Man, all these [Miles] records we've listened to and what are we going to do?' It felt like pressure but Miles was great and didn't buy into that. He said 'We're just going to go out and have fun and we're going to play some good music,'" says Stern. Promoter George Wein certainly appreciated the publicity that Miles's comeback shows generated. "The major event of the 1981 Kool Jazz Festival – New York ... was the reappearance of Miles Davis after a five-year hiatus. Largely as a result, the press surrounding the festival was magnificent."[8]

In early June, Miles sat in on the Mel Lewis Big Band at the Village Vanguard in New York. He played for less than ten minutes and was perhaps using the occasion to steel himself for the comeback concerts. At the end of June, Murphy drove the equipment truck from New York to Boston for the gigs at Kix, while the band flew. But Miles decided to celebrate his return by buying a canary-yellow Ferrari and sharing the drive to Boston with Rose.

The band was booked into a Holiday Inn Hotel, which was close to the club, but Miles insisted on driving to the club every night. "[I] could have just walked across the street every night. A little showbiz don't hurt sometimes," said Miles.[9]

According to Murphy, Kix was a "medium-sized and rather dingy" club.[10]

The club held a little over 400 seats and the band was scheduled to play two short concerts a night, of around an hour each in duration.[11] The tickets cost $12.50 each.

Although this was the band's first outing, the musicians greatly enjoyed playing at the venue. "Kix was perfect and the audience was just ready to enjoy it and they did! It was the kind of band where we got off on the energy of it," says Stern. "It was great. Herbie [Hancock], Quincy [Jones], Richard Pryor were all there. Everybody was there, artists from all over," recalls Cinelu. Miles's partner (and future wife) Cicely Tyson also attended the concerts.

George Butler recalls travelling to Boston for the first night. "When I approached the area near the club, there were lines of people around the block and I thought they were waiting to get into a movie (there was a movie theatre close by), but then I realized – they were hoping to see Miles. Wayne Shorter, Ron Carter and Herbie Hancock were playing close by at the Berklee School of Music [sic], and as soon as they heard Miles was playing at Kix they finished their show real fast and got over to the club. When Miles heard they were in the audience, he called them up on to the stage and everybody went wild!"

"Kix was some of the best nights. It was a very small club and we had that contact with the people – they were so close. At the time Miles wanted me to be right next to him on stage. He'd look at me and say 'Play "Mino".' And I'd do percussion solo every night. It was incredible. Plus we were really all carrying Miles, helping him, because his health wasn't too good at the time," adds Cinelu. Bill Evans recalls that Miles would often stay in bed after the concerts, weak with pneumonia or some other ailment. Miles would say to his young band, "Thanks for pulling me through, guys."[12]

Miles recalls the reaction when people realized he was going to turn up and play. "Man, people were crying when they saw me and crying when I played. It was something."[13] Chris Murphy noticed a change in Miles's on-stage persona. In the 1970s, Miles had been aloof, often standing with his back to the audience and failing to acknowledge their applause. "That pose was all gone now. In its place was something unexpected: Miles was actually reaching out to his audience, as if seeking their approval... This was a whole new Miles, playful and warm," he says.[14]

Miles recalled a dramatic moment when he played a blues solo to a man with cerebral palsy, who was sitting in the front row in a wheelchair. "Halfway through my solo, I looked into this guy's eyes and he was crying. He reached up his withered arm, which was trembling, and with his shaking hand touched my trumpet as if he was blessing it – and me. Man, I almost lost it right then and there, almost broke down myself and cried."[15]

Miles held the man's hand while playing a one-handed solo for three minutes and Miles was so moved by the incident that after the show he went out looking for the man, but he had gone. "I wanted to thank him for what he had done because it meant a lot to me, coming back to play after all I had gone through. It was almost like he was telling me everything was all right and that my playing was as beautiful and strong as ever. I needed that, needed it right at that moment to go on," said Miles.[16]

How long Miles would go on was a question that Columbia Records' executives asked themselves, and after Miles's aborted comebacks in the late 1970s the record company was taking no chances. A mobile recording truck was dispatched to Kix to record all the rehearsals plus each concert. Chris Murphy also recalls the concerts being recorded on video, but at the time of writing none of this footage has emerged into the public domain.[17]

Miles's repertoire at Kix consisted of four tunes, although the band usually played a medley of just three during each set. Two tunes, "Back Seat Betty" and "Fast Track" (the new name for "Aida"), were from *The Man With The Horn*, but the two others were not. One was a new song, "Kix," but the other harked back to the late 1950s when Miles worked with Gil Evans. The track "My Man's Gone Now" was a radical reworking of the tune he had recorded with Gil Evans in 1958 for the *Porgy And Bess* album. It was a classic example of how Miles could both delight and totally wrong-foot his audience at the same time.

Stern was thrilled to be playing with the band's rhythm section. "I thought that was a fantastic band and a very interesting one. Miles used to let his instincts guide him and not second-guess stuff too much. He dug Marcus, he dug Al, even though they were coming from very different worlds. Marcus was more of a funk bass player and Al is a bebop drummer. He knew that stuff would work because they're fantastic musicians and play in their own way. What was so interesting and so fresh was that rhythm section. It had a vibe right away. Al didn't have a big kit. I just knew that whatever the fuck those guys did it would be great for me and it was. It was real loose." "Miles chose us all for a specific reason. He knew how we would all play together," adds Cinelu.

Writer and critic Bob Blumenthal says that on the bandstand Miles treated Stern like an affectionate child, showed benign indifference to Evans, wary approval of Cinelu and casual respect for Miller – while always keeping one eye on Foster.[18] Stern soon learned how Miles's mind worked. "What's funny about Miles was that as soon as something got too tight or too predictable, like he's heard it two nights in a row and it sounds like an arrangement, he'd throw a curve so that he'd change stuff. He didn't want it to be too arranged until later on when he got into the band with more keyboards."

Stern's own role proved highly controversial to some critics, as he mixed rock chords with bebop licks and the blues. "He wanted me to turn up like Hendrix. When he said Hendrix he didn't mean literally Hendrix, but that vibe, that attitude. Miles was always after attitude rather than specific things like 'the bass player plays this and the drummer plays this,'" says Stern. "He wanted a little bit of that but he wanted more of an attitude than anything and if he was getting that he didn't say much. He wanted the cats to feel like they could jam, they could just play and so solos were stretched out. He didn't say much about comping, so it was real loose. Sometimes the band wasn't as good as other times and other times it was just great because there was room for all kinds of things to happen."

Miles was weak and sick; yet, despite his poor physical shape and the long absence from playing the horn, he still managed to make an impact, even though at times it was obvious that he was still undergoing the process of regaining his tone, range, control – and confidence. Teo Macero supervised the Kix recordings and recalls that "It was a helluva mess. It was the first time Miles had played again. I just took everything for what it was. I said 'Okay, we're just going to record it all and get the best sound we can when we're doing it and then later on I'll have a go at seeing what the hell is going on.'" In fact, the band gelled together at Kix and the intimate club atmosphere was so stimulating that some of Miles's best comeback performances occurred here. It is no coincidence that the performances from Kix dominate *We Want Miles*.

On July 5, Miles played two sets at the Avery Fisher Hall. Although Miles had by now played a string of concerts at Kix, the New York concerts were seen as the official comeback event and there was an air of great excitement, anticipation and expectation. The audience was packed with the world's press and jazz critics, as well as a phalanx of artists and celebrities including Bill Cosby, Carlos Santana, Roberta Flack and Cicely Tyson. Writer Quincy Troupe, who attended the concert, reports that those present included Mick Jagger, Dustin Hoffman, Clint Eastwood, Elizabeth Taylor, Woody Allen, Max Roach, Clark Terry, Jackie McLean, Ornette Coleman, Jack DeJohnette, Sonny Rollins, Art Blakey and Dizzy Gillespie.[19] Even Miles felt the pressure of the occasion, telling jazz critic Leonard Feather, "I get butterflies in my stomach before every concert. I can't eat the day before and I really suffer."[20]

Once again, Columbia Records had a mobile recording unit in place, with engineer Don Puluse supervising the recording. "Live albums were usually recorded from a truck, [although] sometimes the CBS guys would set-up a remote in a room in the hall and run a snake [cable] to the stage. I believe that this was the latter situation for these concerts," says Puluse. "Except for final microphone placement, I would not spend much time in the hall, but at the mixing console. I do remember that we had a few of Teo's old reverb tape machines running for effects. Usually we got our sounds and levels together on the first tune of the show."

The start of the first concert was shambolic as the theatre announcer told the audience there would be a delay. There wasn't, and as Miles and his band came on to the stage, half of the audience was milling around in the foyer. Miles was dressed in military-style trousers, a singlet and cap (as shown on the cover of *We Want Miles*) and the band played three numbers, "Back Seat Betty," "Kix" and "Aida." The concert lasted a little over an hour and there was no encore, which prompted some of the audience to boo. The second concert was around twenty minutes longer thanks to the addition of "My Man's Gone Now."

The band's experience at Avery Fisher Hall was not as happy as it had been at Kix. The pressure of the occasion certainly played a part, but so did the venue itself, says Stern: "Avery Fisher Hall is a lousy place to play for electric music – we should never have been playing there at all. It's more geared for strings and orchestra and you can hear the soft things. Otherwise most of the things get lost and it just sounds like a wash. I like to avoid that place whenever possible because it's too live and you can't really feel the kind of music Miles was playing. It's fantastic for acoustic but not for electric. It was a much more difficult situation and more hyped and we were in a kinda hoity-toity kind of venue." Only one track, the opening number of the first concert, "Back Seat Betty," would be included on *We Want Miles* and even this was edited to less than half of its original length.

Reviews for the Avery Fisher Hall concerts were mixed and, while some comments were made about Miles's shaky chops, most of the critics' ire was directed at the band members and in particular Mike Stern, whose loud Fender Stratocaster, long hair and casual attire of tee-shirt and jeans upset many of the jazz *cognoscenti*. Critic Robert Palmer complained that Stern's solos were rife with the most banal of rock clichés.[21] Chris Murphy recalls a review in the *Village Voice* which included a cartoon depicting the band members as Voodoo dolls – with numerous pins stuck into those caricaturing Stern and Cinelu. Murphy adds that Stern was crushed by this review.[22] Stern says he could understand some of the critical reaction. "Some of the first gigs were so hyped and so publicized. We had played a couple of gigs at Kix that were perfect for that band. Then suddenly we're thrust into this other situation. And also critics are like a feeding frenzy – some of them hadn't even been to the gig but read about it somewhere else."

Even so, the comments hurt and threatened to undermine the confidence of Miles's young band members. Chris Murphy recalls seeing Stern close to tears after reading one review and Miles hugging Stern and telling him that he was playing exactly how Miles wanted to hear.[23] Miles would ask his band members who were they going to believe – him or someone who wrote for a newspaper? The bond between the band members was strong and Miles had a sensitive, protective side to his character that was not often glimpsed in public. Miller told writer Sam Freedman, "The Miles the band knows, no one else has ever known. The person is closer, I think, to the real person behind all the stories." Miller recalled how he had spoken to Miles on the phone, telling him that he was feeling uptight about his playing and a little insecure. Miles told him that he had had a similar experience when playing with Charlie Parker. "It meant so much just to see everybody, even Miles, goes through those insecurities," added Miller.[24]

Less than two weeks after the Avery Fisher Hall concerts, Miles played at New York's Savoy Theatre on 44th Street. Miles was booked for two shows at the Savoy and the Savoy's chief audio engineer Ron Lorman was asked by Rose to be the front-of-house sound mixer for the shows. Those attending the show included Mick Jagger and Charlie Watts from The Rolling Stones.

After the show, Lorman was asked to join Miles's road crew as the concert sound engineer. Lorman would remain in the post for the next seven years. Lorman recalls his first meeting with Miles. "It was very apparent that he was all things – opinionated, demanding, understanding, curious, your best friend, your worst enemy with forked-tongue humour – Miles was one of the funniest guys you could meet and he could have an entire room-full of people fall to their knees with laughter. Miles's favourite expressions had to be 'Fuck you,' 'Oh shit,' and 'Say what?' We all experienced his humour, love, compassion and radioactive fire in his eyes."

When Lorman began mixing the sound for Miles's concerts, he faced a dilemma. Half of the audience seemed to comprise older fans that had grown up listening to *Sketches Of Spain* and *Kind Of Blue*, and the rest were younger members keen to hear the louder and more aggressive sound delivered by the new band. Lorman approached Miles and told him about this audio paradox, adding that he was looking for a happy medium. "He looked at me and paused for what seemed like an eternity and said 'Ron. Turn it up – make it loud. I want them to feel it.'"

Each day, Miles seemed to get a little stronger and Cicely Tyson was ensuring that he ate and rested properly. But even so, Miles was still in a bad shape physically and the demands of playing were taking their toll. Writer Cheryl McCall was compiling a major profile about Miles and given unprecedented access to Miles – both backstage and at his home. McCall attended a concert at the Savoy Theatre and recalls her reaction on seeing Miles backstage during the concert. "I was shocked to find Miles in a state of collapse, sweating like a prize fighter between rounds and attended by men with towels, drink, encouragement and aid."[25] The trumpet is one of the most physically demanding instruments and one of the most unforgiving when it comes to relearning how to play it after a prolonged absence.

But despite his frailty, Miles commenced a tour across the US, which began in July and ended in late September, taking in cities such as Washington, Chicago, Detroit, Denver and Los Angeles. For a while, Miles's health improved, but towards the end it deteriorated and he was given oxygen after the concerts. He was also wearing a rubber truss to support his abdominal muscles. Miles's last overseas tour before he dropped out of the music scene in 1975 had been to Japan and he decided that the first overseas tour of the 1980s should start in the same country. Japan had a special place in Miles's heart. He had first visited the country in 1964 and loved both the place and the people. "[They] treated me like a king. Man, I had a ball and I have respected and loved the Japanese people ever since. Beautiful people. They have always treated me great," he said.[26]

Miles and his band flew to Japan on September 29. Teo Macero also joined them, in order to supervise the concert recordings. The first three concerts took place at Tokyo's Shinjuku Nishi-Guchi Hiroba on October 2, 3 and 4. Shinjuku was an outdoor venue and Murphy had arranged for a recording of The Who's "I Can See For Miles" to be played through the PA system at the start of the first concert – a gesture that Miles appreciated.

But Lorman recalls that the concert was memorable in more ways than one.

"I had a traumatic moment during one of the opening shows. It was the first of Miles's return engagements in Tokyo and we were playing outdoors in Shinjuku in front of five to ten thousand people. We had a PA system capable of doing The Rolling Stones twice over. We had more press than you can imagine because it was Miles's first return show in Japan. In the middle of the first performance, the entire PA blew up. It was a full catastrophic technical failure and it all went kaboom! It was rather spectacular. The system turned into a one-tone oscillator that was louder than life – some people were ducking under their chairs."

Lorman did everything he could do at the front of house to shut the system down and was unable to do so. The fault was found to be further down the audio chain and it had blown out the entire PA. Within twenty minutes, the crew had been able to get half of the PA back up and running so the show could be continued. In the meantime, Miles kept playing onstage. "The band were looking at each other and thinking 'What the hell is going on?' Thankfully people seemed to accept it and didn't go crazy," recalls Lorman.

During the course of that night, with winds and rain of a partial typhoon, the road crew rebuilt the entire PA system, speaker by speaker. The following morning Lorman returned to check and reset the system, and when he arrived there were thirty men lined up in front of the PA. The chief of the company told Lorman that the entire organization and staff were resigning. "It was like a hara-kiri type of thing. The event was partially sponsored by Yamaha and I went to the vice-president in charge of production and said 'The crew resigning is not acceptable to me, I do not wish to replace this crew.' I said electronics can fail from time to time – it happens. I explained that a bad crew would not know what to do. This crew did a great job in regaining control of the system during the show and a spectacular job of rebuilding the system under extreme conditions. I said I wanted to do the rest of the tour with this crew. I wanted no other crew in Japan. I believe he thought I was crazy."

The message was conveyed to the crew. "And now they're looking at me like I'm completely nuts. They truly felt as thought they had failed. They looked at each other in bewilderment, bowed at us and they went right on to be the best crew I have ever worked with. The rest of the tour was spectacular. Teo was there and we recorded a lot of that great material," says Lorman.

The Japan-only release *Miles! Miles! Miles!* features the October 4 concert, and the CD booklet includes some photographs of the tour. One shows Teo Macero with his arm around Miles and another is of Miles and Cicely Tyson together. The Japanese photographer Shigeru Uchiyama was given access to Miles on-stage, backstage and in private moments, including Miles's hotel room. Uchiyama would photograph Miles almost every time he visited Japan in the 1980s. In 1993, some of Uchiyama's pictures were published in a book in Japan called *Miles Smiles.*[27]

The book includes a number of shots from the 1981 tour and two of them show Miles with his drummer and close friend Al Foster. In one shot, Foster sits with Miles, who is drinking a can of beer and having a cigarette. A second photograph is more poignant. Shot at a distance, and through the open door of Miles's dressing room, it shows Miles standing and looking straight at the camera. Miles is holding a towel and Al Foster stands next to him, a towel in one hand and a protective arm around Miles's back. Miles looks frail and vulnerable and the image is light years away from his strong, proud Prince of Darkness image.

Miles played further concerts in Nagoya, Osaka and Fukuoka, before returning to the U.S. On October 17, Miles appeared on the *Saturday Night Live* show, where the band performed a seven-minute version of "Jean-Pierre," but, instead of signalling a welcome return, the event proved to be a great disappointment, with the band rushing through the number and Miles looking sick and nervous. But better things were to come and on Thanksgiving Day 1981, Miles married Cicely Tyson, who became his third wife.

Meanwhile, Macero was sifting through the concert tapes and preparing an album of Miles's live performances. Macero explains how he did this.

"The material was chosen on the quality of the performance. [Miles] might make some decision like 'I like that last take or I like some of the stuff that happened in between.' I'd take it back to the editing room, make a copy, I'd listen to it and then come back the next day and do it." This explains why Columbia Records opted for a pick-and-mix approach when it came to the *We Want Miles* album. Rather than simply releasing a complete album, Macero selected a performance from here and another from there and, by using technical tricks such as audience cross-fades and adjusting the equalization (sound balance), he created what sounds like a single concert.

The tracks

"My Man's Gone Now" (20:05)

Composers	Dubose Heyward and George Gershwin
Musicians	Miles, trumpet, electric piano; Mike Stern, guitar; Bill Evans, soprano saxophone; Marcus Miller, Fender bass; Al Foster, drums; Mino Cinelu, percussion
Producer	Teo Macero
Executive producer	George Butler
Arranger	Miles Davis
Recorded	Kix, Boston, June 27, 1981
Engineers	Bud Graham, Hank Altman, Ted Brosnan
Mixed by	Don Puluse, Ted Brosnan
Live performances	June 1981 – July 1982

It is almost a cliché to say that Miles never looked back, but a more accurate observation would be that Miles rarely went back. "My Man's Gone Now" is one of the few occasions when Miles revisited a tune from the distant past. During the last decade of his musical career, Miles only ever included three tunes from his pre-1980s period in his band's repertoire: "Ife," "In A Silent Way" and this tune. "My Man's Gone Now" is the mournful ballad from *Porgy And Bess*, which Miles recorded with Gil Evans in 1958. In that version, Miles played open horn over Evans's elegant orchestration, which includes sections of jazz-swing.

This was the first of three tracks taken from the Kix concert on June 27, and the intimacy of the event can be garnered by the audience chatter that precedes the first note. The piece starts with Miles playing delicately on an electric piano. Bill Evans sometimes played this instrument too, but he says, "That was Miles. I didn't play keyboards until a few months after the band started." The electric piano forms an introduction for Miller's powerful funk bass vamp while Stern plays delicately beneath him and Foster plays an inventive series of accents.

Just after the minute mark, Miles enters on muted horn, which is accompanied by appreciative cries from the audience (someone shouts "yeah man"). Miles may not have been in the best of shape, but his trumpet dominates the piece and he often switches between the mute and open horn. The music seems to drift along with the hypnotic sound of Miles's horn holding the attention, when suddenly it switches into a double-time swing rhythm, with Miller reverting to a walking bass line.

Miles had played jazz-swing on "Ursula," the final track on *The Man With The Horn*, but hearing him play it live is still a great surprise. "He used to sneak in that stuff and he could tell that we wanted to. But he wanted to do it in his own way so that it would fit the music," notes Stern. "The concept of the band wasn't straight-ahead, but we did a couple of straight-ahead things, which had a little more of a swinging kind of vibe. It was interesting the way Marcus and Al made it sound fresh. They weren't going to do it in a traditional way because none of that music was like that. But there was a little glimpse of straight-ahead. I wanted to play more of that."

Bill Evans told Ian Carr how the piece was arranged. "He would just say, 'Let's go into swing on this other section – I'll just cue it.' He would just go into it da, da, da, da, da. He could do it at any point, so the rhythm section would have to keep alert because they might be the ballad part, and then Miles would also go da, da, da, and they'd have to come in right there."[28] "I wasn't even that familiar with the version he had done with *Porgy And Bess* – I didn't recognize it as the same tune!" says Miller. "To me it was some vamp with a straight-ahead middle, but now that I know that stuff it was cool to hear. It's good to hear yourself operating from a place of ignorance!" A trumpet shriek brings the band back to the slower tempo and the funk vamp.

Evans gets to take a long solo (which lasts for more than four minutes) and he plays better than on some other earlier performances, with more control and a smoother tone. At one point Evans even takes the band back into the jazz-swing section. Stern then plays a solo that answers those critics who accused him of playing rock chords and little else. Mixing bebop lines with the blues (and a little rock), Stern plays inventively and imaginatively. Towards the end of the tune, Stern plays a second solo which builds-up dramatically as Foster's drumming crackles and fizzes on open high-hat and snare and Miles joins in on open horn. The jazz-swing section is played for the last time before the music is brought down again and fades out on electric piano and Cinelu tapping his conga drums.

"My Man's Gone Now" is without a doubt a high point on *We Want Miles*. Miles plays for long stretches and, while his playing sounds a little rough in places (most noticeable on the sections that feature open horn), he plays with great energy and passion, and conveys much emotion. It is hard to believe that this is only the band's third gig, following the two concerts of June 26. Everyone listens to each other and responds accordingly. The alternation between ballad and jazz-swing means that neither musician nor listener knows what is going to happen next. The funk bass riff is an inspired touch that brings a new dimension to the original. Despite the long length of the track (it took up a whole side on the LP version) it manages to maintain the listener's interest and concentration – note how little background noise can be heard, despite the close proximity of the audience to the bandstand.

Singer Shirley Horn recalls her reaction when a friend of hers brought *We Want Miles* to her home and she first heard the new arrangement of "My Man's Gone Now." "I went into a little bit of a shock. It was the first time I had heard that drummer Al Foster. He was playing those rhythm patterns. I listened, listened and listened. I got stuck on it. When I used to do 'My Man's Gone Now,' I did it really straight with a little ad libbing and maybe a small tempo change. I hadn't imagined I could do it like on the yellow album and I thought at the time 'I want to do some of that and I want to do it with Al Foster.'"[29] On her 1998 tribute album *I Remember Miles*, Horn sung on "My Man's Gone Now," using Miles's 1981 arrangement – and Al Foster on drums. An edited version of "My Man's Gone Now" was released on a 12-inch single, which lasts a little over seven minutes, but you need to hear the full twenty minutes to appreciate the beauty of this performance.

"Fast Track" (15:13)

Composer	Miles Davis
Musicians	Miles, trumpet; Mike Stern, guitar; Bill Evans, soprano saxophone; Marcus Miller, Fender bass; Al Foster, drums; Mino Cinelu, percussion
Producer	Teo Macero
Executive producer	George Butler
Arranger	Miles Davis
Recorded	Kix, Boston, June 27, 1981
Engineers	Bud Graham, Hank Altman, Ted Brosnan
Mixed by	Don Puluse, Ted Brosnan
Live performances	June 1981 – September 1982

"Fast Track" is the alternative name for "Aida" and the title faithfully describes the character of the tune. "Aida" was the most energetic tune on *The Man With The Horn*, but "Fast Track" has even more power, drive and drama than the original. The track begins, however, with the slow bass vamp from "My Man's Gone Now." Macero may have edited in this section but a more likely explanation is to do with the running order of Miles's set. Miles played his sets as one giant medley, with barely a pause between numbers. "Fast Track" normally followed "My Man's Gone Now" and Miles would abruptly signal the start of "Fast Track" by blowing the tune's ten-note motif, which is what he does here.

The number races along at fever pitch with Miles using open horn throughout. Sadly, the track is marred at times by the sound of Miles's trumpet appearing to get lost in the mix and even suffering from distortion (for example, listen around the 1:37 point). It could be that the high volume of the music overloaded the recording deck, causing distortion. But these technical blemishes cannot obliterate the power and excitement of the performance.

Stern gets to solo at length, offering fast runs and scorching guitar. The tune is also a showcase for Cinelu, who plays his only solo on the album. The most dramatic moment, however, occurs around the seven-minute point, just after Stern's solo, when Miles enters and plays an explosive flurry of notes that soar towards the upper register. Cinelu's solo, around the eight-minute mark, brings the energy level down, before the white-hot funk workout resumes. Miles brings the tune to an end with a scream from his trumpet and the audience applauds wildly.

"Kix" (18:35)

Composer	Miles Davis
Musicians	Miles, trumpet, electric piano; Mike Stern, guitar; Bill Evans, tenor saxophone; Marcus Miller, Fender bass; Al Foster, drums; Mino Cinelu, percussion
Producer	Teo Macero
Executive producer	George Butler
Arranger	Miles Davis
Recorded	Kix, Boston, June 27, 1981
Engineers	Bud Graham, Hank Altman, Ted Brosnan
Mixed by	Don Puluse, Ted Brosnan
Live performances	June 1981 – October 1981

"Kix," of course, is named after the club, where the band played. Like "My Man's Gone Now," "Kix" is a hybrid number that alternates between jazz-swing and another musical form, in this case a section that seems to hover somewhere between reggae and funk, and which is dominated by Miller's powerful bass vamp.

The tune starts off with a reggae-ish flavour with Miller playing the vamp and Miles adding a few stabs on electric piano in support. Stern plays a reggae-like rhythm guitar lick and Cinelu's conga clatter. Stern explains how the number was put together. "Before 'Kix,' we rehearsed it a little, but not much. We were all kinda watching him and listening to each other. There was a loose kind of structure with a little jazz-swing. He wanted that there. I remember him saying in rehearsal that he wanted that there." There may have been just a little jazz-swing when the band rehearsed "Kix" but when it was performed in front of the Boston audience, the jazz-swing section would dominate the tune.

The highlights of "Kix" are the long and impressive solos that Evans and Stern perform. Evans, in particular, really shines on this number and this is doubtless due to the fact that he gets to play the tenor saxophone, his first instrument of choice. "I just picked it up and played. I looked over and Miles was smiling at me. It was an unforgettable moment," says Evans. But this aside, there is little to sustain interest over the eighteen-plus minutes the number lasts and "Kix" could have done with more editing. One suspects its inclusion is more to do with a shortage of material than a desire to devote a whole side of an LP to it. It's no surprise that "Kix" was soon removed from the band's set, with Miles dropping it before the end of his Japan tour in autumn 1981.

"Back Seat Betty" (8:12)

Composer	Miles Davis
Musicians	Miles, trumpet; Mike Stern, guitar; Marcus Miller, Fender bass; Al Foster, drums; Mino Cinelu, percussion
Producer	Teo Macero
Executive producer	George Butler
Arranger	Miles Davis
Recorded	Avery Fisher Hall, New York, July 5, 1981
Engineer	Don Puluse
Mixed by	Don Puluse, Ted Brosnan
Live performances	June 1981 – August 1982

On *The Man With The Horn*, "Back Seat Betty" was a dark, brooding, slow-funk number that overstayed its welcome, but the version on *We Want Miles* is a more satisfying production. This is the only performance from the long-awaited Avery Fisher Hall concerts to be officially released, and Macero did a radical editing job, shortening it to around one-third of its total length (the original master was twenty-one minutes long). Macero's editing is excellent, although two long solos from Stern and Evans were excised in the editing process, and in fact, Evans is not heard at all on this edit.

The performance was taken from the second concert, when the band was more settled after the highly charged opening concert. This live performance also has more power and energy than the album version, with a faster tempo and a greater sense of drama and excitement. One surprise is that one of the most significant features of "Back Seat Betty" – the power chord intro – is missing from this version. Instead, audience applause is used to link it to the previous track ("Jean-Pierre"), designed as a seamless transition between the two tunes.

Miller plays a funk bass vamp and Foster plays cymbals and bass drum. Miller's bass is prominent throughout the mix and it drives the tune along. Miles then enters, playing the theme on muted horn and eliciting cries of delight from the audience. Stern plays some textual chords in the background.

An example of Macero's superb editing occurs at 3:02, the most dramatic moment in the tune, when Miles enters on open horn. In the unedited version, the tension is increased but then the energy level is brought down by Stern, who plays the power chords. As a result, Miles's trumpet blast loses much of its drama. Miles continues playing without the Harmon mute for the rest of the tune, at times pushing himself to the limit. For the most part, Miles plays strongly and convincingly, although there are places where he sounds a little ragged and uneven.

Just before the five-minute point, Macero's reverb tape machine is used on Miles's trumpet blasts and then Miller inserts a new bass line. As the tune reaches its conclusion, the energy level rises even further and Foster plays more aggressively, with splashing cymbals to the fore. Finally, Stern plays the power chords and the track fades out. Macero ended the track just prior to a long solo from Stern, which was followed by a long tenor saxophone solo from Evans, but "Back Seat Betty" greatly benefits from its shortened length and is one of the best tracks on the album.

"Jean-Pierre" (3:56)

Composer	Miles Davis
Musicians	Miles, trumpet; Mike Stern, guitar; Bill Evans, soprano saxophone; Marcus Miller, Fender bass; Al Foster, drums; Mino Cinelu, percussion
Producer	Teo Macero
Executive producer	George Butler
Arranger	Miles Davis
Recorded	Shinjuku Nishi-Guchi Hiroba, Tokyo, October 3, 1981
Engineer	Ted Suzuki
Mixed by	Don Puluse, Ted Brosnan
Live performances	August 1981 – July 1987 (July 1991)

Miles liked "Jean-Pierre" so much that he put it on the same record twice. This wasn't the first time Miles had done this trick. On the 1969 album, *In A Silent Way*, the title track appears twice on side two of the album – sandwiched by "It's About That Time." According to the album credits, this version of "Jean-Pierre" was recorded on October 4 (the same day as the longer version), but discographer Enrico Merlin has discovered that it came from the previous day's performance.[30] The cheering at the start of the track suggests that it could be an encore, but it may also be the result of some sharp editing by Macero. In this version, both Stern and Evans get to solo but their solos are sharply edited. The climactic ending results in whistling and applause from the audience.

"Jean-Pierre" (10:39)

Composer	Miles Davis
Musicians	Miles, trumpet; Mike Stern, guitar; Bill Evans, soprano saxophone; Marcus Miller, Fender bass; Al Foster, drums; Mino Cinelu, percussion
Producer	Teo Macero
Executive producer	George Butler
Arranger	Miles Davis
Recorded	Shinjuku Nishi-Guchi Hiroba, Tokyo, October 4, 1981
Engineer	Ted Suzuki
Mixed by	Don Puluse, Ted Brosnan
Live performances	August 1981 – July 1988 (July 1991)

It is ironic that the best-known tune of Miles's comeback years (and which effectively became his anthem) is also the one whose origins are most shrouded in mystery. No one seems to be quite sure where the song came from, when Miles first played the melody or how he came to play it with his 1981 band. What is known is that it was named after the son of Frances Taylor, Miles's first wife (Taylor had been married to a dancer before she met Miles and Jean-Pierre was the result of that union). According to Chris Murphy and writer John Swzed, it was a melody that Miles had heard Jean-Pierre sing.[31] However, Miles's biographer Jack Chambers claims it is the melody of an old French lullaby, whose words vary from region to region.[32] Mike Stern says "It's probably something he copped in France and it was like a French folk song." Miles seemed to agree with this and once remarked that "Jean-Pierre" was "You know, for kids. The melody is French."[33]

Miles's biographer Ian Carr says Miles first played the motif that became "Jean-Pierre" on April 9, 1960 in Holland during John Coltrane's last tour with the quintet. It was in the sixth chorus of "Walkin'" where Miles played the motif.[34] Miles's discographer Enrico Merlin traces it even further back, to May 26, 1958 (Miles's 32nd birthday), when he played it in a solo of "Love for Sale."[35] And in the closing section of "Petite Machins" on *Filles De Kilimanjaro* (at around 7:27), Miles comes close to playing the theme again. Miles first played "Jean-Pierre" at a concert in Chicago on April 14, 1981, a fitting place to debut such a personal tune, as most of his family lived there.

But members of the 1981 band are unclear as to how the tune was introduced to them. "He played the melody for me at his house one morning when I was visiting. From what I remember, Marcus played a bass line in a rehearsal at his house for this song and that was it. At a concert, Miles asked

'What do you want to play?' and I said 'That little tune you played at your home.' He was not into it at first, but I persuaded him. The rest is history. He thanked me later, saying it was a good idea," says Bill Evans.

But, according to Mike Stern's recollection, "We were rehearsing at Miles's house. Gil Evans came by at a couple of rehearsals. We were just jamming and Gil was playing a little melodica and he said 'Hey Miles, remember this?' He began playing it and it was a melody Miles used to quote a lot in his solos in the 1960s. So Gil started playing this cute little melody and then Marcus started going on his bass and then we had a little groove and then we figured out how to play it. It was very simple." Mino Cinelu supports Stern's version.

Whatever the origins, everyone agrees that "Jean-Pierre" was one of Miles's most simple yet effective tunes. The release of the album *Miles! Miles! Miles!* in Japan gives listeners a rare chance to compare Macero's edited version with the original, as the album contains recordings from the October 4, 1981 concert in Tokyo, from which "Jean-Pierre" was taken. During the concert, "Jean-Pierre" was part of a medley, in which the tune segued from the previous track "Fat Time." Just before the thirteenth minute mark in "Fat Time," Miles starts playing the "Jean-Pierre" melody and the band instantly switches over the tune. The *Miles! Miles! Miles!* version of "Jean-Pierre" shows that Macero edited out the first twenty-five seconds of the introduction, which mainly consists of tumbling percussion sounds and a guitar riff.

On the *We Want Miles* version, "Jean-Pierre" starts with Miller's thundering bass line and the impact is much stronger than on the unedited version. Macero's editing is superb as the bass line is one of the highlights of this track. Bill Evans claims Miller came up with the bass line but Miller modestly says: "You can't really take credit for what you come up with when you're standing in front of Miles. It was two notes, just two funky-assed notes. I was just working on what he played. Those two notes he played with the melody – the bass really works with that."

The child-like melody of "Jean-Pierre" is played by Miles on muted horn, with Evans often doubling up on soprano saxophone and all the band members quote it at some stage. Ian Carr has pointed out that the theme juxtaposes major and minor thirds, which implies the blues.[36] Just before the four minute mark, Stern plays a powerful solo that begins with some dirty, nasty guitar. Foster's drumming becomes more aggressive, Miller plucks his bass strings and Cinelu's conga drums clatter in support. The tension is realized as Miles and Evans resume playing the melody and just after seven minutes, Evans plays a solo, which offers explosive variations of the theme. Miles returns and brings the music down; then Foster's splashing cymbals and Stern's frantically strummed guitar bring the coda to a climax that ends with a cymbal smash from Foster. On *Miles! Miles! Miles!* the audience reaction is almost completely edited out but on *We Want Miles* the applause is used as a bridge into the next number, "Back Seat Betty."

"Jean-Pierre" remained a crowd pleaser for years and the opening phrases of the melody were enough to elicit wild applause. Miller says: "That's a funky little tune. When we played that live you'd think people had just heard it yesterday, they still love that little playful melody." But Macero has mixed feelings about the tune. "He never did finish 'Jean-Pierre.' I kept saying, 'Let's go back and do it again.' But he said 'Ah shit, I don't give a fuck. That's the way it's going.' So I said 'You don't give a fuck? I'll buy that.' It was a nice little piece that could have been a hot one with a little reworking and more energy and more recording. I thought it had a wonderful melody to it and a lot of potential. I don't think he was able to do anything with it." But it is hard to know what else could be added to "Jean-Pierre" without removing its engaging simplicity. Columbia Records released an edited version (four minutes in length) of "Jean-Pierre" on a promotional 12-inch single as a showcase for the album and it was a fitting choice as the track is one of the highlights.

"Jean-Pierre" not only appears on *We Want Miles* twice, but Miles also used it as part of a medley on the *You're Under Arrest* album. It was also the closer for a 1991 concert in Paris, which saw Miles reunited with many old friends on-stage. With "Jean-Pierre" Miles showed that the simplest of melodies can be both beautiful and effective.

We Want Miles – the verdict

Although Miles's studio recording sessions were almost like jam sessions, where the tapes ran constantly and players could stretch out and improvise, there is a world of difference between playing in a recording-studio environment and performing live on-stage in front of an audience. When a band plays in front of an audience, the audience becomes part of the performance, with its feedback often energizing the performers and taking them – and the music – to new heights. *We Want Miles* graphically illustrates this phenomenon.

We Want Miles is a special album in more ways than one, not least because it was the only official live album to be released during Miles's final decade (although two more albums – *Star People* and *Decoy* – would each feature a couple of live tracks). By contrast, between 1970–75, Miles released a string of live albums (*Black Beauty, Live At Filmore East, In Concert, Dark Magus, Agharta, Pangaea* plus *Live Evil*, a mix of studio and live tracks). It would be five years after Miles's death before another live album documenting his 1980's performances was officially released (*Live Around The World* in 1996) and a further six years after that before another emerged (*The Complete Miles At Montreux* boxed set, released in 2002). What is more, at the time of writing, *We Want Miles* still remains the only generally available[37] album to chronicle the live performances of the 1980's touring band featuring Mike Stern, Bill Evans, Marcus Miller, Al Foster and Mino Cinelu.

The cover design for *We Want Miles* is stark, simple and highly effective – it leaps out at you from the record rack. It features a bright yellow background with the album title in large white lettering and a cut-out photograph of Miles taken from the Avery Fisher Hall concert. Inside the LP gatefold sleeve (and CD booklet) is a photograph of Miles taken at Kix, which also features Marcus Miller and Bill Evans – one of the very few times when Miles's albums ever featured photographs of other musicians in the band.

The information on the album sleeve gave little information about the origins of the music, simply reporting that the tracks came from Boston, Kix on June 27, 1981; New York, Avery Fisher Hall on July 5, 1981; and Tokyo, October 4, 1981. It was thanks to the efforts of Miles's discographers such as Jan Lohmann and Enrico Merlin that the location and date of each track was eventually uncovered. The Japanese Master Sound release of *We Want Miles* does give specific track information, although the short version of "Jean-Pierre" is wrongly ascribed to the October 4 gig.

Macero thinks that Miles may have been behind the decision to provide so little information on the sleeve. "Sometimes that was Miles's doing. He didn't want to give any information on the notes or the musicians. In other cases the musicians weren't listed. So I said 'Fine, you're the boss, baby." Macero refers here to *On The Corner*, which did not list the musicians in the initial pressings of the album.

But what really matters is the music and, although Miles was clearly still in the process of regaining his lip, his capacity to move listeners with his trumpet sound remained as strong as ever. The album also highlights his talent to bring musicians from a diverse range of backgrounds and knit them together into a formidable working group. The first band that Miles had was composed of virtuosos, and all of them are given a chance to shine on this record. The lack of preparation brings an excitement and an intensity to the music that is often absent from bands that have extensively rehearsed before the performance. It is the not quite knowing what will happen next that keeps everybody (including the audience) on their toes and everyone responds well to the task. "Within each breath, each note, it was magical," says Cinelu, recalling the band's performances and that is certainly reflected on this record.

We Want Miles has its flaws. Miles sounds a little rough in places and "Kix" is one of the weakest tunes he performed during this period. But tracks such as "Jean-Pierre," "Backseat Betty," "Fast Track" and "My Man's Gone Now" make this one of the best albums of Miles's final decade. It is no surprise that those who played on the album generally have fond memories of the period. Bill Evans thinks it is a very good representation of what the band were doing at the time. "It was very live and none of us knew what was going to happen.

I have great memories from this." "I really like the vibe of *We Want Miles*," says Stern. Marcus Miller likes the album but adds, "The only problem is that Miles isn't that strong; he was getting sick, so that takes away some of it for me but the band had energy!" Mino Cinelu also has some mixed feelings. "At first I was happy to see that album come out but I felt that there were so many magical moments that were not there. 'Jean-Pierre' was a surprise for me because I thought there were some better versions [recorded]. But then it must have been incredibly difficult to find a true selection."

We Want Miles received a much better critical reaction than *The Man With The Horn*, with some critics considering it his "real" comeback album. The album also went on to win a Grammy for Best Jazz Instrumental Performance, Soloist. It is a truism that in the final decade much of the magic of Miles's music happened live on-stage, in real time, and *We Want Miles* is an excellent chronicle of this phenomenon. The great shame is that further live performances from this young, dynamic and imaginative band have (at the time of writing) yet to be officially released.

8 *star people* (59:09)

Columbia CBS 25395

Recorded	(probably) August 1982 – February 1983
Released	Spring 1983
Producer	Teo Macero
Arrangements	Miles Davis, Gil Evans
Executive producer	George Butler
Engineers	Don Puluse (main), Lou Schlossberg, Ken Robertson, Harold Tarowski, Bill Messina, Jay Messina (Record Plant), Ron Lorman (live)
Mixed by	Don Puluse
Tracks	"Come Get It," "It Gets Better," "Speak," "Star People," "U 'n' I," "Star On Cicely"

"I really enjoyed that energy and the confidence that we were playing with." *Marcus Miller, bassist*

For many fans of Miles's post-retirement period, *Star People* represents the high watermark of his post-1980s music. Even writer Jack Chambers, who was less than enamoured with most of the music in Miles's post-retirement period, states that *Star People* "included some tracks that were clearly his best music since the comeback."[1] *Star People* was most certainly a significant milestone in Miles's musical development during the 1980s. It marks the time when his music was developing into a form that writer Paul Tingen has described as "chromatic funk" – a cascade of notes underpinned by linear funk bass lines.[2] The funk bass lines were often accompanied by driving rock rhythms and complex harmonies. There was also a drive, feel and intensity to the music that created a sense of urgency and excitement. It was music that was often abstract, discordant and challenging to the ears. Yet, at the same time, Miles also began playing the blues, both in concert and in the studio. The contrast between the dense chromatic funk tunes, which seemed to shower note after note on to the listener's ears, with the blues, where economy and space are at a premium, could not have been greater.

Star People would also represent the last time when Miles worked productively in the studio with his two long-time musical associates, arranger Gil Evans and producer Teo Macero. It would also be the last time Miles would work in a studio with his band and produce an album out of the sessions. In the future, drum machines and synthesizers would form the basis of backing tracks on to which Miles would overdub his trumpet. It was also the last time that the Foster/Miller/Evans/Stern/Cinelu band would record together, with bassist Marcus Miller being replaced by Tom Barney and a second guitarist, John Scofield, joining the band. *Star People* also saw Miles playing all the keyboards, including the Oberheim OBX-a synthesizer. Miles had grown fascinated by the possibilities offered by the new generation of synthesizers coming on the market.

These new machines were not only smaller and cheaper than their predecessors, but thanks to their polyphonic nature and the inclusion of pre-programmed sounds, were easier to play than the primitive synthesizers Miles's bands had used in the 1970s. However, a certain level of skill was still required to get the best out of the machines. Miles once told writer Bob Doerschuk that when it came to playing a synthesizer "I don't get out of it what it can, because I don't know that much about it."[3]

He also told writer Richard Williams that when it came to using the OBX-a "I haven't read the instruction book yet. It would take someone like Paul Buckmaster or Gil [Evans] or Quincy [Jones] or J. J. Johnson, one of those writers who'd really know what to do with it."[4] Economics as well as creative potential also played a part in Miles's decision to use synthesizers. "That's the only thought I had. What could I get to give me a cheap Gil Evans sound in a small band. That's the way I look at it – not just because it's electric. A synthesizer will sound as long as you pay the electric bill."[5]

Another factor that had a significant effect on the overall sound of *Star People* was that Miles's strength, stamina, confidence and lip were all in the ascendant and this is reflected in the strong trumpet sound that graces this album. But before Miles had even started to record *Star People*, he faced a personal crisis that looked like ending his days as a musician. On November 27, 1981 – Thanksgiving Day – Miles married his long-time friend and companion Cicely Tyson. The wedding took place at the home of actor Bill Cosby and the marriage was conducted by the Rev. Andrew Young. Those present included Max Roach, Dizzy Gillespie and manager Mark Rothbaum.

In January 1982, Tyson travelled to Africa to make a film for the US State Department, and Miles used his wife's absence to over-indulge on cocaine and alcohol. For a healthy person, these are dubious activities at the best of times, but for someone like Miles, who suffered from a range of physical conditions, including diabetes, it was potentially disastrous. One morning, Miles awoke to find that he couldn't move his right hand, which was curled up like a claw. Miles – who seldom liked to publicly reveal feelings of vulnerability – admitted that "This was the scariest shit that had ever happened to me; because with my hand and fingers hunched up and stiff like they were, I thought I would never play again. That was more frightening than death to me; to live with my mind working and not be able to play what I was thinking about."[6]

Miles told Tyson, who immediately realized that he had had a stroke. She flew back immediately and, once again, took control and arranged a battery of treatments and therapies for Miles, including acupuncture, herbal medicines, healthy food and exercise. Road manager Jim Rose also drove Miles to a local hospital three or four times a week for physiotherapy. Eventually, Miles began to regain feeling and control in his paralysed hand and he became fitter and stronger as a result of his new diet and exercise regime. Miles was well enough to resume touring in March, although for a time he needed a mechanical device to help him move the trumpet valves with his stiff fingers. It is a testimony to the loyalty of those who were close to Miles that news of his stroke did not leak to the media and Miles was able to reveal the news himself to jazz critic Leonard Feather some months later.

On August 11, 1982, Miles went into the recording studio and recorded a new number, "Star On Cicely," which was the first sign of a new musical direction. It also saw Miles reunited in the studio with his long-time friend and musical associate Gil Evans. "Gil and I arrange things together — he'd write some stuff out if I composed an interlude or whatever," said Miles in the liner notes for *Star People*, written by jazz critic Leonard Feather.

The liner notes were the only public acknowledgement of Evans's involvement on *Star People*, as the album credits do not list Evans.[7]

But Gil Evans would play a key role in the making of *Star People* and he developed a new way of composing music for Miles. Evans would transcribe solos, most often guitar, which would form the theme for a new tune. John Scofield, who played on the latter sessions of *Star People*, told writer Larry Hicock: "Gil told me 'this is something I've been trying to get Miles to do for twenty years – just improvise on his trumpet into a tape recorder and I'll transcribe it and make music out of it.' Gil would write out twenty pages of music... Miles also taped every gig and he would give those to Gil too. So Gil was walking around during this period listening to Miles's tapes all the time. And they were really working together."[8]

"Gil wrote out many of John's solos from rehearsals and gave them to Miles. Some of the lines became heads [themes] to songs. It was Gil Evans's idea to do that," says Bill Evans. Those present at the sessions have fond memories of Gil Evans. "He was great. He was at all the rehearsals and he had a little melodica with him. Gil was saying very little, maybe 'yeah, yeah, that sounds great.' He was unbelievable. I really loved him," says Stern, adding: "He was really natural, not pretentious at all. He was a very warm guy with all this amazing knowledge but he was very open to any kind of music. If he liked the vibe of it, he loved it and that's what was so great about Gil. There was none of that jazz snob stuff and if anybody was entitled to be one, he was the one. He was knowledgeable about music but he was so far away from that jazz snob attitude."

Engineer Jay Messina, who worked on the sessions at Record Plant Studio, recalls, "Gil was there for most – if not all – of the time. Gil was very cool and mild mannered. He was in the studio with his supply of Perrier and grapes. He had the respect of everyone and always had the answer to any musical question." Mino Cinelu neatly sums up the relationship between Miles and Evans: "There was an incredible osmosis between them. Those two were one."

Teo Macero was also ever-present at the sessions. "He's bad cat, man. He's a real creative guy and an accomplished musician. He was cool in that situation and knew how to work with Miles. He knew how to get that vibe so it was loose like Miles liked it but he would get the job done," says Stern. Jay Messina recalls: "I think the only thing Teo said to me was 'Keep the tape rolling.' He always had a cigarette in his mouth. It was never lit, but he was always chewing on the filter." However, Macero says he and Evans did not work together on the sessions. "If he did the arranging that was it. He never came to the editing room."

Although there was still scope for improvisation, Cinelu noticed that, compared with the loose approach of *We Want Miles*, on *Star People*: "Miles wanted a tighter concept, not as loose as what we used to do. He had more information [music charts] for us to share. The blues were really present on that album. He'd say to me 'Think of the blues, think of the blues.' And I remember that the synth was on those sessions – it was like a new toy!"

The first public indication of a shift in Miles's musical development occurred on August 28, 1982 at two concerts held at the Jones Beach Theatre in Long Island, New York. The usual opening number, "Back Seat Betty," was replaced by a new tune, "Come Get It," and this live performance would appear on the *Star People* album. During the two concerts, Miles's band played three more numbers that appeared on the album, "U 'n' I," "Speak" and "Star People." Miles recorded two tunes, "U 'n' I" and "Star People," probably on September 1 and then resumed touring the US. It was toward the end of this tour that Miles acquired a second guitarist, John Scofield. Leonard Feather says Scofield was hired because of "some problems Miles was having with Stern."[9] In his autobiography, Miles said: "I felt that two guitarists with two different styles would create a tension that would be good for the music."[10]

But the reality was that Stern had serious drink and drug problems, which were beginning to affect his playing. "During that whole time I was going through an awful lot of excessive stuff. Drinking a whole lot and taking everything I could," says Stern. "That shit had been going on for years. I was amazed Miles hired me because he knew what was going on. He put up with a lot from me. He wasn't exactly sober himself at the time, but he wasn't anything close to where I was. I was really pretty strung out. I was just getting more and more out and finally I missed a flight and was showing up at gigs pretty lit up. Miles was trying to get sober at that stage because he had some real health scares and here I was carrying on like that."

Miles asked Bill Evans to recommend another guitarist and he suggested John Scofield. Scofield was almost thirty-one at the time and had a wealth of experience, recording and playing with artists such as Charles Mingus, Chet Baker, Gerry Mulligan, Dave Liebman, Gary Burton, Billy Cobham, George Duke, Tony Williams and Ron Carter. In other words, by the time Scofield joined Miles's band, he had developed his own style. Scofield's playing often contained strong elements of jazz, blues and rock and showed great versatility, whether it was laying down graceful, melodic lines or aggressive rock chords. He also had the ability to surprise listeners with unexpected chords sequences or lines.

Bassist Darryl Jones, who later joined Miles's band and played with Scofield, recalls, "Miles used to call John 'the out man' because of his style of playing." "With John Scofield in the band, I started playing more blues," said Miles.[11] Miles had already began playing the blues with "Star People" months before Scofield joined the band, but there is no doubt that the presence of Scofield stimulated Miles to record a second blues number on the *Star People* album, "It Gets Better."

"I got the gig because Miles was a recovering drug addict himself and Mike was pretty much into it. Miles loved Mike but had some new music he wanted to play and he told me that Mike couldn't even rehearse the stuff – he was really in the throws of addiction," says Scofield. "At the time, Mike was strung out on drugs of all kinds. Miles got me in the band because Mike wouldn't – couldn't – learn the new tunes. Not that he couldn't play them, because he could improvise on them, but there was a lot of written music and he wanted me to play. And that's why I was in the band in the first place."

On December 20, 1982, the group, which now included Scofield, recorded some music at Columbia Records' studio in New York, although at the time of writing none of this material has been publicly released. Although Miles would include two live tracks on the album, this was done more for creative purposes than as a result of a shortage of material. *Star People* clocks in at just under one hour, stretching the recording limits of the vinyl LP record, which, in 1983, was still the dominant music carrier.

According to Cinelu, the album could have been much longer. "We recorded a lot of things. You could have done about ten *Star People* [albums] from what we did." Another session on January 5, 1983 saw "It Gets Better" being laid down, the last studio track. It also saw Miles record at the Record Plant, New York, rather than Columbia's studios (in fact, Miles's next two albums would also be recorded at the Record Plant). The last track to be added to the album was "Speak," which was probably recorded in February 1983. *Star People* was complete and the music from this album would dominate Miles's live performances for the next eighteen months or so.

The tracks

"Star On Cicely" (4:30)

Composer	Miles Davis
Musicians	Miles, trumpet, electric piano; Al Foster, drums; Bill Evans, soprano saxophone; Marcus Miller, bass; Mike Stern, guitar; Mino Cinelu, percussion
Producer	Teo Macero
Executive producer	George Butler
Arrangers	Miles Davis, Gil Evans
Recorded	Columbia Studios, New York, probably August 11, 1982
Engineer	Don Puluse
Mixed by	Don Puluse
Live performances	October 1982 – July 1984

"Star On Cicely" was of course named after Miles's third wife, Cicely Tyson, and was probably Miles's way of publicly thanking Tyson for helping him get back to health after his stroke. Miles's discographer Enrico Merlin has identified three themes that make up "Star On Cicely."[12] The first theme would inspire another Davis tune "Hopscotch," which Miles included in his live repertoire from October 1982 until July 1982. According to bassist Darryl Jones, a bass line from "Hopscotch" turned out to be the inspiration for yet another tune, "What It Is" (for more details see the entry on "What It Is," p. 140). If all this wasn't enough, Merlin claims that the second theme from "Star On Cicely" was the inspiration behind yet another tune, "Wrinkle," although "Wrinkle's" co-writer Randy Hall disputes this connection – see Chapter 13. What is clear though, is that "Star On Cicely" was the inspiration behind at least two other tunes played by Miles in the 1980s.

The inspiration for "Star On Cicely" itself came from a Mike Stern solo, which was transcribed by Evans. "The band were all complaining about how hard it was to play!" recalls Stern. Macero's editing of "Star On Cicely" involved removing the first theme and starting the track at the end of the second theme, which is why the tune starts abruptly, with Evans's soprano saxophone accompanied by Foster's driving drum pattern and Miller's energetic bass line. Cinelu plays a variety of instruments, including conga and timbale throughout the tune. The result is a powerful groove that propels the tune along.

Miles plays a solo on muted horn, as well as playing a series of keyboard stabs that are down in the mix. Just after the first minute, the band reverts to the third theme, with Evans and Stern playing in unison and Miller overdubbing a second bass line. The second theme, introduced by a slurred bass line from Miller, occurs at the 1:49 mark, with Stern's guitar the dominant instrument before Miles joins in. The opening section is repeated and then Miles plays a second solo. The third theme is repeated again and the track fades out. "Star On

Cicely" is one of the highlights of *Star People*, although surprisingly Miles would not play it live on-stage for more than two months after the studio recording. The long gap between recording and performance has led Miles's discographer Jan Lohmann to question the recording date given by Columbia Records.[13]

"Come Get It" (11:03)

Composer	Miles Davis
Musicians	Miles, trumpet, electric piano, synthesizer; Al Foster, drums; Marcus Miller, bass; Mike Stern, guitar; Mino Cinelu, percussion
Producer	Teo Macero
Executive producer	George Butler
Recorded	Jones Beach Theatre, Long Island, New York, August 28, 1982
Engineer	Ron Lorman
Mixed by	Don Puluse
Live performances	August 1982 – June 1983

Any musician will tell you that there is a world of difference between recording in a studio and playing live on-stage. In the studio, constraints such as the studio environment, the recording process, and pressures such as studio time and recording budgets can all conspire to create tension and remove a lot of the looseness of the performance. "Generally, it's a rule of thumb that when they play live it's a whole different world," says Stern. "Joe Henderson once told me recording in a studio and playing live are just two different things. When you're in front of a live audience it's a cool thing – you're not in a room in a studio, so there's a certain kind of energy. It's like the acoustic album *Four and More* and when Miles used to play 'So What.' On the record it's very cool, but live, he'd play it uptempo." "Live recordings are really special. People aren't hung-up about the recording process; they're just playing," says engineer Jay Messina. That was why Macero would simply let the tapes roll in the studio, with two tape recorders set-up in such a way that as one tape reel approached the end, the other recorder would automatically start recording, so that nothing was lost.

The energy, excitement and experimentation offered by a live performance was one reason why Miles was so keen to mix live recordings with studio recordings. For Miles, it was about getting the best take and the tightest performance and that didn't matter whether it was live on-stage or in a studio. Miles had mixed live and studio recordings on his 1970 album *Live Evil*, and he would repeat the trick on this album and on the follow-up, *Decoy*.

Two tracks, "Come Get It" and "Speak," would be taken from recordings made by the front-of-house sound engineer Ron Lorman. "I believe those two tracks are [from] front-of-house cassettes that I did for Miles. I recorded every performance for Miles and would give them to him after every show," says Lorman. "And, oh yes, he listened to them. He would grab the guys one by one in the morning in hotel lobbies, airports, buses – anywhere, and tell them what he thought. 'You got to play like this,' 'Play like that,' 'I want it to sound like so and so.' He kept us all on edge and he liked it that way. I had no idea he used my board tapes on the album until I heard it. It caught me by surprise too."

Yet, somewhat surprisingly, Miles claimed "Come Get It" was a studio recording. "In the fall of 1982 I took the group into the studio to record *Star People*," he said. "That was the session when we recorded 'Come and Get It' [*sic*], which was the opening number at our live performances."[14] But "Come Get It" was indeed the new opening number, replacing "Back Seat Betty." However, the latter's opening power chords were retained, along with Foster's swirling cymbal and Cinelu's clattering percussion.

Foster lays down a heavy backbeat and Miles adds a few keyboard stabs on the electric piano, then Miller enters with a hyperactive bass line, which Miles says was inspired by an old Otis Redding riff.[15] "I have no idea where that bass line came from," says Miller. When Miller first played on "Aida," Miles had told him to "play F and G and then shut up," but on this track he seemingly instructed Miller to play every note on his bass. Miller thumps, plucks, pops and slurs his bass strings throughout the track, with his fingers moving all over the fretboard.

Miller's bass line is already prominent, yet at around the 56-second mark it seems to jump even further out of the mix. Stern plays a combination of funky riffs and edgy lines and Cinelu pounds away on percussion. The intense rock rhythm, frenetic playing and swirling synth lines from the OBX-a create a tension and an energy that is almost exhausting to listen to.

And if all this wasn't enough, Miles then enters with a screaming trumpet, seemingly pushing himself and his instrument to the limit. The tension is unrelenting until just before the seven-minute point when Stern plays an extended solo (it lasts for almost four minutes) and brings the energy level down. Stern ends his solo by playing the power chords again and then Miles plays a short section on the OBX-a, although it is not certain whether this was overdubbed at a later late. Macero edited the track at this point, excising a scurrying soprano sax solo from Evans in the process. On *Star People*, the Oberheim section was used as a bridge for the second track "It Gets Better."

"Star People" (18:47)

Composer	Miles Davis
Musicians	Miles, trumpet, electric piano, synthesizer; Al Foster, drums; Marcus Miller, bass; Mike Stern, guitar; Bill Evans, tenor saxophone; Mino Cinelu, percussion
Producer	Teo Macero

Executive producer	George Butler
Recorded	Columbia Studios, New York, probably September 1, 1982
Engineer	Don Puluse
Mixed by	Don Puluse
Live performances	August 1982 – July 1991

Funk may have been the music of the 1980s, but Miles never forgot his musical roots and that meant the blues. "The blues was always around you in St. Louis," Miles told Leonard Feather. "I played it because I heard blues played by the bands that came up from New Orleans on the river boats and by the musicians from Oklahoma and Missouri and Kansas."[16] As Miles's chops improved he gained the confidence to play more of the blues in his live sets and noticed the effect it had on his audiences. Miles told Leonard Feather, "You can play the blues right now and see where people in the audience are coming from. We do it as our second number every night now and you'll hear these shouts of 'All right.' Black people in particular react to it every time. I remember one night in Dayton a while back, some woman was having a running conversation with my trumpet."[17]

Like all the studio tracks on *Star People*, the music was played live in the studio and Cinelu recalls that this was "A challenge for the engineer, because Miles was moving from mike to mike and he had to open up some and close some others." "Star People" begins with a short interlude recorded on another occasion (probably at the later Record Plant sessions) with Miles on the Oberheim and Stern on guitar.

According to Feather, Miles and Macero came up with the idea of inserting the interlude at the beginning of "Star People,"[18] but Macero's recollection is somewhat different. "I was making the final master and he [Miles] calls me up and says 'I'm sending you a cassette; I want it to go somewhere.' I said 'I'm making the master today.' He said 'I don't give a shit, I want this in there.' So I said 'Okay, send it on to me.' And I put some of the cassette stuff in the final master."

In the circumstances, Macero did a fine job in grafting the interlude on to the track, but the Oberheim/guitar section clashes with the rest of the music. Miles and Macero also employed another technical trick, which Feather described as "a unique and indefinably different sound to Al Foster's drums, creating a sonic illusion, the exact nature of which is known only to Davis and Macero."

But the result is that Foster's drums sound artificial and somewhat lifeless. But on the plus side, Miles plays for very long stretches on muted horn and sounds in fine lip. "I really think I got into the solos I play on it," said Miles[19] and he's right. Around the six-minute mark, Stern plays the first of two solos, starting off aggressively and using some sustain. Miles solos again before Evans plays a stirring solo on tenor saxophone – one of his best on record.

Miles resumes and then, at the 12:40 mark, a second Oberheim/guitar interlude is inserted and is apparently used to stitch together a second separate performance. After the interlude, Miller plays a bass riff which marks the introduction to Stern's second – and more powerful – solo. Stern begins his solo almost tentatively but then builds up to a searing pitch. "Mike does his B. B. King on 'Star People,'" said Miles.[20] Miles plays a little more and finally the tune comes to a complete stop, ending with a cymbal smash and thumped bass. Miles then says "Teo" – the last time he uttered his long-time producer's name on a record.

"U 'n' I" (5:55)

Composer	Miles Davis
Musicians	Miles, trumpet; Al Foster, drums; Marcus Miller, bass; Mike Stern, guitar; Bill Evans, soprano saxophone; Mino Cinelu, percussion
Producer	Teo Macero
Executive producer	George Butler
Recorded	Columbia Studios, New York, probably September 1, 1982
Engineer	Don Puluse
Mixed by	Don Puluse
Live performances	August 1982 – May 1983

In 1975, Miles and Gil Evans worked on the arrangement for a tune called "You And I," which was recorded by Miles's then wife Betty Davis. This tune has no relationship with that. After almost twenty minutes of playing the blues, Miles lightens the mood with this playful mid-tempo number that is dominated by Miller's thumping bass line and Foster's pounding drum beat. Miles plays the child-like melody on muted horn and there is a playful feel to the whole tune. Stern supports all of this with some fine rhythm-guitar playing.

Both Stern and Evans get to play short solos and Evans plays particularly well on soprano saxophone, with good tone and none of the shrillness that had bedevilled some of his earlier recordings. Miles plays the melody repeatedly and the tune comes to a graceful conclusion before fading out. Turn the volume up at this point and you can hear some nice interplay between Miles and Evans that is lost in the fadeout. "U 'n' I" is hardly groundbreaking music and, while it has a certain charm, it lacks the depth and substance found on the other numbers on the album. No surprise, then, that Miles dropped this number from his live set the following spring.

"It Gets Better" (10:06)

Composer	Miles Davis
Musicians	Miles, trumpet; Al Foster, drums; Marcus Miller, bass; John Scofield, guitar; Bill Evans, soprano saxophone; Mino Cinelu, percussion

Producer	Teo Macero
Executive producer	George Butler
Arrangers	Miles Davis, Gill Evans
Recorded	Studio A, Record Plant Studios, New York, possibly January 5, 1983
Engineer	Jay Messina
Mixed by	Don Puluse
Live performances	December 1982 – December 1984

"It Gets Better" was the last studio number to be included on the album and is a showcase for John Scofield. The tune was a result of collaboration between Miles, Scofield and Gil Evans. "Gil was hanging with Miles. They were best buddies and they working together all the time," explains Scofield. "At one point Miles called me and said 'Come on over' and I went to Miles's apartment and Gil was there and we jammed. Gil and Miles both played the piano and I played guitar. Miles had this chord sequence that was the same as a 12-bar blues if you don't play the first four bars. If you turn it into an eight-chord sequence and start on the fifth bar and go from five through twelve over 12-bar blues it's like a brilliant thing. He just subtracted four bars from the blues. Gil made up a bass line and Miles said 'Improvise over it.' The next day we went into the studio and Gil had this music written out and he came up to me and said 'That's your solo that you took yesterday.' And Miles said 'Gil, don't tell him that, he'll get a big head!'"

The genesis of "It Gets Better" begs the question as to whether Evans and Scofield should have shared writing credits for the tune. "I should have gotten a credit for that one, but okay, it's not my tune, it's me improvising," says Scofield.[21] Scofield told writer Larry Hicock: "I remember once, I asked Gil, 'How come Miles does that – take the tunes and puts his own name to them when you or I were involved in it?' And Gil said, 'Well, it's just fame, Miles wants fame.' And I said 'Well, that's funny because he's so famous already,' and Gil said 'Yeah, but he *really* likes that fame.' And the way he said it, he wasn't judgemental at all."[22] Miles also claimed that he got the chord sequence for "It Gets Better" from the blues singer/guitarist Lightnin' Hopkins.[23]

Miles had recorded the bulk of *Star People* at Columbia Studios, but for "It Gets Better" he decamped to the Record Plant studios in New York. Engineer Jay Messina, who worked on these sessions, recalls that Miles and his band spent around two weeks at Record Plant and recorded a number of tunes, although at the time of writing only "It Gets Better" has been officially released. Most of the sessions took place in Studio A, with a little overdubbing and some extra recording occurring in Studio B.

In Studio A, Foster's drums were placed on a platform with a low wall around them. Marcus Miller's bass was recorded by a method known as direct injection, with the bass plugged directly into the recording console. Miles had a clip-on microphone and his trumpet was recorded as a separate track. Miles also had an amplifier that was enclosed in a booth and another microphone recorded the sound from this and fed it to another track.

Miles was increasingly interested in studio technology (hence his use of digital effects on Al Foster's drums) and for "It Gets Better" he wanted to use a click track, a type of metronome that is used for tightly controlling the tempo. The musician hears the click track through a pair of headphones. "So Miles comes into the control room and gives me the tempo by snapping his fingers," says Messina. "It takes me about ten seconds to get the tempo and find a good starting point. I start the click track generator and on the second click, Miles says 'No man, that's not the tempo' and walks back into the studio. I looked at Teo, who said, 'Don't worry about it.'"

Miles put on his headphones and then took them off. He stopped playing and counted off the tune again and the band played. "The count has no relation to the click. By now, everybody has forgotten about the click, except Al Foster, who is still wearing headphones with the click track on them," continues Messina. "About an hour later, we took a break and I went into the studio to check a few things. When I checked the drum set-up, I could hear the click coming from Al's phones. I was amazed and impressed how he had played all that time while hearing a click that had nothing to do with the tempo of the tune."

Macero spent most of the time in the control booth with Messina. "He didn't have much interaction with the guys. He just let it happen and I respected him for that. I do remember thinking that with the tapes just rolling and all this material to listen through, it was going to be a major job editing it all," says Messina.

Mike Stern was present for some of the Record Plant sessions, but he is absent on "It Get Better." Stern thinks that this may have been because he was also playing with drummer Steve Smith, who was recording a new album, *Vital Information*. Yet, strangely, Miles said that "On *It Gets Better*... John is featured as lead soloist with Mike playing in the background."[24]

"It Gets Better" segues with the opening number "Come Get It," with an Oberheim interlude used as a bridge between the two tracks. If you program your CD player to play the second track from a standard CD release of *Star People*, the interlude is included, but the Japanese *Master Sound* version of the album rectified this mastering error and "It Gets Better" starts at the right position.

The blusey tune is underpinned by a three-note bass riff and Foster's light touch on the cymbal – although it sounds as if his drums have had some digital reverb added to them as well. Scofield plays the theme and then Miles enters on muted horn. The track essentially alternates between Miles and Scofield playing the theme. There is a relaxed feel to the music and plenty of space around each instrument – it is a stark contrast to the high density of the opening number, "Come Get It." Around the nine-minute point, Miller adds an additional slurred note to the bass line and then briefly switches to a walking bass line as Miles plays on top. Scofield then plays the theme again as the track fades out.

Macero edited the track from a 19-minute performance that has emerged on a Japanese bootleg. The unedited version shows that little was lost by trimming the track by almost half and, in fact, "It Gets Better" is measurably improved as a result. One wishes a similar approach to economy had been made to the 18-minute title track.

"Speak" (8:33)

Composer	Miles Davis
Musicians	Miles, trumpet, Oberheim synthesizer; Al Foster, drums; Tom Barney, bass; John Scofield, guitar; Mike Stern, guitar; Bill Evans, soprano saxophone; Mino Cinelu, percussion
Producer	Teo Macero
Executive producer	George Butler
Recorded	Cullen Auditorium, Houston, Texas,[25] February 3, 1983
Engineer	Ron Lorman
Mixed by	Don Puluse
Live performances	August 1982 – February 1988

Marcus Miller was just twenty-one when he joined Miles's band, but he was already a veteran on the New York session scene and was also writing material for artists such as David Sanborn, Luther Vandross and Aretha Franklin. He was also touring extensively and becoming increasingly interested in studio production. Even when Miller was a member of Miles's band, he was still touring with other artists and doing numerous sessions. Miller described his punishing schedule to writer Gibson Keddie. "I would do Aretha's gig, then catch a plane to Boston before I missed my gig with Miles and get fired! Or I'd be playing with David Sanborn, who'd have two gigs in L.A., then Miles would have two gigs in Chicago and Detroit; they'd be on consecutive days of course, so I would fly back and forth three or four times to make all the gigs."[26] Miller never missed a gig, but there were one or two close shaves. "I once came in at the last minute to a Miles gig and he gave me that look, like 'Don't do that shit again.'"[27]

It was a situation that could not persist and so Miller nervously approached Miles with the news that he was leaving the band. "I was in the band for around two years and eventually I said to Miles, 'Miles, I want to get into the studio and produce. I want to learn how to compose and I can't do it if I stay in the band. I just need to grow." Miller told broadcaster Alyn Shipton, "You can imagine how frightening that was just to even approach Miles at twenty-two, twenty-three years old and tell him that I'm leaving the band. But he was really supportive and he said 'Man, I wish you all the best and you're one of the best musicians I ever had in my band and whenever you need something let me know.' Now anybody who knows anything about Miles knows that for him to say that to somebody was like the ultimate compliment."[28] Miles explained how sad he was to lose Miller. "Marcus Miller was leaving and this hurt me a lot, because Marcus was the best bass player I had in a long, long time. Plus he was a funny motherfucker who kept everyone in the band loose."[29]

Miller recommended bassist Tom Barney as his replacement. Barney was born and raised in New York and grew up with Miller. "Marcus and I are old buddies. He used to live across the street from me," says Barney. It was inevitable that Barney would gravitate to the bass – his father, Tom H. Barney and foster father Bob Cranshaw were also bassists. Barney is a highly accomplished player on both acoustic and electric bass and his influences include his fathers, Ray Brown, Ron Carter, Richard Davis, Willie Weeks, James Jamerson, Chuck Rainey and Larry Graham. "I grew up surrounded by bassists like Ray Brown, Ron Carter and Richard Davis," he says.

Barney would later go on to play with a wide range of artists, including Eric Clapton, Herbie Hancock, Dizzy Gillespie, George Duke, Chaka Khan, Aretha Franklin, Burt Bacharach, Santana, Wynton Marsalis, Liza Minelli, Frank Sinatra and Michael Jackson, as well as becoming the musical director for Steely Dan. At the time he received the call from Miles, he was playing with David Sanborn. "It was a situation where both my bassists [Miller and Barney] had ended up with Miles," says Sanborn.

Barney recalls his audition with Miles. "I went up to Miles's house and for what was supposed to be a half-hour audition. I ended up staying something like six hours! Gil Evans came over and we played a bunch of tunes. We had a good time." Talking about Miles, Barney says: "He was hilarious. It was like dealing with a schizophrenic and I kinda dug it. You'd get calls from him at four or five o'clock in the morning asking if you were asleep. You'd hang out with him. You'd have some really nice conversations with him but then there were moments when he would flip and you didn't know what to expect."

However, Barney would only remain in Miles's band for a few months, although one of his performances – on "Speak" – would end up on *Star People*. Like "Come Get It," "Speak" is a live track and, like much of the music on *Star People*, it was transcribed from a John Scofield solo. " 'Speak' was just me soloing on an existing tune, but they didn't play the other melody," he recalls. Oddly, Miles is credited as sole composer of "Speak," but on the *Decoy* album the track "That's What Happened" is in fact the second theme of "Speak" and credited to both Miles and Scofield. The second theme of "Speak" was also used for the tune "Street Scenes" on the *You're Under Arrest* album, but here Miles is credited as sole composer.[30]

Speak was probably recorded live in Houston on February 3, 1983 and is the only track on *Star People* to feature both Stern and Scofield (at the time of writing, it remains the only official release featuring the two-guitar line-up that Miles had from November 1982 to June 1983). The tune, a funk-rock workout, starts dramatically, with Miles playing a series of trumpet blasts that are accompanied by keyboard stabs on the Oberheim (Miles often performed with a trumpet in one hand while simultaneously playing keyboards with the other in concert). Evans and one of the guitarists play the first theme while Barney busily pops and thumps his bass strings. Stern plays the first solo above a boiling cauldron of notes. The energy level is intense and is increased further as Barney's playing becomes even more aggressive and Miles's trumpet screams.

Scofield enters just after the three-minute mark and plays the second theme, bringing the energy level down in the process. Barney uses his fingers rather than his thumbs and Miles plays some under-stated lines on the Oberheim. At the end of Scofield's solo, the first theme is played again and then Barney's bass is briefly highlighted as he plucks and pops strings – it's the closest thing to a bass solo on the entire album. Miles blows above the bass and plays some more keyboard stabs. Cinelu's percussive sound also becomes more prominent before the tune fades out.

Star People – the verdict

Star People was released in the spring of 1983 with an eye-catching cover that held two surprises. The first was that the cover art was by Miles – "all drawings, color concepts and basic attitudes by Miles Davis" the cover informed us. The second was the return of liner notes which had last appeared on Miles's 1970s albums *Live At Filmore* and *Jack Johnson* – Miles had penned the notes to the latter album. *Star People* gave the public their first glimpse of Miles's art and the covers of several more albums (*Decoy*, *You're Under Arrest* and *Amandla* and the tribute album *Endless Miles*) and videos (*Miles in Paris* and *Live In Munich*) would also be graced by the presence of Miles's art. It also marked the start of Miles's parallel career as an artist, which would see his work being exhibited around the world and at least several art books published.[31]

Miles had always liked drawing, as he explained: "I've been painting and sketching all my life. As kids we would do comic books that could be turned upside down to get something different. And all through growing up, I'd always be sketching."[32] When Miles had his stroke in 1982, his doctor recommended that he hold a pencil and take up drawing to improve the strength and flexibility of his paralysed hand. Cicely Tyson also encouraged Miles, buying him sketch pads and pencils. In time, art became a mental as well as physical therapy for Miles. "More and more I have been drawing and painting. I do it several hours a day now when I'm at home. When I'm on the road too. It's soothing for me to paint and I just love seeing what comes out of my imagination."[33] Indeed, Miles was rarely seen without his sketchpad and pens when he was at an airport, in a hotel or hanging out in a studio.

Joanne Nerlino, a close friend of Miles and whose Nerlino Gallery in SoHo was home to Miles's first New York exhibition in 1989, describes Miles's art as 'Figurative Expressionist.' "It's a term I've made up because they are expressionist paintings with figures merging through them. What makes Miles's art so special is the same as what makes his music so special – him. Like his music, Miles's artwork was a creative vehicle for what was going on inside him, but instead of a trumpet he was using a paint brush." Miles's artistic development was also profoundly influenced by the artist Jo Gelbard (who later became Miles's partner).

The cover of *Star People* features three, brightly-coloured, abstract figures set against a white background. One of the figures looks like a trumpeter and the other two could be dancers.

Leonard Feather, the author of *Star People*'s liner notes, was also a friend of Miles (he attended Miles's 60th birthday party). Feather had been born in London in 1914 but moved to the US in the late '30s. He was a producer, promoter, musician and composer – he had written tunes for artists such as Sarah Vaughan, Ella Fitzgerald, Cannonball Adderley and Sonny Stitt. But Feather was best known for his role as a jazz critic and writer and was one of the few critics that Miles respected (the others were Nat Henthoff and Ralph J. Gleason). Miles had been impressed by the fact that Feather had been one of the few critics to appreciate bebop and to recognize the talents of Charlie Parker.

Feather may have liked Miles but he wasn't afraid to criticize him, and Feather panned a performance that Miles gave on September 26, 1981 at the Hollywood Bowl, which he described as musically barren. Yet this didn't stop Miles from granting Feather an exclusive interview with him and Cicely Tyson (when he revealed that he had suffered from a stroke) nor from getting Feather to write the liner notes for *Star People*.

Feather listened to the *Star People* tapes with Miles and Macero and, from his conversation with the men, compiled his notes. Feather gives little away in terms of what he thinks about the album and, indeed, his opening sentence asks whether "It Gets Better" refers to Miles's band, his playing, his health or simply life at large. But on the plus side, he gets some interesting insights out of Miles in terms of how he approached the music on the album.

Star People marked the end of two long musical collaborations that Miles had had with Gil Evans and Teo Macero. After *Star People*, Miles simply did not contact Macero and initially decided to produce himself. Miles retained his friendship with Evans and attempts were made to get Evans involved in Miles's later projects, most notably the *Decoy* album and a planned album of pop ballads.

But none of these projects would come to fruition. *Star People* set the musical direction Miles would take for almost the rest of the decade, mixing funk tunes with the blues. In fact, the opening two tracks of *Star People* were the template for most of Miles's concerts in the 1980s, which almost invariably began with a heavy funk workout before segueing into a blues number. The addition of John Scofield to the band also takes the music to a new level and clearly invigorated Miles.

There is much to enjoy on *Star People*. The two live tracks ("Come Get It" and "Speak") bristle with energy and excitement, while it's a joy to hear Miles playing for long stretches on the two blues numbers. "Star On Cicely" has a strong groove and is the parent of two or three other numbers that featured in Miles's repertoire. Teo Macero believes that *Star People* is "A great album," and it is certainly one of his best of the era.

But the album suffers from two major problems. The first is Miles's and Macero's use of studio technology to "enhance" the sound, particularly on Foster's drumming. It would have been better to have let the instruments speak for themselves. But a bigger issue is the editing. Macero had time and time again shown himself to be a superb producer and editor whose post-production work was often an inherent part of the compositional process. On *The Man With The Horn*, Macero had managed to construct tunes out of what effectively were studio jams. On *We Want Miles*, his editing tightened up the music considerably. But, on *Star People*, some of the edits are crude and the title track should have been trimmed back considerably.

Bill Evans recalls: "I do remember being a little upset with Teo for editing so much of it. He did not need to do any of that on this music. He did a lot of editing of Miles's stuff in the early 1970s because they just had lots of grooves and not many songs, so Teo would have to create something. But we had songs – that was the difference and he did it anyway. I was happy to be part of it none the less." Stern says *Star People* was: "A fun record," but Cinelu found the album to be: "A bit strange for me because compared to the energy we had on stage, it was more subtle." Marcus Miller played on the first three of Miles's comeback albums and feels that *Star People* is the best of them. "I really enjoyed that energy and the confidence that we were playing with. The whole thing for me is a journey and after *We Want Miles* we'd been around the world and now we were back."

Star People is not as instantly accessible as, say, albums such as *Tutu* or *You're Under Arrest*. The highly chromatic nature of the music and the high degree of abstraction can be off-putting on initial hearing. But it is an album that really does get better the more you play it. Many had hoped that Miles would build on the foundations laid by *Star People*, and while the album dictated much of his future musical direction it also marked the end of a creative process that Miles had used for years.

It is tempting to speculate as to why Miles no longer worked with his band in the studio to the same degree as on this album. Was Miles running out of energy? Had he got bored with making music this way? Did the potential for synthesizers and other electronic instruments to replace live instruments excite Miles to the degree that he preferred working with them in a studio than with a band? Was the *Star People* band the last to be composed of virtuosos that enabled Miles to work in this way? The answer is probably a mix of many of these factors. What is clear, though, is that *Star People* represents an important chapter in Miles's last musical decade.

9 *decoy* (39:34)

Columbia CK 38991

Recorded	June–September 1983
Released	May 1984
Producer	Miles Davis
Co-producer	Robert Irving III
Assistant producer	Vince Wilburn Jr.
Executive producer	George Butler
Engineer	Ron Lorman
Tracks	"Decoy," "Robot 415," "Code MD," "Freaky Deaky," "What It Is," "That's Right," "That's What Happened"

"I think Miles wanted to move into a new era, new sounds, and embracing new technology. He wanted a more progressive sound. He wanted a different feel to it." *Ron Lorman, engineer*

"Miles Davis had me so focused in a way that I'd never really experienced before." *Branford Marsalis, saxophonist*

Background to the album

In 1983, Miles's personal life spilled over into his professional life, fracturing several long-term relationships in the process. The problems seem to have been largely caused by Miles's deteriorating relationship with his third wife Cicely Tyson, her tightening grip on his business affairs and the conflict between Tyson and several key members of Miles's entourage. Barely six months after their wedding in November 1981, Miles was complaining about Tyson's behaviour on a European tour in spring 1982. "Since Cicely had become a star actress, her personality had changed. She demanded everything, gave a lot of people a hard time, treated a lot of people like they were nothing," he said.[1] Miles was so upset by Tyson's behaviour that he got his road manager Jim Rose to book the couple in separate hotel rooms while they were staying in Rome. So far, Tyson has refused to speak publicly about her relationship

129

with Miles, so her version of events is missing from the following chronicles. But from the descriptions provided by several parties, there was clearly a lot of tension in the air during this period of Miles's life.

Slowly but surely, Tyson was exerting a greater control over Miles's life, a problem he recognized later on in their relationship. "What really bothered me about Cicely was how she wanted to control everything in my life," said Miles, "like who I saw, who my friends were."[2] The first casualty of this interpersonal conflict was Chris Murphy, who had been a member of Miles's road crew since 1973 and had got on well with Miles.

The split happened on a European tour in April 1983, where relations between Murphy and Tyson had been deteriorating for some time. During an argument between the two of them in Torino, Italy, Miles sided with Tyson. Murphy decided to leave. The next person to go was Miles's manager Mark Rothbaum, who had managed Miles's affairs since the mid-1970s. In a power struggle between Tyson and Rothbaum, the latter lost out and he left Miles. "It was nothing personal between me and Miles, but between Cicely and her business staff. There were financiers from Philadelphia called the Blank brothers and Cicely was taking control over Miles's day-to-day stuff. And at that time she wasn't treating me with the respect I deserved. It wasn't like I quit or got fired; it was just obvious that I had no more interests. I was supposed to report to the Blank brothers and I just thought 'I don't need this shit.'"

On Tyson's advice, Miles made Blank and Blank his new management team, an arrangement Miles later described as a "horror show,"[3] as they apparently had problems getting Miles a sufficient number of gigs. As a result, money became tighter. John Scofield told writer Ian Carr: "When I joined the band, the money was more than when I left the band. It was one of those strange situations when the money went down. When I joined the band, we were picked up in limousines to go the airport and we were treated incredibly well... After he got new management, the money went down."[4]

Another key person to exit around this time was Teo Macero, who had worked with Miles for almost a quarter of a century, editing and producing Miles's prodigious output since 1960. But when Miles came to record his next album, he decided to dispense with Macero's services. "He decided he wanted somebody else. I guess I was giving him a hard time," says Macero. However, Macero also suspects that Tyson got Miles to fire him, and, while there may be some truth in this, it is not the full story behind the breach between the two men.

In an interview with Gene Kalbacher, Miles was asked why he no longer worked with Macero. His response was brutal: "He's like an old woman, man. I'd say 'Teo, do this, do that.' He'd say 'Well, Miles, you know my wife.' Shit. Fuck it. No more. I should have done it a long time ago." When Kalbacher tried to get Miles to elaborate, Miles refused to, but added: "It's a different ball game now, so it lets Macero out. He's always complainin', always sick..."[5]

Whatever Miles's complaints about his erstwhile producer, it is extraordinary that he never informed Macero of his decision to end what had been a long, fruitful and highly productive partnership. "That's what Miles would do. If he didn't want somebody he just wouldn't bother to call them up. I was very hurt," says Macero. But *Decoy* wasn't the first time Miles had considered using a different editor, explains Macero. "It wasn't a pleasant atmosphere when some guy is trying to get somebody else to do the editing. I remember he wanted Herbie Hancock to do the editing on one of the records. I said 'Fine,' so Herbie Hancock came into the studio – I wasn't there – he tried for an hour or two and then ran out the goddamn door. I guess he figured he couldn't do it. It takes some skill."

Bill Evans believes that Miles's new music required a different approach to production and editing. "I can't speak for Miles, but from what I understand, a lot of the time Miles used to go into the studio and play vamps that would last for a long time, so Teo had to edit it down so that they would fit on to a record. From the 1980s on, Miles was recording more songs that had a beginning and end, so Teo's editing approach wasn't used as much. But, remember, Teo was there for a long time, so he must have been doing something that Miles liked."

Robert Irving III, who would be drafted in to help Miles produce *Decoy*, adds: "Teo's name never came up and I had no idea that I was producing the recording until the project was well under way. I think that, until this time, Miles had only exercised a hands-on involvement in the creative side of making his records and that Teo had taken care of every technical detail so that Miles didn't have to be concerned with any such issues. Also, before *Decoy*, it seems that a lot of Miles's electronic excursions had been loosely formatted during the recording. Teo would do a lot of editing to create what was later heard as 'arrangements.'"

Irving has his own theory as to why Miles decided to stop working with Macero. "I was not told the reason why Teo was no longer involved, but it was my sense that at that time Miles was ready to shift his direction musically, and that he needed someone who could handle the technical aspects. He seemed to like the idea of taking control of his projects." Ron Lorman, who was also brought in to engineer the recording sessions, adds: "I think Miles wanted to move into a new era, new sounds, and embracing new technology. He wanted a more progressive sound. He wanted a different feel to it."

Lorman believes that Miles's approach to *Decoy* was a logical development. "I don't think he ever changed. Miles was always looking for something new. Miles always had an ear out for new sounds. Miles kept track and listened to everything. He never wanted to do anything old and surrounded himself with young musicians because he loved it and loved working with them. Miles embraced new, he loved new. Working with Bobby [Irving], Darryl [Jones] and everyone else was exciting and he embraced them. He certainly taught them and he loved playing the music with them."

During the making of *Star People*, there were already signs that Miles was taking a greater interest in the production side of things. Don Puluse, the recording and mixing engineer on *Star People*, says: "Miles surprised me in a mixing session for *Star People*. He came to the editing room and got involved, asking if we could replace a bar from a repeated phase, if we could raise the pitch of the whole recording a quarter-tone and so on. For twenty to twenty-five years Teo had made those decisions, but not that night." John Scofield adds: "I had only worked with Teo on one thing [*Star People*] and Miles was telling the producer what to do. People talk about Teo's input and I'm sure he did a lot, but when I was there Miles was really involved in the production. I guess [with *Decoy*] he wanted to call the shots completely."

But before Miles could start working on his next album, he needed to find a new bass player. Tom Barney had only been with the band for several months, but already felt that it was time to leave. "There were a number of things going on that had nothing to do with me. It was getting a little weird and if you're not having fun it's time to move on," he says. John Scofield believes the problem was one of personality rather than Barney's playing ability – Scofield describes Barney as an incredible bass player. "I don't think Miles and Tom got on."

Mike Stern agrees. "Tom was playing good. I guess they had some kind of disagreement. Tom played his ass off." Miles turned to his nephew Vince Wilburn Jr. for advice. "We were in New York and I think Uncle Miles was fed up with Tom Barney. He asked me to recommend a bass player from Chicago. I suggested three names: Darryl [Jones], Felton [Crews] and Nathaniel Phillips, the bassist with [soul/funk group] Pleasure. Darryl was home when we called," recalls Wilburn.

Darryl "The Munch" Jones got his nickname in high school as a result of his short stature. "I was a late bloomer and when I got to high school I was only about five feet tall. There was a group of people who gave everyone a nickname and, believe me, 'The Munch' was one of the better ones and I decided to stick with that!" recalls Jones. Presumably those who gave Jones his nickname decided he was a "little munchkin," or so small you could munch him up with one bite. Jones had known Wilburn for some years and, whenever Miles played in Chicago, Jones would attend his concerts. "I remember I used to watch Miles play and almost had tears in my eyes thinking 'I could do that,'" he says.

Jones was only twenty-one when he got the call,[6] but he had already gained a reputation around Chicago as a phenomenal bass player. Jones's technique included a ferocious thumb action that slammed, slapped and popped the bass strings almost to destruction. Jones's playing was funk with a hard edge, bass playing that was aggressive, upfront and in your face – and it was exactly what Miles was looking for.

When Wilburn called, Jones initially thought he was joking. "Vince said 'Miles wants to hear you play over the phone.' Now for some reason, my bass was in the trunk of my car, so I told Vince that I'd go outside and get it, but Vince told me to hold on. The next voice I hear is Miles's, who asks me when I could be in New York. This was like on a Monday and I was trying not to seem too eager – I thought I'd be cool! So I said I could be there on Wednesday, and Miles says 'What's going to take you so long? Are you gonna walk?' So I said I could be there tomorrow morning. Before he hung up I asked Miles if he still wanted to hear me play on the phone and he said 'No, you can play, can't you?'"

In May 1983 Jones flew to New York and met Miles at a house that belonged to a relative of Tyson's (at the time, Miles's home was being gutted and refurbished on the advice of Tyson). Miles did much to make the young bassist feel relaxed, joking around and telling Jones that if he failed the audition it wasn't because he couldn't play, but simply that Miles was looking for something different. "I just settled right into it and wasn't nervous," says Jones.

Miles asked Jones to play a B-flat blues. "He kept stopping me and saying 'No, real slow,' so I'd say 'Okay.'" Miles then asked Jones to play along to a concert tape. "He said, you don't have to follow the bass line, just play how you feel." Miles then left the room and Wilburn walked in to tell Jones he had got the gig. "I said to Vince, 'I want him to tell me!' So Miles walks in and punches me on the shoulder and says 'You got it.'"

The arrival of Jones changed the whole dynamics of Miles's band and the rhythm section of Foster, Jones and Cinelu was one the strongest of Miles's comeback years. This was a rhythm section that could whip up a collective storm, driving the music along at a furious pace and pitch. When the section was in full throttle, a cascade of notes showered the audience, with a blur of arms and hands moving furiously to create a powerful and exhilarating groove. Cinelu says he was thrilled to have Jones in the band, and Scofield adds: "Darryl had such a tremendous groove." In his autobiography Miles said: "I really loved the way he played."[7]

Jones made his debut on June 7, 1983 at the Fox Theatre in St. Louis in a septet that consisted of Miles, Mike Stern, John Scofield, Bill Evans, Al Foster and Mino Cinelu. The two-guitarist line-up continued until the end of June, when Stern's drink and drug problems finally overwhelmed him. "Basically, I was just out," says Stern. "I was just getting drunk and showing up drunk and Miles was trying to get sober. He told me he was not happy about it. He offered to pay for me to go into rehab – he had a sweet side and he understood what I was going through. He told me to let him know when I wanted to come back and said 'You got to take care of yourself.'"

At the end of June, Miles took his band into A&R Studios in New York for several days to lay down the first tracks of his new album. These sessions were a landmark because, for the first time, Miles took on the role of producer. On June 30 and July 1, Miles, Evans, Scofield, Jones, Foster and Cinelu were present at the sessions, but on the July 2 sessions, the saxophonist Branford Marsalis (brother of Wynton) replaced Evans. Branford Marsalis was born in New Orleans in 1960 and plays both tenor and soprano saxophone, although on *Decoy* he would play the latter instrument exclusively.

In addition to being a highly talented musician, Marsalis is also one of those artists who happily straddles the jazz, pop and classical worlds, working with artists from Art Blakey to Sting and from the Orpheus Chamber Orchestra to The Grateful Dead. He's also played music that combines elements of rap and hip-hop with a jazz sensibility. Miles had heard Marsalis play at a concert in St. Louis on June 7 in a tribute band called VSOP II that had included Ron Carter, Herbie Hancock, Tony Williams and the Marsalis brothers.

"I was playing with VSOP and Miles was opening for us, which is not really true because we were opening for Miles, but he plays before everyone so he can get the hell out," recalls Marsalis. "We were in the airport and that was the first time I met him." Marsalis remembers the effect Miles's presence had on the musicians. "Being on the road with Herbie [Hancock], Ron [Carter] and Tony [Williams], I would ask them questions constantly about Miles. They had gotten older and little more defiant and trying to be as honest as they could about him. When they saw him in the airport, it was amazing. He had some kind of mythic sway – on Tony and Herbie more so than Ron – but it was interesting to watch from a distance because I was trying to think of a musician who would have that kind of influence on me and I couldn't think of one."

Marsalis adds: "Miles came up to me and said 'I hear you can play,' and I said 'No, not me, man.' And Herbie said 'Yeah, he can play.' And Miles said 'I got my eye on you.' That's still kinda deep for Miles Davis to say that kind of shit to you. But I kinda tempered that with the fact that at the time Miles was playing with a whole lot of musicians who didn't knock me out. So it wasn't like Miles was saying 'I had [John] Coltrane in the band, then I had Wayne [Shorter] and now I want you.' That being said, it's still Miles Davis. It was one of those things where I was flattered but I didn't hold no stock in it."

When VSOP II were in San Francisco on a day off, Marsalis received a phone call in his hotel room. "There was a guy who sounded like Miles Davis saying 'I want you to do my record. You wanna do a record with me?' and I'm like 'Yeah, man.' And he said, 'Get on a plane and come to New York.'" But Marsalis was wary because Herbie Hancock – who can imitate Miles's voice with uncanny accuracy – had previously played some tricks on Marsalis, including a number of fake telephone messages purporting to come from Miles.

"So when the phone rang it was 'Right, whatever, right,' and Miles said 'It is me' and I said 'I don't believe you.' So he asks what he has to do to prove it and I say 'Get me a first-class ticket to New York.' Twenty minutes later, American Airlines confirms the first-class ticket. Man, I would never have asked Miles for that – he could have sent me on a horse and buggy, I would have come. But I didn't think it was him and I was very brazen, which probably worked out to my benefit," adds Marsalis.

Marsalis flew to New York, staying at his brother Wynton's apartment. Despite a growing rift between Wynton Marsalis and Miles over Miles's decision to play funk (see p. 198), Branford Marsalis says it never caused any difficulties between him and his brother. "Wynton knew I was playing with Miles and he was all for it. He said 'Man, all the shit you're going to learn from that bad motherfucker.' Wynton was like 'Man, he's too great a musician to let all that shit get in the way.'"

Miles called Branford Marsalis and asked him to be at the studio the next day. It is not quite clear why Miles brought Marsalis in while Evans was still in his band, but Evans says he was relaxed about Miles bringing in another saxophone player. "Miles was known to have more than one horn player from time to time, [for example] Cannonball and Trane. I was okay with it."

The next day, Marsalis arrived at A&R Studios and went to the studio where Miles was with his band. "He was in real Miles form, cussing up musicians. So I'm standing behind him while he's cursing the musicians and I know he knows I'm there because he's Miles. He let me stand behind him while he's telling the musicians they ain't shit and some sad motherfuckers, and then he turns to me and says 'And you, didn't your momma raise you with no manners?' I'm like 'Well yeah,' and he says 'Don't you know you ain't supposed to come into somebody's house unless you knock first?'"

Marsalis's instant reaction was "'Okay, test time.' Because having played with Art Blakey and spending some time with a guy like [drummer] Michael Carvin, they fuck with you that way. It's like a test to see how much of a punk you are. So I said 'I'm sorry,' and I left the studio. I'm smart enough to know that a studio door is about three feet thick and there's no way you're gonna hear me. I knock on the door, no answer. I knock on the door again, no answer."

Marsalis went into the studio foyer, where an American Grid Iron college game was being shown on TV. He watched it for about an hour and then left and went back to the apartment. Later that night Miles called him. "He said 'Where the fuck were you?' And I just said, 'Well Miles, my momma did raise me with manners and I knocked and I knocked and no one was home, so I left.' And then he laughed and said 'That's that New Orleans shit, huh? Come back tomorrow.' And I said 'Will you be home tomorrow?' He said 'Yeah motherfucker, I'll be home tomorrow.' And he hung up the phone."

Marsalis says a combination of experience and being a student of jazz had helped prepare him for Miles's test. "I'd heard tons of these stories about the mysterious barracuda. So if you went on the road, for instance, and your suit jacket has a hole in it, the other guys would say 'The barracuda's got an eye on your coat,' meaning 'Replace the coat or else.' And after sufficient warning, if the coat is not replaced, you'll come back and find the jacket has been ripped to shreds, which forces you to replace it."

Marsalis encountered the barracuda while touring in Europe with Art Blakey in Europe. "I had my clothes in a bag and we were a week away from Italy. And I thought I'd buy a suitcase in Italy because leather's cheaper over there. Suddenly I hear a motherfucker saying 'The barracuda's got an eye on your bag, man,' and I say 'Tell the barracuda to wait until I get to Italy.' But that's not the rule: you're supposed to replace the shit once the 'cuda has spotted it. So we were at Frankfurt airport and I picked up my bag and all my shit fell out because somebody had cut the bottom and so I had to buy a new suitcase at the airport. So this is like part of the folklore of jazz; it's like guys fuck with you and test you."

Marsalis adds that he had also encountered these dog-and-pony tricks while growing up in New Orleans. "That's just the kind of thing people do, so when Miles did it I was up to the task but I think a lot of the other guys in the band who didn't grow up in that environment really didn't know how to take it. So they stood there and took it while he berated them and poured beers on their head and smacked them around. When he joined Charlie Parker's band, he was not prepared for that level of intimidation and it affected him to the extent that he was determined to do the same to every motherfucker he had in his band. But when he said that shit to me I said 'Fuck it, I'm out.' And we were cool from that point and he never tried to do anything after that." Marsalis played on the July 2 session, but so far, the only music to be released from those three days in the studio is the track "Freaky Deaky."

In early July, the band, now pared down to a sextet (and with Evans still in the saxophonist's chair), played a number of gigs in the U.S. and Canada, including one on July 7 at the Theatre St. Denis in Montreal, Canada. Parts of this concert would appear on *Decoy*. On August 29, Miles and his band were back in the recording studio, although this time at Record Plant Studios in New York, a studio popular with rock artists (Hendrix and The Who had recorded there). No music has been released from these sessions, suggesting that they were either unproductive or that Miles was unhappy with the results.

Miles already had Ron Lorman assisting him in the studio, but he still needed some extra help. He decided to keep it in the family and work with his nephew Vince Wilburn Jr. and family friend Robert Irving III, both of whom had worked with Miles on *The Man With The Horn* album. Irving recalls: "Miles phoned me and asked me if I knew how to mix a record. By that time I had done quite a bit of demo work and a few recording projects and I felt I had good ears and enough technical knowledge to assure him that I knew what I was doing. He asked me only to mix his next record and invited me to bring some tunes for the band to record." Miles also tried to get his old friend Gil Evans involved, but Evans decided that Irving didn't need any help in handling the project.

Miles's usual method of working was to go to the studio with his band and develop the music organically, but *Decoy* would see two radical changes in the way Miles produced his music. First, electronic instruments such as synthesizers and drum machines would be used to create the music from the ground up rather than simply being used to add colour or texture to the sound. But, more controversially, Miles would spend little time in the studio, preferring to delegate much of the work to Irving and Wilburn, who assumed the roles of co-producer and associate producer respectively.

Irving says: "Miles hated the studio. He felt it was cold and impersonal. He liked playing live because of the audience feedback. Nevertheless he would come into the studio primarily for overdubs (his own or overdubs by other musicians), but he would seldom attend any live tracking sessions that involved the entire band. I think he didn't want to get involved in the social interaction that can be distracting. He preferred to work one-on-one in a workshop type of scenario. In this way he would feel more comfortable working out ideas. He once entertained the idea of having a party in the studio and making the recording a 'performance' for friends. It never happened."

Under Miles's direction, Irving handled all the arrangements and rehearsals. The 24-track master tapes were always rolling even during rehearsal. At the end of each session Miles got cassette copies of everything. Wilburn adds: "When Miles would leave the studio, Bobby and I would hash-out the tapes and distribute them. Miles would also be on the phone a lot and say things like: 'Do this and do that and then bring me the mixes at the end of the night.' We did the legwork under his direction. When Miles had heard the mixes we would get a list of things to do and we would do them. We were like the foot soldiers. He loved it because he planned so much."

There is no doubt that the hand of Miles loomed large over the making of *Decoy*, but equally, there is some degree of disconnection if you are not present in the studio while the music is being rehearsed or put down on tape. Even so, Miles's influence was still making a strong impact on the musicians, as Marsalis recalls. "I didn't know what the hell I was playing on – the songs didn't have names. They were kinda cobbled together in that Miles Davis fashion, 'Here, play on these changes.' There was one instance where I was playing on some changes and he said 'Damn man, I gave you the changes, but I don't want you to play on the changes' which, of course, fucked me up, because when you talk to jazz musicians they always talk about the changes being sacrosanct. But Miles was like 'I don't want you to play the fucking changes.'"

Marsalis didn't understand what Miles meant and, after he had scrabbled around for a while, Miles told him to just play A-flat. "I was so intimidated that I wasn't thinking straight, so he takes the music [chart] and throws it on the floor and says 'Now play,'" says Marsalis. "And it wasn't until then that I understood what he meant. The changes are like the basis of the song, but my job is to play the song, not the changes and he wanted me to play solos that were based on the melody. It's something I never forgot."

In early September, the first track to be recorded under the Irving/Wilburn partnership was one of the shortest tracks Miles had ever recorded, "Robot 415," a piece that lasted barely a minute. However, Miles did attend this session, playing keyboards along with Irving. Further sessions would result in three more tracks, "Decoy," "Code MD" and "That's Right." But after these sessions Miles only had around thirty minutes of music, enough to fill a single side of an LP record but insufficient for a full album. So Miles repeated a strategy he had carried out on his previous album *Star People* and included a couple of live recordings, "What It Is" and "That's What Happened" from the July 7 Montreal concert.

This fleshed out the album, although *Decoy* was still less than forty minutes in length, almost two-thirds the length of *Star People*. Irving was heavily involved in both the recording and post-production work, as he explains: "The mix-down sessions were quite intensive and lengthy, usually one track per day with subsequent tweaking and remixing sessions. Once the project was completed, Vince and I were also responsible for compiling the album credits for Miles to review and approve." One puzzle in Miles's autobiography is that he claims that *Decoy* won a Grammy for Best Album,[8] but in fact *Decoy* was nominated for a Grammy but did not win (although it did win some magazine polls).[9]

The tracks

"Freaky Deaky" (4:30)

Composer	Miles Davis
Musicians	Miles, synthesizer; John Scofield, guitar; Darryl Jones, bass; Al Foster, drums; Mino Cinelu, percussion
Producer	Miles Davis
Arranger	Miles Davis
Executive producer	George Butler
Recorded	June 30/July 1, 1983
Engineer	Ron Lorman
Live performances	July 1983

"Freaky Deaky" is slang for someone strange or weird and is often used in the context of sexual behaviour. In 1988, the writer Elmore Leonard published a novel using the same title. The song title was inspired by a phrase that Miles's old friend Richard Pryor (the black American actor/comedian) used at the time. Pryor is renowned for his off-beat sense of humour. In this context, "Freaky Deaky" is well named because it can only be described as an off-the-wall recording.

Writer Paul Tingen goes even further, describing it as "one of the most bizarre tracks [Miles] ever recorded."[10] Like the track "Rated X" from *Get Up With It* (which also saw Miles abandoning his trumpet for the keyboard), "Freaky Deaky" almost defies description. It is also a track that divides listeners down the middle – they either love it or wonder what on earth Miles was thinking of when he went into the studio.

"Freaky Deaky" saw Miles taking on the role of producer for the first time and the track also marks the first time Darryl Jones went into the studio with Miles. Almost at once the young musician found himself facing the daunting task of finding an elusive bass line that Miles was looking for. "He kept talking about a bass line that went on forever and he kept trying to get me to come up with something. He was sitting at the piano and I was trying so hard to be on the same page as him. It went on for a while," remembers Jones.

John Scofield says: "Miles said he was looking for a bass line from a record he had heard as a kid in St. Louis." Writer John Szwed reports that Miles was looking to add an umpah bass line from German composer Kurt Weill to a blues.[11] "At one point I asked Miles when he had heard the bass line and he said it was back in the 1930s! So I said to him 'That's why I don't know it!'" recalls Jones. "Miles said 'It should just keep rolling, I want something that keeps rolling.' I just scratched around with different stuff and eventually I came up with that one."

"Freaky Deaky" starts with a fade-in and the first instruments heard – Miles's synthesizer and Jones's bass – are the dominant sounds throughout the track. Scofield (who for some reason is not credited on the CD liner notes but can clearly be heard), Foster and Cinelu play a solely supportive role to the Miles/Jones combination, adding colour and atmosphere to the overall sound. Scofield's guitar sounds like it is being played through a wah-wah effect. Cinelu and Foster add various percussive sounds while Miles's synthesizer meanders throughout the track as Jones sticks resolutely to his rolling bass line.

The music is atmospheric, with an almost trance-like feeling and Jones recalls that: "We played for a long time. We must have done it for a couple of hours and there were a lot of takes." Scofield recalls one take that featured Miles on the horn. "We recorded it once with a trumpet solo and a guitar solo – I thought it was an incredible Miles solo, but he didn't like it because it sounded like the old Miles. It reminded me of 'Walkin.' But in the end he decided to play it without the horn and got a lot of weird sounds." But Irving believes the released version is the better one. "I did hear the Miles version. It didn't have the same amount of space with the horn. The version that we used had the 'vibe,'" he says.

Miles once said: "My music is influenced by today's sounds. When it comes to synthesizers, there's always something new."[12] Even so, Miles's playing is rudimentary, even when he occasionally uses a second keyboard to support the main one. Close to the four-minute mark, Jones briefly switches out of the rolling bass line for a few bars and then switches back, although this time leaving a short pause between each riff. Finally, the track ends, almost seemingly from exhaustion, and Miles can be heard saying: "I definitely want to hear that...Freaky Deaky."

"What It Is" (4:32)

Composers	Miles Davis, John Scofield
Musicians	Miles, trumpet, synthesizer; John Scofield, guitar; Darryl Jones, bass; Al Foster, drums; Mino Cinelu, percussion; Bill Evans, saxophone
Producer	Miles Davis
Co-producer	Robert Irving III
Associate producer	Vince Wilburn Jr.
Executive producer	George Butler
Arranger	Miles Davis
Engineer	Guy Charbonneau
Recorded	July 7, 1983
Live performances	June 1983 – December 1984

Miles was known for mixing live and studio tracks on the same album (for example on *Live Evil* and *Star People*) and so he returned to this well-worn formula for *Decoy*. Miles's decision to include live tracks was partly down to a shortage of material, partly because of a tight recording deadline and partly because Miles loved the sound of the band live. "The band always played at its best when it was live. Miles realized the intensity that he and his bands delivered to the audience. I feel the same way, I loved the interaction between the audience and band. Miles truly loved these live cuts and wanted to use them," says Lorman.

"We had to complete the record in time for the fall tour. Miles would often listen to recordings of previous live concerts. Miles had the idea of using some of these live versions with the idea of improving them. And we were also listening for performances that would complement the studio tracks already recorded and he particularly liked this one," says Irving.

"What It Is" is a hard funk number and one of two performances taken from a concert at the Festival Internationale De Jazz in Montreal. At this point, the group had just become a sextet following the recent departure of Mike Stern. This track is also the first of three numbers where Miles and John Scofield share the composing credits. In all cases, transcriptions of Scofield's solos formed the foundation of a theme used in the tunes. The fact that Scofield became one of a select group of members of Miles's 1980s working bands ever to get a composer's credit on a Miles Davis album (Robert Irving III was another), shows how much influence the guitarist had on Miles's music at the time.

Another prominent feature is Darryl Jones's ferocious bass line that drives the tune along. In fact, Jones's playing helped to inspire the track. "The bass line came from the first night I played with Miles. I did it on 'Hopscotch' and wanted to find this bass line that just bounced. Miles didn't say anything then, but the next day he called me and said 'If you don't play that bass line you played on 'Hopscotch' last night, it's curtains for your ass!"

"What It Is" begins with a thumping bass line followed by some heavy backbeat support from Foster. Miles enters soon after, playing a few phrases on open horn that end with an almost banshee-like screech. Scofield begins repeatedly playing the melody while Cinelu pounds away furiously in the background on a variety of percussive instruments. The music is full of energy and everything is played at a furious pace – there's an overwhelming feeling of urgency.

Miles plays strongly, often shifting to a high key. The tempo drops just prior to Evans playing his only solo of the album on the soprano saxophone. Scofield plays the main melody again and Miles returns on open horn, this time double-tracking a second trumpet to support the sound. Irving explains how this came about. "Miles liked 'What It Is,' but he wasn't sure he liked the trumpet solo. This was a problem because we were working with a pre-mixed stereo recording, [and] everything was etched in stone. He asked me 'What if we added to the trumpet solo in the spaces?'"

Miles played along with the track, just practising the phrases while Ron Lorman worked on the sound. "Ron recorded the rehearsal as Miles always insisted. Miles had played a whole new solo that overlapped the original one at times. After hearing it back, I commented that it sounded great with the two horns, but with no intention of using them both. Miles obviously liked it and decided to use it. He joked, 'They'll get two for the price of one,'" says Irving. At around the four-minute mark, the track starts winding down, before ending with Miles playing a few notes on electric piano.

The unedited version of the track shows that almost three minutes were removed and there are some interesting changes in the construction and juxtaposition of the instrumentation. During the concert, "What It Is" is segued with the previous track ("Star People") with Scofield repeatedly playing the main melody. Jones's bass line comes later and, what is more, is never isolated as it is at the start of the album version. Jones says no over-dubbing was involved on the album version. "There's no way I could have repeated that bass line in the studio!" In fact, the intro was edited in by Irving and Lorman in the studio. Starting the track with Jones's pounding bass line was an inspired piece of post-production work. So was the decision to add a second trumpet, which really does fill out the sound.

Evans's sax solo was cut by about half on the album and sounds better for it. The sheer power and energy of "What It Is" make it an exciting tune to listen to, but it also clearly illustrates the sharp contrast between the music Miles played in the studio and what he played live on-stage. Finally, where did the title come from? Apparently Miles often used this phrase when greeting friends – usually with a smile.[13]

"That's What Happened" (3:31)

Composers	Miles Davis, John Scofield
Musicians	Miles, trumpet, synthesizer; John Scofield, guitar; Darryl Jones, bass; Al Foster, drums; Mino Cinelu, percussion; Bill Evans, saxophone
Producer	Miles Davis
Co-producer	Robert Irving III
Associate producer	Vince Wilburn Jr.
Executive producer	George Butler
Arranger	Miles Davis
Engineer	Guy Charbonneau
Recorded	July 7, 1983
Live performances	July 1983 – November 1987

Whenever live tracks are used on an album, they are almost invariably edited, but with "That's What Happened" Miles came up with a novel concept – chopping off the last section of a tune and then giving it a new name. "That's What Happened" is actually the second theme from "Speak," a funk track that first appeared on *Star People* (and which incidentally was also a live performance). Scofield explains how he got the co-writer's credit on the track: "It was from a transcription from my solo in 'Speak,' which turned into a melody for 'That's What Happened.' That's why I got the credit."

Like "What It Is," the track came from the Montreal Jazz Festival and once again finds the band whipping up a storm. The track starts abruptly with Miles playing a series of stabs on synthesizer. Jones thumps away on his bass and Foster plays his usual combination of hard snare and splashing cymbals. Cinelu plays furiously on percussion while Scofield repeatedly plays the melody. Evans is barely heard and his role is confined to doubling up on the melody with Scofield. Miles's trumpet playing simply consists of a series of blasts and stabs.

This track is full of drive and energy and the only clue that it is a live performance is a faint "Whoo!" that can heard from someone in the audience at around the 2:20 mark. "We wanted the live tracks to melt in with the studio tracks so the audience noise had to go. That particular audience response had to stay because the music had not completely decayed naturally. To cut it off sooner would have sounded abrupt and unnatural," says Irving.

The track continues to rush along until just towards the end, when it starts winding down. Jones plays some funky licks on bass, Scofield and Evans play the melody together, before the track ends in the same way as it began – abruptly.

The full version lasts for more than twelve minutes and the track really smokes. Miles plays some powerful open horn, Scofield gets to solo at length and Evans plays some blistering tenor sax. It is a great pity that Miles didn't include the complete version on *Decoy*. As well as extending the album's overall playing time, it also would have done justice to a band that was tight on the night.

"Robot 415" (1:09)

Composers	Miles Davis, Robert Irving III
Musicians	Miles, trumpet, synthesizer; Robert Irving III, synthesizer, electronic drum programming; Mino Cinelu, percussion
Producer	Miles Davis
Co-producer	Robert Irving III
Associate producer	Vince Wilburn Jr.
Executive producer	George Butler
Arrangers	Miles Davis, Robert Irving
Engineer	Ron Lorman
Recorded	September 5, 1983?[14]
Live performances	None

"Robot 415" saw Miles move to Record Plant Studios, where he would complete the rest of the album (and its successor, *You're Under Arrest*). "We stayed predominantly in Record Plant, 44th Street NYC. It was a great studio, with some of the most talented engineers and staff in the business," says Lorman. "Miles was comfortable there because many of his counterparts were walking through and the studio treated him with the utmost of respect. We worked in Studio A. It was the right place for Miles to be. It was like home for all of us."

Like "Freaky Deaky," the inclusion of "Robot 415" perplexed some listeners. Jazz writer Barry McRae wrote: "One cannot help but wonder why 'Robot

415' was included at all. It runs for a bare one minute and, just as Davis commences his solo, it is faded out. The inclusion of such items does suggest [a] novelty appeal and infers [sic] that jingles are acceptable if 'catchy' enough."[15] "Robot 415" sounds like a fragment of a longer piece, but Irving says it was deliberately short. "This tune was meant to be an interlude. Miles had been listening to some albums that had utilized a lot of interludes, which were cross-faded between longer cuts as transitional pieces."

"Robot 415" may be short, but it was also a complicated track to record, recalls Irving: the core of the track came from a 6/8 blues taken from a live concert. "If you listen to the melody alone, you can hear a simple 6/8 blues track (with Al Foster's drums in the background) improvised in half time in relationship to the 4/4 rhythms that we superimposed over the blues. It was a challenge to get the 4/4 drum pattern to feel locked over the 6/8," explains Irving.

Indeed, on close listening, "Robot 415" reveals itself to be quite a complex tune. In addition to the drum machine, which gives the whole sound a mechanical feel, a myriad of synthesizers are layered on top, with one of them playing the main melody, another playing a simple (and funky) bass riff and a third, played at a higher key, dancing on top of it all. Add to this a series of keyboard stabs, Cinelu's clattering conga plus the different time signatures and the result is an intriguing brew. Then, just as the track fades out, Miles plays a few phrases on open horn before "Robot 415" has gone.

Very little of the music Miles made in the 1980s was ever covered by other artists, and "Robot 415" would appear to be a highly unlikely candidate for a cover version. But in fact the classical violinist Viktoria Mullova did no fewer than five versions of "Robot 415" on her album, *Through The Looking Glass*[16] including an original version, with the violin replacing Miles's horn, plus solo, duo, psycho and waltz versions.

The album's recording producer and arranger Matthew Barley, who with his wife Viktoria Mullova selected the tracks, explains how she got to record "Robot 415": "When I bought *Decoy* I was really fascinated by that track. It was so quirky and it just turns around and circles back on itself. It was as if they had latched on to an idea and said 'Why turn it into a piece? – let's just put it on the album.' I originally didn't have the intention to turn it into five different pieces, but I found that I could arrange it in so many ways. That's why it ended up being like the refrain for the album." Irving says: "I enjoyed hearing these arrangements. From the perspective of an arranger, there are infinite possibilities for the arrangement, interpretation and orchestration of a melody. Mullova found some special ways to achieve this."

The track's title is an intriguing one and it could be that the robotic feeling of the music inspired Miles, but where did the 415 suffix come from? Irving says: "We never questioned Miles about the meanings of his titles. At that time 415 was the telephone area code for San Francisco. I thought it might have been related."

"Decoy" (8:33)

Composer	Robert Irving III
Musicians	Miles, trumpet; Robert Irving III, synthesizer, electronic drum programming; John Scofield, guitar; Branford Marsalis, soprano saxophone; Darryl Jones, bass; Al Foster, drums; Mino Cinelu, percussion
Producer	Miles Davis
Co-producer	Robert Irving III
Associate producer	Vince Wilburn Jr.
Executive producer	George Butler
Arranger	Robert Irving III
Engineer	Ron Lorman
Recorded	September 10 and 11, 1983
Live performances	June 1984 – October 1985

The story behind "Decoy" has some uncanny parallels with the tune "In A Silent Way," written by Joe Zawinul for Miles's landmark 1969 album of the same name. That album featured three keyboardists (Herbie Hancock, Chick Corea and Zawinul) with Tony Williams on drums, Dave Holland on bass and John McLaughlin on guitar. In February 1969, Miles called Zawinul, inviting him along to a recording session. Zawinul said he would be there. A few minutes later, Miles called again and asked Zawinul to bring along some music. The tune he brought was "In A Silent Way." Miles modified the track, removing many of the chords. During the recording session, he also instructed guitarist John McLaughlin to "play like you don't know how to play guitar."

Fast forward fifteen years and Miles asks Irving if he would help him mix his new album. Miles also asked Irving to bring along some music. "I immediately composed a tune entitled 'Outer Space,' which he later renamed 'Decoy.' I went into Paul Serrano's studio in Chicago and recorded the demo with a drum machine and keyboards, and Felton Crews on bass," says Irving.

Later on, Henry Johnson, a former guitarist with Joe Williams, came in to overdub his part. "I asked Henry to play a solo. He sounded great playing inside the changes using a blues-based pentatonic approach. I asked him to try it again, approaching it as a beginner who had just found the guitar and was playing it for the first time," recalls Irving.

Irving says he never knew the story about Miles and McLaughlin. The result of Irving's instructions was Johnson playing a melody that caught Miles's attention. "Miles loved what he did so much that he asked me to transcribe it as a saxophone/guitar solo for Branford [Marsalis] and John [Scofield]. It appears as a 16-bar passage near the end of the track [at 7:22] just after the guitar solo. As Branford and John were sight-reading the transcription 'on the fly', they staggered a couple of the phrases by mistake. It worked contextually, so we kept it." Johnson was thanked in the album's credits. "When Miles heard the demo he called Al Foster and told him, 'Bobby wrote some shit that sounds just like our band!'" recalls Irving.

Miles's genius for arrangement was clearly illustrated when, at the last moment, he asked Jones to thumb the bass. Jones remembers gearing himself for the first take when Miles talked to him on the phone. "It was just before the recording, it was like during the countdown 'one, two,' when Miles suddenly says: 'Darryl thump it!' so I say 'The whole thing?' and Miles says 'Yes.' It was one of those moments when Miles asks the musician to do something that's not in his consciousness." Jones says that this instruction had a profound effect on him. "I had been doing tunes with Bobby's bass lines in Chicago, so I was familiar with them. When Miles said that to me something clicked – it made me play beyond my capabilities."

Irving adds: "The bass line was originally mostly fingered, which sounded more conservative. Miles didn't attend the original tracking session, but he would listen to playbacks of the rehearsal/recording over the phone. Miles knew from Darryl's work with him in live performances that he was a master of the thumped bass technique, so he suggested that Darryl thump the bass. It was a great choice and this change of approach to the bass changed the entire character of the track, making the bass a featured instrument rather than a background part. Darryl told me years later that sound put him on the map. In retrospect it did become a showcase for his 'thunder thumb' technique."

From its dramatic five-note intro on the synthesizer and Cinelu's rattle-like percussive effect, "Decoy" is a track that grabs your attention. A drum machine lays down a metronomic beat that drives the track along, supported by some offbeat accents by Foster and the steady jangling sound from a triangle. Miles liked the combination of a drum machine and live drums. "You use the drum machine like a metronome. When you put a drummer with it, it starts to breathe," he said.[17]

An explosive note introduces Jones's hard percussive bass line, which is mixed upfront – you can almost feel his thumb thumping the strings. Miles plays muted horn and sounds fresh and vibrant. At around the one-minute mark, he plays a melody line, which is supported by Irving on synthesizer. Throughout the track, Cinelu plays a range of percussion including timpani, sticks and conga.

Marsalis begins his solo at around the four-minute point and it's an excellent one, fast, fluent and showing a high degree of control. Marsalis attributes the presence of Miles to his fine playing. "I am notorious for not practising, so my playing was really hit or miss. But the presence of Miles Davis had me so focused in a way that I'd never really experienced before. I had never been tired before after playing and that was another thing I learned from him. Miles just had me on point, man [on my toes]; it's the best I've ever played. Wynton was like 'You don't play like that in my band,' and I said 'You hire Miles to stand in the room while we're doing the record and I have a feeling I will.'"

Marsalis solos for the best part of two minutes and then there is shift in the music as Miles and Cinelu both start to dominate proceedings. Instruments begin to disappear from the mix until only a triangle and a synthesizer can be heard. Cinelu taps a conga drum, Jones thumps the bass and Scofield begins his solo, supported by Cinelu on chugging percussion and triangle.

Scofield plays fast, fluently and inventively, with notes dancing off his guitar. Marsalis re-enters with his second solo, which is bisected by a long rising note on a synthesizer. Marsalis fires off a stream of notes before the track fades with Jones playing some funky lines on the bass. Without a doubt, "Decoy" is one of the album's highlights and, as Irving notes, it is a landmark recording in Miles's musical development: "One jazz critic really got the point and said that it was a pivotal track that bridged the two phases of Miles's comeback era."

The presence of Branford Marsalis has a positive impact on the music and seemed to inspire Miles. It is no surprise that Miles wanted him to join his band (sadly, Marsalis would decline the offer – see pp. 153-54). Of the many tracks Miles recorded in the 1980s, there is no doubt that "Decoy" stands amongst the best of them.

One puzzle. How did "Outer Space" become "Decoy"? The answer is that Miles liked the title. Prior to working with Irving, Miles had asked musician Randy Hall (who worked with him on *The Man With The Horn*), to write a song for The Rolling Stones. Hall came up with a song called "(Let Me Be Your) Decoy." However, The Stones never recorded it: "Keith Richards said it's funky, but it wasn't The Rolling Stones," recalls Hall. However, Miles decided to use the title for his new album. "When *Decoy* came out I thought 'Oh, Miles has used my song,' but when I heard the track I realized he had just used my title," says Hall. Irving says he only discovered this fact twenty years after the track was recorded. "I never asked Miles about the concept of the title, but I thought it was cool and somewhat intriguing."

In the 1980s, the MTV music video channel was changing the face of popular music. Now it wasn't enough simply to release a new album or single: you also needed a video to go with it. And so *Decoy* saw Miles record his first music video.[18] The video was directed by the British director Annabel Jankel, and partner Rocky Morton, who had directed music videos for artists such as Elvis Costello, Talking Heads and Tom Tom Club. Their trademark was the mixing of computer animation with video footage.

Jankel admits that she and Morton were surprised when Columbia Records called to commission them for the shoot. "We said, THE Miles Davis?"

She also recalls the first meeting with Miles to discuss the project. "It was in a big board room at the record company. We had to wait for what seemed like ages and he eventually came in, sort of hunched and holding a walking stick." The young film directors had obviously met Miles on a bad day because, after the pleasantries were exchanged, Miles gripped his walking stick tightly as if he was strangling it and exclaimed that he wanted to die.

One delicate subject was the concept for the video. Miles wanted something glamorous, with dancing girls in a desert, but Jankel and Morton diplomatically suggested that this was not a good idea. "We had to imply that, in our opinion, it wasn't dignified for the world's greatest trumpet player to devalue his iconic status with a bunch of gallumping girls. We wanted something that was more abstract but still suggestive." Despite the rocky start, Jankel says: "Miles was extraordinary to work with. Once he accepted he was working with white, Jewish, English people who were as committed to their approach to filming as he was about his music, we had his total trust."

Once the commission was confirmed, Jankel and Morton asked to see Miles's wardrobe and trumpets to decide what to use in the video. "We went to Miles's apartment and were led into his bedroom. He pulled out various clothing options, which we decided on pretty quickly. But then came out the trumpet and – horror – it was anodized turquoise! We rejected it and insisted that he brought out a trumpet that befitted the world's greatest trumpet player. He then brought out two more anodized trumpets that looked more like kids' trumpets."

The next day, when the first shooting sessions were taking place, Jankel and Morton sent a props person to a nearby pawn shop to find a more suitable trumpet for Miles to play in the video. The props person returned with an old, bashed-up trumpet. "Miles tried playing it but it obviously hadn't been played for years and was all gummed up – nothing worked," says Jankel. "Miles painstakingly took it apart, lovingly restored it over two days and put it back together again so he could play it. When the shoot was over, we returned it to the pawn shop, with the mythic Miles infused in it for the next lucky person who would inherit it."

The video is shot in black and white because: "In our minds, Miles lived in a black-and-white world," says Jankel. It starts with Miles sitting in a chair, wearing a pair of sunglasses, a cap, baggy pants and a short leather jacket. Miles gets up from the chair, removing his sunglasses and, as he does so, he glares into a Hot-Head camera (a remotely-controlled camera that can be panned and tilted through 360 degrees at various speeds) that is almost in his face. "We thought it was a timely juxtaposition of a musician who favoured playing with his back to an audience, and the technology that was perfectly designed to rotate around him, allowing him the freedom to play in his own space," says Jankel.

Miles puts down his sunglasses, picks up a trumpet and licks his lips in preparation for playing the horn. For much of the video, Miles is either standing on a turntable or the Hot-Head camera is revolving around him. For some sections, Miles plays his horn, but in others he blows an imaginary horn or rotates his arms in front of him and then flicks out his fingers, creating a shower of dancing coloured graphics (added during post-production). During the guitar solo, there is also a shot of a guitarist's hand on the fingerboard, with each note generating more coloured graphics (that was John Scofield although we never get to see his face).

Also featured is the hand of a percussionist tapping a conga drum (this is a stand-in as Cinelu didn't take part in the video). At the end of the video, Miles sits back down, puts on his shades again and then stares straight ahead with his hands clasped together. The video then fades out. The shooting, which took place over two days in New York, was followed by several weeks of post-production work, which involved editing and combining the animation with the live footage. Another version, using pixel effects in place of animation, was also produced, but Jankel and Morton decided that the animated version had a more organic feel. Asked how she feels about the video today, Jankel says she still loves the video.

Sadly, Miles wasn't so keen. "That wasn't nothing," he told writer Bob Doerschuk when asked about the video. "I didn't like that so much."[19] It is a shame that Miles didn't like the video because even today, more than twenty years after it was shot, it stands up well. Many music videos produced in the 1980s were over-blown, over-produced and suffocated under a surfeit of fancy digital effects that were often seen as a substitute for a good concept or imaginative direction. Many now look dated. By contrast, the "Decoy" video still looks fresh, puts Miles at the centre of things and captures much of his persona.

"Code MD" (5:56)

Composer	Robert Irving III
Musicians	Miles, trumpet; Robert Irving III, synthesizer, electronic drum programming; John Scofield, guitar; Branford Marsalis, soprano saxophone; Darryl Jones, bass; Al Foster, drums; Mino Cinelu, percussion
Producer	Miles Davis
Co-producer	Robert Irving III
Associate producer	Vince Wilburn Jr.
Executive producer	George Butler
Arranger	Robert Irving III
Engineer	Ron Lorman
Recorded	September 10 and 11, 1983
Live performances	October 1983 – November 1985

Irving wrote "Code MD" under some pressure and after the recording sessions had already started. Like some tunes (and Paul McCartney's "Yesterday" is probably the most famous example), "Code MD" came to the composer in a dream. "I had only had time to compose one tune prior to going to New York for the project. Miles liked 'Decoy' and wanted some more material from me," recalls Irving. "I didn't have access to a piano at the hotel, but, as often would happen, I woke up from a musical dream in which the main melody phrase for 'Code MD' was the theme that permeated my thoughts. I would keep a small tape recorder for this purpose and hummed the melody onto tape."

The next day Irving went over to Miles's place for their morning pre-session meeting and used Miles's piano to develop the rest of the tune. "Miles liked the basic idea, but said I should develop the rhythm basis for it so that he could hear it in context. He had already rented a Linn drum machine and a keyboard for me to work on so I worked out the rhythm foundation for the track at the studio. Then I did a quick sketch chart for the musicians and we played live with the drum machine pattern," adds Irving. When Dave Liebman came to record his tribute album to Miles, *Miles Away*,[20] he chose "Code MD" as the track to represent Miles's 1980s period.

"Code MD" starts with Miles's raspy voice saying, "Go ahead" (the track "Full Nelson" on the album *Tutu* would use exactly the same beginning) before a synthesizer begins playing the theme, with a drum machine and bass synthesizer laying down a mid-tempo groove. Scofield and Marsalis play on top of the electronic backdrop, often doubling up on the main melody. Scofield also gets to take a short solo, while Marsalis plays a few phrases at times but never solos.

Throughout the track Cinelu can be heard playing various percussive instruments but it is hard to discern the contribution of the rest of the rhythm section, with Jones and Foster playing a purely supportive role to the drum machine and bass synthesizer. It is not until two-thirds of the way into the track that we hear Miles on open horn (listen carefully and you'll also notice a second horn buried deep in the mix). Miles plays well, occasionally letting out a series of screams. Irving says: "When Miles overdubbed later, he opted out of stating the melody and instead he improvised over the track. He liked the sound of guitar and sax playing the melody together and felt he would be redundant." However, less than two minutes after Miles makes his appearance, the track fades out.

The main problem with "Code MD" is that electronic instrumentation dominates the track, giving a slightly cold, mechanical feel to the music. On the track "Decoy," Irving showed that he has the talent to successfully combine electronics and live instruments to create music that sounds fresh, exciting, engaging and energetic, but "Code MD" lacks this vibrancy. It is for this reason that live versions of "Code MD" – where the music is much looser – offers a much more satisfying execution of the tune.

Even so, Ron Lorman thinks the music would have made an ideal movie theme. "I thought it would have made a great James Bond theme song. I remember suggesting this to George Butler. That maybe they could ask Mick Jagger to sing the vocals. I regret that I didn't push the idea any further. What could be cooler than Miles Davis doing a James Bond movie theme, with Mick Jagger singing?" At the time we had also discussed the strength of 'Decoy' to be used for possibly an NFL theme song – on the opening long-pass shots. I believe there was serious thought and conversation of Miles opening up for a Stones tour. That would have been a blast. Maybe a bit of that came true with Darryl Jones now playing with The Stones."

"That's Right" (11:11)

Composers	Miles Davis, John Scofield
Musicians	Miles, trumpet, synthesizer; Robert Irving III, synthesizer; John Scofield, guitar; Branford Marsalis, soprano saxophone; Darryl Jones, bass; Al Foster, drums; Mino Cinelu, percussion
Producer	Miles Davis
Co-producer	Robert Irving III
Associate producer	Vince Wilburn Jr.
Executive producer	George Butler
Arrangers	Miles Davis, Robert Irving III
Engineer	Ron Lorman
Recorded	September 10 and 11, 1983
Live performances	October 23 and 25, 1983

Anyone who reads CD liner notes will see that the arrangement for "That's Right" is credited to Miles Davis and Gil Evans, but in fact it was Miles and Robert Irving III who did the arranging. Irving explains how the album credits came about. "Gil would often visit Miles and just hang out talking about life and music. Miles asked Gil to bring me some of his scores to study. It was amazing to see how much space he left open for interpretation or spontaneous direction during performances. Gil told me, 'You are a piano player so it's all right here' (motioning with his fingers). He also said: 'If it sounds right, it is right; it's all about your feeling and your vocabulary to convey that feeling.' He invited me to sit in with his big band. It was quite an experience. I can't believe I never even took a photo of him and Miles together. It's something you take for granted when people are here with you."

On his solo album *Midnight Dream*,[21] Irving would list Miles and Evans among the seven masters whom had made a significant contribution to his musical development through their instruction and inspiration. Irving remembers that, during the recording for *Decoy*, Miles tried to get Gil to come into the studio and take an active part in the project. "The three of us sat and listened to the tracks we had already done. In one sense, Gil didn't have the energy, and secondly he would say, 'Bobby has it all together…he's doing a fine job.' It was my impression that Gil would not have known what to do with the direction the project was taking. His forte as an arranger was to create and develop a concept from start to finish. It was not his nature to join in to reinvent the wheel. Instead, Miles ended up using archived tracks from some previous live performances to fill out the album. Miles had Gil thinking about doing the next project, which would be a ballad album. So when we finished the *Decoy* project, Miles asked me to give Gil some kind of credit for the inspiration he had given us. I decided to give him an arranging credit for my arrangement of 'That's Right.' I felt that Gil deserved it and that it didn't take away from my contribution to the project."

It was a nice gesture and, more to the point, the arrangement on "That's Right" has Evans's inspiration written all over it. A bluesy number, "That's Right" is the longest track on the album and, along with "Decoy," the most successful. There are three reasons for this. First, at more than eleven minutes in length, the extended time means that the music has a chance to breathe and the musicians have an opportunity to stretch out. Second, the electronics are kept to a minimum, with Foster, Jones and Cinelu laying down the rhythm track rather than a drum machine. Third, it was recorded live in the studio and Miles's presence seems to have inspired the musicians – and he in turn sounds inspired by their playing. The result is a virtuous circle that is reflected in the resulting sound and feel of the music.

Starting with a long note on the synthesizer, which decays gracefully, Miles enters almost immediately on open horn. There is a relaxed feel to the music and Jones shows that, in addition to being a superb funk player, he is also a master at playing the blues. Marsalis puts much of the track's laid-back feeling down to Jones's playing. "Darryl Jones is such a monster. One of the big arguments I had with New York guys like [keyboardist] Kenny Kirkland and [drummer] Poogie Bell was that when Miles played with Marcus Miller, they would say, 'Marcus Miller is a great bass player,' and I would say 'He's not a bass player, he's a bass guitar player.' They would ask 'What's the difference?' and I'd say 'Bass players hold down the tempo in a way that drummers like Al Foster – who have a tendency to rush – don't rush. Bass players play in a way that is so simple and yet so weighted that it doesn't allow you to rush – they lock you in."

Marsalis adds: "Marcus is such a phenomenal virtuoso – he's amazing. But I think a lot of it is because he's from New York and not a country boy, so he's urban and hip and there's a certain weight and density to the sound that us country boys have that you don't hear in New York generally. But when Darryl joined the band, Al stopped rushing and we have it on records to prove it."

Foster plays a simple drum pattern that occasionally includes some open high-hat, and Cinelu supports with tambourine and conga. Miles plays with much feeling and at around the two-and-a-half-minute mark, he plays a flurry of notes that culminate with someone letting out an appreciative "Whoo!" After this, Scofield and Marsalis play an arranged melody together, which writer Paul Tingen says was transcribed from a Scofield solo.[22] Soon after, Scofield starts a long solo (it lasts for around two and a half minutes) and like much of Scofield's playing is angular and inventive, throwing in a few surprising twists and turns and at times using a little sustain; at others, some distortion.

Scofield and Marsalis then play the arranged melody again and at around the seven-minute point, Marsalis gets to solo, with Foster playing a series of rim shots combined with some open high-hat. "There was no real preparation for that and that's because it's the blues and Miles's feeling was 'If you can't play the blues, you don't belong here,'" says Marsalis. "I was just sitting there and the song started and when he pointed at me, I started playing. And then they had these changes I hadn't heard, so I was trying to find it, so there's a part of solo where I was playing these funky New Orleans licks and then they got these changes I hadn't heard and you can hear me trying to find it" [around 7:59].

Once again, Marsalis plays strongly, with good tone and control, while a synthesizer plays beneath him (some keyboard stabs sound like Miles's playing) and Jones pops a string or two. Miles re-enters on open horn, again playing with much feeling and emotional impact, and at the ten-and-a-half-minute mark, the music begins to slowly wind down, ending on a couple of synthesizers playing into the fadeout.

"That's Right" is a gem of a track that leaves you wishing Miles had made more music like this on the album. It also showcases Irving's fine arrangement skills and the band plays excellently, especially Scofield and Marsalis. Indeed, Miles was so pleased by the musical contribution of Marsalis that he asked him to join the band, seemingly with the aim of having two saxophone players as he had in the late 1950s with John Coltrane and Cannonball Adderley.

But Marsalis did not join the band. At first, Miles suggested that he had turned down Marsalis. "He just did the record," Miles told writer Ian Carr. "He wanted to join, but he's not really there for me."[23] Talking about the incident years later, Miles had changed his story. "I wanted to have Branford in my band, but he couldn't do it because he was committed to playing with his brother Wynton."[24]

It seems that Miles's first quote was more an act of bravado to cover up hurt feelings because Branford Marsalis actually turned down the offer to join Miles's band, deeply upsetting Miles in the process. Marsalis explains why he refused to play in Miles's band: "When Miles Davis was a child, he used to listen to Louis Armstrong and Duke Ellington and so funk was not music that was natural to him. When I hear old guys play funk, it's just pretty funny to me. There's a couple who really like it and are really curious about it, like [the late] Walter Davis Jr and James Moody and it's just incorporated. And then there's other people like Miles who just never wanted to see a situation where he wasn't considered a hipster. It was really difficult for him to accept that time passes you by. When he started playing funk, that's not the shit that made him what he is."

Marsalis adds that this doesn't mean Miles shouldn't play funk. "But when you listen to him playing 'My Funny Valentine,' it's just phenomenal, and when you hear him play on *Bitches Brew* the shit is phenomenal, although the band concept is more phenomenal than the shit he's playing. When you hear him play 'Human Nature,' it's not phenomenal. There's not a trumpet player in the world who aspires to play jazz who puts that record on to try and learn the solos. When you hear him play on 'Time After Time,' you take one of the greatest jazz instrumentalists in history and he's suddenly become Herb Albert. That was some shit I didn't want to do, I didn't see how that was going to help me become a better musician. I didn't grow up listening to jazz, I grew up listening to rock 'n' roll and R&B. And there wasn't anything about this shit that I didn't already know."

Miles was angered by Marsalis's refusal to play funk with him. "He didn't call it popular music, he called it social music and he said I was a snob because I didn't want to play social music. I said 'That's bullshit, man. I just don't want to play social music with you.' Then he said 'What do you think about Prince?' and my response was 'Don't do it.' I said 'I love Prince, but I don't think you should be trying to play like Prince.' Two years later I joined Sting's band and then he was really pissed off! He said 'You wanted to play with Sting but you wouldn't play with me.' And I said 'If Sting wanted to play "My Funny Valentine," I wouldn't play it with him.' I said 'Sting grew up on this and he's one of the best at it.' Miles was one of the greatest conceptualists, but in his mind that wasn't enough for him."

Marsalis's ultimate reason for not playing live with Miles was to do with his development as a musician. "It's not my place to tell Miles what he should do with his life, but when he wants to include me there are only a few things I'm willing to do with Miles and they're things that will make me better as a musician. Playing 'Human Nature' would not have made me better. Playing that *Decoy* shit – I could have done that all the time, but it was clear to me that Miles was moving away from that. I think he wanted to be popular. He liked to be popular."

Marsalis's attitude sums up the problem Miles faced throughout his musical career. Miles's refusal to stand still and his need to play the music of today rather than yesterday left behind many fans and critics, and, judging by Marsalis's view, some musicians too. It is a shame that Marsalis never did join Miles's band as the evidence on this album suggests that he would have inspired Miles to even higher heights as a musician. Robert Irving III, for one, is sad that Marsalis never joined the band.

One surprise is that despite the highly successful outcome of the recording session that produced "That's Right," Miles hardly ever played live. "We did actually play it twice, [but] the arrangement on 'That's Right' was never transcribed so when it was performed it never sounded as good as the original version," says Irving.

Decoy – the verdict

When *Decoy* was released, the compact disc had been launched in the US and Europe barely a year and, at the time, few jazz releases were available on CD. So when *Decoy* first appeared it was on LP vinyl record and on pre-recorded cassette. In fact, this turned out to be an advantage in terms of how the record was packaged. Although *Decoy* was only a single album, Columbia Records artfully packaged it into a gatefold sleeve, which did justice to a striking portrait shot by the photographer Gilles Larrain (whose past subjects had included John Lennon and Salvador Dali).

Larrain has vivid memories of the shoot. "It took place at my studio in SoHo, New York, and it was around mid-July 1983 and really hot. It also happened to be the time when my air conditioning had broken down, so there were fans working away. I had got the commission through someone at CBS Records who had liked my work. I remember that, before the shoot, people from the record company were saying things like 'Don't worry if it doesn't work out. He'll be late, you have to be flexible.' I was thinking 'Is there a monster coming to see me?'"

At 1.30 pm, there was a knock on Larrain's studio door. "There was this blond chauffeur – it was like something out of James Bond – who announced that he had Mr Davis in his car. I told him to bring him in. So Miles walks in and says 'I'm Miles and I've got five minutes!' I asked him whether he was thirsty and he said he was always thirsty. I had prepared some nice wines for him and some spicy food."

Miles and Larrain then went downstairs to where the shoot was to take place. Larrain (whose father was Spanish Basque) was playing some Flamenco music on a tape. "I knew that Miles liked Flamenco music and he asked me why I was playing it. I told him that I played Flamenco guitar and he said 'Go and get your guitar,' and I said 'You get your trumpet,' and we played together. He liked the sound of my studio because it had a high ceiling like a cathedral and there was lots of reverberation. I remember apologizing about the heat and lack of air conditioning and Miles said: 'Don't worry, I come from Africa a long way back.'" The photo session lasted five hours and Miles even came back a couple more times for further shots. "If Miles liked you, he'd stay around, but if he didn't, he'd leave. I took lots of shots, colour and black and white. Miles was playing his trumpet, messing around, looking at the camera – all kinds of shots," recalls Larrain.

Larrain's photograph (sepia-coloured – the result of Larrain's printing techniques) shows a serious-looking Miles looking over his left shoulder and staring hard into the camera lens. Robert's De Niro's famous line from the film *Taxi Driver*, "Are you talking to me?" fits Miles's expression perfectly. Miles wears a hat and a short jacket, gripping a trumpet in his left hand. "The watch is prominent and I thought 'Oh no, it's too shiny!' But then I thought the picture had it all. You had the soul of Miles in his eyes, the trumpet representing music and the watch representing time or tempo," explains Larrain. "If you look at the picture, you see that the trumpet valves are up because he was just about to play some music. And if you look at his clothes, he is like a man for all seasons and could be dressed for the summer or the winter."

The portrait was also used for the front and back covers of Miles's autobiography. "Miles and [co-writer] Quincy Troupe liked the picture and pushed for it to be used on the cover," explains Larrain. The same shot was also used for a poster, brochure and catalogue for "Miles Ahead: A Tribute to an American Music Legend," a special event celebrating Miles's life and music, which was organized by Columbia Records and the Black Music Association in November 1983. Indeed, the photo session with Larrain was very productive, because another shot would be used for the cover of another of Miles's albums, *Aura*, released in 1989. "Miles asked for a photograph from the *Decoy* shoot to be used, even though it had been taken years earlier," says Larrain.

Sadly, the impact of Larrain's image is lost on a tiny CD sleeve, which only shows the top half of Miles's body.[25] Larrain has fond memories of that time. "He was an amazing person and it was so intimate – it was just Miles and me. I find that if you have all kinds of assistants for lighting, make-up, etc., it becomes more like a fashion shoot. I know people from Columbia Records wanted to come along but we said no. The only other person present was Miles's wife Cicely Tyson. It was an extraordinary occasion – I really liked the guy." Inside the LP and CD booklet are some coloured abstract-like drawings by Miles, although some CD booklets feature a different drawing in black and white.

At just over thirty-nine minutes in length, *Decoy* is rather short, especially when one considers that Miles's previous two studio albums, *The Man With The Horn* and *Star People* were fifty-two and fifty-nine minutes long respectively and, like *Decoy*, were LP releases. Quantity, of course, is no indicator of quality, but nevertheless one wishes *Decoy* offered more music, especially as John Scofield claims more tunes were available: "There's some good stuff in the can. There was another tune that was really hip and Miles played it to George Butler. Somebody told me that Butler had said to Miles that it wasn't commercial enough and that he'd never sell any records with it, so it was left off. I know there was another tune with Branford."

Irving doesn't recall this tune, although he adds that they did record a jam session/rehearsal that was a variation of "Decoy." But the main problem seems to have been a lack of time. "We had to finish and deliver the master to Columbia on a deadline prior to Miles's fall tour (my first tour). There was no time to edit and mix any more material," says Irving.

Decoy is a disparate mix of music combining live heavy funk tracks, with the bluesy "That's Right," Irving's electronics-dominated tracks and Miles's quirky offering, "Freaky Deaky." But despite the patchiness of the music, *Decoy* has many redeeming features, not least some excellent tunes as well as some inspired performances and arrangements. The rhythm section, bolstered by Jones, is superb; Marsalis shows a gift for melody and Scofield is, as ever, imaginative, inventive and exciting. Irving deserves much credit for his arrangement skills.

At around the time of "Decoy," Miles's musical powers were in the ascendant, and his stamina, range, tone and control are noticeably stronger than on previous albums. All this means that *Decoy* is an album that can't be ignored when considering Miles's musical odyssey of the 1980s.

But what do the musicians think of the album? Irving points out that: "It would be the only time Branford Marsalis performed with Miles. The chemistry between Branford and Scofield was electrifying. The polyrhythmic foundation with the drum machine, Al Foster and Mino Cinelu was powerful. This, to my knowledge, had never been done before. 'Decoy,' is, of course, my favourite track. When Miles came into the studio to play over the track there was only one take and it was magical."

Marsalis rates his playing with Miles as one of the most important developments in his musical career. "Absolutely. Playing with Miles and playing with Sonny Rollins. Those were the two periods when I really learned what it meant to be a jazz player philosophically. Standing next to them and watching their eyes as they processed information did wonders for me. It made me understand the creative process a lot better than before I met them."

Jones and Scofield are also positive about the album. "I remember thinking with *Decoy* 'Wow, this is really happening, this is great,'" says Scofield. But Cinelu expresses some disappointment: "I thought it could have been more powerful. There were some good moments on it, but it didn't have the power and strength." Bill Evans says he thought it was interesting at the time but adds: "I always thought we could do a great live record if they just recorded one of our good concerts and put it out that way." On the evidence of "What It Is" and the full version of "Speak/That's What Happened" one has to agree with this sentiment. Ron Lorman's verdict is: "I love it. It's a different album. It's not over-produced, it's not over-engineered, it's not over-played; it's a very subtle, straight-ahead album. It's very easy to listen to and if you turn it up loud, you will feel it."

As with *The Man With The Horn*, *Decoy* finds Miles at the musical cross-roads, moving towards a new phase of music and, more crucially, a new way of making music. In fact, *Decoy* would set the template by which Miles would create music for almost the rest of his life, often using younger musicians who were comfortable with electronics and whose ears were sharply attuned to the contemporary sounds of the day. It marked the time when Miles took a step back from the active creative process in the studio.

In the future, much of Miles's creative input would be reactive rather than proactive. Miles would often hear music that was created by another musician rather than music that was developed by him and his band in the studio. In the past, the studio had been a living laboratory, a workshop for exploring musical ideas and concepts, but that role had now changed. This isn't to suggest that Miles was no longer a creative force in his music. In fact, there would be many times when a suggestion from Miles would transform an ordinary piece of music into an extraordinary one (witness his suggestion for Jones to thump the bass on the title track). But there is no doubt that *Decoy* marked the moment when Miles's energies began to focus less on the music he made in the studio and more on the tunes he played live on-stage.

10 *you're under arrest* (42:02)

Columbia CK 40023

Recorded	Early 1984 – January 1985
Released	Autumn 1985
Producers	Miles Davis and Robert Irving III
Co-producer	Vince Wilburn Jr.
Executive producer	George Butler
Engineer	Ron Lorman, Tom Swift
Mixed by	Ron Lorman, Tom Swift
Tracks	"One Phone Call/Street Scenes," "Human Nature," "MD1/Something's On Your Mind/MD2," "Katia Prelude," "Katia," "Time After Time," "You're Under Arrest," "Medley Jean-Pierre/You're Under Arrest/ Then There Were None"

"[Miles] was always observing rhythms in the natural and urban environments. He was bubbling with rhythms." *Robert Irving III, producer*

"Miles listened to everything. He listened to all kinds of things and there were songs that he heard that had something about them." *Steve Thornton, percussionist*

Background to the album

It is ironic that after years of complaining about the way Columbia promoted his albums to a mass audience, *You're Under Arrest* would become one of Miles's most commercially successful albums. But the journey of *You're Under Arrest* was a long one, involving studio sessions which began in late 1983 and ended in early 1985. What is more, Miles would lose two members of his band just before the first sessions began, another key member would walk out in the middle of the sessions and Miles would go on to make two radical changes to the album's concept.

On November 6, 1983, saxophonist Bill Evans and percussionist Mino Cinelu played their last gig together with Miles at the Radio City Music Hall in New York (although Cinelu would return to the band in January 1987). Evans was finding it increasingly frustrating on the bandstand, with Miles giving him little space to play. It wasn't unusual for an uncomfortable-looking Evans to spend almost the entire set standing on the sidelines while the rest of the band played on. And even when Evans did get a chance to play a solo, it would almost invariably be cut short by a sharp blast from Miles's trumpet.

Whether Miles had got tired of Evans's playing or had simply fallen out of love with the saxophone is not clear. However, on the previous album, *Decoy*, Miles had decided to use Branford Marsalis in place of Evans and had even asked Marsalis to join the band. Evans decided to leave Miles and join John McLaughlin's band. But despite their musical differences, Evans and Miles parted amicably and the two men remained friends – Evans would be one of a select group of musicians invited to play at a special concert for Miles in Paris in 1991, which saw him reunited with many former players.

Mino Cinelu had joined Miles's band in early 1981, at a time when Miles's chops were down and the band members were given lots of space and much scope for improvisation. But since then, Miles had regained his chops and was playing much more. Also, the music had changed, with more funk, more notes and less space being the dominant characteristics. Cinelu felt unhappy and decided to leave. "It was a combination of things. There was a change of management and I was not enjoying the music as much, so it was time to go," he says. Cinelu went on to join Weather Report.

Miles's next project might well have been entitled "Miles Play Pop," as his musical director at the time, Robert Irving III, explains. "Miles's idea was to take the current popular songs and arrange them in the way that he and his contemporaries had rearranged the popular music of their era. His vision for this project was to have Gil Evans arrange the album, with Miles and I co-producing." "We did a ton of pop tunes," says John Scofield. "Gil [Evans] transcribed a bunch of tunes that Miles wanted to do. He had me transcribe a DeBarge tune that he really liked. Bobby Irving did some too. And then we went into the studio and we recorded all these pop tunes. I'm not sure whether it was the result of [executive producer] George Butler telling Miles that the stuff we had done with Branford [on *Decoy*] wasn't going to sell."

According to Scofield, around forty pop tunes were recorded, including Cyndi Lauper's "Time After Time," Tina Turner's "What's Love Got To Do With It?," Dionne Warwick's "Déjà Vu," Kenny Loggins's "This Is It," plus several Toto tunes and songs by the British guitarist/songwriter Nik Kershaw.[1] Miles wanted to do some tunes from Kershaw's album *The Riddle* and Irving transcribed a tune called "Wild Horses (Can't Drag Me Away)." "I rehearsed it with the band maybe once, but some other music distracted Miles and we never recorded this tune," says Irving.

Other tunes were considered from artists such as Roberta Flack and Chaka Khan – Irving says Khan's "Through The Fire" was played live but never recorded.[2] Jazz acts have a long tradition of covering the pop tunes of the day and Miles himself had recorded songs such as "My Funny Valentine," "If I Were A Bell," and "Bye, Bye Blackbird." In 1969, guitarist George Benson released *The Other Side Of Abbey Road*, an album of jazz interpretations of the tunes found on the classic Beatles' album. Miles's initial album concept explains why *You're Under Arrest* would be so commercially-oriented.

Miles spent three sessions at Record Plant Studios in New York at the end of 1983 (on November 17 and 18 and December 17 and 21) but then the project was put on hold because Miles had a hip operation and also suffered from a bout of pneumonia. On January 26, 1984, Miles was well enough to resume the sessions, but a decision was made to bring a percussionist in on the rest of the sessions. Steve Thornton was born in Brooklyn in 1954 and was inspired by Mongo Santamaria's playing of Herbie Hancock's "Watermelon Man" (Thornton would go on to tour and record with Santamaria). A highly talented musician, Thornton has played with many artists, including Roy Ayers, Dizzy Gillespie, McCoy Tyner and Grover Washington Jr.

"At the time I was doing sessions for George Butler. Vince Wilburn and Bobby Irving were in New York doing the song 'Time After Time' and they wanted percussion on it – I think that was the first number I played on. I believe George Butler gave my number to Vince and Bobby and they called me and asked me to go down to the studio and do a session," recalls Thornton. "So I went down and it was nice. We recorded different takes of every song. Miles said to Jim Rose, the road manager, 'I think he adds a nice element to the band.' And then they called me for more sessions and then Miles asked me to go on tour." Thornton would remain in Miles's band for almost three years.

There would be seven more recording sessions (all held at Record Plant) that year, with the last one taking place on April 14, 1984, before Miles decided to radically change the musical direction of the new album. "Gil's energy was quite low for this type of endeavour. He was not doing any new projects outside of his own big band. Miles tried to pull Gil into the project repeatedly. We would get together with Gil, and Miles would show examples of the tunes he wanted to do," recalls Irving. "As time went on, Miles was contemplating his move away from Columbia. He was quite anxious to finish the project because it would be the last one required on his contract."

Irving jointly produced the new album with Miles, and Vince Wilburn Jr. was promoted from assistant producer on *Decoy* to co-producer. Miles asked Irving whether he thought that some of the tracks from a recent live recording would work well if they were mixed in with some of the pop ballads.

"After listening to the tracks, I told him that I liked the live tunes but I felt that it would be a completely different album from the one he had envisioned. He didn't care about that and so we proceeded without Gil and without more ballads," adds Irving (even so, Gil Evans would receive thanks in the album's acknowledgements).

Irving's comments suggest that Miles had already decided to leave Columbia Records in early 1984, although he didn't sign the contract with his new record label Warner Bros until May 1985. Miles's rush to complete the album may also help explain the rather haphazard method involved in the completion of *You're Under Arrest* (more on this below). The change in direction coincided with the recruitment of a new saxophonist, Bob Berg.

The contrast between Berg and his predecessor Bill Evans could not have been more marked. Whereas Evans had been a new talent whose musical experience had been limited to college bands and a few gigs around New York and Boston, thirty-three-year-old Berg was an established player who had played with Horace Silver, Cedar Walton and Al Foster (he appears on Foster's 1979 album *Mr. Foster*). And by the time Berg joined Miles's band, he had already released two albums as a leader, *New Birth* and *Steppin' – Bob Berg Live In Europe*.

Berg's main instrument was the tenor saxophone and he combined fast, fluent playing with a rich, muscular sound. Berg was initially invited to attend a rehearsal. "Miles arrived late and after playing a few tunes and not saying much he packed up and left. I stayed for a while hanging out with a few of the cats. Al Foster and John Scofield were friends and we just rapped a bit and then said our goodbyes. The next day, Jim Rose, who was tour manager at the time, called and asked if I could make a block of dates," recalled Berg.

But before the tour started, Berg would attend another recording session at Record Plant, in early May 1984. "When we first went into the studio we recorded for hours. Miles wanted the tape to run continuously and everything went down, warts and all. I don't particularly remember what tunes we did, but they were all funk oriented. Most of the stuff was improvised and not very structured. I don't think anything was issued from the first sessions I was involved in," said Berg.[3] After this session, Miles would embark on an extensive touring schedule covering the U.S. and Europe. There would be another recording session at Record Plant on September 22 before Miles resumed his European tour. On December 14, Miles was in Copenhagen to receive the prestigious Sonning music award and play in a concert that showcased an orchestral piece composed in honour, "Aura" (see the chapters on *Tutu* and *Aura* for more on this).

According to engineer Ron Lorman, Miles's new album was more or less completed when he decided to scrap it and start again. "The album was put together over a one- or two-month period. Miles turned around somewhere prior to Christmas and decided he wanted to change the whole album. I believe the album was stripped back to drums and we re-did the entire album. He wanted to come in on Christmas Day and re-do it. I don't know why, maybe he heard something new and wanted to do it. We had our twelve or fourteen tracks and we were just about ready to start mixing and he says 'We're starting over. Erase it all,'" he recalls, adding that: "I told George [Butler] and he was like 'what?' We slammed the album together in another two- or three-week period around Christmas. I didn't know whether I was recording or mixing. We were then leaving for a tour."

One reason for Miles's change of heart seems to be that he was dissatisfied with the tempo of the music. Miles had an uncanny ability to notice the slightest change in time and the smallest shift in tempo would disturb him. "We had to re-make everything we did in the studio," he told writer Gene Kalbacher, "because there's different tempos, or it wasn't fat enough and we had to put in new sounds. So I just said, 'Fuck it.' The numbers I thought would carry the album – when I heard 'em back, you know… I have perfect time, you know, near perfect time. I can tell when tempos go off. If they go off for a bar, I can tell because I have to play against 'em … Say you're runnin' a long run or some thing, and behind you the tempo changes in the middle, your eighth notes become uneven." Miles added that a drum machine was widely used in these sessions in order to maintain perfect time.[4] Irving explains how Miles changed the album's structure. "The focus on ballads didn't work for Miles, with the exception of "Ms. Morrisine," "Human Nature," "Time After Time" and "Something's On Your Mind" (which had originally been much slower). This is when we started listening to the live tracks. This was technically Miles's last album for Columbia as he was already planning not to renew his contract. He now wanted the record to have a little more edge, which was more akin to what he did in live concerts. This was something that he desired later after signing with Warner, but they pushed him into a different direction."

Miles dropped the other ballads and added the tune "You're Under Arrest." I transcribed the melody [from a John Scofield solo] and overdubbed it on Hammond organ. "We mixed it to sound like I was part of the live band," says Irving. Also added to the new album mix was the "Then There Were None" medley and "One Phone Call/Street Scenes." " 'One Phone Call' had been the opening of our live concerts so we recorded it and added elements to the track," says Irving.

This suggests that "Time After Time" was recorded before the December 26/27 sessions when the bulk of the new tracks were recorded. Miles did new versions of "Something's On Your Mind" (with a faster tempo) and "Ms. Morrisine" (using John MacLaughlin rather than John Scofield on guitar.)

The addition of "Then There Were None" seems to have been influenced by 1984 being such a dramatic year, both socially and politically. In November, Ronald Reagan was re-elected as President of the United States in a landslide victory. The cold war between the U.S. and the then Soviet Union was escalating as relations between the two countries became frostier. A year earlier, Reagan had committed the U.S. to its controversial Star Wars project, which was designed to destroy Soviet missiles from space.

The Russians boycotted the Olympic Games held in Los Angeles that year. In the same year, there was a severe famine in Ethiopia, which inspired Band Aid's "Do They Know It's Christmas?", the US equivalent, "We Are The World" and, in 1985, the Live Aid concert. The AIDS virus was discovered, British society fractured as mine workers went on strike and battled against the State, and in Bophal, India, a catastrophic disaster resulted in a leakage of toxic chemicals that killed thousands of people.

Miles had always been politically aware, and he now decided that on this album he wanted to wear his political conscience on his sleeve. In effect, Miles had decided to mix pop tunes with political statements about race, pollution and war. "The concept for *You're Under Arrest* came out of the problems that black people have with policemen everywhere," said Miles. "The police are always fucking with me when I drive around in California. They didn't like me driving around in a $60,000 yellow Ferrari, which I was doing at the time I made this record. That's where the concept of *You're Under Arrest* came from: being locked up for being part of a street scene, being locked up politically, being subjected to the looming horror of a nuclear holocaust – plus being locked up in a spiritual way. It's the nuclear threat that is really a motherfucker in our daily lives, that and the pollution that is everywhere. Polluted lakes, oceans, rivers; polluted ground, trees, fish, everything."[5]

Miles told Kalbacher that the full title of the album was *You're Under Arrest, You Have The Right To Make One Phone Call Or Remain Silent, So You Better Shut Up*,[6] and indeed those words appear on the front of the album cover. "Miles wanted to do a parody of his own past run-ins with the police and the problem of police brutality, which was prevalent. He wanted the title to reflect the entire concept," says Irving.

Most of the new tunes were recorded over a frenetic two days on December 26 and 27, as well as the first two weeks of 1985. In the latter sessions, Miles's former guitarist John McLaughlin played on three tracks. Even when the new tracks were laid down, Lorman's problems weren't over. "We finished tracking about four days before we were due to leave and I remember telling George Butler 'It's in the can. Everything's under control. I'll take the tapes with me on tour, listen to them and then, when we come back, I'll mix it.' He said, 'Ron, that's a good idea, but have it done before you leave.' So it got mixed together in that short period of time. I guess at times it might sound a little rough around the edges. But the music on the album is fantastic."

The tracks

"Time After Time" (3:37)

Composers	Cyndi Lauper, Rob Hyman
Musicians	Miles, trumpet; Al Foster, drums; Robert Irving III, synthesizers; Darryl Jones, bass; John Scofield, guitar; Steve Thornton, percussion
Producers	Miles Davis, Robert Irving III
Co-producer	Vince Wilburn Jr.
Executive producer	George Butler
Arrangers	Robert Irving III, Miles Davis
Recorded	Record Plant Studios,[7] early 1984
Engineers	Ron Lorman, Tom Swift
Mixed by	Ron Lorman, Tom Swift
Live performances	June 1984 – August 1991

In 1983 a young and relatively unknown American female artist called Cyndi Lauper released her debut album, *She's So Unusual*. The album sold millions and spawned four top-five hits including a beautiful ballad "Time After Time." Miles heard the tune and liked it so much that he decided to cover it, much to the surprise of some of his band members, including Darryl Jones. "He came to me one day and said 'Do you know that Cyndi Lauper tune "Time After Time?"' I said 'Yeah' and he said 'Learn that, because we're going to play that.' I remember thinking 'Oh man, not with the pop tunes!' But then I heard him play on it and it was 'Oh!' It was apparent I was wrong."

The album version opens with a plaintive cry from Miles's trumpet, which is immediately joined by the rhythm section. Thornton plays shaker and triangle, Jones lays down a solid and unfussy bass line, and Foster plays gentle rim shots. Scofield's rhythm-guitar playing alternates between gentle figures and reggae-like off-beat comping. Miles's trumpet takes on the role of the lead vocalist and he sounds in good lip. The arrangement is sparse, simple and highly effective. According to the Japanese SACD version of *You're Under Arrest*, Gil Evans arranged this track, but Irving says this is incorrect: "Gil didn't actually arrange anything on the project." Miles's album version sticks closely to the original and the track fades out all too soon after three and a half minutes.

"Time After Time" was released as a 12-inch single, with the record's cover decorated by some colourful drawings by Miles. The cut is also longer (5:32), continuing on from the fadeout section, with Miles playing a few more verses. This version is also found on several albums, including *This Is Miles! Volume 2 The Electric Side*. A third studio version has emerged and is much more interesting. It lasts for more than eight and a half minutes and sounds like an early mix (Miles plays different phrases at various points and Steve Thornton's congas are more pronounced). This version sounds more the way Miles played "Time After Time" live, as, at around the six-minute mark, he plays open horn, adding even more poignancy to the sound. The track also comes to a complete end with no fadeout. It's a shame this longer version was not included on the album.

"Time After Time" became one of the most enduring songs in the final decade of Miles's life and once he added it to his set list it remained there right up until his final concert, some seven years later. It became a crowd favourite and Miles often greatly extended the track. Even so, not everyone was impressed. "This becomes a matter of personal taste. Miles and just about anyone else in the history of jazz played a lot of current pop tunes. If you think about Miles's Prestige records, they're full of standards, which were basically the pop tunes of the time," said Berg. "Almost invariably the tunes were played in an original and organic style that made them sound fresh and contemporary. I guess I felt that tracks like 'Time After Time' and 'Human Nature' sounded like direct interpretations of covers. The rhythm section's role seemed somewhat static, and I think with a bit more imagination the hipness factor could have been raised." Berg had a point when it came to the album versions, but on-stage it was a different story.

"One Phone Call/Street Scenes" (4:34)

Composer	Miles Davis
Musicians	Miles, trumpet; Al Foster, drums; Robert Irving III, synthesizers; Bob Berg, soprano saxophone; Darryl Jones, bass; John Scofield, guitar; Steve Thornton, percussion, Spanish voice; Sting, French policeman's voice; Marek Olko, Polish voice; James Prindiville, Handcuffs
Producers	Miles Davis, Robert Irving III
Co-producer	Vince Wilburn Jr.
Executive producer	George Butler
Arranger	Miles Davis
Recorded	Record Plant Studios, December 26/27, 1984
Engineers	Ron Lorman, Tom Swift
Mixed by	Ron Lorman, Tom Swift
Live performances	November 1984 – February 1988

Miles Davis may have grown up in a privileged middle-class environment; he may also have been one of the greatest names in jazz, but that didn't totally isolate him from the poison of racism. As Stevie Wonder once said, no matter how high you reach and no matter how much money you earn, if you are black you cannot cash in your face.[8] It matters not to the racist whether you are a black shoeshine or a black heart surgeon. Throughout his life, Miles had had various confrontations with the police, one of the most notorious occurring on August 26, 1959, when he was coshed on the head by a police officer while smoking a cigarette outside the Birdland club. Miles also liked to drive flamboyant cars such as brightly-coloured Ferraris, which attracted a lot of police attention. "The police fuck with me by stopping me all the time. That kind of shit happens to black people everyday in this country," said Miles.[9]

Miles included his nephew Vincent in that group of people. "My nephew said he was driving out in Beverly [sic] Hills with the drummer from Earth, Wind & Fire [Fred White] ... and the police pulled them over. They were drivin' a Mercedes. They [the police] said 'What're you doin'?' They do that all the time!"[10] Wilburn confirms the story: "Freddie and I used to get stopped coming down to Malibu. Freddie had a Mercedes and the car would be jacked up. I rented a Jaguar in Chicago and got stopped."

So Miles decided to create a musical mini-drama in which he played the role of himself being hassled by the police. The backdrop to "One Phone Call/ Street Scenes" is a frenetic rhythm track based around two older tunes. "One Phone Call" is based on the riff played at 18:49 on the track "Right Off" from the album *Jack Johnson*. In fact, the track begins in a similar fashion to "Theme from Jack Johnson" on the album *Agharta*. "Street Scenes" is based around the second theme from "Speak" on the album *Star People*.

"One Phone Call" opens with the sound of Miles snorting cocaine and muttering under his breath "What the fuck was that for?" Synthesizers are used to create the sound of wailing police car sirens and Miles utters "Uh-uh" as screeching car tyres pan from left to right across the stereo soundstage. The officer – Handcuffs – reads Miles his rights and informs him that the police have been watching him, adding that Miles has "got that girl in there ... smoking that marajaroney." "'Girl' is used in this context as the old slang terminology for cocaine ('Boy' was used for heroin)," explains Irving. "The symbolism was that 'girl' makes you speed."

Just after this point (around 55 seconds), "Street Scenes" begins and in the background Scofield plays a heavily distorted guitar riff. Miles's dark sense of humour pervades throughout the track; at one point, he asks whether the handcuffs are cuff links, and in another he suggests that the police have been following a cab and not, as they say, his yellow Ferrari. Miles joins in muted horn and tells the police to "call George" (presumably Columbia vice-president George Butler), before switching to open horn. Scofield then plays a short solo before the first of three voices emerge.

First is Marek Olko, who was a friend of Miles. "Marek Olko was a Swedish-born concert promoter who lived in Poland. I'm not sure, but he may have been the one to bring Miles to the Jazz Jamboree in Warsaw in October 1983. He had been working long and hard to book Miles in Russia after Russian President Leonid Brezhnev was asked, 'Despite your differences with the West, what do you like about Western culture ... ?' He replied, 'Rolls Royce, Jack Daniel's and Miles Davis.' Marek came very close to sealing an agreement for Miles to play there," says Irving. But the problem was funding. Apparently, the amount that the Russian audience would then pay to see the concert would have been about the equivalent of five US cents. "Coca Cola was approached about partially sponsoring the trip. The Russians offered to fly us (on jumbo jets) to anywhere in the country we wanted to visit for sightseeing. There were also plans for Roman Polanski to make a documentary film on this trip. But it never made good business sense so it never happened," adds Irving.

During this time, Olko was spending a lot of time in New York hanging out with Miles. "Whenever Miles invited me over Marek was there. So, when Miles had the idea of doing voiceovers, Marek was probably the first inspiration for Miles to use a foreign voice," explains Irving. Olko tells Miles in Polish: "You just sit quiet, just sit there and be quiet."

Next comes Steve Thornton. "Miles called me at my house and said 'Steve, come down to the studio,' and I asked 'What do you want me to bring?' and he replied 'Don't bring nothin', just bring your voice.' Then Bobby came on the phone and I asked him what was going on and he said Miles was being serious and wanted me to speak some Spanish on the record. When I heard that, I asked a friend of mine to come down to the studio with me and help me out with my Spanish. Miles told me that he wanted me to say that I come from Miami and this is part of my religion."

The third voice was supplied by the rock star Sting, who just happened to be visiting the studio with Darryl Jones. "I auditioned for Sting at Studio Instrument Rentals in New York," recalls Jones. "I think Sting had already told me I had got the gig. I was leaving the rehearsal and I think he may have asked 'Where are you going?' and I said I had a record date with Miles. And he just kinda looked at me! I asked him if he wanted to come along and he said 'Yes.' So I called Miles, who said it was cool. As soon as Sting gets in and is ready to say hello to Miles, Miles cuts him off and says 'You know, Sting, can you speak French?' And Sting says, 'Well, a little bit.' Two minutes later he was on the phone translating with someone and getting this monologue together."

Irving takes up the story. "Miles gave him the words to translate and it turned out that Sting wasn't very fluent in French. So he called his girlfriend in London who was fluent and had her do the translation for him over the phone." Sting says in French "You have the right to remain silent, so shut up [tais-tois]!" Miles then says "Tais-toi some of this," and, according to those present, grabbed his crotch as he spoke the words. Then the track fades out.

Miles enjoyed himself immensely during the making of "One Phone Call/Street Scenes" as Thornton recalls. "I remember Miles was in the studio with handcuffs – if you listen to the album you can hear them. And he had Jim Rose [Miles's road manager and the album's production co-ordinator] handcuffing him while he was talking. He was playing the role!" But according to Irving's recollection: "Miles wanted the sound of the handcuffs but Jim didn't actually handcuff Miles, although he would have enjoyed doing so." "One Phone Call/Street Scenes" is a piece of self-indulgence from Miles, but behind the play-acting and the humorous asides lies a serious message.

"You're Under Arrest" (6:14)

Composer	John Scofield
Musicians	Miles, trumpet; Al Foster, drums; Robert Irving III, synthesizers; Bob Berg, tenor saxophone; Darryl Jones, bass; John Scofield, guitar; Steve Thornton, percussion
Producers	Miles Davis, Robert Irving III
Co-producer	Vince Wilburn Jr.
Executive producer	George Butler
Arrangers	Miles Davis, John Scofield
Recorded	Record Plant Studios, December 26/27, 1984
Engineers	Ron Lorman, Tom Swift
Mixed by	Ron Lorman, Tom Swift
Live performances	November 1984 – July 1985

"You're Under Arrest" is based around a riff played by John Scofield, which is why he gets the writer's credit. It's a storming funk number which starts in a similar way to "That's What Happened" on the *Decoy* album, with a sharply edited introduction. Right from the start, the power and the energy of the track is unrelenting. Jones plays a furious funk riff, Foster slams into the snare drum as if it has offended him and Thornton's timbale drums rattle along. Irving and Berg play the theme together, and just before the ninety-second mark Miles enters on open horn, emitting a series of shrieks and adding more excitement to the sound.

Berg then plays an all-too-brief powerful solo. "[It's] a short edited excerpt of a longer solo I played at the date," said Berg. Miles plays more open horn, before Scofield enters with a fast, agile solo. Irving and Berg play the theme again and the tracks begins winding down, before coming to a complete stop. "You're Under Arrest" is undoubtedly one of the album's highlights. Everyone plays with great focus and intensity and, what is more, everyone seems to be having fun.

It is an observation that is confirmed by those who played on the track. "We really liked that version of 'You're Under Arrest.' I remember Al saying it really smoked. The groove we got on the tune was so strong and Miles played his ass off," says Scofield. Irving adds: "The title track was fun to play in live concert, making it my favourite track." "You're Under Arrest" has such a powerful groove that saxophonist Gary Thomas (who joined Miles's band in late 1986) was inspired to do a cover version on his 1989 album, *By Any Means Necessary*, featuring John Scofield on guitar.

"Medley: Jean Pierre/You're Under Arrest/Then There Were None" (3:23)

Composers	Miles Davis, John Scofield, Robert Irving III
Musicians	Miles, trumpet; Al Foster, drums; Robert Irving III, synthesizers; Bob Berg, tenor saxophone; Darryl Jones, bass; John Scofield, guitar; Steve Thornton, percussion

Producers	Miles Davis, Robert Irving III
Arrangers	Robert Irving III, Miles Davis
Recorded	Record Plant Studios, December 26/27, 1984
Engineers	Ron Lorman, Tom Swift
Mixed by	Ron Lorman, Tom Swift
Live performances	June 1985 – November 1986

Miles did not often explain the rationale behind his music, but with this track he made an exception. In his autobiography he explained how the tune was written as a reaction to global events. "They're just fucking up everything because they're so fucking greedy," he said. "I'm talking about whites who are doing this, and they're doing it all over the world. Fucking up the ozone layer, threatening to drop bombs on everybody, trying to always take other people's shit, and sending in armies when people don't want to give it up. It's shameful, pitiful and dangerous what they're doing."[11] Irving says: "Miles wanted to make an artistic/socio-political statement with this piece and so we approached it like a piece of art, taking several days to brainstorm about the elements that would go into it. The idea was to summarize some of the other tracks like a 'life review' before the 'ending' (nuclear holocaust)."

Like "One Phone Call/Street Scenes," the medley is a mini drama, although this time Miles and Irving used library tapes to create many of the sound effects. The track starts with Jones playing the bass line of the child-like tune "Jean-Pierre." Miles and Scofield then play the theme together before Scofield switches to play the theme to "You're Under Arrest." Both versions are fractured and distorted and there is a sinister undercurrent to the sound. Next we hear a countdown for a missile launch. "Then There Were None" starts at the 1:17 mark, when Irving plays a beautiful melody on a Celeste. Miles told Gene Kalbacher that he was inspired to include the Celeste on the track because "Somebody, my daughter or my wife, gave me a music box for Christmas. It plays 'My Funny Valentine' on Celeste."[12]

As Irving plays, children can be heard playing together in a playground. Then a bell tolls, helicopters hover above the skies, a baby cries and suddenly bombs start exploding. There are screams and cries, as Irving continues to play the Celeste and Miles plays the "Jean-Pierre" theme. The sound effects end, leaving just the sound of Irving and Miles playing together. Miles's horn drops out of the mix and Irving continues to play the melody and then stops. Miles can then be heard whispering "Ron, I meant for you to push the other button." A bell tolls and the track ends. "Miles was hearing sound effects that would create an atmosphere of the contrast between child-like innocence (the Celeste) and ominous implications of the sirens and bombs," Irving says.

Miles also explained why he had used the various effects on the track. "I have the synthesizer creating sounds like flaming, howling winds which were supposed to be a nuclear explosion. Then you hear my lonely trumpet, which is supposed to be a baby's wailing cry, or the sad cry of a person who has survived the bomb's explosion. That's why those bells are there in that tolling, mourning kind of sound."[13] The juxtaposition of the children's screams and the explosions is unsettling, and the contrast between the innocence of childhood and the horrors of the world has been widely used throughout art. The James Cameron 1991 movie *Terminator 2: Judgement Day*, for example, contains an opening scene that could have been written for "Then There Were None," when an idyllic playground scene suddenly turns into a nuclear holocaust.

"George [Butler] told me you can't listen to that but once. It's like a political statement. It might happen!"[14] said Miles. Ron Lorman, who engineered the track, also found the music hard to listen to. "That's a very spooky song. I was uncomfortable doing it and I'm uncomfortable listening to it. I think Miles was expressing concern about politics and world affairs," he says. "The music is all sort of mixed with 'Jean-Pierre' and Bobby's keyboard. Miles was fascinated with children's nursery rhymes. It then crossfades into this scary image with children playing and the bells and there's an atomic bomb. The vision of the children playing in the playground and the bomb going off was what he wanted. The effect may not be as strong today in terms of what you can get technically but the music is so haunting and so weird with the bells going off. When I hear it I feel I'm watching children in a playground and the bomb goes off and it's just killing them. My hand was shaking at the console trying to record that thing. I still get shivers. At the very end of the track Miles whispers – 'Ron, you pushed the wrong button.' I'm still not sure but I figured that was our President [Reagan] and not me."

"Human Nature" (4:30)

Composers	Steve Porcaro, John Bettis
Musicians	Miles, trumpet; Vince Wilburn Jr., drums; Robert Irving III, synthesizers; Darryl Jones, bass; John Scofield, guitar; Steve Thornton, percussion
Producers	Miles Davis, Robert Irving III
Co-producer	Vince Wilburn Jr.
Executive producer	George Butler
Arrangers	Robert Irving III, Miles Davis
Recorded	Record Plant Studios, probably December 26/27, 1984
Engineers	Ron Lorman, Tom Swift
Mixed by	Ron Lorman, Tom Swift
Live performances	April 1984 – July 1991

Michael Jackson's album *Thriller*, released in 1982, was a phenomenon, selling more than fifty million copies, winning eight Grammy awards and spawning seven hit singles. One of them was "Human Nature," a song with a beautiful melody and catchy 'why, why, tell them that it's Human Nature' hook. But fate had played a hand in the track making it on to the *Thriller* album.

"Human Nature" was originally written by Steve Porcaro, keyboardist with the rock band Toto. "I had written the song for my daughter Heather. Something had happened at school and it just inspired me. I wrote the song while we were mixing [the hit single] 'Africa' and was just tinkering on the piano and wrote 'Human Nature.' It was one of a batch of three songs I had written in a certain time period. I had written the lyrics, which were the same verse I was singing over and over again. I had the 'why, why' chorus with the slap echo. Like most of my songs it was an unfinished song."

Porcaro and fellow Toto member David Paich worked with producer Quincy Jones on the *Thriller* album, doing some synthesizer programming and playing. "Quincy had been asking David for songs and he was sending a messenger almost every day to David's house – where I was living at the time – to pick up anything David was working on. And so David was sending him stuff. One time, he had gotten a call that the messenger was on his way and he called down to me and told me to throw something we'd been working on onto a cassette. I didn't have any blank cassettes, so I took a cassette that had 'Human Nature' on one side and turned the B-side over, rewound it and put on these two songs of David's and then gave them to the messenger," recalls Porcaro.

Jones played both sides of the cassette and was excited about "Human Nature." "Quincy called David the next day and I remember David telling me that Quincy was raving about this tune that went 'why, why.' It took David half an hour to tell Quincy that it wasn't his song! But the song was incomplete lyricwise and Jones asked Porcaro to finish them. "I forced myself to write the lyrics and Quincy was less than thrilled with them and he asked if I would mind if he brought in John Bettis to finish them. I was completely thrilled with what John did with the lyrics." Bettis, one of America's leading songwriters, has worked with many artists, including The Carpenters, Madonna and Burt Bacharach.

Like "Time After Time," "Human Nature" would become one of Miles's best-known tunes in the 1980s and remain in his set-list until the end. But the sessions for "Human Nature" saw the departure of his long-time drummer and good friend, Al Foster. Miles explained why Foster left in the following way: "He wouldn't play the kind of drums I wanted him to play. He never did like that rock thing. I used to ask him over and over again to play that funky backbeat, but he just wouldn't play it and so I brought in my nephew, Vincent Wilburn, on drums because that was his thing. I hated to see Al go because we were close, but music comes before everything."[15]

"Al loved Miles and they offered so much for each other musically. They were like brothers, for maybe twenty years or more," explains Lorman. "Miles couldn't say goodbye to anybody, maybe he didn't have that capacity. It was awkward for Miles to change relationships and I don't think Miles could face the fact that the relationship, for whatever reason, had come to an end. So he shut it down like a light switch. It was his way of handling the separation. At the time, Miles was looking for a pushier and pushier drummer and so he was forcing Al to play harder. Al Foster is an amazing drummer. Al is the most fluid, natural drummer I know. This guy could push a band like you'd never believe and yet Miles wanted something else. I guess Miles wanted a more rock-and-roll type of drummer."

Certainly Miles's reference to Foster's reluctance to play "that funky backbeat" will have surprised many who had heard Foster play with Miles over the years. One of the main reasons was that as Miles got into synthesizers and electronic music, he became fascinated by drum machines and in particular their ability to keep perfect time. Miles wanted his drummers to lock into a groove, and so on many tracks he employed a drum machine and a click track for the drummer to play along to. A click track is designed to keep the drummer at a constant tempo and involves the drummer wearing a pair of headphones and playing in time to a pulse that is generated by a metronome or rhythm box. Some drummers complain that a click track stifles their creativity and makes their drumming stiff. Foster was clearly unhappy with this process of recording drums.

But then Miles often gave his drummers a hard time. Irving recalls an incident that occurred when the band was playing in Pompeii, Italy [probably July 21, 1984]. "Miles had his back to the audience and was singing drum rhythms to Al Foster and motioning with his hands how he wanted them played. Miles was a frustrated drummer himself. He was always hearing rhythm cadences. Foster obviously felt insulted by Miles telling him what to play, so he stopped playing in the middle of the concert and just sat there with his sticks in his lap and arms crossed while Miles begged him to resume. The audience of about twenty thousand people in this old Roman theatre was silent during this stand-off. It was amusing!"

The stand-off lasted for around five minutes, and when the band finally re-started, the audience went wild as Miles gave Foster a solo – in fact, says Irving, Foster got a solo every performance after this. "This incident was the precursor to Al walking out of the studio during the tracking of 'Human Nature,'" he adds. Vince Wilburn Jr. was in the control room when Miles asked him to play on the track. "I loved Al and I hated to see him go, but when Uncle Miles asked me to play I did not hesitate," says Wilburn.

"Human Nature" starts with Wilburn counting off and tapping his drum sticks together. If you have heard the track sung by Michael Jackson, you'll notice that the arrangement sticks very close to the original, with Miles's muted trumpet taking on the role of Jackson's vocals. A special mention should be made about John Scofield's excellent rhythm-guitar playing, which is double-tracked in places. Miles's version adds little to the original, except of course the magic sound of his horn. But when "Human Nature" was played live it was a different story. The song's arrangement evolved into a tour de force, with the final section turning into a showcase for a blistering guitar or saxophone solo.

Steve Porcaro was thrilled when he first heard Miles's version of his tune. "My father was a jazz musician and when I was growing up most of the music we heard in our household was classical music and jazz – Miles Davis. He was my father's hero. My brother Jeff learned to play drums listening to 'Bag's Groove.' Miles Davis was ingrained in all of us, so I was completely thrilled. I was so honoured. I remember doing a session with the bassist Neil Stubenhaus about six months after Miles did *You're Under Arrest*. He just cornered me and said 'Do you realize how great it is to have Miles do one of your tunes? Do you have any idea what it means?' I certainly did. It's one of the things I'm most proud of out of everything I've done."

"MD1/Something's On Your Mind/MD2" (7:17)

Composers	Miles Davis, Hubert Eaves III, James Williams
Musicians	Miles, trumpet; Vince Wilburn Jr., drums; Robert Irving III, synthesizers; Darryl Jones, bass; John Scofield, guitar; Steve Thornton, percussion
Producers	Miles Davis, Robert Irving III
Co-producer	Vince Wilburn Jr.
Executive producer	George Butler
Arrangers	Robert Irving III, Miles Davis
Recorded	Record Plant Studios, December 26/27, 1984
Engineers	Ron Lorman, Tom Swift
Mixed by	Ron Lorman, Tom Swift
Live performances	December 1984 – November 1986

D-Train was a duo comprised of keyboardist Hubert Eaves III and vocalist James "D-Train" Williams, which had a number of disco/funk hits in the 1980s, including "You're The One For Me," "Keep On," and "Music," all designed to get you grooving on the dance floor. The tune "Something's On Your Mind," however, was something of a departure for D-Train, being a ballad, complete with female background singers.

Miles's first cover version stuck close to the original ballad arrangement (you can hear this arrangement on discs three and four on *The Complete Miles Davis At Montreux* boxed set, which cover the 1984 concerts). But Miles later decided to up the tempo. "Miles liked the way it grooved with the faster tempo," explains Irving. "He was right, the syncopated accents inherent within the rhythm section parts were somehow more emphasized at the faster tempo. This was the whole appeal for this tune, which was otherwise not very complex harmonically or melodically. Rhythm concepts were at that time the main inspiration for much of what Miles created. I remember when he was questioned by a talk show host who asked, 'I've seen you at the Lakers' basketball games...so are you a Lakers' fan?' Miles responded, 'I'm not there for the game – I'm there for the rhythm.' It was true. He was always observing rhythms in the natural and urban environments. He was bubbling with rhythms."

There was also another reason for the increased tempo, adds Irving. "He felt that the faster tempo allowed the tune to serve as a bridge between the pop ballads we had recorded ('Human Nature' and 'Time After Time') and the more fusion-oriented tunes like 'You're Under Arrest.'" "Something's On Your Mind" is sandwiched between "MD1" and" MD2." The former consists of the sound of a bell and a steam train waiting at the station, which leads into the tune.

The drum machine is most pronounced on this tune and there is a some-what mechanical and stiff feeling to the rhythm track, although Jones plays a supple and funky bass line. The increased tempo gives the music a strong groove and Miles plays well on muted horn. "I remember how Miles used to move when he heard that song – he loved that groove," recalls Thornton.

The most interesting section occurs around the three-minute mark when Scofield plays a short solo and then Miles briefly resumes playing. Scofield solos again but, this time, Miles returns powerfully on open horn. The track continues to groove along, Miles switches back to the mute and then the tune ends. "MD2" immediately follows and simply consists of some wailing notes played on a synthesizer, accompanied by a rattling percussive sound.

Incidentally, Miles wanted to call this tune "D-Train," and Irving asked the group if they could use that title on the album, but they refused. However, they were happy for Miles and Irving to put additional music at the beginning and end of the tune and that is how "MD1" and "MD2" came to be written.

"Ms. Morrisine" (4:57)

Composers	Morrisine Tynes Irving, Miles Davis, Robert Irving III
Musicians	Miles, trumpet; Robert Irving III, synthesizers; Darryl Jones, bass; John McLaughlin, guitar; Vince Wilburn Jr, drums; Steve Thornton, percussion
Producers	Miles Davis, Robert Irving II
Co-producer	Vince Wilburn Jr.
Executive producer	George Butler
Arrangers	Robert Irving III, Miles Davis
Recorded	Record Plant Studios, early January 1985
Engineers	Ron Lorman, Tom Swift
Mixed by	Ron Lorman, Tom Swift
Live performances	April 1985 – November 1985

Miles and Cyndi Lauper had been in communication because he was record-ing her song "Time After Time" and whenever Miles was in contact with a pop artist he would typically offer to write a song for them, often delegating the task to singer/guitarist Randy Hall or Robert Irving III. Irving and his wife Morrisine wrote a tune for Lauper called "I Can't Stay Away From You." This number would become the precursor for two tunes that appeared on *You're Under Arrest*, "Katia" and "Ms. Morrisine."

In early 1985, Miles discovered that the guitarist John McLaughlin was in New York with his partner Katia Labèque, the French concert pianist. Miles had always been close to McLaughlin, who had played on a number of classic Miles's albums, including *In A Silent Way*, *Bitches Brew* and *Jack Johnson*. "When McLaughlin called Miles to say hello, Miles invited him to come to the studio and play on a track. There was nothing for him to play on," explains Irving. "Miles suggested that we do a variation on 'I Can't Stay Away From You.' I transcribed the flute passage from the intro and the chords. When John saw the music he decided right away that there were too many notes that would have to be played too fast for guitar. I tried to convince him to try it anyway, but this part remained a keyboard flute passage and John played a rhythm guitar part and solo instead."

Miles and his band had in fact recorded an early version of the tune on September 22, 1984, featuring John Scofield on guitar, but when Miles discovered McLaughlin was in town he was keen to include him on his new album and so decided to cut another version of "Ms. Morrisine," this time using McLaughlin on guitar. Scofield, in typically gracious fashion, says: "I don't think I knew John was coming in. McLaughlin was always my idol and was very nice to me, so I didn't feel so bad about being replaced by him. I guess that Miles just loved McLaughlin and wanted to play with him again."

"Ms. Morrisine" is a reggae-tinged tune which uses a synthesizer to play the main rhythm rather than the chopping rhythm guitar usually employed on reggae music. Miles starts off the track by blowing a few phrases on open horn before the rhythm section starts up. Wilburn pounds away on Simmons electronic drums, and at around the twenty-second mark there's a lovely flute sound played by Irving on keyboards. McLaughlin then plays a driving guitar riff beneath Miles's horn. Miles plays strongly, occasionally soaring towards the upper register and there is a joyous, upbeat feel to the music – it's a sharp contrast to the darkness of "Then There Were None." Just before the four-minute point, McLaughlin plays a gritty solo, which he double-tracked. The solo fades out and leads into the next track, "Katia Prelude."

"Katia Prelude" (0:40)

Composers	Miles Davis, Robert Irving III
Musicians	Miles, trumpet, OBX-a synthesizer; Robert Irving III, DX-7, Korg Poly-6 and OBX-a synthesizers; Darryl Jones, bass; John McLaughlin, guitar; Vince Wilburn Jr., Simmons drums; Steve Thornton, percussion

Producers	Miles Davis, Robert Irving III
Arrangers	Robert Irving III, Miles Davis
Executive producer	George Butler
Recorded	Record Plant Studios, early January 1985
Engineers	Ron Lorman, Tom Swift
Mixed by	Ron Lorman, Tom Swift
Live performances	None

Fans of LP vinyl records will tell you that the old analogue format had a lot going for it, not least the fact that there were two sides to a record. This gave artists the opportunity to put two strong opening numbers on the same album – one for each side. Another feature was the ability to put a link track or prelude at the end of side one. For this reason, "Katia Prelude" works better on an LP than on a CD, where it immediately precedes the full version.

"Katia Prelude" segues on from "Ms. Morrisine" and fades up on McLaughlin playing some scorching guitar licks over a busy rhythm section and assorted synthesizer sounds, before it fades out after less than a minute. Miles described the track as follows: "What happens is that the other side of the LP, the A side, ends with like Bap! Like I cut loose the chord on the synthesizer and it goes chromatically up. Then, with a couple of rat-a-tat things on the drums, real sharp rolls, crisp rolls, we changed the mood. John comes in at the end on the A side. And when you turn over to the B side, he's already playin'... The start of the B side is on A. When we got through with the last tune, to change the mood I let the synthesizer go, Wa-aa-aa-aa-ah like that, and John starts playin'. You hear two or three bars, then you turn the side over and John's right into it already."[16]

"Katia" (7:47)

Composers	Miles Davis, Robert Irving III
Musicians	Miles, trumpet, OBX-a synthesizer; Robert Irving III, DX-7, Korg Poly-6 and OBX-a synthesizers; Darryl Jones, bass; John McLaughlin, guitar; Vince Wilburn Jr., Simmons drums; Steve Thornton, percussion
Producers	Miles Davis, Robert Irving III
Arrangers	Robert Irving III, Miles Davis
Executive producer	George Butler
Recorded	Record Plant Studios, early January 1985
Engineers	Ron Lorman, Tom Swift
Mixed by	Ron Lorman, Tom Swift
Live performances	April 1985 – August 1985 (July 1991)

French-born Katia Labèque is a classical pianist who often performs in concert with her sister Marielle, who is also a pianist. Labèque met McLaughlin after a concert and later joined his band, playing piano and synthesizer on tour. She also performs on several McLaughlin albums, including *Belo Horizonte* and *Music Spoken*. She and McLaughlin also became romantically attached. Labèque also has an interest in jazz and has recorded an album of jazz tunes, *Little Girl Blue*, which features artists such as Chick Corea, Herbie Hancock and Joe Zawinul.

Katia Labèque also became close to Miles. "Miles did not attend many classical music concerts, but he came to all our concerts in Los Angeles and New York. Miles was an amazing man," she explains. "One day he arrived with the record [*You're Under Arrest*] and I said 'Thank you, that's very nice,' and then he showed me the cover with 'Katia Prelude' and 'Katia.' I was so happy, even though the tune is almost like a jam session." But when Labèque came to record the tune on her album *Unspoken*[17] she found that "there were a lot of elements we could use."

Miles was always keen for McLaughlin to record with him, explains Labèque. "They had a close relationship – there was a love between them." Miles called McLaughlin and asked him to bring his guitar and come to the studio. "It was a complete surprise and we had no idea what was going to happen," says Labèque. "Of course, when I got the studio, I had no idea that Miles would name the music after me." "Katia" was written and recorded very quickly, explains Irving. "We needed to take advantage of John McLaughlin's presence in the studio. It was all so spontaneous that there was not time to write any more new music. Miles suggested that we isolate a motif from 'Ms. Morrisine' [in the fifth bar] and use that as a vamp for 'Katia.'"

Ron Lorman describes how the recording of "Katia" precipitated some frantic activity in the studio – and why the track starts as a fade-in. "I was getting ready to remix a song when Miles unexpectedly walked in with John McLaughlin. We were totally patched [plugged into the studio console] for a remix and he went into the studio and started playing. I'm tearing the patch bay apart and we started recording that tune channel-by-channel as I'm pulling the patches out of the console and then we'd get a kick drum on [one] channel, then the snare, then the trumpet – the whole tune came up bit by bit, channel by channel, they played for about half an hour." Miles said: "I wrote this thing right quick for John, and we just played behind; I'm playin' synthesizer and Bobby's playin' synthesizer. Then I punched in a lot of brass parts – bap, bap ba-da da da-da, that kind of shit. It turned out good. That's a strong number."[18]

"Katia" may start with a fade-in, but the intensity and the energy are there right from the start. The track has a similar feel to "Speak" on *Star People* and there is an abrasive quality to the sound. It is music that keeps you sitting at the edge of your seat. The track is driven by McLaughlin's powerful rock-like guitar chords, Wilburn's pounding Simmons drums, Thornton's clattering percussion and Jones's funky bass riff (which is a close variation to the one he plays on "Ms. Morrisine" at around the 38-second mark).

Supporting this are an assortment of keyboard stabs, lines and chords played by Miles and Irving. Throughout the track, Miles plays a series of trumpet blasts which are accompanied by cymbal smashes from Wilburn. Miles also plays some short, powerful solos on open horn. Just after the seven-minute mark Miles brings the energy level down with a short flurry of notes, which are followed by some "spacey" sounds played on a synthesizer. Then Thornton blows a whistle and the synthesizer fades out. "Katia" was one of the tracks performed at Miles's concert in Paris in July 1991.

At almost eight minutes in length, "Katia" is the longest track on *You're Under Arrest* and Miles explained how he edited it from a master tape that was almost twice as long. "When I went into the studio to edit 'Katia,' everybody acted like somebody died. It was so good they wanted to leave everything on... They said, 'We're not gonna touch it till you get there.' So I went down there and edited it. Every time John starts some runs on guitar, and ends this and ends that – you know, that staggered start – I just took it out."[19]

"Katia" is essentially a high-energy jam and there are many moments of drama and excitement, but after almost eight minutes of such intensity the following track on the album, "Time After Time," comes as something of a relief.

You're Under Arrest – the verdict

Once again, Columbia Records' art department did Miles proud by releasing *You're Under Arrest* in a gatefold sleeve, despite the album being a single disc like *Decoy*. The cover photograph, taken by black photographer Anthony Barboza, features Miles holding a gun. Barboza had known Miles since the 1970s, when he first photographed him for *Essence* magazine. "Miles and I got on really well. He used to cook for me. He was a brilliant cook. I remember he had this giant French cook book – it must have had around 2,000 pages. Miles also used to send me his girlfriends to photograph – I remember shooting Mayisha and Betty Davis – man, she was something else."[20]

In December 1984, Barboza had also directed Miles in two thirty-second commercials for the Japanese drink company Van Aquavit. One of them had Miles blowing into an empty bottle as if he was playing a horn and the second had Miles walking around and playing in an empty room. "I remember they bought Miles some clothes and he didn't like them, so he went out and spent $7,000 on his own clothes for the shoot!" says Barboza. Barboza also introduced Miles to writer Quincy Troupe, who later became Miles's autobiography ghost writer.

Miles and Barboza discussed the concept for the album cover and decided to have Miles holding a gun. Barboza went out and bought a toy gun for the photo-shoot. The image seems to be based on the vision of white America's worst nightmare – a black man with a gun. The album design was memorably described by writer Ian Carr as one which "boldly combines camp with kitsch. Against a red background, a colour reminiscent of the décor of a Toulouse Lautrec brothel, Miles – wearing a black homberg and the black garb of a Spanish dancer – holds an automatic gun in both hands."[21] Incidentally, Barboza had Miles hold the gun as if he was left-handed for artistic reasons.

As with Miles's two previous albums – *Decoy* and *Star People* – *You're Under Arrest* also featured his artwork. The inside cover featured a coloured abstract drawing of a female dancer, while the LP's paper inner sleeve featured a large black and white drawing by Miles that included pianists, couples, people sitting at a bar and two signatures of Miles. "[On] the inside cover I did some black dancers; you can frame the picture. The sleeve – I got forty or fifty people doin' a lot of different things. It looks like an orgy, but it isn't. I drew all that stuff," said Miles.[22] This artwork did not appear in any other format.

So much for the cover, what about the contents? *You're Under Arrest* combines many different elements: pop tunes ("Time After Time," "Human Nature," and "Something's On Your Mind") with political tracks ("One Phone Call," "Then There Were None"), hard funk ("You're Under Arrest," "Katia") and reggae influences ("Ms. Morrisine"), yet, despite this wide variation in theme and genre, one has to agree with Irving's assessment that: "It's an eclectic mix of music and despite the way it came together I feel that it has cohesion."

The cohesion and the coherence are much stronger on this album than on *Decoy*, which also mixed various genres. The public certainly seemed to think so and *You're Under Arrest* sold more than 100,000 copies after just a few weeks of its release. The *Penguin Guide to Jazz* describes the album as: "Entertainment-wise, perhaps the best of the late albums."[23] "Certainly the album was uneven, but it seemed to define Davis in the 1980s as *Bitches Brew* had in the 1970s and *My Funny Valentine* in the 1960s," was the verdict of critic Stuart Nicholson.[24]

You're Under Arrest does have its faults. Bob Berg noted that: "It's not my favourite album...it sounds a bit canned," but in view of how little time Lorman had to mix the album, he did a creditable job. At this point in his career, Miles was fascinated by synthesizer and drum machine technology, both for its sonic characteristics and its ability to keep perfect time. The album's soundscape is dominated by the Yamaha DX-7 synthesizer. On the album, *Tutu*, Miles would go even further, replacing his band with an electronic orchestra.

The political tracks may lack the power and subtlety of those produced by other artists, such as Marvin Gaye ("What's Going On") and Gil Scott-Heron ("The Revolution Will Not Be Televised," "B-Movie") but they are heartfelt.

Miles: JVC Festival, New York, July 5, 1981

Miles: Beacon Theatre, New York, with Mino Cinelu, Marcus Miller, Al Foster and Bill Evans, December 31, 1981

Miles: Jones Beach, New York with Bill Evans and Marcus Miller, August 28, 1982

Miles's long-time friend and musical associate Gil Evans helped with some of the arrangements on *Star People*

Miles: JVC Festival, New York, June 26, 1983

Miles: JVC Festival, New York, with Al Foster and John Scofield, June 22, 1984

Miles: Hartford, Connecticut, June 22, 1985

Bob Berg: North Sea Jazz Festival, July 12, 1985

Miles with Darryl Jones: North Sea Jazz Festival, July 12, 1985

Miles with Angus Thomas: The Pier, New York, August 17, 1985

Miles: The Pier, New York, August 17, 1985

Robert Irving III: Danbury, Connecticut, August 31, 1985

Miles with Mike Stern: Danbury, Connecticut, August 31, 1985

There is much to enjoy and admire on *You're Under Arrest*, not least any album that features the superb guitar playing of both John Scofield and John McLaughlin.

You're Under Arrest is probably Miles's most accessible album of the 1980s and, indeed, if you were going to recommend one album from Miles's final period to someone who wanted to get into this era of music, *You're Under Arrest* would be close to the top of the list. It is also significant because it represents the last time when Miles's working band would be present on so many album tracks.[25] *You're Under Arrest* has its flaws, but it is also a powerful mix of funk, rock and pop – and there is much to enjoy when listening to it.

11 *aura* (66:59)

Columbia CK 63932

Recorded	January 31 – February 4, 1985
Released	Autumn 1989
Producer	Palle Mikkelborg
Executive producer	George Butler
Musicians	Miles, trumpet; John McLaughlin, guitar; Vince Wilburn Jr., electronic drums; Thomas Clausen, Ole Koch-Hansen, Kenneth Knudsen, keyboards; Bjarne Roupe, guitar; Bo Stief, fender and fretless bass; Niels-Henning Ørsted Pedersen, acoustic bass; Lennart Gruvstedt, drums; Marilyn Mazur, Ethan Weisgard, percussion; Niels Eje, Oboe/Cor Anglais, Lillian Tørnqvist, harp; Eva Hess Thaysen, vocals; Benny Rosenfeld, Palle Bolvig, Jens Winther, Perry Knudsen, Idrees Sulieman, trumpet/flugelhorn; Vincent Nilsson, Jens Engel, Ture Larsen, trombone; Ole Kurt Jensen, Axel Windfeld, bass trombone/tuba; Jesper Thilo, Per Carsten, Uffe Karsov, Bent Jaedig, Flemming Madsen, saxophones/woodwinds; Palle Mikkelborg, additional trumpet/flugelhorn
Soloists	John McLaughlin, guitar on "White," "Orange" and "Violet;" Niels-Henning Ørsted Pederson, acoustic bass on "Green" and "Indigo;" Bo Stief, fretless bass on "Green;" Thomas Clausen, acoustic piano on "Indigo"
Engineers	Henrik Lund, Og Niels Erik Lund
Mastered by	Rune Persson (original), Darcy M. Proper (re-issue)
Tracks	"Intro," "White," "Yellow," "Orange," "Red," "Green," "Blue," "Electric Red," "Indigo," "Violet"

"He was like a crystal in a way. There were so many beams to him, both as a person and as a musician." *Palle Mikkelborg, producer*

"I think it's a masterpiece, I really do." *Miles talking about* **Aura**[1]

In late 1984, Miles would participate in an event that would ultimately result in him recording one of his best works for years. It would also see Miles perform with a big band, something he had not done for almost twenty years. The event which sparked all of this was the Sonning Music Award, which Miles won in 1984. The award, which comprises a diploma and money (in 2004, it was roughly the equivalent of US$40,000), was founded by Leonie Sonning, the widow of Danish writer Carl Johann Sonning, and is given in recognition of a significant contribution to music. The first award was made in 1959 and the first winner was Igor Stravinski. Other past winners include Leonard Bernstein, Isaac Stern, Dmitri Shostakovitch and Yehudi Menuhin. Miles became the first jazz artist and black person to win the award.[2]

But getting Miles to accept the award had not been easy. The Sonning Committee had written to Miles on several occasions, but he had not replied to their letters. Finally, the committee decided to send one of its musical consultants, Erik Moseholm, to New York to talk to Miles personally. Moseholm eventually managed to arrange a meeting with Miles and talked to him about the award. When Miles saw the list of winners, he was impressed and accepted the prize. One of the rules of the Sonning Award is that the winner must perform (play or conduct) at the award ceremony, but as Miles was the first ever jazz winner they weren't initially sure how this rule should be interpreted. They decided that Miles should perform for at least five minutes. Miles agreed and was even prepared to perform solo if need be.

But the Sonning Committee wanted to commission a work especially for the award ceremony. Gil Evans was asked to write something, but never managed to complete anything, so the Committee then asked two composers based in Denmark. One of them was the American composer Ray Pitts and the other was Palle Mikkelborg, a native of Denmark and a highly accomplished trumpeter, composer and conductor. Mikkelborg's main influences were Miles, Gil Evans, and the composers Charles Ives and Olivier Messiaen (the latter won the Sonning Prize in 1977). "One composer who was very important in the Miles story that Miles may or may not have been aware of was Olivier Messiaen. The reason being is there are convergences and similarities in the harmonic language. The use of similar kind of scale structures. The diminished scale is very prevalent in jazz and very focused, and developed and advanced in Miles's music," notes arranger/composer Paul Buckmaster, who worked with Miles in the 1970s and 1980s.

Mikkelborg was influenced by jazz, classical and avant-garde music and had also used electronics with the trumpet. He had also been a band leader and had played with an impressive roster of jazz artists that included George Russell, Dexter Gordon, Bill Evans, Don Cherry and Gil Evans.

Mikkelborg composed a piece comprising seven movements, which he called "Aura." The inspiration behind the piece was Miles's musical and personal aura. Many people who have met Miles talk about the incredible presence he had. The guitarist Bobby Broom, who played with Miles in 1987, recalls: "I was rehearsing in a large room, and playing with my head down and my eyes closed. Then I felt this thing, a change in the atmosphere. I looked around and there was this little guy walking into the room. You could feel Miles's presence, his aura. It was pretty wild." Patrick Murray, who was Miles's concert sound engineer in the late 1980s, adds: "Miles had quite a powerful aura. He was one of the few artists that I have worked with that you immediately felt his presence the moment he entered the room. He didn't have to say a word. You just felt it."

Mikkelborg chose an unorthodox system to compose "Aura." First, he assigned a chromatic note to each letter of the alphabet and then using the letters that make up Miles's name – M.I.L.E.S.D.A.V.I.S. – he created a theme. "It was like an orchestral tribute or homage to his life in these seven colours," says Mikkelborg. There were seven movements to "Aura" – "Yellow," "Orange," "Red," "Green," "Blue," "Indigo" and "Violet" – and Miles was supposed to play only on the last movement. "When I wrote the piece I hadn't met Miles, I had only heard the stories and of course had been to all his concerts in Sweden and Copenhagen," says Mikkelborg. "My inner voice said I should do it in seven movements, these prime colours. Miles was fascinated by the idea although I'm not sure he fully understood what I did or maybe he wasn't that interested! He just found it interesting that someone described his life in colours."

Miles flew into Copenhagen in December 1984, accompanied by his nephew and drummer, Vince Wilburn Jr. "We first met at the airport and he was very reserved. He wasn't that healthy at the time and Denmark wasn't showing its best side with the weather – it wasn't even snowing even though it was December. It was just dark and wet," remembers Mikkelborg. "Vince was very sweet. Things loosened up in the limo. One of the first things Miles said to me was that Gil was at home 'listening to overtones,' meaning he would never finish anything. But he said it in a sweet way as if he was protecting a friend."

The award ceremony and concert was due to take place at the Falconer Centre concert hall. Supporting Miles was the Danish Radio Big Band, which was part of the Danish Radio Orchestra. Miles attended the rehearsal and was surprised by the size of the orchestra. Mikkelborg had also arranged for some coloured lights to shine on to the stage. "He was happy with what we had done with colours and oboe and harp and things he hadn't worked with for many years – I don't think he was prepared for that. I think he was impressed with what he saw," says Mikkelborg. The original plan was that

Pitts's composition would be played in the second half, with "Aura" being the opening piece. But when Miles heard the music he decided that although he liked Pitts's music, he didn't want to play on it. As a result, "Aura" became the centrepiece of the concert.

It was during these rehearsals that Miles was introduced to Marilyn Mazur, a percussionist Mikkelborg had invited to play at the concert. Mazur was born in New York to an African-American father and a Polish mother, but was raised in Denmark from the age of six. As a child she studied ballet and classical piano and later on became a percussionist and composer. Mazur soon became well-known on the Danish jazz scene. "I'm sure Miles was impressed by the way Marilyn plays and the way she looks when she plays because she looks fantastic. She was also just one of two black people present and I think he was amazed to see her playing percussion," says Mikkelborg.

"I was thrilled to be invited by Palle to play in 'Aura,' as I wasn't an actual member of the Danish Radio Big Band, which was the main body of the orchestra," says Mazur. "I was seriously inspired by Miles's music, which I had listened to from my early teens (such as *Bitches Brew*), and I would really have felt left out of something great if I hadn't been a part of 'Aura'! Anyway, in one of the first rehearsals, with Miles listening to the music from the concert hall, I was told that Miles wanted me to come down and say hello to him. I remember feeling rather shy but honoured. Of course all us Danes were in total awe of this incredible icon and did our best to play this heavenly music together." In fact, Miles was so impressed with Mazur's playing that he would later on invite her to join his band.

The award ceremony took place on December 14, 1984 and Mikkelborg had invited Miles's guitarist John Scofield along as second soloist. Danish Radio recorded the event and later broadcast the concert. As expected, Miles played in the final movement "Violet," but such was the crowd reaction that "Violet" was repeated as an encore, then John Scofield began playing "Jean-Pierre," and Miles and the Big Band played it for almost seventeen minutes. Finally, Mikkelborg surprised Miles by getting the band to play "Time After Time." "He ended up playing for more than an hour – he just went on and on! He started off by not knowing who the hell we were, but it ended up being a very happy evening," recalls Mikkelborg. Mazur says: "I enjoyed the Sonning prize concert very much, and when Miles came back to record the piece I wasn't surprised at all, since I felt that it was a wonderful project that Palle had created."

Miles left Denmark and went back to the U.S., where he made two adverts for the Japanese drink company Van Aquavit. He also completed the recording of the *You're Under Arrest* album. But the experience of performing "Aura" had had a great impact on Miles and he decided he wanted to record the work. In the late 1950s and early 1960s, Miles had worked with Gil Evans on *Porgy And Bess* and *Sketches Of Spain*, two orchestral works that rank amongst some of his finest music. Miles and Evans also worked on a new orchestral work, *Quiet Nights*, in 1962/63, but the project was never finished and Miles was unhappy when it was released. "The last thing Gil and I did on *Quiet Nights* ... just wasn't happening. It seemed like we had spent all our energy for nothing and so we just let it go. Columbia brought it out anyway ... .but if it had been left up to me and Gil, we would have just let it stay in the tape vaults. That shit made me so mad that I didn't talk to Teo Macero for a long time after that."[3]

The last time Miles worked with the Gil Evans Orchestra was on February 16, 1968, when they recorded the track "Falling Water" at Columbia Studios in New York. Miles had always hoped to work with Evans again on a major project and "Tosca" was often mentioned as a possible work, but it never happened. Evans had helped arrange much of the *Star People* album and Miles had also tried to get him involved in the *Decoy* album and a planned album of pop ballads, but nothing ever came to fruition.

But the "Aura" concert had clearly whetted Miles's appetite for recording with a big band again, and so in mid-January 1985 he called Mikkelborg one morning at 3 am Danish time. "He called me and said 'I'm coming back, we're doing it. Put the band together. Two weeks from now I'm here.' That was very surprising to me," recalls Mikkelborg. When Miles called, the Danish Radio Big Band weren't even in the country, but Mikkelborg managed to organize things within the two-week time frame.

Miles arrived back in Copenhagen and was again accompanied by his nephew Wilburn Jr. Miles and Mikkelborg began working together on an album version of "Aura." "The record is quite different from the first performance on stage," explains Mikkelborg. "Working with Miles meant he more or less guided us. He used his intuition – which was the biggest lesson I took from him. He could immediately say 'I like that, I don't want it.' Even though I don't think he ever studied the score, he captured the atmosphere of the piece. He was very sweet. He'd say things like 'I have nothing against saxophones but I'm not sure I like them so much in groups.' In other words, 'Take that part out.' He was very careful about what he said. I knew what he could be like but he was very sweet to us."

Mikkelborg describes how Miles shaped the music on the album version. "He played much more and cleaned out much more of my written material. The live performance was also much longer than you could get on one CD as well, so we had to cut anyway. But he did some interesting things that he didn't do in the concert. The 'White' movement, for example, was not in the concert. Everything that Miles did was clever in the best sense of the word. He always said 'There's a beginning, a middle and an end.' He already saw the end when we begun things, he knew where it would lead to."

Mikkelborg says he didn't approach the album with any preconceived plans and so was prepared for the unexpected. One of Miles's surprises was to bring in Vince Wilburn Jr. on electronic drums. " I just went along to be with Uncle Miles and the next thing I know he's got these Simmons drums and gets me to play on the album," recalls Wilburn. "We had a drummer who already knew all the time signatures for the pieces and it would have been impossible for anybody to learn all the parts in just a few days so I think Miles decided Vince should be like a colour," adds Mikkelborg.

Mikkelborg would usually meet Miles at his hotel room to discuss the music, but the day before recording was due to start the two men met at CBS Records' offices in Copenhagen. "He asked me to play the tape from the concert and bring the score. We were sitting in a small office and I had a cassette. Miles looked at the score and then he looked at me and said 'I want some bassoons.' I said 'Miles, it's too late.' He said 'What do you mean, too late? Gil could do it in a day. I need some bassoons and low flutes.' I said 'It's impossible. We're record-ing tomorrow morning at 9 am. We can't put it in.' He looked at me with those eyes of his and said 'Okay.' It was like a little test or Miles just seeing how far he could go. It was like 'Does he know what he wants?' It was very nice and very strong. I said 'We have to stop here, this is the material. I can't do it. We have to work with this' and there were no problems."

Mikkelborg recalls the effect Miles had in the studio. "Everybody was quiet when he came in. All the musicians were completely quiet. He walked into the studio and put a strange hat on. He walked around and looked at all the musicians and he gave the characteristics of many of them just by looking at them. It was very strange. The big lesson I learned from Miles was to dare to believe in your intuition – trust in your intuition. When I was compos-ing most and thinking less, it was not as good as when I composed less and mediated more. Miles was a very spiritual person. I said 'You're like a Zen master to me.' He asked 'What do you mean?' I said, 'I haven't a clue what you mean, but I know that it's right.'" Some the sessions at Easy Sound Studio in Copenhagen were recorded by Danish TV and parts of the film were used in a programme about the making of *Aura*.

During all their time together, Mikkelborg never talked to Miles about the trumpet, except once, several years later, when he asked Miles how he managed to get his amazing sound on the soundtrack for *Siesta*. "I said, 'That sound is incredible – how did you do it?' He said 'A good microphone,'" recalls Mikkelborg. He also remembers a "beautiful incident" in the studio. "One of the young trumpet players wanted to show Miles his trumpet. He said 'Miles, I'd like you to see my trumpet' and Miles said 'It looks great.' And the guy said 'Miles, it's from before the war.' Miles looked at him and said 'I prefer peace.' It was so sweet."

Marilyn Mazur recalls that: "I was more daring at those recording sessions, where I also had a lot of musical functions to experiment with. Miles decided to play on top of most of the composition, and so we got the chance to work more closely together. It was very exciting to experience the man at work. He enjoyed experimenting and also having such a different musical playground to the American scene."

The recording sessions took place between January 31 and February 4 and it was during the recording sessions that Miles heard that John McLaughlin was in town with his band. "Miles asked John to come up immediately. He didn't even have a guitar but I had a good friend who had a guitar and an amp. McLaughlin came along with his partner Katia Labèque," recalls Mikkelborg. Katia Labèque says "Miles always wanted John to play with him wherever he was, but the problem was that Miles usually wanted John to play electric guitar, which he rarely carried around with him." "John came and had no idea what was happening," notes Mikkelborg. "Miles said 'Play downtown New York, John, you know what I mean?' Then they put on the tape and John played fantastically – wild and strong. They were very close and it was nice to see them together. There was such a strong intuition between them. I think they were like father and son at one time."

Miles and Mikkelborg spent a further five days working together on the music and Miles asked the Dane to produce the album. "I told him that I felt unqualified. I had co-produced my own CDs, but this was on a different scale. He said 'What's wrong with you? I told you, you produce.' He had confidence in me. There was a lot of cleaning to do. He did so many solos and cracked so many notes. We needed one solo and we had ten. So I decided I would keep him informed about the process. Some of the lines he had played were so beautiful that I wanted to use them as themes. So with a couple of keyboard friends and myself on flugelhorn, I whistled something from *Live Evil* and asked if we could use them [the lines] as a theme. So we did another session," says Mikkelborg.

Mikkelborg worked hard on the music. "I had a very good engineer. I felt blessed and I felt comfortable enough to produce it," he says. Mikkelborg eventually sent Miles the final mixes on cassette. "I called him one night and Cicely Tyson took the phone. She said, 'It's nice to hear from you, Miles is thrilled with what he's heard.' It was like, phew! Then Miles came to the phone and said 'You've done a motherfucker job. I like what you did.'" Miles was indeed thrilled with the results and was soon telling everybody about the new album he had made. "It'll be a two-record [i.e. two LPs] set on Columbia," Miles told writer Richard Cook. "This music will be like nothing you ever heard."[4]

But Columbia seemed less than keen to release the album. Timing seems a more likely explanation. Around this time, Miles's plans to leave Columbia for Warner Bros Records were well advanced, and it is possible that once Columbia discovered that Miles was planning to leave them the company's interest in the *Aura* project rapidly cooled.

But Columbia Record's then vice-president George Butler thinks the real reason was that "The marketing department didn't understand the album and I think they felt it would be difficult to sell *Aura*. It wasn't the melodic kind of stuff that Miles was doing, so I guess they felt 'Let's sit on it for a while.' I insisted that we put it out." Mikkelborg says: "I had a feeling they didn't want Miles to go in this direction," adding: "[but] even to record with Miles had been a treasure and I remember thinking that if nothing happens, it's still great. Of course I'm very pleased that the album came out."

The first time Mikkelborg discovered that *Aura* would be released was when he received a surprise call from Butler. "He said 'I just went through some of Miles's tapes and I haven't heard Miles play like this for years and I love it. We're going release it,'" recalls Mikkelborg. So, after sitting in Columbia Record's tape vaults for more than four years, *Aura* was finally released. And when fans and critics heard the album, they realized that Miles was right – it sounded like nothing they had heard before.

The tracks

Note: all music is written by Palle Mikkelborg. All tracks were recorded at Easy Sound Studio, Cophenhagen.

"Intro" (4:47)

The opening movement begins with several seconds of silence. This desolate aural landscape is slowly brought to life by a sustained note played on a synthesizer that creeps along like a slow-moving glacier. As it advances, the sound gradually increases, both in volume and intensity. Then John McLaughlin enters, playing the ten-note theme on guitar. His final notes are sustained and mixed with the rising synthesizer note, increasing both the tension and the expectation.

Suddenly, the band enters dramatically with two trumpet blasts introducing a syncopated rhythm produced by keyboard stabs, drums (both electronic and acoustic) and Mazur's frenetic percussion. McLaughlin plays the theme again and then Miles enters powerfully on open horn, his sound soaring over the bubbling rhythm section. The complex time signatures add drama and excitement to the sound and McLaughlin plays a fine short solo, displaying both speed and agility. Miles plays again, at times seemingly pushing himself to the limit. Then the track appears to come to a complete stop, before McLaughlin repeats the theme. The track ends with his final sustained notes decaying gracefully.

"White" (6:05)

It is highly appropriate that "White" should be the first colour to appear on the album, because when white light is passed through a prism it splits up into the seven colours of the rainbow – the names of the movements that follow this track. However, "White" was not originally written as part of *Aura*, but as background music on a tape that was played before the start of the concert. "That was a tape I made to introduce people to a certain sound and a certain scale when they came into the hall," explains Mikkelborg. "Miles had heard that tape. One afternoon, all the horn section had gone home and there were only Marilyn, myself and an oboe player, who was about to pack up and go. Suddenly Miles said 'Do you have that tape?' Mikkelborg asked what tape Miles was talking about and then realized it was the one he had prepared for the concert. Fortunately, Mikkelborg had the tape in the studio and he played it for Miles.

"Miles was sitting in the corner and it was very dark. He played two solos on top of that tape. That was a very magical moment. I said to the oboe player, 'When I do like this, you play the first part of this theme and when I do this, you stop.' I said to Marilyn 'Just hit what you have.' And it became one of the strongest movements. Miles was also very surprised himself and at the end he said 'Did you like my rhumba?' Then he said, 'You clean up the solos, you know what to do.'"

Miles's opening phrase on muted horn is so powerful that it was used as the theme for two major radio series about him, *The Miles Davis Radio Project* on American Public Radio and an eight-part BBC Radio 3 series, *The Music Maker*, which was presented by Ian Carr. Both series were broadcast in the 1990s. The movement has a haunting quality, with a stark soundscape that includes bells, a warm oboe sound and synthesizer notes that dance across the sparse aural backdrop. Miles plays beautifully and with much tenderness. The use of double-tracking and echo effects on Miles's horn is reminiscent of Teo Macero's studio post-production work of the 1970s.

The track is full of space and silence, which provides the perfect backdrop to Miles's haunting sound. "'White' is the sound of nothing. The tonality is very open," says Mikkelborg. "White" is also a classic example of the "less is more" principle, which often guided Miles's musical philosophy. Mikkelborg's arrangement is superb and everyone involved makes a valuable contribution to the overall sound. "I remember hearing a Wayne Shorter interview in which he said, 'I hate music that sounds like music,'" recalls Mikkelborg, "and I almost leapt up from my seat, because that is exactly how I feel about music. Too much music gets in the way of the music."

"Yellow" (6:49)

"Yellow is like the sun rising. We say good morning to the sun and nature in all its beauty," explains Mikkelborg. The opening combination of harp and oboe creates an atmosphere of calm and serenity and evokes the feeling of a new day dawning. Just after the two-and-a-half minute point, the serenity is disturbed by an abrasive guitar riff, followed by a blast of horns that burst out of the mix. The brass section, now joined by pounding drums, creates drama and tension. Serenity is revived but then the brass section returns, before the energy level is taken back down again and the track fades out.

"Orange" (6:38)

A peel of bells marks the entrance of the next movement, a mid-tempo number that is dominated by a heavy backbeat provided by Wilburn's electronic Simmons drums, a funk bass line, Mazur's percussion instruments and some lively guitar playing from McLaughlin, who at times plays aggressively. Miles joins in muted horn and later changes over to open horn. "Orange is when life starts. There's some yellow reflection and some red. Life starts, people go to work. In that movement we're taking a walk or driving slowly through a city of the prize winners," says Mikkelborg. "The small themes in the bass line and the orchestra are themes of the previous prize winners. It's as if they're all standing on the corner and we're driving through and they're waving at us with their little themes – Janet Baker, Stravinsky, Messiaen. I made this movement using the same system as I used for Miles," says Mikkelborg.

Around the five-and-a-half-minute mark, the bass line changes, increasing the tension, and some funky chords are played on an electronic piano. Then the tempo increases and a blast of horns and a driving bass line propel the music along. The mix of frantic guitar playing, wah-wah effects, muted horn stabs and busy electric piano are reminiscent of some of the music Miles played during his electric period of the 1970s. Just before the fadeout the horn section almost quotes the theme from Miles's tune, "Wrinkle," and the energy remains high until it fades out. "Orange" is powerful piece, spoilt only by the addition of electronic drums, which give the music a dated feeling. Miles's musical instincts were more often than not proved to be right, but sadly on this occasion they were not.

"Red" (6:05)

The first sound heard is Miles's open horn, to which some reverb has been added in post-production. He plays over a shimmering synthesizer line. Then the heavy rhythm section starts up, dominated by pounding electronic drums, some slapped bass and an edgy guitar riff. Miles plays strongly and just after the four-minute point, a distorted guitar chord marks the end of the first section. The second section is made up of the syncopated rhythm from the "Intro." "Red" has energy and intensity, but Mikkelborg was not completely satisfied with the final result. "The energy is there, but it could have been heavier in my opinion. But we couldn't make it any heavier, because the more we put on, the less it sounded."

"Green" (6:12)

After the high energy of "Red" comes the introspective "Green," an atmospheric piece that begins with some delicate playing on fretless bass by Bo

Stief, whose notes dance over swirling synthesizer lines. An English horn plays the theme. The music is beautifully recorded and mixed – you can hear Stief's fingers move along the fretboard. Just before the four-minute point, there is a short pause before the second movement begins. Now we hear Miles's muted horn, this time supported by some fine playing by Niels-Henning Ørsted Pedersen on acoustic bass.

The sounds are joined by a sixteen-voice choir which in reality is the voice of vocalist Eva Hess Thaysen overdubbed many times. " 'Green' is a tribute to Gil. It consists of two slow movements, one light green and the other dark green," says Mikkelborg. The arrangement of "Green" certainly evokes the spirit of Gil Evans and it was only much later that Mikkelborg discovered a striking synchronicity between the title and the subject of his tribute. "After *Aura* was released, two female graduates from north Denmark asked if they could do their research on *Aura*. I agreed and then one of them said to me: 'Regarding the "Green" movement, did you know that Gil Evans was born with the name Gilmore Green?' I had had no idea."

"Blue" (6:36)
" 'Blue' is intuitive of Miles's late acoustic period before he started using electronics," says Mikkelborg. Swirling synthesizers fade in, Miles blows a few phrases on open horn before an infectious reggae-like rhythm starts up in 7/8 time. The catchy three-note bass riff and chopping guitar riff are supported at times by muted horns. Miles plays strongly and there is an uplifting feel to the music – you get the impression that everyone played this tune with a smile on their face. Just after the four-minute mark, the music undergoes a dramatic transformation as the reggae rhythm fades out of the mix and Miles switches to muted horn. Miles plays along with a horn section, but then the supporting horns disappear to be replaced by music-box-like sounds played on a glockenspiel and a synthesizer. Miles plays tenderly over the fragile notes and then the track ends.

"Electric Red" (4:17)
Miles was not averse to repeating tunes that he liked on the same album – witness "In A Silent Way" from the album of the same name or "Jean-Pierre" on *We Want Miles*. Miles liked "Red" so much that he played two solos on it – one with open horn and the other with a Harmon mute. "I said to him 'What do I do? You've done two fantastic solos!' He said 'Use them both'," says Mikkelborg. "Red" was played with open horn and on "Electric Red" he puts in the mute. The track is almost two minutes shorter than "Red" but still makes a strong statement and ends with a screaming guitar and a heavily distorted chord. In the words of Mikkelborg, " 'Electric Red' is a powerful movement."

"Indigo" (6:05)

When Aura was re-issued in 2000, this track contained a little surprise for anyone who had heard the original version of the track – a new five-second brass
intro. Even Mikkelborg was unaware of the change. "It was never mentioned to
me by [re-issue producer] Bob Belden. They asked me to do new liner notes.
But they also said they wanted the freedom to do what they felt. It was never
planned in the original, but I have nothing against it," says Mikkelborg with typical generosity. He explains the background to the tune. "I wrote this as a tribute
to Herbie Hancock, Tony Williams and the rest of the band Miles had at the
time [the second great quintet of the 1960s]. It was in their loosest, freest time
period, around the time of *Filles De Kilimanjaro*. Miles didn't want to play on it."
Miles told Kheprha Burns: "The piano player was playing enough music."[5]

"Indigo" is indeed a showcase for pianist Thomas Clausen, who plays fast
and fluently over a fizzing rhythm section that includes a walking bass line,
energetic cymbal taps and furious and inventive percussive work from Mazur.
Clausen's piano dominates the music to the extent that it is hard to see a place
for Miles's horn. The Hancock influence is clearly evident as Clausen races up
and down the keyboard spraying chords in the process. A wild guitar and frantic
horn section bring the track to an abrupt end.

"Violet" (9:05)

Aura ends with the music of Miles's childhood – the blues. "There were two
Messiaen chords that had been on my mind for years, bluesey chords. I took
the two organ chords from Olivier Messiaen's book *My Musical Language* –
which was my bible at the time – and used them as my basic chords; combined
with Miles's theme and the scale, I created his name," explains Mikkelborg.
"We used three soft synthesizers." Miles is joined by McLaughlin on guitar on
this track. Both solo well over a laid back and abstract bluesy rhythm section,
with Miles on muted horn for most of the time and McLaughlin playing some
searing lines. As the track draws to a conclusion, Miles takes out the mute
and blows a flurry of notes over pounding drums and tinkling percussion. He
finishes with a scream and the track ends in a dream-like manner as harp,
synthesizers and organ fade out.

Aura – the verdict

Aura finally appeared in the autumn of 1989, around the same time that
Miles's autobiography was published and coinciding with the release of his
third album for Warner Bros, *Amandla*. Sadly, it was released a year after the
death of Gil Evans, but there is a possibility that Miles had played Evans the
tapes Mikkelborg had sent him. It would have been interesting to have heard
Evans's thoughts about *Aura* and it may even have motivated him to work
with Miles again on a major recording project.

When many people first heard *Aura*, their reaction was "Why have Columbia Records held on to this gem for so long?" *Aura* was released as a double-LP album (in a single-album cover) and as a single CD. Both records featured the same cover shot by Gilles Larrain, a sepia-coloured photograph showing Miles wearing a hat and looking downwards as he blows a muted horn. The shot was taken from the same photo-shoot that produced the cover shot for the *Decoy* album.

Columbia Records had had more than four years to prepare for the release of *Aura*, all of which somewhat compounds the shoddy album packaging on the original release. In the first instance, you had to look hard to find any mention of Palle Mikkelborg's contribution to this momentous project. Mikkelborg's name does not appear on the front or back cover. When Gil Evans helped arrange and orchestrate albums such as *Porgy And Bess* and *Sketches Of Spain*, his name was rightly on the cover alongside Miles's. When Marcus Miller produced and arranged the soundtrack to *Siesta*, his name was as large as Miles's on the album cover and deservedly so.

All this makes the lack of prominence given to Mikkelborg's name nothing short of scandalous. Miles had long left Columbia Records by the time *Aura* was released, so the decision to relegate Mikkelborg's significant contribution to two small credits on the inside of the CD cover and a small personal note on the background of the album must have come from the record company.

There are no recording dates and, what is more, an error in the mastering process resulted in the first section of "Green" being wrongly positioned at the end section of "Red," giving "Red" a total running time of almost ten minutes and "Green" one of just four minutes. The only redeeming features were Khephra Burns's informative liner notes and, of course, the music itself. The mastering error was corrected in the 1997 and 2001 Japanese *Master Sound* versions of *Aura* and in a new remastered release in 2000 on Columbia/Legacy.

The latter release also improved the packaging, including several photographs taken from the recording sessions (including two featuring Miles and Mikkelborg) and Mikkelborg contributing some extended liner notes. The back of the CD cover also contained the information that: "*Aura* was the product of Danish composer/trumpeter/flugelhornist Palle Mikkelborg." Overall, Mikkelborg is pleased with the new version. "They remastered it rather than remixed it," he points out. "Some intros and outros are a bit rough [on the original release], which the remastering softened and I was pleased with that." The new five-second brass introduction to "Indigo" adds some interest but is still indicative of a somewhat cavalier approach to this body of work by Columbia Records (now owned by Sony Music) – if you are going to make changes to this music, however subtle, why not get Mikkelborg involved?

Fortunately none of this detracts from the music itself, which is a triumph both for Miles and Mikkelborg. The combination of Miles's trumpet sound, a big band and electronic instruments saw Miles playing the kind of music many had thought he had long left behind. The influences of Ives, Evans and Messiaen coupled with Mikkelborg's respect and awareness of Miles's musical heritage combined to produce a body of work that shows both new and old sides to Miles's playing. Miles, of course, was highly influential in the overall sound, feel and direction of the music.

Overall, *Aura* was well received (although critic Stanley Crouch described it as "an over-blown fusion piece."[6] Critic Angus McKinnon described *Aura* as: "Davis's most important recording since his 1981 comeback,"[7] adding that "Davis was fifty-eight when this album was recorded and the intelligence, power and spontaneity of his playing hardly imply a man who was disinterested or idly flattered by Mikkelborg's composition." He concluded that: "*Aura* is not an absolute artistic statement in the order of Davis's *Kind Of Blue* or *Miles Smiles*; instead, like *Bitches Brew*, *On The Corner* or *Dark Magus*, it offers tantalizing possibilities any of which most musicians would be content to spend a lifetime exploring."

Writer Paul Tingen says that *Aura* "contains some of Miles's best playing of the decade,"[8] while critic Gary Giddens said that the album was "his most satisfying recorded work in several years – perhaps since the 1983 *Star People*."[9] The critic Francis Davis concluded that *Aura* was "so shockingly good that you're slightly disappointed in it for not being perfect."[10] Quincy Troupe, who helped Miles write his autobiography, believes that "all in all, it is a wonderful album."[11] *The Penguin Guide to Jazz* stated that: "Unique among his later records, *Aura* has an unexpected power to move."[12]

Aura went on to win two Grammy awards in 1989, for Best Jazz Instrumental Performance, Soloist (on a Jazz Record) and Best Jazz Instrumental Performance, Big Band. "I was very pleased for Miles because he really went for it and he plays great on it. He was very brave in doing what he did," says Mikkelborg.

Miles had warned Mikkelborg that *Aura* would change his life and it certainly did raise his profile throughout the musical world. It also affected Mikkelborg's subsequent approach to music. "After *Aura*, I felt I had used up my interest in the big band sound for a while. I didn't write anything for a large ensemble. I did some orchestral things and some choir things but I didn't do anything with a similarity to this," says Mikkelborg. The Dane kept in touch with Miles in the years afterwards, often meeting in hotel rooms when the two men were in the same city. Mikkelborg recalls one of his last meetings with Miles, just when the latter was showing an interest in hip-hop. "He was interested in the new technology. I had the feeling he was moving into a new period. He liked techno-drums and electronics."

Aura was not the last time Miles would work with a big band. Miles surprised everybody by appearing in concert with the Gil Evans Orchestra and

The George Gruntz Concert Jazz Band at the 1991 Montreux Jazz Festival. Quincy Jones conducted the music, which consisted of Gil Evan's original arrangements for albums such as *Miles Ahead* and *Sketches Of Spain*. But while the Montreux concerts were about looking back, *Aura* represented a fresh approach to the music of Miles. It was also recorded at a time when Miles was close to the peak of his powers, whereas at Montreux he was weak and sick and just two months away from his death.

In his liner notes for the 2000 edition of *Aura*, Mikkelborg wrote: "I still thank my guardian angel for giving me the marvellous present of meeting and working with this true master." Doubtless many of those who play this album are giving their thanks too.

12 the road to *tutu*: the background

"[Miles] felt that Wynton was the darling over there and that he was like old news." *Tommy LiPuma,* Tutu's *executive producer*

"He left for the money." *Miles's ex-manager Mark Rothbaum on why Miles left Columbia Records*

Background to the album

In 1985, Miles shocked the music world by ending his thirty-year association with Columbia Records and signing for Warner Bros. Miles never publicly revealed the full story behind his decision to leave Columbia, and even those close to him at the time (like his nephew Vince Wilburn Jr. and musical director Robert Irving III) say he never talked to them about the motives behind this momentous decision.

But from the interviews Miles gave around the time and comments made in his autobiography, it seems that a combination of factors led Miles to make the move, some of which had been running like a festering sore for months. Finally, they erupted and drove Miles to cut loose. The reasons behind Miles's breach with Columbia can perhaps be summarized in three words: *Aura,* Wynton and money. Miles was clearly irked by the refusal of Colombia Records to release *Aura,* an album Miles had made with Palle Mikkelborg (see previous chapter). "Columbia was supposed to release the album [*Aura*] but they reneged on me and I had to get a grant from the National Endowment for the Arts to finish the album. That was the beginning of the end of my relationship with Columbia. That and the way George Butler was treating me and Wynton Marsalis," said Miles.[1] On another occasion, Miles elaborated a little more on his reasons for splitting with Columbia: "When we did this [*Aura*] I wanted $1,400 for a digital remix and Columbia wouldn't pay it. And then [Columbia Jazz vice-president] George Butler calls me up. He says to me 'Why don't you call Wynton?' I say 'Why?' He says ' 'Cause it's his birthday. That's why I left Columbia.' "[2]

George Butler admits asking Miles to do this, adding that: "I think Miles called Wynton, said 'Happy birthday' and then hung up." Miles and Wynton Marsalis were both highly talented trumpeters, but that was where the similarity began and ended. Marsalis was everything Miles was not: young, celebrated by critics who believed that jazz had died after the mid-1960s, and playing music that was closer to Miles's early 1960s period than his 1980s repertoire. And whereas Miles wore flamboyant stage costumes and played funk, Marsalis wore a suit and tie, and eschewed electric instruments.

Wynton Marsalis was born in New Orleans in 1961 and was given his first trumpet when aged six. He received classical training when he was twelve. Marsalis heralds from a musical family – his father is a pianist and his three brothers are all jazz musicians. One brother, the saxophonist Branford, played on Miles's 1984 album *Decoy*. Marsalis was a trumpet protégé and was soon attracting a lot of attention in the jazz world. At the age of eighteen he joined Art Blakey and the Jazz Messengers, and the following year he toured with the rhythm section from Miles's great 1960s quintet, featuring Herbie Hancock, Tony Williams and Ron Carter.

Butler signed Marsalis to Columbia and the young trumpeter recorded classical and jazz albums, which were heavily promoted by the record label. In 1983, when aged just twenty-two, Marsalis became the first artist to win Grammys in both the Jazz and Classical categories in the same year. He repeated this achievement the following year. With Marsalis riding so high both critically and commercially, it would have been hard for Miles not to feel a little envious. And Miles would not have been human if he had not felt that George Butler, the man who had helped get Miles back into the music scene, was now focusing his attention elsewhere.

With so much talent and so much success at such a young age, and with critics lauding almost everything he did, it is perhaps not surprising that Marsalis developed strong views on the jazz scene. These included some highly critical comments about Miles's current music. "I resent what he's [Miles] doing because it gives the whole scene such a let-down," he once said. "He's just co-signing white boys, just tomming."[3]

Butler says there was an uneasy relationship between him and Miles as a result of Wynton's high profile. "I think Miles thought I was more interested in Wynton, which wasn't the case. I also believe that Miles had the utmost respect for Wynton on the classical side, but I think he was more distant when it came to saying fantastic things about Wynton's jazz side." The two trumpeters were also guarded towards each other. "I remember Miles and Wynton were performing at an event in Atlanta and CBS sent a TV crew over to interview them. The producer asked if he could interview Miles and Wynton together," says Butler. "I said I'd see if I could arrange it."

Butler first asked Marsalis, who was initially reluctant to be interviewed with Miles, but then relented. Butler then asked Miles, who didn't say much but eventually muttered an "okay." Butler took Marsalis into Miles's dressing room, where the TV crew was set up. "Wynton walks into Miles's room and the two men embraced as if they were the greatest of friends – I was shocked. They started talking and saying complimentary things about each other and that session was fantastic. But as soon as Wynton got out of Miles's room he said 'Man, let me out of here.'"

On one infamous occasion on June 28, 1986, Marsalis walked on-stage in the middle of a Miles's concert in Vancouver without invitation, causing Miles to stop the band and ask him to leave. The story goes that Miles threatened to sack anyone in his band who played along with Marsalis. Wynton Marsalis's brother, Branford, commenting on the rift between the two men, says: "I remember when he was saying shit about my brother 'He's just a scholarly cat and does all this imitation' and it's like Wynton was very young and he was clearly a scholar but Miles should know that where you are at twenty-one is not really a fair indicator of what you will become. But to talk about someone in that fashion when they are twenty-one is irresponsible and it's manipulative and it's smart if you're trying to shore up your position as the pre-eminent genius."

Branford Marsalis also believes that Miles's reaction to his brother walking on-stage is most telling. "It was an interesting thing that when the bully got bested when Wynton walked on the stage in Vancouver, Miles cut off the band. Wynton walked out and said 'How can you all fall for this? He's just a bully.' He said that with his actions. People always said Miles Davis was the authority but the authority is the one that plays the most not what says the most, and Miles cut the band off because Miles already knew what Wynton knew – Miles couldn't play the trumpet anymore. And Miles wasn't going to stand there and have Wynton tear him to shreds. But if Wynton was the punk he said he was, he should have played, it should have been easy."

Marsalis adds: "So there's this dichotomy. There are people who are willing to accept that everything he [Miles] says is the truth instead of dogma. So when Wynton went on the stage – which is a tried-and-tested system that the jazz community has, that all disputes are settled on the bandstand – everybody turned on Wynton, 'How dare he disrespect Miles,' but this had been the code of the bandstand before Miles Davis. But suddenly, now, nobody does it anymore."

Miles had initially looked upon Marsalis favourably, acknowledging his talent and inclined to believe that interviewers were setting-up Marsalis to criticize him. But as the criticism grew stronger, Miles's mood changed from irritation to anger: "All these white people are praising Wynton for his classical playing and that's all right. But then they turn around and rank him over me and Dizzy in jazz, and he knows he can't hold a candle to all the shit we have done and are going to do in the future."[4] Musician/producer Randy Hall recalls: "Miles called me one day and the [1986] Super Bowl was on. Wynton was playing the "Star Spangled Banner" and Miles said 'Ain't that some sad shit!'"

Miles bitterly noted that: "George Butler was the producer for both of us and I felt that he was more concerned about Wynton's music than he was about mine."[5] Writer Quincy Troupe recalls Miles telling him about "the trouble he was having with George Butler and Wynton Marsalis and that he was thinking of leaving Columbia for Warner."[6] Tommy LiPuma, the producer of Miles's first three albums at Warner Bros, is blunt: "He felt that Wynton was the darling over there and that he was like old news."

Another thing that seems to have got under Miles's skin was the reluctance of Columbia to release yet another recording by him. This time it was Miles's version of the Cyndi Lauper pop hit "Time After Time," which Miles felt would have made a good single. Miles had been playing his version of the song at concerts in summer 1984, and the combination of Miles's beautiful and haunting trumpet coupled with the song's gorgeous melody was wowing the crowds.

Miles's version had much cross-over potential, but he was having problems getting it released: "I told George [Butler] I'm getting a strange reaction from the crowd when I play 'Time After Time.' He ignored it because he was so busy with Wynton Marsalis. He heard it at the Montreux Jazz Festival last year. He said, 'We gotta do it!' I said 'George, I told you, man, we already did it!' And he still didn't release it. International CBS told me 'Man, if we had had that tune we'd have sold millions of records.'"[7]

Miles also complained that Columbia kept filing his album releases under the label of Contemporary Jazz, which he felt restricted his potential audiences. "I'm tired of 'jazz.' If they want to call it 'popular music' – OK. In the old days, they would call it funky, but nobody would buy it. If they're going to call it and stay there and promote it, that's another thing. I don't like labels, but if they do it so you can find it, great. But jazz, they just pass it by."[8] One thing is clear from all of Miles's complaints – he wanted commercial success and his remarks suggest that he believed that Columbia was putting less effort into promoting jazz releases than it did for pop and rock recordings.

However, Butler sees things differently when it comes to examining how Columbia treated Miles. "No one had done as much for an artist as we had for Miles. This is comparing him to what would be done for rock-oriented artists in terms of parties, promotional campaigns and the like." Butler added that Miles's move to Warner Bros was because Miles wanted "a change of scenery. It was not personal. He just wanted to get away and maybe do something other than jazz."[9]

Money was another factor that had prompted Miles to sign-on with Warner Bros. After an acrimonious split with his previous management,

Blank and Blank, Miles had been forced to sell his beloved house in West 77th Street to pay off the Blank brothers. Miles's new manager was David Franklin; Miles's wife Cicely Tyson also managed at that time. The negotiations with Warner Bros involved a signing-on fee, believed to be around $1 million, and Miles was feeling good about the deal. He told Troupe: "They gave me all the money I need and some more. I'd be a fool *not* to go."[10]

Mark Rothbaum, who managed Miles from 1978 to 1983, believes that the so-called rivalry between Miles and Marsalis was a smokescreen to hide Miles's main motivation for moving to Warner Bros. "He left for the money. If anything, the rivalry between him and Wynton was good for business."

Butler agrees. "Miles's manager at the time – David Franklin – was about money and mega-dollars and had done this deal with Warner Bros that gave Miles a lot of money. Whenever you told Miles about any big money deals, he was interested." Butler adds that Columbia was not given the opportunity to match Warner's offer. "We had gotten word of rumours that Franklin was putting together a deal with Warner Bros, so when Miles's contract with Columbia ended, I said to [CBS President] Walter Yetnikoff, 'I think we should have dinner with Miles and talk because I have a feeling his attorney is talking to Warner Bros.'" Yetnikoff agreed and a dinner was arranged the next evening.

But the next day, Franklin called Butler to inform him that Miles had signed with Warner Bros. "I called Yetnikoff and said 'Forget about the dinner.' Miles has already signed to Warner Bros, and of course there was nothing we could do because Miles had signed on the dotted line," says Butler.

Miles may have thought he had got a good deal with Warner Bros, but when the ink had dried on the contract, the resulting deal didn't look so great. The contract that Franklin negotiated with Warner Bros' music publishing arm, Warner Chappell Music, was generous towards the publishers to say the least, and when Miles found out he was not happy. "David fucked up the negotiations by giving up too much to Warners, like the rights to all my publishing. They [Warner Bros] gave a lot of money to come over to Warner Bros, in seven figures, just to sign. But I don't like the idea of giving up my publishing rights to them. That's why you don't see my own songs on my new albums."[11]

Rothbaum adds: "I don't want to second-guess the people who were advising Miles at the time, but he had one of the greatest catalogues of all time. Even an unsophisticated businessperson could have made a deal that made Miles fabulously rich without giving away his publishing rights. I know [producer] Tommy LiPuma and [Warner Bros chairman] Mo Ostin are really fine people, but so were George Butler and the people running Columbia at the time. If Miles had stayed at Columbia he could have made a deal like Michael Jackson or Janet Jackson that would have made him rich beyond his wildest dreams and let him keep his own publishing companies. Artists can be desperate without knowing the viability of their catalogue."

It also seems that Miles soon regretted his decision to sign with Warner Bros, because a year later Butler was contacted by one of Miles's managers. "He said to me 'Miles wants to come back.' I said I didn't think we could do anything about it. Miles's first album for Warner Bros [*Tutu*] was a huge success and we were all happy for Miles. But it seems that amidst all this success Miles wasn't happy and wanted to come back to Columbia," says Butler.

Columbia has always treated Miles well, such as the time when they set up a special fund for him when he stopped recording in the mid-1970s. "Miles had gotten used to Columbia treating him as a kind of celebration that I knew he enjoyed, because he could do no wrong," says Butler. "He could get money any time he needed it and the company always responded to him and gave him whatever he wanted. He was selling [back] catalogue as well and the company was always making money. When he went to Warner Bros, they knew who he was and I'm sure they were awestruck by him, but they stayed their distance and he was not used to that."

Tommy LiPuma, then head of Warner Bros Jazz division, was given the responsibility of handling Miles. "I had some trepidation at the beginning because I had heard horror stories about how he dealt with people. But at the same time this was someone I had been listening to all my life. *Birth Of The Cool* changed the way I listened to music," he says.

LiPuma met Miles briefly at the 1985 Montreux Jazz Festival and the two of them met again at LiPuma's home in New York. "We spent two or three hours together just playing music and talking. He loved art and I collect early twentieth-century American art and he just flipped out." When Miles left, he stopped at the doorway, gripped LiPuma by both shoulders and looked him straight in the eye. "He had these incredible eyes – as black as coal. He looked at me as if to say 'Yeah, everything is cool.' From that point on that cat was a very good friend and that's the way it stayed until he died. There's no one who could make me laugh as much as Miles, he was the funniest cat on two feet. I really miss the time we had. We had great times. We laughed a lot."

LiPuma was also impressed by the way Miles communicated with his musicians. "The first time I saw this was when we had just signed Miles and he was at a rehearsal. Miles's guitar player – a fabulous guitarist called Mike Stern – was playing a solo and he was playing lots of notes. At the end of the rehearsal Miles went up to Mike and said 'I'm gonna send you to Notes Anonymous!' He didn't need to say 'You're playing too many notes,' or anything – that said it all."

Warner Bros now had a jazz legend on their hands, but the question was: what were they going to do with their new superstar signing? During the initial stages, LiPuma was content to take a backseat role in the album's development. "Let's just say that when you come to work with a musician of Miles's pedigree, it's not fitting to try and tell him what to do," he said.[12] So despite LiPuma's considerable production experience (amongst the many artists he'd produced were George Benson, Al Jarreau, David Sanborn, Earl Klugh and Randy Crawford – LiPuma's work had also won him Grammy awards), the plan was to let Miles choose the direction of his first Warner Bros album. It was a strategy that would result in Miles calling on some old friends, cutting some new and radical stuff – and recording an album that would break new boundaries.

The September sessions

Miles's first sessions as a Warner Bros artist saw him take his current band into the Record Plant Studios in Los Angeles on September 23 and 24, 1985. The band members were: Miles on trumpet and keyboards, Bob Berg on saxophone, Mike Stern on guitar, Robert Irving III on keyboards, Angus Thomas on bass, Vince Wilburn Jr. on drums, and Steve Thornton and Marilyn Mazur on percussion. Steve Thornton recalls Tommy LiPuma being present some of the time.

The first tune recorded was a nine-minute version of "Maze," which had featured in Miles's live set since March 1985 – it remained there until March 1987.[13] "Maze" is so-called because it was inspired by a track from the soul/ funk band Maze called "Back In Stride," a hit from the band's album *Can't Stop The Love*. Maze's keyboard player Wayne Linsey had written the horn line, which Miles liked so much that he based "Maze" on it. "Maze" is a furious funk workout that includes some heavy-duty bass playing and frenetic percussion. Miles plays fast, open trumpet, with some energetic solos that at times verge towards the upper register. Around the two-minute mark, the tempo slows and Miles and Berg double up on the melody.

Another tune Miles recorded was "Broken Wings," a song by the rock/pop group Mr Mister. "Miles called me and said, 'Have you heard that track "Broken Arrow?" So I said 'You mean "Broken Wings"?' and Miles says 'Right. It's a motherfucker,'" recalls LiPuma. "Broken Wings" is a haunting ballad and Miles's arrangement was close to the original, with his trumpet playing the part of the lead vocals. Vince Wilburn Jr. describes the recording as "awesome" and it's a shame that at the time of writing, "Broken Wings" has not been officially released. Miles did play the tune live several times during the closing stages of his 1985 European tour, and the audience reaction was ecstatic. The live version also includes some beautiful open trumpet playing from Miles.

But for some reason, Miles decided not to continue pursuing this musical direction, which could well be described as *You're Under Arrest* Part Two. Whether Miles simply wanted a change or whether there was pressure from Warner Bros (subtle or otherwise) to explore a different musical path is unclear. Miles's musical director at the time, Robert Irving III, believes this was the main reason. "There was an entire body of music that Warner Bros would not allow Miles to record under his new deal. They (Tommy LiPuma and others) wanted the music to continue to have a certain structure and polished aesthetic, without too much edge. Warner was going for 'smooth jazz' radio airplay, but ironically, the 'smooth jazz' radio format in the US didn't play [Miles's] Warner music, yet 'Human Nature' from *You're Under Arrest* is still played even now."

LiPuma says he isn't sure why Miles didn't continue recording more material in this vein but adds: "I think what happened was once we started this thing [*Tutu*], he just said 'This is happening' and he didn't feel the need to go back." The problem with this observation is that Miles did not begin working on *Tutu* until a good four months after these sessions.

In late 1985, Miles went into the studio with Robert Irving III and percussionist Steve Reid to record some music that was used as the soundtrack for an episode of the TV series *Alfred Hitchcock Presents*. But these excursions into the studio would be almost the last time Miles would use any of his regular band for recording new material for well over a year. The exception was drummer Vince Wilburn Jr., who would play on some of the sessions of one of the most controversial and yet largely undocumented episodes in Miles's 1980s recording career – the *Rubberband* album.

13 the road to *tutu*: *rubberband* – the lost miles davis album

"My concept for the album was 'Miles meets Trevor Horn.'" *Randy Hall, co-producer of the* Rubberband *album*

"He was so easy to work with, he was a classic clown. I've never had more fun with any other artist." *Zane Giles, co-producer of the* Rubberband *album, talking about Miles*

Miles claimed that the deal with music publisher Warner Chappell (which resulted in the company gaining the rights to half his song royalties) had left him with little appetite for writing his own music. But in practice, Miles was not a prolific composer, nor was he a composer in the conventional sense of someone who sat down to write a complete score or charts for his musicians.

Although Miles had composed some great tunes (and here the *Kind Of Blue* and *Bitches Brew* albums spring to mind), he was more a shaper of ideas. Part of his genius was in being able to take a musical fragment, a chord here or a vamp there, and turn it into something special, even magical. In other words, Miles's creative inspiration often came from his interaction with the sounds and the musicians in the studio. Miles once said: "I always write for musicians, I can't write for myself."[1]

Even on albums such as *Kind Of Blue* and *Bitches Brew*, most of Miles's compositions were created organically in the studio. "I didn't write out the music for *Kind Of Blue*," said Miles, "but brought in sketches for what everybody was supposed to play because I wanted a lot of spontaneity in the playing."[2] Miles described how he directed the *Bitches Brew* sessions like a conductor, so that "the recording was a development of the creative process, a living composition."[3] Drummer Jack DeJohnette, who played on the *Bitches Brew* sessions, recalls that "as the music was being played, as it was developing, Miles would get new ideas."[4]

Miles's working method has parallels with the British film and theatre director Mike Leigh, whose productions include *Abigail's Party*, *Naked*, and *Secrets and Lies*. Leigh's productions almost invariably start with each member of the cast being given a bare outline of the character they are to play, along with a brief scenario. Then through a process of exploration, improvisation and experimentation, the actors develop their roles. It is only after this process of discovery that Leigh then begins writing the playscript.

But since *Star People*, Miles had more or less abandoned this way of working, spending less time in the studio and preferring to delegate the act of composition to others. So Miles went looking for songs and, in doing so, he called on some old friends and musical associates. Robert Irving III, his musical director at the time, recalls suggesting that Miles record a song from the past: "He was looking for material for his new recording. I suggested 'Burn' [a tune recorded during *The Man With The Horn* sessions] and this reignited his interest in the tune and we began to revive it for live performances."[5]

However, "Burn," a rock/funk track, was never recorded in the studio because as Irving notes: "The vision of his new producer [Tommy LiPuma] and label was for a much more accessible recording without too much 'edge.'" As we shall see, Irving's observation was not only perceptive but it explains why there was to be a major change of direction for Miles's first Warner Bros album.

In his search for new tunes Miles contacted the English producer/composer/arranger Paul Buckmaster, who had helped arrange the *On The Corner* album and had also worked with Miles during his retirement period. "Miles called me in London and asked me to write some material for him," recalls Buckmaster. Miles hummed a bass line over the phone and Buckmaster used this to construct the music. Working at his eight-track home studio, Buckmaster constructed two "spacey, science-fictiony" tunes, "Outpost" and "Mission."

Buckmaster used synthesizers to create bass, drum, keyboard and horn parts. "I thought 'Right, I'll borrow and incorporate Stockhausen's idea of short-wave radio-tuning.[6] Finally I'll be able to show some of what I meant about Karlheinz Stockhausen back then on *On The Corner*.' I had a portable boombox with short and medium wave (AM) dials, and used the tuning pot [dial] to slowly scan through the radio stations. I was also thinking that here was an opportunity to move towards what I'd always been hearing in my imagination, about Miles in this beautiful, strange and sometimes disturbing odyssey," he says, "so I recorded the transmissions on to one of the tracks and then mixed it with the music, so you had the transmissions swirling in and out of the music." After transcribing the music and copying it on to cassette, Buckmaster sent the package to Miles's management office in New York, but it never reached Miles in time.

Another person Miles called was the bassist/producer Bill Laswell, who had worked with Herbie Hancock on the 1983 album *Future Shock*, which included the smash hit "Rockit." But Laswell wanted to do a complete album with Miles rather than just one or two pieces and so declined the offer.

Steve Porcaro, keyboard player in the rock band Toto, was also considered. Miles, LiPuma and keyboardist Adam Holzman went to meet Porcaro at the home of David Paich, one of Toto's keyboardists. Porcaro had known LiPuma for a while and the two men had a lot of mutual friends, so it was logical that when Miles was looking for material LiPuma would recommend the man who had co-written "Human Nature," the Michael Jackson song Miles had covered on his last album, *You're Under Arrest*.

Porcaro remembers waiting hours for Miles to arrive at Paich's home. "When he showed up, he was wearing the most amazing alligator-style trousers," says Porcaro, "and the first thing he asks is whether me and him could spend some time alone together around a piano." Paich had a grand piano in another room, and as Miles and Porcaro walked through the hallway of the house they passed several large mirrors. "Miles did a double-take and saw himself in the mirror," says Porcaro, "and he pulled up his pants, turned to me and asked 'What do you think of these?' I said 'They're fucking incredible.' They were the hippest pants I'd ever seen."

Porcaro had prepared two tunes for Miles, "Exist" and "Walk of Life." Both songs had been written at the same time as "Human Nature" and, melodically, were in a similar vein to it. "I figured that they would be right for Miles," says Porcaro. The recording sessions took place at the studios of Jeff Porcaro, Steve Porcaro's brother and Toto's drummer.

But the sessions with Miles did not gel, recalls Steve Porcaro. "I really don't know why things didn't work out, but Miles never really settled into the tunes. I think the problem may have been that I was trying to bend Miles to my will. He was trying to play my melodies and it just didn't flow naturally. I think the problems were more to do with the tunes than with Miles."

"Exist" was the tune that Miles came closest to finishing but, after this, the project was abandoned. Porcaro says "Tommy was present and if there had been any way that he could have made things happen, I would have been more than happy to have stepped back and let him take control. I would have loved my songs to have been on Miles's new album. But despite what happened, it was a great experience." However, as a result of the visit, Miles would agree to play on a Toto song, "Don't Stop Me Now."

Miles also made contact with two artists then signed to Warner Bros, George Duke and Prince, although with the latter it is not certain who was first to make contact. Both men would compose songs for Miles, although only Duke's work would appear on the album that eventually became *Tutu*.

Another person Miles contacted was Randy Hall, one of the original members of The Chicago Group who had worked on Miles's comeback album *The Man With The Horn*. After his spell with Miles, Hall went on to become a successful singer/producer, and by the time Miles called, in summer 1985, Hall was recording his new album, *Love You Like A Stranger* at

Ameraycan Studios in Los Angeles, owned by the artist/producer Ray Parker Jr. When Hall received the call he instantly recognized the raspy voice at the end of the line – it was Miles. "He said 'Randy, I want you to produce my next album,'" recalls Hall.

Hall believes that Miles called him because he wanted his next album to be a commercial success. "*The Man With The Horn* had done a lot for Miles commercially – he was getting air play on black radio all over the country. He knew with me he'd get the three-minute pop song!" Bassist Cornelius Mims, who played on many of the *Rubberband* sessions, adds: "I believe Miles wanted a more commercial record, a more radio-friendly album."

Miles invited Hall to attend a gig at the Greek Theater in Los Angeles on September 19, 1985. After the gig, Hall went backstage to meet Miles. "He was sitting there all regal, surrounded by these journalists asking him questions. I just stood at the back watching," recalls Hall. "Then Miles points at me and says 'And by the way, that guy over there is Randy Hall and he's producing my next record.'" Despite this public invitation, Hall was still unsure whether Miles really was serious about him producing the new album, but a few days later Miles called and confirmed his offer.

At the time, Hall was working with the musician/producer Zane Giles on his new album. Hall asked Giles if he would like to co-produce the next Miles Davis album with him. Giles was ready. Giles played guitar, bass, drums and keyboards, and had worked with artists such as The Jacksons, Dionne Warwick, Earth, Wind & Fire, and Gladys Knight and The Pips. Hall and Giles asked engineer Reggie Dozier (brother of Lamont Dozier, one of Motown's legendary Holland-Dozier-Holland songwriting team) to work with them on the project. Dozier had no hesitation in accepting the offer. "My reaction was, of course! It made me feel good and honoured when they asked me to work with such a great musician," he says.

Hall and Giles then set about writing songs for Miles, and their inspiration was the work of an English record producer who was making great waves in the 1980s. "My concept for the album was 'Miles meets Trevor Horn,'" says Hall. If Phil Spector was famous for his "wall of sound" productions, then Horn's productions could best be described as a "brick wall of sound." Synthesizer and drum-machine-driven, with a driving rhythm and a bass sound that went straight to your chest cavity – a classic example is the hit "Relax," by Frankie Goes To Hollywood – there was no mistaking the Horn sound.

Hall wanted some of this on Miles's new album. "It was fat grooves, really funky, Miles talking. It was street and funky and dirty. We didn't go after writing a great jazz song, Miles wanted the street thing; he wanted the chord changes [that] he wanted to play. The basis was to take it to the street like *On The Corner*, it was Miles taking more chances." The term "taking chances" often crops up when you talk to Hall and Giles about *Rubberband*. Their aim was for Miles to take chances by moving into musical directions that encompassed a variety of genres, from funk to Latin, and pop/rock to Caribbean. Giles says, "Miles kept saying 'I don't wanna do my usual stuff. I wanna do something different.'"

One of the new directions was for Miles to talk on some of the tracks. Miles's voice can be heard on many of his recordings, but these are little more than brief asides (for example, on *The Man With The Horn*, Miles can be heard talking to Teo Macero at the end of "Fat Time" and at the conclusion of "Ursula"). But on *Rubberband*, Miles's voice would be more upfront. "Miles was introducing one of the tracks and saying things like 'This is for all the lesbians and non-lesbians.' He was just goofing off, but it was so cool. I don't think people had heard a record where Miles was talking like that, which was a classic within itself," adds Hall.

Hall also wanted the album to feature an all-star cast of artists with singers such as Al Jarreau, Chaka Khan and Teena Marie joining Miles on some of the tracks. Prince had also written a song for Miles, which would have been included on the album (see next chapter).

Hall and Giles would usually work together at Giles's home studio on a tune and then play it to Miles (often over the phone), who would listen and then sketch an idea and give the two writers the direction of where he wanted to go. "So we'd go back to the drawing board and put the track together and then present that to him. Miles wanted a more youthful thing. When we played something he liked he'd come in and say: 'We need to do that,' and once the track was down in the studio, he'd come in and put his thing on top. A lot of the tracks had funk things on the bottom and Miles thing on top. That's why it was an interesting mix," says Hall.

Giles also describes how the tunes were put together: "Miles would say 'I like it, leave it alone,' or 'Give me something with a little calypso feel or play it, but make that a "B" or a "C".'" Hall and Giles would do a lot of bass and drum programming on a Linn sequencer and often played rhythm guitar together on the same track. "We would pick up our guitars and lay down a kind of James Brown, Sly and The Family Stone funky style over hard funky bass and drums. They were the grooves and Miles was loving it," says Hall.

The *Rubberband* writing and recording sessions at Ameraycan Studios took place from late 1985 to early 1986, with the first tracks laid down in October 1985 and further sessions taking place the following November, December and January. The recording sessions were spread out over several months because Miles was touring Europe in late 1985, and so the sessions had to fit around his schedule.

The first session took place on October 17, 1985, with the album's title track, "Rubberband." "We wrote Rubberband, which was a funky kind of thing, and I played it to Miles and he said 'That's it! We'll start recording tomorrow!'

It was just like what happened in Chicago [when Hall and co-writer Robert Irving III were composing tunes for *The Man With The Horn*] and after he had heard the first song, he'd just say 'Keep writing, keep writing'," says Hall.

The musicians on the *Rubberband* sessions were Miles, who played trumpet and keyboards; Randy Hall on guitar and programming; Zane Giles on guitar, bass, drum programming and keyboards; Adam Holzman, Neil Larsen and Wayne Linsey on keyboards; Cornelius Mims on bass; Glenn Burris and Mike Paolo on saxophone (the latter only played on one tune, "I Love What We Make Together"); Steve Reid on percussion and Vince Wilburn Jr. on drums. Dozier says Wilburn was only present at a few sessions, with most of the drums programmed by Giles on a drum machine.

Mims recalls the intensity of the recording sessions: "We assembly-lined it – it was a 24/7 operation. Randy and Zane were working pretty feverishly. Sometimes we'd start at 3 am in the morning, other times it would be 10 am. Randy and Zane would call me to do a bass overdub or sometimes they'd have three or four tracks knocked out for me to play bass on. I spent a lot of hours asleep on a couch in the studio. Other times a group of us would be sitting in the lobby with Miles watching boxing on the TV."

Mims, who was twenty-four at the time, recalls being somewhat overwhelmed by the experience of working with Miles. "I remember being intimidated by him because he was such a strange character, but he also was the coolest and the most comical dude I'd met – he was very funny. But at the same time he's Miles and he had this presence. He had the same effect on me as I had when I was working with Michael Jackson. You're thinking, 'Wow, that's Michael Jackson and he's standing just five feet away and he's digging what I'm doing.' It was the same with Miles and it was pretty overwhelming."

Mims also observed Miles. "He had a low tolerance of bullshit – you were on egg shells around him. If you didn't perform to the ability he expected you were fired or you could end up in a fight with him. I recall the engineer rubbing Miles up the wrong way and Miles was ready to beat him up. It took everybody to save that engineer's ass because Miles was ready to go all the way with him."

Linsey had got to know Miles through his role as keyboardist for the soul/funk band Maze and met Miles at a Peabo Bryson concert. "We became friends and I'd hang out at his home and he'd call me on the phone. When Miles was making *Rubberband* he asked me to join the sessions. I wrote a couple of things and played on some other tracks."[7]

When Steve Reid joined the *Rubberband* project he was already a veteran percussionist on the session scene, but despite his wealth of experience Reid was both anxious and excited about being on a Miles's gig. "I was scared to death. Being a white guy I thought I was going to last ten seconds and then Miles was gonna go 'Fuck you, get outta here!'"

When Reid finally met Miles for the first time, he must have thought his worst fears had come true. "We waited about four or five hours for Miles to arrive. I had set up my instruments around 8 pm, but Miles didn't appear until about 3 am. He turned up with a small entourage and I stood up and my heart was racing – I was excited. So Randy introduced me 'Miles, this is my friend Steve Reid. He's a wonderful percussionist.' Miles looked at me with these angry eyes and said 'Fuck you!' then he looked right through me, walked to a corner, sat down and started drawing. He didn't say another word to me. Zane and Randy laughed because they knew what was going down. I laughed too, but I was shocked."

After this unusual introduction, Reid started to work on a tune. "I was pretty inspired and I think I did a really good job. I went into the recording booth and listened to the playback then did two more passes [recordings]. On the third one, I was in the booth with my back towards Miles, standing in front of the console. Then I felt this hand grip my shoulder tightly. Just as I was turning around to see who it was, Miles nestled his mouth to my ear and said, 'You ain't bad for a fucking white boy!' and that kinda broke the ice."

But if Reid thought that the ice was well and truly broken he was in for a rude awakening. "The next day the same thing happened and we waited about five hours for Miles to arrive. Only this time I was feeling okay and I'm happy, thinking things were cool with Miles. So Miles walks in and I say 'Hi Miles, how are you doing?' and he goes 'Shut the fuck up!' and looks right through me. This time I laughed for real. He loved reaction and he would judge you by the way you dealt with him. He didn't say another word to me for two or three hours then he came up and said 'Yeah man.'"

It was during these sessions that Reid learned how Miles operated. "Miles would sometimes fuck with me. I remember I was feeling inspired and Miles could see in my face that I was really digging whatever I was doing. So he'd go 'Steve, I know you really dig this stuff, but I want you to forget about it and try searching for something else.' It not only challenged the hell out of me but it made me realize that Miles was about pushing the envelope. At no time did you settle with Miles and that was the magical thing. I learned not to settle for the first thing you think about and not look any further. Miles also taught me about space. There were times when Miles would tell me not to play when I thought it would be a good place to play. But when I looked back, it was a good thing."

Reid ended up being tight with Miles. "It was a time when Cicely had cleaned him up and he was probably the nicest and most compassionate he'd been for years. He would sit down and talk to me about life. He was like a father figure to me. He even let me drive his car."

Also present in the October sessions was guitarist Mike Stern. Stern had played on Miles's first three 1980s comeback albums and had toured with him from 1981–83. He rejoined Miles's band in August 1985 (he stayed with the band until spring 1986). "I asked for Mike," says Hall. "I love Mike's playing and although Miles wanted me to do it, I felt it needed what Mike does. Zane and I played rhythm guitar. Miles wanted me to play more and said I should be more like Hendrix. Miles wanted to have the blues, Jimi Hendrix and that's why he got [black lead bassist] Foley." Stern enjoyed the session. "It was fun. I wish we could have done more stuff like that," he says.

Reggie Dozier has no problem recalling the first time he met Miles at the studio: "I can tell you exactly what happened that day – it was so weird. Miles came into the room [recording booth] with Zane, who introduced me. Miles didn't say a word – he didn't even look at me. He was looking around and he saw the console and said 'There's a lot of shit in here,' and I said 'Yeah, we've got a few things in here,' but he still didn't say anything."

Miles then asked Dozier to play something and so he played a track that had been prepared by Hall and Giles. Miles went into the studio with his horn and then donned a pair of headphones. "I was playing the tape and it was weird. He started going in the corners and he'd blow a little bit and then wander around the room and then work his way back to the microphone literally blowing at the floor. I'm freaking out thinking 'Oh my God, what's he doing?'"

An increasingly anxious Dozier was wondering how he could get Miles to the microphone when Miles asked for the tape to be stopped. Dozier used the break to make a suggestion. "I said, 'Miles, the microphone is right on top of you,' and he says 'I can see the fuckin' microphone,' so I says 'Okay.' Then Miles says 'Reggie Dozier – that's your name?' and I says 'Yeah,' so then Miles says 'Fuck you.' I thought 'Oh my God, how do you approach this guy?'"

Miles recorded his part and then returned to the recording booth, where he explained the rationale behind his seemingly bizarre behaviour in the studio. "When Miles was wondering around the room I had no idea that he was working on the reflection. He was looking around the floor and finding a reflection off the floor that would bounce into the microphone and smooth out the tone he wanted to hear," says Dozier. "Later on when I went to his house he explained it a little more. There were certain overtones that he loved to hear, and that's why he played like that. He said people thought he was out of his mind playing to the floor like that but he could hear the reflection and stay in pitch a lot better. Nowadays, we have screens that go around the microphone that reflect so you can hear the pitch, because it's hard to hear a horn that's shooting out."

But if Dozier thought Miles's mood had mellowed following the explanation, he was wrong because when Miles heard the playback he asked Dozier to turn up the recording level to capture more of the reflection. "He said 'I'm going back in to do something else, I don't like what I've done. Turn the damn thing up sonofabitch.'" Later on, when Miles was talking to Hall and Giles about another tune, his mood was no better, recalls Dozier. "I think it was Randy who said to Miles 'Can you play more of this melody?' The melody went something like [sings] da, da, da, daah, but Miles was going like da dara da dah da da dara dara. It was crazy!' So Randy says 'We're trying to make it more melodic,' and Miles says 'That's as melodic as I'm going to get it. That's me, I'm playing me,' and Zane and Randy go: 'Okay Miles.'"

Miles went in and recorded another part and then came back to the booth, but his attitude was still no warmer towards Dozier. "He said something else to me and after hearing fuck you all day I snapped back 'Fuck you too, Miles!' I thought he was going to have my tail but he just cracked up and started laughing and said 'Nobody has said "fuck you" to me before, you must be crazy!' and I said 'No, I'm just trying to stay with you, man. That's the rule of the session – I wanna be with you!' After that we got along pretty good. I think this was the best approach to him."

Around a dozen songs were recorded during the *Rubberband* sessions, although not all of them were completed. The song titles (with the composer credits provided by Hall and Giles) were "Rubberband" (Miles, Hall and Giles), "Wrinkle" (Miles, Hall, Giles and Linsey), "Carnival Time" (Larsen, Hall and Giles), "Give It Up" (Miles, Giles and Hall), "This Is It" (Miles, Hall and Giles), "Let's Fly Away" (Miles, Hall and Giles), "See I See" (Miles, Hall and Giles), "No Time For Showtime" (Miles, Hall and Giles), "I Love What We Make Together" (Miles, Hall and Giles) and "It's Not A Waste Of Time" (Linsey).

Adam Holzman describes the *Rubberband* songs as a "broad range of styles, some funk, a Caribbean-type track, some vocal things, some Miles-ish experimental grooves, with 'Rubberband' maybe being the hardest-hitting one." In fact, *Rubberband* is the most diverse album Miles ever recorded. *The Man With The Horn* mixed pop, rock, funk and jazz-swing, but not even this comes close to the diversity of *Rubberband*. Miles seemed to be moving in a dozen different directions at once, exploring new sounds and trying out numerous musical genres.

The *Rubberband* recording sessions were special for Holzman in more ways than one. Holzman had got the gig through a chance meeting with Hall. "Adam was working in a music store down the road from Ray Parker's studio and demonstrating some keyboards to me," recalls Hall. "I said 'Man, you're a good player, how would you like to play on my album?'" It was through this that Holzman ended up on the Miles sessions. Holzman brought along a PPG Wave synthesizer to the sessions. The PPG Wave was a very popular instrument and its users included David Bowie, Steve Winwood and Stevie Wonder. Hall probably didn't know it at the time, but Trevor Horn had also used the instrument with Frankie Goes To Hollywood.

Miles was fascinated by the sounds Holzman was getting from the PPG Wave and was keen to have Holzman in his band. Hall says: "Miles asked me whether he should have Adam in his band. I said 'Yes.'" Dozier adds: "Miles said to Adam, 'Where are you working?' and Adam tells him and then Miles says 'You make pretty good [money]?' and Adam says 'Yes.' So Miles says 'Well, I want you to work with me – be here tomorrow,' then he walks out. Adam's going: 'What was all that about?' and we all say: 'You better be here tomorrow!'" Three days later Holzman was touring Europe with Miles's band and the keyboardist stayed with the band for four years, eventually becoming its musical director.

The *Rubberband* tracks

"Rubberband" (6:12)
Live performances   October 1985 – December 1985

"Rubberband" was given its title by Miles, says Randy Hall, after he had heard the groove. Sometimes written as "Rubber Band," Hall says the title is in fact a single word – on the *Doo-Bop* sleeve notes it is written as "RubberBand." "Rubberband," a funk track lasting some six minutes, begins with an electronically distorted voice saying "Rubberband, rubberband, rubberband." A drum machine, heavy bass line and James Brown-like funky rhythm guitar played by Hall and Giles form the backbone of an infectious groove. Weaving throughout the track are weird sounds and chords, many of them courtesy of a PPG Wave. Miles alternates between muted and open trumpet, playing the same simple theme on both. Early in the tune, Miles plays open trumpet and then says "Rubberband, rubberband, rubberband" – Giles had sampled Miles's voice using an Akai MD28 sampler.

During the bridge, Mike Stern plays a solo that features all his trademarks including fast runs and blistering guitar. While Stern rocks away, Miles plays short blasts of open horn in the background. Miles is then back upfront on muted horn and the tune continues on in a funky groove until near the end, when the music stops. This is followed by a short guitar riff, more of the electronically distorted voice and swirling synthesizer sounds, which rise and then decay. Two more mixes of this track have emerged.

A shorter version (5:10), originally set for inclusion on the abandoned *The Last Word* boxed set (see note 18), places the swirling synthesizers at the start of the track. Other changes include the removal of Steve Reid's tambourine, additional keyboard stabs and percussive effects, new rhythm guitar licks, the removal of Miles's horn stabs during Stern's slightly extended solo and an echo effect added to the end of the guitar solo. An even earlier mix of this track has more striking differences. First, many overdubs are missing but the biggest change is that Mike Stern's guitar solo lasts for two minutes rather than the forty seconds or so on the final mix.

By coincidence, William Bootsy Collins, bassist with George Clinton's P-Funk collective of Parliament and Funkadelic, had a group and an album called *Rubber Band*, and the music Miles recorded on this session would have fitted well with the style of music played by the P-Funk groups. Miles obviously loved this tune because it was part of his live act within a week of the recording. "Miles was digging it and his band were learning it even while it was being recorded," recalls Giles. Reggie Dozier says: "That was a song. I remember when we were mixing it and thinking 'This is going to be a big song. It should have been one of his biggest songs.'" However, Miles only played "Rubberband" on his European tour until the end of 1985, after which it was replaced by tunes from *Tutu*.

"It's Not A Waste Of Time" (6:40)
Live performances   None

"It's Not A Waste Of Time" was written by Wayne Linsey while he was on tour with Maze. "Miles had accidentally heard the tune while I fast forwarded through a cassette, looking for another song. He heard just a piece of it and made me play it from the beginning...I sang it and in an effort to get me to relax, Miles coached me by saying, 'Don't pay attention to those motherfuckers. Zane is tall and Adam is white.' Bill Withers sang it on the album I did for Virgin in '91. 'Perfect Love,'" recalls Linsey.

With a dream-like opening that includes whistling and harp-like sound effects from a synthesizer, "It's Not A Waste Of Time" is a ballad that begins with a serious message for young people who feel disenfranchised from society. It then widens its scope to cover the plight of people living in lands without any rights (South Africa) before covering the topic of infidelity. The overall theme is about trust. Some thirty seconds into the tune, there is a dramatic blast of orchestral sound from a synthesizer. Listen carefully and you can hear Miles talking in the background, "Zane is tall and Adam's white." Linsey then begins to sing the tune's opening lyrics, gently, tenderly and accompanied by Giles, who whistles in the background.

During the middle section, Miles plays tenderly on muted horn on top of some gentle synthesizer sounds as Linsey whistles along. The track fades to the sound of Miles's horn and more harp-like sounds. "It's Not A Waste Of Time" is clearly a work in progress (at one point, Linsey can be heard asking the engineer "...which one are we?"). Giles says: "Miles was trying to stretch out, though we never really got to finish it."

"Carnival Time" 5:58
Live performances   March 1986 – April 1989

"Carnival Time" is a bright, uplifting tune with a Latin feel and a lovely bossa nova-like opening. Fifteen seconds into the tune, there is a dramatic staccato-like switch to the sound with a bank of synthesizers playing the main theme, accompanied by popped bass strings. A drum machine drives the tune along and Miles plays an open horn. Neil Larsen had written most of the tune (originally called "Carnival") and Hall and Giles's main contribution was to include a bridge, during which the groove settles down and Miles plays along with some strong open horn (sadly, this section was never played live).

Miles included this tune in his live act for three years and when you hear "Carnival Time" you know why – it's a song that lifts the heart and the spirit. Note that Miles played many variations of this tune, with some versions lasting under four minutes and others stretching out for more than twenty minutes, with the percussionist given plenty of space to solo. "Carnival Time" eventually appeared on *The Complete Miles Davis At Montreux* collection in 2002.

"Wrinkle" 9:13

Live performances   March 1986 – August 1991

"Wrinkle" is a fast and furious funk workout that, when played live, tested the agility of both drummer and bass player. "Miles used to make me work during 'Wrinkle'," recalls bassist Richard Patterson, who played with Miles during 1990/91. "I'd be looking at him and thinking 'Give me a break!'" When played live, "Wrinkle" would start at breakneck speed, but on the *Rubberband* album, there is long, slow atmospheric build-up with Miles playing softly on muted trumpet over swirling synthesizer strings. Miles's trumpet is also put through some form of processing, which causes it to drift from the left to right speaker, creating a trance effect.

A minute and a half into the track and a funky bass riff kicks in, closely followed by a drum machine and the tempo increases. This version has a harder edge to the live versions and at around the six-minute mark, Randy Hall plays some wild rock guitar that weaves in and out of the track until the fadeout – live versions of the tune omitted this guitar part. "Wrinkle" is one of the best tracks from the *Rubberband* sessions with a powerful funky groove.[8]

Miles's discographer, Enrico Merlin, says the song's origins can be traced back to the second theme on another Miles song, "Star On Cicely," which appeared on the 1983 album *Star People*.[9] Adam Holzman also believes that "the main melody of 'Wrinkle' was derived from the song 'Star On Cicely' on *Star People*."[10] Certainly the guitar riff played by Mike Stern at 1:49 on "Star On Cicely" on the album *Star People* is found again in "Wrinkle" (Miles plays it repeatedly during the tune's fadeout). But Hall disagrees with Merlin: "No, his views are totally off. As talented as Miles was, he still had certain riffs he would play over and over again just like any other musician soloist. So that is why you would hear certain melodies repeated."

"Wrinkle" is one of the few tracks from the *Rubberband* sessions that has been officially released (it's on *Live Around The World* and the video and DVD *Miles In Paris*) and was initially credited to Miles's son Erin Davis. However, the credits were later changed, with the names of Hall, Giles and Linsey added. These three, along with Miles, had in fact written the tune during the *Rubberband* sessions.

"Give It Up" (6:16)
Live performances   None

And the funk goes on with this uptempo, energetic number that sees Miles's trumpet scurrying on top of a funky mix of drum machine, synthesizer, bass and rhythm guitar – bassist Cornelius Mims can be heard busily popping and plucking his strings. The track revolves around a simple and playful three-note theme ("give it up"), played on keyboards and at times by Miles. Miles plays muted trumpet almost continuously throughout the track and his speed, range and stamina are impressive. Incidentally, "Give It Up" was the title of a song and album from the soul/funk group Pleasure, which Randy Hall joined after working with Miles on *The Man With The Horn*. The two tunes, however, are different.

Untitled (possibly "This Is It") (4:40)
Live performances   None

This is a mid-tempo track, with the rhythm section dominated by drum machines and a funky guitar riff. If you can imagine Miles's version of "Something On Your Mind" (from *You're Under Arrest*) being played at a more sedate pace, you'll have some idea of how the basic rhythm track sounds. The most interesting aspect of the tune is the sound of Miles's trumpet, which at times sounds as if it is being played through a wah-wah. Towards the end of the track, Miles plays his muted horn without any effects over a wash of synthesizer sound, then the funky backing track returns along with the trumpet sound effect, before the track ends abruptly.

"Let's Fly Away" (7:05)
Live performances   None

Another highlight from these sessions, "Let's Fly Away" is a Caribbean-tinged mid-tempo number with a heavy backbeat and steel drum sound effects courtesy of drum machine and synthesizer. The bass strings pop and snap and there is a joyous feel to the whole sound. Miles plays some great open trumpet throughout the track and the groove is strong. A special mention should be made of Steve Reid's inventive use of an array of percussive instruments. The sound may be closer to pop than jazz, and no doubt many of Miles's fans would have raised an eyebrow or two over the direction he had taken, but Hall and Giles got a strong and inspiring performance out of Miles – and it's a lovely tune.

"See I See" (6:00)
Live performances   None

Giles describes "See I See" as being a "typical Miles tune," and the tune certainly has a dark, mysterious quality to it. Beginning with a high-pitched note on a synthesizer, it is followed by swirling sounds and atmospheric sound effects. In the background, Cornelius Mims or Zane Giles lays down a funky bass line and Steve Reid's percussive effects add colours to the sound as Miles plays muted horn on top of the mix. The mix destined for *The Last Word*, Warner Bros' boxed-set retrospective, was shorter (5:18), had a different opening section, Mim's popped bass line is less prominent and the track had a false ending, after which Miles played a flurry of notes that are absent on the longer version. Note that Adam Holzman claims that Miles wrote this tune alone at his home, with Holzman providing some support.[11]

"No Time For Show Time" (5:26)
Live performances   None

Hall and Giles had plans to include several guest vocalists on the *Rubberband* album and one of them was Chaka Khan, the ex-lead singer of the soul/funk group Rufus, who had found subsequent success as a solo artist. She was also an old friend of Miles. However, Khan says she never knew anything about the project, nor did she ever hear the tune. "Miles and I wanted to work together, but he didn't tell me about this project. I would have loved to have heard it," she says. Khan is famous for her belting delivery and this tune would have been an ideal vehicle for her vocal style.[12] This demo track was sung by soul singer Vesta Williams, a friend of Hall and Giles, and a singer with an uncanny ability to sound like Khan. The song, an upbeat pop/soul track dominated by drum machines and synthesizers, is about a woman who plans to cut loose from her vain partner.

The song starts with Williams noting that every time she's in the street with her man he thinks every woman is looking at him. The chorus has Williams declaring that it's her time for showtime. In the middle section, Hall and Giles play some real funky guitar (causing Williams to ad lib "It's funky, baby"). "No Time For Show Time" is one of the most commercial tunes on the *Rubberband* album and the song's catchy hook line coupled with Miles and Khan's participation would have garnered a lot of airplay.

No doubt many jazz purists would have said that Miles should not have been doing this type of music, but this overlooks the fact that Miles had guested on a number of pop/soul records during this period, for artists such as Cameo and Scritti Politti. Miles's horn cannot be heard on the track, although he may have played some keyboards. Even so, this demo is pretty close to how the finished article would have sounded and Williams even double-tracks her vocals to also sing the background vocals. If Miles wanted something with commercial potential, he certainly got it with this number.

"I Love What We Make Together" (4:43)
Live performances   June–July 1986

Another vehicle for a guest singer, "I Love What We Make Together" was written with Al Jarreau in mind. A happy-sounding, mid-tempo tune, the demo has Zane Giles singing the guide vocals. Giles captures Jarreau's vocal style really well, throwing in ad-libbed scat lines and other Jarreau trademark mannerisms. Giles laughs when you tell him how close he sounds to Jarreau: "That's why I laugh at the beginning of the tune. I was brought up with the view that as a producer you fit the sound to the artist, whereas, today, the artist fits in with the producer's sound." The song sings the praises of a girlfriend and begins with Giles singing about waking up with his woman and getting excited about all the things they're going to do. The chorus, sung by background vocalists, is simply the song title, with Giles singing scat-style on top.

In June and July 1986, Miles played "I Love What We Make Together" in his concerts, although it was called "Al Jarreau" and done as an instrumental. The tune formed part of a set shown on the 1986 documentary *Miles Ahead*. Recorded at the New Orleans Jazz Festival, the song really swings and it's a mystery why Miles only played the tune for a couple of months before dropping it. An instrumental version (called "Al Jarreau Tune") is on *The Complete Miles Davis At Montreux* boxed set. With regard to the version recorded on the *Rubberband* sessions, the demo is virtually complete, with Miles playing strong, open trumpet on many sections of the tune. Indeed, all you need do is to replace Giles's vocals with Jarreau's and the song would be just about finished. Let's hope this happens one day.

At the sessions

Miles had a lot of fun during the *Rubberband* sessions, says Giles. "He was so easy to work with, he was a classic clown. I've never had more fun with any other artist." Miles had a routine for every time he turned up for a session, adds Giles. "He'd come to the studio and he'd ask us how much was he wearing, from his shoes to his necklace. He came to work clean, like he was performing and sometimes he'd be wearing $150,000 of stuff on him." Miles had long been a boxing fan and during the sessions he would sometime come up behind a musician and hit him in the kidneys while he was playing: "He'd say to me 'Boy, if I had you in the ring, I'd take you apart.' Now I'm six feet seven and I'd be like 'Man, you're a little ant, I'd smash you up!' We had a lot of fun."

Reid also remembers Miles doing a lot of drawing during the *Rubberband* sessions: "A lot of the great art he did was sketched during those sessions. A lot of the stuff I see in galleries I watched him sketch. He drew at least one hundred wonderful drawings during those sessions." Miles also had a favourite routine whenever a musician flunked something. "Miles had a classic line if you screwed up. He'd say 'Get me my pen so I can draw you and erase you.' He'd be there erasing you and tearing up the paper and we'd be peeing in our pants!" recalls Giles. Miles was also a powerhouse of ideas and suggestions in the studio. "Sometimes he'd put his arm on the keyboard because he had so many chords in his head and two hands weren't enough for him, so he used his arm," adds Giles.

Dozier recalls the first time Miles met Holzman in the studio. Holzman had brought a PPG Wave from his music store and was playing some sounds on it when Miles walked over to the electronic instrument muttering: "Wow! What the fuck is that? That's great!" Miles began playing on the PPG Wave and at one stage kept his finger pressed down on a single key. Holzman tried to stop him, saying: "The note will sustain until you stop it." Miles grabbed Adam's hand and said: "That's what I want, let go." He had hit the tonic note and the tonic went through the whole song. We're all freaking out and thinking, 'Man, that fits!' It was a genius at work," says Dozier.

Miles and Dozier would talk a lot about music together. "He once said that jazz fusion was confusion. He said everyone was saying how this [fusion] band was good or that band was good, so he did it to show how much better he was. He wasn't egocentric, it was just that if he didn't think he was good, nobody else could. That was what made him so good." Dozier adds: "I had worked with a lot of people in the business but this was different. I had heard about Miles, listened to him, but had never met him. It freaked me out. Miles taught me a lot. He didn't know it, but I know it!"

When the *Rubberband* sessions were almost completed, Miles, Hall and Giles felt they had a great album in the making. "As far as we were concerned, the album was almost finished," says Hall. Miles, Hall and Giles may have been pleased with the fruits of their work, but one person was less than happy with the results – Tommy LiPuma.

When asked about his reaction to the *Rubberband* material, LiPuma says: "I didn't hear anything. To me it didn't sound like nothing was going on. They had done *The Man With The Horn*[13] and I guess that's the way he connected with them." Hall and Giles say they had no idea at the time that LiPuma was underwhelmed by the results of their work. "Tommy came to a session we were mixing and said 'Man, that's happening.' We thought we were cool with Tommy and we just wanted to do what Miles wanted to do," recalls Giles.

Hall adds that: "Tommy acted like he liked them [tunes]. We had done the record but towards the end just as Miles was putting on some solos – that's when the bottom fell out." Dozier adds: "Tommy never said a whole lot. He was really nice and that's what shocked me – he had seemed impressed." Miles's ex-bass player Marcus Miller would eventually be given the job of writing the material for and co-producing most of *Tutu*.

During the making of *Tutu*, Miller played almost every instrument, with synthesizer technology and studio effects replacing a live band. Whereas *Rubberband* was conceived as an all-star album, *Tutu* was basically a one-man band [Miller] with Miles playing on top. "Tommy started his own sessions with Marcus Miller and so he had Marcus in his camp. Marcus is bad, I love Marcus, but we were at a disadvantage because he was on the inside," says Giles, adding, "I don't blame Marcus at all, he didn't know what was going on."

When Randy Hall attended a boat party to celebrate the launch of Miles's first Warner Bros album he must have felt that history was repeating itself. Back in 1980/81, Hall and Robert Irving III had written more than a dozen songs for Miles's comeback album on Columbia Records. The original plan was that Miles's new album would consist of songs mainly written by the two young musicians from Chicago, but, as things turned out, only two tunes were used on the resulting album *The Man With The Horn*.

But what was about to unfold would be even worse for Hall, who at least had had the consolation of getting a couple of his tunes on Miles's comeback album. "They're playing the new Miles album and none of our stuff is there! So I'm going through the whole thing again!" Hall says Miles found the situation somewhat embarrassing: "Miles came up to me and said 'Randy, I want to apologize to you. The record company felt I should be doing this.'"

Hall adds: "Tommy wanted the say-so of what was on that record. This [*Tutu*] was in his concept of what a Miles record should be. I thought *Tutu* was incredible and I told Miles that I loved it, but at the same time I was shocked because it was a different direction to what Miles had been telling us to take. To me, *Tutu* was a very political record. When we were in the studio I remember Tommy was kind of left out and he wanted to be there. The music industry is political and people will smile in your face at the same time they're stabbing you in the back. Nothing is done until the cheque is in the bank and you've cashed it to make sure it doesn't bounce."

Dozier confirms that LiPuma was rarely present during the *Rubberband* sessions: "The first time I saw Tommy was when we were mixing [the tune] 'Rubberband' at Ocean Way [studio]. I knew who he was and I thought 'Oh, I didn't realize he was involved,' because he had never been present when I was in the studio, although I hear he was there a few times when I wasn't.

I remember too that George Benson – who was working in another studio – also came in and listened for a while."

Steve Reid has a theory as to why the *Rubberband* sessions took place: "I think Tommy did a power move. He let us complete that album knowing full well in his mind that he wanted Marcus to produce that record. It had to be some kind of business thing. Warner didn't have any back catalogue and this was a way of getting some." But if Reid's theory is correct, surely Warner Bros would have released the *Rubberband* album by now? "I thought the album would come out a few years after Miles passed away because there's some incredible stuff on it and Miles is gonna be a legend for the rest of our world. But it didn't, which doesn't make sense to me from a business point of view," admits Reid.

Giles adds: "When a record company puts someone like Tommy over a project, Tommy is in a position to say 'You need to be over here,' but Miles was like 'I want to do this.' So we're having problems with Tommy over negotiations and what we wanted to do. For a long time Miles was belligerent and putting Tommy on his heels. Miles was saying 'I wanna work with these guys, I like what I'm doing in LA and I'm gonna do it.' Tommy was losing his mind because Miles was vibing with us. It basically became a wrestling match."

But LiPuma insists there was no bust-up between him and Miles: "It was so funny how this happened. I said 'Miles, I've got this idea to bring Marcus in. Let's do some things and see what happens.' Marcus came to L.A., we did *Tutu* and that was it – bam. And that's basically what happened." LiPuma says he does not like confrontation and prefers a more subtle approach: "I don't think Miles disliked it [the *Rubberband* album] as much as I did, so if there was anything it was that he didn't think they [the *Rubberband* tunes] were that bad. Instead of saying 'Look, this stuff sucks, let's do something else,' I said 'Let's try this with Marcus.' I didn't say I wanted to dump it – it never got to that. I think Miles was so blown away by *Tutu* he decided to go that way."

In his autobiography, Miles says nothing about the *Rubberband* sessions and nor does he directly address any differences that emerged between his musical direction and Tommy LiPuma's. However, Miles does make an oblique reference to some tensions at the time: "Tommy LiPuma's a great producer for the kinds of things *he* wants to hear on a record. But I like raw shit, live, raunchy, get down, get back to the alley shit and that isn't really what he likes or understands."[14]

In an interview Miles did around 1989, there is a telling moment where the interviewer reminds him that when they had previously spoken (probably around 1985), Miles had mentioned that if he was going to work with any singers, they would be Chaka Khan and Al Jarreau. For just a brief moment, Miles looks nonplussed before replying: "I was going to do that [pause] ... but it was too heavy." Miles then quickly changes the subject to his forthcoming album (*Amandla*).[15]

Hall doesn't believe that Miles decided that the music from the *Rubberband* sessions was not good enough. "If Miles had not loved it, we would have only recorded one or two songs instead of spending three months or so recording in the studio." In fact, Miles had even gone as far as to commission two comic artists to design the album cover. If Miles's plan had gone ahead, it would have seen a return to the days when Corky McCoy's cartoon characters graced album covers such as *Big Fun*, *In Concert* and *On The Corner*.

In one of the few occasions when Miles ever publicly mentioned the *Rubberband* album, he recalls how he tried to get an unnamed French comic artist to draw the cover. "I told him I'm doing a record, it's going to be called *Rubber Band* [*sic*]. And I want you to draw this cover the way you draw in your comic." Miles invited the artist along to one of his shows, at a time when his group included the female percussionist Marilyn Mazur. When the artist told Miles that his idea for the cover was a drawing of Miles beating up Mazur (!), Miles decided to draw the cover himself.[16]

Miles's concept was a man dressed in a jumpsuit raising a fist and saying "We Want *Rubberband*." There would also be thunder flashes, mountains crumbling, lots of guns and bullets raking the man's chest. Miles worked on the drawing for two weeks but was never happy with the results. However, Miles also says he asked an Italian artist to draw the cover. This time it would feature a drawing of a huge man holding his arms up in the air with the caption "We want to hear *Rubberband*!" Next to him would be a drawing of Miles.[17]

The fact that Miles used a number of tunes from the *Rubberband* sessions in his live act also supports the view that he was happy with the results of the *Rubberband* sessions. Furthermore, Giles also says that Miles asked him, Hall and Burris to join his band, but Hall had a solo career to promote, and, at the time, Giles had two small children and didn't want to be out on the road. This act doesn't sound like a man who was unhappy with the music produced by Hall and Giles. In fact, it's likely that Miles loved both *Tutu* and *Rubberband*, but perhaps felt, at the time, that *Tutu* was the best direction to follow.

Miles was renowned for his strong character and for his refusal to take bullshit from anyone, so if he was so keen to have the *Rubberband* tunes released, why did he capitulate over such a major issue? "Artists are very fickle in the sense that they will fight for what they want for one minute and give up the next. Miles had just left Columbia and he's smart enough to know that if Tommy and the team want to pull him in another direction and he doesn't go that way, he's not going to have the full support of the label. In that sense it was a business move," says Giles.

Giles is convinced that: "If *Rubberband* had come out it would have smashed. Herbie [Hancock] was doing the break-dance type of stuff but still [keeping] his [own jazz] thing. Miles would talk about doing Herbie's stuff."

This probably also explains why Miles initially approached Laswell. Hall adds: "*Tutu* was a different approach to what he wanted to do. With us, Miles was doing different stuff he had never done before. It was definitely putting Miles in other directions where Miles wanted to go." Glenn Burris, who was present at many of the *Rubberband* sessions, says *Rubberband* was "a totally different direction, a totally different musical background to a huge degree. There were so many different writers on the project. [On *Tutu*] You've got Marcus Miller. He's a great guy, but how much imagination can one man have?"

Hall adds: "I loved *Tutu*, but to me it was not really groundbreaking. Our material was funky, it was Miles taking more chances." Giles says: "Marcus's stuff was really nice and it was easy for Miles. Miles was a sucker for great musicians and Marcus is a very talented guy." Steve Reid adds: "There was some amazing stuff on that [*Rubberband*] album. Miles wanted a fresh R&B approach on the record and Randy and Zane came from the school of funk while Marcus was from the school of jazz-funk and that was the difference. *Rubberband* wasn't as slick in production terms as *Tutu* but what you did have was this raw, funk, street thing. Some of my best playing is on that stuff and it's criminal that Warner haven't released both [the *Tutu* and *Rubberband*] albums."

But Linsey says he's not totally surprised that Warner Bros released *Tutu* because: "I loved the *Tutu* album. It was a lot more structured and focused in a sense. *Rubberband* was more experimental. We didn't really try anything in terms of a live band; it was more drum machines. We did some great stuff at the time. A lot of the tunes were kinda vampish, with a less formal structure, but that was fine for Miles. That's what he wanted, but I guess Tommy wanted something else."

Mims believes that the music from the *Rubberband* sessions was just too commercial and radio-friendly for Warner Bros' taste. "We could have done more avant-garde stuff, but the concept was to get Miles on to mainstream radio. It was pretty funky stuff and I was proud to be a part of it. The general consensus was that we had done a good job – it was mission accomplished."

Glenn Burris adds: "*Rubberband* would have been awesome. That was the most incredible stuff. We just went for broke and tried so many things from a technical standpoint, like using the harmonizer [an effect that electronically changes the pitch] on the horns. I don't think Tommy LiPuma was with it. He's more of a traditionalist and he couldn't hear that. But I tell you what, it was out there, it was cutting-edge stuff."

And that probably explains Warner Bros' decision to take Miles in another direction: *Rubberband* was a leap too far. The tracks recorded for the *Rubberband* album had a rougher edge, were closer to the sound of the street but, as far as Warner Bros was concerned, had less polish and less crossover potential than *Tutu*. *Rubberband* was also hampered by the fact that it was experimental and that, like all experiments, some things worked well and others less so. "We were searching and some of the things came out well and others didn't. That's what you do. We were gonna go back and change some of the songs but Tommy snatched the project from us," says Giles. As Linsey notes wryly: "It's all about record companies. You can make a great album, but if it's not flavour of the day, then nobody's going to play it."

Dozier remembers the day when he heard that the *Rubberband* album was being shelved. "I was in Ray Parker's studio when Randy and Zane told me. They said 'It's not happening man, it's a done deal, it's over.' They're very talented musicians and I think that was the turning point for them. I think it really hurt them because that would have put them in another area of music. *Rubberband* was a really good album and should have made it on to the street." Reid adds: "They were devastated. It was quite a blow. We put a lot of time into that record. I personally spent around 200 hours working on the tracks. There was a lot of waiting around and experimentation."

Experimental or not, it's a shame that virtually all of the music produced during the *Rubberband* sessions has so far remained in Warner Bros' vaults, even though some of it invariably sounds a little dated today.[18] We will never know what would have happened if Miles had released the *Rubberband* album rather than *Tutu*. *Tutu*, of course, was hugely successful for Miles, winning plaudits and awards and crossing over to a wider audience. One of the saddest episodes of the *Rubberband* saga was that Hall and Giles, two talented writers, musicians and producers, never got the credit, recognition or the reward they both richly deserved, even on the *Rubberband* tunes that did make it on to the stage or record.

In a postscript to the *Rubberband* episode, Miles's trumpet playing was stripped out of two tracks from the *Rubberband* sessions and used in two songs on Miles's posthumous album *Doo-Bop*. But as we shall see in the chapter on *Doo-Bop*, far from placating Hall and Giles, this move rubbed even more salt into their wounds.

14 the road to *tutu*: miles and prince

"For me, he can be the new Duke Ellington of our time if he just keeps at it."[1] *Miles talking about Prince*

The Prince connection

In 1985, Prince was a superstar. The previous year, the diminutive performer had released the single "Purple Rain," a rock ballad featuring scorching guitar playing from Prince. On August 24, it reached number one in the US charts, staying in the charts for twenty-four weeks. The album would go on to sell more than thirteen million copies, make him an international star, win three Grammys and spawn a handful of top-ten smash hits such as "When Doves Cry." Prince's music was a blend of jazz, rock, pop and funk, whose influences included James Brown, Jimi Hendrix, Sly Stone, George Clinton, and The Beatles. Prince's androgynous image had its roots in the 1970s style of David Bowie.

And, like Stevie Wonder, Prince was a gifted and prolific composer, as well as a multi-instrumentalist who often played drums, guitar, bass and keyboards on his own songs. On-stage, Prince danced like James Brown, played guitar like Hendrix and sang like Marvin Gaye – it was an awesome sight. But despite the extrovert stage manner, Prince was an intensely private person who gave few press interviews, all of which added to the mystery of the man. He also had a strong independent streak and created his own studio complex in Minneapolis called Paisley Park Studios. Prince also had his own record label (Paisley Park Records), which was distributed by Warner Bros.

Prince Rogers Nelson was born in Minneapolis in June 1958, the son of jazz pianist John Nelson (who was known as Prince Nelson) and jazz singer Mattie Shaw Nelson. He taught himself to play piano, guitar and drums and would soon master many other instruments. At the age of nineteen, he signed with Warner Bros records. When Miles signed with Warner Bros, Prince was on the same record label, and this may have influenced Miles's decision to join the record company.

Miles clearly admired Prince. "I really love Prince and after I heard him I wanted to play with him sometime," he said.[2] Miles was also intrigued by Prince's image of sexual ambiguity. "He's got that raunchy thing, almost like a pimp and a bitch all wrapped up in one image, that transvestite thing," remarked Miles.[3] Miles says Prince wanted them to do an entire album together and talked about the possibility of them touring together,[4] and it is no coincidence that Prince is the last person Miles quotes in his autobiography.

The admiration was mutual. Quincy Troupe says that Miles "loved Prince's music and his attitude and the young star idolized Miles."[5] Prince held Miles in much respect and musician Randy Hall recalls that during the *Rubberband* sessions: "I picked up the phone and it was Prince calling Miles. He was very polite and said 'Can I speak to Mr Davis? This is Prince.' Miles loved Prince and he liked that funk and tempo."

It is no surprise, then, that when Miles joined Warner Bros a collaboration with Prince should be high on the agenda, although Tommy LiPuma had initially expressed some reservations about a collaboration between the two superstars. "I felt Prince might not be conversant with certain idioms pertaining to Miles's playing, but his work on *The Family* album displayed a keen awareness of the dynamics inherent in bebop, so, yes, indeed, Prince was ideal," he said.[6]

How Prince came to write some music for Miles's new album is not entirely clear. In one version, Miles said: "Prince wrote me a letter and also with the letter he enclosed a tape of instrumental tracks he'd recorded by himself in his studio. And in this letter he wrote 'Miles, even though we have never met, I can tell just from listening to your music that you and I are so exactly alike that I know whatever you play would be what I'd do. So if this tape is of any use to you, please go ahead and play whatever you feel over it because I trust what you hear and play.'"[7]

Prince sent Miles a vocal and instrumental version of a song he had written, which perhaps explains why Miles has given an alternative explanation of how he received the song. "Prince sent me two tapes. He wrote me a letter that said 'We think alike. I know how you feel, I know what you're doing and these tapes you can put on with or without a vocal'... So I sent him what we took out, what I put in. He loved it. So he sent it back and put some more words on the end of it."[8] The resulting track "Can I Play With U?" was slated to go on Miles's new album, which at the time was going to be called *Rubberband*. The album's co-producer Randy Hall says: "His tune fit with the concept of what we were doing. At the time, Prince was super-hot and I was proud to have his song on the CD."

"Can I Play With U?" was never officially released, although unofficial sources such as bootlegs have brought it into the public arena. The tune appears on numerous Prince bootlegs, most notably an album called *Crucial*, where for some reason the track is called "Little Red Riding Hood." The version on *Crucial* is a poor-quality recording spoilt by a muddy mix and being recorded at too fast a speed. As a result, Prince's vocals are in the wrong pitch. The track is also shorter (3:45) than a superior-sounding 6:37 version that has also emerged. The mixes are also different – on the *Crucial* take, Miles's voice is heard at the beginning of the track saying "Prince, Prince," but this intro is missing on the longer version.

Prince plays most of the instruments on "Can I Play With U?" including guitar, drums, bass and keyboards, as well as providing vocals (often double-tracked). Eric Leeds, the saxophonist in Prince's band, supplied the horn section. Christmas 1985 proved to be a short holiday period for Prince, because on December 26 he started recording the basic tracks for "Can I Play With U?"[9] Eric Leeds says: "When I heard that Prince was interested in doing something for Miles, I was gonna make damn sure that I was involved."[10] Leeds was on holiday in Florida at the time, but immediately flew back to California to record his saxophone parts on December 27. Miles and keyboard player Adam Holzman overdubbed their parts on at least two sessions, which took place on February 26 and March 1, 1986. Percussionist Steve Reid, who had played on the *Rubberband* sessions, says he also overdubbed some percussion on the track.

"Can I Play With U?" begins with a screeching guitar and Miles's muted trumpet. A James Brown-style horn section kicks in and the track settles into a fast funk groove. The lyrics seem to be about Prince spotting an attractive woman standing alone by a wall, and offering her the proposition of a night of fun. "Can I Play With U?" has a stop-start structure with a chorus that brings down the funk rhythm. Then Prince asks if he can talk, walk, stay and play with the girl tonight, before the funk bubbles up again.

Miles plays simple phrases, alternating between muted and open horn, while Prince plays two main guitar pieces, a funky riff à la James Brown, and strangulated rock guitar chords that are deep in the mix. Towards the end of the track, Prince lets rip with the vocals before everything comes to an abrupt stop. Miles then plays a flurry of notes and the track ends. The overall feel of the music is rough, raunchy and raw.

By the time "Can I Play With U?" was being completed, Marcus Miller had taken over the main production role for Miles's new album, which would become *Tutu*. Miller was sent a copy of the Prince track and realized that it was different from the material he was preparing. As a result, Miller wrote a new tune, "Full Nelson," that was designed to act as a transition or bridge between his music and Prince's track. In the end, it wasn't necessary, because as Miles explains: "When we sent him [Prince] the [*Tutu*] tape and he heard what was on there, he didn't think his tune fit."[11]

It was a wise decision because "Can I Play With U?" would have stuck out like a sore thumb had it appeared on *Tutu*, even though Miller had provided a bridging track and was even involved in the mixing (but not the recording) of "Can I Play With U?" Listen to a track like "Rubberband" and then "Can I Play With U?" and you can hear the connection, but play any track from *Tutu* and then Prince's tune, and the mood, dynamics and feel are significantly different. What's more, "Can I Play With U?" sounds like a work-in-progress, with some sections requiring their rough edges to be smoothed out. Prince discographer Per Nilsen describes the tune as a "fairly mediocre funk outing highlighted only by a funky saxophone riff by Eric Leeds and Prince's frenzied guitar playing," adding that the lyrics are "uninspired."[12]

It is to Prince's credit that he resisted the temptation to have one of his songs on Miles's first Warner Bros album. No doubt, he and Miles thought there was plenty of time for future collaborations, but although Miles would live for another five years the two artists would spend little of that time working together on music.

Alan Leeds, Prince's tour manager, told writer Alex Hahn that it was Prince's working methods that prevented the two artists ever working productively together. Although Miles was by now spending less time in the studio and essentially playing over pre-prepared music, he was still an active participant in the creative process. He would listen to the music that had been developed for him, make suggestions and give directions. In other words, although Miles had moved towards the periphery of the music-making process, there was still some degree of interaction between him and those creating the music.

But while Miles was looking for some form of face-to-face creative collaboration with Prince, the latter seemed to prefer a more arms-length approach. "Up until his illness and death, Miles continued romancing the idea of an eventual album collaboration with Prince – an idea Prince never rejected but never brought himself to take seriously enough to commence writing and recording together. Instead, Prince made periodic offers of various tracks. Miles held out, wishing for the opportunity to actually work together. Alas, it never happened," says Leeds.[13]

Reports of Miles and Prince playing together, recording together and composing songs for each other are littered with rumour, misinformation and even downright lies. The Prince bootleg *Crucial*, for example, says on its cover "Prince with Miles Davis and Friends," suggesting that Miles appears on most if not all of the tracks. In fact, apart from "Little Red Riding Hood"/ "Can I Play With U" and "Amandla" (given the title "The H Man") Miles is absent. Even the inclusion of "Amandla" is down to a rumour that Prince wrote this track – he didn't, it was Marcus Miller.[14]

But Prince has confirmed that he and Miles have recorded together, probably in jam sessions rather than on individual songs. "I've actually recorded some indescribable music with Miles Davis – long improvisations that I will release at some point. But again, I want to wait until the spirit moves me, you know. Bring those recordings to the public when it feels right. Like release it on his birthday or his death day, when Miles was released from the circle of life and death."[15] At the time of writing, none of this music has been released.

Miles and Prince appeared on stage together on New Year's Eve 1987 at Paisley Park Studios when Prince hosted a $200-a-ticket concert for Minneapolis's homeless. Four hundred people, including Prince's parents, attended the event and Miles was the guest artist. Although the event was recorded and filmed, it has never been officially released, but a high-quality bootleg, *Miles From The Park*, has emerged.

The album consists of two discs, an audio disc containing most of the concert and a CD-ROM with a video of the same event. The album's title, plus the fact that the cover consists of a portrait shot of Miles, with the same image on the audio CD label, together with the CD booklet containing several pictures of Miles and quotes from his autobiography (all referring to Prince), suggest that Miles was much involved with the project. But, in fact, Miles can only be heard for around four minutes on the 78-minute music disc.

Miles's appearance takes place during the long medley "It's Gonna Be A Beautiful Night," when he enters at around five and a half minutes into the tune, soberly dressed in a suit and playing open horn. Prince directs operations as the band whips up a groove and Miles plays on top of it. Although Miles's chops are good, his presence is less than imposing, and his body language lacks the confident swagger one is accustomed to seeing when Miles is on-stage. The interaction between Miles and Prince consists of a short section where Prince copies Miles's trumpet phrases with scat vocals. In less than four minutes, Miles has blown his horn and gone.

Miles and Prince appeared together the following year on Chaka Khan's album *CK*. Prince wrote, arranged and played most of the instruments on the track "Sticky Wicked," with Miles overdubbing horns and vocals at a later date (Eric Leeds and Atlanta Bliss form the horn section). However, Prince had not written the tune with Miles in mind, confirms Khan: "Miles just happened to be around."

"Sticky Wicked" is instantly recognizable as a Prince track, with a funky jangling rhythm guitar and a drum machine providing the main beat as Khan sings some typically cryptic lyrics penned by Prince about the subject of urban deprivation. Miles's contribution mainly consists of using his muted horn to add colour to the sound and occasionally whispering "Sticky Wicked, yo Sticky Wicked." At the end of the track Miles can be heard saying "Eeh! Eeh! Don't this sound like one of those crows or somethin'?" before blowing a couple of quick blasts on his horn.

Although Miles and Prince did not play together much, they did meet socially and Miles did perform a number of Prince tunes from the late 1980s up until his final concert in August 1991.[16] In 1987, Miles began featuring Prince's song "Movie Star" in his concerts and it remained in his repertoire until the end of 1988. With a staccato-like keyboard intro and a mid-tempo groove, "Movie Star" is a workman-like tune that fails to excite.[17]

Around early 1991, Prince sent Miles several tunes, some of which had been written in the late 1980s for a jazz album project called *Madhouse 24*. Miles hoped to include some of these tunes on his next album (which was to be *Doo-Bop*). Miles performed four of the tunes at several concerts in Germany in March, and then went into a studio to record several of them. But as we shall see in the chapter on *Doo-Bop*, Miles never got to finish them.

Prince is also rumoured to have written a number of songs inspired by Miles. Several Prince bootlegs contain performances or songs written by Prince with a Miles connection. "Letter4Miles" (also known as "Miles Isn't Dead") was recorded two days after Miles's death on September 30, 1991. "A Couple Of Miles" is a tribute which has Prince playing keyboards, synth-bass and electronic drums, and Eric Leeds on tenor and baritone sax. It was recorded on December 27, 1985, the same time as "Can I Play With U?"

On March 24, 1987, Prince and Eric Leeds recorded an untitled instrumental for Miles, although it is not clear whether Miles even heard the finished results. Recordings of Miles rehearsing "Movie Star" at Paisley Park Studios have also emerged, and a Miles's bootleg, *Jailbait*, contains three Prince songs – the title track, "Penetration," and "R U Legal Yet?" And if any more proof was needed on the influence Prince had on Miles, two of his paintings were called Penetration and R U Legal Yet?

15 *tutu* (42:22)

Warner Bros 925 490-2

Recorded	c. January–March 1986
Released	Autumn 1986
Producers	Tommy LiPuma and Marcus Miller; Tommy LiPuma and George Duke ("Backyard Ritual")
Executive producer	Tommy LiPuma
Engineers	Peter Doell and Eric Calvi; Erik Zobler ("Backyard Ritual")
Mixed by	Bill Schnee, Eric Calvi, Eric Zobler
Tracks	"Tutu," "Tomaas," "Portia," "Splatch," "Backyard Ritual," "Perfect Way," "Don't Lose Your Mind," "Full Nelson"

"There's no such thing as wrong music." *Miles Davis speaking to musician Zane Giles*

"When Miles played on Tutu, it was the best solo I had heard him play for twenty years." *Tommy LiPuma,* Tutu*'s executive producer*

Tutu was an album made more by accident than design. The fact that it achieved such critical acclaim and commercial success is largely down to the magic sound of Miles and the creative talents of Marcus Miller, who was responsible for the most of the music. But if one tune can be said to have been the template for the album and influenced its overall feel and direction, it was George Duke's "Backyard Ritual," the first track to be recorded for the album. When Miller heard a recording of "Backyard Ritual," he realized that Miles was interested in using synthesizers and drum machines and this helped formulate his approach to composing the tunes that formed *Tutu*. "['Backyard Ritual'] did give me an idea of the direction that he [Miles] was going. I knew Miles wanted to get into a more modern thing, which was cool."[1]

George Duke: one phone call

The keyboard player/producer George Duke had known Miles since the days when he played with saxophonist Cannonball Adderley (1971), who had been a member of Miles's band in the 1950s. "Miles used to show up at gigs and whenever I played in New York," says Duke. "I also remember him coming to the Village Gate [theatre] when I was with Frank [Zappa] at the time. For some reason Miles and I always got along. I can't explain, but Miles either liked you or he didn't like you. It wasn't like he grew to like you – it was instant. If he took a liking to you, you were cool, but if he didn't, you were out! Miles was always cool with me. I found him to be very funny, not as mysterious as everyone says he was. He had a sense of humour but I've seen him dis [disrespect] people he didn't like. There were times during his comeback years when I was the only one backstage with him because he didn't want to see anyone else. I'd knock on the door and he'd let me in. I can't tell you why."

By the mid-1980s, Duke had a long track record as an artist, composer, arranger and producer, with some of his productions with artists such as Stanley Clarke, Deniece Williams and Jeffrey Osborne crossing over to the pop and R&B charts. Duke was also comfortable playing a wide range of musical genres as illustrated by his association with Frank Zappa and Cannonball Adderley, so it's perhaps no surprise that Miles called Duke when looking for material.

But Miles's recollection of his collaboration with Duke is one of the biggest errors in his autobiography. Miles says *Tutu* "started with some music that George Duke, the piano player, sent to me. As it turned out, we didn't use George's music on the album, but Marcus heard it and wrote something off it."[2] Miles adds that Duke arranged a lot of the music on *Tutu*.[3] This again is another glaring error, as Miller arranged almost all the music on the album.

Duke notes that Miles's recollections are: "Not directly true. What happened is that Miles called me and asked me to write some songs. He just called me out of the blue and said 'Hey, this is Miles,' and I said [sarcastically], 'Oh yeah, okay,' and he said 'No, motherfucker, this is Miles. Write me some tunes.' I said 'Okay,' and hung up. I thought it was one of my friends fooling around and so I didn't do anything." A week later, Miles called back. "He said, 'Hey this is Miles, where are my tunes?' I said, 'Oh man, I didn't know it was you,' and he cussed me out." Duke adds: "Miles called me and told me to just write. He said 'I'm not dead yet – just write.' So whenever I had a spare moment I would write some stuff. I had an idea of starting with some sounds and then something with a groove he could just play off."

To give Duke some idea of the direction he wanted to go, Miles sent him a tape of the Cuban band Irakere, whose music is a mix of jazz, rock and Cuban music. Duke wrote three songs that would be sent to Miles, "Backyard Ritual," "Tribute" and "Fumilayo." "Backyard Ritual" was the only tune that wound up on *Tutu*. But what happened to the other tunes Duke composed for Miles? They were not wasted.

"Tribute" appeared on the album *Forever Yours* by the group 101 North, which Duke had helped sign to Capitol Records: "I wanted something that was in the pocket, with the drums laying the law down and Miles floating on top, but Miles never had time to finish it. I needed some tracks and just took the track I'd sent him. I told Miles 'I'm gonna write you some other music.'"

101 North consisted of three vocalists, Annette Jones, Angel Rogers and Carl Carwell, with Everette Harp on saxophone. Duke, plus a host of session players, also play on the record. "Tribute" appears on the album as "Tribute (to Miles Davis)" and, like "Backyard Ritual," it begins in a mysterious fashion, with dark synthesized sound and a sampled horn that sounds like Miles in his *Sketches Of Spain* period. "Tribute" has a similar mid-tempo groove to "Backyard Ritual," albeit slightly funkier, and the two tunes were probably felt to be too similar to appear on the same album.

"Fumilayo" was the result of Duke listening to the Irakere tape Miles had sent him. "He began to change his concept and asked me to write something like Irakere. So I wrote the tune and he said he was going to use it on his next album." But "Fumilayo" would end up on an album by Duke's cousin, the singer Diane Reeves. "I was working on the tune and Diane came in and said 'I've got to have this song.' I said 'I'm writing it for Miles,' so she said 'Call Miles back and get it back.' I said 'You must be out of your mind!'

"So she harped on me and eventually I called Miles and I said 'Miles, you know this young singer Diane Reeves?' Miles says 'Who's the bitch?' So I said 'She's my cousin and she really wants to do the song, but I've got more ideas in that Irakere groove and I'll write you another.' So Miles says 'Tell the bitch to get another song.' But then Miles calls me back and gives up the song! He said 'Okay, write me something else – but it had better not be bullshit.'" "Fumilayo," which appeared on Reeve's album *Never Too Far*, is a bright, happy Latin-jazz number that even includes the lyrics "Ore Tutu Fumi Lashe."

Duke wrote a fourth number for Miles, although Miles never got to hear it. "Bag Lady," a slow-groove track with a bluesey feeling and lots of sound effects, ended up on 101 North's debut album, released in 1988. Duke would go on to collaborate with Miles on his next but one album, *Amandla*, and, once again, Miles's working methods would surprise him.

"Backyard Ritual" (4:49)

Composer	George Duke
Musicians	Miles, trumpet; George Duke, keyboards, synclavier, samples; Marcus Miller, bass; Steve Reid and Paulinho DaCosta, percussion
Producers	Tommy LiPuma, George Duke
Arranger	George Duke
Engineer	Erik Zobler
Recorded	Capitol Recording Studios,[4] February 6, 1986
Live performances	None

Duke had composed several tunes for Miles in his studio in California using a synclavier, a combined synthesizer, sampler and multi-track recorder. Duke says it took around a day to create the track: "I did everything on a synclavier. I put the drums together and came up with a bass line and kind of stacked it as I went." The samples included a trumpet and what Duke describes as "a stupid little saxophone."

As far as Duke was concerned, the music he sent Miles was simply a rough draft. "I just did a little demo and sent him them to get an idea, then I'd send him the charts. I figured he and his musicians and Tommy LiPuma were going to record it and that would be the end of it. I hoped they would allow me to play piano on it."

But Miles had other ideas. "Miles called me back and said how he dug one of the tunes. I said 'When are you going to record it?' and he said 'I'm not. I want to use what you got, it sounds funny to me and I like it.' And he said to me 'You think that's the way I play trumpet?' and I said 'That's the way it sounds to me!' Of course they took my trumpet sample off but they left my saxophone sample that was just a demo for Kenny Garrett or somebody!"[5] Duke tried talking Miles out of simply using the demo, but Miles could not be persuaded.

The album credits on *Tutu* list Paulinho DaCosta as the sole percussionist, but this is an error. "I was mis-credited on 'Backyard Ritual'," says Steve Reid. "They screwed it up and I was so bummed because of all the credits to screw up it was on a Miles Davis record. Tommy LiPuma told me they'd put things right in the reprint, but they never did. I played almost all the percussion on that track, and Paulinho added a little magic afterwards."

George Duke says the song's title is deliberately vague. "After I'd written the song I had to figure out what to call it. I didn't want anything obvious like 'Love In The Afternoon.' I was thinking about Miles and the history of Miles. There was nothing specific – it just sounded right. I wanted something that was interesting and Miles Davis-ish. So I came up with 'Backyard Ritual' – whatever that is."[6]

"Backyard Ritual"'s introduction has a mysterious quality to it, almost sounding as if it appears out of thin air. Miles blows a few notes on muted trumpet and, underneath them, the synclavier's glassy sound swirls around. Twenty-one seconds into the tune, a drum machine kicks in, setting down a mid-tempo groove which is maintained for the rest of the track. Marcus Miller's overdubbed popped bass, Steve Reid and Paulinho DaCosta's tasteful percussive effects, and some sampled "mmm" vocals add various moods and textures to the sound. The sampled sax can be heard playing beneath Miles at around the 2:25 mark. Miles was right – it does sound funny.

Shortly after this Miles plays a few phrases with an open horn – one of the few times he plays without a mute on *Tutu* – as the sax solo continues.

The track ends in a similar way to the intro, with Miles playing a flurry of notes accompanied by the swirling sound from the synclavier. Because "Backyard Ritual" was essentially a demo it obviously sounds less crafted than the other tunes on *Tutu*, but this seems to enhance rather than detract from the overall performance. "Backyard Ritual" also appeared on a 12-inch single in two versions, a short version with both the atmospheric introduction and the ending edited and the track beginning on the first beat of the sampled drum rhythm. The second version is identical to the album track.

So what does Duke think of the track today; for example, does he wish some things could have been changed? "There's always something I would have preferred to change and since it was a demo and not meant for release there are things I would have changed. I love the way Miles played on it and what Marcus and Tommy did with it, but I would have preferred to see a real drummer and have a real saxophone, but Miles was his own man."

Marcus Miller and the *Tutu* project

In the three years since Marcus Miller had left Miles's band, his compositional, arrangement and production skills had blossomed. Miller had evolved from being a superb bassist to a multi-talented multi-instrumentalist, who could write, arrange and produce for a diverse range of artists and musical genres. After his stint with Miles, Miller produced his second solo album (called *Marcus Miller*) as well as a string of artists including David Sanborn, Luther Vandross and Aretha Franklin. Miller also got heavily involved into playing synthesizers, and he was extending the range of instruments he played on recording sessions – it wasn't unusual for Miller to play at least several instruments on the same track.[7]

Miller also moved to the other side of the glass in the recording studio, learning the craft of mixing and engineering tracks and becoming skilled in a variety of studio technologies. All this experience would mean that Miller was well equipped for what would turn out to be his most challenging project to date: to almost single-handedly compose, play, arrange and produce *Tutu*.

Miller's involvement in *Tutu* came at a critical time for both Miles and LiPuma. With LiPuma rejecting the music from the *Rubberband* sessions, he now only had two potential album tracks in his hands – "Can I Play With U?" and "Backyard Ritual." Quite simply, Miles and LiPuma had reached a creative impasse. LiPuma suggested working with the British keyboardist Thomas Dolby (who had had pop hits with songs such as "Hyperactive" and "Einstein a Go-Go") and Lyle Mayes, who played keyboards with jazz guitarist Pat Metheny.

"Lyle Mayes was one of the most talented keyboard player/programmers alive and I always wanted to work with him," says LiPuma. "In fact, I called Lyle and had a conversation with him, but at the time he was – still is – tight with Pat Metheny and I think they were going on the road or something, so that didn't work out. I had heard a few things Thomas Dolby had done and he was working with machines and it seemed like he had the science down on them." Thomas Dolby recalls: "I heard via my management that he was thinking of covering [the hit song] 'Hyperactive' at one time. Then it went quiet."

Miller became part of the *Tutu* project when he heard that Miles had moved from Columbia Records to his then current record label, Warner Bros. "I was thinking: 'Wow, man, I wonder if he's going to do some new music?' So I called Tommy LiPuma up."[8] After Miller had enquired whether Miles was looking for any material, LiPuma encouraged him to send some music. LiPuma notes: "I had been working with Marcus on a few different projects like the albums with Bob James and David Sanborn, and George Benson and Earl Klugh. Marcus had played on them and had written a few things.[9] Marcus is a fabulous musician and his melodies just stand out. It just seemed to make sense. Plus the fact he had worked with Miles so it wasn't like I had to convince Miles, because he knew the guy's talent. It seemed like a natural." LiPuma's hunch was right because the two musicians worked well together on the project. "Miles and Marcus had a great relationship. I think he really loved the way Marcus played," says LiPuma.

Miller agrees with the view that *Tutu* would turn out to be a musical odyssey for both him and Miles. "Miles said he wanted to do something new and the guys in his record company said they wanted to do something new. And so it seemed like a good time to do something that was a product of now, which was 1985/86." Miller's involvement in the making of *Tutu* grew gradually, which in retrospect made life easier for him. "It was definitely easier knowing that I was just going in there with a specific project of creating three songs I had written because I didn't have to worry about the overall thing. That meant somebody else would be worrying about the whole picture and I could just provide my own little contribution," he says.

Miller adds that he was unaware of any disagreement Miles and LiPuma may have had over the aborted *Rubberband* album. "Somebody might have made a reference to some of the other stuff that Miles was working on, but because my music wasn't the only thing being commissioned for the album I just assumed there was going to be other stuff." Even when Miller was asked to write more material for *Tutu*, he still assumed that contributions from other writers and producers would appear on the final album: "I was still under the impression that Prince was going to have something and who knows? I wasn't making the executive decision on the album. My job was just to write what I could do."

But Jason Miles, a keyboard player, programmer and producer, who worked closely with Miller on *Tutu*, says: "The vibes that I was hearing before Marcus got involved was that Miles was doing some recordings that weren't coming together. I think *You're Under Arrest* was one of Miles's weakest records except that it did spawn a couple of tunes that got a lot of radio play like 'Human Nature' and 'Time After Time.' There was always a little magic on every Miles album, but was it the direction he should be in and one that Tommy LiPuma should be sticking his neck out for?"

He adds: "I think they were looking for Miles to lead the way but who knows what he was thinking about because his sense of the synthesizer sound was what we called the 'Oberheim A1 sound' [a synthesizer pre-set mode]. We came in and started to create something completely different. Marcus knew what he wanted to do and I think Tommy liked that. Tommy was like 'Here we go – I get it.' He knew what it was and he's a very intuitive guy. I don't think Tommy was going to release a Miles album just on chance. He was going to make something happen."

LiPuma also sent Miller a tape of "Backyard Ritual." "Tommy said, 'Let me send you this so you can get an idea of what Miles is doing.' I heard it and thought 'I don't have to operate with the parameters I had originally thought I would operate with, which was what Miles had been doing up to that point with live instruments and a band. So I pulled out the synths and started adding colours – it was exciting because that's what was going on at that time," says Miller.

Miller then set about creating several tracks, enlisting the help of Jason Miles. Jason Miles had first met Miller in 1979, when he hired the young bassist for a recording session. Over the years, the two men would collaborate on numerous projects and spend many hours together in the studio. "When MIDI [Musical Instrument Digital Interface] and synths really started to get into fashion and people started using them I got a call from Marcus asking me to come to the studio and work on some stuff he was doing with a band that included Lenny White and Bernard Wright [The Jamaica Boys]," recalls Jason Miles.

"When I realized there was an opportunity to use some more modern sounds I called Jason and said 'Listen man, I need you to bring your emulator to my house.' He brought his emulator and he had a bank of sounds that were really new to me. I have never heard an orchestra stab just start from under a key on a keyboard – it was pretty fascinating at the time," recalls Miller. Miller would work through Jason Miles's sound bank until he found things that were interesting to use for the demo.

Jason Miles remembers going to Miller's home with an array of equipment that included a PPG Wave, Emulator and an Oberheim Matrix-12 synthesizer. "Marcus had a [Yamaha] DX7 in a little loft in his home and we'd work together. We'd start using different sounds. He had sketches for the tunes and when he was putting it down I would come up with some interesting sounds and then he'd adjust the music to the sound he wanted to use," says Jason Miles. A funny incident occurred when Miller first played Miles the demos that he'd created in New York. Jason Miles had sampled Miles's trumpet from a record: "Marcus said 'Yeah man, that's the vibe.' So Marcus plays Miles his trumpet sample and Miles goes 'Who's that on trumpet? Sounds like Nat Adderley.' We laughed our asses off over that," says Jason Miles.

Jason Miles says working on the *Tutu* project was: "A culmination of all I had worked for. Since 1965, when I was fourteen I'd been listening to Miles, though it was when I heard *Bitches Brew* that Miles had a real effect on me. I became a total Miles freak." Using a combination of synthesizers, samplers, drum machines and multi-track recording, Miller composed several pieces – "Tutu," "Portia" and "Splatch" – and then contacted LiPuma when he was ready to send him the tapes.

But to Miller's surprise, LiPuma suggested he flew to LA bringing the tapes with him. So Miller travelled from New York to LA, unsure how he would fare at his audition with Miles and LiPuma. But when he arrived at the Warner Bros studio, he was in for several more surprises. First, there was no sign of Miles, and when Miller played LiPuma the demos, LiPuma said "This is great. Let's go." When Miller asked "Go where?" LiPuma replied "Let's begin recording!"[10] When Miller then enquired about a band, LiPuma suggested he record the tracks in the same way he had done the demos, by overdubbing the instruments.

"It was a time when drum machines were starting to hit the scene and I had been doing a lot of things with synths at that time," recalls LiPuma. "I would use them to set up a pulse with percussion and have the band play along to them. The pulse you get from a drum machine is a different feel from what you get from live players. It's not a question of one being better; it's just how you utilize these tools to your advantage." LiPuma says it was George Duke's track that got him thinking about using machines with Miles. "The first thing I had gotten and had any sense of 'Gee, this would be something great to do' was George Duke's 'Backyard Ritual' and that was done with machines for demo purposes. That started it. I said 'George, basically all we have to do is put Miles on here and take the synth trumpet off,' because it seemed to make sense just the way it was."

Miller had spent a lot of time programming the drum machine to make it swing and this had a profound effect on LiPuma. "The difference with Marcus was what he had done. It was the first time I had heard someone program a drum machine where he was having the snare playing like a drummer would play his left hand in a bebop situation. The left hand played loose. It just wasn't played with a 2/4 or a 4/4-rhythm feel and I thought that was really novel – I had never heard anything like that. And that was basically how he had programmed it." Jason Miles adds: "We took the demos to a place where they were right in your face. You knew something was happening when you heard it because Marcus and I were starting to get things together where I understood his music and his genius and let him flow so he could achieve his fantasies."

Miller admits that when LiPuma suggested he dispense with a live band he was surprised, but adds: "But I was only surprised for a couple of minutes and then it seemed like 'Hey, this is the way I've been making music all my life.' You've got to understand that you're dealing with people like myself who lived through Stevie Wonder playing every instrument on some of the greatest albums of the 1970s. You're dealing with a guy who came through Prince who basically did the same thing. This overdub technology allows you to create music in a different way. So it was like 'We're going to do it the way I do any other album – that's cool. Let's try that, it could be interesting.' I already knew what the music was going to sound like so what it really did was to take away any of the variables, meaning, now I'm sure what the music's going to sound like because I'm gonna be doing everything. It was going to be a better-recorded version of my demos with Miles putting his magic over it."

Until the arrival of overdubbing technology music had happened in a continuum, adds Miller: "It started and you played and that was it. But with overdubbing, you played and then sat back and looked at it like you would with a painting. You'd keep adding little bits and it became a different way of making music. But what you're not going to change is the original inspiration. That's what we did with Miles. When he played it wasn't like we changed things there and then."

So, like a painter surveying his canvas, Miller would add extra colours to the sonic palette of sounds that he and Jason Miles had created, until, finally, the finished track would emerge. It was an approach that Miles could relate to, now that he was creating his own paintings. "Miles would paint something, look at it, eat, watch boxing on the TV and then return to it. It was going in the same direction as Miles's life," adds Miller. The analogy with painting is an apt one, not least because Miles once told his keyboardist Robert Irving III that "a painting is music you can see and music is a painting you can hear."[11]

Jason Miles says he wasn't surprised that LiPuma basically wanted Miller to re-create the demos. "I felt the basic fibre of the demo was there. It didn't surprise me because I knew the melodies were just amazing and I knew Marcus was on to something." There is a balance between a live, real-time performance and music that is created by a step-by-step process, says Miller. "When you don't have the opportunity to step back and look at things, there's a magic that happens and that's what jazz has been, 'This is it, right here and now.' But there are so many art forms when that magic is enriched by the ability to go back and create what's exactly in your mind."

LiPuma's suggestion to dispense with a live band was, in hindsight, an inspired one, but at the time making a Miles Davis album and using electronic instruments and studio technology as the main instruments was highly controversial. In the mid-1980s, a phalanx of technologies was at the disposal of artists and producers, including synthesizers, samplers, drum machines, MIDI technology and multi-track recording. It was a time when the music industry debated whether real instruments would soon be replaced by computers.

Supporters of the new technology even predicted that synthesizers would replace guitars and those extolling the virtues of drum machines pointed out that, unlike humans, they didn't drop time. In the studio, music could now be electronically manipulated with just the touch of a few buttons. With so many new toys at their disposal, it was no surprise that some artists and producers were seduced by them and spent more time tweaking the technology than crafting the music. All too often the electronic music that came out of the techno-driven 1980s was cold and clinical, lacking both soul and content.

But although Miller was interested in the technology, his first priority was always to make good music. Miler says he saw *Tutu* as a "combination between technology and humanity"[12] and, as a result, *Tutu* sounds warm and musical rather than cold and mechanical. Even so, eyebrows were raised when Miles decided not to take his working band into the studio and they were raised even higher when Miles explained why. "I have found that taking my working band into the studio is too much trouble these days. The band might not feel good that day at the recording session or at least some people in the band might not... You've got to teach them what you want them to do, show them right there in the studio... that holds things up. Doing it the old way, recording like we used to, is just too much trouble, and takes too much time."[13]

Miles also dismissed complaints that playing to a tape rather than a musician risked losing spontaneity. "Maybe that's true; I don't know. All I know is that the new recording technology makes it easier to do it the way we have been doing it."[14] This seems astonishing when one considers how much of Miles's musical creativity and inspiration came from working with musicians in the studio. It seems to suggest that Miles had grown tired of making music the way he done so for more than several decades, but a more likely explanation is that Miles's energy levels were not what they used to be.

LiPuma confirms that Miles was not concerned about using his band. "One of the great things about Miles was that he was always looking to experiment and do things, so he didn't have any problems. He didn't ask 'Why don't we do this with a band?'" An incident during the recording of "Portia" – where Miller suggested that Miles bring his regular saxophone player to the studio to play the soprano sax parts – supports this view. Miles rejected the idea of using his own sax player and insisted that Miller record the saxophone parts (see below).

Even so, one of Miles's greatest skills was his ability to inspire musicians (both on-stage and in the studio) to play beyond their skills and expectations. Numerous musicians who have worked with Miles in the studio talk about his awesome working methods and Miles, in turn, was often inspired by what was going on around him. A simple chord or riff played by a musician in the studio could spark off new ideas and take the music off in new directions. But none of this was possible when playing to music recorded on tape.

Miles's previous albums, *Decoy* and *You're Under Arrest* had been largely created in the studio by Robert Irving III and Vince Wilburn Jr. under Miles's direction. Miles would often be absent from the studio, but his involvement in the direction and overall feel of the music was much greater than with *Tutu*. Even so, Miles was not merely a passive agent on *Tutu*, and after initially having little say in the musical direction he would start making suggestions to Miller. Miller recalls times when Miles would say, "'I don't like that piano, take it off' or 'You need to write another section.'"[15]

It is interesting to note that the decision not to use a band was LiPuma's alone. Miles was not present when the suggestion was first made to Miller to overdub the instruments himself, and Miller had originally written the tunes with the assumption that Miles and his band would record them. By the time Miles had arrived to survey Miller's work, it was a *fait accompli*, because Miller was well into the process of creating the tracks. It is likely that Miles went along with the decision to record *Tutu* without his band because a) he liked what he had heard, b) he trusted and respected Miller's musical ability, c) he wanted to experiment and d) he didn't want another disagreement with LiPuma.

So how did Miles's working band feel about being left out of the project? Bob Berg said he felt "bugged" by not being involved with the making of *Tutu*.[16] However, on further reflection he added: "Whenever I've been involved with a working band, I've been involved with the recordings, at least on some level. When I found that the new record was done without the participation of the band members, I was a bit disappointed. Now, in retrospect, I don't have any negative feelings about the situation. Miles was just trying something different and I don't take it personally. I guess I was a bit surprised that a 'heavy' saxophonist wasn't employed." Vince Wilburn Jr. is sanguine about the decision: "It was weird because it was Marcus with Miles on top. That shit was bad because Marcus is bad – he's a motherfucker. I guess that was the way it was. There was never any questioning about it. We just learned the songs and played them live."

Miller is quick to acknowledge the role Tommy LiPuma played in the making of *Tutu*. "First of all I didn't have to deal with any money, which as a producer that's what you normally do – Tommy dealt with the budget. He would make suggestions about the music, he would sit and listen to the performances that Miles was doing. When we finished [the track] 'Tutu,' Miles ran it down twice and Tommy said 'Man, that first one – Marcus, listen to the first one!' He was a step away from the active process so he could make the kind of assessments that might have been difficult for me."

A rumour surrounding *Tutu* was that Miller was pushed into making a highly commercial album with Miles, but Miller says this wasn't the case: "Commercial success wasn't even a thought. If somebody had told me 'You know what? Miles doesn't want to sell any records, Marcus, so make sure it's not commercial,' I would have done the same thing because there was no guarantee in my mind that this was going to be something that everybody loved. There was nothing on the radio like that at the time, so there was no way I could go 'Yeah man, this is going to be Miles's shit.' I didn't realize until people reacted to it."

Tutu was a product of Miller's experience that embraced many musical art forms. "In that era I was involved in hit records. When I was working with Aretha Franklin and with McCoy Tyner I loved both sides of the music and had always wanted to combine them. The music that changed my life was Herbie Hancock's *Headhunters* – 'Chameleon' and all that great stuff. My whole world was evolved around this combination of jazz and R&B and funk and taking the things I love from these kinds of music and creating something new. There's an inherent commercialism in that because it's so cool."

With its lush electronic soundscapes and Miles essentially soloing over pre-prepared music, *Tutu* has been compared to some of Miles's earlier works with Gil Evans, most notably, *Sketches Of Spain*. But Miller says he was inspired more by Herbie Hancock's *Speak Like A Child*. Years later, Miller would read the sleeve notes to *Speak Like A Child* only to discover that Hancock in turn had been influenced by the work of Gil Evans. "Now I understand why people tell me that *Tutu* was like the *Sketches* for the 80s."[17] Miller saw *Tutu* as "developing a conversation between me and Miles. You know how jazz musicians wanted the album with the big band: they'd play the melody, then solo for sixteen bars and then play the melody again. That's how I envisioned these albums."[18]

Miller had wanted to use Jason Miles on the *Tutu* recording sessions, but for some reason Warner Bros wouldn't stump up the expenses, so Adam Holzman, who had recently joined Miles's band as a keyboard player and programmer, became involved in the project. Writer Paul Tingen reports that Miles recommended Holzman for the *Tutu* gig[19] although Miller recalls LiPuma making the suggestion. "Tommy said 'Get Miles's keyboard player down here because he's got some unusual synth things that he's doing, so Adam came in and played on *Tutu* and he came up with some cool sounds particularly for the middle-section interval part [on the track 'Tutu']. He did some beautiful things and put in some weird things and he played on 'Splatch'. His solo is crazy and sounds like glass is breaking. He was operating on a creative level. He was a performer like you would have a sax player come in and perform a solo on a track." When asked whether he realized at the time that he was helping to create something special, Holzman says: "Definitely. I had never been part of anything that heavy before. The songs 'Tutu' and 'Portia' are classics and Miles played great on them."

Although Holzman was working with Miller in L.A., Jason Miles was still involved in the project, even though he was on the other side of the U.S. coast. "We did a lot of shit on the telephone. Marcus would call me up and say 'Hey man, when I'm doing this, what about this?' I knew these machines with my eye closed so I'd go 'Press this, go to six, balance that out.' We had that great vibe," says Jason Miles.

It wasn't until a couple of days after Miller had received the go-ahead from LiPuma that he saw Miles. "Miles walks into the studio and the first thing that struck me was 'This guy looks fantastic!' Because when I left the band two years ago he was real frail and I wasn't sure he was going to make it through. But the guy's vibrant, his eyes are shining and you could just feel this energy. I kept commenting on it until he finally said 'Just shut up, will you? I know I look good!'"[20] Miller had been apprehensive about how Miles would react to the music, but when he played the track Miles simply said "That's great. Keep going. Bye!"[21] And with that, Miles left the studio.

When the tracks were ready for Miles to overdub his trumpet, Miller faced another challenge: adopting the role of being the producer of Miles Davis. "It was a completely different relationship and it had to grow into that. When I presented the music to him, I presented it as his former bass player, but essentially we couldn't operate like that. It had to become a more equal relationship."[22]

During his first recording session with Miles, Miller sat next to him in the studio, both of them wearing headphones and listening to the music. Miller simply watched Miles as he played around on the horn trying to make sense of the music – Miles often didn't know what he was going to hear until he arrived at the recording sessions because Miller wanted to keep some spontaneity in the proceedings. After a few minutes of scratching around, Miles told the engineer to stop the tape and then turned to Miller, saying: "When are you going to tell me what the fuck to play? You know the music, I don't know the music."[23] After a while, Miller became more comfortable about directing Miles, cueing him when to play and even writing out parts for him when necessary.

When the three tracks were completed, Miller felt pleased with the results and assumed his work was done. He thought: "This sounds really nice. It's not *Kind Of Blue* but it's for now, it's what going on. [Miles] was working with a lot of producers and I assumed it was a nice little contribution from me. I figured my job was done. I felt pretty good about it."[24] But when Miles and LiPuma listened to the results of the Miller sessions, they knew they had something special. Tommy LiPuma said: "I remember when I left the studio in the early hours of the morning, I must have played the track ['Tutu'] ten times on the way to the hotel. I couldn't get over it. When I got up in the morning,

I immediately played it again. It had a magic quality about it. I hadn't heard Miles play like that in a long time. It blew me away."[25] He adds: "'Tutu' was so great I said 'Marcus you've got to write more stuff.'"

At last, LiPuma and Miles could both agree on a musical direction for the new album. Both men decided that Miller should take over the project. Miles knew that Miller was on a creative high and was more than happy for him to take charge. "If a guy's in his creative period, you let him write whatever he wants. I did Wayne like that, Herbie, Bill Evans," he said.[26]

LiPuma adds: "When you hit on something that feels right, why go any further? As far as I was concerned, it was the right chemistry at the right time." Back in New York, Miller received a call from LiPuma asking for more material. So Miller went back into the studio with Jason Miles and worked on several new tunes. *Tutu* the album was born.

The tracks

"Splatch" (4:45)

Composer	Marcus Miller
Musicians	Miles, trumpet; Marcus Miller, bass, guitar, synthesizers, soprano sax, drums; Adam Holzman, synthesizer solo; Paulinho DaCosta and Steve Reid, percussion
Producers	Tommy LiPuma, Marcus Miller
Arranger	Marcus Miller
Recorded	Capitol Recording Studios, Los Angeles, February 10, 1986
Engineer	Peter Doell
Mixer	Bill Schnee
Live performances	March 1986 – November 1988

Miller showed great subtlety and restraint when applying sampling and synthesizer technology to the other *Tutu* tracks, but he seemingly abandoned this strategy when it came to "Splatch." The track sounds as if it's had everything but the kitchen sink thrown at it – a battery of synthesizers, an array of samples (including voices, grunts, gunshots and broken glass), not to mention two percussionists. The track title aptly describes Miller's approach to the music: "'Splatch' was a word I used to describe where you take something from one area and put it on to another," says Miller. "It's like splicing only more sloppy – like if you moved mud or clay. I envisioned I was making music at the time by taking this from here and that from there and splatching it all around."

"Splatch" is a funk/rock number that is something of a shock to the ears after the sublime "Portia," which precedes it on the album. An opening rock guitar chord and a hard snare sound launch an aggressive, edgy number which Miles's trumpet playing echoes in its character – he sounds angry. The video for "Splatch" has Miles stalking along a corridor while playing a series of stabbing notes, an image which really captures the mood of the tune.

Miles mostly plays with a Harmon mute, but there are a couple of nice short sections of open horn. Miller's bass playing is in-your-face, with strings popped, thumped, slapped and plucked – he sounds like he's had a bad day at the office. In the background, samples and synthesizer lines fight it out for space. Adam Holzman plays a short sharp solo created by linking several synthesizers and MIDIing them up to an emulator. Jason Miles says: "Adam probably had the most input on 'Splatch'. When I heard his solo I said 'That makes a lot of sense, it's not just some dude throwing his stuff on there.' He did a good job on that."

The solo got Holzman a playing credit on the *Tutu* album, although interestingly he had also played a little on "Tutu" – although he was not credited on the album sleeve. Holzman says there's a fine line between programming and playing. "I did play a little bit on the song 'Tutu' – there's a synth interlude in the middle with a couple of swells and filter sweeps that I played. But overall, when it says 'programming,' it means (or it used to mean) that you actually created the sounds from scratch (using samples or waveforms), or did some slick tricks combining different sounds, or had some cool ideas regarding sound design. "These days 'programming' means sequencing, that is, running the computer. There were no computers involved in the sessions I worked on for *Tutu*. Guys like Jason Miles were more known for their sound-programming skills, and guys like Bernard Wright (who I think is very funky) are known as players. I was kind of an odd bird, a player who could program synths, too, so I sort of blurred the line a little."

"Splatch" saw Paulinho DaCosta and Steve Reid adding various percussive effects – the two percussionists overdubbed their parts on separate occasions in the studio. "Steve Reid was a guy Miles had seen and he said 'This guy's really cool, you should bring him in,' and so we did to have him add some colours. That was nice," says Miller. In fact, Miles had once described Reid as: "One of the most imaginative percussionists of the decade." "Miles wrote that on a photograph of him and me in the studio. I'm very proud of that," says Reid, who played most of the percussion on this track.

Reid recalls an interesting incident from this session: "Whenever Miles came in and felt inspired, Tommy would stop everything and put up a microphone so Miles could blow. I was playing on a tune at the time and Tommy said 'Why don't you take a break and have Miles blow?' So Miles starts blowing then stops and says 'Steve, come on in here.' I go in and he says 'I want you to grab a shaker and play along so it feels live.' So I grabbed a shaker and I'm thinking 'This is just a vibe.' Well, the engineer is just tearing his hair out saying 'I can't record this way. You can't have this shaker leaking through the microphone.' So Miles goes: 'Fuck you. This is my take and I want the shaker on there. This is it – print [record] it!' We did two or three things this way."

"Splatch" may not have been subtle when compared with the other tunes on *Tutu*, but it is a funky number and, when played live, it got audiences jigging in their seats. Even so, today, Miller has a few reservations about the finished article. Ask Miller which parts of *Tutu* he would change if he had the chance now, and he says: " 'Splatch' was probably the most heavy use of all that technology stuff. When I hear that song I think it was dying for a drum, just something to balance it, because I think it's a little unbalanced in terms of technology versus reality. I still get a kick out of it, but when you're asking me about things I would change, I would probably do that."

"Tutu" (5:15)

Composer	Marcus Miller
Musicians	Miles, trumpet; Marcus Miller, bass, synthesizers, soprano sax, drum fills; Paulinho DaCosta, percussion
Producers	Tommy LiPuma, Marcus Miller
Arranger	Marcus Miller
Recorded	Capitol Recording Studios, Los Angeles, February 11, 1986
Engineer	Peter Doell
Mixer	Bill Schnee
Live performances	March 1986 – July 1991

Edited single version released (4:04 in length).
A live version of "Tutu" appears on *Live Around The World*.

"Tutu" was named after Archbishop Desmond Mpilo Tutu, the South African cleric who was at the heart of the struggle against apartheid. In 1984, Tutu won the Nobel Peace Prize, and the following year he became the first black Anglican bishop of Johannesburg. As a black man growing up in America, Miles was acutely aware of the issue of racism[27] and one of his earliest memories was of being chased down a street by a white man shouting "Nigger! Nigger! Nigger!"[28]

Talking about the situation of blacks in America, Miles said "America is such a racist place, so racist it's pitiful. It's just like South Africa only more sanitized... I have always had a built-in thing for racism. I can smell it. I can feel it behind me, anywhere it is."[29] In 1985, Miles had recorded on several tracks for an album called *Sun City*, featuring a group of musicians called

Artists United Against Apartheid.[30] One of the tracks Miles played on was called "Revolutionary Situation" and featured the voices of Nelson Mandela and Desmond Tutu.

In 1989, when the South African apartheid regime was still in place and Nelson Mandela was still imprisoned, Miles was asked whether he would go to South Africa and perform. He replied "I wouldn't go there unless it was cool... I would play for Bishop Tutu but I'm not gonna play for the prejudiced white people – racists. I wouldn't be able to play one note."[31]

"Tutu" also has another meaning, which has great relevance to Miles's personality, as the singer Cassandra Wilson explained why she decided to record "Tutu" – under the title "Resurrection Blues (Tutu)" – on her tribute album *Traveling Miles*: " 'Tutu' also means 'cool' in the Yoruba language and there's a whole concept around coolness that really for me describes Miles Davis's music and Miles Davis's persona and it's about graciousness under pressure. Always a cool delivery."[32]

Miller recalls that as soon as he had hung up the phone after speaking to LiPuma about the possibility of writing some music for Miles, he had the idea for "Tutu": "The idea came at that moment. It often does when I come up with music for somebody else. I was in a hotel in L.A., I hung up the phone and said 'Man, this will be great,' and the bass line from 'Tutu' was right there. Of course I had imagined it with a band and I figured I'll have the bass player in Miles's band playing this and I'll play another bass part higher on the fretless bass. I heard the whole lot of it right then and there. If you hear 'Tutu' there's a low bass playing the main bass line and there's a fretless bass above it dancing around it, and that's how I originally heard it."

Miller had no doubt that he could create something special for Miles. "I never had any self-doubt about whether I could come up with something good. I felt pretty confident about that plus I always knew that it's not like Miles is just going to accept any old thing that I presented to him. So I know my job was to come up with something I thought was basically cool and if Miles dug it we could present it together."

When Miller began composing "Tutu," he had a number of ideas inside his head, which included the workers of South Africa. Miller also wanted the tune to reflect various elements of Miles's musical heritage, as well as the personality of the man himself. Miller, ably assisted by Jason Miles, used a variety of synthesizers and a Linn 9000 drum machine to compose the basic track. Later on, Adam Holzman would add some additional sounds to the track.

Miller also wanted to use a New Orleans beat Miles had taught him and Al Foster in the early 1980s, a shuffle with a half-time backbeat. Miller began by recording a ride cymbal effect from the drum machine to create a wash over the sound.[33] He also wanted to recreate the sound of a bebop drum rhythm and used the casaba sound on the drum machine to achieve this. Next came a bass drum sound to funk-up the track. The drum machine programming by Miller and Jason Miles was so subtle that it managed to avoid the monotonous mechanical beat that bedevils so many drum machine sounds; indeed the drum sounds were so natural that some listeners thought they were being played by Omar Hakim.

But a drum machine cannot recreate the fluency of a human drummer, and so Miller added yet another element to the drum sound by going into the studio with a snare drum and cymbal, and adding some press rolls and cymbal crashes. The result is a rhythm that really swings. The next element was the bass line, which consisted of sampled voices played on a synthesizer. Miller then added his electric bass, popping and plucking strings to lay even more funk on to the track. The playing of Herbie Hancock during his time with Miles's 1960s quintet inspired the melody on "Tutu." Miller also used sampled trombones and played soprano sax to create a sound that harked back to Miles's late 1940s *Birth Of The Cool* period. When the track was ready, it was time for Miles to do his thing.

"The first thing we did was to transfer the programming from the drum machine on to a 24-track analogue [recorder]. That took us about a day. Then Miles did his thing on top," recalls LiPuma. Miller went into the studio with Miles and a soprano saxophone and played him the melody. When Miles was ready, the tape ran. Miller initially felt intimidated about directing Miles, until Miles told him to direct him by tapping his shoulder when he wanted him to play and holding up his hand to stop playing. Miles played just two takes and the effect on Tommy LiPuma inside the control room was electric: "I won't forget when we did 'Tutu' and he put his solo on. That was like the first time down – bam! That was it. I kept looking around the [tape] machine, making sure it was recording because it was so good. The next day I told him how excited I was over what we had gotten."[34] He adds: "When Miles played on 'Tutu,' it was the best solo I had heard him play for twenty years."

During editing and post-production, Miller and LiPuma listened to the solos and decided that the first one was the one to go for. "Tommy made the combination of Miles's performances and I think it was all take one, except for a couple of beautiful phrases from take two. We were careful not to chop up every performance of Miles's so it becomes a Frankenstein thing with parts from here and parts from there," explains Miller. "Usually one spirit went through and then just maybe you add a couple of lines from another performance. That wasn't anything new. Producers in the 1950s – even on *Kind Of Blue* – weren't doing anything different. If the tag at the last head [theme] on a certain take fell apart but the performance was great, they'd simply pick up a tag on a good last head. That's the thing with music – it's closer to painting than people think, especially recorded music.

You want to present people with the best of what you have to offer and that sometimes means playing it twice."

The day after Miles had recorded his parts, LiPuma asked him if he was coming to the studio to hear the playback, but Miles said he needed a couple of days off. "I realized he had given his all, to the point of exhaustion," added LiPuma. "There's nothing else you can ask of any artist – just to give everything he's got."[35] LiPuma elaborates: "He said 'Tommy, man I'm tired. That took everything I had just to do that solo.'" LiPuma believes that Miles was sicker than anyone really knew at the time: "Miles would always try to hide how bad he felt."

Miller didn't simply want Miles reacting to a tape: he also wanted musicians reacting to Miles, so he brought in some session musicians. "When you become a producer you become a casting director and you think 'Which players would you like to have who could contribute to this thing?'" says Miller. One of those chosen by Miller was Brazilian-born percussionist Paulinho DaCosta, whose recording credits include Madonna, Michael Jackson, Ella Fitzgerald and Sting. DaCosta had worked with Miller and LiPuma before and Miller explained why he called him: "He's one of the most musical percussionists you'll ever hear. He just reacts in a real sensitive way to the music he hears."[36]

"My role is to add a little flavour, a little support that glues together certain tracks," says DaCosta. "I put a little spice on the top." DaCosta was thrilled when he received the call from Miller and LiPuma. "I was very excited at the prospect of working with Miles. When I heard about *Tutu* I knew it was going to be a great project and I was glad to be involved." On most sessions, DaCosta sat in the studio with Miller and LiPuma, although there were occasions when it would just be him and Miller.

The session would start with DaCosta listening to the music and then talking with Miller and LiPuma about what he planned to do. "They didn't give me much direction – they trusted me. I'd go in and maybe do a couple of things that we might touch up here and there. Of course I listen to what Marcus is doing and try to fit in with him or the melody. It's really a collaboration," says DaCosta.

Tutu used drum machines and lots of music technology rather than a live band, but DaCosta says this wasn't a big challenge. "I can adapt easily to electronic instrumentation or a live band – it's not a problem. With a live band some drummers play on top of the beat or lay back and I just go with what I hear. Machines are very synchronized and you have got to make sure you're not pushing the other way." After DaCosta had recorded his parts he would listen to playback with Miller and LiPuma: "We listen to see if the tempo is right and so on. If it's good, you see lots of smiles, but if it's bad, it's a case of 'go back in there' or 'you're fired!'" he laughs.

A highlight of the sessions was meeting Miles, says DaCosta: "The first time he came in and looked through the glass [in the recording booth], but later on he said hello. He was very nice and very positive. I thought he was a special person – you could feel his vibe. He was so young in his thinking, in his dress and the way he conducted himself in the studio. He still had the drive for the youthful feeling."

DaCosta used a variety of percussion instruments including drums, shaker, tambourine and conga, to add yet more colours to the sound (he can be heard to good effect in the interlude at around the 2:12 mark). Finally, Miller got Adam Holzman to add some synthesizer sounds, and for this Holzman used an Oberheim Xpander and PPG Wave 2.2 – the latter's glassy descending sound can be heard during the interlude. Just before the five-minute mark, the tune begins to end, eventually fading out. However, if you turn up the volume at this point, you'll hear Miles play a delightful flurry of notes before the sound ends.

When you're creating music like a painting there is the danger of adding too many colours and textures and then cluttering the various elements, says Miller. The secret, he adds, is knowing when to stop. On "Tutu" he showed that he certainly knew when that point was reached.

So how does "Tutu" stand up as a Miles Davis track? One has to agree with Holzman's verdict – it is a classic. Miller wanted to capture something of Miles's Prince of Darkness image and in this he ably succeeds, from the track's dramatic explosive opening chord to the fadeout. The atmosphere is dark, brooding and menacing, but the swing is so infectious that it's difficult to listen to "Tutu" without at least tapping your feet along with it. Miles's playing sounds fresh and invigorated – you know he just digs the music.

Miller's arrangement is spacious, with synthesizer sounds subtly weaving in and out of the track. But perhaps his greatest success is in making it hard for listeners to tell whether humans are producing many of the sounds heard on *Tutu* or whether it's a machine. LiPuma says it was one of his favourite tracks and the same goes for DaCosta: "My favourite track was 'Tutu' and I felt it should be the title track. Of course, I had no say in this, so I was so pleased when it happened," he says.

Miles's new album was originally going to be called *Perfect Way*, after the Scritti Politti tune Miles also recorded. But LiPuma suggested that "Tutu" should become the title track. "Miles and Marcus were coming up with titles for the songs. My take on album titles is that the shorter they are the more to the point they are. The title doesn't even have to have a direct relationship to the music. As it turned out, Desmond Tutu was all over the papers. This was prior to there being a black government in South Africa and he was championing for the rights to be given to all South Africans. As for the Yoruban word, I didn't even know it at the time. *Tutu* felt right and that basically was how it worked."

And what did Archbishop Tutu think of the tune named in his honour? "He sent Miles a note saying he was happy that Miles was assisting the cause. Miles was proud of that note," says Miller. And Miller was to experience for himself the impact *Tutu* had had on black South Africans when he visited the country for the first time in 2001. "Before I went over I did an interview with a South African radio station and the DJ asked me what I was expecting to get from my visit, adding 'and don't give me any of that back to the motherland stuff,' and I laughed because I understood what she meant. When a lot of African-Americans get to the continent of Africa they want to kiss the ground even though the likelihood is that you're not descended from South Africa but from the west coast of Africa. So I thought 'It's just a place. I'm glad they're getting closer to an equal situation. I'm just going to enjoy myself.'"

But Miller was in for a shock when he reached South Africa. "I didn't realize the impact that the music we did with Miles had over there. I did 'Tutu' assuming it would be banned in South Africa and I didn't realize that people would get hold of the stuff. They did and it meant a lot to them. A guy said to me 'How does it feel to have made the most important African-American musical contribution to the cause?' and that just capped the whole thing for me. I realized it had helped give people hope and it fortified people who were struggling for their freedom. It's just unbelievable.'"

"Tutu" became a central part of Miles's act almost until his final concerts, and the opening bars always elicited a huge reaction from the crowds. "Tutu" still sounds like it is the music of today and has since become Marcus Miller's anthem, often forming part of the encore in his live shows. In short, "Tutu" is a creative triumph that simply shows that man and machine really can swing together.[37]

"Portia" (6:18)

Composer	Marcus Miller
Musicians	Miles, trumpet; Marcus Miller, bass, guitar, drums, synthesizers, soprano sax; Paulinho DaCosta, percussion
Producers	Tommy LiPuma, Marcus Miller
Arranger	Marcus Miller
Recorded	Capitol Recording Studios, Los Angeles, February 13, 1986
Engineer	Peter Doell
Mixer	Bill Schnee
Live performances	March 1986 – July 1990

The name Portia is believed to have originated from the Latin for 'sharing,' and was the name of Shakespeare's heroine in *The Merchant of Venice*. It was also a name that Miller thought was beautiful and a fitting title for this tune. He was right, because "Portia" is one of the highlights of *Tutu*. "Portia" would see Miller adding yet another instrument to his recording credits – the soprano saxophone. "I had always played these instruments on the demos for the different artists that I work with – I'd play saxophone on my David Sanborn demos and guitar on my Luther Vandross demos. I'd play all the instruments and I was always getting kidded by the musicians because we'd come to the sessions and they'd go 'Man, why did you call us?'"

He adds: "With Miles it was the first time I began to seriously consider putting these on tape for everyone to hear. Miles was encouraging me, he said 'Look, you're the composer. You got the sound in your head. Why not do it if you already know it rather than get somebody else to interpret what you got?' When he said that, I understood what he was saying, but I also know that some of the magic also comes from somebody else interpreting what you're explaining to them. But then I thought this was a great opportunity to work on that initial theory that Miles had – when the guy who has the music in his head performs it."

Miller had initially brought the soprano sax into the studio to demonstrate the melodies to Miles, but then Miles pushed him towards the microphone when the tape was recording. "I was a little nervous," admits Miller, who at one stage even asked Miles to bring his regular sax player (Bob Berg) into the studio. But after a while Miller began to feel more comfortable and Miles would ask him to play more. "He started saying, 'Look, I want you to just copy my phrases. When I play something, I want you to play the same thing behind me.'"[38] Miller adds: "I'm glad it happened because it released me from that whole thing of 'you have to be registered in the union as a sax player in order to perform it on a recording.' It opened up a whole new world for me."

"Portia," a Spanish tinged ballad, is the most beautiful tune on *Tutu*, and like all the music written by Miller was composed with Miles in mind. "With that whole album when I'm trying to come up with music, I'm thinking about Miles and what I know of his life. I knew he was really connected to that Spanish sound," says Miller. Miles's first wife Frances Taylor, a classical dancer, had introduced Miles to Spanish music in the 1950s, which ultimately led to Miles recording *Sketches Of Spain* with Gil Evans. "So 'Portia' has a lot of that Spanish sound in it, particularly the scale. It uses a scale where the first step is a half step, and it was really me just trying to provide Miles with something that he could relate to."

"Portia" was one of the first tracks Miller created with the assistance of Adam Holzman. "The main pad [sustained chord] on 'Portia' was a combination of Emulator voices and PPG," says Holzman. The tune begins with a synthesizer fading in, creating an almost eerie atmosphere – it's like a ghost ship appearing through the mist. A hard snare sound, programmed on a drum machine, kicks in, joined by cymbal and shaker effects. Miles's initial trumpet playing is so soft and delicate that it sounds almost tentative. The Emulator voices are also used to create a breath of sound. Miller's fretted and fretless bass playing is wonderfully melodic and, at times, the bass is played almost like a Spanish guitar (listen at 4:15 to 4:27). A soprano sax frequently repeats Miles's phrases and Miller plays three short sax solos. Also in the mix are a chugging rhythm guitar and a battery of percussive sounds from Paulinho DaCosta, created mainly with conga and shaker.

Close to the five-minute mark, the track slowly begins to draw to a close, with an ensemble part that leads towards a long fadeout – Miles had suggested this section: "He came in and listened to 'Portia' and said 'You need another section at the end, you need an ensemble ending.' So he left and I sat down at the piano – it was like my assignment! That section is my favourite part of the song," says Miller. Close to the end of the track, the music almost comes to a complete stop, then Miles plays a few short phrases, before the track finishes.

"Portia" is probably the closest that *Tutu* ever gets to the smooth jazz sound of Tommy LiPuma. But Miller's elegant arrangement and Miles's lyrical trumpet playing mean it avoids verging into the realms of muzak. At his concerts, Miles often used "Portia" for the final encore and sometimes the band members would play a short solo, leaving the stage one at a time, until there was just a lone keyboard player. He too would eventually exit, leaving his synthesizer programmed to repeatedly play the closing notes. Such was the power and the beauty of "Portia" that audiences would be left wildly applauding an empty stage.

"Tomaas" (5:32)

Composers	Miles Davis, Marcus Miller
Musicians	Miles, trumpet; Marcus Miller, bass, guitar, synthesizers, soprano sax, bass clarinet; Omar Hakim, drums; Bernard Wright, synthesizers
Producers	Tommy LiPuma, Marcus Miller
Arranger	Marcus Miller
Recorded	Clinton Recording Studios, New York, sometime between March 12–25, 1986
Engineer	Eric Calvi
Mixer	Eric Calvi
Live performances	March 1986 – February 1990

"Tomaas" was one of the second batches of recordings Miller did back in New York (assisted by Jason Miles) and was co-written with Miles. Miles had sent Miller a pile of tapes containing ideas and melodies, and Miller took some of the pieces he liked and crafted a new tune around them. Miles also contributed to the song's title – it was the name he called Tommy LiPuma. "The funny thing about the name is that I never presumed to think it was named after me, and I didn't find out until much later that it was, even though Miles called me Tomaas," notes LiPuma.

It was during these sessions that Jason Miles met Miles for the first time. "Marcus had said to me 'You're either gonna be here four minutes or four weeks and there's nothing I can tell you.'" Miles was alone in the studio when Jason Miles introduced himself: "I walked in and said 'Miles, I just want to introduce myself. My name is Jason Miles, I work with Marcus and do all the synth programming. I just wanna tell you it's an honour to be here and whatever you want me to do I will do it for you.' And he said 'What's your name?' and I said 'Jason Miles,' and he replied 'Good name.'" Later on, Miles would give Jason Miles a sketch which he signed "Miles to Miles." "Sounds like a law firm," quipped Miles. "We'd probably make more money from that than from this shit!"

On this track, Miller also plays soprano sax and bass clarinet. Not many people know that Miller's first instruments were the recorder (which he learned when he was eight) and the clarinet (he starting playing this at ten) before he switched to bass guitar at thirteen. "I worked in the bass clarinet on this one," said Miller. "I really love that instrument. You never really hear it anymore and I think it's beautiful. It's so sinister sounding, but warm at the same time. I mainly used it for doubling; if you play an octave below something it's like having this cushion of air beneath the melody, and Miles really likes that."[39] Back in 1970, Miles had used a bass clarinet (played by Bennie Maupin) to add an array of textures to the sound on *Bitches Brew*.

Once again, Miller played almost all the instruments, although he also used two session musicians on this track, both of them boyhood friends. Omar Hakim is a superbly agile drummer with an ability to set up a powerful groove and lock on to it. His credits include Sting, Weather Report and Gil Evans. "'Tomaas' was laid down with a heavy drum machine beat and I just wanted something going on behind the drum machine that was more reactionary. The biggest problem with a drum machine is that it doesn't change. You can do different things but it's not going to react. I asked Omar to come in and just react to stuff and we just mixed it subtly so there's something going on to help it grow," explains Miller.

Miller also used keyboardist Bernard Wright because: "He's got great feeling." Miller had also asked Wright to play acoustic piano on the track. "Miles had made it perfectly clear that he wasn't interested in any acoustic piano in the music at that point. So I said to Bernard, 'Man, put the acoustic on there anyway and if it's good enough Miles will just say 'Man, leave it on.'"

Following on from that, LiPuma recalls a funny incident involving Wright and Miles. "Bernard was in the studio booth and then Miles walked into the studio. He looked into the booth and motioned with his head for me to go into the studio, so I went in and Miles says: 'Who's that cat?' and I said 'That's Bernard Wright, he's a keyboard player and a friend of Marcus's.' So Miles goes into the booth and Marcus introduces Bernard. But then Bernard, who was in awe of Miles, made the mistake of going 'Oh Mr. Davis, you're my hero.' Miles says 'I don't wanna hear any of that shit.'

"Bernard had played piano and Marcus said 'Hear this thing.' So we started playing the tune and it couldn't have been more than two bars in when Miles turns to the engineer and says 'Take the piano off!'" Miller adds, "We [Bernard and I] both had a laugh about it. It wasn't like anybody's feelings were hurt. We respected Miles's view." But Miller notes that when he was making a second album with Miles (*Siesta*), Miles asked him to add acoustic piano to a track: "He said 'Marcus, this needs an acoustic piano,' so it's not like his edicts were set in stone."

"Tomaas" begins with a rising synthesizer note followed by a drum machine programmed to a mid-tempo beat. Ten seconds in, Miles can be heard saying "Yeah." The drum pattern on "Tomaas" sounds more mechanical than the swing of "Tutu" and, thanks to the subtle mixing described by Miller above, Omar Hakim's presence on drums is hard to determine. His contribution seems more designed to create an underlying feeling or mood rather than to add some straight-ahead percussive effects. Miller adds some James Brown-style funky rhythm guitar to good effect and his soprano sax and bass clarinet can be clearly heard in the mix. Miles's playing is fluent and economical and, just before the three-minute point, he lets rip with a flurry of notes. In several sections, Miles overdubs a second trumpet.

"Tomaas" is a deceptive track to listen to. On initial hearing, it sounds simple in structure, but listen carefully and you find all kinds of sounds weaving in and out or rising and falling – there is a lot going on in the background which adds to the overall mood and atmosphere. Once again, Miller shows his forte in adding just the right combination of sounds and effects. "Tomaas" is one of Tommy LiPuma's favourite tunes on *Tutu*: "Not because it was named after me but because I liked the melody. It had this slow manner of creeping along," he says. Although "Tomaas" was part of Miles's live act for four years, he performed it intermittently. Sometimes the tune would drop out of his live performances for months, only to reappear. However, on some live performances, the tune was extended and Bob Berg or Kenny Garrett would play a long sax solo during the closing section.[40]

"Don't Lose Your Mind" (5:49)

Composer	Marcus Miller
Musicians	Miles, trumpet; Marcus Miller, bass, guitar, synthesizers, soprano sax, bass clarinet, drums; Michal Urbaniak, electric violin; Bernard Wright, synthesizers
Producers	Tommy LiPuma, Marcus Miller
Arranger	Marcus Miller
Recorded	Clinton Recording Studios, New York, sometime between March 12–25, 1986
Engineer	Eric Calvi
Mixer	Eric Calvi
Live performances	August 1986

Miles goes dubbing. Everything from the playful title to the intriguing mix of reggae, African and dub influences tells you that this is a fun track. Many artists have been influenced by reggae (such as Paul McCartney, Stevie Wonder and Sting) and Miller may have been inspired when he played with those master exponents of the art, Sly and Robbie, on *Mobo II*, an album by Japanese guitarist Kazumi Watanabe.

Miles had even flirted with reggae on the track "Ms. Morrisine" on *You're Under Arrest*. With its off-beat chopping rhythm guitar, heavy bass lines and syncopated percussion, "Don't Lose Your Mind" has a relaxed, lazy feeling. Miles and Miller often double up on trumpet and soprano sax, with a bass clarinet lurking beneath them at times. "'Don't Lose Your Mind' could have been called 'Splatch Two,'" says Miller, "because it's got this reggae feeling down, but the melody could have been on *Kind Of Blue*, where it's just three horns playing that three-part harmony. But it's just a little abstract, fractured almost, where all this stuff is coming in and going out."

An explosive interval (which includes a sampled car crash and a cry of "Miles" recorded dub-style) heralds the arrival of Michal Urbaniak's lively electric violin solo – just listen to how it reaches a pitch towards the conclusion. "I said 'Man, I need a solo but I don't want it to be some guy with a tenor playing some traditional thing. So what's an unusual thing? A violin," says Miller.

Michal Urbaniak's route to *Tutu* was a long and convoluted one. Polish-born Urbaniak moved to the US in 1973 and over the years has played with many artists including Quincy Jones, George Benson, Elvin Jones, Ron Carter, Billy Cobham and Jaco Pastorius. Miller had also known Urbaniak for some years and once told Urbaniak that he liked playing with him because he was the only producer at the time that gave him music to read during a session. Miller says: "I said 'Michal, you got to come down here and give me something for Miles.'"

Michal Urbaniak started out as a sax player but health reasons forced him to switch to the violin. "Basically I play jazz violin like a saxophone," he says. "I was always looking for attachments to make the violin not so sweet." One of these add-ons included a vocoder, a voice-controlled synthesizer. "In the early 1980s, I was doing a lot of travelling between Europe and New York and my kids were in Sweden, so I was riding the trains a lot. I would take my keyboard and records on the train and one day I listened to Jermaine Jackson's 'Take Good Care of My Heart,'" he recalls. "I called pianist Horace Parlan from the train and said 'Listen, I got a couple of other good songs plus this talking violin.' The violin would not produce a sound unless I blew into it or sung." Parlan was so enthused by the idea that he met Urbaniak at Copenhagen station and the musicians immediately went to a studio and recorded "Take Good Care of My Heart" in a couple of hours.

When the album was finished, Parlan sold about 150 copies to US importers and one of them ended up at a Californian radio station. "It was a smooth jazz station and they were giving the tune a lot of airplay. Johnny Carson heard it and told his producer he wanted me on the show. I got to play on *The Tonight Show* three times as a result of that song. About a year before Miles made *Tutu*, he saw me on *The Tonight Show* and, although he normally didn't like the violin, he liked my sound. He said to Tommy 'Get this fucking Polack, he's got a great sound!'"

In late 1985, Urbaniak moved from New York to California and in early 1986 called Tommy LiPuma's office by chance. "They said 'Oh it's you, Michal. Tommy's been looking for you. Give him a call.' So I call Tommy and he asks 'Where are you?' and I say 'In California,' and he says 'Well, we're here in New York and Miles wants you on his new record, so come on over.' Then Marcus speaks to me. So my wife and I go back to New York and end up staying in a hotel next door to our old apartment!" Urbaniak had been influenced by Miles's music ever since he was fifteen and swapped a treasured and hard-to-get Louis Armstrong record for some Miles Davis recordings with a school friend. He had also met Miles prior to the *Tutu* sessions, although few words had passed between them. Recalls Urbaniak: "I met Miles at the Montreux Jazz [Festival] and I said to him 'I love you' he replied 'Yeah,' and that was it!"

Waiting at Clinton Recording Studios was Marcus Miller and an engineer. Urbaniak's musical equipment surprised Miller. "I figured a violin was unusual enough but he came in with a microphone strapped around his head and the violin was somehow shaped by the sounds he was making with his mouth through the microphone – it was kinda like a vocoder. There was weird stuff and it was perfect for the song. That's what Miles does. He just makes musicians react and come up with something new." I heard the track and we talked about the music and I asked 'What happens after me?' and Marcus said 'Miles will solo,' so I thought about it and that was it."

Urbaniak's solo was done in a single take and he says he arrived the next day to do some more recordings. "I played on three tunes; two of them are in the can," he says.[41] On the second day, Urbaniak met Miles again at the studio. "He said 'How did you play?' and I said 'I think it's exactly how you want it.' Then he did an incredible thing: he went behind me and rubbed my neck and said 'How does it feel?' I had tears in my eyes. He also took to me a piano and showed me some chords."

After the *Tutu* sessions, Miles invited Urbaniak to a concert at the Beacon Theatre in New York (Miles played four concerts there on March 5 and 6, 1986). "I went into Miles's dressing room and he said 'Where's your violin?' and I said 'It's at home,' and he told me to go and get it. I ended up playing on-stage for the part of the concert. I played several times with Miles's band, although only in parts of the concerts. I didn't know what was happening, whether I was in the band or not, but soon after Miles cut the tour short."[42]

When Miles switches to open trumpet after Urbaniak's solo, he is clearly inspired by the groove. "I really liked the solo he played. I liked it to the point where I actually went in with my bass clarinet and doubled some of it," says Miller. Miller and Jason Miles had fun making this track, as the latter recalls: "It was really flipped out. When we got to the spot where we would be throwing all these samples in, we turned the lights down low, and man we went crazy. I had horn hits, sampled orchestras, car noises; it was sort of like Miles meets Steel Pulse."[43] He adds, "I think [rapper] Queen Latifah was going to cover it."

Miles performed this track only a few times in his live concerts, including a ten-minute version played at Chautauqua, New York on August 27, 1986. The song is opened up and extended with gutsy solos by guitarist Robben Ford and saxophonist Bob Berg.[44] And as for the title, Miller says: "People had to deal with *Tutu* first and then get past 'Portia' and 'Splatch.' It was like, don't lose your mind!" "Don't Lose Your Mind" is one of Miller's favourite tracks on *Tutu* – and it's not hard to see why.

"Full Nelson" (5:05)

Composer	Marcus Miller
Musicians	Miles, trumpet; Marcus Miller, bass, guitar, synthesizers, soprano sax, drums
Producers	Tommy LiPuma, Marcus Miller
Arranger	Marcus Miller
Recorded	Clinton Recording Studios, New York, sometime between March 12–25, 1986
Engineer	Eric Calvi
Mixer	Eric Calvi
Live performances	August 1986 – November 1989

Single remixes released (5:53 and 4:00)

There's more to this title than meets the eye. "Full Nelson" is a triple entendre referring to Nelson Mandela, Prince (his surname) and "Half Nelson," a tune Miles cut with Max Roach and Charlie Parker in 1947.[45] And if you want to take the Nelson connection even further, Darryl Jones, Miles's bass player for much of the mid-1980s, has Nelson as his middle name. The partial reference to Prince is apt as the tune was written in response to Miller hearing a tune Prince had written for Miles called "Can I Play With U?" (see previous chapter). Miller, realizing that his tunes and "Can I Play With U?" were both different in mood and character, decided to write "Full Nelson" as a link between the two. But, as Miller notes: "I don't think either of them was totally happy with the way it ['Can I Play With U?'] turned out. So now the tune is a transition to nothing."[46]

So does Miller feel that "Can I Play With U?" would have been the right track to follow "Full Nelson"? "Probably not, especially since the album has grown roots now. But at the time I didn't know what was happening. You know how you're in the middle of the jungle, you don't have a perspective of the whole thing. And to me it was 'It's Prince. I'm sure I'll grow to like it and figure out what's great about it.' I ended up doing a mix on it so I got to hear the whole thing. The only problem with it was it didn't seem like Miles had a lot to do on it. It sounded like he was rising over it as opposed to being in it. I think if he and Prince had spent more time together that would have been different."

"Full Nelson" starts in a playful fashion, with Miles and Miller doodling around together on trumpet and soprano sax respectively. After the briefest of pauses, Miles's raspy voice commands: "Go ahead," followed by a Prince-like jangling rhythm guitar and a heavy backbeat courtesy of a drum machine. The tune has an almost marching band feel to it, and Miles and Miller are clearly having lots of fun together. Miller's bass playing – complete with popped strings and slurred notes – combines force with fluency and at times you can almost feel Miller's fingers snapping the Fender bass strings. Miller was always reluctant to solo when he was a member of Miles's band, and on *Tutu* he was careful to avoid using the tunes as a showcase for his own considerable musical abilities.

On most of the tunes, Miller leaves virtually all of the soloing to Miles or guest musicians, but on "Full Nelson" Miller stretches out a little and plays a short soprano sax solo at around the one-minute mark and a funky bass solo just after the three-and-a-half-minute point. Miles plays a solo that sounds almost playful, and samples of his voice are inserted in several places. Upbeat and uplifting, "Full Nelson" leaves *Tutu* finishing on a high.[47]

"Perfect Way" (4:32)

Composers	Green Gartside, David Gamson
Musicians	Miles, trumpet; Marcus Miller, bass, guitar, synthesizers, soprano sax, bass clarinet, drums
Producers	Tommy LiPuma, Marcus Miller
Arranger	Marcus Miller
Recorded	Clinton Recording Studios, New York, sometime between March 12–25, 1986
Engineer	Eric Calvi
Mixer	Eric Calvi
Live performances	August 1986 – August 1991

Miles's taste in music could surprise even his closest friends and colleagues, but his mind and ears were always open to all kinds of music. Cheryl Davis remembers growing up in a home full of all kinds of music: "There would be classical music playing, Spanish guitar, but no jazz." Zane Giles recalls Miles saying to him, "There's no such thing as wrong music."[48]

One of the artists Miles took a shine to in the mid-1980s was the British band Scritti Politti (a rough translation of 'political writings' in Italian), fronted by vocalist Green Gartside and keyboardist David Gamson. Scritti Politti's music was a blend of blue-eyed soul and electro-pop, coupled with some intriguing lyrics. Miles decided to use "Perfect Way" after Tommy LiPuma had sent him a pile of albums and asked Miles to find a track to cover. "Miles loved pop music and I don't think many people realized that. When he played the Scritti Politti track he called me and said 'Spitti Politti – he couldn't say it right – that's a motherfucker.' I once said to Miles 'Man, if you ever want to go into A&R [artists and repertoire] I'd definitely hire you,' because he had great ears."

Miles settled on "Perfect Way" and called Miller. "He played me this song and I had no idea how we were gonna do it because, basically, the song is the arrangement. The way the synths and the drums work together is what makes the song. I don't think the melody by itself would make it identifiable. Since I was locked into the arrangement, I basically re-created it and stretched it out in a couple of places."[49]

Green Gartside recalls his reaction when he first heard that Miles had covered the tune: "One day I got a phone call. Someone said 'Do you know that Miles has covered "Perfect Way"?' At first I thought it to be a joke… I was incredibly surprised." Later, Davis called Green and asked him about the possibility of working together in the future.[50] In fact, Gartside and Miles struck up a good friendship and it wasn't unusual for Miles to call him in the middle of the night. Miles also played on the track "Oh Patti (Don't Feel Sorry For Loverboy)" on Scritti Politti's 1988 album *Provision* (the album had a strong *Tutu* connection – it also featured Marcus Miller and Jason Miles).

Gartside says there was even talk of Scritti Politti appearing on Miles's next album, adding: "He is such a great and extraordinary human being. Miles is still up to date musically. He's listening to all the new trends and checks them out. He's got a great ear for sounds. I guess he likes the way we are working with the latest technology. He's simply hip!"[51]

Miller's arrangement creates a bright, upbeat, pop sound, with Miles's trumpet taking the place of the lead vocals. The drum machine's heavy rhythm clatters along throughout the track. One striking development is Miller's increasing prowess as a soprano sax player – you can almost hear his growing confidence being sucked into the instrument and emerging as strong, lyrical phrases. Miller also adds some lines from the bass clarinet to support the sound.

At 4:10, there's a neat little sample of Count Basie's trademark cry of "One mo' time" which Jason Miles had taken from the album *April In Paris*. "Jason said 'Check out these samples' and I went 'Whoa! Let's throw that in there!' There was so much of that stuff going on in pop music at the time that it wasn't even that unusual for us to do it. Except that the people who were listening to the Miles record had never heard that mess before, so it was funny to hear their reaction. I thought 'Have you ever heard of Art of Noise? What world are you living in where this is something unusual for you?'"

Many of the *Tutu* sessions were filmed and some short footage of Miles struggling to get to grips with this tune has emerged. "They filmed a great deal of the sessions," recalls Miller. "I remember them having the cameras in and Miles was pissed off because 'Perfect Way' was in some weird key like B or C-sharp and Miles said 'Man, why they got to come in here when I got to play in B?'" One hopes that more of this footage will emerge on a "Making of *Tutu*" DVD some time in the future.

"Perfect Way" has a nice groove, but is the least satisfying track on *Tutu*, mainly because of the limitations placed on Miller in terms of extending or enhancing the original tune. Even so, Miles obviously enjoyed performing "Perfect Way," because it remained a part of his live set until his final concerts, and from late 1989 it became the concert opener.[52] Two trivia points: "Perfect Way" was originally going to be the album title (see the section on the "Tutu" track) and it was set to appear on Miles's posthumously released live album, *Live Around The World* but, although a master was created, it was left off at the last moment.

Tutu – the verdict

When *Tutu* was released in September 1986 it hit the music world like a whirl-wind. In every respect, *Tutu* was a milestone recording and everyone seemed to be talking about it. The reason could be put down to the M-factor – Miles, the music and the marketing. Every new Miles Davis record was eagerly awaited by the jazz world, but with *Tutu* the excitement and expectation was at fever pitch. Miles had moved from Columbia to Warner Bros – just what was he going to deliver? The music on *Tutu* not only stretched your ears, it also challenged your perception of what jazz was – and of the kind of music you expected Miles to play. Although Miles's music had always been constantly changing, the change was generally evolutionary rather than revolutionary.

Albums such as *Miles In The Sky* and *Filles De Kilimanjaro*, for example, showed Miles going through a period of transition as he moved from acoustic instruments to electric jazz. Change would often be characterized by a change in band personnel, as older members left and fresh musicians were drafted in to help Miles achieve the new sound he was looking for. By the time an album such as *Bitches Brew* appeared, listeners had a pretty good idea where Miles had been coming from. Even an album as fresh and challenging as *On The Corner* contained elements that could be found in some of Miles's earlier electric albums, such as using an ensemble of musicians and tracks that were underpinned by powerful grooves.

In the 1980s, anyone who bought, say, *Decoy* would not find it difficult to adjust his or her ears to the follow-up album, *You're Under Arrest*. But *Tutu* was out on its own; Miles had never made an album like this before. There was no audible connection with *You're Under Arrest*. The only points of reference with Miles's earlier works were orchestral albums such as *Sketches Of Spain*, but even then Miles had played on top of live instruments. Miles's bands had used primitive synthesizers and rhythm boxes in the mid-1970s, and in the 1980s synthesizers and electronic drums could be heard on many tracks. But Miles had never released an album where electronic instruments dominated so much, with no involvement from a live band or orchestra.

Warner Bros' marketing department went into overdrive when it came to promoting *Tutu*. The celebrated American portrait and fashion photographer Irving Penn (whose previous subjects had included Alfred Hitchcock, Picasso and the Duchess of Windsor) was commissioned to take the cover shots and the results were stunning. *Tutu* consists of a black-and-white portrait of an unsmiling Miles, shot close up and sharply lit from the front so that the sides of his head are in shadow. The cover looks like an album from the 1950s which perhaps explains why the film *The Talented Mr. Ripley* mistakenly used it in one of its scenes. The film is supposed to be set in the late 1950s and Tutu, of course, wasn't released until almost thirty years later...

On the back cover is another stunning photograph of Miles, with his eyes closed, lips pouting as if blowing an invisible horn. The black film director Spike Lee was hired to direct a video consisting of a medley of tunes from *Tutu* – the title track, "Portia" and "Splatch."[53] There were 12-inch singles including remixes of "Full Nelson," huge poster campaigns in cities such as New York, and the airwaves were saturated with the sound of *Tutu*. *Tutu* would go on to win two Grammies for best jazz instrumental performance and best recording package.

Tutu saw Miles reaching audiences beyond jazz, drawing in people who normally listened to pop, rock or funk. But what did Miles think of the music? Marcus Miller believes that Miles dug the music, but then adds: "I think for Miles it was no big deal, because he's been involved with amazing music all his life." But there are signs that suggest that Miles loved the music and was proud of the results. An amusing example of this occurred on a jazz radio programme hosted by saxophonist David Sanborn. The programme, which involved Miles, Marcus Miller and Tommy LiPuma, was a discussion about the making of *Tutu*. At one point, David Sanborn described the music as "stuff," and Miles immediately shot back: "That's not stuff!"[54]

But the proof of the pudding was in the playing and, almost as soon as *Tutu* was recorded, Miles began including the tunes from it in his concerts in March 1986, some six months before the album was released. Even "Rubberband" was sacrificed for tracks from *Tutu*. From mid-1986 until early 1988, the songs from *Tutu* dominated Miles's live sets, with each concert featuring four or more tunes from the album (some concerts would include up to six tunes). Miles continued to play at least one or two tunes from *Tutu* right up until his final concerts.

Miller says Miles was certainly pleased with the attention *Tutu* received. "He said to me 'Marcus, thank you for bringing me back.' For him to say that, man, there's nothing that can take it away from me." Miles's profile was certainly elevated as a result of the success of *Tutu*. He began getting invitations to appear on other artists' albums and even appeared in an episode of the cop TV programme *Miami Vice*. Companies such as Honda and Gap would use him in their adverts. *Tutu* evoked strong emotions from its listeners, a reaction that pleased Miller. "What was great about *Tutu* was it got people to take sides. So people would come up to me and say 'Man, I love that album; it changed my life.' [Other] people would come up to me and say 'Man, you ruined Miles's career!' It was fantastic to me because that was how it was supposed to be."[55]

Argument raged over whether *Tutu* was really a Marcus Miller album in all but name, with Miles simply playing the part of a guest musician. One critic went as far as to say, "Basically, *Tutu* is the finest Marcus Miller album to date."[56] Miller is sanguine about such comments. "*Tutu* was like the albums Miles did with Gil or when Quincy [Jones] arranged Sinatra. Their sound was very much part of those records and my sound is very much part of Miles's records. But I think what most people don't realize is that when I worked with Miles there was a freedom to use harmonies that I would never use with any other artist because it was Miles. There was the knowledge that any melody I wrote was going to be performed by Miles and that no one else could approximate because Miles was playing the melody. All these things made it Miles's album. I don't deny that I played an important part in the album, but what you hear is his silver sound on the whole album. It was Miles's record and he played a big part in it."

But some music critics were less than impressed with the results, especially certain jazz critics who dismissed *Tutu* as a bland pop/funk record. *The Penguin Guide to Jazz* said: "Miles's first post-CBS albums were an uneasy blend of exquisite trumpet miniaturism and drab cop-show funk, put together with a high production gloss that camouflaged a lack of real musical substance."[57]

In the updated version of the book *Milestones: The Music and Times of Miles Davis* by Jack Chambers, which runs to close to 800 pages, Chambers devotes barely a paragraph to talk about Miles's Warner Bros albums. "The studio productions that resulted, *Tutu*, *Siesta* and *Amandla*, found an audience on the fringe of pop, ran their course and turned up in delete bins" was almost all he could muster.[58] In one of the most vicious critiques of Miles's work, jazz critic Stanley Crouch declared that "His albums of recent years

– *Tutu*, *Siesta*, *Amandla* – prove beyond doubt that he has lost all interest in music of quality."[59] Music critic Barry McRae complained that *Tutu* was "distinctly disappointing, with Davis set as 'product,' his trumpet parts anonymous and … the overall impression was one of commercial awareness."[60]

Jason Miles says, "The people that said that are only living in the past, and wanted Miles to go back, but that was something Miles would never ever do." Tommy LiPuma adds, "The jazz police think I'm a pariah. I'm so amazed that I run across this a lot. They put music on an altar and God forbid if you do anything that doesn't fit into this niche. I grew up right up in the thick of that music. I used to buy bebop and I love all this music. If you want to go back and listen to that music, go and play a record. But if you keep doing the same thing, it just gets tired. You have to keep moving forward."

George Duke says *Tutu* is his favourite Miles post-retirement album because "It made a statement. People are forgetting that any musician's greatest works are more likely to come during their early days when they're hungry, and their middle period when they're mature. As people get older they lose their chops. Having said that, Miles only looked ahead and you can't dismiss that period because Miles never stopped looking forward and he's still making music that was challenging and interesting. That's more than you can say for the majority of jazz musicians who get in one rut and stay there. You have to be able to find one track and say 'Man, that's some classic Miles' and, if you don't, you're dismissing a whole period of his life and not giving him the credit he's due." Singer Chaka Khan agrees: "*Tutu* is my favourite album of Miles's 1980s period. In fact, I have written lyrics to many of the songs and intend to perform them on a tribute album to Miles."

Marcus Miller says he can understand to some degree why certain jazz critics dismiss the music on *Tutu*. "Music is really powerful and when you connect with a certain music it becomes an important part of your life. I think when an artist changes it's a sign to you that part of your life is over and it's not as important as it was before. The guy who's into the music of Miles's group with Wayne Shorter, Tony Williams and Herbie, well, that music affected his life. It's pretty tough in 1986 to have Miles move away from that sound." Miller points out the dangers of trying to compare like with like: "Contemporary music is always going to be hard to judge because it hasn't been around long enough for you to develop the confidence to judge it. It's easy to judge if someone's playing Mozart well [because] it's been around long enough for everyone to digest and understand what's good and what's bad about the way people perform Mozart. The thing about *Tutu* in 1986 is how do you judge it? You can't judge it by the rules of 1965 because they obviously don't apply and if you try and apply those rules you're wasting your time."

This problem isn't unique to jazz, or even music for that matter. Critics of art and architecture will often dismiss modern art or a new building by comparing it with glories from the past. The irony is that some of the paintings and buildings that are so often admired today were heavily criticized in their day for being too radical or in poor taste.[61] Keyboardist Kei Akagi, who played with Miles in 1989–90, and later became professor of music at the University of Los Angeles, says: "This music has influenced a generation of younger musicians, who now treat 'Tutu' as having the same significance as 'So What,' and this acceptance too is now becoming a historical fact, in the same way that hip-hop rhythms have found their way into all manner of recent acoustic jazz works." The biggest danger with wanting to keep to the rules of the past and stave off the present is that an art form will stagnate and ultimately become redundant in today's world. As Miller remarks: "Some jazz people are trying to make it like the language of Latin. It's a beautiful language, but it's not like we use it today. If a language isn't being modified or added to, it won't be in tune with what's going on today. It's being preserved but it's not going to advance."

But many critics did get it. The perceptive British music writer and critic Charles Shaar Murray (who awarded *Tutu* five stars in his review) noted that: "In direct contradiction to the popular misapprehension that old age brings with it stagnation, rigidity and general hardening of the creative arteries, Miles Davis shows [that]… passing 60 means an increased sense of playful confidence, a willingness to take chances born of the knowledge that long ago [he] proved everything [he] had to prove."[62] Charles Shaar Murray went on to declare that *Tutu* was superior to anything in Miles's comeback years, with the possible exceptions of *We Want Miles* and *You're Under Arrest*. He concluded, "Maybe he don't make records like he used to in the 1950s, but NOBODY makes records like this. Except Miles Davis."

Down Beat magazine gave the album four stars and reviewer Bill Milkowski concluded his review: "Skeptics may dismiss *Tutu* as hip muzak. But if they would forget about labels, ease up on the jazz fascism, and listen to the horn, they'd hear the man is still blowing. And more power to him."[63] Critic Mike Zwerin declared that "The best jazz record of the decade is *Tutu* by Miles Davis. Absolutely no doubt about it. It is the soundtrack to the movie of our lives."[64] Zwerin, who played trombone with Miles in *The Birth Of The Cool* period and who now lives in France, says: "I stand by that statement. It was clear to me that the music was the sound of our contemporary urban environment. Whenever I look at the St. Martin Canal [in Paris] and the gentrified buildings along its banks, I can always hear *Tutu*. *Tutu* is midtown Manhattan, still now."

Tutu's immense popularity resulted in many of its tracks being played as background music in public places, and this led some to suggest that *Tutu* was simply muzak or wallpaper music. As Miller noted: "A guy told me once he'd heard *Tutu* being played in a restaurant. He didn't mean it as a compliment."[65] But as writer and critic Richard Williams points out, "*Tutu* was a record of outstanding beauty, and there was no shame in the fact that it could sound as much at home as a background to the hubbub of a busy coffee house as on an expensive domestic stereo system. What was wrong with that? Miles Davis never thought that music should be above functionality."[66]

Tutu was another example of Miles's refusal to stand still and how he always wanted to make music for now. As Miller notes, "To even create music at sixty that's still relevant and still controversial is incredible. How many sixty-year-olds were creating that kind of activity and that kind of reaction? He changed the face of jazz five or six times and he's sixty years old and he's still doing it. I think that's amazing in itself – he remained relevant to the end of his life. Miles was still searching, he was still vulnerable and he was still making mistakes at sixty. I find it almost unbelievable that anybody could find that something to criticize."

When you listen to *Tutu* with open ears and an open mind, you can appreciate the timeless beauty of Miles's playing and realize that you're listening to an album that is destined to become one of his classics.

16 *siesta* (37:55)

Warner Bros 925 655-2

Recorded	January 1987
Released	Autumn 1987
Producer	Marcus Miller
Executive producers	Tommy LiPuma, Gary Kurfirst
Engineers	Ray Bardani (Minot Sound Studios), John "J.C." Convertino (Sigma Sound Studios) and Steven Strassman (Amigo Studios)
Mixed by	Ray Bardani
Tracks	"Lost in Madrid Part I," "Siesta/Kitt's Kiss/Lost in Madrid Part II," "Theme For Augustine/Wind/Seduction/Kiss," "Submission," "Lost in Madrid Part III," "Conchita/Lament," "Lost in Madrid Part IV/Rat Dance/The Call," "Claire/Lost in Madrid Part V," "Afterglow," "Los Feliz"

All tunes composed by Marcus Miller, except "Theme for Augustine," written by Miles Davis and Marcus Miller

"I love that album. I think he [Miles] played beautifully." *Marcus Miller,* **Siesta***'s producer*

Background to the album

Miles was no stranger to the world of movie soundtracks, having recorded the soundtrack to the film *Ascenseur L'echafaud* in 1957. In 1970, Miles was asked to write the music to *Jack Johnson*, a film about the life of a black American boxer whose love of the high life, fast cars and pushing against authority no doubt strongly resonated with Miles's own attitude to life.

The soundtrack to *Jack Johnson* included the musicians Michael Henderson, Herbie Hancock, John McLaughlin and Billy Cobham, and comprised just two long tracks, the rocking "Right Off" and "Yesternow," a moody, intro-spective tune. Aided by some creative editing by producer Teo Macero, *Jack Johnson* is considered to be one of the classic albums from this era of Miles's music. In October 1986, Miles played on sessions for the soundtrack to the film *Street Smart*, although Robert Irving III, Miles's keyboardist and musical director, composed the music.

In late 1986, Miles received a call from the producers of a film called *Siesta*. The film was largely shot in Spain (in Madrid and Barcelona) and so, natu-rally, the producers wanted the soundtrack music to have a strong Spanish flavour. The producers had used Miles's 1960 album *Sketches Of Spain* (which was arranged by Gil Evans) as a temporary track and when they couldn't get permission to use the music for the movie soundtrack, they asked Miles to compose some new music for *Siesta*.

Siesta was based on a novel by Patrice Chaplin (daughter-in-law of Char-lie) and was directed by Mary Lambert, who had previously directed music videos for various artists, most notably Madonna. The film had a fine cast of actors including Ellen Barkin, Gabriel Byrne, Julian Sands, Isabella Rossellini, Jodie Foster and Martin Sheen. *Siesta*, a cross between a psychological thriller and a surrealistic fantasy, begins with Claire (Ellen Barkin) waking up next to an airfield in Spain. She is covered in cuts and bruises and her red dress is torn and soaked with somebody else's blood. But Claire suffers from amnesia and doesn't know whether she has been involved in a terrible accident or, worse, killed somebody. And so begins a frantic journey through Madrid to find the answer.

The film then goes back to five days earlier, where we learn that Claire is a daredevil skydiver, who is planning to free-fall into a giant net strung across an extinct volcano in Death Valley on July 4th. She has a husband Del (Martin Sheen), who is also her manager and promoter, and she has a lost lover in Spain, Augustine (Gabriel Byrne). Augustine has written a letter to Claire to inform her that he is now married.[1]

Acting on impulse, Claire packs her bags and flies off to Spain to find Augustine. But, after finding him, her mind goes blank. In her journey to discover what has happened to her, Claire encounters a number of strange characters, including a deranged cab driver (Alexei Sayle), an English society couple (Jodie Foster and Julian Sands) and an enigmatic diva (Grace Jones). It is only in the final scene that Claire discovers the truth – although there are several clues signposted along the way.

Siesta uses a non-linear structure to tell the story, with many flashbacks and inter-cuts. The present suddenly becomes the past; night becomes day; and a moment of extreme tenderness instantly transforms into a scene of vicious violence. The overall mood of the film is dark, desolate and despond-ent, with even the few lighter moments tinged with an aura of bittersweet emotion. The melancholic nature of the narrative weighs heavily on the shoulders of the viewer and the most powerful feeling is one of regret, of looking back at better days and mourning lost opportunities.

Siesta was released on November 11, 1987 and almost universally panned by critics. *The Washington Post*, for example, declared that: "[*Siesta*] is so preposterously aggressively half-baked that it practically dares you to march out of the theater. Starring Ellen Barkin… it takes place in a kind of timeless purgatory in which the character, wearing a scanty, bright red dress, must run around in a panic, trying to figure out what's happened to her."[2]

Miles turned to Marcus Miller to help him on the project. "Miles called me and asked me to write two songs for a couple of scenes," recalls Miller. "He also asked the producers to send me a tape of the film. When I saw it I called Miles and said 'Miles, this movie is kinda strange,' and he said 'Yeah, it's got a few wrinkles in it,' and then he made some suggestions about the music." In January 1987, Miles and Miller went to Sigma Sound Studios in New York and recorded two tracks, "Siesta" and "Theme For Augustine," with the former also including John Scofield on guitar and Omar Hakim on drums. The two tunes were then sent to the film's producers for approval.

Miller recalls what happened next. "I considered my job was done and then the director called me up and said 'Those two tunes are wonderful, and now for scene three…' and I said 'Wait a minute – am I doing the whole thing?' and she said 'Oh yes – didn't Miles tell you?' So I stepped into the whole thing gingerly, not really knowing what was going on and when I realized that this was something I was doing, I had to get the whole thing together in just a couple of weeks. So it all happened very surprisingly and very quickly."

Miller and synthesizer programmer Jason Miles decamped to Amigo Studios in North Hollywood to complete the rest of the soundtrack, mainly because the American film industry is based in Hollywood and Miles was living in Malibu for much of the time. Amigo Studios was a big studio facility that had been owned by Warner Bros (they sold the studio to some private investors just prior to the recording of *Siesta*). It had three major rooms and several smaller rooms. Some of the rooms were big enough to accommodate an orchestra, but *Siesta* was recorded in two smaller rooms, Studio E and Studio B. Work commenced in Studio E, a medium-sized room with a large control room and a small TV monitor, which was used for viewing the movie.

"Back then, there were very few studios in town that incorporated big screens in their control room," recalls Steven Strassman, who engineered most of *Siesta*. "Most film scoring that involved orchestras were done on [sound] stages that had big screens, but at that time things were getting switched to electronica and so much more was being done in the control room." Also in the studio was an industrial U-Matic video tape deck that was locked to the studio tape recorder.

Miller, Jason Miles and Strassman worked long hours in the studio – sometimes from nine in the morning until 2 am the following day. But Strassman says he always looked forward to coming to work because the atmosphere was so good. "Marcus was the nicest man I had ever met. He was soft-spoken, and as accomplished as he was and – not knowing me from Adam – was totally open to any suggestions I'd have, be it musically or sonically."

Strassman recalls a couple of times when he made suggestions to Miller. "I always liked tape slap [echo] and the sound you get when you rewind the tape back. I said 'Let's use that on something' and we used it at the end of 'Afterglow.' The bass clarinet turned out to be my most favourite instrument to record – I just love the sound of it. Before Marcus would start to blow he'd rattle the keys with his fingers and at one point I said 'Don't blow, just give me you rattling the keys' and we used that sound throughout."

Strassman adds, "Jason was like a clown. He was just so happy all the time and [as] far as synthesizer prowess [went], he was the best I had seen at the time. Marcus would say 'Give me this sound or that sound' and Jason would just have it up in a second." Strassman had worked with many famous musicians, including Paul Simon and Eric Clapton, but even he felt something when he was first introduced to Miles by Miller. "When I first met Miles he said 'This must be a monumental occasion for you!' Miles was a groove. I had heard the horror stories, but I certainly didn't experience that from him."

Whereas *Sketches Of Spain* had been created with a large orchestra, *Siesta* would be mainly composed with electronic instrumentation: synthesizers, drum machines, samplers and sequencers. Bibi Green, one of the production coordinators, explains her role in the making of the soundtrack and album: "The job included getting the studio, booking the musicians, making sure the tapes are moved to the right place, paying everybody and filing musicians' contracts. Basically, to help Marcus get what he needs, so he can focus on the music."

With Miller and Jason Miles now holed up at Amigo Studios, they began putting together the new tracks. There is an art to creating a movie soundtrack that requires many skills and disciplines. The usual process is to sit with the director (and sometimes the producer and the film's sound editor) and run through the movie, marking off cue points where the music is to be inserted. The director also decides the type of mood he or she wants the music to convey (happiness, sadness, suspense and so on). In addition to the demands of composing music that fits an allotted sequence to within fractions of a second, there is an extra layer of creative approval involved. The composer may be happy with a particular piece of music, but if the producer or director are not, it must be junked and the work started afresh.

Miller viewed the film on a video tape that was marked with a SMPTE ("simtee") timecode,[3] which gives each frame a unique time reference code, allowing for precise synchronization between music and pictures. The SMPTE code was fed to a linking unit which in turn was synchronized to a multi-track tape recorder. Sometimes, Miller would watch the film, create the cue using keyboards and then add Miles's horn, bass guitar or bass clarinet where appropriate. Whenever Miller needed some horn parts, he would call Miles and the only other musicians involved in the Amigo Studios sessions were guitarist Earl Klugh and flautist James Walker.

But Strassman recalls how Miller mostly worked on the soundtrack. "A lot of times when you're scoring a film, you're constantly running the film, but with this one Marcus had so little time that he was literally writing it on the fly. He was based at a hotel and he would come in each morning with the stuff written on scraps of paper or in a notebook. Then we'd lock into the film so he could see how many bars it would be and how much he could fit on the film. Very little music was performed to film."

Strassman adds that *Siesta*'s unusual structure and complex plot meant that "We had a lot of fun with the film because we spent a lot of the time trying to figure out what it was about. Plus we weren't watching it in the right order and so seeing it out of context was something else. We made up the song titles as we went along, so we might call it after the dialogue that cued it."

The first two days of recording were spent in Studio E. "That was the most interesting session from a technical point of view," says Strassman. "Miles would walk around when playing and he was so comfortable doing that, that I didn't want to inhibit him. On-stage he used a wireless microphone strapped to his trumpet but I wasn't going to go with that. So in Studio E I had six pressure-zone microphones, which are basically flat panels that you tape to a wall or a window and it becomes the microphone. So I used six microphones, one on each surface (the ceiling, floor and four walls) and told him he could walk around when he wanted and I just followed him with the faders as he walked towards a particular microphone. I think it was with 'Lost In Madrid' [Part V, the opening theme] where you can hear the tone change as he walked around the room and he loved that."

Sadly for Miles, Studio E was booked by the rock band Metallica and so the rest of the recordings were done in Studio B, which had a small control room and tiny vocal overdub booth. "It was about four [feet] by eight. Marcus and Jason were comfortable in the small studio, but when we got the talent to come in and record their parts, they'd say 'You're sticking me in that booth?'" says Strassman. Miles's recording experience in Studio B was in stark contrast to the freedom he had experienced in Studio E. "Marcus had written out the music for Miles to play on pretty much everything. Miles was sitting in a little folding chair, wearing headphones and with a music stand and a microphone placed at floor level. I remember on one piece he did a scale and was so close to the microphone that he was overloading it and he said 'I like that: let's keep it.'"

Miller worked under intense pressure, as Jason Miles recalls: "A lot of what we did was improvised on the spot. Marcus would go to the piano, sit down, and write up changes. The tune we just finished the other night, he wrote in twenty minutes."[4] He adds: "Most of the pressure was squarely on Marcus, who had to write the score. I know he was under a lot of intense pressure, yet Marcus always had an idea. I did a lot of sitting around and playing video games while he constructed the score. I would then spend time with him crafting the synths to the track to make his ideas match with the picture." Mary Lambert would occasionally come into the studio with her associates to see how things were going.

With so little time and such much intense pressure, does Miller wish he had had more breathing space for planning and preparation? "No, being a jazz musician means there are certain decisions you make when under pressure that you might not make if you had more time. I enjoy hearing the decisions. It's like an athlete – you like watching somebody having to make a decision right there in a split second. I enjoy hearing how I reacted to the situation."

When Gil Evans arranged and conducted *Sketches Of Spain*, he used an orchestra playing "real" instruments, so does Miller wish he could have used the same? "There were certain budget issues and there were time issues," he says. "I didn't have the time to arrange the whole thing and then have musicians come and play it. And it was also a creative decision. It didn't need to be *Sketches Of Spain*. *Sketches Of Spain* doesn't need to be re-created because it exists well on its own. Also, I thought what would make this unique would be a kind of alternative electronic sound and that went particularly well with the movie. But, having said that, there were certain things that needed humanity, like a guitar player or marching snare drums."

Around halfway through the production process, Miller was in for another surprise, because Warner Bros decided to release the soundtrack as a CD. "I think Warners heard the music and decided it was really nice and so they wanted to put it out as an album," says Miller. Miles was not present at all the sessions but Strassman recalls that, when he was, "Miles was having a great time. He was obviously super-comfortable with Marcus. I always had the impression that whatever Marcus did, Miles was behind him. I remember when we were sitting in the control room and Marcus was working on the sound and Miles turned to me and said 'This guy's brilliant, isn't he!'"

Miles would often sit with his sketch pad all the time, but Strassman remembers an occasion when Miller and Jason Miles were working together on a sound. "Miles suggested we take a walk. We would occasionally hear sounds from other studios coming through the wall and he'd ask who it was. I remember us walking into a Metallica session and we were standing in the back of the control room and the music is super-loud. Miles leaned over to me and screamed in my ear 'These guys really suck!' I couldn't hear him and so he repeated what he said – just as the music stopped!"

After two weeks' intensive work, with Miller and Jason Miles practically living in the studio, the *Siesta* soundtrack was completed. But Miller's work was only half done – he now had to construct an album out of the collection of cues he had created for the movie. Miller took the *Siesta* master tapes back with him to New York and, working with engineer Ray Bardani, set about constructing and mixing the album at Minot Sound Studios in Whiteplains, New York. "We had mixed the music in ultra-stereo, which at the time was the state-of-the-art surround-sound system. A lot of the stuff was pre-mixed before by the time Ray got to it. I think the mixes he did were very true to what we did in the studio," says Strassman.

"I think they only had about three or four days mixing the album," recalls Green. In some cases, Miller would extend a cue or remix it so that its sound was optimized for a home stereo system rather than a movie theatre. Some of the cues were very short, so Miller resolved this problem by stringing several of them together to make a medley. But even this wasn't enough. "After I had put the cues together, back to back, I listened to it and thought 'I need one thing that's longer to give it a little more continuity and that's when I composed 'Conchita.' I wrote it just before I completed the album, when I still had a feeling of the movie in me. That's why Miles isn't on it," says Miller.

With the *Siesta* album completed, Miller's then manager Patrick Rains decided that his client needed more recognition and credit for his efforts. "He insisted on it. He heard it and said to me 'This is as much you as it is Miles and I'm going to ask them to put your name on it.' I said to him 'Miles doesn't do that kind of thing,' but by then Miles and I had a pretty good relationship. Even so, I was pretty surprised that Miles let it happen. I was very pleased, because not many people got that." In fact, Miller shares with Gil Evans, Michel Legrand and Quincy Jones the rare distinction of having his name on the cover of a Miles Davis album.

However, when Bibi Green checked the proofs for album cover credits, she discovered that Miles and Miller were also sharing all the compositional credits. "I looked at the credits and all the songs had 'written by Miles Davis and Marcus Miller' next to them," recalls Green. "It wasn't even as if they had put Marcus's name first. Now I don't know whether this was Miles's doing or his management or the record company or maybe even somebody at the film company thought Miles had also written the songs. Anyway, I called Marcus and said 'Do we need to call the lawyers?' and he said 'No, leave it to me,' and, sure enough, he sorted it out with Miles."

Siesta – the tracks

The first New York sessions
These sessions took place on January 7 and 8, 1987 at Sigma Sound Studios in New York. The musicians who participated on these sessions were: Miles

(trumpet), Marcus Miller on keyboards, bass guitar and bass clarinet, with John Scofield on acoustic guitar and Omar Hakim on drums on *Siesta* only.

"Siesta" (5:06). The title track is one of the few tracks to feature additional musicians: in this case, guitarist John Scofield and drummer Omar Hakim (who also played on "Tomaas" on *Tutu*). Scofield had been a member of Miles's band between 1983 and 1985, appearing on several albums, *Star People*, *Decoy* and *You're Under Arrest*. He was well known for his imaginative and at times idiosyncratic style of playing on electric guitar, but on "Siesta" he played acoustic guitar. "Miles asked for John," Miller recalls. Scofield takes up the story: "I had played some stuff with Miles on acoustic guitar that never came out. I had used Miles's Ovation acoustic guitar and Miles said to me 'Now you've found your sound.' I eventually made a record of my own called *Quiet* because of Miles. It was so nice that he invited me back. I can't tell you what it meant to me – Miles was my idol."

"Siesta" starts with Scofield strumming his guitar in dramatic fashion, then Omar Hakim joins in with some military-style drumming, which he maintains throughout the track. Miller plays some dark, brooding lines on bass clarinet and then Miles enters, playing on open horn, with a rich tone and occasionally soaring towards the upper register. Clicking castanets add to the Flamenco flavour of the tune, which is one of the most uplifting pieces in the movie. A special note should be made about the mixing of this track, which resulted in a clear, crisp sound, with all the instruments given their own space to breathe.

"Siesta" appears at several points in the movie, at approximately the twenty-eighth-minute mark (where there is a fight at the art gallery), at fifty-four minutes (when Claire, Kit and Nancy run from the art gallery), sixty-eight minutes (when Claire jumps onto the top of a bus and is then taken through the town to the airport) and around eighty-three minutes (when Claire runs down the road and is passed by police cars with wailing sirens).

"Theme For Augustine" (4:20). A bass clarinet introduces this haunting ballad, with background vocal effects courtesy of a synthesizer. Miles plays with a muted horn and Miller joins him on bass clarinet. Electronic percussion beats away gently in the background and Miller also plays piano – Miles had suggested that the track needed it. The bass clarinet's rich deep sound is used to good effect, with some echo occasionally added. The tune, which expresses Claire's feelings towards Augustine, beautifully conveys her painful longing to be a part of his life again.

"Theme For Augustine" appears at a number of points in the movie, at around sixteen minutes (when Claire sees him for the first time at the trapeze school), just before the twenty-minute mark (when Claire and Augustine's wife are at a café bar), at the dinner table scene at around thirty-one minutes, and around seventy-five minutes, when Claire and Augustine meet at their secret location.

The North Hollywood sessions
In these sessions, Miles played trumpet and Marcus Miller on bass, bass clari-
net and keyboards. Earl Klugh played classical guitar on "Claire" and James
Walker on flute on "Los Feliz."

"Lost In Madrid Part V" (2:03). This was the only track from these sessions to
be recorded in Studio E and the one on which Miles got to wander around
the studio as he played. A plucked harp (played on a synthesizer) plays the
melancholic theme, with Miles joining on open horn and Miller on fretless
bass. This version is played over the opening credits, although the harp introduction is edited out in the movie.

"Lost In Madrid Part I" (1:47). The album's opening track has a suitably dramatic beginning with an explosive chord followed by wind blowing over a
desolate landscape. Scraping sounds are joined by a moan that sounds like a
dark beast rising from the depths of the earth and then what appears to be
the sound of pouring rain. Then we hear Miles's trumpet, sounding so ach-
ingly mournful that it conjures the vision of "a little boy who has been locked
out," as so memorably put by Kenneth Tynan's daughter. The background
sounds subside, leaving Miles's trumpet isolated, then the wind reappears
and Miles repeats the melancholy phrases before the track fades out. This
track appears around two minutes into the movie, as Claire lies unconscious
next to the airfield.

"Kitt's Kiss" (0:15). A short piece with Miller playing solo bass clarinet, with
some added echo effect. In the film credits, Julian Sands's character is billed
as Kit rather than Kitt, suggesting that the producers had not yet decided on a
final spelling until after the soundtrack was completed. The music appears at
around fifty-two minutes, when Kitt kisses Claire on the bed.

Lost In Madrid Part II (1:30). A harp (created on a synthesizer) is plucked gently
against a backdrop of a tumbling percussion sound and some rock-style guitar
buried deep in the mix. Miller also plays some melodic lines on fretless bass,
and the whole effect is to produce a track with a dream-like feeling. The music
appears approximately 3:30 minutes into the movie, when Claire washes the
blood out of her dress at the river bank.

"Wind" (0:13). A synthesizer-generated sound effect that is used as a bridge
for the next track.

"Seduction" (0:48). The sweeping sound of a synthesizer creates a deeply melancholy sound. Although the title of the tune is "Seduction," the overall feeling
is one of desperation. The music appears at around seventy-six minutes when
Claire cries in Augustine's arms.

"Kiss" (1:11). "Kiss" is sequenced exactly as it is in the film – running seamlessly on from "Seduction." Opening with cello-like sounds, the track's highlight is the beautiful sound Miller produces on bass clarinet, played over a background of synthesized strings. This is followed by Miles, who evokes a strong feeling of tenderness on a muted horn. Yet, despite the beauty of the music and the tenderness of the moment (it's played in the seventy-seventh minute when Claire and Augustine embrace), there is a feeling of desolation, of two lovers who know they are probably meeting for the last time. All this makes "Kiss" one of the most hauntingly beautiful tracks on the album.

"Submission" (2:41). Miller plays bass clarinet over an electronic vocal chorus and some gentle playing on (electronically generated) chimes. Hovering over all of this is a sustained note. Miller begins by playing softly, tenderly, but towards the end he plays with a greater urgency, pushing out notes that also have some echo effect added to them. This music is used for the love-making scene between Claire and Augustine at around seventy-eight minutes in the movie, but it is also intercut with a rape scene between Claire and the cabby.

"Lost In Madrid Part III" (0:43). A short section comprised of the theme played on a synthesizer to create a ghost-like sound. Flowing water, which pans from the left to right speaker, marks the ending of the track. The music occurs at around the 5:30 mark in the movie, where Claire is in the back of a cab and desperately trying to recall what has happened to her.

"Lament" (0:53). A simple chord sequence played on a synthesizer which creates a suitably dark mood to match the title. It appears at around seventy-four minutes into the movie, when Claire gets out of the scene of a car accident and discovers the shattered remains of a photograph of her on the ground. It was added to the end of "Conchita" on the album.

"Lost In Madrid Part IV" (0:19). This very short segment consists of Miles playing the theme on open horn. It appears at about sixty-one minutes, when Kit rests his head on Claire's shoulder in the back of a cab.

"Rat Dance" (0:45). Pounding drums and massed vocals are used to create a sense of urgency. The music occurs at around fifty-eight minutes, when Claire storms out of the airport. The title was suggested by Steven Strassman, who says the tune was originally written for the scene where the Grace Jones character Conchita holds a rat (around sixty-four minutes) but the music was not used here in the final cut.

"The Call" (0:36). This tune has Miller playing solo bass clarinet, switching to a lower key towards the end to give a rich, deep sound. It's played when Claire

calls on Augustine's home at night, at around the sixty-one-minute mark in the movie.

"Claire" *(2:35).* This track features Earl Klugh on classical guitar. Miller had played with Klugh before, on the album *Collaboration*, which also featured George Benson. "Earl happened to be in L.A. and I needed some classical guitar and asked him along to the session," says Miller. Klugh plays beautifully on this ballad, caressing each string on his guitar and playing over a background of synthesizer strings.

But Strassman expresses some disappointment over the CD version when compared with the movie version. "Earl Klugh got a great sound with his gut string and the vocal booth had a very bright sound. The one thing I was most disappointed about the record mix was that I had used a lot of backward echo on Earl's acoustic guitar. You can barely hear it when the record starts in the album mix." Miles joins in on muted horn with Miller supporting on fretless bass. Once again, Miles shows his great gift for melody and the tune conveys a strong feeling of fragility. A brief snippet of the tune is heard at around sixty-three minutes, when Claire and Augustine arrange their secret assignation.

"Afterglow" *(1:40).* This keyboard-dominated track also features some background percussion. It's a sparse arrangement although it switches towards the end, when Miller plays a simple but catchy chord sequence on keyboards. In fact, the last forty-seven seconds of this tune are not in the movie and the tune may well have been extended by Miller when he was putting together the soundtrack album. The tune is heard at around seventy-one minutes following the rape/love-making scenes.

"Los Feliz" *(4:34).* "Los Feliz" was the last track to be recorded for the film soundtrack (but not the CD) and the one that caused Miller the most difficulty. "This was the last piece and, because of that, it had to emotionally tie the whole movie together. It was the kinda movie where you don't know what's going on until the end of the movie, so this piece had to explain everything," he says. Miller composed one piece but Lambert said it wasn't quite what she was looking for. He wrote a second piece and Lambert rejected that too. "So now I'm beginning to run out of ideas and so I say to Miles 'Man, I'm striking out on this last piece,' and he invites me to his house and puts me in one of his rooms with a lot of Spanish music. He said 'Just sit and listen to it for a while.' So when I come out of the room and I go back to the room [studio] and write this piece."

The track starts with the gentle sound of lightly plucked harp strings (courtesy of a synthesizer), which are joined by James Walker on flute. "James played really good on that tune," says Miller. Walker's flute sound was triple- or quadruple-tracked to make it sound like a flute section. The combination of harp and flute works well and they are joined by Miles on open horn, whose playing once again conveys a deep sense of desolation. There's also a feeling of finality about the sound. The track ends with the plucked harp and some synthesized strings, before coming to a final conclusion. "When I played the music to the director, she started crying – in fact everybody was crying," says Miller. It's easy to see why, as "Los Feliz," like much of the music on *Siesta*, has a haunting quality. The music is heard at around eighty-five minutes, when Claire and a group of villagers converge on a building, where the truth is finally revealed. The music is also used in part of the closing credits.

The Minot Sound Studio session
"*Conchita*" (5:50). "Conchita" is named after the character played by Grace Jones, who, like Martin Sheen, makes a cameo appearance in the film. This tune does not appear in *Siesta*, which is a shame because it's one of the best on the album. After Miller had compiled the various audio cues to create the soundtrack album, he decided that a longer piece was required and so wrote this tune to give the album more coherence. Bibi Green recalls how Miller left it up to the last minute before recording "Conchita." "The mixing was all done in a very short time and I called Marcus at the studio and said 'Have you recorded the new song yet?' adding that he had two days to finish all the remixing. I call back two hours later and ask again and Marcus says 'No, not yet. Ray [Bardani]'s still mixing; but don't worry, Bibi, I know what I'm doing – it's in my head.' I replied 'It's no good in your head – it has got to be on tape and you've only got another day to do it!' Anyway, I call the next morning and he still hasn't recorded the song, and you know what? They recorded and mixed 'Conchita' in a day."

An eerie note played on a synthesizer rises up and starts off the track, reminiscent of the introduction to "Portia" on *Tutu*. Then follows some syncopated percussion and breath-like synthesized vocals. A dramatic section that conjures up visions of a matador confronting a bull comes next. Sloshing water and bell effects are added to the mix before Miller plays some rich, deep bass lines. The next section, with Flamenco-like figures and bell effects, adds to the drama. Miller then plays some melodic bass guitar, adding some bass clarinet to the mix before the Flamenco-style section returns, increasing both the tension and the intensity of the sound. Miller plucks some strings on a fretted bass and the music, like a mad bull, becomes wilder.

The tension is released by a short percussive break before the dramatic section returns accompanied by more plucked bass strings from Miller. Then some inventive playing on fretless bass follows before the dramatic section returns. The tune finally fades. "Conchita" combines drama, intensity and passion, creating a real sense of excitement. Such is the power and the dramatic quality of "Conchita" that the American skater Nancy Kerrigan used it for her routine in the 1992 Olympics (she won a bronze medal).

Green recalls her reaction. "When I saw it on the TV, I called Marcus and said 'You're not going to believe this, but your music's being used by the skater Nancy Kerrigan in the Olympics!' And all Marcus could say was 'Did she fall over when the bass clarinet came in?'"

Siesta – the verdict

Siesta was released with a record cover that gave no indication that it was a soundtrack album. Instead of using the film's publicity shot (of Barkin and Byrne together), Warner Bros opted for a painting by the American artist George Tooker, "Mirror," painted in 1962. The picture shows a round-faced woman looking into a hand mirror, with a skull glancing over her left shoulder. Tooker is sometimes described as a "magic realist," an artist who combines everyday reality with elements of fantasy, and the strange, slightly unsettling image he produced for "Mirror" fits well with the surrealistic quality of the film. On the CD version, the film credits are tucked away at the back of the booklet. Warner Bros may have hoped that these tactics would have distanced the music from the film but, alas, *Siesta* suffers from the "great soundtrack, shame about the movie" syndrome. Savage reviews coupled with limited theatre distribution means that few people have seen the film.

As a result, the *Siesta* album has never got the recognition it deserves and is something of a quiet classic. "I love that album," says Miller. "I think I get as many comments about that album as I do about *Tutu* and *Amandla* because the people who love it really love it and make a point of telling me about it." One of the undoubted highlights of the album was Miles's playing. "I think he played beautifully," adds Miller, "and I remember the aspect I enjoyed the most was that he wasn't playing a lot with the mute, which he had been doing up until then. He was playing full open horn and showing that glorious tone and he sounded really comfortable." Indeed, some of Miles's finest playing in his comeback years can be found on *Siesta*. The album is also infused with the spirit of Gil Evans– little wonder that the album is dedicated to "Gil Evans – The Master."

Although the film's overall mood is dark and much of the music is created to reflect this quality, the beauty of it is also uplifting. It seems incredible that Miller was able to create such powerful and evocative music in such a short time. Credit should also go to Miles of course and Jason Miles, whose excellent programming turned Miller's aural fantasies into reality, and the session musicians who, in the words of Miller, added some humanity to the electronic-based music.

Bibi Green recalls seeing the impact the music has on people first-hand, when she attended a screening of *Siesta* before it went out on general release. "The film had started and Ellen Barkin walked into the screening room with a friend and sat next to me. I'm sure she must have seen the film rushes or even the final cut, but she hadn't seen the film with the music. I remember that every time the music played she would gasp and turn to her friend and say "Wow! Did you hear that? It's beautiful."

What is also surprising is that *Siesta* was the first soundtrack project Miller had worked on (since then he's worked on almost a dozen film projects, including *House Party*, *Boomerang* and *The Trumpet of the Swan*). It would be interesting to see what Miller could create if given the opportunity to tackle the soundtrack for a major Hollywood film. What also makes *Siesta* stand out is that, like Isaac Hayes's *Shaft* and Curtis Mayfield's *Superfly* soundtrack albums, it has a life of its own beyond the movie for which it was written. "I was real disappointed that the soundtrack wasn't nominated for an Oscar because the music in this film blew away anything else that was going on at that time," says Strassman.

Meanwhile, Miller plans to do further work on *Siesta*. "I'm trying to convince Warner Bros to let me do a limited edition of *Siesta*," he says. "When I was putting together [the cues] they had a certain length [given] to them, so [they] didn't all sound like ten-second snippets, but there are a couple of things in the movie that are not on the album and I was hoping that Warner Bros would let me back in there and include some of the other pieces that weren't on the original album. Miles just played so well on the whole thing and I was in a space too, because I gave myself completely to the movie, which is what you've got to do when you compose for a movie. There are some colour and things that I used then that I haven't used since and I'd like the people to get a chance to hear."[5]

17 *amandla* (43:27)

Warner Bros 925 873-2

Recorded	June and September 1987, September 1988 – January 1989
Released	Autumn 1989
Producers	Tommy LiPuma and Marcus Miller except "Cobra" (also produced with George Duke) and "Jilli" (John Bigham, associate producer)
Executive producer	Miles Davis
Engineers	Eric Calvi, Bruce Miller, Eric Zobler ("Cobra" only)
Mixed by	Bill Schnee
Tracks	"Catémbe," "Cobra," "Big Time," "Hannibal," "Jo-Jo," "Amandla," "Jilli," "Mr. Pastorius"

"If I could have only one album I would take the song 'Tutu' and put it at the front of *Amandla* and I think that would be a very good representation of where I started and what I wanted to achieve." *Marcus Miller,* **Amandla***'s co-producer*

Background to the album

Amandla would be the third and final collaboration between Miles and Marcus Miller and an album that began life in the same way as *Tutu*, with Miller writing all the tunes and playing most of the instruments himself. Once again, Jason Miles was responsible for almost all of the synthesizer programming. But in early 1987, Miles acquired three new band members whom he was very excited about: alto saxophonist Kenny Garrett, drummer Ricky Wellman and lead bassist Joseph "Foley" McCreary, who took on the role of guitar player. All would dramatically alter the sound of Miles's music. Miles had not wanted to take his working band into the studio during the recording of *Tutu*, but he was keen to include his new trio of musicians on *Amandla*. "They had discovered Kenny Garrett at that time, and they felt they had Miles's other voice," said Jason Miles to writer Stuart Nicholson. "I mean, Kenny come on the scene and I heard him play and I knew that this guy was a monster."[1]

The inclusion of the band members resulted in some major changes in *Amandla*'s musical direction, says Miller. "The difference [between *Tutu* and *Amandla*] came with how many people we brought in to add to it. On *Tutu* I left it to the drum machine a lot; with *Amandla* we would replace it with Ricky Wellman or Omar Hakim. And with *Tutu* I played the saxophone, but now we have Kenny Garrett so I don't need to bother with that anymore. Then we got into it and started to enjoy bringing different people into the sound and the album grew that way." Jason Miles adds, "Marcus did not want to create another CD like *Tutu* that just basically relied on all synths creating the parts. The concept was to expand the sound of *Tutu* using live musicians."

Kenny Garrett was twenty-six when he joined Miles's band, and at the time he was one of the rising young stars of the jazz world, having played with acts such as Freddie Hubbard, Woody Shaw, the Mercer Ellington Orchestra and Art Blakey's Jazz Messengers. In 1984, Garrett also released his first album as a band leader, *Introducing Kenny Garrett*. Garrett's playing combined superb range and tone with enormous power and stamina. During a solo, the rush of air from the lungs would cause Garrett's neck to almost double in size and his body would rock wildly as notes sprayed out of his saxophone. Garrett was initially hired for just four days and joined tenor saxophonist Gary Thomas on the bandstand. But after just four gigs of playing together, Thomas left the band, leaving the solo sax spot to Garrett.

The departure of Thomas meant that the tenor sax would almost disappear from Miles's music both on-stage and in the studio. "I guess Miles wanted to go back to that Charlie Parker sound," says Garrett.[2] From now on, whenever Miles embarked on a new project, such as film score (e.g. *Dingo*), a special concert (such as the 1991 Montreux retrospective concert) or a one-off event (such as a John Lennon tribute concert in Japan in 1990), Garrett would almost invariably be at his side. "There are a few young guys out there developing their own style," Miles said. "My alto player Kenny Garrett is one of them."[3]

Ricky Wellman got the Miles gig through John Bigham, a young black guitarist Miles had met in early 1987. "I played Miles some of my demos and on the other side of the tape was Chuck Brown and the Soul Searchers, who Ricky Wellman played with. When Miles heard that, he wanted Ricky Wellman immediately. He said 'Who's that dude? I gotta have his number.' A week later Ricky was in the band," recalls Bigham. The music that had attracted Miles was go-go, which was developed in Washington D.C. The godfather of go-go is Chuck Brown, who with Wellman made go-go a worldwide phenomenon. Go-go was developed in the 1970s, partly as a reaction to the explosion of disco music. Brown noticed that club DJs had a habit of segueing songs so that the music ran continuously, so why not do the same for live music? "We had go-go girls and Smokey Robinson's 'Going To A Go-Go,' so I figured why not have go-go music?" recalls Brown. In addition to a constant beat, go-go music incorporates African, Latin, jazz and soul elements and uses a rhythm pattern that creates a skipping-like beat.

Ricky Wellman's father James F. Wellman had been Chuck Brown's original drummer and Ricky Wellman joined the band in 1974. "Back then, go-go was about a constant powerful rhythm groove played with percussion instruments while Chuck rapped to the crowd as we're going into songs. The music was non-stop. After performing a song, it laid back into a percussion groove that was hot and exciting both for us and the crowd," recalls Wellman.

"Ricky sat in on a tune and I told him to play this particular beat," says Brown, "and he played it like no other. It was like an old church beat that I heard when I was a kid. Grover Washington Jr. had a similar feel on the tune 'Mr. Magic.'" The rhythm played by Wellman formed the basis of the go-go sound. Brown also had a party trick whenever Wellman played a solo. "He nicknamed me 'Ricky Tricky Sugarfoot Wellman' because whenever I took drum solos there was a point where I used one foot pedal to do a roll which sounded like a horse galloping and I used my snare drum to accent the rhythm. The crowd chanted 'Go Sugarfoot! Go Sugarfoot!' and Chuck would stick his microphone in my bass drum and create a monstrous sound that came out from the speakers. Everyone could really feel the rumble in their chest," says Wellman.

After Wellman agreed to join the band, Miles sent him a concert tape to learn the music – there was no audition or rehearsal. "I love the beat," said Miles when talking about go-go. "Go-go is like Max [Roach] used to play; the beat swings."[4] "I was honoured and surprised when Miles got into go-go," says Brown. But if Miles was happy to have found a new drummer and a new sound, he was distinctly less happier about having to sack his current drummer and nephew Vince Wilburn Jr. "One of the most painful things I had to do in 1987 was let my nephew go," said Miles. "I had known for a long time that I was going to have to let Vincent go because he kept dropping time," he added.[5]

The move was especially painful for all parties because the next gig on the tour was in Chicago – Wilburn's home town and a gig that was always well attended by his family and friends. Miles waited a few days before calling Wilburn's mother – and his sister Dorothy – to tell her about the sacking. The move caused a temporary split in the Davis family.

"It was tough," admits Wilburn, "but I didn't have a problem with Ricky coming in and doing the go-go thing. I love Miles and I love the fact that I was with him – I wouldn't have traded it for the world." However, the charge of dropping time clearly irks Wilburn. "I never thought that I dropped time – that was bullshit. I prided myself on keeping the groove," he says. Indeed,

Miles once commented that "I got Vince up there – he's got a nice touch; he doesn't lose time."[6]

In another interview, Miles observed that "Somebody like my nephew Vince, he plays drums and he don't vary the time. The time stays the same; even if he drops it a little bit, it stays the same."[7] Ron Lorman, who engineered the album Wilburn played on *You're Under Arrest*, adds, "Vince has great timing. He is solid as a rock. I remember times we would use a click track in the studio. I would turn it off and I turn it back on after twenty measures or so. Vince would never drift. He was still in perfect time with it. All our jaws dropped at the console."

The third new member, Joseph "Foley" McCreary, was born in Columbus, Ohio in 1962. He acquired the name Foley from his time as a baby. "It came from the four-legged walker you put a child in to teach it how to walk. I was a hyper baby and they used to call me 'Four Legs.' My sister couldn't say that and called me 'Foley,' and so everyone started calling me that." Foley grew up influenced by the sound of George Clinton, Sly Stone and bassist Bootsy Collins and he learned to play a variety of instruments including drums, keyboards and bass. But Foley wasn't satisfied with a conventional bass sound and so he developed a new concept – lead bass.

Leo Fender introduced the first electric bass guitar in 1951, the Fender Precision Bass. Although jazz bassist Monk Montgomery was quick to embrace the electric bass, the jazz world still generally viewed the acoustic bass as a "proper instrument," with the electric bass seen as a pale imitation. Even Miles, who was so often at the cutting edge of jazz, didn't start using an electric bass in his music until 1968, when Ron Carter played it on "Stuff," the opening number to the *Miles In The Sky* album. However, on the rest of the album, Carter played acoustic bass. Carter's successor Dave Holland joined Miles's band in 1968 and switched between acoustic and electric bass. In 1970, Miles employed funk bassist Michael Henderson and the acoustic bass effectively vanished from Miles's music from that point.

The 1970s saw the bass guitar undergo a revolution in terms of technique. Until then, the bass guitar was essentially a background instrument, albeit one that could have a significant impact on the sound – such as bassist James Jamerson's glorious bass lines on countless Motown hits. But the bassist was essentially the musician who stood at the back of the stage laying down the groove. But then Sly and the Family Stone bassist Larry Graham developed a technique of using the thumb to thump the bass strings and fingers to pluck them – slap bass had arrived on the electric bass.[8]

Stanley Clarke developed Graham's technique further on the groundbreaking tune "School Days." Meanwhile, bassist Jaco Pastorius revolutionized electric bass playing with his imaginative and innovative use of harmonics on a fretless bass. Bassist Anthony Jackson also transformed the bass sound by using a six-string bass and electronic effects (best heard on the O'Jays' track

"For The Love Of Money"). Soon, other bass players such as Bootsy Collins, Louis Johnson and Mark King were playing the bass guitar more like a lead instrument.

The techniques developed by Graham, Clarke and Pastorius have influenced every electric bass player today, but in the mid-1980s Foley began developing his lead bass concept. "I was about twenty-one, twenty-two when I started messing around with the bass," recalls Foley. Like Stanley Clarke, Foley used a Piccolo bass, which is tuned an octave higher than a conventional electric bass and so sounds more like a guitar. "I was a bass player that wanted his instrument to sound more like a guitar or a horn and play a lead instrument role. I didn't like guitar at the time because it had too many strings and the B and E switch you have to make when you play guitar used to freak me out, so I said 'I'm gonna stay on my bass and figure out how to sound like a guitar.'" Foley achieved this by turning up the volume, using a pick and employing a Roland guitar processor. Later on, he would add a whammy bar, a metal plate that is used to bend the guitar strings to change the pitch.

"I turned it up very loud to the point of distortion and used guitar pedals – anything that would make me sound like a guitar. The main thing though was the phrasing, the mind-state, because everybody sounds like a Piccolo bass player when they play a Piccolo bass, but I didn't because I was playing the bass as a lead instrument," explains Foley. "It didn't sound like Stanley, it didn't sound like Larry, it didn't sound like Bootsy – it sounded like a guitar. You literally had to do a double-take sonically. I would phrase just like Jimi [Hendrix], or Jeff Beck or [Eddie] Van Halen, [John] Scofield – I would try and sound like a guitar player in my mind, even though I knew it was a bass. I would have to work harder than a guitarist because I only had four strings. Lead bass is a state of mind and nobody has really challenged that shit since. I remember at Miles's memorial, Stanley came up to me and told me I had taken the bass as far as it's going to go." On *Amandla*, however, Foley is listed in the credits as a guitarist and not a lead bassist.

Working at home, Foley composed a tune using the lead bass called "The Senate." "I wrote it for Miles never thinking that he ever would get to hear it let alone play it," says Foley. Playing all the instruments himself, Foley recorded the tune onto tape and sent copies to some of his favourite bassists including Stanley Clarke and Marcus Miller. "A good friend of mine was calling up all the numbers to all these people she'd met and that included Marcus. We called him but no one was home. I had Marcus's number for a year before I called him. I told him who I was and Marcus was really nice. He said 'Send me a tape,'" says Foley. "Two months later Marcus called me back and said 'Yeah the tape was jamming; it sounds really good. I'm going to go to the Knicks [New York Knicks basketball] game. I'll call you back.' But I never heard back from him; however, two weeks after that call, Miles called and said 'Send me the tape you sent Marcus' and wanted to know if I wanted to play with him."

It was purely by chance that Miles called Miller at the same time as he was playing Foley's tape. "What had happened was that Marcus had been listening to my tape and Miles called him around ten in the morning Malibu time and 'The Senate' was playing the background. They're just talking and Miles said 'Who is that? What is that?' and Marcus explained and then Miles asked Marcus to hold the phone to the speaker so he could hear it better. He then said 'Get me that kid's number.' He didn't know it was a lead bass; he liked the song and the energy and hired me over the phone," says Foley.

When Miles first called, Foley thought it was the singer/producer Bobby Taylor, who had discovered The Jackson Five and also hailed from Columbus. "Bobby had a similar voice to Miles; so when I picked up the phone I was like 'Hey Bobby you motherfucker, what's going on?' And this voice says 'No, this ain't Bobby, this is Miles Davis.' I thought 'Shit, it cannot be Miles.' It freaked me out." When Miles called, Foley was still developing the lead bass concept, but Miles was more than happy with his new guitarist, whom he described as playing funky blue-rock funk, almost like Hendrix. "I truly had finally found the guitar player that I had been looking for," said Miles.[9] Indeed, Miles was so pleased with the playing of Garrett, Wellman and Foley that the three young musicians would remain in the band right up until Miles's death almost five years later.

Another element Miles wanted to see included on *Amandla* was zouk, a musical decision that was inspired after hearing the music of the group Kassav. Zouk is French Creole for "party" and the music originates from the French Caribbean islands such as Guadeloupe, Martinique and Dominica. Zouk is a mixture of African, Caribbean, jazz, funk, salsa and several other musical genres. It is highly rhythmic music with a strong driving beat, layered percussion and uses a mixture of modern instruments (such as electric guitars and synthesizers) and traditional ones such as accordia, conga drums and shakers. The overall feel to the music is joyous and uplifting.

Miles was introduced to zouk by writer Quincy Troupe, who helped Miles produce his autobiography. "I remember bringing the music of Kassav for him to listen to one afternoon," recalls Troupe. "As soon as he heard them, Miles almost jumped out of his skin with excitement."[10] Troupe adds that hearing Kassav "freaked Miles out" and Miles spent the next three days listening to the group's CD before directing Miller to write something for *Amandla* that was based on Kassav's rhythm and feeling. Miles also wanted to include music from John Bigham and from George Duke, who had written "Backyard Ritual" on *Tutu*.

Miller says he wasn't daunted by the prospect of somehow combining all the disparate elements together – electronic instruments, the inclusion of Miles's new band members, the go-go sound, zouk, plus musical contributions from George Duke and John Bigham. Nor was Miller concerned about any great expectations for what was effectively the follow-up to the highly successful *Tutu* (*Siesta* had of course followed *Tutu*, but that was a sound-track). "I wasn't feeling that much; I really wasn't affected by that because when you're in the middle of it, it doesn't seem as big a deal as it does. To me it was just a question of where do we go from *Tutu*? Let's try to make this thing grow; make it a little bit more multi-dimensional," says Miller. But Jason Miles admits to feeling the pressure. "I felt there was more pressure because now the word was out. There was more and more pressure to make something on the same level."

Work began on *Amandla* in early June 1987, when Wellman, Garrett and Foley recorded three tunes live in the studio – "Big Time," "Hannibal" and "Catémbe." Work resumed in September for around a week and then the project was put on hold for almost a year, before work recommenced in September 1988. The delay was due to Miller and Jason Miles's punishing work schedule – both were much in demand for their playing, producing and pro-gramming prowess. "Marcus had to do a Sanborn record, then Luther Vandross called me to do some stuff with him and then there were other records; then we'd do another Luther record so that's another three or four extra months. Marcus was all over the place and trying to get [his band] The Jamaica Boys off the ground," says Jason Miles. And during this period, Miller was also the musi-cal director of a television show, *Night Music*, presented by David Sanborn.

"Miles was touring a lot because *Tutu* was big so there wasn't that pressure to get back in the studio and record another album," adds Miller. In addition to his live work, Miles was also recording with a number of artists including Cameo, Chaka Khan and Scritti Politti, and he also played on the track "We Kings of Orient Are," which appeared in the movie *Scrooged*, starring Bill Mur-ray. Miller says that it wasn't hard to get back into the music after such a long absence. "I don't think it was that difficult because even if I wasn't working on it, I was listening to that stuff all the time and planning on what I would do when I got back to the studio. I was living with it the whole time."

Once again, producer Tommy LiPuma worked with Miller on the *Aman-dla* project. "There were some different players. It was a combination of real players and machines, which is basically how we had been doing things on the other albums. It was just a question of Marcus coming up with tunes and going in and doing them," says LiPuma. "Tommy was sitting behind that desk, saying 'Yes, that sounds great,' or 'We might want to try that again' and just helping to make things happen," says Miller. "He took on all the budget considerations and it was nice. I just dealt with the music and he just let me create. If he felt like I was running off in the wrong direction, he let me know! He'd coordinate when Miles would come to the studio. We had a great relationship."

"Tommy LiPuma really called the shots – he was in the studio all the time. Tommy has got a great ear and a great knowledge of how things work together," adds Jason Miles.[11] Engineer Bruce Miller, who was present at many of the *Amandla* sessions, had also collaborated with Miller and LiPuma on other record projects, and recalls how LiPuma works in the studio. "I saw Tommy work differently depending on the musical style, artist and production team. Sometimes he would be very directly involved in choosing takes, and sometimes he would allow the team he had assembled to 'do their thing,' but kept them in line by making comments that would shed new light on the subject. In the midst of a discussion Tommy would make a single statement that helped others not only see his point of view but also incorporate that viewpoint when making production decisions. Tommy was always able to give people enough rope to be creative without letting go of the reins himself."

Another major development since the recording of *Tutu* was the advancement in synthesizer technology. "The first thing about *Amandla* was that the technology had been updated since we did *Tutu*. There were new synthesizers out there, new things making new sounds. We were upping the level and the intensity of the sound, so we could make it more lush and do more interesting things, because we had better equipment. Not better, but it was just more advanced – a year in the synthesizer world back then was a huge step. And if you notice on the record, the textures are much deeper on the synthesizers, like on 'Hannibal,'" says Jason Miles. "There was a new synth out by Roland called the D-50 that had sounds that were amazing to program. I was able to create some really unique sounds, and Miles really loved it."[12]

In addition to using several of Miles's band members, Miller also drafted in a number of seasoned session players, such as drummer Omar Hakim (who had also played on *Tutu* and *Siesta*), percussionists Don Alias, Paulinho DaCosta and Bashiri Johnson, guitarists Jean-Paul Bourelly and Billy "Spaceman" Patterson, as well as Joe Sample on piano. Also participating were Rick Margitza, who would replace Kenny Garrett on saxophone during Miles's 1989 European tour, and keyboardist Joey DeFrancesco, who joined Miles's band in autumn 1988. Two ex-members of Miles's 1980s bands, Al Foster and Mino Cinelu, also played drums and percussion respectively. According to engineer Bruce Miller, guitarist Steve Khan was also present at the sessions, although his contribution was edited from the final mix.

"I remember feeling that it would be better if we could use the guys from Miles's group as much as we could, because that's who people are going to hear when Miles goes on tour," says Miller. Yet, strangely enough, the three musicians only appear on two tunes together ("Big Time" and "Jilli") although Jason Miles recalls that: "A few of the tunes were cut live in the studio using Foley, Ricky Wellman and Marcus. The ones I remember were 'Big Time,' 'Hannibal' and 'Catémbe.' We recorded them live with the rhythm section, then we overdubbed on that."[13]

Yet Wellman's drumming is missing from two of these tracks ("Catémbe" and "Hannibal") and he only appears on two tracks ("Big Time" and "Jilli"); Foley is on three ("Hannibal," "Jilli" and "Big Time"). Kenny Garrett fares much better, appearing on seven of the eight tracks (the exception being "Mr. Pastorius"). It could well be that the diverse range of music – from zouk to go-go – called for different players with different skills, or that when Miller came to work on the original three tracks a year later, he had altered his concept of how the music should sound.

When *Tutu* was being created, Miles spent relatively little time in the studio, but Miller says this was different on *Amandla*. "I think Miles was in the studio more for *Amandla* than *Tutu*. On the day that we needed trumpet, Miles would come early and hang out, with headphones on in the studio, fooling around with his horn and listening to what was going on. He'd usually spend the whole day there and he'd tell me 'Take that out! I hate that sound!' or 'You need to add something to this.' So when he was there he got involved and I sent him tapes of what was going on. He was the one who wanted the Caribbean/African feel on the album. Knowing he had Ricky Wellman in the band, I knew we had to go for the go-go sound." Jason Miles also points out the influence Miles had on the album. "Miles always heard the tapes every day – he was digging the shit out of it. It was his idea to use more musicians, so we were able to integrate more of his people [band] into the project."

"I know that Marcus and Tommy were in constant communication with Miles," says Bruce Miller. "There was a funny story Marcus told me about how Miles woke him up in the middle of the night and told him that he wanted to change the tempo of a particular song. Miles said 'I think the tempo should be like this,' and then tapped the new tempo on the phone to show him!"

Even when Miles was absent from the studio, he would still give directions; as Don Alias recalls, on one session: "Marcus rang Miles basically to say hello and he mentioned that I was present, so Miles asked to speak me. He said 'Don, I want this to sound like a whole band of drummers – I want it to sound like 500 drummers.' That's all he said. Miles never gave you any serious instruction on how to play or what you should do – he left it up to you. The fact that Miles wasn't always present in the studio shows how much he trusted Marcus. Marcus is a consummate producer and Miles trusted Marcus's process of recording implicitly."

Engineer Bruce Miller recalls his first day in the studio working on *Amandla*. "When I walked in, Marcus pointed to a version of 'Amandla' and asked me to make some arrangements by editing the two-inch tape. So there I was, day one of a Miles Davis album and I was cutting up the master [tape]!" As Bruce Miller sat at the control desk with Marcus Miller, he was holding a razor blade, preparing to make the edits, when he suddenly had a perverse thought to run the razor blade over the tape and destroy it. He immediately put down the razor blade.[14]

Bruce Miller also remembers the focus and concentration of Marcus Miller in the studio. "Marcus was recording lead bass through a Marshall

Head [amplifier] for a little grit, and in the middle of a phrase the head blew. I took about an hour to fix it and then we punched in exactly where the head had fried. Marcus continued playing with the same intensity and feeling as if there had been no pause!" Recalling the incident, Marcus Miller says: "A lot of the music exists in your head. I was focused on what I had to do. It's all about staying focused."

Most of the sessions took place between 11 am to around 7 pm, says Bruce Miller. "Whenever Miles was there of course we recorded horn. He would play for a few hours and we captured everything he did." Miller had heard stories that Miles was a difficult artist to record because he liked to move around the recording studio while he played, but this wasn't how Bruce Miller found things. "He was a pleasure to record and stayed focused at his microphone. The first day I recorded him, we were starting with the horn tracks of a new song and since I didn't have to match a sound that was already on tape I decided to record him the way I record vocals, with no EQ [equalization] and no compression[15] but lots of careful level riding to tape. I know others would have compressed Miles and recorded him at a lower level to be on the safe side, in case Miles played something unpredictable, but I wanted a strong signal on the tape."

Bruce Miller found that by carefully listening to what Miles was doing and watching his breathing he was able to predict Miles's volumes and ride the fader accordingly. "In the entire album, he only surprised me once when I thought he was going to be louder and he was quieter instead. After I recorded him the first time, Miles came into the studio and listened. Then he turned to me and said 'Nice horn sound.'"

But it wasn't all hard work on the sessions. Bruce Miller also recalls a number of times when Miles would sit around the sessions telling stories. And on another occasion: "We were working on my birthday and Miles, Marcus and Tommy presented me with a sea bass loaded with candles!"

"Catémbe" (5:37)

Composer	Marcus Miller
Musicians	Miles, trumpet; Marcus Miller, bass, keyboards, drums, guitar, bass clarinet, soprano saxophone; Kenny Garrett, alto saxophone; Don Alias and Mino Cinelu, percussion
Producers	Tommy LiPuma, Marcus Miller
Arranger	Marcus Miller
Recorded	Clinton Recording Studios, September 1988 – January 1989
Engineers	Eric Calvi, Bruce Miller
Mixed by	Bill Schnee
Live performances	None

Catémbe is located across the Bay of Maputo, Mozambique and is a popular tourist destination, with a long, sandy beach. Not long after *Amandla* was completed, Marcus Miller would play on the 1990 album *Collaboration* featuring George Benson and Earl Klugh. Miller wrote the opening number, "Maputo," suggesting that he has some affinity to this part of Africa. "I have a friend whose father led the revolution there and he was assassinated when she was about ten years old," explains Miller. "She was telling me about it and I was just fascinated about that whole southern part of Africa and the South African struggle – it was really at the centre of my mentality at that time." The Mozambique revolution, which started in 1964 and ended with independence from Portugal in June 1975, was led by Frelimo (Front for the Liberation of Mozambique), and on Miles's 1974 album *Get Up With It* there is track called "Calypso Frelimo."

"Catémbe" starts off *Amandla* on an upbeat note. Driven along by a pounding bass drum and snare drum combination, plus a myriad of percussive effects from Don Alias and Mino Cinelu, the tune opens with a joyful scream before Miles enters playing the melody on muted horn. Sneaking in and out the track are the dark textures and tones of a bass clarinet played by Miller. He also plays some fine rhythm guitar.

At around the 2:40 mark, there is a short percussive break, followed by some intense playing by Miles and Miller which increases the tension and forms an introduction for Garrett's powerful alto sax solo, which is supported by a (sampled) ghost-like vocal choir. Miles then resumes playing the melody as Garrett continues to blow. At around the five-minute mark the track begins to wind down and an echo effect is added to Miles's trumpet sound, reminding one of the introduction to the track "Bitches Brew." The music then fades out. "Catémbe" is one of the stand-out tracks on *Amandla*, with a strong melody, glorious arrangement and each player making a strong contribution to the overall feel of the music. The surprise is that Miles never got around to playing this tune live, because "Catémbe" has it all: power, energy and excitement.

"Big Time" (5:41)

Composer	Marcus Miller
Musicians	Miles, trumpet; Marcus Miller, bass, keyboards, bass clarinet, soprano saxophone; Kenny Garrett, alto saxophone; Ricky Wellman, drums; Foley, guitar and guitar solo; Jean-Paul Bourelly, guitar; Don Alias, percussion
Producers	Tommy LiPuma, Marcus Miller
Arranger	Marcus Miller
Recorded	Clinton Recording Studios, September 1988 – January 1989

Engineers	Eric Calvi, Bruce Miller
Mixed by	Bill Schnee
Live performances	None

Wellman's go-go influence is most apparent on this track, a playful number with a child-like "na-na-na" theme, which Miles plays on muted horn, often with support from Garrett. The second guitarist Jean-Paul Bourelly adds some funky rhythm guitar licks (heard best at around the 2:12 mark) and the mid-tempo track skips along happily. The only real moment of interest occurs just before the three-minute point, which marks the start of a triple sequence of solos, starting with Garrett, followed by a rough-and-ready solo from Foley, who bends notes and adds some echo effects. Miller's bass solo is next, a funky combination of thumped and popped strings. Miles plays the theme again and then Garrett gets to solos once more, before the number starts winding down. "Big Time" is pleasant, inoffensive music, but one expects more than just pleasantries from a Miles Davis performance.

"Hannibal" (5:51)

Composer	Marcus Miller
Musicians	Miles, trumpet; Marcus Miller, bass, keyboards, bass clarinet, blues guitar; Kenny Garrett, alto saxophone; Omar Hakim, drums; Foley, guitar; Paulinho DaCosta, percussion
Producers	Tommy LiPuma, Marcus Miller
Arranger	Marcus Miller
Recorded	Clinton Recording Studios, September 1988 – January 1989
Engineers	Eric Calvi, Bruce Miller
Mixed by	Bill Schnee
Live performances	April 1989 – August 1991

Miller played on an album by the trumpeter Hannibal Marvin Peterson, *Visions Of A New World*. During the sessions, Miller asked Peterson about the origins of his first name and he heard the story about the great African warrior and military genius Hannibal Barca, famous for crossing the Alps with his army and a herd of elephants. But while the title of the tune was inspired by the great warrior, its overall feeling was influenced by the loss of a close friend of Miller's, the drummer Yogi Horton. Although Horton was best known as an R&B funk drummer, who played with artists such as Luther Vandross and Aretha Franklin, he was a versatile musician who also played with acts such as The B52s, Talking Heads, Jean-Michel Jarre and Martha and the Muffins.

On June 8, 1987, Horton committed suicide by jumping out of a hotel window. He was thirty-three years old. On the day Horton died, Miller was in the studio putting together the backing track for "Hannibal". Miller was told the grim news. "That was pretty rough. Tommy LiPuma asked me if I felt like working and I said 'Yeah, I gotta work,'" recalls Miller. "I went in the studio and I was working on the melodies and I remember Foley was hanging out with me that day and he was like 'Man, there's a lot of soul going into that song.' That song is as much about Yogi as it is about Hannibal now." "The one thing that sticks out in my mind in those sessions was how Marcus was going through it that day," says Foley.

All this helps explain the bittersweet nature of "Hannibal," which combines bright, happy, sampled Caribbean steel drums with a mournful theme played by Miles on muted horn. Hannibal opens with a dark, menacing bass line and rock-like guitar licks from Foley, followed by a shuffling rhythm pattern played by Omar Hakim using a combination of high-hat, rim shots and strong kick drum. The steel drums enter, followed by Miles on horn. Once again, Miles shows his great ability to convey emotion, evoking a strong feeling of sorrow and loss.

At around the two-minute mark, Garrett plays a sombre solo, with Miles joining in as it approaches its climax. The tension is released and then Miles plays for a long stretch, with some support by Miller on bass clarinet. Garrett plays another solo and once again he and Miles take the music to a peak before the tension is released again. The track ends with Miles playing a series of phrases which are copied by Garrett right into the fadeout.

"Hannibal" is music written and played from the heart and it sounds like it. It is no surprise that Miles played this tune right until his final concert on August 25, 1991. By then, it had evolved into a *tour de force*, often lasting the best part of twenty minutes. When Warner Bros released the posthumous live album *Live Around The World* in 1996, the final track was an edited performance of "Hannibal" played at Miles's final concert at the Hollywood Bowl. It was more than fitting that a tune written in memory of a lost friend should conclude an album celebrating Miles's life on-stage.

"Jo-Jo" (4:51)

Composer	Marcus Miller
Musicians	Miles, trumpet; Marcus Miller, bass, keyboards; Kenny Garrett, alto saxophone; Rick Margitza, tenor saxophone; Jean-Paul Bourelly, guitar; Paulinho DaCosta, percussion
Producers	Tommy LiPuma, Marcus Miller
Arranger	Marcus Miller
Recorded	Clinton Recording Studios, September 1988 – January 1989

Engineers　　Eric Calvi, Bruce Miller
Mixed by　　Bill Schnee
Live performances　　July 1989 – April 1990

In 1984, Miles met a young woman in an elevator. She was thirty-four-year-old Jo Gelbard, an artist and sculptor. Later on, she became Miles's art teacher and then his artistic collaborator. She also became his lover and stayed close to Miles right up until his death.[16] When Miles wrote his autobiography, published in 1989, he made a couple of oblique references to Gelbard, including their initial meeting in an elevator and an incident with his then wife Cicely Tyson.[17] And later on when their relationship had developed, he wrote: "I have met another woman whom I really feel comfortable with. She's a lot younger than me, over twenty years younger [Miles was twenty-four years older than Gelbard]...I don't want to mention her name because I want our relationship to stay out of the public eye. But she's a very nice, loving woman who loves me for myself."[18] The only clue to the woman's identity was the name "Jo Jo" buried within the acknowledgements section.[19] Miles and Tyson divorced in 1989.

Miles and Gelbard did talk openly about each other in another book *The Art of Miles Davis*, although the subject was about art rather than their personal relationship. "I'm Jo's biggest fan," he said. "I think she's a great artist, I really do."[20] After talking about how she and Miles work together on paintings, Gelbard concluded with the observation that she and Miles were "kindred spirits."[21] Miles and Gelbard worked together on *Amandla*'s album cover art, a brightly coloured picture of Miles's face and a horn superimposed over an outline of the African continent.

"Jo-Jo" is based around an attractive go-go rhythm, programmed on a drum machine, with support from a burbling synth-bass and some catchy keyboard riffs and stabs. Miles plays the melody on muted horn and there is a happy feeling to the music, no doubt reflecting Miles's feelings towards Gelbard. Two saxophonists are used on the track, although only Garrett gets to solo, with Margitza forming part of the horn section that can be heard as the tune winds down.

The track also features guitarist Jean-Paul Bourelly. Bourelly was born in Chicago and was good friends with many of the musicians who played in Miles's 1980s bands, including Vince Wilburn Jr. and Darryl Jones, both of whom would play in Bourelly's basement. Bourelly, whose musical influences include B.B. King, Jimi Hendrix, John McLaughlin and James Blood Ulmer, moved to New York when he was nineteen and played with artists such as Roy Haynes, Elvin Jones and Pharaoh Sanders. He was also a close friend of Marcus Miller. "We used to play basketball together," recalls Bourelly.

Just before the two-minute mark, Bourelly plays a short, gritty solo that has clearly been edited. Bourelly recalls seeing Tommy LiPuma's head fall as he played a solo and instantly knew that this was not the sound LiPuma was looking for on the album. "I don't recall this incident, but I think we had Jean-Paul play some stuff that might have been too outside for Tommy's taste," says Marcus Miller.

"I was happy to be a part of it. I had met Miles a few times when I played with Elvin Jones's group. Miles would come down to the Vanguard [theatre] and see us and so to do the record was really special," says Bourelly. But he adds: "That was the '80s, it was a reflection of the times. The '80s were so superficial and I knew that when Warner picked Miles up, for them to sell the type of records they needed to sell during the '80s, that shit had to have that production sound on it and so that's what it ended up being. There was a lot of fading down of solos, fading shit up. There were one or two times when they let me do something, but then they quickly cut that shit!"

Bourelly describes *Amandla* as a "pleasantly listenable record," adding: "But my experience with Miles's music was live shit, you know when a solo comes up, you let the shit hang out. And some of my contemporaries like Mike Stern and [John] Scofield had a chance to do that; they were the last cats to do that. But by the time I got close to this production gig, it was already in this production vibe. That's where my disappointment is. With Miles you do have expectations and he did set a standard. It's like playing with [basketball star] Michael Jordan and you get on the court and the motherfucker never passes you the ball! Looking at it objectively, it was a nice period for Miles. He kept up with the times, he had something new to say, but as a guitarist and a person who understood the institution of what were Miles and his groups, it was a little disappointing."

"Amandla" (5:21)

Composer	Marcus Miller
Musicians	Miles, trumpet; Marcus Miller, bass, keyboards; Kenny Garrett, alto saxophone; Joe Sample, piano; Omar Hakim, drums; Don Alias and Bashiri Johnson, percussion
Producers	Tommy LiPuma, Marcus Miller
Arranger	Marcus Miller
Recorded	Clinton Recording Studios, September 1988 – January 1989
Engineers	Eric Calvi, Bruce Miller
Mixed by	Bill Schnee
Live performances	July 1989 – July 1991

Amandla means "power" in Xhosa, a language that is mainly spoken by groups of people living in the former Transkei, Ciskei and Eastern Cape regions of

South Africa. *Amandla* was also a cry often used by members of the African National Congress (ANC) during the struggle against apartheid.[22] It was also a title Miles wanted to use for a track on his new album. "That was Miles. I think he had been doing his own research and he said 'I need you to write a song called "Amandla"' and he wanted to call the album *Amandla*. I said 'No problem.' I had this ballad and I thought 'Amandla' would be a great name for it," says Miller.

"Amandla" fades up on a rattling sound, before Miles enters on muted horn. Miles plays beautifully with good support from Omar Hakim, who uses brushes to create a softer, gentler sound on the drums. Jason Miles also programs a variety of atmospheric sound effects that form a backdrop to Miles's horn. Just after the one-minute mark, the tension increases but is soon released as Garrett begins playing his solo. Garrett is given plenty of space to solo and makes good use of it, with strong, elegant phrases and conveying much feeling.

Garrett is immediately followed by Joe Sample, who plays a fluent solo on acoustic piano – an instrument rarely heard in Miles's 1980s music. Miles then resumes playing the melody, with Garrett in support and then, just before the four-minute mark, there is what sounds like a sample of an electric guitar playing a sustained note, which adds some drama to the sound. Garrett plays another short solo before he starts copying Miles's phrases and the track fades out. "Amandla" is one of the highlights of the album and it's no surprise that Miller concludes: "That came out well; Joe Sample, Omar Hakim and Kenny Garrett played really well on that."

"Mr. Pastorius" (5:41)

Composer	Marcus Miller
Musicians	Miles, trumpet; Marcus Miller, bass, keyboards, bass clarinet; Al Foster, drums; Jason Miles, synthesizer programming
Producers	Tommy LiPuma, Marcus Miller
Arranger	Marcus Miller
Recorded	Right Track Recording Studio, probably January 1989
Engineer	Bruce Miller
Mixed by	Bill Schnee
Live performances	April 1989 – July 1991

It sometimes seems that the price paid for genius is to face a battle against the ravages of severe mental illness. Classical pianists John Ogdon and David Helfgott both suffered from it, as did artists such as Salvador Dali and Vincent van Gogh. And so did John Francis "Jaco" Pastorius, undoubtedly one of the most influential bassists of all time. As guitarist Pat Metheney – who played with Pastorius – puts it: "Jaco Pastorius may well have been the last jazz musician of the twentieth century to have made a major impact on the musical world at large. Everywhere you go, – sometimes it seems like a dozen times a day – … you hear Jaco's sound; from the latest TV commercial to bass players of all stripes copping his licks on recordings of all styles, from news broadcasts to famous rock and roll bands, from hip hop samples to personal tribute records, you hear the echoes of that unmistakable sound everywhere."[23]

Pastorius suffered from manic depression which led to a downward spiral towards drink, destitution and ultimately his death on September 21, 1987 after being beaten up by a bouncer at a club he was trying to gatecrash. He was just thirty-six years old. Like so many bass players, Miller had been profoundly influenced by Pastorius. The two men had also known each other personally and even jammed together on occasions.

"It was really sad when he passed. I wrote 'Mr. Pastorius' for him and played it for Miles," says Miller. "Miles liked it and we began recording it. He asked me what the title was. I wasn't sure how Miles felt about Jaco at the time. We didn't discuss him much. I told Miles 'I named it "Mr. Pastorius." I can come up with another title if you're not cool with that.' Miles said 'No, I think that's really nice to name this for Jaco.' I felt great about that because now I could honestly feel like the tune came from me and from Miles too. Miles's playing was fantastic on this piece. 'Mr. Pastorius' is one of my favourite Miles performances from when I was with him and I really think that he laid a fantastic gift on Jaco with that piece!"[24]

"Mr. Pastorius" is indeed a beautiful piece, but its initial structure was somewhat different from the finished piece, as Miller explains. "I'd been playing with Miles on and off for seven years and knew that the 4/4 straight-ahead thing [jazz swing] was something he didn't want to do that much, because it brought him back too much to the past. I was reluctant to even hint at it. I wrote this ballad and the most obvious thing to do after we played the melody was to go into a four but I wasn't going to do it, so I figured we'd figure something else out. I recorded the intro with some string synthesizers and he played the melody against those synths."

Miles and Miller were in the studio together and Miller had his bass ready so that when the orchestral part was over, Miles could do some improvising and Miller could just play a little bit of bass so that Miles would have something to work off. "So I'm just sitting there and I'm playing and the melody's over and I'm thinking 'Maybe I'll just play a funky blues, something with a little backbeat that Miles can play off of.' But instead of going to the blues, Miles went up to the top of the tune to play off the changes. I didn't even know if he still did that kind of thing. It was almost as if he was playing back in the '40s and '50s and I was like 'Man, I know this isn't happenin'!' and I'm still playing this kinda funky two-beat on the bass and that's when he held up four fingers, meaning 'Play in four.' I went to four right away – he didn't have to tell me twice! He just kept blowing, man, he blew chorus-after-chorus-after-chorus. We rolled the tape back and he blew another four or five."

At the end of the day when Miles had left, Miller called Miles's ex-drummer Al Foster. "I said 'Man, you gotta get over here and hear what Miles just did!'" When Foster arrived, Miller first played him the track "Amandla." "Al was like 'Man, you brought this cat back,' and then I said 'Listen to this!' and I played him 'Mr. Pastorius' and man, Al gets a little weepy when Miles does his thing. Al's eyes start tearing up and he says 'Alright, let's put some drums on these things.' And I played along with Al to support him. So Al's just sitting there with his headphones [on], as loud as he could get them, so he could vibe with Miles who was probably at home watching TV!"

After the drum part was laid down, Miller sat at the piano. "I listened to Miles's solo and tried to figure out how to comp for him and make it make sense and that's how it all happened. It was beautiful. And then I called Bill Schnee who was a mixing engineer and I said 'I want you to edit every chorus of Miles's and add them all together – I don't want to leave anything on the cutting-room floor.' I told him exactly how to edit it all up and that's how we got each chorus on there. It was pretty cool because I don't think people had heard Miles play like that in a long time."

"Mr. Pastorius" begins with a pinging sound that reverberates, added to which are running-water effects and a few lines of bass clarinet. Then Miles starts playing, on open horn and with a glorious tone. His horn sings beautifully and majestically. Just after the one-minute mark, the jazz-swing section starts, with Miller's walking bass line accompanying Miles's horn. Al Foster's drumming fits perfectly and it is hard to believe that the drums were almost the last instrument to be recorded on the piece.

Miller's bass lines are supple and engineer Bruce Miller notes: "When people have asked me what the 'chorus effect' was that I used on some of Marcus's bass lines in that song and I have explained that it was no effect but him doubling parts, they are amazed." After the long jazz-swing section, the tune reverts back to a ballad, with Miles finishing on a flurry of notes. Writer Ian Carr has noted that although "Mr. Pastorius" was written for Pastorius, the memory of Gil Evans was also in Miller's harmonies.[25] Evans had died on March 20, 1988 and *Amandla*, like *Siesta*, was also dedicated to him. Miles was deeply affected by the death of his long-time friend. "I saw Miles backstage in London in 1989," recalls Paul Buckmaster, "and all he spoke about for twenty minutes was Gil." "Mr. Pastorius" is not just one of the highlights on *Amandla*, but of all the music Miles played in the last decade of his life – it's a classic.

"Jilli" (5:06)

Composer	John Bigham
Musicians	Miles, trumpet; John Bigham, drum programming, guitar, keyboards; Marcus Miller, bass, additional keyboards, bass clarinet; Kenny Garrett, alto saxophone; Foley, guitar; Ricky Wellman, drums; Billy "Spaceman" Patterson, wah-wah guitar
Producers	Tommy LiPuma, Marcus Miller
Associate producer	John Bigham
Arrangers	John Bigham, Marcus Miller
Recorded	Right Track Recording Studio, probably January 1989
Engineer	Bruce Miller
Mixed by	Bill Schnee
Live performances	April 1989 – July 1991

John Bigham was born in Chicago in 1959, but left the city when he was fifteen. Originally wanting to play the drums, he took up the guitar at thirteen, inspired by guitarists such as Hendrix and Led Zeppelin's Jimmy Page. After a spell in the airforce Bigham moved to Los Angeles, where Wayne Linsey, an old school friend and musician, also lived. Linsey introduced Bigham to Jillian Menges, who later became his girlfriend and was also a friend of Miles. "Jillian was a singer and had met Miles on a cruise," says Bigham. "She was a feisty person and wasn't intimidated by Miles – she'd go toe-to-toe with him! Miles liked her because she was a great person, and she used to run errands for him."

One day, Menges played Miles some demos that Bigham had created at home and Miles liked what he heard. As a result, Miles met Bigham. "I got a chance to audition as the guitarist in Miles's band, but I wasn't that good, especially when it came to playing jazz. I just didn't have enough musical knowledge to do that gig. So I didn't get the gig but a call from Jillian saying Miles wanted me to write some music for him." Miles became Bigham's mentor, putting him on the payroll and asking him to write songs. "John Bigham [is] just a great musical writer," said Miles. "He writes beautiful, funky music. He's a guitarist. He writes off a computer ... he just hears sounds that are unbelievable."[26] Bigham wasn't a trained musician and this had much appeal to Miles. "I want that street sound and John has it ... He doesn't know that much about theory. I told him 'Don't worry about all that, I'll show you.'"[27]

"Once I started writing, I wrote songs for him all the time. All I did all day long was write songs," recalls Bigham. Bigham remembers the first time he and Miles recorded some of his music together. "In the first session, it was just me and him and the engineer at Sunset Sound [studio]. He came in and said 'What do you want me to do?' I'm thinking 'I don't know!' We hung out and had a lot of fun. There are four or five tunes in the can, including one called 'Naked'."

Bigham would often hang out at Miles's home, either playing demos or listening to music. "Miles had me listening to a lot of zouk music. He said 'I want something like this, an island kind of feel, happy-sounding tunes,'" says Bigham. As work progressed on the *Amandla* album, LiPuma put Bigham in touch with keyboardist Jeff Lorber and the two of them worked together at Sunset Sound. "Jeff Lorber helped me program beats. I knew Miles was into African rhythms and I was listening to a lot of go-go stuff. I decided to fuse go-go with the jazz and put in a lot of rhythms. I was pushing the boundaries, pushing rhythms against other rhythms and Miles thought that was great. Not knowing a lot about music principles means I'm going to do things that are not correct, but which work," says Bigham.

The resulting tune, "Digg That," was recorded on December 21, 1987. "Digg That" is a mid-tempo number with clear influences from zouk. Although the tune has some interesting polyrhythmic patterns, a nice groove and a few neat touches (such as Miles's sampled vocals and a Hawaiian-style guitar chord at its conclusion), Miles fails to stamp his mark on it. "Digg That" was left in the can.

Miles also introduced Bigham to Marcus Miller. "They flew me to New York and I worked at Right Track [studio]. I went into studio with Marcus and Tommy. Marcus was pretty much running the whole thing. I asked for an Atari ST1040 computer plus some little gadgets and they just let me do the track. And then Marcus played on it and called in some others. He just spiced it up and organized it to make it work. I called it 'Jilli' because I wanted to do something for Jillian for hooking me up with Miles. It was an opportunity to immortalize her," says Bigham.

If Miles wanted Bigham to write some "happy music," he certainly got it with "Jilli." With its quirky go-go beat and catchy synthesizer riffs, "Jilli" skips along merrily. The tune's opening (sampled) horn section was dubbed "The Camel Horns" by Miller, who asked Jason Miles to program some "desert sounds." "I always had this vision of a North African big band in the desert, with music stands. And whenever I was looking for that sound I'd say 'Pull me out some of that camel.' They always had that kind of safari sound to them," says Miller.

But, as with "Digg That," Miles seems to struggle to make much impression on the music. Kenny Garrett fares better with a solo just after the two-minute mark. Following the sax solo, Miles continues blowing his horn, Miller plays a short bass solo and then, soon after, the tune fades out as Garrett blows a little more.

"Jilli" is a more successful recording than "Digg That," but seems to suffer from the problem of reconciling Bigham's street sound and abstract musical ideas with Miller and LiPuma's sleek, clean and more formalized production values. The result is an uneasy compromise which doesn't quite ignite the creative spark. Even Bigham admits that: "It's not my favourite song. I didn't get a chance to do as much as I would have liked on it. I don't think my mind was ready to take it to where it needed to go. I know that it needed more work in my mind. That song is a little too happy for me."

"Cobra" (5:16)

Composer	George Duke
Musicians	Miles, trumpet; George Duke, keyboards and synclavier; Marcus Miller, bass, additional keyboards and bass clarinet; Michael Landau, guitar; Kenny Garrett, soprano saxophone; Joey DeFrancesco, additional keyboards
Producers	George Duke, Tommy LiPuma, Marcus Miller
Arranger	George Duke
Recorded	Le Gonks West 1988–89 (backing tracks), Right Track Recording Studio (overdubs)
Engineers	Eric Zobler (Le Gonks West), Bruce Miller (Right Track)
Mixed by	Bill Schnee
Live performances	None[28]

Miles would often ask George Duke to write him some music and, when it came to recording *Amandla*, Duke submitted a number of tunes. "I sent a bunch of songs including a beautiful ballad called 'That Feelin'.' They didn't have space for it, but Kenny [Garrett] wanted to use it. But I told him I needed it for a group I was producing, 101 North." When Miles didn't have space for the track "Tribute" written for the *Tutu* album, Duke used it on 101 North's *Forever Yours* album. That is where "That Feelin'" can be found too. A soulful ballad, played predominantly on saxophone, it would have been interesting to hear how Miles would have played it.

But one track that did make it on *Amandla* was "Cobra." Duke explains where the title came from. "I used to look at some Miles Davis pictures and I remember there was one picture where he had his tongue stuck out and he was sweating and I thought 'He looks like a snake.' So I said 'What kind of snake would Miles like?' and I said 'Cobra.' It's exotic and [in the picture] Miles had this interesting shaped head with his tongue sticking out. I just thought that was a good title for the song."

Although Duke hoped Miles would use a live band rather than his demo, he took no chances. "I spent more time on the demo. I felt like I got trapped in that 'Backyard Ritual' thing, so I spent a little more time on 'Cobra' to get it the way I thought it should be. Miles basically just told me to do whatever I wanted. He was that free. He said 'Just go!' and I went!" Once again, Duke used a synclavier to build up the track, although this time he also employed the services of guitarist Michael Landeau to add some guitar lines to the tune. "Michael is a great guitarist. I had used him for a long time and he has a way of playing like Steve Lukather [of Toto]. He fills up holes; he's an incredible kind of glue in a track and that's why I've always liked to use him," says Duke.

Duke sent the demo to Miles and, as he suspected, it was used as the basis for the complete track. However, Miller overdubbed bass, bass clarinet and keyboards. Miller also brought in two extra musicians, Kenny Garrett on soprano saxophone (the only time he foregoes the alto sax on *Amandla*) and Joey DeFrancesco on additional keyboards.

Like "Backyard Ritual," "Cobra" is a mid-tempo track, with a rhythm track driven by a drum machine and some funky bass lines from Miller. The main focus is the interplay between Miles and Garrett, who often double-up or repeat phrases with each other. Just after the two-and-a-half-minute mark, Garrett plays his solo, and begins by quoting the theme from "It Ain't Necessarily So." "That's one of my biggest memories of the sessions," says Bruce Miller. "Nobody expected Kenny to play that and the whole control room went nuts when he started playing it." And no doubt Duke approved of Miles using a real saxophonist on his track rather than the sampled version he'd left on "Backyard Ritual." The track ends with Garrett repeating Miles's phrases into the fadeout.

Amandla – the verdict

Contemporary music invariably reflects the tastes, trends and technology of the times and *Amandla* is no exception. The 1980s saw the music industry move from an era of punk – where the power and the energy of the music was more important than a polished production – to an age where production values soared. The 1980s were the age of the record producer. There had always been producers who had made a significant mark on the musical landscape, such as Phil Spector, George Martin and Arif Mardin. But in the '80s, producers such as Trevor Horn, Nile Rogers, Jimmy Jam and Terry Lewis, Quincy Jones and Stock, Aitken and Waterman became household names, often identified by their distinctive sound, no matter who the artist was that they were producing. Indeed, producers were often sought out by artists (or their record companies) wanting to have a particular sound on their next album.

The 1980s was also the era of adult-orientated rock (AOR), MTV and the compact disc. The latter offered consumers a digital music medium for the first time and the record industry was keen to exploit the CD's greater audio clarity and extended dynamic range. The CD's arrival coincided with the explosion of digital technology in recording studios – synthesizers, samplers, sequencers, drum machines and MIDI (Musical Instrument Digital Interface) equipment. As a result, more and more time was spent on the production side of the recording process.

It is fitting that one of the albums launched at the start of the 1980s was Steely Dan's *Gaucho*. Steely Dan's Walter Becker and Donald Fagen were famed for their keen attention to detail and their quest to create the "perfect take," even if it meant their studio musicians playing the same chord sequence ad nauseum to get it. The days when Teo Macero could leave the sound of a bottle accidentally falling over in the studio in the final mix (as on *In A Silent Way*) were long gone. The emphasis now was on achieving a clean (and at times clinical) sound with any grit taken out. The result was often music that was easy to digest aurally, if somewhat bland.

The writer Ian MacDonald concluded that the modern recording process was in danger of taking the heart out of music. "Modern records, rather than embodying a *performance*, are usually built up as they go along using a layering principle which, apart from eliminating any possibility of a natural balance between instruments, leaves no pores through which the sound can respire," he said.[29]

The driving force behind the modern recording ethos is automation (such as the use of signal-processing, sequencing and mixing), added MacDonald, pointing out that "These functions, while convenient, tend to distance artists from the integrity of the material they are building... It's hard to infuse real feeling into music so synthetically constructed, and easy...to lose a sense of proportion during a process less akin to traditional live recording than to what's known in the cinema world as 'post production.'"[30]

But Miller says such outcomes are not always inevitable. "Unless you're telling me you haven't seen a film that had heart and soul in it, you can't tell me that automation and mixing and the other things automatically means that it takes this stuff out of the music or the art. It's not the tools; it's the people operating the tools and while it is very easy for you to allow the computers and the mixing board to overwhelm your music so that your music begins to reflect the technology more than it does the humanity, it's not a given. If you're comfortable and good enough with those instruments, you can get some heart. It's going to be different. But what I end up doing when I'm piecing things together is that I'm showing you the best of what happened in a period of time. It's like in a movie. You don't show the entire scene, you show the things that tell the story in the best way."

Miller points out that this process of recording was not novel for Miles. "With Miles, it's nothing new. If you listen to anything he did after 1971, I hate to tell you that that stuff was highly constructed and Teo would be the first one to tell you. Because he was experimenting, because he was working new things out in the studio, the studio became an easel. You have to show the successes, the thing that really worked. That's what we did."

"It's important to point out that Marcus worked in a very 'organic' and natural way," says Bruce Miller. "Even when musicians were playing together to tracks already on tape, Marcus made sure that the performances were real musical performances between musicians rather than simply 'playing to tape.' This was his way of combining the expressiveness and communication of natural performances with the control and precision of the available technology."

There is no doubt that Miller managed to combine humanity and technology on *Amandla* and there are many stirring performances to prove it, but one wishes that – to paraphrase Bourelly – there had been greater scope for the musicians to play with more grit and adventure. Jason Miles refutes Bourelly's complaints about over-control. "I have to disagree with him. Experimentation was always going on and every player I saw come through those sessions was given a lot of freedom to express themselves, [although] I was not present for Jean-Paul's session." However, most of this experimentation seems to have remained on the cutting-room floor.

Jason Miles found much to like on *Amandla*. "I really liked 'Big Time,' that sounded Gil Evansey to me. I also loved 'Hannibal'; I think the textures and the movement of the chords on that tune were really interesting. I also liked 'Catembe' a lot too and the horn part on 'Jilli'."[31] But there was one aspect he was unhappy about – the mixing. "Marcus's wife was about to give birth to their first child and he couldn't make it to L.A. for the mixes. I felt that if Marcus was present there would have been more energy in the mixes. I felt the rough mixes had more of an edge," he says.

Miller declares himself to be more than satisfied with the final mix. "I wasn't around for most of *Tutu* either. I kinda dug that, after laying down every single note and being around for every single thing, hearing somebody else's musical perspective at the end. I'm sure there are some things that would have been better presented if I had been there but on the whole I was pretty happy with it."

Despite *Amandla*'s wide range of musical influences and the various musical collaborators involved in it, some have found many of the tracks too similar sounding. "Somewhat over-produced, the overall impression is of monotony of tone, not helped by short solos and emphasis on studio-generated ensemble textures," says writer Stuart Nicholson.[32] Paul Tingen declares that: "The motifs, arrangements and atmosphere of many of the tracks on *Amandla* are too similar."[33] Part of the problem is Miles's apparent reluctance to play more with an open horn, which is why "Mr. Pastorius" is such a gem of a track.

But Miller believes that *Amandla* represents the best of the three albums he made with Miles. "I'm really happy musically and, for me, *Amandla* and *Tutu* are the same period of time. If I could have only one album I would take the song "Tutu" and put it at the front of *Amandla* and I think that would be a very good representation of where I started and what I wanted to achieve. Because we had never done anything like *Tutu* before you could hear a few tentative steps. With *Amandla* you could tell we were much more comfortable with the idea of electronics and Miles and the whole concept. But it didn't have that thing that you get when you hear a sound with *Tutu*. So I'm very happy with the combination of the two."

There is indeed much to enjoy and admire on *Amandla*, not least on tracks such as "Catémbe," "Hannibal," "Mr Pastorius" and the title tune. And Miller shines as a composer, player, arranger and producer. Miles, as ever, adds his glorious tone to the music. But *Amandla* is just a little too smooth and a little too well refined. Up until this album, Miles's records had had a degree of rawness and edge to them. And as Mike Stern points out, the great thing about Miles was he knew that a performance didn't have to be perfect to move you. "He didn't over-work, he had funkiness; it's not all pristine," says Stern. "The best of Miles was the raw stuff that he did – it didn't have to sound like Hollywood."

18 *doo-bop* (40:04)

Warner Bros 7599-26938-2

Recorded	c. July 1991 and c. late 1991
Released	1992
Producer	Easy Mo Bee
Associate producers	Gordon Meltzer, Matt Pierson
Executive producer	Gordon Meltzer
Engineers	D'Anthony Johnson, Eric Lynch
Mixed by	D'Anthony Johnson, Eric Lynch, Matthew "Boomer" Lamonica, Roy Hendrickson
Tracks	"Mystery," "The Doo-Bop Song," "Chocolate Chip," "High-Speed Chase," "Blow," "Sonya," "Fantasy," "Duke Booty," "Mystery" (Reprise)

"That's a bad motherfucker right there – how you do that? I like that. You gonna do that on my album. You do that for me." *Miles talking to producer/rapper Easy Mo Bee*

"I like playing with young musicians. I want to keep creating. Changing. Music isn't about standing still and becoming safe."[1] *Miles*

Background to the album

As Miles entered what was to be the final year of his life, he was busily making plans for his next album. Miles's plans were ambitious and he was keen to work with a wide range of musical collaborators and explore a variety of musical genres. Indeed, Miles's creative juices were flowing so strongly that he envisioned his new record as being a double album. Miles had a number of musical collaborations in mind. Prince had sent him a selection of tracks, several of which were destined for the new album.

John Bigham, a young black guitarist whom Miles had met in 1987 (and who briefly joined Miles's band as a percussionist in late 1989), was also preparing material. And if Miles had lived longer, his long-time and close musical collaborator Marcus Miller might also have contributed to the new album. But Miles's most radical – and controversial – decision was to record a series of hip-hop tunes.

Hip-hop started out as the sound of the street and went on to become a global phenomenon. So it was no surprise that Miles – whose ears were always sharply attuned to the music of the day – should have been interested in playing hip-hop. But it was also no surprise that some of Miles's fans and critics would be shocked by his decision to explore hip-hop. Part of the reason was that hip-hop is so fundamentally different from jazz. The foundations of hip-hop music are the beats – everything else, such as the melody, is built up from them.

But Miles had always been fascinated by rhythm and so hip-hop presented a new and interesting musical direction, as well as a means of reaching a wider audience. Miles once said, "I've been experimenting with some rap songs because I think there's some heavy rhythms up in that music. I heard that Max Roach said that he thought the next Charlie Parker might come out of rap melodies and rhythms. Sometimes you can't get those rhythms out of your head."[2]

The mainstays of hip-hop music are drum machines, electronic keyboards and samplers, and many hip-hop tunes also feature rapping, where the rhyme, rhythm, accent and intonation of the rapper's vocals are designed to flow with the beat. And like the English language, hip-hop borrows from many sources: pop, soul, rock, jazz – even opera – have been incorporated into hip-hop.

And hip-hop is more than just music – it is a culture that encompasses music, dance, fashion, language and graffiti. Today, the influence of hip-hop can be found in many facets of modern culture including music, film, sport, fashion, art, advertising and technology (think digital samplers).[3] It has also crossed all age, social and racial barriers. In the late 1980s, the New York-based record label Def Jam was one of the major driving forces behind the spread of hip-hop across the USA and ultimately the world.

Russell Simmons and Rick Rubin founded Def Jam in 1984 and the label had its finger firmly on the pulse of the street.[4] Def Jam artists, such as LL Cool J, Public Enemy, Slick Rick, and The Beastie Boys, were amongst the biggest names in hip-hop. Def Jam's empire included an artists' management company, Rush Artist Management (Rush was Simmons's nickname, because he was a bundle of energy and always rushing about), and Rush Producers Management (RPM), which had producers such as Prince Paul, Daddy O, Sid Reynolds, Sam Sever and The Bomb Squad (producers of Public Enemy) on its books.

By the time Miles decided to work with hip-hop, various artists had already integrated elements of hip-hop into their music. In 1983, Herbie Hancock released "Rockit," a mixture of techno, jazz, funk and hip-hop featuring Grandmixer DST. The following year, Chaka Khan's "I Feel For You" featured the rapping of Melle Mel. Producer Quincy Jones's 1989 album *Back On The Block* included the rappers Ice-T, Melle Mel, Big Daddy Kane, and Kool Moe Dee. By coincidence, Miles also appeared on the same album and the track "Jazz Corner Of The World" featured Miles, James Moody, George Benson, Sarah Vaughan, Dizzy Gillespie, Ella Fitzgerald and Joe Zawinul, as well as rappers Big Daddy Kane and Kool Moe Dee.

It could be that this experience had planted the seeds in Miles's mind to explore hip-hop. In 1991, the group A Tribe Called Quest released *The Low End Theory*, an album which mixed hip-hop and jazz and even featured the bass playing of Ron Carter, who had played in Miles's second great quintet of the 1960s.

One factor that almost certainly did motivate Miles to explore hip-hop was his friendship with Russell Simmons, and the two men would occasionally meet to discuss music and business matters. Miles's previous three albums – *Tutu*, *Siesta* and *Amandla* – had been slick, polished studio productions nurtured by Marcus Miller and Tommy LiPuma. But Miles's next album would be produced in a completely different way.

The decision to play hip-hop was dictated by both creative and business reasons, says Gordon Meltzer, who at the time was Miles's tour manager. "The artistic and the financial aspects worked together in Miles's mind to make that decision. On the one hand he was a friend of Russell Simmons and he talked to Russell about how the hip-hop records were made. So Russell is giving him insights into the cost of producing monster hip-hop hits. Then Miles gets the bill for *Amandla* and he sees that maybe he got an advance of $450,000 from Warner Bros, and maybe the producers of the records spent $650,000 making it because they camped out at Right Track studios every day for three years, doing remixes and just putting it on the record budget."

The records produced by Miller and LiPuma involved a great deal of over-dubbing, multi-tracking and mixing, which in turn required much studio time and a high degree of control and coordination during the recording process. Meltzer says Miles was not happy with his role in this production process. "A couple of years later [after starting work on *Amandla*] they called Miles and said 'It's time to do your tracks' and Marcus would coach him, phrase-by-phrase. That's what really pissed him off at the end. He never did a take. He would come in and Marcus would stand over him and have him blow a phrase. And then have him blow it again and then again, and then they'd blow another phrase and do it again and again. And then Marcus and Tommy would tell Miles 'Go back to the house,' and then they'd edit it and mix it and work it. And a couple of years later *Amandla* came out and Miles said 'I want to play a whole song.' So there was the ridiculous cost and out-of-pocket losses of making *Amandla* (and *Tutu*) that really bothered Miles."

But Miller refutes this assertion. "We only had Miles play complete takes. We did have him do his solos again and a lot of the time this was because it was the first time he had heard these things – it was not like he had the sheet music to take home. He had so many ideas that I didn't want to waste or lose any of them, so we'd roll back the tape and let him play all the crazy ideas he had. We could have done what you do on pop records, which is to take the best phrase of the best performances and put them together, but there would have been no continuity. Miles had a ball in those sessions."

There is no reason why both of these contradictory versions of events are not true. Miles's views on a situation could change like the weather and his feelings towards people could oscillate wildly. "Miles would love me one day and hate me the next," recalls Teo Macero. What is certain is that when it came to making *Doo-Bop*, Miles wanted a much simpler production process and he also wanted to be much closer to the creative process. But it's also true that Miller would remain a close part of Miles's life until the very end, with Miller being one of the few people outside of Miles's immediate family to visit him when he went into hospital for the last time. And shortly before he died, Miles also invited Miller to participate in *Doo-Bop* – proof that any ill-feeling Miles may have had over the making of *Amandla* had dissipated by then.

But Meltzer adds that Miles had another major concern about his music. "It bothered him none of it got played on the radio. He wanted the kids to play his records. He would ask everyone around him 'Why isn't my stuff on the [urban] radio?' and you'd have to say 'Well Miles, when you make songs that are twelve minutes long and nobody's doing remixes, they're not going to get on the radio.' So you have this high cost and you have the fact that he wanted to be heard by the kids. He wanted to be on the radio."

Meltzer recalls hanging out with Miles: "I remember sitting in his apartment one day in summer and Miles – who hated air conditioning – had the windows open, even though it was like one hundred fifty degrees with one hundred and ten per cent humidity. And he hears kids walking down the street carrying radios and there were lots of tunes that were on Russell's label, a lot of hip-hop stuff and nothing of his. He wanted his stuff to be out there and he wanted to record it in full takes, instead of this coaching phrase-by-phrase way."

Miles asked Simmons to recommend some hip-hop producers he could work with and Simmons delegated the task to Francesca Spero, who ran RPM. "I remember that Russell used to go Hawaii every New Year and Miles would vacation there around the same period," she says, "and a couple of seasons in a row, Miles would be like 'I want to make a hip-hop record.' Finally Russell took him seriously and said to me: 'Miles really wants to do this thing.' So I got Faith Newman, who was vice-president of A&R [artists and repertoire] for Def Jam records, to put together producer reels, selections of tracks that had been produced by various people signed to RPM." Meltzer recalls that: "Francesca was the day-to-day contact, passing tapes between Miles and Def Jam. Miles picked tracks that were on those tapes and said 'I want to do that one and that one and that one.'"

Spero says that most of the music that Newman put together for Miles wasn't hardcore hip-hop, but was in a more musical, melodic jazz style. Miles whittled down his selection to several potential collaborators. Two of them – Chuck D (real name Carlton Ridenour) and Flavor Flav (William Drayton) – were members of Public Enemy. Another was Sid Reynolds, but one name stood out when Spero and Newman analysed Miles's selections. "On one of the tapes Miles had said 'I want number two, three, four, five and seven, and when we looked at the label it was like 'Oh shit, Mo Bee produced like every one of these tracks.' So we hooked him up," says Spero.

Easy Mo Bee was a young and relatively unknown rapper/producer when Miles called for him. Mo Bee – whose given name is Osten S. Harvey Jr. – was born in Brooklyn in 1965. His moniker Easy Mo Bee is based on the name of a musical hero, the rapper Kool Moe Dee, and Harvey's childhood nickname, Bubee. Mo Bee's musical heroes were the neighbourhood DJs with their sound systems comprising a twin record deck, speakers, mixer and microphone. Amongst them were the DJs that pioneered hip-hop such as DJ Kool Herc, Grandmaster Flash, Afrika Bambaataa and DJ Grand Wizard Theodore. These DJs would develop the techniques that formed the foundations of hip-hop, such as scratching, mixing and sampling. They also assumed the role of an MC (master of ceremonies) and used a microphone to talk over the music, often indulging in braggadocio or exhorting the audience to dance or wave their hands in the air.

When Mo Bee was a teenager he began DJ-ing, putting together his own system, which included two BSR turntables and a microphone salvaged from a dump. From there he progressed to performing and producing. He formed his own vocal group with two friends, JR (Darron Strand) and A. B. Money, called Rappin' Is Fundamental (RIF), and he joined Cold Chillin' records, where he co-produced an album for the hip-hop artist The Genius (real name Gary Grice, now known as GZA), called *Words From The Genius*. But Mo Bee's prime aim was to become part of Def Jam's roster. "Everyone was on Def Jam. That was the place to be for a hip-hop artist or producer," he says.

Spero recalls: "I brought Mo Bee into Def Jam. I came back from lunch one day and someone I was working with told me 'There's a kid outside in the lobby, I think you should check him out.' So there's Mo Bee sitting there, writing out all his songs on a yellow pad. What Mo Bee didn't know is that I had been at Cold Chillin' for a while, so I knew who he was and I was a big fan of his. We pulled him in. All I needed to do was to send his music out and people responded to it. He was great; he had such a unique style."

Mo Bee says he was aware of Miles's musical heritage through records such as *Bitches Brew* and Miles's Blue Note recordings, but Spero's recollection suggests that, at the time, Mo Bee found the situation hard to comprehend. "When I called Mo Bee and told him, I was so excited. I had grown up in the 1970s following people like Sun Ra and Miles and going to Miles's concerts. It was like 'Now I'm going to talk to Miles Davis and be in the studio with him?' That was crazy to me and I was so excited. So I rung Mo Bee up with all this excitement and so he gets excited. Twenty minutes later he calls me back and he's like 'Who's Miles Davis? Is he that jazz guy?' So I go over to his place and give him a little history." Spero also remembers when Miles called her on the phone to enthuse about Mo Bee: "He said 'I never met a cat like this who starts with the drums and rides around the drums. You know what I'm talking about?' Miles was fascinated by it."

Miles invited Spero around to his home. "He lived in this crazy place on the Upper West Side. He had paintings that were like twelve feet high, these huge canvasses around his apartment. He had very little furniture and he was just painting. He was very casual and he just wanted to talk and show me around the place and tell me about Mo Bee. It was a very cool, very casual thing. I knew that he was this amazing historical voice from before I was born. But when you got around him and hung out with him, he was just Miles. He was very sweet and he was very humble – just a regular guy."

Another thing Spero noticed about Miles was that: "You could tell that he loved women. He was a flirt. I seem to remember this white woman in the studio with him, constantly around, rubbing his shoulders and neck. She was very sweet. I remember him teasing me. I would go to the studio and he would be in the vocal booth, calling my name. I'm like 'Why don't you sample my name and put it on the record and make me famous?'" The white woman Spero refers to was probably Joanne Nerlino, a New York art dealer and close friend of Miles. Spero recalls that it was also a time when Miles had cleaned himself up. "He had cut down on drinking, he was clean and he was very proud of the fact that he was. He would offer me champagne and liqueur and say 'I don't indulge.'"

Miles also invited Mo Bee to his home. "I went up there and he had his personal chef and he asked me 'What do you want to eat? Are you hungry?' So I asked for some fried chicken. Miles told the chef to prepare some chicken. When I arrived two other producers were already there. They were playing Miles some music and I noticed that he was real quiet while the music was playing. After it had finished, he didn't say too much and then he dismissed them. When they had left he said to me: 'I didn't like that shit.' I thought 'Whoa! All the things they said about this man are true!'"

But it was a different story when Miles listened to Mo Bee's music. "The song that got me the Miles gig was the tune 'True Fresh MC' from the *Words*

From The Genius album. Miles kept playing that again and again. When he played the song he said to me 'That's a bad motherfucker right there – how you do that? I like that. You gonna do that on my album. You do that for me.' I thought 'Oh shit. He really wants to get down with hip-hop.'"

Miles also decided that he wanted Meltzer to help him produce the album, taking on the role of associate producer (Meltzer would later become the album's executive producer too). "I don't know anything about music and I think it irked some people a lot that Miles had me in the studio. It irked some of the musicians because I've no musical understanding or talent and yet Miles said 'Mix these records,'" says Meltzer. "When we did *Siesta* and the final mixes of *Amandla*, Miles had me in the studio and he was trying to teach me how to do things. How lucky was I to have Miles say 'Go into the studio and help with the records.'" But Miles's approach to music was often unorthodox, as Susan Rogers, who engineered many of Prince's records in the 1980s, discovered in a conversation with Miles. Miles asked Rogers whether she was a musician and when Rogers replied in the negative, Miles said: "That's okay, some of the best musicians I know ain't musicians."[5]

But one of Meltzer's less happier tasks was contacting Warner Bros chairman Mo Ostin and informing him that Miles wanted his next record to be a double album. "This bothered me and made me embarrassed because I knew Mo was right from a business standpoint and yet Miles said 'Get Mo on the phone.' So I'm saying 'Miles is here, Mr Ostin, and he's telling me to call you and tell you that *Doo-Bop* has to be a double album.' Mo said what he said and Miles grabbed the phone when he heard that it wasn't going well."

Miles also wanted his band's keyboard player Deron Johnson to be involved in the recording sessions. "I can play a little bit, but Deron's job was to lace [sweeten] the album on every song that needed it. That keyboard layer would make it the complete musical song and give it structure," notes Mo Bee. "It was Deron's job to give it the quality. Miles didn't want to play with just straight beats. With Deron there was some musical structure, some integrity. If you ask me, there was nothin' wrong with that. I don't think Miles was going to play his horn on top of something like 'Peter Piper' [a tune by Run-DMC]."

When Johnson got the call to play on *Doo-Bop*, he had only been with Miles for several months and Johnson would become the last member of a Miles Davis band ever to work with Miles in the studio. "It all happened in the summer when we were off tour," says Johnson. "I was based in L.A. and I would fly like, three or four times back and forth to New York. I played on at least four songs. I wish everybody [else in the band] would have experienced what I did, but it probably wouldn't have been the same. When it's just you in the room with Miles and Easy Mo Bee and an engineer – just to watch him work was so intense in that setting."

Johnson describes his role during the *Doo-Bop* sessions. "I did some synth bass stuff, some organ stuff, guitar stuff on the keyboards. The *Doo-Bop* stuff was just one take and then Miles would ask me to play background stuff with his horn and I'd have to figure out what he was doing and this was all on the spot, nothing was written out. So it was – just go! It was great. And at that point I was hanging with him a lot by myself."

Before Miles went to the studio with Johnson and Mo Bee he had also invited Chuck D and Flavor Flav separately around to his home to listen to their music and see whether there was any potential for a musical collaboration. Meltzer recalls a memorable occasion when Flav was working at Miles's home: "Miles was living in a duplex on Central Park West. Upstairs was Flavor Flav, who was working on some music with Deron Johnson. Downstairs was one of Miles's girlfriends. Quincy [Jones] and Claude Nobs [founder and promoter of the Montreux Jazz Festival] were also there, trying to get Miles to agree to do a Montreux show featuring the old Gil Evans music."[6]

Miles spent much of the time moving between the two floors, checking out the music with Flav and Johnson while simultaneously negotiating a fee for the Montreux concert with Jones and Nobs. Meltzer continues: "At the end of the evening, Flavor came downstairs, kissing and hugging everybody and saying goodnight. When Flavor hugged Claude, Miles said (and to this day I'm still not sure whether it was tongue-in-cheek or not) 'What are you hugging and kissing him for? That's a white motherfucker. What are you kissing him for?' And Flavor looked at him and said 'Miles. There is no other – there is only brother.' And Miles went 'Agh!' Bam! It was as if he had been hit with a good left hook."

The *Doo-Bop* album was recorded at Unique Recording Studios, located on the top three floors of the Cecil B. DeMille building on 47th Street and Seventh Avenue in the heart of Manhattan. Most of the sessions took place in Studio B, which included a twelve-foot by six-foot vocal booth. However, the mixing and some overdubbing was done in Studio A. The sessions were intimate affairs and often only Miles, Mo Bee and an engineer were present.

The engineers who recorded and mixed almost all of *Doo-Bop* were D'Anthony Johnson (no relation to Deron Johnson) and Eric Lynch. Johnson had worked before with Mo Bee and the men had become good friends. Lynch was drafted in by Johnson after the latter found that other commitments clashed with the *Doo-Bop* sessions. Studio B was set up like a live performance room, says Johnson: "We treated Miles's horn like it would be a vocal and so we had a basic vocal set-up. We treated it like it was Chaka Khan singing and let Miles do his thing."

Mo Bee says much of the music was composed before they arrived at Unique. "Believe it or not, I came with a bunch of tracks that were already created and Miles said yea to some and nay to others. 'The Doo-Bop Song' was an instrumental and he liked it straight away. 'Mystery' was another. 'Sonya' was already created before he accepted it." Most of the recording sessions began in the early evening and would usually start with Mo Bee using an SP1200/S900 drum machine and sampler combo to lay down the beats of the backing track for Miles to play over. After Miles had played his part, Johnson would put down some additional keyboards followed by any vocals.

Lynch recalls his first meeting with Miles, which was on a session for the track "Sonya." "You always hear about Miles and his temper; however, from day one, you never saw that side of him. He was cordial and polite," he says. An illustration of Miles's good mood occurred when he came to the studio and wanted to go into the vocal booth with his horn and try something out. "So now, it was time to get ready for Miles to record," says Lynch.

Lynch began putting together a microphone set-up while the backing track was playing in the studio. As the music was being played over the studio monitors, Miles began blowing his horn over it and Lynch assumed that Miles was simply warming up for a take. "So I'm doing the usual engineer thing, getting a nice sound before tape and Miles is playing and it sounds really nice. The song plays through – all six minutes of it – and so I'm now ready to record and Miles turns and says 'Let me hear that back.' So I had the pleasure of telling Miles that I wasn't recording and I thought 'This is where I get the Miles Davis attitude,' but he just said 'You didn't get it? All right, I'll do it again.' And from that day on, if anyone stepped into the vocal booth for any reason at all they'd get recorded!"

Spero says Miles and Mo Bee became very close during the recording sessions. "The chemistry was really with Miles and Mo Bee. I would go by the studio and they were just doing their thing. Mo Bee would lay the beats. There wouldn't be a tremendous amount of overdubs on it and Miles would go into the vocal booth with the horn and play it like a vocal. He was riding the beat like an MC would. He would pull the melody out of the beat and just created it with the horn. It felt so very freestyle [improvised]. It didn't feel like anyone was sitting down and writing these compositions. Mo was playing the beat and Miles was feeling it and he was just spitting out on the trumpet what he felt melodically. A lot that stuff was very raw. You had the raw track with Miles over it and you mixed it. It was very similar to the way we were making hip-hop records at the time." Mo Bee says he learned a lot from playing with Miles. "One thing I learned is that you don't have to always be perfect. Some of your imperfect qualities can become standout features. And the way he would just throw off notes, like on 'High Speed Chase,' he got some notes up there that are so abstract."

Meltzer describes how much Miles enjoyed doing the sessions: "The thing that Miles loved is that he would listen to the tape once or twice and then say

'Okay I'm ready.' And then he'd have the headphones on and he'd have the horn and he'd blow the track all the way through. Then we'd play it back and listen and a couple of times he said 'That's it,' and a couple of times he said 'Do it again.' But nothing was mixed. There was no mixing out of two takes. The whole tune was blown in one take and that's how he wanted it and he was very happy. That's how *Doo-Bop* got built and then came the mixing and the fixing and the sweetening."

However, Lynch says recording an acoustic instrument, such as the trumpet over an electronic backing track with a steady beat, was a challenge: "It was definitely something new. It was a challenge because every bar that Miles played had a different shape, a different feeling. With R&B and hip-hop music you're working with complete choruses, complete bars, complete hooks and when you're mixing for R&B songs you create two environments, a hook and a verse. But when Miles was playing you had to be aware that in any moment you could get a completely different feeling and you have to mix to his playing."

D'Anthony Johnson recalls how happy Miles was at the sessions. "I just think he loved being back in New York again – it was his kinda town. He'd be hanging out with the [hip-hop] guys and there would be times when he would talk to us about the old days and tell us about Coltrane and Quincy and others. And if there was downtime in the studio, he would sit and draw in his sketch pad."

Miles and Mo Bee recorded six tracks together and, around the end of July, Miles was preparing to fly back to the West Coast to resume touring. Lynch says: "Miles didn't hear the final mixes, except for 'The Doo-Bop Song,' which was finished while he was here, but he did hear the rough mixes with the trumpet and the raps." Johnson adds: "Miles always took the rough mixes home with him. The rough mixes were still good mixes and he was happy with everything."

Lynch recalls his last meeting with Miles. "I remember coming into the studio and saying hello to Miles and he said he was going back to L.A. and was then coming back. He went to L.A. and never came back." Mo Bee also remembers the last time he saw Miles. "We were in Studio A and Miles was in a good mood. He was in the booth recording and he was telling me 'I got my girl coming by.' He had two white girls come by the studio. He was in the booth, cutting it up and playing around and joking and lifting his shirt and showing his chest."

But Mo Bee had noticed occasions when the energy seemed to slip away from Miles. "Even in the sessions where he was playing around, there always came a time when he would say 'Right, Easy, I'm getting tired. That's it for today, I'm not playing anymore.' He would become tired and lethargic. The last time I was with Miles, Gordon came up to me and said 'Okay, Easy. That's it for today. Miles has got to go out of town on the tour, we'll see you again.' That was the last time I saw him. Then they called and told me he was in hospital and then they told me he had died."

The times when Miles would get tired in the studio brought back memories of Mo Bee's initial visit to Miles's home. "You know, the first time when I thought he could be sick or physically going through anything was the first time he had invited me to his apartment. For a while he was standing up or sitting on the couch and listening to my music. And then after a while he let me control the tape deck. I had my back to him and I was changing tapes and really into the music. After a while I looked back over my shoulder and Miles was lying there on the couch, with his arm across his forehead like he had a headache. I remember going over to him and saying 'Miles, are you all right? You okay?' and he just lay there so I kept playing the music. Then I went back again and asked if he was all right and he said 'That's it for today. Just leave the tapes. I'll listen to them later.'" Mo Bee quietly left the room and, glancing back, saw Miles lying on the couch, alone, vulnerable and sick.

Not long after Miles finished playing the last gig of his U.S. tour, at the Hollywood Bowl in Los Angeles on August 25, he was hospitalized. For years Miles had suffered from various physical ailments, including diabetes and sickle cell anaemia. He also had problems with his hip joints and suffered from bouts of pneumonia. So it wasn't unusual for Miles to go into hospital, which explains why no one was unduly worried about his latest visit, least of all Miles who told people he was merely going in for a tune-up. One of Miles's visitors was Marcus Miller. "I got a message that Miles had asked for me and wanted me to do something on the hip-hop album he was making," recalls Miller. "When I saw Miles in hospital he was playing mixes of the *Doo-Bop* material and I said to him 'You have got to get better man, because I've got some ideas for this thing.' It didn't happen of course, but I'm so glad that Miles wanted me involved."

Miles's condition deteriorated and he had a stroke before falling into a coma. He died a few weeks later on September 28, 1991 at the St John's Hospital and Health Care Center in Santa Monica. Miles's death certificate records that he died as a result of a stroke, pneumonia and respiratory failure, although this hasn't stopped rumours suggesting that he died from an AIDS-related condition.

Miles's death sent shock waves around the world and those who had only recently seen Miles were extremely shocked. "He was still very beautiful and looked very healthy. I was surprised when he passed away," says Spero. Miles's death hit Mo Bee especially hard because he felt they were on the verge of a long and fruitful musical partnership. "I was real sad when he died. Before he died he told me: 'Easy, you want to take your shit on the road with me? I want you. You gonna tour with me.' I said 'What? [Take] my SP 1200 and all that and come on the stage with you?' He said 'Yeah.' I was so sad because I thought it would probably have evolved into more albums, more songs and just touring with him would have exposed me to so much more of the jazz world."

Although Miles had planned working with a range of musicians, his failing health and touring commitments had left little time for any actual collaboration. In the summer, Miles had also met hip-hop producer Sid Reynolds and they had even spent time together at Miles's home. "He was doing splash art, which was splashing paint on to a large canvas. The paintings looked simple to do, but when he explained how they were put together it was pretty difficult," says Reynolds. The two men also met at Unique Studios one day, along with the female rapper Nikki D, although nothing was recorded on that occasion.

However, Miles and Reynolds were due to record two tracks together, "Time Frame" and "Mr. Cool." Both tracks were going to feature a young female rapper from Brooklyn called Ces Nieves. She had a day job as a swimming-pool attendant at the apartment building where Miles lived. Miles used to go swimming there and that was how he and Nieves got acquainted. Nieves, who was also a dancer, wanted to get into the music business and it seems that Miles was prepared to help her achieve that goal. "There were talks about using Nikki D but Miles had Ces and wanted me to include her on the project," recalls Reynolds. "Nikki laid a rough vocal at one of the sessions, but Miles told me to put Ces on the tracks instead of Nikki. Ces laid vocals on the 'Time Frame' track and Nikki was on 'Mr Cool.' Ces had lyrics ready to 'Mr Cool,' which were definitely gonna be used instead of Nikki's lyrics."

Reynolds cut the two backing tracks at Chung King Studios in New York, but Miles got sick and never played on them. Reynolds describes the music as having the "same feel as Mo Bee's music. It had a more jazzy essence but was still hip-hop. I'd even included a sample from a Donald Byrd record, which Miles really liked."

Miles's death also meant that plans to work with John Bigham had never progressed much further than the drawing board. "The week Miles went to the hospital, John was supposed to be in the studio with Miles. We had finished the Hollywood Bowl show and everyone was staying in L.A. and Miles was at his house in Malibu," explains Meltzer. "John lived in L.A. and on Monday we had studio time booked and John came up to Miles's house but Miles felt too sick. John came back Tuesday and Miles had bought a new big-screen TV and didn't want to go. And then on the Wednesday or Thursday, Miles went into hospital."

John Bigham adds: "We already had the working relationship. So it was like, 'We're off the road and we need some songs' or 'This is what I'm working on, have you got any music?' I was always writing tunes for Miles. I remember writing him some music for a John Lennon tribute in Japan. He took some music I did for him on a DAT [digital tape], which he played over, although I have never heard him play it."

Bigham says that *Doo-Bop* was a work in progress. "I don't even remember what tracks I had for him. I had tracks but they were so early in the developmental stages. We hadn't recorded them yet, except maybe I had them on a cassette." Bigham describes the confusion on the day Miles was hospitalized: "The day he went into the hospital, we were supposed to meet at his house. So I was at his house with my friend Jillian and we're sitting out there waiting for him to come home. He had apparently gone in for a routine check-up because he had bouts of pneumonia all the time. He'd go out on a tour and come home and be exhausted. So it was quite a regular thing for him to go to the hospital, I certainly wasn't too worried about it. I talked to Gordon Meltzer who said 'He's at the hospital and he's gonna be back later on today so hang loose.' Later on I got a call saying they've checked him in. I never saw him again."

Even the tracks Prince had sent to Miles were unfinished. The music supplied by Prince had its roots in a project called Madhouse.[7] Madhouse was essentially a collaboration between Prince and his saxophonist Eric Leeds playing a set of jazz-inspired tunes. The Madhouse project was shrouded in secrecy and when the first album, 8, was released in January 1987, the album sleeve contained no personnel information, and to throw everyone off the scent there was even a reference to the fictitious Madhouse studios in Pittsburgh. Even the eight tracks on the album were simply titled "One" to "Eight." A second Madhouse album, 16 (with tunes entitled "nine" to "sixteen"), was released in late 1987, although this time it was more funk-orientated and featured several more musicians. In June 1988, Prince started work on a planned third Madhouse album to be called (not surprisingly) 24. But for a variety of reasons, this album would be shelved, even though Prince had prepared the basic tracks.

But these tracks would not be wasted. In January 1991, Prince sent Miles a number of tunes on a 24-track tape for consideration, including four from the aborted 24 album. The 24-track recordings consisted of Prince playing a variety of instruments, with several tracks left free for Miles's horn. Prince's idea was that once Miles had recorded his parts he would return the tapes to Prince for mixing and sweetening. The songs Prince had sent to Miles from the aborted 24 project were "17" (now re-named "Penetration"), "18" ("R U Legal Yet?"), "19" ("Jailbait") and "20" ("A Girl and Her Puppy").[8]

Prince had certainly sent Miles an eclectic mix of music. The strongest number, "Penetration," was a mid-tempo funk track with a catchy riff. "R U Legal Yet?" was a frantic, edgy tune that rushed along at breakneck speed, while "Jailbait" was a laid-back, 12-bar blues. The title "A Girl and Her Puppy" perfectly describes the tune, a syrupy ballad with a strong melody. Incidentally, both of the Madhouse album sleeves had featured a picture of a woman playing with a puppy.

But Miles would not touch Prince's 24-track recordings. Instead he opted to rehearse the tunes with his band live on-stage and then record them with the band. Those fortunate enough to attend one of several gigs Miles played in Germany and Switzerland between 13 March and 26 March 1991 were amongst the privileged few who ever got to hear the Prince tunes being played live. A gig at the Stadhalle in Gutersloh, Germany, on March 13 was especially memorable because it would be the only time when Miles and his band would play four Prince tunes in the same set. More unusually, Kenny Garrett, who normally played alto sax and flute, played a deep, growling baritone sax on "Jailbait" and "R U Legal Yet?" and soprano sax on "A Girl and Her Puppy." At the start of "A Girl and Her Puppy" Miles announced that: "On our next album, Prince wrote four songs. We played three of them, this is the fourth."

Not long after that gig, only "Penetration" would remain in Miles's set. A comparison between Prince's original backing tracks and the music played by Miles and his band shows that Miles kept close to Prince's original arrangements, although the live versions pack more punch and sound better by being played with live instruments rather than the drum machines that dominated Prince's versions.

On the evening of March 27, 1991, Miles took his band into the Bauer Studios in Ludwigsburg, Germany, to record several of the Prince tracks, most probably, "Penetration," "Jailbait" and "A Girl and Her Puppy." "After one of those shows he went to a nice little studio and the band was like 'Couldn't we just go to bed?'" recalls Meltzer. "Miles said 'No, we're going to go to the studio and we're going to record this and you motherfuckers are going to be on my record.'" But the session was not as productive as Miles had hoped, adds Meltzer. "We went to the studio and Miles was so weak and sick he just couldn't play. He did play what he called guide tracks. He felt too weak to play really well enough for a record and he said 'I'm just going to blow a little and we'll take these tapes back to New York and we'll use them as a guide for when I can really play.' Matt Pierson [then head of Warner Bros jazz] told me Warner Bros cleaned up the tapes and processed them and that some of them were okay and decent."

In fact, Prince was asked if several of the tunes could be included on *Doo-Bop*, but he refused to grant permission. By this time, the relationship between Prince and Warner Bros had deteriorated badly[9] and this may help explain his reluctance to give his approval, but it could also be that Prince felt that the tracks were simply not up to standard. Sadly, Prince's refusal to include the tracks even on the (abandoned) Miles boxed-set retrospective, *The Last Word*, means that at the time of writing few people have had the opportunity to judge for themselves.

Miles's death meant that, ironically, the problem of having too much material for the *Doo-Bop* album had now become an issue of having too little. Miles had recorded just six tracks with Mo Bee, Prince was refusing to release his music and the rest of the music planned for *Doo-Bop* either hadn't been recorded or Miles had never got around to recording his parts. Fortunately, a piece of lateral thinking would present a way out of the impasse. "It wasn't my idea, it was my wife's, Dorothy Weber [who was also one of Miles's lawyers]," says Meltzer. "I remember walking down the street with her and saying 'This is really terrible because we've now got an EP – we don't have an LP.' It was about the time that Natalie Cole had just done an album with her Dad's music. Dorothy said 'Why don't you do something like that? The first time you took Easy Mo Bee's music and Miles played on it. Why don't you take Miles's music and have somebody play on it?'

The album Meltzer refers to was Natalie Cole's *Unforgettable With Love*, a tribute to her father Nat King Cole released in the summer of 1991 and which saw Cole use studio technology to perform a "duet" with her late father on the title track. More controversially, five years after the death of Jimi Hendrix in 1970, producer Alan Douglas created a series of new albums (including *Crash Landing* and *Midnight Lightning*) by taking original Hendrix recordings and using session musicians to build new music around them.

Meltzer admits that business considerations also called for the situation to be resolved. "I was concerned about the royalty rates – not for me because I didn't have any points [which determine whether you get royalties] – but for Miles's family and [feared] that Warners wouldn't put it out. We didn't make an ambitious record in *Doo-Bop*. We didn't know what the hell to do. We had part of a record and we wanted to make it a real record and part of that is a business decision because without an LP Warners was going to treat it like shit and the family wouldn't get the royalty money."

Lynch recalls how the atmosphere in the studio became highly charged after Miles's death. "When Miles passed away it became very stressful here. You had a lot of people coming out of the woodwork trying to put their two cents into a record that had been controlled by Miles and Mo Bee. The record company people started coming in and saying what they wanted the record to sound like. When Miles was around we didn't have any problems. It was just a communication between Miles and Mo and how they wanted the sound. You now had to deal with other voices. You had new people in the studio and there were a couple of times when they tried to remix songs. It just got very stressful at that point."

But Weber's inspired suggestion had offered a way of dealing with the shortage of suitable material for *Doo-Bop*. "I thought it was a good idea and went to the Warners people and said 'What do you have in the vaults?'" says Meltzer. Warner Bros had the *Rubberband* sessions (recorded in late 1985 and early 1986) in the vaults, plus a number of concerts that had been recorded during 1986. There was also a sprinkling of unused tracks from various sessions, such as John Bigham's "Digg That" and "Maze" from sessions held in September 1985. But none of this music in its current state would have fitted well with the hip-hop tunes played by Miles and Mo Bee.

Meltzer also approached Miles's estate, which now had control over Miles's music and it approved of the strategy. Matt Pierson also became closely involved in the project, taking on the role of associate producer alongside Meltzer. Adam Holzman, Miles's ex-musical director and who had played on the *Rubberband* sessions, helped Meltzer select the music to be used for the additional tracks. "Adam really knew the music and that's when I said 'Adam, let's listen to all this unreleased stuff and come up with some things that are going to work'," says Meltzer.

When Meltzer and Holzman examined Warner Bros' tape archives, the tunes from what became known as the *Rubberband* sessions seemed to offer the best potential. After sifting through the most promising tracks from these sessions, Meltzer and Holtzman selected two pieces, "Give It Up" and (probably) "Let's Fly Away," which Mo Bee would use to construct two new tracks. Mo Bee recalls: "They [Meltzer and Pierson] gave me two unreleased songs. They said 'We're looking for you to remix these songs and these two songs plus six will make a complete album.'" After Mo Bee had completed the two new tracks, *Doo-Bop*'s running time was now extended to forty minutes. At last, *Doo-Bop* was now a complete album, but its release in 1992 would result in Miles generating yet more controversy, even from beyond the grave.

The tracks

All tracks recorded at Unique Recording Studios.

"Mystery" (3:55)

Composers	Easy Mo Bee and Miles Davis
	Includes a sample of "Running Away" by Chocolate Milk
Musicians	Miles, trumpet; Easy Mo Bee, keyboards, samples; Deron Johnson, keyboards
Producer	Easy Mo Bee
Associate producers	Gordon Meltzer, Matt Pierson
Executive producer	Gordon Meltzer
Arranger	Easy Mo Bee
Date of recording	c. July 1991
Engineer	D'Anthony Johnson
Mixed by	D'Anthony Johnson
Live performances	None

"Mystery" was one of the tunes Easy Mo Bee had composed before his meeting with Miles and one that the trumpeter was keen to play on. It was also the first tune they recorded together. The title "Mystery" came from a feature of the tune. "Miles didn't name one single song on the album," explains Mo Bee. "After we had done a song I would ask him 'What do you want to call this, Miles?' and he'd say 'I don't know. What the fuck are you asking me for?'"

So Mo Bee decided to name it after a sustained note that runs through the entire track and can be heard almost as soon as the music starts – you can hear it as a high note dancing over the opening electric piano/bass sound. "That tone just held there and hovered over the track," he says. "It just hung there and didn't change and to me it created like a mysterious vibe." "Mystery" begins with a gentle electric piano/bass riff, with Miles entering almost immediately on muted horn. Then a bass drum and ride cymbal drum loop kicks in, playing throughout almost the entire track, giving it an acid jazz feel. "Mystery" is one of the most melodic tunes on the album and Miles plays beautifully, pulling strong melodies from the beat – there is a lot of feeling in his playing.

Towards the end of the tune, a funky keyboard riff adds extra support to the backing track, before the music subsides and then stops. "Mystery" is one of the most successful collaborations between Miles's horn and hip-hop music, and anyone who thinks that hip-hop and jazz can't mix should have a good listen to this tune. And when you listen to the intensity of Miles's playing, you can hear that he treated hip-hop as seriously as he did the music from his other eras. Miles was clearly not just going through the motions or simply trying to be hip – he cared far too much about the music ever to do that.

"The Doo-Bop Song" (5:00)

Composers	Easy Mo Bee and Miles Davis
	Includes samples from "Summer Madness" by Kool & The Gang, "The Fishing Hole" (Theme from *The Andy Griffith Show*), "Running Away" by Chocolate Milk and "La-Di-Da-Di" by Slick Rick
Musicians	Miles, trumpet; Easy Mo Bee, keyboards, samples; Deron Johnson, keyboards; Rappin' Is Fundamental, vocals
Producer	Easy Mo Bee
Associate producers	Gordon Meltzer, Matt Pierson
Executive producer	Gordon Meltzer
Arranger	Easy Mo Bee
Date of recording	c. July 1991
Engineer	D'Anthony Johnson
Mixed by	D'Anthony Johnson
Live performances	None

Easy Mo Bee's group Rappin' Is Fundamental (RIF), which included rappers A. B. Money and JR, had developed a style of singing that combined doo-wop with hip-hop. Doo-wop is the street corner/staircase style of singing that became popular in the 1950s with artists such as The Platters, The Flamingos, and Frankie Lymon and the Teenagers. "The style of what we did we called it doo-hop because we sang doo-wop and we rapped," says Mo Bee. "We created a new word right there." RIF would go on to record an album called *Doo-Hop* on A&M Records in 1991.

Mo Bee then coined another new word doo-bop, when it came to recording the tune with Miles. "You have hip-hop, a style of jazz bebop and doo-wop. When we worked with Miles and jazz it was my idea to take it a little further and call it doo-bop." Before playing the tune with Miles, RIF had sung, harmonized and rapped on "The Doo-Bop Song" at home and the group had planned to record it one day. But then Miles decided he wanted to use it. However, "My group liked it so much that I got the idea to sing on it and Miles was cool on it," says Mo Bee.

"The Doo-Bop Song" has a lazy, relaxed feeling and that's because its inspiration is a tune by Kool & The Gang called "Summer Madness." Although Kool & The Gang are best known as a dance/funk band, with hits such as "Jungle Boogie," "Hollywood Swinging" and "Ladies Night," the group began life as a jazz quartet, The Jazziacs, with its main influences being John Coltrane, Thelonious Monk and Miles. "Summer Madness," which first appeared on the band's 1974 album *Light Of Worlds*, has become something of a classic and saw the band returning to its jazz roots.

"Summer Madness" is a mellow jazz instrumental that begins with a soft electric piano riff, followed by some gentle guitar figures and a thundering electric bass that sounds more like an upright bass. The tune also includes sweeping synthesizers, a catchy series of ascending notes played on a synthesizer and some fine jazz guitar playing. All combine to create a truly evocative piece and it's no surprise to find that others have been inspired to use the music including DJ Jazzy Jeff and Fresh Prince (aka the actor Will Smith), who sampled "Summer Madness" for their 1991 hit "Summertime." The hip-hop/house violinist Jerald Daemyon recorded a cover version (complete with rap) in 1996.

The opening electric piano riff on "Summer Madness" forms the basis of the melody for "The Doo-Bop Song" (listen closely and you can hear it being played continuously on top of a drum track that was itself in part inspired by the track "You're A Customer" by rap duo EPMD). "The Doo-Bop Song" starts with the electric piano/drum track combination and almost immediately Miles joins in on muted horn. Miles plays with feeling and with great economy – not a note is wasted and he leaves plenty of space between each phrase. Miles plays for almost a minute before being joined by backing vocals singing the chorus "just taking that doo-bop sound." Miles plays some more before JR sings the first verse. Each member of Rappin' Is Fundamental wrote his own lyrics and, although the printed song lyrics for the opening verse talk about Miles's music being around for a long time, JR actually raps about Miles being around for a long while, an ironic statement in view of the fact that Miles would be dead in less than three months after these words were recorded.

JR's lyrics pay homage to Miles, who is described as a "multi-talented and gifted musician." The chorus is sung again although this time "with Miles Davis" added at the end of the last line and sung in doo-wop style. A. B. Money then takes over the next verse with Mo Bee coming in on the third, with lyrics that describe the uniqueness of Miles's style. In one line, Mo Bee talks about the 1960s American situation comedy *The Andy Griffith Show* and then whistles the theme song. "We had to clear that as a sample just because I whistled the theme. It's still sampling!" recalls Mo Bee. Mo Bee's rap is followed by the chorus, which is repeated until the fadeout.

The quality of rapping on the *Doo-Bop* album has been dismissed by some critics as banal, who argue that the lyrics do little more than glorify Miles, but such criticism overlooks the fact that rap covers a wide spectrum of styles and content. Rap can be frivolous (for example, Sugarhill Gang's "Rapper's Delight"), serious (Grandmaster Flash and the Furious 5 "The Message"), overtly sexual (2 Live Crew "Me So Horny") or controversial (Ice-T "Cop Killer").

In the case of the *Doo-Bop* album, the members of RIF simply opted to pay homage to Miles. "There were the critics who like hip-hop but who felt that it was just so self-aggrandising, you know with Easy saying Miles's names over again in some of the raps. You know Eminem does it today and nobody says he's self-aggrandising because maybe as society as evolved, Miles was just a little ahead of his time! If the evolution of society can be tracked by hip-hop, Miles was way ahead. Miles liked it: 'I'm an old dude and here's this young guy rapping my name and let the kids hear it'," says Meltzer.

Fortunately it is possible to hear what "The Doo-Bop Song" sounds without the rapping thanks to "The Doo-Bop Song" being released as a single (there are two CD versions and a 12-inch vinyl record). Five mixes were released (although only one of the CDs has all five; a second CD and the 12-inch single have four each) including an extended version that lasts 6:50 (it was extended by repeating one of the sections from the album version).

Two other mixes are edits but there is also an instrumental version of the album track, which only retains the chorus parts. And while the instrumental version sounds good, it definitely lacks something without the rapping. A video was also made of this tune, featuring the three members of RIF performing while images of Miles were projected on a video screen behind them.

"Chocolate Chip" (4:38)

Composers	Easy Mo Bee, Miles Davis and Donald Hepburn Includes samples from "Bumpin' On Young Street" by Young-Holt Unlimited and "Thanks For Everything" by Pleasure
Musicians	Miles, trumpet; Easy Mo Bee, keyboards, samples; Deron Johnson, keyboards, samples
Producer	Easy Mo Bee
Associate producers	Gordon Meltzer, Matt Pierson
Executive producer	Gordon Meltzer
Arranger	Easy Mo Bee
Date of recording	c. July 1991
Engineer	D'Anthony Johnson
Mixed by	D'Anthony Johnson
Live performances	None

"Chocolate Chip" is the heaviest number on the album, with a rhythm section that sounds like a giant sumo wrestler or heavyweight boxer lumbering into a ring. Miles's trumpet dances around, its melody ducking and diving, swerving and weaving on top of and around the heavy backbeat. The contrast between the powerful groove and Miles's melodic trumpet sound is especially sharp on this number. Deron Johnson's contribution is most noticeable on this track, with some James Brown-style funky rhythm guitar at around the 30-second mark and some delightful comping just before the three-minute point.

At around the one-minute mark, a sample loop from "Bumpin' On Young Street" by Young-Holt Unlimited is added. "I got the main groove going and then changed the beat and threw in a sample before going back. It always had to be a smooth transition," says Mo Bee. The combination of a raw sound, a powerful groove and Miles's nimble trumpet playing makes "Chocolate Chip" one of the most satisfying collaborations on *Doo-Bop*.

"Blow" (5:08)

Composers	Easy Mo Bee and Miles Davis Includes a sample of "Give It Up Or Turn It Loose" by James Brown
Musicians	Miles, trumpet; Easy Mo Bee, keyboards, vocals, samples; Deron Johnson, keyboards, samples
Producer	Easy Mo Bee
Associate producers	Gordon Meltzer, Matt Pierson
Executive producer	Gordon Meltzer
Arranger	Easy Mo Bee

Date of recording	c. July 1991
Engineer	D'Anthony Johnson
Mixed by	Matthew "Boomer" Lamonica
Live performances	None

On the album credits "Blow" is said to contain a sample from James Brown's "Give It Up Or Turn It Loose," but, as Mo Bee explains, Brown's tune forms the basis of the whole track. "'Blow' is based upon James Brown's 'Give It Up Or Turn It Loose,'" he says. "There's an original version, made in the late '60s on King Records and a second version made in the 1970s on Polydor. The one I took was the Polydor version. We brought it up an octave or so higher." "Give It Up Or Turn It Loose" is a classic James Brown tune, dominated by a highly infectious rhythm guitar riff that gets under your skin, with just drums and bass in support. This trio of instruments is occasionally joined by a series of short stabs from a horn section and added on top of all this are Brown's trademark explosive vocals, complete with grunts, screams and yelps.

It is more than fitting that James Brown should be the inspiration of a hip-hop tune played by Miles, as the latter had been a long-time admirer of Brown's music. In the 1970s, the music of James Brown, Sly Stone, Aretha Franklin and Motown had inspired Miles to play funk in order to reach young black kids,[10] and Miles says that he was thinking about Sly Stone and James Brown when he entered the studio to record the *On The Corner* album.[11] "I love James Brown because of all the great rhythms he plays," Miles said.[12]

What is more, Brown is one of the most sampled artists in the history of hip-hop music, with more than 650 samples taken from just a dozen of Brown's tunes. The drum pattern from just one James Brown number, "Funky Drummer," has appeared on more than 150 tracks.[13] Miles had even borrowed the bass line from Brown's "Say It Loud, I'm Black And I'm Proud" for the track "Yesternow" from the album *Jack Johnson*.

"Blow" starts with an answer-machine message from Miles declaring that: "Easy Mo Bee and Miles Davis are gonna blow." The message was actually taken from Miles's personal answer machine. Miles had given Mo Bee his home number and Mo Bee would occasionally call Miles and play his music over the phone. When Mo Bee called one day he was greatly surprised when he heard the answer-machine message. "He must have really been impressed with me because the take-home demo version of 'Blow' formed the greeting of his answer machine. He had that playing in the background and that was his greeting. I said 'Aw man, that's it! Everybody who knows Miles Davis, from Lionel Hampton to Marcus Miller or whoever is calling his house, and now they know about me!' He thought of me and what we did in the studio that much that he put it on his answer machine." The idea to use the message at the start of "Blow" was Gordon Meltzer's.

Straight after the answer-machine message, the heavy backbeat of the rhythm track kicks in, with Miles's playing on top of it. Miles's playing is accompanied by what sounds like a sampled saxophone, which pans between the left and right speakers. This sound was probably produced by Deron Johnson, along with a number of keyboard textures that are buried in the mix. Mo Bee starts rapping soon after the intro, informing the listener that "Here I am, Easy Mo Bee, kickin' it loud with the legendary Miles Davis." Mo Bee also refers to Miles as "chief," a name used by many of Miles's musicians.

Although many elements are missing from "Give It Up Or Turn It Loose" (including of course Brown's vocals) both tracks have the same tempo and feel. "Blow" is one of the album tracks with the greatest commercial potential, so it was no surprise that it was chosen as the first single from the album. "Blow" was released as a 12-inch single and a CD single, with the latter containing additional mixes. The singles contain a series of remixes and edits. Mo Bee produced one remix entitled "New Orleans Hip-Hop Mix," which also featured vocals from fellow rapper JR. The remix features a different rap, along with some scratching effects and additional keyboards. There is also an edited version of this remix.

More radical remixes were produced by remix specialists David Shaw and Winston Brown (both had worked together on Chaka Khan's 1989 album *Life Is A Dance – The Remix Project*). Shaw and Brown created three remixes, a "Shadowzone Extended Club Mix," an "R&B Mix" and an "Extended Mix." The remixes added vocals from Karen Pernod and Cathy Brown, as well as piano, scratching effects and other additional keyboards. Shaw and Smith also gave more punch to the sound, with an even heavier backbeat than the original, a more upfront bass line, and, on the "Shadowzone" mix, open high-hat samples.

The CD single also features the album version minus the rap and a track called "Miles Alone." The latter isolates Miles's horn track so all you hear is Miles playing alone with no accompanying backing track. The two-minute track shows that Miles was in good lip, with strong tone and control. And the fact that Miles would be dead in less than three months after making this recording adds some pathos to the naked sound of his trumpet.

"Sonya" (5:29)

Composers	Easy Mo Bee and Miles Davis
Musicians	Miles, trumpet; Easy Mo Bee, keyboards, samples; Deron Johnson, keyboards, samples
Producer	Easy Mo Bee
Associate producers	Gordon Meltzer, Matt Pierson
Executive producer	Gordon Meltzer
Arranger	Easy Mo Bee

Date of recording	c. July 1991
Engineer	Eric Lynch
Mixed by	Eric Lynch
Live performances	None

It was Mo Bee's girlfriend at the time who inspired the song's title. "I thought it was real pretty and so I named it after her," he explains. "Skyy drummer Tom McConnell had a studio downtown [New York] and I originally recorded it there. I was hoping to get the tune on an album of the late Gwen Guthrie, but it never got accepted. When I played it to Miles he loved it." Mo Bee played all the music on the demo track, laying down a piano track and strings, along with a strong bass line. "I really wanted a solid slap bass – I wanted it to sound like a real bass. I used a keyboard bass. As I was putting the track together, I had no idea what I was creating," adds Mo Bee.

"Sonya" is one of the best tracks on *Doo-Bop* and Miles plays some of his strongest trumpet on this tune. The track starts without any introduction, with Miles and the rhythm track playing in unison. The dominant elements are the strong groove courtesy of the backing track, a powerful bass riff and Miles's imaginative and inventive trumpet playing. Playing underneath this are swirling synthesizer strings, a catchy synth line (it starts at around the 20-second mark and then disappears and reappears throughout the track) and some jazz-style playing on an electric piano by Deron Johnson. "Deron added some nice piano work, but everything else was created by me on the keyboards," says Mo Bee.

"Duke Booty" (4:53)

Composers	Easy Mo Bee and Miles Davis
	Contains a sample of "Jungle Strut" by Gene Ammons
Musicians	Miles, trumpet; Easy Mo Bee, keyboards, samples;
	Deron Johnson, keyboards, samples
Producer	Easy Mo Bee
Associate producers	Gordon Meltzer, Matt Pierson
Executive producer	Gordon Meltzer
Arranger	Easy Mo Bee
Date of recording	c. July 1991
Engineer	D'Anthony Johnson
Mixed by	D'Anthony Johnson
Live performances	None

Mo Bee named this track after rapper/producer Duke Bootee (real name Ed Fletcher), who was a session musician at Sugarhill Records (the label that released "Rapper's Delight" by The Sugarhill Gang). Bootee was also the driving force behind the hit record "The Message" by Grandmaster Flash and The Furious 5. In fact, Bootee and Miles had even appeared on an album together, *Sun City*, by Artists United Against Apartheid (both men were featured on the track "Let Me See Your ID"). "I always thought his name was cool. He must have been dookin' a lot of booty! It's one of the funkiest songs on the album; that's why I gave it a funky title," says Mo Bee. There was also another Miles connection via the sample used by Mo Bee, "Jungle Strut," which was written and performed by the tenor saxophonist Gene Ammons. Both Miles and Ammons had played together in Billy Eckstine's Orchestra, back in the late 1940s.

"Duke Booty" begins with Miles giving instructions to keyboardist Deron Johnson. "Deron, you're goin' to play behind me and then whatever...," but before he completes the sentence the music breaks in, a chugging rhythm track interspersed with a looped sample of the word "Strut." Once again Miles plays a muted horn, which is double-tracked in sections. Miles's playing is both strong and lyrical and at times he comes close to quoting the themes from "A-Tisket A-Tisket" (at around 1:04) and "Wrinkle" (4:00).

Deron Johnson's deft touches on the keyboard add many interesting textures to the sound and in one section he doubles up with Miles's horn (at one point Miles can be heard saying "Break it up, Deron"). Johnson's contribution deserves special mention because he never over-plays and the sonic backdrop he creates to support Miles's horn really enhances the tune. At the end of the track, the music comes to a stop, before a synthesizer finally fades out. Mo Bee isn't sure whether Duke Bootee was pleased to have this tune named after him, but on the aural evidence there is a very good chance that he would have appreciated the gesture.

"Mystery Reprise" (1:23)

Composers	Easy Mo Bee and Miles Davis
Musicians	Miles, trumpet; Easy Mo Bee, keyboards, samples; Deron Johnson, keyboards, samples
Producer	Easy Mo Bee
Associate producers	Gordon Meltzer, Matt Pierson
Executive producer	Gordon Meltzer
Arranger	Easy Mo Bee
Date of recording	c. late 1991/early 1992
Engineer	D'Anthony Johnson
Mixed by	D'Anthony Johnson
Live performances	None

In the days of the LP record, reprises were fairly common, particularly on albums by soul artists (such as Barry White and Marvin Gaye). The reprise was usually tucked away at the end of side two and marked the conclusion of a record. Mo Bee decided he wanted to use the same device on this album. "That was my idea. I really used to like that on an album. On an Earth, Wind & Fire album they used to do interesting things, like there would be a song on one side of the album and later on there would be a short version that was slightly different. I was just trying to make the album sophisticated. You don't see people doing stuff like that any more. I wanted to follow in the tradition of the great albums." So Mo Bee went back to the original master tape and decided to do a little overdubbing and editing.

"Mystery Reprise" opens with a fade-in of a cheering crowd followed by the same opening bars from the full version. "I wanted the cheering to give the effect of an audience calling for an encore," says Mo Bee. At the 34-second mark there is a sharp edit point where the closing keyboard riff is inserted followed by a series of edits of Miles's horn, to which some echo has been added. In less than a minute and a half, the track fades out.

"High Speed Chase" (4:40)

Composers	Easy Mo Bee, Miles Davis and Larry Mizell
	Contains horn track taken from "Give It Up,"
	written by Miles, Randy Hall and Zane Giles
	Contains sample from "Street Lady" by Donald Byrd
Musicians	Miles, trumpet; Easy Mo Bee, keyboards, samples
Producer	Easy Mo Bee
Associate producers	Gordon Meltzer, Matt Pierson
Executive producer	Gordon Meltzer
Arranger	Easy Mo Bee
Date of recording	c. late 1991/early 1992
Engineer	Eric Lynch
Mixed by	Eric Lynch
Live performances	None

With Miles dead and just six completed tracks in the can, *Doo-Bop*'s total playing time was little more than thirty minutes; enough, as Gordon Meltzer has said, for an EP but not enough for an LP. After trawling through Warner Bros' archives, Meltzer and Adam Holzman selected two tracks from the *Rubberband* sessions, which were then given to Mo Bee to develop. It was the solution to the problem of a shortage of material, but such practices also throw up serious ethical considerations, such as were the original composers consulted and did they approve? And was it right to issue music under the name of Miles Davis when he was no longer around to approve of it?

The tracks used to extend *Doo-Bop* were taken from sessions produced by Miles, Randy Hall and Zane Giles, and the trio also wrote the bulk of the material, including the two songs that were destined for *Doo-Bop*. Neither Giles or Hall knew anything about the decision to use their tracks until *Doo-Bop* was released and they read the credits and heard the horn tracks used on "High Speed Chase" and "Fantasy." If you look carefully at the album credits, you'll see that Hall, Giles and Reggie Dozier (who actually engineered the *Rubberband* sessions) are credited under "additional engineering." Hall and Giles were already upset over the fact that none of the music produced during their months in the studio with Miles had ever been released, with producer Tommy LiPuma deciding to use the music of George Duke and Marcus Miller on the album that became *Tutu*. When Hall and Giles heard *Doo-Bop* they were outraged.

"They were so wrong in what they did. They took tracks that we produced, and melodies that we wrote. A lot of times we would come up with the basic melody for the trumpet and Miles would embellish it. They also described me as an engineer – I had never been described as an engineer," says Giles. With admirable candour, Meltzer admits that mistakes were made. "In hindsight they should have had more credit. I'll confess to charging ahead ignorantly at the time and just saying 'Gee, these are tapes and it's Miles.' I didn't really give the thought to how these tapes came to be – I just knew I didn't like them. But they had Miles's trumpet. It was just Miles and I didn't give sufficient thought to who recorded this stuff and how much blood, sweat and tears went into getting these tapes into the can and into the hands of Warner Bros so that they could sit there and we could use them years later. I didn't even know at the time who had written, recorded or produced the stuff. I just knew we had clearance to use it."

Mo Bee was unaware of all the controversy behind the music. "I had no information as to where the music had come from and nor did I ask," he says. Meltzer adds that there was never any consideration given to releasing the original music complete. "It sounded so dated and terrible."

The other question is whether music that was never heard by Miles, let alone sanctioned by him for release, should ever have gone out under his name. Before going ahead with the plan to use the *Rubberband* tracks, Meltzer consulted the Miles Davis Estate, which comprised of Miles's sister Dorothy, brother Vernon, daughter Cheryl, youngest son Erin and nephew Vince Wilburn Jr. Meltzer is more comfortable about this decision. "Dorothy and Vince and Cheryl and Vernon said 'Make the record.' Erin was too young and in shock to really say anything. They handed me the authority to do it and that's what happened. As regard to stuff coming out without Miles approving the finished tracks, I swear that Miles would have loved it because that's where he was going and that's what he wanted. He would have been fine with it."

When Mo Bee first heard the music, he asked for Miles's horn track to be stripped away from the rest of the music and put on to a DAT digital tape. "I took the tape home and practised with it. I just let the horn play and kept trying to do different things. The number one rule when you're working with an acappella vocal or instrument is that whatever you put there has got to be in tune or it's not going to sound right. So I tried a couple of things and then came up with the final beat and said 'That's it.'"

"High Speed Chase" is one of Mo Bee's favourite tracks. "I like it because of the tempo. I was trying to make like a mood [you get] in an action movie – a high-speed car chase. You know when you look at the old movies and hear that background music they use when there's a police car chase? As soon as I heard the track I thought of that. That was created just for Miles."

A blast of horns creates a dramatic opening for this track and the effect is certainly reminiscent of soundtrack music. A sampled yelp, which is looped throughout the track, is joined by traffic sound effects (blaring horns, fast-moving cars and so on) and a frenetic rhythm track. The groove is based on "Street Lady," a track written by Larry Mizzell, which is why he shares co-writing credits with Miles and Mo Bee. Miles's muted horn enters around the 30-second mark and you can hear him playing the theme to the original track, "Give It Up" at the 33-second mark. The pounding rhythm track is augmented in sections by some fast, fluent keyboard playing and Miles's playing is both agile and strong. A looped saxophone sample appears just after the four-minute point, followed by some more nimble keyboard playing, before the track ends with some more car sound effects.

Mo Bee did an excellent job in marrying Miles's horn with the new backing track and, as Meltzer points out in *Doo-Bop*'s liner notes, it's hard to spot which are the two posthumous tracks. Mo Bee was also ably assisted by the engineers at Unique Studios in creating a seamless recording out of the old and new music tracks. D'Anthony Johnson describes the work involved in stripping off Miles's horn track and adding it to the new backing track: "We didn't have computers in those days and we had to use a SMPTE [time code] track to lock the horn track to a drum machine. With all the technology that's around today, this can be done fairly easily, but at the time it took a lot of hard work." Eric Lynch adds: " 'High Speed Chase' and 'Fantasy' were interesting tracks because they were part of another track and Miles's playing had all kinds of rhythm to it and so editing that track was tough. I think I edited like every alternate second of 'High Speed Chase.' It took me two days to complete it so it sounded like a solid performance."

"Fantasy" (4:30)

Composers	Easy Mo Bee and Miles Davis
	Contains horn track probably taken from "Let's Fly Away," written by Miles, Randy Hall and Zane Giles
	Contains a sample of "Love Pains" by Major Lance
Musicians	Miles, trumpet; Easy Mo Bee, keyboards, samples

Producer	Easy Mo Bee
Associate producers	Gordon Meltzer, Matt Pierson
Executive producer	Gordon Meltzer
Arranger	Easy Mo Bee
Date of recording	c. late 1991/early 1992
Engineer	Eric Lynch
Mixed by	Eric Lynch
Live performances	None

"Fantasy" was the second track created by Mo Bee after Miles's death and it starts with a long introduction comprised of a chugging rhythm track and synthesized strings that are used to create an orchestral-like effect. A strong bass line kicks in, adding weight to the sound. This is the only track on *Doo-Bop* where Miles plays open horn and for this reason its most likely origin is a track called "Let's Fly Away" from the *Rubberband* sessions. As on *Doo-Bop*, "Let's Fly Away" was the only track on the *Rubberband* sessions where Miles played open horn exclusively, although the mix destined for the aborted *Rubberband* album would use a different take.

While "High Speed Chase" was created as an instrumental, "Fantasy" features a sexually-charged rap from Mo Bee, who talks about his "big fat stick" and notes from Miles's horn "causing ladies get freaky like sex" – although the climax is in their minds rather than in their panties. "I guess I was kinda cocky back then!" says Mo Bee. "I was just basically telling people that I'm about. I never rapped about gangsta-ish things. To me rap always started off being bragado-ish [boastful]. I thought I hadn't got raunchy on this album yet so I'll pick this song to do that! There were a couple of women who commented about that! That song was geared towards the ladies to create a little bit of mystery. It was all just talk. Prince, Marvin Gaye and different people over the years had made sexy records."

It is good to hear Miles play without a mute and he performs with power and precision. It shouldn't be forgotten that when Miles originally recorded his horn part it was in late 1985, when he was at his peak in terms of energy and stamina, and it certainly shows on this track.

Doo-bop: the verdict

Doo-Bop was released in late 1992, almost a year after Miles's death. The album cover featured a picture of Miles taken by photographer Annie Liebovitz, who shot Miles against a backdrop of two large, brightly-coloured cushions and a couple of his paintings. Miles is naked from the waist up and looks very thin. He's wearing leopard skin-style trousers and sits with his legs wide apart, holding a red trumpet to his lips, staring at the camera without expression.

There are many parallels between *Doo-Bop* and the album *On The Corner*, which was released twenty years earlier. In both cases, Miles wanted to reach the same audience. "It was with *On The Corner*...that I really made an effort to get my music over to young black people,"[14] said Miles. Both Gordon Meltzer's sleeve notes for *Doo-Bop* and Columbia Record's press advertisements for *On The Corner* talked about Miles being influenced by the sound of the street, and the two albums were based around repetitive grooves over which Miles played. Last, but not least, the two albums sparked much controversy and criticism. Writer Paul Tingen's assessment that the tunes on *Doo-Bop* were "mostly bubblegum teenage music"[15] summed up the view of a number of critics.

"That album fell under the heaviest criticism," says Mo Bee. "The jazz purists and reviewers – some of them tore it to pieces. I guess it was because that whole collaboration, that hybrid hip-hop and jazz was very new. I guess the jazz purists didn't accept hip-hop making its way into jazz – they felt it had no place. But when you think about it, the early wild be-bop by Charlie Parker and Dizzy was also looked down upon and fell under as much criticism as hip-hop. So I kinda understood the criticism because these jazz purists have a certain idea of what jazz should be."

Some jazz critics might have preferred Miles to have created music that was closer to *Kind Of Blue* or *My Funny Valentine*, but Miles wanted to do hip-hop, adds Mo Bee. "There are tones of R&B on *Doo-Bop*. 'Sonya' is jazzy but has R&B overtones. 'Blow' was basically New Jack Swing [a mixture of R&B and hip-hop] when you really listen to the drum programming. 'High Speed Chase' sounds like some straight jazz. 'Chocolate Chip' was 70's hip jazz, the shit that Donald Byrd and the Blackbyrds and Ronnie Laws and different people were doing," says Mo Bee. "I didn't get too mad at the jazz purists because what did jazz purists ever think about Grover Washington Jr. when he did 'Mr. Magic'? Or Donald Byrd? Where else could Miles go? He had done everything else. Every other form he fused into music and even made up a couple of styles of his own. What the critics forget is that if people had never experimented, we wouldn't have had the records we have today. There has always got to be freedom for experimental."

Doo-Bop wasn't only just criticized by sections of the jazz establishment; some of those in the hip-hop sector were none too impressed either, recalls Mo Bee. "I fell under a lot of heavy hip-hop criticism too. I remember reading a reviewer who commented that my hip-hop jazz hybrid was more of a commercial pop type version of hip-hop jazz, like Greg Osby or Ronny Jordan. But Gangsta [rap] had dabbled with hip-hop jazz too and the hip-hop critics felt that *Doo-Bop* could have sounded more underground. But you know what, that was not what Miles wanted." Any artist who tries to fuse two disparate art forms always faces the danger of falling between two stools and being neither one thing nor the other. But Miles had faced the same issues when he had fused jazz with rock and with funk.

Disliking a piece of music is one thing, but some critics of *Doo-Bop* have a more fundamental objection to the album, namely that, like oil and water, jazz and hip-hop do not mix. Music critic Stuart Nicholson makes a strong case against the fusion of the two. "Ultimately, however, jazz and hip-hop can never be anything more than an uncomfortable liaison between man and machine. Never part of the music's internal construction, the collage of beats and samples assumed an independent existence as a rhythmic, rather than musical, medium, thus musical considerations in hip-hop were subservient to the message," he says. According to Nicholson, the jazz musician is robbed of his story-telling role and so remains an outsider who is never central to the performance created by the machines. "His role [is] that of an occasional participant, with a solo here, a solo there, or an obbligato, ingredients of decoration rather than an integral part of the music's overall construction."[16]

Jazz producer and promoter Milan Simich brought together jazz keyboardist Bob James and hip-hop DJ Rob Swift, but even he believes that jazz and hip-hop are mutually exclusive. "They don't work together because sampling is simply the notation music of the twenty-first century. People learn music by listening to records and now, rather than making a notation, they just sample a figure here and maybe another one from there, and when you do that it's hard to fit an instrument on top of it. You can probably do something with a keyboard, but a horn is really contradictory to what is going down. It's a contradiction to have a sample with a live instrument. The only way you can blend hip-hop and jazz is to have a band and a DJ, and, even here, if it's not done right the DJ ends up like being a bongo player in a band. Plus hip-hop artists are not musicians, so that's a problem as well." But in Simich's eyes, *Doo-Bop* is not a total failure. "There are a couple of tracks where Miles did some hip things and he was able to put some momentum in it. You could hear that he was driving something, whereas everyone else who tries to do this with hip-hop sounds so static."

Branford Marsalis was one of the first people to add jazz samples to hip-hop music, when he worked with hip-hop duo Gang Starr on "A Jazz Thing," a tune that appeared in Spike Lee's *Mo' Better Blues* film, released in 1989. "Some English critic tried to credit me and DJ Premier [one half of Gang Starr] with being the inventors of hip-hop jazz, because we mixed jazz samples with hip-hop, but I don't buy that. When you take a sample of a jazz record and remove it from its environment that it was created in and it repeats itself over and over – which jazz doesn't do when it's played well – it's more not like jazz than jazz," he says.

Marsalis believes that the constant backbeat of the hip-hop rhythm track also makes it an alien environment for jazz to thrive in. "The backbeat limits the shit you can play, so it becomes less like jazz. The thing that makes jazz 'jazz' is the constant motion of the band and this allows you to play in a way that is always evolving, but when you get rid of the constant motion it limits the things you can play."

Marsalis adds: "There are very few jazz songs that have one chord – they exist and Trane [Coltrane] used to do it all the time – but on *Doo-Bop* those one-chord songs limit what you can do. Listen to Miles play on *Doo-Bop* and then listen to him solo on his Prestige records and you'll see what I mean. Jazz and hip-hop don't really mix, but sensibilities occur, like a lot of the shit we do has hip-hop sensibilities, but we're not playing hip-hop." In the mid-1990s, Marsalis was behind a couple of albums from an act called Buckshot LeFonque,[17] which included rappers and DJs. But Marsalis prefers to describe the albums made by Buckshot LeFonque as combining a jazz sensibility with hip-hop influences, rather than as straight jazz or hip-hop albums.

So how does he describe *Doo-Bop*? "If you listen to that record, there's not a lot of jazz being played on it. The only reason they call it jazz is because Miles Davis is on it. If [trumpeters] Tom Browne or Chris Botti had played on *Doo-Bop* they wouldn't have called it jazz. I can understand why popular culture would want to appropriate jazz, because it gives it an elevated view, but jazz doesn't benefit by being associated with *Doo-Bop*."

As far as Marsalis is concerned, *Doo-Bop* is: "A couple of disparate ideas that never reached fruition because Miles died. It was something that was just cobbled together and Miles never really got his brain around it in order to make it something cohesive and I don't think he ever would, but it was worth trying because Miles always wanted to align himself to youth – he never wanted to be old."

Few would argue with the notion that simply adding a few jazz samples to a hip-hop track makes the resulting music a combination of jazz and hip-hop. There is also no doubt that improvisation lies at the heart of jazz and that the way the rhythm section responds to the soloist can be inspiring, motivating and challenging, often taking the music down new, exciting and uncharted pathways. But equally, there is no law that says that improvisation is only possible when there is a high degree of fluidity and flexibility within a rhythm section. The constant backbeat of a hip-hop track calls for new skills of improvisation, where much of the inspiration comes from within rather than from the interaction with other players. It could be argued that such improvisation is less exciting or offers narrower musical horizons, but that does not make it less valid or, indeed, less of a jazz statement.

Certainly, many of those who played with Miles believe it was natural for him to turn his attentions to hip-hop. Percussionist Don Alias rejects the notion that Miles sold out when he played hip-hop music. "Miles never compromised on anything where music was concerned. It wasn't like 'If I record this Michael Jackson track I can make some bread.' Miles always succumbed to the integrity of the music, to the honesty of it. He was always being innovative, always looking for the contemporary situation. Miles had a lot of good things to say about rap. He thought that the times when a rapper would come in and just say things off the top of his head was like the way be-bop players would just get on the bandstand and improvise. Miles really liked that stuff."

Miles's decision to explore hip-hop was no surprise for bassist Dave Holland either. "His music was all about integrating it with the current developments in the music and it's clear that hip-hop was one of the major developments. The younger generation of musicians I'm working with have grown up on hip-hop and have brought some of that language into the music I'm playing. To me popular music has always been part of the language that jazz has drawn on. In the past it was Irving Berlin, Cole Porter, Gershwin, the classic Ellington tunes and things like that, which were the language of the music. As jazz has evolved it's always drawn on to the popular culture to integrate that language in its language, so it didn't surprise me at all. It's also been one of the most significant contributions of the African-American community in America and Miles was very much cognizant of that."

Chaka Khan adds: "I love merging two really interesting and unique things together and trying to come up with something beautiful. Art is made for that – it screams for collaboration and that's what Miles loved to do." "I don't think Miles sold out," says guitarist Jean-Paul Bourelly. "I think Miles was a cat that was always trying to be with the times. *Doo-Bop* wasn't cutting edge – there were younger groups doing that kind of thing – but I saw it as contemporary. Miles had an internal hipness that attracted people. He never got old and that's always a challenge for a musician. There are very few musicians who didn't settle into a certain style and just stay there. Miles's horn playing was still the same, but he put it into different contexts and it really fit. The hip-hop shit seems natural as anything, but other artists of his generation wouldn't have dreamt of doing that. For me that's a real purist – not the guy who's now playing 40's and 50's jazz. The purist is the guy who takes the shit and wants to change with the times. Miles was definitely a symbol for us all."

Those who participated on *Doo-Bop* certainly believe that Miles was on to something special. "I was definitely feeling the music. Even now, they're [musicians] still trying to go on [from Miles], trying to play instrumental stuff over hip-hop grooves. It was Miles over hip-hop and that combination sounded amazing," says Deron Johnson. "I remember reading that if you listened to all of Miles's music from *The Birth Of The Cool* to *Doo-Bop*, if you took away all the background music, Miles would be playing exactly the same shit he played for fifty years. His playing style didn't change, it was the stuff that was around him. I thought it was brilliant." Gordon Meltzer believes that: "Those tracks hold together well with the new stuff."

"*Doo-Bop* is probably one of the few albums that I've worked on that I listen to constantly," says Spero. "I love that album and I think it definitely works. There have been a lot of other combinations [of jazz and hip-hop] but when it came to Mo Bee and Miles it wasn't merely a blending of two genres, it was two musicians who were really feeling each other. Miles always got a lot of criticism. When Miles went from doing *My Funny Valentine* to *Bitches Brew*, the jazz purists were up his ass, so why should this be any different?"

Eric Lynch believes that: "For that time it was groundbreaking. That's the chance you take. It's one of those records where either you love it or you don't. Miles was very happy doing it. You can relate *Doo-Bop* to *The Wizard of Oz*. Right after the film was produced the studio didn't like the movie, and today it's a classic, so who knows? Twenty years from now it could be renowned as a classic." D'Anthony Johnson describes *Doo-Bop* as being the greatest project he ever worked on. "When I present my resume, Miles's name is the first thing people see and their eyes pop out. Eric and I were the last engineers to work in the studio with Miles and I'm proud of that fact."

Doo-Bop would go on to win the award for the best R&B instrumental performance at the 35th Annual Grammy Awards, but what is its lasting legacy? "Miles was more than five years ahead of his time," says drummer Ndugu Chancler. "There are still people just starting to do what he did on that album."

By putting his horn on to hip-hop music, Miles gave a high degree of integrity to the notion of fusing jazz and hip-hop and that encouraged many others to go down that same road. In the ensuing years since Miles's death, there have been many attempts to combine hip-hop with jazz. In some cases, jazz artists have added elements of hip-hop to their music, such as Greg Osby (*3D Lifestyles*), Gary Thomas (*The Kold Kage* and *Overkill*), Stanley Clarke (*1, 2 to the Bass*), Bill Evans (*Push*), Barry Finnerty (*Irazz!*) and Roy Hargrove (*The RH Factor* – described on the cover as " 'Neo-Soul Jazz,' an organic musical street party at the corner of hip-hop and bop").

Hip-hop artists have, in turn, incorporated jazz into their music, including Guru's album *Jazzmatazz*, which featured contributions from Roy Ayers, Lonnie Liston Smith, Donald Byrd, Ronny Jordan, Courtney Pine and Branford Marsalis. Volume two included Freddie Hubbard and Kenny Garrett. The British band Us3 combined Bluenote classic tunes with hip-hop, and Bluenote Records would go on to release an album featuring hip-hop artists and producers such as Easy Mo Bee, Diamond D and DJ Smash, remixing classic jazz titles from artists such as Horace Silver, Donald Byrd and Cannonball Adderley.

The US group Coolbone developed the concept of brass-hop, which combined a jazz brass sound with hip-hop. In the UK, trip-hop, a combination of jazz samples and electronic music, emerged in the mid-1990s from UK acts such as Tricky, Massive Attack, Portishead and Coldcut. The 1994 album *Stolen Moments: Red, Hot and Cool* saw jazz musicians such as Donald Byrd, Ron Carter and Ronny Jordan collaborate with hip-hop artists such as Guru and MC Solaar.

Jazz has never stood still. The jazz we have today is due to artists such as Armstrong, Parker, Coltrane and Miles pushing at its boundaries and daring to challenge the accepted norms of the art form. Even today, more than a decade after Miles's death, jazz musicians and hip-hop artists are still trying to find ways of forging links between these two musical forms. Some collaborations have been more successful than others. It is possible that like two magnets whose ends have the same polarity, jazz and hip-hop will come close to making contact but ultimately repel each other. But it is only through trial and error that we will discover the answer. It is tempting to wonder how *Doo-Bop* would have turned out had Miles lived long enough to complete it, but at least it does provide us with an idea of where Miles was going musically. "I think Miles would have gone on to drum-and-bass, the sort of Aphex Twin[18] kind of stuff," says Foley, the lead bassist in Miles's last band.

Doo-Bop has its flaws, but that is no surprise given the circumstances under which it was made. Miles was sick, he was at the start of new musical explorations and he never managed to achieve all his musical ambitions. But there are enough magical musical moments from Miles on *Doo-Bop* to more than justify its release. As Branford Marsalis puts it: "A record with Miles Davis on it is better than one without him."

Equally important, *Doo-Bop* reminds us of the essence of the man. Miles always wanted to develop as a musician, and despite his monumental past achievements he never lost his innate musical curiosity or his capacity for change. He never stopped challenging either himself or his fans or his critics. It is easier to play music that your fans and critics like hearing you play than it is to play music that forces them to re-evaluate their expectations. Writer Ron Frankl put it well when he wrote: "For Miles Davis, music was a lifelong journey, with no final destination. He never ran out of ideas; he just ran out of time in which to realize them."[19]

19 *miles alive*

"To understand Miles's work of the 1980s, the studio albums are of less use than a shelf-load of concert tapes." *Brian Priestley, critic* [1]

"[Miles] really wanted music to be from the heart and soul and nowhere else; he was very adamant about that." *Benny Rietveld, bassist*

The final phase of Miles's live performances lasted almost exactly ten years – beginning with a gig at the Kix club in Boston on June 26, 1981 and ending on August 25, 1991 at the Hollywood Bowl in California. Miles toured extensively during his final decade, criss-crossing the US, Asia and Europe. During this period, both the music and his bands underwent a considerable transformation.

Miles's bands varied in size from a sextet to a nonet. At times, Miles's bands included two guitarists, saxophonists or percussionists. Many line-ups also had two keyboard players, with Miles also playing keyboards. Sometimes, other band members, such as Bill Evans and Bob Berg, would occasionally play keyboards as well. Yet, at other times, the band's line-up would have no specialist keyboard player or percussionist. On some occasions, Miles would play for less than an hour at an event; other times he would be on-stage for over five hours, doing two performances on the same day.

The music Miles played live on-stage had a power, energy and excitement that could not be reproduced in a studio, even during a jam session. That was why Miles liked to include recordings of live performances on his studio album and why he tried to recreate the live atmosphere in the studio by simply letting the tapes run. Live performances also gave Miles the ability to extend and enhance the music, which he often did. Miles would experiment with new arrangements and a new band member could radically change the direction and the feel of the music. In many ways, the studio was the preparation ground for Miles's live performances, as Ian Carr notes: "His studio albums…seemed like blueprints for the looser live performances where the magic and the music really happened." [2]

Miles's first band comprised of Mike Stern on guitar, Marcus Miller on bass, Bill Evans on tenor and soprano saxophone (and occasionally flute and keyboards), Al Foster on drums and Mino Cinelu on percussion. The way each member was recruited by Miles has been chronicled in the chapters on *The Man With The Horn* and *We Want Miles*. When Miles first went back on the road he was in a bad shape, both physically and emotionally. He was weak and was still taking alcohol, cocaine and painkillers. He was also acutely aware that his embouchure was not what it once was. As an insurance against his weak chops, Miles could have toured with an all-star band that would have provided him with lots of support, but instead he chose a band that was largely composed of unknown and relatively inexperienced members. This decision not only demonstrates Miles's considerable courage but also his uncanny instinct for finding the right combination of musicians to create the right musical chemistry. But while the chemistry is important, Miles had a more fundamental rule when it came to what made a band successful. Miles was once asked, what made a good band? His answer was simple. "In the first place you've got to get the drummer. No drummer, no band."[3] This helps explain why Miles was so determined to work with Al Foster again.

When discussing Miles's live performances, mention should be made of Miles's road crew and in particular Jim Rose, Chris Murphy, Ron Lorman and Patrick Murray. The first three worked with Miles from 1981 and Murray joined the operation in 1986. These men did much to ensure the smooth running of Miles's touring operation and to improve his concert sound. One of the most radical developments was a wireless amplification system for Miles's horn, which included a miniature transmitter/receiver. This was connected to Miles's horn with a mounting system fabricated out of brass tubing.

Later on, the brass tubing was replaced by Plexiglas tubing to reduce the weight. This also improved the removal of unwanted resonances and handling noise. Another bonus was it didn't bend, as Miles was always banging the microphone into things, bending the brass tubing in the process (this is why sometimes the sound on Miles's live recordings has "pops" and "bangs"). The plastic tubing, however, would simply spring back into place. The biggest impact, though, was the freedom the wireless system gave Miles to wander around the stage and beyond, while continuing to play and be heard through the PA system.

The road crew often had to contend with sound systems that were not up to the task, as Murray explains: "At that time in Europe – where the majority of our touring took place – we would, more often than not, show up to do a gig in a soccer stadium with a PA from the '70s that was designed to do acoustic jazz. It was a constant challenge. We were really a large rock band from a technical standpoint playing for promoters who had a jazz act mentality. We would spend the better part of the day rewiring and fixing whatever they had provided and somehow we always pulled it off."

Miles's first gigs were at Kix and at the Avery Fisher Hall in New York. Each concert typically lasted for less than an hour and the set comprised of "Back Seat Betty" and "Aida (Fast Track)" from *The Man With The Horn* album, plus "Kix" or "My Man's Gone Now." The set would be played as a medley, with Miles cueing the band for the next tune, usually by blowing a phrase that marked the end of one tune and the start of another. "It was kinda cool that he wouldn't go for 'Okay, the song's ended now, we'll get applause,'" says Stern. It meant that there was no time for the musicians to rest, something that Stern enjoyed. "I loved to play – that was the easy bit. It's getting to the gig that's the exhausting part."

After these gigs, Miles embarked on a tour across the U.S. that included a gig at the Savoy Theatre in New York on July 17, 1981. Here, Miles received a surprise as Dave Liebman joined him on-stage. "I just went on the bandstand, grabbed Bill's [Evans] soprano and started playing. Miles was playing keyboards with his back to me. He turned around, saw who it was and put his hand out to me. He said 'What are you doing here?' I said 'I'm here to check you out.' He then said, 'Man, no one ever sits in on me,' and I said 'I think it's okay after all these years; you've got my student up there, for God's sake.'"

In August 1981, Miles introduced two new tunes to his repertoire, "Fat Time," from *The Man With The Horn* and "Jean-Pierre," which would become his signature tune of the 1980s. The band toured Japan in late 1981, but Miles's health was deteriorating. However, the band returned to North America and played several more gigs. It was during this period that Miles added another tune to his set and, like "My Man's Gone Now," it was a song from his past. "Ife," recorded in 1972, was a moody, introspective piece, with a creeping four-note ostinato that bassist Michael Henderson would sometimes play for more than twenty minutes.

In early 1982, Miles suffered a stroke, which paralysed his right hand, putting him out of action for several months. After a health routine that included exercise, physiotherapy and a change of lifestyle, Miles was well enough to resume touring in April. His tour began in the U.S. and then moved to Europe in mid-April. When Miles played at the Hammersmith Odeon in London on April 20, 1982, the second gig was recorded by the new commercial TV station Channel 4 and broadcast later in the autumn. Miles's appearance was a shock to those who recalled the fit-looking, Afro-haired man that had stalked the stage back in the 1970s. Now, Miles looked thin and weak and he wore a white jacket and a woollen hat pulled over his head. He also had a moustache and a wispy goatee beard. Miles would spend long stretches of the concert perched on the stool at his electric piano, watching and directing the band.

On the opening number, "Back Seat Betty," Miles's tone sounded weak and his playing lacked power, but, as the gig progressed, Miles's playing improved.

The band swung on the second number "My Man's Gone Now," and on the third, "Aida," the energy level was taken to new heights, with Stern playing some scorching guitar. Cinelu also performed his party piece, a solo that involved him sitting aside an upturned conga drum and playing it with his hands and bare feet.

This performance came as a result of Cinelu explaining to Miles about some of the traditional drumming in Martinique, where Cinelu had been born. "I told him how you sit on a drum and can change the pitch of the drum with your foot. As I explained this to him he had that look and then three days later when we were on-stage he invited me to the front! Sometimes I'd do it three or four times a night. I didn't want it to become a gimmick, but he would say to me 'Come on and play,'" says Cinelu.

In the second set, the band played "Ife," with Evans playing an extended solo on flute and Miles supporting him on electric piano. The next tune, "Fat Time," was taken at a much brisker pace than on the album and the Spanish influence was also much greater. Stern played more searing guitar before the band started playing the final number, "Jean-Pierre." Unusually, Miller played a solo, something he never really felt comfortable with when he first played with Miles. But Miller played as if he was enjoying the moment and even smiled over at an encouraging Miles.

After the London gigs, the band flew back to continental Europe, where they played in Belgium, France, Italy and The Netherlands. The gig in Paris on May 3 was a memorable occasion, not least because the PA system blew during the second set, just as the band was playing "Fat Time." "There's no silence like the sudden silence in the middle of a show and the crowd began to murmur," says Murphy. "Then out came Miles walking to centre stage. He picked up the plaintive melody again, and the crowd hushed. The acoustics were so good; they could hear his unamplified trumpet in the upper seats." Foster swapped his sticks for brushes; Miller picked up one of Evans's saxophones and played the bass line on that – the only musician that couldn't be heard was Stern. "This was one of Miles's finest hours. He took a potential disaster and turned it into a triumph. When the last note sounded, the crowd exploded, jumping to their feet for a standing ovation. The band was as jubilant as the audience, flocking to Miles and high-fiving him. We all knew we had witnessed something rare and precious."[4]

After a two-month break, the band was back touring the US, playing the same repertoire. But at a gig at the Jones Beach Theatre in Long Island on August 28, 1982, half of the concert was taken up by four new tunes that would map out Miles's future musical direction for years to come. The usual concert opener, "Back Seat Betty," was now discarded and replaced by a new opening tune, "Come Get It," a driving rock-funk number that retained the opening power chords from "Back Seat Betty." This performance would be used as the opening track for Miles's forthcoming album, *Star People*.

The other new additions were "U 'n' I" and "Speak," and "Star People." The latter was a revelation because it was a blues number. Miles also started playing the Oberheim OBX-a synthesizer in concert. "Ife" was dropped from the set. Later that month, Miles introduced another new number, "Hop-scotch," a funk track with a catchy theme that was derived from "Star On Cicely," which appeared on the *Star People* album.

On November 7, 1982, Miles added a new member to the band, the guitarist John Scofield. Scofield's recruitment has been reported in the chapter on *Star People*, but it is worth repeating that he was added to the band because of Stern's growing problems with drink and drug addiction. When Stern missed a flight to a gig, Miles asked Bill Evans to recommend another guitarist and he suggested Scofield. Instead of sending Scofield a tape of the band's live performance in order to learn the music, Miles simply asked him to watch the band from the side of the stage for three nights, before bringing him out on the fourth.

This was the first time Stern was aware that he was no longer the solo guitarist in the band. "So I show up at a gig and Scofield's there and then we did about four or five gigs. Sco just played a little – he was basically hanging out. He was just for insurance at first and then we started playing together and Miles kinda snuck him in more and then we started playing with two guitars together," recalls Stern. Stern had mixed feelings about the situation, but most of them were positive. "For me it was a total treat to play with Scofield. Of course I was kinda pissed off with myself but I couldn't really stop what I was doing – I just couldn't get it together. So I was disappointed that it came about that way, but at the same time I was really happy musically to be playing with John, because that was fun, man. I've always loved the way he played and I used to check him out in Boston."

Scofield explains how he was integrated into the band. "In the first few weeks I was playing these written melodies and Mike was doing all the stuff he'd do. Then we just kinda divided it. I think maybe Miles would say 'You solo here.' We tried not to comp too much to get in each other's way. Mike and I had played together at a club called 55 Grand Street in a two-guitar band with bass and drums. We played together a lot and were really good friends. It evolved and then I got to solo too and Miles just worked me in to give me new features as things came up."

One result of Scofield's recruitment was that Miles added a second blues number to his set, "It Gets Better." The new two-guitar line-up played the last gig of the year at the Felt Forum in New York on New Year's Eve. The band played a 70-minute medley comprising of "Come Get It," "It Gets Better," "U 'n' I," "Star On Cicely," "Star People," "Hopscotch," and "Jean-Pierre." The band was in fine form and Miles started proceedings by playing a long electric piano introduction on the opener "Come Get It."

The highlights of the gig include Scofield's sharp soloing on "It Gets Better," and on "Star People," where Miles solos for long periods and plays strongly. Mike Stern also solos well on this number. Bill Evans gets his chance on "Star On Cicely," and lets rip on tenor saxophone. Finally, Miles plays some elegant Spanish-type figures on the closer "Jean-Pierre," and Stern plays a blistering solo. Miller also plays a solo. This gig, incidentally, was Miller's last with the band, although he would remain with Miles for a little longer and play on the session that produced "It Gets Better" on *Star People*.

Critic Lee Jeske was at the Forum gig and noted that Miles "soloed long and frequently and was in control the entire time." He also reported on a piece of theatre that Miles had begun playing with Evans, namely pushing a seemingly reluctant Evans up to the electric piano to play. Evans, who learned to play classical piano as a child, would duly oblige and play for several minutes, much to Miles's and the audience's delight.

But the other revelation for Jeske was the addition of Scofield to the band. "Scofield, with his hollow-bodied guitar, played the kind of music he has been playing for the past few years – scorching clear blues-drenched jazz, with a little smidgen of avant-garde and a small dollop of rock 'n' roll," he said. "He is one of the finest guitarists around these days and his playing brought a new hue to the band – he is a think-on-his-feet soloist who presents Miles with a challenge. If Miles scuffles, Scofield has the equipment to blow him away."[5]

Miles resumed touring again in the New Year (1983) and the band's new bassist, Tom Barney, had been recommended by Marcus Miller (see the *Star People* chapter). Barney toured with the band in the U.S., Europe and Japan during the spring of 1983. Only one performance of Barney's – a live recording of "Speak" probably recorded in Houston Texas on February 3, 1983 – has so far been officially released, appearing on the album *Star People*. However, when the band toured Japan in May, a performance at the Yomuri Land Open Theatre in Tokyo on May 29, 1983 was broadcast by Japanese radio.

The broadcast reveals a tight band in sparkling form, with Stern and Scofield complementing each other superbly and Miles playing extensively. Barney's bass is also a prominent feature, although the bassist did not find it easy to settle into the band, not least because his preparation had been minimal. "It was something I wasn't accustomed to. At that point in Miles's life I'm not sure how important things were to him because I never had a rehearsal. You just went to the gig and you did the gig," says Barney.

Barney adds that the dynamics of the band at the time were also unsettling for him. "There were times when the interaction between Miles and Stern and Scofield wasn't fun. I just came into a situation where there was a lot of turmoil going on at the time – it was like walking into a whirlwind. People were not happy and there was alcohol and drugs. But what amazed me was that once we went on-stage and the curtain went up, it was magic.

But once the curtain came down, the issues would start up again." However, he adds: "It wasn't all bad. There were times when I had a lot of fun and things were nice." Even so, Barney only stayed with the band for around five months, leaving soon after the Japan tour. Barney says the reason was that: "When Miles originally asked me to join the band, he made a deal with me. But, later on, the management tried to change things." But, according to some of those close to the situation at the time, Miles and Barney also never really hit it off on a personal level.

But, despite the nature of his departure, Barney has warm feelings towards Miles. "The thing I really learned from being with Miles was that he was brutally honest about his music in terms of his playing and his performance. If he played something he didn't like, he'd look at his horn and say 'Damn.' That kind of honesty in your own playing is great."

Barney's replacement was Darryl Jones, who was recommended by Miles's nephew Vince Wilburn Jr. Jones gave the rhythm section more focus and more attack and was the foundation for the funk sound that dominated Miles's music. Producer and promoter Milan Simich describes Jones's playing as being like "A Mack [massive] truck just tearing down the highway at you – it's unstoppable." "I went into it with the attitude 'I'd better just have some fun, because it might be over,'" said Jones. But Miles clearly loved Jones's playing. "He said a lot of amazing things to me. I remember once he called me to his room one night and said 'If I played bass, I'd wanna play just like you.' I was able to really enjoy the compliments but not get too hung up on it. But it helped me to play a certain way when I was playing with Miles."

Miles paid a lot of attention to Jones on-stage, as the bassist recalls. "At one point he'd be looking at me thinking 'When am I going to catch this cat sleeping?' And it went on for a long time before one night he caught me sleeping! And he busted me and he just laughed like 'I finally caught you!' That was one of the things that endeared me to him." Jones adds that Miles still influences his playing today. "Sometimes when I'm playing I'll get something that he said to me all those years ago. And I'll go 'Oh shit, that's what he was talking about.' I didn't understand everything when I first started playing with Miles. When I played with Miles I learned the lesson that when what you're doing with the band doesn't seem to be working, you over-play to compensate. Miles was always telling me that you can't fix it like that. What you have to do is to play even less. I'm constantly learning that."

The septet that had included the two guitarists ended on June 26, 1983, when Stern's drink and drug problem was so severe that Miles had to let him go. But the parting would not be permanent and Stern would rejoin the band in 1985 after cleaning himself up. "Obviously when Mike left I had more space to play," says Scofield.

Miles's set was still dominated by the music from *Star People*, with tracks such as "Speak," "Star People," "It Gets Better" and "Star On Cicely" forming the centrepiece of the proceedings. These were supplemented by the funk tune "Hopscotch," and the usual concert closer, "Jean-Pierre," now the only track remaining in the set from Miles's first two comeback albums. But the influence of Jones's hard-funk playing was already being felt in late June, when Miles introduced a new song to the set, "What It Is," a driving funk tune that was inspired by a bass line Jones had played one night during "Hopscotch."

In August and September 1983, Miles was in the studio laying down tracks for the *Decoy* album. The recording sessions saw the return of keyboardist Robert Irving III, who had worked with Miles on *The Man With The Horn*. Irving was also asked to join Miles's band and became its musical director.

"My gig was simply to act as a liaison between Miles and the other musicians in the band, to confer with Miles on new music arrangements, write the scores, extract the parts and to schedule and conduct rehearsals, which Miles never attended," explains Irving. "If I told him that the band was ready with a new arrangement, we would try it live on-stage that night. If not, we would keep working until the music was tight. Miles liked the charge that comes from playing without a rehearsal."

Irving became the first keyboardist in Miles's band since Lonnie Liston Smith, who had left in May 1973. Irving would sit on-stage surrounded by a battery of synthesizers and other electronic keyboards and took on the role of an orchestral player. Irving's main role was to set a mood, to create an atmosphere over which the rest of the band would play. Miles once said of Irving's role in the band: "If you can hear him, he was too loud. You're supposed to be able to feel him, not hear him."[6]

However, there were occasions when Irving could be both seen and heard. "Miles had two pet peeves when it came to the music, playing too loud or playing too much. I, like many musicians in the group, would get in trouble for both," says Irving. "When Miles would break the band down to a whisper, I would turn my volume down to one, but then the house mix engineer would push my volume level up to compensate. Because Miles was standing right next to the front speaker he would still hear me, while in my own monitor there was virtually no sound. One day, in Japan this happened and he came over to the keyboard rig and started to pretend to strangle me. There had been a quote in a Tokyo newspaper where Miles had said 'I'm gonna kill Bobby Irving for playing so loud!'"

In autumn 1983, the band, now consisting of Miles, Evans, Irving, Scofield, Jones, Foster and Cinelu, set off for a European tour that included a gig on October 23 at the Sala Kongesowa concert hall in Warsaw, Poland. This was a time when there was no sign of a thaw in the Cold War and few Western artists ventured behind the Iron Curtain. Miles was clearly touched by the reception he got in Poland. He was waived through customs, everybody was wearing "We Want Miles" badges and he was driven everywhere in a limousine provided by the then Soviet leader Yuri Andropov. "This tour was something special because the people were so happy to see me, and they really got into the music," said Miles. "They put me up at the very best hotel in Warsaw and treated me like a king."[7]

The band's set now included "That's Right" and "Code MD" from *Decoy* and the concert was recorded by Polish television. A limited edition album of the Warsaw gig was also released for members of the Polish Jazz Society's record club that included a selection of tracks. Starting off with the driving funk of "Speak," the energy level is brought down with "Star People," which finds Miles playing with both power and passion. Scofield also plays a superb solo over Jones's punchy bass line and Foster's driving beat.

Bill Evans gets to solo on soprano saxophone on "What It Is," and tenor saxophone on the next number, "It Gets Better." This track also highlights Scofield's playing, who solos with imagination and grace, and at times he even plays unaccompanied by the rest of the band. Miles's European tour also included Spain, Germany and France, before ending with a gig at Radio City Hall in New York on November 6, 1983. Both Evans and Cinelu left the band after the gigs, with only Foster now remaining from Miles's original 1981 band.

The rest of 1983 was spent recording at the Record Plant Studios in New York with a pared-down band consisting of Miles, Scofield, Irving, Jones and Foster. These were the initial sessions for Miles's next album, *You're Under Arrest*. But when Miles suffered a bout of illness in late November, it put the recording sessions on hold. The sessions resumed in January 1984, when the studio band was augmented by percussionist Steve Thornton.

In May, a new saxophonist Bob Berg joined the band and Miles resumed touring in June 1984 in the U.S. Berg's main instrument was the tenor saxophone, but Miles also wanted him to play soprano saxophone a lot. "When I first joined the band, I didn't even own one, but I bought a [Selmer] Mark VI immediately and shedded [practised] like a maniac for a week," said Berg. "By the time we hit the road I felt completely comfortable with the instrument. My main axe is the tenor and I gradually snuck it in. Once in a while Miles would say 'Bob, play the little horn.' So I did, but after a while he had no problem letting me blow on the tenor as much as the soprano."

Berg added that Miles gave him very little musical direction. "I basically played what I heard, the way I would normally approach anything. Of course I would take a cue from the direction Miles would outline. Most of the tunes were centred around one tonality, but Miles had this uncanny chromatic approach and I took some inspiration from this. Miles gave me the freedom to play whatever I felt at the time. He never told me what to play."

Berg had joined the band at a time when Miles's health and technique were in the ascendant. "I always say that the greatest impact of playing with Miles was to stand up there night after night and witness his approach to playing," said Berg. "When I joined the band, his chops were way up. I remember the first gig we did in L.A. at a packed theatre [the Beverley Theatre on June 2, 1984] Miles was playing his ass off. I had heard him a few times since the comeback, but what I heard far surpassed his recent playing. It was quite impressive and completely inspiring. It reminded me of what I heard as a teenager, when I used to sneak into clubs to hear Miles in the mid-1960s."

Miles's band now comprised of Miles, Irving Scofield, Jones, Berg, Foster, and Thornton. It was around this period that Miles began playing two new tunes in his concert, Cyndi Lauper's "Time After Time," and D-Train's "Something's On Your Mind." These pop-oriented tunes marked the beginning of a new musical direction for Miles, which would see more pop songs creeping into his repertoire over the next year or so. "Time After Time" would remain in Miles's set right up until his final concert seven years later.

A sign of Miles's increasing strength was the fact that he would now sometimes play two full-length concerts on the same day. An example of this occurred at the Montreux Jazz Festival on July 8, 1984. Incredible as it may seem, Columbia Records never released a live album of this band. Until the release of the Montreux boxed set in 2002, the only way of hearing recordings of the band was via radio or television broadcasts or bootlegs.

Miles played two concerts at Montreux, in the afternoon and evening, each lasting around ninety minutes. Miles's set now consisted of funk tunes ("Speak," "What It Is" and "Hopscotch"), blues numbers ("Star People" and "It Gets Better") and pop tunes ("Time After Time" and "Something's On Your Mind"). Also added to the mix were "Jean-Pierre" and a new tune, which has been called "Lake Geneva." The latter number is a surprise as it is basically a smooth-jazz number. The main focus of the piece is a duet between Miles and Berg, with the latter playing soprano saxophone. The number was soon dropped from the band's set.

The afternoon concert found a band fizzing with energy, with the opener "Speak" dominated by Jones's pounding bass line. Miles plays beautifully on the thirteen-and-a-half-minute "Time After Time," and Scofield's melodic guitar playing is the perfect complement. The version of "Something's On Your Mind" has a stronger groove than the album version, with a funky bass line and a tempo that is closer to the original ballad by D-Train. Miles also plays it on open horn rather than with a mute, another sign of his growing strength and confidence. It is also reprised in the encore. Darryl Jones's bass solo from "Hopscotch" is given a track to itself and Jones ably demonstrates his virtuosity, popping and slapping his strings in the process. The evening concert retained much of the repertoire of the afternoon event, the main difference being the inclusion of "Code MD" in the encore.

Miles's 1984 tour included two concerts in London and part of the afternoon concert as broadcast on UK radio. One of the tunes played was "Hopscotch," which included a solo by Jones which was more adventurous than the ones played at Montreux. Jones's on-stage rig included a host of effects pedals, which he used on this solo. One effect involved playing a riff and then looping it through the PA system and using it as the background to play more riffs on top. "I was using a lot of effects back then," says Jones. "I first got the inspiration to use effects pedals when I saw [friend and bass mentor] Angus Thomas using a fuzz pedal. It was like 'I don't want to play regular bass any more!' I was also inspired by Jaco [Pastorius] and [Jimi] Hendrix."

In July 1984, "Freaky Deaky" was added to the set list, but the number was soon dropped. Miles's summer tour moved from Europe to the U.S. and ended in August. In September, the band was back at Record Plant Studios, where they recorded "Ms. Morrisine." The tour resumed in November 1984 in the U.S. and then Miles was back in Europe. The band's opener was now the short medley "One Phone/Street Scenes," which was followed by "Speak." Tina Turner's "What's Love Got To Do With It?" was also included in the set, although it would be dropped before the end of the year. Miles went with John Scofield to the Sonning music award ceremony in Copenhagen, and afterwards he flew back to the U.S. to continue working on the *You're Under Arrest* album.

Miles spent most of January 1985 in the recording studio, where he completed the last sessions for *You're Under Arrest* before flying back to Denmark to record the album *Aura* with trumpeter Palle Mikkelborg. Touring resumed again in April 1985, but this time with a new drummer, Miles's nephew Vince Wilburn Jr., who replaced Al Foster. Foster had been associated with Miles since 1972, when he played on the *Big Fun* album. When Foster joined Miles's band in September 1972, he thought he was going to play jazz, but found himself playing jazz-rock with Miles in the 1970s and funk in the 1980s. Foster had been the one constant in Miles's bands until he left in January 1985 and it says something about his devotion to Miles that he did not like much of the music he played. "A lot of what I played in the '70s was not tasteful and some of the music I didn't care for," he said.[8] When it came to Miles's 1980s material, Foster had liked the *We Want Miles* album and the track "Mr. Pastorius" on *Amandla* (recorded in 1989), which saw Miles playing jazz-swing. Foster recalls a conversation with Miles. "When he called me for the album [*Amandla*] I asked him 'What kind of music are we doing?' and he said 'Jazz, motherfucker!' and he hung up. He knew I was tired of playing that backbeat with him."[9]

In the light of these comments, it is not surprising that Foster left Miles's band at this stage, because Miles wanted his drummer to lock into a heavy backbeat, something that Wilburn was happy to oblige with. Wilburn may have been Miles's blood relative (Miles called Wilburn "Nefdrum") but that didn't make him immune from the pressures of playing with Miles, who would often spend much of the time on the bandstand with his back to the audience, staring hard at Wilburn and directing him. "It was tough, but I learned from it and I wouldn't have traded it for the world," says Wilburn.

When the spring tour started in April 1985, Miles was still a Columbia Records' artist, but in May he signed with Warner Bros records. The tour began in the U.S. and three new tunes were added to the set – the heavy-funk workout "Maze," the fiery "Katia," and a reflective version of John McLaughlin's "Pacific Express," which was based around a hypnotically slow bass pulse. Part of a concert at Theatre St. Denis in Montreal on June 28, 1985 was broadcast on television and later appeared on a video and a DVD, *Live in Montreal*. The blues number "Star People" and two funk tracks "Maze" and "Hopscotch" were omitted from the broadcast and DVD, but the rest of the set was included.

The concert began with a storming version of "One Phone Call/Street Scenes," and included the three pop tunes, "Human Nature," "Time After Time" and "Something's On Your Mind." The arrangement of "Human Nature" was similar to the album version but, on "Something's On Your Mind," Scofield solos and Berg plays an extended solo on soprano saxophone. Miles was clearly happy with Berg's performance, pointing to him at its conclusion and encouraging the crowd to applaud Berg.

But Miles was not always enamoured by his saxophonist's playing as he once recounted: "Bob Berg I used to tell, 'Bob, why do you play in this spot? You're not supposed to play this spot.' He said 'It sounded so good, Chief, I had to play it.' I said 'The reason it sounded so good is because you wasn't playin'.' As soon as he jumps in, he fucks it up. It's a hard thing playin' with a group."[10]

On "Time After Time" Berg plays keyboards. "I was trained early as a classical pianist, but my role on keyboards was just to play pads [sustained chords] occasionally, to beef things up," said Berg. Berg plays another long solo on "Code MD," and the concert finishes with the "Jean-Pierre/You're Under Arrest/Then There Were None" medley, one of the highlights of the gig. The tune begins almost tentatively and builds up to a searing climax.

An interesting thing occurs in this tune (it's about fifty-two minutes into the DVD), when Jones can be seen shaking his head at Scofield as if to say "No, not yet." So was Jones directing Scofield? "Definitely not! John Scofield had been in the band longer than me and I certainly wouldn't direct him. Miles was the only one who did any directing. I've seen that thing myself and I've been trying to figure out what was going on. I think John perhaps asked me something and I communicated in a non-verbal way," says Jones. The tension increases at around the 55-minute mark when Miles switches to open horn and there is a shift in modulation, preparing the way for a blistering guitar solo from Scofield. As Scofield's guitar screams, Jones thumps away on his bass and the end is signalled by a blast from Miles's trumpet.

The band travelled to Europe in July and, once again, played two sets at the Montreux Jazz Festival on July 14, 1985. Miles sounds healthier than he did the year before and the band sounds tighter. The concert set consisted of "One Phone Call/Street Scenes," "Star People," "Maze," "Human Nature," "Something's On Your Mind" (now played at a faster tempo and sounding more like the version that appeared on *You're Under Arrest*), "Time After Time," "Ms. Morrisine," "Code MD," "Pacific Express," "Katia," "Hopscotch," "You're Under Arrest," "Jean-Pierre/You're Under Arrest/Then There Were None," finishing with "Decoy" for the encore.

This is a superb concert with many highlights including a rousing version of "Ms. Morrisine," which features Berg playing a gutsy solo on tenor saxophone; Scofield lets rip on "Katia," and Jones performs a hard, driving solo on "Hopscotch," with more fluency and drive than the 1984 version. Another sign of Miles's growing energy is the number of funk tracks that feature in the set. In the last five tunes, the energy level is kept high, save for the intro to the "Jean-Pierre" medley. Miles went back again in the evening to do it all again, playing the same set, but with many different interpretations.

When Miles appeared at the Royal Festival Hall in London on July 20, 1985, he played two concerts and was on-stage for more than five hours. "The current ensemble is the most exciting and empathetic Davis has been involved with since before his six-year layoff," wrote critic John Fordham, reviewing the first concert. "It is much looser in approach than the new pop-flavoured album (*You're Under Arrest*) lets on, and the leader is clearly enjoying himself."[11]

Miles played for long stretches at both concerts and Miles's biographer Ian Carr was able to see the effect of Miles's physical exertion at close hand. Carr had a backstage pass and watched as Miles came off the stage at the end of the second concert, after playing the encore. "As soon as he got down the two short flights of stairs and out of the audience's sight, two large men were waiting for him, and each grabbed an arm and supported him as he suddenly sagged and almost caved in," observed Carr.[12]

Miles had been back on the road for four years and during that time had only used two guitarists in his band, Stern and Scofield. But around the middle of 1985, Miles was looking for a new guitar sound. "I thought I might get fired because he kept saying 'Check out Eddie Van Halen,' and I was thinking 'I don't want to do Eddie Van Halen, I've got my own thing,'" says Scofield. "I kept thinking, maybe he's getting bored with my playing, because Miles went through people – everybody does. You need more sounds around you to spice it up." Miles once talked about one of the problems he had been having with the guitarist's playing: "John Scofield ... used to play so far behind the beat, I'd say, John, goddamn!'"[13]

Scofield went on to tour with Miles in Japan and one gig – at the Yomuri Land Open Theatre in Tokyo on July 28, 1985 – was broadcast on radio. Ironically, on the closing number "Katia," Scofield plays a superb solo, sounding more like a rock guitarist than a jazz player. Scofield left the band soon after to pursue a successful solo career.

Scofield has many great memories of playing with Miles, but notes: "On one hand I was a little frustrated because I felt that when we'd go out and play on tour, we wouldn't play that much. But by the end of the tour, we'd be in such good shape that I'd wished we'd recorded that. The music on certain nights was incredible, but at the time I played with Miles he was also getting his stuff together with Cicely Tyson and they had a kinda busy social life and stuff. Which was great, because I guess Miles needed to do that, but I was used to playing every day with a band, like going on tour and playing thirty concerts and then going in the studio and stuff. Here I was in my early thirties and Miles was late fifties and he was cooling out and I wanted to go forward. It just seemed like we could have gotten more happening."

By 1985, Mike Stern had cleaned himself up and kicked his drink and drug habit. The guitarist was also literally a shadow of his former self, having lost around fifty pounds in weight – Fat Time [Stern's nickname] was no more. "Mike is one of the greatest guitarists," notes Scofield, "but as great as his music is, what he did to pull himself out from being strung out is the greatest lesson, because this cat was near death. He's fine now and it's a really good message to the young musicians that you can come back from that."

With Scofield now gone, Miles needed a replacement and top of his list was Stern. "When I left Miles he said 'Let me know when you want to come back.' He called me back and I ended up playing with him for another year," says Stern. It may seem strange that Miles should go back to Stern rather than look for a fresh guitarist, but Stern has a more rock-orientated approach to his playing than Scofield and Miles knew that Stern would be able to quickly fit in with the band.

The new band was very different from the first one Stern had played in. "That was a totally different concept; there were keyboards and there was more arranging. It was a thicker sound but it was definitely fun, although I enjoyed the first band the most, just because of the looseness, but I liked the second one a lot too," says Stern. Miles also used the opportunity to add a second percussionist to the band, Marilyn Mazur, the American-born Dane he had met in the rehearsals for the performance of "Aura."

Mazur got the Miles gig by chance. "In July, I went to Molde jazz festival with Pierre Dørge's New Jungle Orchestra. I was airsick on the trip and we arrived just as Miles's concert started. It was sold out, so we were allowed to sit in front of the audience right beneath the edge of the stage. Suddenly Miles spotted me and talked to me through his trumpet microphone:

'Marilyn, come on up here, don't you want to play a song with us?' I was too tired, but he came back again later in the concert and said: 'Play this reggae with us.' So in spite of me being not well and also rather terrified by the circumstances, I felt that I had to get up and sit in, so I played along on Steve Thornton's timbales."

Back home in Denmark the next month, Mazur heard rumours from other musicians that Miles wanted to talk to her. "I thought they were joking, but then Miles called me and said: 'When can you be here? [in New York] Be here on Wednesday!'" Mazur had never returned to her birthplace New York since leaving it at the age of six. She flew back and started rehearsals with Miles's band. Two days later, on August 17, 1985, she made her debut at Hudson River Pier. "Miles sent me out to buy a more hip-looking costume and told me I could dance if I wanted to, which I did a bit – he must have heard about my wild dancing from Palle [Mikkelborg]." Miles explained why he had recruited Mazur: "I like pop rhythms and they're buried in Marilyn. I like to hear undercurrents and, rather than have one drummer play them, I like to have one drummer playing and another drummer playing another pattern. When she sees me look at her in a certain way, she knows what to do."[14]

Mazur used many instruments on-stage. "I had a large set-up with lots of bells and gongs, mixed drums, congas and cowbells, temple blocks, water drum and a Prophet 2000 sampler with my own home-made sounds, which I played from a Roland Octapad. For my dance solo, I used a specially-made trigger-mat connected to the same sampler and footbells and a talking drum. In a few tunes, the musical director would require some specific sound for, say, the tunes from the record *Tutu*. I would make my home-made versions of them in order to avoid stuff like standard synth-drum sounds, which I didn't like!"

Mazur noticed a difference between American and European musicians. "Musically it was never a problem as I always felt in touch with the magic of Miles's universe, although playing with those musicians was very different from the more open and communicative styles I had worked with in Europe."

Miles gave Mazur little direction verbally, so she and Thornton had to work out their own parts. "I would react to Miles's look and vibe, and that was a wonderful way of playing together. The musicians didn't really talk about how to share the roles in the rhythm-section – that was supposed to be Miles's decision. And Miles would tell Vince a whole lot about what to play, which didn't sound easy! But Steve and I would play as we each felt like. The one time I tried to talk about dividing the instrumentation between us, Steve felt that I intruded on his work, so instead I did my best to find my own role and space, playing a lot of colours and sounds."

Thornton says Mazur's "technique and style were quite different from what I did. I think what Miles liked was how we sounded together. He put it together and it worked for him – we sounded pretty good together." Miles said he kept Thornton in the band because he gave him the African sound he liked.[15]

Mazur became the only female ever to be a member of a Miles Davis band, so did he treat her differently? "Miles might have been a little more gentle with me – he was always very nice and inspiring, but sometimes provocative! I had heard rumours about how he sometimes treated women, and had also heard him go off on some of the other musicians, so I mostly kept a certain distance. I regretted this later, because the times when we actually did talk were close. He was fantastic and he even invited me to compose some music for him, but I never really got it together, mainly because I'm not the type that writes on tour and also I wasn't into making demos at that time, which he preferred."

Miles could also be a calming influence, she recalls. "I remember once being furious after a concert where a speaker had fallen down and smashed my talking drum, and he heard me banging doors. He called me into his dressing room and we had a great discussion about the music in some abstract way. This seemed to be our form of communication."

The band – now an octet – started touring the U.S. in August 1985, and that month Darryl Jones left the band. The British pop star Sting had disbanded his hugely successful group The Police and started to pursue a solo career. Sting had started his musical career playing in jazz bands in the northeast of England before forming The Police, a pop/rock band, with traces of punk. Now Sting was going back to his roots and was in New York holding auditions to find jazz musicians for a new jazz-pop band. Jones passed the audition for the bass player's chair.

In was in late July, when Miles was on a short tour in Japan, that Jones had approached Miles with some trepidation and informed him of his intention to leave the band and play with Sting. "That was a tough time in my life. At the time I was really devastated," says Jones. "I finally went to Miles and I told him 'I just really need to do this, man. I feel this is the right thing to do and I want to come back and play for you again.' He told me 'Darryl, it's not so hard having somebody back if you've asked them to leave in the first place. But for me to have you back will be tough.' When he said that it really saddened me, but I was young and I didn't believe him. I said 'No man, I'll just be back.'" Jones was right – he would return in October 1986.

In his autobiography, Miles recalls walking to his hotel room in downtown Tokyo, with the headphones from his personal stereo player dragging on the floor. When Jones told him about the trailing headphones, Miles snapped back: "So fucking what? You're not with us anymore, so what does it mean to you? Go tell that shit to your new leader Sting!"[16] Miles added that he was mad with Jones because "I really loved the way he played … Darryl had grown to be almost like a son to me."[17]

Miles said he understood from an intellectual point of view why Jones was leaving, but emotionally he was hurt. This helps explain why Miles was scathing about Jones's decision to leave the band when he spoke to writer Nick Kent. "I had to let him go ... That boy ... I liked him too. He could play so good and hell, I felt kind of paternalistic toward him in a way. But then Sting comes along, offers him more money, high-class accommodation and all that stuff. And Darryl, he's so damned confused. I just said to him, real diplomatic and cordial like 'Man, what do you really want?' You know what he said to me? 'Miles, I wanna do cross-over.' God I almost threw up! Here's a boy with real potential and yet he is falling for that white man's corporate bullshit. Cross-over, my black ass! Don't mean nothing! Anyway, the boy has made his choice."[18]

However, later on Miles called Jones to his room for a long talk and ended it by saying: "Hey Darryl, I understand man. God bless you in everything that you do man, because I love you and I love the way you play."[19] Miles's words have echoes of what he said to Marcus Miller, another bassist whose departure had greatly saddened Miles.

Jones's replacement was his old friend and bass mentor from Chicago, Angus Thomas, although Thomas did not get the gig as a result of a recommendation from Jones. Angus Thomas's name came from a Scottish slave owner who had given it to his great grandfather. Thomas also acquired the nickname "Bangus" because of his habit of banging his bass guitar on stage. He first took up trumpet and then switched to the bass guitar when he was aged around fifteen. Before joining Miles's band, Thomas had played with artists such as John Mayall, Buddy Miles, Albert King and Harvey Mandel. "I was always into Miles – *Bitches Brew* brought me into Miles. I was saying back then that I was going to play with Miles," he says.

Thomas was in Chicago in August 1985 when he got a message saying that Miles would be calling him from Japan. "I was just helping a band around town, moving their gear and all that. Miles called my girlfriend, who called me. I think I had another three or four deliveries to do and I said 'Sorry guys. You're going to have to get your own shit together – I'm off to play with Miles Davis." Thomas was given a tape of the band to learn the music and then met Miles at a rehearsal with the band. "Miles came in on the second day. I played a couple of tunes, did a solo and then Miles gave Vince the high-five and the low-five to say I was cool and had got the gig," recalls Thomas.

Thomas's first gig was at the Hudson River Pier in New York. "We were playing on a huge floating barge. George Clinton was there, Cicely [Tyson] was there. About fifteen minutes before the gig, Miles calls me over to his trailer," says Thomas. "I go there and he asks me whether I have any questions about the music. Then he says 'Damn, didn't I tell you we wear show clothes?' I had gone out and bought these baggy pants and a leopard-skin shirt. Then he says 'Take this shit off.' So I'm standing there in my underwear ten minutes before the gig. Then his dresser comes in and Miles tells him to take his clothes off. Miles tells me to put the guy's clothes on, which was like a Japanese bad-ass white suit. I put it on and Miles asked whether I felt good. I said 'Yes,' and then I went off to do the gig."

Thomas believes Miles did this to stop him from being overwhelmed by the prospect of playing his first gig with the band. It did the trick. "I remember there was a moment when a boat went by and it blew its horn and I immediately went to that note and Miles did the same thing!" Miles would sometimes call Thomas at three or four in the morning to discuss his performance. "He always wanted my bass to sound like his voice and I used a lot of distortion with my playing. Miles wanted his voice sampling long before samplers came on the scene."

In October 1985, the band gained yet another new member, the keyboardist Adam Holzman, who had worked with Miles on some of his first recording sessions for Warner Bros Records. The addition of Holzman as a second keyboardist resulted in the band becoming a nonet. Holzman explains how he and Irving played together. "At first he played the main chordal parts and I added reinforcement, doubling lines, playing Minimoog bass, covering clavinet and brass parts. It eventually developed into an even sharing of roles, plus we had this 'spontaneous orchestration' thing going after a while. We would improvise semi-orchestral sections as an alternative to standard comping. I learned a lot from Bobby."

The band was now composed of Miles, Berg, Stern, Irving, Holzman, Thomas, Wilburn, Mazur and Thornton. Thomas describes the nonet as: "The baddest motherfucking jam band on the planet," and a performance at the Falkoner concert hall in Copenhagen on October 28, 1985 bears this out. The concert was broadcast on Danish radio and reveals a band in sparkling form.

By this time, several new tunes had been added to the set: "Burn" was a rock-funk track originally recorded at *The Man With The Horn* sessions – Miles was now considering using it on his first album for Warner Bros. "Stronger Than Before" was a song written by Burt Bacharach, Bruce Roberts and Carole Bayer Sager and covered by Chaka Khan on her 1984 album *I Feel For You*. "Rubberband," a funky number written by Miles, Randy Hall and Zane Giles, had been recorded barely a week earlier by Miles. "Katia" was dropped from the set.

There was also a new and radical arrangement to "Human Nature," which turned the tune into a *tour de force* performance. Irving explains how this came about. "At that time, during performances we had a lot of freedom to create live on-stage. On one performance, during the normal vamp of 'Human Nature,' Miles changed the modality from major to minor. We responded and what happened was very interesting; it opened up a completely new realm of expression. When we reviewed the tape, Miles suggested that I play 'Milestones' over this vamp. Ironically this vamp was already in A-minor, the same key as the section of 'Milestones' which he had made reference to. In order to make it work, I had to play the phrase with a half-time triplet feel superimposed over the 4/4. When we played it again, it kept driving the vamp forward as it seemed to keep turning and evolving as a solo vehicle for Miles and the saxophonist."

In fact, at this stage, Miles was still experimenting with the new arrangement and couldn't decide whether to use the solo spot as a showcase for the saxophonist or guitarist. In this show, both Berg and Stern play solos over the vamp, but Miles later decided to let the guitarist play the solo spot alone. This situation would remain until early 1987, when thereafter the solo spot on "Human Nature" was always played by saxophonist Kenny Garrett. Another development was Miles quoting themes or melodies from other tunes in his solo, such as Ella Fitzgerald's "A Tisket, A Tisket."

While Miles is undoubtedly the star of the show, playing with grace, power and elegance, other band members also get to shine. Berg, for instance, plays a powerful and fluent solo on "Ms. Morrisine." Stern lets rip with a scorching guitar on "Something's On Your Mind," but his most powerful performance is saved for "Jean-Pierre/Then There Were None," one of the highlights of the concert. Beginning at around the five-and-a-half-minute mark, his solo begins slowly, gradually building up to a searing climax four minutes later. During the intro to "Decoy," which was played as an encore, Thomas displays some agile bass playing. Miles was very pleased with this concert and played the tape to writer Mark Rowland, stating that it was planned to be released by Columbia as his last contracted record for the company.[20] At the time of writing, the concert is still officially unreleased.

The nonet was also featured on another broadcast, although this time on both radio and television. The concert took place at the Philharmonica concert hall in Berlin on November 1, 1985 and, once again, changes were made to both the repertoire and arrangements. "Decoy" and "Jean-Pierre" were dropped and a new song "Broken Wings" was tried out for the first time. For some reason, Miles would revive "Jean-Pierre" on an intermittent basis until July 1988. For the Berlin concert, Miles was dressed in a flowing blue top and baggy red satin trousers. He also wore his trademark sunglasses and during the concert acknowledged the audience on numerous occasions.

The one-hour television broadcast featured pop tunes "Time After Time" and "Something's On Your Mind," but there were also several tracks that have never featured on any official Miles Davis studio album. During "Pacific Express," Miles played to several female members of the audience and even left the stage to flirt with a blonde woman in the second row. And in this number, Stern swapped his Fender Stratocaster for an amplified acoustic guitar, and Miles and Irving played a short reprise together. "I enjoyed playing 'Pacific Express' because I got a chance to play piano and it allowed for a great amount of freedom of expression," says Irving.

"Hopscotch" probably featured the most flamboyant performance ever given by a Miles Davis band. The tune begins ordinarily enough, with Miles playing the theme on open horn and Berg playing the melody on soprano saxophone. But halfway through the performance there is a dramatic change in mood as Miles blows a few phrases and the rhythm section starts playing with a greater intensity. This is a signal for Thornton to move his conga drums to the front of the stage, where he plays hyperactively.

Behind him, Thomas plays a stirring bass riff and Miles jabs at the keyboards. "I was so happy that Miles had heard something that he really wanted to hear and he didn't want me standing back and playing my solo. He wanted me to come out and when he brought me out to the front I think I played like I have never played before and I think he knew that would happen," says Thornton. During Thornton's solo the camera cuts away to Miles, who at one point springs back from the keyboards as if he has had an electric shock. Then with a dramatic flourish, he stretches out his arms in front of him, like a zombie rising up from the ground.

Thornton continues to play at great speed and then the energy is brought down, leaving the percussionist to solo unaccompanied for a brief period. The band starts cranking up again and Mazur moves from behind her kit and advances to the front of the stage, holding an African talking drum. She then proceeds to dance wildly, before joining Thornton for a duet. Then Thomas moves to the front of the stage, Mazur does some more dancing, before retreating back to her normal position. Thomas plays a stirring solo, which Miles brings to an end with the trumpet blast. On hearing this, Thomas throws himself to the floor in front of Miles, gets up and then marches up to a speaker cabinet at the back of the stage and rubs his fretboard against it – this seems more like a rock show than a jazz performance.

The next number, "Rubberband," has a strong groove and finds Miles playing trumpet with one hand while stabbing out chords on a synthesizer with the other. Stern grins at Miles and everybody is having a good time, including the audience who are seen jigging in their seats and clapping along with the beat. The tune ends and Miles acknowledges the audience, stretching out his arms and waving to those up in the balcony. The encore, Mr Mister's "Broken Wings," was only broadcast on radio. Thomas plays a catchy riff during the intro, which encourages the audience to clap along and then Miles enters on open horn, which he plays with much tenderness and feeling. The nonet toured Europe until the end of the year, but Miles would then spend the next two months laying down tracks for what would be his new album, *Tutu*.

When Miles resumed touring in March 1986, his band had a new bassist, Felton Crews. Crews was yet another bass player from Chicago and a close friend of Miles's nephew Vince Wilburn Jr. Crews had also played on the early *The Man With The Horn* sessions. Thomas explains how he discovered he was no longer with the band. "I did the dates in America and then in Europe. We got off the road and were supposed to go back in February. But I didn't hear anything until a journalist from Sweden called me and told me that I wasn't on the tour." But Thomas was not bitter. "I was just thankful that I got to spend my moment in life with the man. People ask me 'Don't you wish you could have stayed longer with Miles?' It's like a relationship – would you rather have six happy months with a person or go on for longer and be miserable? I was always very happy with Miles. That experience you cannot buy."

Miles also revised his set list, dropping "Rubberband," "Stronger Than Before," "Pacific Express," "Broken Wings" and "Ms. Morrisine." In their place were three tracks from the forthcoming *Tutu* album, "Tutu," "Portia" and "Splatch," plus a Neil Larsen tune "Carnival Time," which had been recorded in sessions with Zane Giles and Randy Hall that took place in late 1985 and early 1986. But after just a few gigs, in March 1986, there would be another change in personnel, as Mike Stern left for a second and final time.

"At that point I wanted to do some other stuff and I was feeling that it was time to move on. I had been there about three years and now another year. I had just done my first record[21] and I think Miles also felt that it was time [for me] to leave," recalls Stern. "He was in one of those moods – sometimes he would get in those moods where he would just dog on everything. We were in Chicago and the electronic hook-up on his trumpet broke and they had to stop the gig and the band had to play without Miles for a while. And then he came back and played. It was a good gig but he was in a nasty mood about it. I went to his room after the gig – everybody said 'Don't go to his room tonight!' – I wanted to play him my new record [*Upside Downside*] and he was in a terrible mood, so we had a little bit of a fight and I just said 'Look, that's it, I've got to cancel.'"

But Stern says he felt bad about this situation later on. "At that point I was sober and I realized what he had put up with for so many years. I was grateful for what he had done. So I didn't really want to leave that way, so I sent him a piece of jewellery – a little silver trumpet – and I heard he got it and really dug it. I sent him a letter – I was very grateful for the gig."

Reflecting on Miles the person, Stern adds: "He could be a piece of work sometimes and he was a pain in the ass, really unpredictable and crazy in some ways – hot and cold. Some days he was really happy about everything, other days there was nothing about anything and he'd just get into a dark mood and that's always difficult. But everybody gets like that to some degree, but it was over the top with him because he was always taking some kind of drugs – codeine and some prescription stuff – so that messes with you. But as difficult as it was sometimes, it was an absolutely amazing experience for me."

Stern's replacement was Robben Ford, who had been introduced to Miles by Warner Bros producer Tommy LiPuma. Ford was (and is) a superbly talented guitarist and his versatility can be discerned by the range of artists he has played with, which include Burt Bacharach, Kiss, George Harrison and Joni Mitchell. Ford made his debut on April 4, 1986 at Constitution Hall in Washington D.C. "I met Miles about forty minutes before we played," recalls Ford. "He took one look at me (in my very conservative clothes) and said 'Robben, whatcha gonna wear on stage?' He didn't ask me about the music and left me to hang myself [find my feet]. He was smiling after my first solo though. I was terrified the first night I played and thought he would want someone who could play a lot and fast, so basically I was in knots. I decided from that point on to relax and be myself. I learned that lesson straightaway."

Ford was a great find for Miles, a musician who could play the blues and was also comfortable with jazz, rock and funk. Playing with Miles was an intense experience recalls Ford: "Miles just left you out on a limb. It seemed that you had to be on 'ten' at all times. That almost seemed unmusical and I'd never know if that was exactly what he wanted." Given the amount of space Miles gave Ford it would appear that he was giving Miles exactly what he wanted.

Many band members who played with Ford, and many others, who joined the band after he had left, recall how much Miles would talk about Ford. "Miles loved Robben," says Thornton. Miles told writer Roy Carr: "Robben has the knack of playing the right things in the right style at the right moments. Another thing he has got going for him – he doesn't over-play. He's an exceptional musician ... a rare find. Some nights I just end up listening to him."[22]

Parts of a concert the band played at the New Orleans Jazz Festival on April 25, 1986 was broadcast on a programme about Miles, "Miles Ahead: The Music of Miles Davis." The featured tunes were "One Phone Call/Street Scenes," "Time After Time," "Human Nature," and a new tune entitled "Al Jarreau" on the programme but in fact is called "I Love What We Make Together." During the performance of "Time After Time," we see Miles calling Ford forward to play along with him. Sadly, the excerpts are short and the closing number "Human Nature" ends just as Ford is about to take his solo.

Marilyn Mazur left the band soon after this concert. "We were supposed to go to Martinique and something happened about a missing contract, so that all the gear was sent ahead but the gig was cancelled. So it cost a fortune and someone had to go to save money!" recalls Mazur. "So after being kept in the U.S. between all the tours for about a year, I was sent home. This turned out to be very important for me, because I got to see my mother shortly before she died unexpectedly. To me it seemed to be another aspect of the magic intuition that Miles possessed." Mazur would rejoin the band in 1988.

The band, now composed of Miles, Ford, Irving, Holzman, Berg, Crews, Thornton and Wilburn, played at the Amnesty 25th anniversary concert at the Giant's Stadium in East Rutherford, New Jersey on June 15, 1986. The band played a short set featuring "One Phone Call/Street Scenes," "Speak," "Tutu," "Splatch" and "Burn." The latter tune saw Miles's old friend Carlos Santana join him on-stage. This was a sizzling performance with Berg's driving saxophone and the two guitarists (Ford and Santana) trading scorching licks.

Miles also played the Montreux Jazz Festival that year, an event which was recorded by both TV and sound crew. The full concert was eventually released on *The Complete Miles At Montreux* boxed set in 2002. The set consisted of "One Phone Call/Street Scenes," "New Blues," "Maze," "Human Nature," "Wrinkle," "Tutu," "Splatch," "Time After Time," "Al Jarreau/I Love What We Make Together," "Carnival Time," "Burn," "Portia" and "Jean-Pierre."

"New Blues" is the alternative name for the blues tune "Star People," which always followed the frenetic opening number. Miles's discographer Enrico Merlin has pointed out that, over the years, Miles performed this tune more than 350 times and that it slowly evolved,[23] while maintaining the original feeling. Irving explains how "New Blues" developed: "The meter and style of the blues would change maybe once a year. This usually coincided with the changing of bass players. Miles would want to try different things with the new players coming in."

The concert was especially memorable because the Montreux Jazz founder and promoter Claude Nobs had asked Miles if keyboardist George Duke and saxophonist David Sanborn (who were also performing at Montreux with their bands) could sit in separately on some numbers. Miles agreed. George Duke played on two tracks, "Tutu" and "Splatch," using a portable synthesizer that was hung from his shoulders like a guitar. "I was milling around backstage and Miles asked me to come in and I said 'Cool.' I remember Miles holding the neck of my instrument until he was ready for me to play," recalls Duke, who plays some scorching keyboard on "Splatch." After the concert, Duke went back to his hotel room, when the phone rang. "It was Miles asking me to join his band! I said if he'd asked me six months earlier I would not have hesitated, but at the time I was too busy with production work and other kinds of stuff," explains Duke.

Earlier on in the festival, Sanborn had met Miles backstage and Miles asked him if he would like to sit in with the band a couple of nights later. "I was actually supposed to be in Peruga later that week and the travel arrangements were such that the only way I could do it was to leave on the day I was going to play with Miles. I remember Claude Nobs really wanting it to happen and Claude said 'I can arrange to get a jet to fly you from Geneva to

Peruga,'" recalls Sanborn. Bibi Green, who was working with Sanborn at the time, recounts how it all happened at the last minute. "We had checked out the hotel and our bags were packed in the cars ready to take us to the airport when Claude suddenly appeared with this proposal to hire a jet for us all. After a short discussion, we unpacked all the bags and checked in again at the hotel."

Claude Nobs recalls that, for Sanborn "it was a dream come true for him to play with Miles Davis... Sanborn was very nervous on-stage, but Miles whispered to him 'Relax, man, we got time!'"[24] Sanborn played on three tunes "Burn," "Portia" and the closer "Jean-Pierre," and, after the initial stage nerves, thoroughly enjoyed the experience (he plays particularly well on "Portia"). "It was great because my good buddy Bob Berg was playing with Miles. It was fun and we had a great time," he says.

"That was actually one of my favourite shows," says Ford. "George and David were a bit mystified by the whole thing – it took a while to be comfortable out there. Montreux was the greatest jazz festival at the time and I'm glad I got to play it with Miles." Once again, Ford got plenty of space to play and he delivers a number of solos. On "Splatch," he quotes the theme to "I Like To Be In America," the song written by Leonard Bernstein and Stephen Sondheim from the musical *West Side Story*, and on "Burn" he quotes Hendrix's "Purple Haze."

Miles was gradually bringing more tunes from the *Tutu* album into the set and by August 1986, "Tutu," "Splatch," "Tomaas" and "Perfect Way" were becoming concert regulars. What is more, Miles wanted the songs on-stage to sound like the recorded versions and so the music became more highly organized and tightly arranged. On the bootleg CD *The King Of Priests*, the band can be heard rehearsing "Tomaas" and "Perfect Way." On both recordings, the band spends much of the time repeatedly going over short sections of each song for more than twenty minutes. Ford was feeling increasingly uncomfortable about Miles's new musical direction and he left the band at the end of August 1986.

According to Miles, Ford left because he was getting married and wanted to make his own record,[25] but that is only part of the story. "I had just signed with Warner Bros and was about to embark on my solo career," recalls Ford. "I might have been able to put the two things together but he started playing more music from *Tutu* and tightening up the arrangements to be more like the record. I felt it was time to go."

But Ford has many good memories of Miles. "Miles was always very supportive and complimentary to me. And I did hear that he said good things about me after I left his band. He told me the last night I played with him that if I ever wanted to come back, just come. Miles increased my self-confidence. He made me laugh a lot. I learned a harmonic device that became very important in my playing and I also found some things that were rhythmically fresh to me. He liked musicians and creativity. He was a true artist and responded to genuineness. What a guy."

Between June 1981 and April 1986, Miles had only ever used two guitarists – Mike Stern and John Scofield – in all his bands. But between April 1986 and May 1987, Miles would try out seven guitarists. This "hunt the guitarist" strategy was a result of Miles looking for a particular guitar sound. Ford recommended a friend, Garth Webber, who sent Miles a tape of him playing a live gig with his own band. Like Ford, Webber's playing was steeped in the blues, but he too was a versatile performer – he has played with artists such as Greg Allman, Boz Scaggs and John Lee Hooker. "I met Miles at the back door of a hall where the band was playing in Detroit," recalls Webber. "The door opened and there was Miles. He grabbed my hand and pulled me into the building and we started walking down the hall. Miles said to me 'You sound good on those tapes.'"

Webber was given a cassette featuring a couple of live shows and then spent the next three days holed up in a hotel room, where he practised the tunes. "There were no charts or instructions, just the cassette. Miles said nothing about what he wanted from me. When I was given the cassette, there were no titles and there were never any set lists on stage – it was all memorized. It was only in reviews and stuff in print that I began to glean the names of the songs. I bought the *Tutu* CD and that had some names on it. There was just one rehearsal – which Miles did not attend – and that was to work on a specific new tune that the band was learning, so we didn't go over the set."

Miles liked to use this "sink or swim" approach with his new musicians because it challenged them to play beyond their expectations and capabilities, and it is a sign of Miles's uncanny instinct that most members of his bands were up to the task. Webber made his debut at Rio De Janiero in September 1986. "I was actually quite comfortable just before the gig and felt that I would be able to do a good job. After the set, Miles said to me 'You played your ass off,' and I thought I had gotten off to a decent start," says Webber.

Webber enjoyed his time with Miles. "I did feel comfortable in the band and Miles was always very nice to me. We were playing the *Tutu* songs and I loved them. I love Marcus Miller's writing and it was great to play those songs, especially with Miles. I totally dug 'Tutu,' 'Carnival,' 'Full Nelson' and 'Portia.' When I first went to see the band knowing I was being considered for the gig, I loved the way it sounded and how the set went from one song to another without any stopping between songs. I thought that continuity really kept the mood happening."

Webber also recalls how Miles would direct the band on-stage and, in particular, how Miles would get the band to seamlessly move from one tune to the next. "He would sometimes count for the drummer. He had these hand signals that he flashed at Vincent to give him the tempo and to suggest a particular figure to play. He had ways of cueing the band for ending solos by starting lines [series of notes] mostly. Then the rest of the members would fall in. Usually we caught on within a note or two. Sometimes I could successfully guess when Miles was going to cue something and come in right with him on the first note – you could sort of feel that he was going to give the cue." Miles rarely communicated with band members verbally when it came to giving musical directions, adds Webber: "When I asked him how he would like me to play a particular song we were adding to the set, he responded 'Play it like you're salutin' the flag,' which I thought was an interesting suggestion."

Webber often played extensive solos on "Star People/New Blues" and "Human Nature." For the latter, Webber would use effects pedals to produce a "spacey" guitar sound. "When I had soloed for what felt like long enough for me, I would start listening for Miles. But the length of the solos was determined by Miles and not you. At one time he left Bob Berg 'flapping in the breeze,' for what must have been five minutes. Bob kept turning around and trying to get Miles's attention, but Miles wouldn't even look at him, much less stop him playing. The same happened to me once to a lesser degree. It was good for me in that I discovered a place to go with the solo that I wouldn't have found otherwise. When Miles wanted me to play for a long time, however, I generally took it as a compliment. Poor Adam [Holzman] used to get through the preamble of his one solo of the night and Miles would cut him off and end the song."

In October 1986, Darryl Jones returned to the band. "The following year, I ran into Steve Thornton and I said 'Man, tell Miles that I love him,' and he said 'Darryl, you call him and tell him yourself,' so he gave me Miles's phone number and I called him. He said 'What are you doing?' I said I'd just finished playing with Steps Ahead and he said 'You wanna come back?' I said 'Yeah man, you know I want to!' He said, 'Okay, come over right now, I wanna have a look at you and see if your ass ain't no junkie!'"

The band and the music had changed since Jones last played with Miles. "Sometimes it would be the same song, but it would be arranged differently. We'd go to a rehearsal and I'd play the bass line I had found [when playing in the last group] and which I thought was the slickest thing I could play over this tune. He'd hear it and say 'Don't play that, play something else.' You'd be confused but out of that something really new would come. It was like 'how to get lost and then find your direction another way.'"

Not surprisingly, Jones's playing had developed since he had left Miles. "Playing with Miles and having him dig what I was doing created a lot of confidence. Then I played with Sting and that created more confidence. And when I came back to Miles, he would comment sometimes on my confidence and I couldn't see what he was talking about. But after you've been in the band a while and you see a new guy come in and gain confidence, that's when I was able to see what he meant. Miles also used to say that 'guys don't play the same when their ladies are in the audience.' He was talking about ego."

Webber recounts what it was like to hear Miles play on-stage: "I remember the very first solo he played at the first gig I did with him. He started out his solo with the 'ugly duckling' of all notes. I thought 'Oh my God, what is he doing?' Then, as he held this long note, he worked it until by the time he finished it was this thing of beauty that just sailed out into the room – this golden note. It was almost as if he had thrown a shapeless lump of clay on to a wheel and then made a beautiful work of pottery out of it. He really had a way with the tune 'Time After Time.' He used the most fragile tone to evoke the sweetness that was very beautiful and endearing. Miles really loved ballads and I remember that quote where he was asked 'Why don't you play ballads anymore?' and he said 'Because I love them so much.' I think I understand that."

In November, a new tune was added to the set, Toto's ballad "Don't Stop Me Now," which Miles had recorded with the band. The band spent much of the remainder of 1986 touring Europe before playing in Canada and the U.S. in December. Music critic Dave Gelly saw the band play in London on November 17, 1986. "Going to a Miles Davis concert is very much like going to one by Frank Sinatra," he wrote. "You know there will be a fair amount of dross, some outrageous posing, quite long periods of appalling dullness, but also a few moments of true and perfect eloquence." Gelly also noted that "the first ten minutes are usually the worst, as the whole band go flat out in an apparent bid to test the acoustics to destruction." He added: "the drummer Vince Wilburn Jr. deserves some kind of award for stamina. He was the only one who had to play non-stop throughout, often very hard indeed, yet his beat never faltered. In more than two hours of non-stop performance, perhaps thirty minutes were sheer perfection, another thirty absolute screaming boredom and the rest, a strange edgy mixture of the two."[26]

In late December 1986, Webber was sacked from the band. "I was called by the manager and told that they were going to try somebody from Funkadelic. I had considered the whole experience to be so fortunate for me that I was in no way unhappy when they let me go." Like almost everyone who played with Miles, Webber has fond memories of him. "He was very bright and intense and liked to play around with people. He would be doing stuff like rolling the limo window up while I had my arm through to shake his hand. Once when I was soloing with my eyes closed, I felt something on my foot. I opened my eyes and there was Miles two inches from my face with those big sunglasses on, standing on my foot!"

Webber adds that he learned many things from working with Miles. "One thing I learned is that you can make any song groove at any tempo you have to. He would call some of the tunes at radically different tempos from night to night and the band would just find a way to make it sound good, even if it meant changing the melody or lines on the spot. I am very grateful to have had the chance to play with Miles. There were many guitarists who perhaps deserved it more than I, but what are you gonna do?"

Webber's replacement was Dewayne "Blackbyrd" McKnight, who became the first black guitarist to join Miles's band since Reggie Lucas and Pete Cosey in the summer of 1975 (from now on, all the guitarists Miles hired for his bands would be black). McKnight had played in George Clinton's Funkadelic band and with Herbie Hancock. McKnight earned his nickname from members of the local bands he used to play in around Los Angeles. "I would not stay in a band for very long and was always moving from band to band, so they said that you never knew when I would fly away," he recalls. In the light of what happened during his tenure with Miles, it was an ironic choice for a nickname.

Many members of Miles Davis bands say they had a premonition that one day they would play with Miles and McKnight was no exception. "It's a funny thing, but I knew at one point I was going to play with Miles. I used to joke with my girlfriend 'Did Miles call today?' One day I came home to my answer service and somebody from Miles Davis called. I thought it was a joke. It was [road manager] Jim Rose and I spoke to him on the phone and he said 'Miles is getting ready to call you.' He hung up the phone – I thought it was a prank. Then Miles called." Miles wanted McKnight to send him a tape of him playing. "I don't know who told Miles about me, but I think [drummer] Dennis Chambers may have been responsible," says McKnight.

McKnight prepared for the gig by buying the album *Tutu*. "I had seen Miles play a couple of times, so was familiar with the band. I also had a live tape and practised with it. It didn't feel challenging because it was always something that I wanted to do – it was nothing that I couldn't do. I just tried to enjoy it." But McKnight found his initial meeting with the band an unsettling experience. "It was a shaky relationship from the start – it was really weird. They gave me Adam Holzman's number and told me to tell him that I was in the band and I said 'Don't you think you should do that? I don't know this guy.' We had started rehearsing before I met Miles – Miles was never at the rehearsals. The rehearsals were stressed and the relationship with the group wasn't good, with the exception of Bobby Irving and Vince Wilburn – they were cool. I think maybe the band didn't care for the way I played. The only good vibes I got were from Miles on-stage."

The first time McKnight met Miles was at a Christmas dinner that Miles had laid on for the band. The dinner came as a result of a joke by Patrick Murray, then the band's keyboard technician and lighting director. "It was late December 1986 and we had just found out that we were going to be doing a double bill of shows with Al Jarreau at the Universal Amphitheater in Hollywood from December 28 to 31, 1986. Miles flew us out to L.A. on December 23 and we had to rehearse on Christmas Eve! Of course Miles doesn't show, so I jokingly said to Vince Wilburn 'So Vince, is Miles gonna have us all over for Christmas dinner or what?' Vince immediately gets on the phone and says 'Hey Miles, Pat says you're having us all over for Christmas dinner.' I could have killed Vince. I guess Miles thought about it for a while and said 'Sure, come on over.'"

The next day, the road crew arrived at Miles's home. "We had decided that we were going to be fashionably late because the last thing we wanted to do was be the first ones there, so we arrived about an hour late. Of course we were the first ones there and when we got to the door of his place on the beach in Malibu his valet Mike answered the door and we heard Miles's voice from upstairs 'Hey Mike, who's that? The crew? Must be the white contingent. Quick, open up the doors, they're smellin' up my house,'" says Murray

Murray surveyed the meal, set out on tables. "Miles and Cicely had a huge catered spread with everything from turkey and salmon to Miles's favourite – corned beef and cabbage. He loved to watch people eat and was always trying to get you to try some of his food. Later on, as the sun was setting, Miles sat up on his balcony and serenaded us with a little solo trumpet music. Later on, we ate popcorn and watched the movie 'To Live And Die in L.A.' and then videos of old boxing matches. It was one of my most memorable Christmas dinners ever." McKnight recalls feeling "terrified" at the dinner because "I didn't know what to do or what to think. I didn't ask him all the things I wanted to ask him like a fan would do. I tried to be cool."

At this point, Miles also added another member to the band, the tenor saxophonist Gary Thomas. Thomas is a large man (six feet five tall) with a large sound. Thomas, whose influences include Woody Shaw, Eddie Harris and Billy Harper, plays with a ferocious power and intensity. Thomas had opened for Miles's band in Baltimore on August 30, 1986, but Miles had failed to notice him then. It was through a mutual acquaintance that Miles heard about Thomas and he asked the saxophonist to send him a tape of him playing. But the tape got lost in the post, so Miles telephoned Thomas and asked him to play a tape over the phone. After listening for just a few minutes, Miles invited Thomas to join the band.[27]

His recruitment saw Miles touring with a twin saxophone line-up of Berg and Thomas. "I learned that Gary was playing when he appeared on a gig. He's a great player. Miles didn't need to explain anything – it was his band. At this point it was obvious to me that he was looking for another sound, which after three years is completely understandable," said Berg. But at the time it must have been unsettling for Berg, something which Miles once alluded to: "Bob's feeling a little funny now that Gary's there. Only because my road manager – who talks too fucking much – says to him 'Hey, Miles has got a new sax player.' So then Bob says to me 'The guy's playing my shit.' I said 'Look, Bob, I had Coltrane and Cannonball together!'"[28]

McKnight and Thomas made their debut at the Universal Amphitheater in Los Angeles on December 28, 1986. The band was now composed of Miles, Berg, Thomas, McKnight, Irving, Holzman, Jones, Wilburn and Thornton. McKnight features prominently on several tunes, including the opener "One Phone Call/Street Scenes," where he plays a sharp, fast solo that begins in the eighth minute, and on "Splatch" and "Human Nature." On the latter tune, McKnight plays a strong solo that lasts for almost two minutes. He's also given plenty of space on "Star People/New Blues," and the last three minutes of this performance are taken up by another solo from McKnight.

McKnight acquits himself well on the faster tracks and has a strong sense of rhythm, but while there is some fine, expressive playing on "Star People/New Blues," it is also a little disjointed at times. A highlight of the concert was a rousing version of "Wrinkle," which saw both Thomas and Berg trading explosive solos over a ferocious bass riff. If Miles had wanted the presence of Thomas to energize the band, he had certainly succeeded on this number. "During the first gig I had butterflies, because it was an element I wasn't used to – you're playing with Miles Davis. I was anxious and hoping that I pleased him. A friend who was at the gig tells me I got several standing ovations," recalls McKnight.

But Miles was not entirely happy with McKnight's playing. "I like the way McKnight plays guitar," he said, "and when he finally hears the sound that's in his head, he's going to be something else."[29] "He'd call me every morning after the show and he'd tell me what he would like to hear from the guitar. They told me he was pretty particular about what he wanted to hear from a guitar. He didn't yell like I'd hear people say, he was pretty cool and down to earth," says McKnight. But by the December 31 gig, the guitar solo spot during "Star People/New Blues" had been replaced by a saxophone and Miles curtailed McKnight's solo spots. The band went off the road and resumed touring on January 24, 1987. By that time, McKnight had been sacked.

"It was probably one of the greatest shocks I had," recalls McKnight. "I called the road manager because it was coming up time to go back on the road and nobody had called or said anything. So I guess they didn't expect me to call. I called Jim Rose and I asked him, was I going on the tour? And he said 'No' and then I asked him why. He couldn't answer – I never got a valid answer from him. I gave him a bunch of suggestions, but I never got an answer to that question. The only thing he said was that it wasn't the sound that Miles was looking for, which didn't tell me anything. I asked, was the answer new gear? What are you talking about? The same thing with Miles. I called Miles. He couldn't give me an answer. Miles's last words to me were 'I'll call you when I need you.' Then he hung up the phone."

Darryl Jones, who has the distinction of playing with almost every guitarist Miles had in his bands during the last ten years (the exception was Robben Ford), says: "With Blackbyrd, it did not concern his playing. I think it was an equipment thing, but then you never really knew with Miles. I think Blackbyrd can really play." McKnight says the incident greatly affected his confidence as a guitarist for a long time afterwards. "It hurt. I had always wanted to work with Miles."

In January 1987, Miles began looking for a new guitarist. One of those auditioned was a young black guitarist John Bigham, who by his own admission was not ready to play with Miles. Miles also considered Barry Finnerty, who had played on *The Man With The Horn*. "Jim Rose called me and said Miles was thinking about having me in the band. They asked me to send a tape," says Finnerty. "I said 'But Miles knows what I sound like.'" Finnerty sent a tape. "I got a message later on from Jim Rose saying that Miles thought that all white guitarists sounded like Mike Stern, which was bullshit." Miles's new guitarist was Hiram Bullock, an exciting and extrovert player who had been born in Osaka, Japan. Bullock spent much of his early childhood travelling around the world because his father was in the CIA. As a child, he learned to play piano, saxophone and bass, before switching to guitar at sixteen.

Bullock is a versatile performer who has played with many artists including Gil Evans, Paul Simon, James Brown, Barbara Streisand and Eric Clapton. He also appeared as the barefoot guitarist on *The David Letterman Show*. Bullock is also closely associated with David Sanborn, who discovered him. "Hiram was playing with a group of friends in a club in New York that was across the road from the club where I was playing. I saw him and asked him to join my band," recalls Sanborn. "I'd known Miles for several years since about 1983. I met him through Gil Evans. He needed a guitar player, he called and I accepted," says Bullock. Bullock was contracted to play for four gigs, and made his debut on January 24, 1987. There was also another change to the line-up at this time, with Steve Thornton being replaced by Mino Cinelu, the third member of Miles's bands to return for a second stint.

Thornton recalls how he heard the news that he was no longer in the band. "Jim [Rose] called me and said 'Miles is not going to take you out on the next tour.' It wasn't like a surprise or a disappointment for me. I think he said that Mino was going to come back or that Miles was going to try something else. So I called Miles and he said 'Don't worry about it man, we'll get back together. I'm hearing something else and I want to try it.' Who's going to argue with Miles about what he hears and what he wants to try? I just wanted to let him know that I was thankful for the time I had worked with him and I had learned so much from him. I wanted him to know that I appreciated the fact that he had chosen me to be in his band. I really wanted him to know that."

Looking back at his time with Miles, Thornton says: "The one thing that I carry with me most from my experiences with Miles is just to play and just to feel as relaxed and as comfortable as you can. One thing about Miles was if you didn't know what he was going to play, he felt very good about it! So sometimes, just play and see what happens." Cinelu explains how he returned to Miles's band. "He called me when I was in Weather Report and asked me to come back. I asked him 'Who's on bass?' and he said 'Darryl,' and he laughed because he knew I would say yes, because Darryl could hold a groove like no one else."

The new band, now composed of Miles, Bullock, Irving, Holzman, Berg, Thomas, Jones, Wilburn and Cinelu, made its debut on January 24. The set now comprised "One Phone Call/Street Scenes," "Speak," "Star People," "Perfect Way," "Human Nature," "Wrinkle," "Tutu," "Splatch," "Time After Time," "Full Nelson," "Don't Stop Me Now," "Carnival Time" and "Tomaas." The encore was "Maze" and "Portia."

The following night the band played in Indianapolis. On the opening number "One Phone Call/Street Scenes," Bullock injects some dirty, nasty guitar chords and on "Human Nature" he plays a superb solo that has his guitar screaming and soaring. "I didn't really see the music as a challenge – it was just music with a definite jazz sensibility," says Bullock. "Miles was a bit cryptic and aloof. He could be difficult at times, but at other times he was very sweet and charming. He could be manipulative, not what you'd call a nice guy, but certainly interesting. One thing I learned from him was to trust my musical instincts."

One of the standout performances was made by Bob Berg, who played a moving soprano saxophone solo on "Tomaas." This was Berg's last gig with the band. "At this point my playing time was reduced to very short segments [and] the addition of another saxophonist reduced it even more. I also knew that after someone was in the band for a long time, Miles had a hard time letting them go, so he'd just bring in someone else on the same instrument. I also felt that I'd hit a wall regarding self-expression in Miles's band and it was time to move on. I really did feel a static quality in the band that became more pronounced with time. I guess it became more of a show than an organic, searching musical experience. As they say, each to their own," said Berg.

Berg got to see Miles in concert a few times after he had left the band. "I always paid my respects to one of the masters of the music. The highlight of my experience with the band was to get to hear Miles play night after night and to be around one of the pioneers of jazz," he said. Berg went on to pursue a successful solo career but his life was tragically cut short when he died in a traffic accident in December 2002.

Berg was soon followed by Bullock, who left after playing his allotted four gigs with Miles. "He wanted me to continue with him, but I turned him

Marilyn Mazur and Steve Thornton: Danbury, Connecticut, August 31, 1985

Miles in London, 1987

Miles's former guitarist John McLaughlin made guest appearances on *Aura* and *You're Under Arrest*

Felton Crews: Lehman College, Bronx, New York, March 22, 1986

Vince Wilburn Jr. with Miles: Lehman College, Bronx, New York, March 22, 1986

Robben Ford: Beacon Theatre, New York, April 6, 1986

Gary Thomas played in two line-ups that featured two saxophonists

Miles with Kenny Garrett, who played with Miles from 1987 to 1991

Miles and Foley in London, 1987

Miles at the Apollo Theatre, Manchester, 1989

Miles and Chaka Khan at the 1989 Montreux Jazz Festival

Miles's self-portralt

Miles at home

Dave Holland was one of Miles's former band members who played at the July 1991 reunion concert in Paris

Easy Mo Bee, Sid Reynolds, Miles and Nikki D at the *Doo-Bop* sessions at New York's Unique Studios

down," says Bullock. "I didn't play with Miles because I didn't want to. I was doing a lot of freelance work at the time and I really didn't want to be tied down to one group. Also there was a 'weird power vibe' in that organization that wasn't my style. I was contracted for four gigs and that's what I did." The "weird power vibe" Bullock alludes to is a period of great upheaval in Miles's life as he parted with his manager David Franklin and his friend and road manager Jim Rose.

One of Rose's many tasks was to collect the band's money after the gig. According to Miles, when he asked Rose for the money he had given it to Franklin's assistant. Miles was concerned about "funny things going on with his money" at the time and he punched Rose in anger. Rose left. It was a sad end to what had been a close friendship and professional relationship. Patrick Murray describes the situation at the time. "At the beginning of 1987, I went on the road with Wayne Shorter for about three months and missed about half a dozen gigs. In that time period Miles fired just about everybody on the crew, management and many of the band members. Only Ron Lorman (front-of-house sound), Ves Weaver (lighting director) and I were asked to return. At that time, I began mixing monitors and stage management which eventually rolled into the production manager job. I always wore a few different hats while working with Miles." Miles appointed lawyer Peter Shukat as his new manager and Shukat recruited Gordon Meltzer as Miles's road manager.

Gordon Meltzer entered the music business by accident. Meltzer's hobby was electronics and in 1983 he started a small business in New York, which involved visiting people's homes to fix their hi fi systems. One day, an acquaintance of Meltzer's explained that a friend of hers needed her stereo fixing. The person was a then little-known singer called Cyndi Lauper. Lauper was about to go on tour and Meltzer was asked to accompany the band on the road. He never went back to his hi-fi repair job after that. After the Lauper tour, Meltzer started working for the rock group Foreigner and was soon promoted to tour manager. He later worked for the rock band AC/DC.

In early 1987, Meltzer was unemployed and kicking his heels when a friend informed him of a new job opportunity. "He told me to go to the offices of Peter Shukat and when I got there, Peter said 'Ever heard of Miles Davis?' and I said 'I've heard the name...' He then told me that Miles had punched out his last road manager and he needed a new one for a month." Meltzer agreed to take the job, but before he could be given it he had to meet Miles for approval. Meltzer was to meet Miles at Shukat's office and, when Meltzer arrived, Shukat and two other business associates of Miles were waiting for him. "Miles came in wearing these big wrap-around shades and a beautiful silk shirt and silk pants. He had so many gold chains and what came to mind was an Egyptian Pharoah," says Meltzer. Miles asked to be left alone with

Meltzer. "He's staring at me and he was drinking a bottle of Perrier," says Meltzer. "Miles then said 'I look good, don't I?' I said 'Yes Mr Davis, you look great.' 'Yeah,' Miles said, 'and I drink a lot of water, but when I come, it's white powder!' He just cracked me up, it was so perfect." Meltzer got the job.

Meltzer decided that Miles's touring arrangements needed an overhaul. "I knew how successful rock bands lived and the kind of lifestyle they liked to maintain on the road. I don't think it went over-well with the band because the deal was that the artist and his partner lived one way in one set of hotels and the band lived a different way," he says. "Miles loved being separated from the band, travelling differently and being in a separate hotel. He'd never really done that before. That's what I tried to bring to the party, to give him a lifestyle that isolated him from reality and gave him as much luxury as possible. It gave him the space to do what he wanted to do."

If Miles wasn't playing music, he was spending a lot of time painting. "Sometimes we'd come to pay the hotel room bill and they'd say 'That will be $2,000 for the carpet and the suite Mr Davis painted last night.' Sometimes he wanted to stay with the guys in the band but other times he wouldn't and so this gave him that space," says Meltzer.

The game of guitarist musical chairs saw the arrival of Bobby Broom in the band. Broom was born in New York, but later moved to Chicago. Before joining Miles's band, Broom had played with Tom Browne, Sonny Rollins and Kenny Burrell. Broom was renowned for his "smooth-jazz" style of playing, and so the decision by Miles to recruit him to a band that was playing a mix of jazz, rock and funk was a surprising one. "At the time I got the Miles gig, most of the guys in the band were Chicagoans – Darryl Jones, Bobby Irving, Vince – so I knew these guys. The three of them came to see me play in an instrumental R&B band I had in Chicago at the time and they told me to get a tape together because Miles wanted to hear me."

Broom compiled a tape. "I knew that Miles wanted rock guitar. I knew that he loved Hendrix and Stern and that kind of thing. The guitarist that was closest to me that had been in his band was John Scofield. My inclination is not to play with any distortion and I hadn't really got my sound together at the time, so it wasn't going to be a comfortable experience for me. But there was no way that I was not going to take this opportunity." Broom's demo tape included some guitar played with heavy distortion. "The word I got back was that Miles had said 'Tell him to come to New York. He sounds good but tell him don't play so far behind the beat.' I thought 'What's he talking about? Scofield plays behind the beat!'"

Broom travelled to New York, where he still had an apartment, and prepared himself for the gig. He was given live tapes to learn the music from. "I also had *Tutu* so knew some of the music. I had several rehearsals with the band, although Miles only turned up for the last one. I felt comfortable with the band until Miles turned up!" Miles was aware that the music he wanted Broom to play was not something the guitarist was accustomed to playing. "I think he really knew what kind of guitarist I was. I'd just put out a record with Kenny Burrell,[30] so if he was paying attention he'd have known my style. "He said to me 'I know the music's really loud, just go ahead and play.' But I said 'Yeah, but this is really loud!' Another thing he said to me was 'Have you ever tried playing with your eyes open? You play more shit with your eyes open.' I was once comping on a tune at a rehearsal and he said to me 'Don't be so obvious.'"

Another new member was alto saxophonist Kenny Garrett, who Miles had seen playing with Dizzy Gillespie on a video. "When Miles saw the video, he was asking around 'Who is that alto player?'" recalls his wife Sayydah Garrett. "He tracked him down and called our house one day and I picked up the phone and just about fainted. He said 'Is Kenny there?' and I said 'Yes, who's calling please?' and then he said 'Miles Davis.'" Garrett was originally contracted to play for four gigs (Miles seemed to give every new musician four gigs to gel with the band), but would stay with Miles for almost five years, remaining in the band right up until the end. "When Kenny came off the phone he was very excited, although he's not one for jumping up and down," says Sayydah Garrett. "He was very honoured and thrilled of course, but very humble. Miles was obviously someone Kenny admired very much."

Kenny Garrett told writer Fred Jung how he was inducted into the band and his first impressions of Miles as a person. "When I got to the band, he was a different person from all those stories I heard, about him being so rough on people and stuff. We had a great relationship. I played four gigs. The first two gigs, Miles never even heard what I was playing because my microphone wasn't working. By the third gig, he finally heard what I was playing and in disbelief he took off my sunglasses because, of course, at that time I was trying to dress like Miles. I had my glasses on. I had to be cool because I'm part of this unit."[31]

Garrett went on to explain how he and Miles played together on-stage: "What happened is, we developed this relationship without even having to verbalize it. It's basically how we did this call and response thing. He played something and I played it back. I guess he didn't believe it, so he played it and I played it back. This became part of the show. A lot of the things were communicated just through the music. It was nothing like 'You do this, I do this.' It was just communicated through the music. To me that was the greatest thing, that we didn't have to talk about what it was we were going to do ... we just did it."[32]

Garrett was not only technically equipped to play with Miles, but his musical history also gave him an edge in understanding Miles and his music. "I understood the bebop. I understood the James Brown that he was doing at that time. I understood the Prince that he was doing at that time also. I grew up on James Brown and I was listening to Prince, so it was actually a perfect vehicle for me. Not only that, some of the other musicians...were only from the R&B genre [or] go-go genre, so they were kind of limited in what they could do, but, as far as my experience with Miles, it was great. I learned so much. I was like a sponge. I tried to absorb as much as I could in those five years."[33]

Miles was clearly delighted with his new find and once said that: "There are a few young guys out there who are developing their own style. My alto player, Kenny Garrett, is one of them."[34] Sayydah Garrett recalls that: "The first words Miles said to me when we met were 'Kenny plays his ass off.' Kenny and Miles had a tremendous love and respect for each other." She recalls an incident which illustrates the regard Miles had for Garrett. "Miles called a lot of people the 'MF' word and Kenny is so proper – he never swears. The first time Kenny rehearsed with Miles, Miles says 'blah, blah motherfucker.' And Kenny was so shocked that he just looked at Miles and said 'What?' That was the first and last time he ever said that to Kenny!"

The band was now composed of Miles, Garrett, Thomas, Irving, Holzman, Broom, Jones, Wilburn and Cinelu. The set was unchanged except now the solo on "Human Nature" was played by the saxophonist rather than the guitarist. Broom vividly recalls his first gig with Miles. "It's the first tune and I'm coming up to my first guitar solo with Miles Davis when, pow! My string breaks! So Miles walks over to hand it off to me, sees what has happened and so cues the band to play on while the tech guy comes on-stage and replaces it. So now it's time for my solo. You can imagine the pressure – I was thoroughly flustered."

On March 25, 1987, the band's line-up was changed again, when Miles sacked Wilburn and brought in a new drummer Ricky Wellman from Washington D.C. "I performed with Miles without any auditions or rehearsals. He sent me a show tape and asked me to learn the material, which I did. I was very nervous my first time out with Miles and the group. Apparently, it all worked out because I was his drummer until the end of his life. I felt very fortunate and blessed because out of all the drummers in the world, he looked down and chose me! He really liked my style for some reason," says Wellman.

Miles and Wellman developed a close relationship. "He would invite me up to his hotel room after concerts and we would eat and talk and share ideas about the concert or how to improve my grooves to enhance his original ideas. He used to hum nursery rhymes to me in order for me to better understand different rhythms in the music. If a song was in 4/4, I would have to play a 3/4 pattern inside a 4/4 beat. Sounds odd but it worked. He loved musicians to improvise on the spot, to change the music to various peaks of excitement. He was a man of few words but, when he spoke, you listened. He was a powerful man in that his insight of creativity was unbelievable. If you really tuned in and listened, you could really learn and exploit your creativity to achieve what he wanted – to make you a better musician." The arrival of Wellman changed the nature of the rhythm section, which became looser and less confined to a constant backbeat.

But despite these changes, Broom was feeling uncomfortable. "I wasn't cutting the gig as far as I was concerned. My voice hadn't developed. I was twenty-six years old and wanted to be a jazz guitarist. By the fourth gig I was bored. It wasn't an environment where you got a bunch of interaction going on. It was very prescribed and I felt confined. Maybe with bass and drums you lock up on a groove and that's something. There was plenty of solo space, but it was more like recording in a studio – 'Here's this groove and I want you to record your stuff on top of it.'"

Broom faced a dilemma soon after joining Miles's band, which meant he had to choose between two gigs. "The Kenny Burrell record had come out. It was quite a thing because he was with two young black guitarists, myself and Rodney Jones. And now the record was out and we've got our first gig as 'The Jazz Guitar Band.' At the same time, Miles has got a gig at the Auditorium Theater in Chicago. So now I'm in a quandary. I remember calling Sonny Rollins up and telling him about the problem. I said 'There's a part of me that wants to do the Miles gig,' and Sonny simply said 'What part is that?', which wasn't that helpful! Then I had to call Miles and tell him I've got another gig. I said 'Can I call you a sub?' Miles was cool about it."

Broom recommended another Chicagoan guitarist Alan Burroughs. "I thought 'If I recommended Alan for the gig, I should be prepared to lose the gig with Miles because Alan was and is in that genre and one of the baddest dudes. A perfect fit for Miles." Burroughs took up the guitar when he was thirteen and his musical influences include The Beatles, Jimi Hendrix, Kenny Burrell, Wes Montgomery, George Benson, Sun Ra – and Miles. "I heard *Live Evil, On The Corner, Big Fun* and *Agharta* when I was at high school and I just knew that I wanted to play with Miles real bad," says Burroughs. "I went to see Miles in 1975 but he got sick and stopped playing. I was praying he'd get well so I could play with him! When he got back in the 1980s, a lot of my friends were playing with him. So that gave me hope."

Burroughs was ecstatic when Broom called him about standing in on the Miles gig. "Bobby said he'd send me a concert tape and that there would be no rehearsal – I would just show up at the gig, which was in two weeks' time. My mind was blown. Funnily enough, before I got the call, I had started practising a lot and listening to *Tutu*. So when Bobby called I was ready. I literally turned up at the sound check before the gig. Bobby Irving went over a few things and that was it."

Burroughs did not meet Miles until the last moment before the start of the performance. "I first met Miles in the wings as we were walking on to the stage. We didn't exchange a word – we just shook hands. It was an awesome feeling. I had my mother and my friends in the audience. I had bought new clothes to wear, real slick New York-style. I had my dreadlocks untied. I was completely excited. But I knew I was prepared so I wasn't worried about clamming up or freaking out. Right after I finished my first solo, Miles walked up to me and pulled me up the front and I felt so comfortable after that." Burroughs' experience echoes that of other musicians who played with Miles, such as saxophonist Azar Lawrence and guitarist Dominque Gaumont, whose audition occurred on the bandstand at a concert at New York's Carnegie Hall on March 30, 1974.

Although he would only play the one gig with Miles, Burroughs says he learned an important lesson that night which still impacts on his playing today. "I remember Miles came up to me in the middle of the show when we were playing an uptempo number and he whispered 'Play one or two notes.' I was excited and probably busier than the soloist I was accompanying! That's all he had to say to me and it's affected me ever since. Now, when I'm supporting somebody I might just push them a little bit, but basically I try to construct my accompaniment around a simple idea. That came from Miles."

Burroughs and his mother met Miles in his dressing room after the gig. "After the concert, he told me how good I was. My mother told him I was [pianist, composer, and arranger] Fletcher Henderson's nephew and Miles said that was where I got my sound from. We started talking music theory. He was basically saying you could play any triad over any chord. Basically you're liberated to do whatever," says Burroughs.

Broom was convinced that Burroughs was a more suitable guitarist for Miles's band than him, so he was surprised to find himself going back to playing again with Miles. But this was to be his last performance with Miles. "I saw Miles before the start of the gig and we hugged. Then we played and that was the last time I saw him. I didn't hear anything after that, but I knew it was over. I was cool about it and glad that it was over," he says. Burroughs recalls: "I got a call from Bobby Irving a few days after my gig, saying 'Miles wants you to join the band.' I had a bitter-sweet feeling because that meant Bobby [Broom] was going to get fired. They told me to get my passport and when the tour was going to start – on my thirtieth birthday on April 19. I had to get a passport quickly and they told me about all the countries we were going to – I had never been out of the country, apart from to Jamaica. My head was just bursting with possibilities – endorsements and interviews. More than all of that was that I knew Miles would just bring the best out in people. This was what I really wanted – to be with Miles. That's when I was really freaking out."

But as the date for the tour got closer, Burroughs had heard nothing. "I called Darryl Jones and he said 'I think you'd better call this number.' That's when I found out that Foley had been given the gig. The rug was pulled out from under me. For the next few months I kept asking myself 'What could I have done differently?' Later on, I went to New York just to talk to Miles. I saw him after a show at Avery Fisher Hall. [His assistant] Finney had just done his hair and Foley was in the group. Miles asked me what I thought about his new guitarist? I said 'He's okay.' In the end I had to move on and say to myself, 'Well, at least I'm in that unique group of people who have played with Miles.'"

Another change in the band's line-up occurred when Gary Thomas left after playing just four gigs with Garrett. Those close to the situation at the time say "musical differences" between the saxophonist and Miles prompted Thomas's departure. But around this time, Miles recruited yet another new member to the band. Joseph "Foley" McCreary was just twenty-three when he joined Miles's band and had developed a unique style of playing the bass which he called "lead bass."

The full story of how Miles recruited Foley and how Foley developed his lead bass concept can be found in the chapter on *Amandla*. By using a Piccolo bass tuned up an octave, along with various effects pedals, Foley made his bass guitar sound more like a lead guitar. "With the lead bass, I was doing a lot more than a guitarist would have to do with only four strings," he says. Miles called Foley and invited him to join the band after hearing him on a tape. "When I got the call from Miles I was still experimenting with the lead bass concept, so I honed a lot of that while I was in the band," he says.

Foley made his debut on May 15, 1987 in Philadelphia and, not surprisingly, he found the experience overwhelming. "It was weird trying to play with a king like that. If you doodle around a bit and then Picasso wants you to join his ranks, it's overwhelming if you know all you're doing is doodling and learning how to become an artist. You're a doodler, but Picasso sees something in your doodles and puts you out there to do it in front of everybody. It's overwhelming to think that you're in a long tree [from] Charlie Parker to Coltrane and then you're standing next to the same guy who dealt with them. Miles was there on a revolving stage theatre wearing the same jacket as in the 'Tutu' video. It was very surreal."

Miles's directed Foley on-stage and often called him to the front of the stage, where the two musicians would play close together, with their foreheads almost touching each other. "I may have looked cool, but I was scared to death," admits Foley, adding that, "the hardest part was growing up in front of people."

In an echo of the days when Mike Stern started out in Miles's band, Foley's raw-guitar-style playing also came under some harsh criticism. "A lot of people used to blast me, 'He's no Scofield or whoever.' But they didn't understand that I was learning how to play. A lot of guitar players hated me but a lot of bass players respected me, because I was putting their instrument out there. I don't think the guitar players understood that I had just started learning how to play, much less experiment with that lead bass shit," recalls Foley. "There was a lot of personal shit on musicians' message boards but I actually got a lot of good reviews. Those guys would rather hear me play my funny little notes that were honest as opposed to running down 'bop lick forty seven.' They knew whatever I played was going to be honest. Miles hated somebody to hear people playing bop licks – he'd heard it done by the guys who created it. When he heard it second-hand you were sent out of there."

Foley may have been an up-and-coming musician, but he had a mature approach when it came to knowing his position in the band. "Some of the guys in the band were amazing players, but they had to understand where they stood musically. They were still an after-thought, because people came to see Miles; they didn't give a fuck who was on stage with him. I don't think a lot of those guys realized that. Their attitude was 'I'm with Miles Davis, I'm the shit,' and I'm like 'No, Miles is the shit, you're lucky to be up there.' It's not like any of us were Coltrane, who really played with Miles. He played with you, you didn't play with him. Being up there didn't make you as great as Miles."

Miles was thrilled to have Foley in the band, saying he had finally found the guitarist he was looking for.[35] "Maybe I was close to what he was looking for with rhythm as well – I could play really good rhythm. I was new, I wasn't some hot-shot just coming in. I was new blood, new life and he lived for that.

"He treated me like a son. Everybody had a different relationship with him, just like any band leader. Some of the guys in the band you'll be okay with, some you may not like at all. I think he saw the ghetto part of me in terms of me being a street person and I think he connected with that. He also saw I was a young kid who was still trying to learn," adds Foley. Holzman says: "For the later period ('87 onwards), Foley was really the perfect mix of creativity and funk."

Foley and Garrett got on well. "I was closest to Kenny. At high school I had done drugs and all that shit and at the age of seventeen I stopped doing drugs and concentrated on music. Kenny didn't do drugs; he was married and he didn't screw around. He was really good to hang out with," he says. Foley noted that Miles didn't like continuity – he lived for change and he liked to see his musicians stretch themselves. "Miles liked you to play differently every time, so every song always seemed new to you. That's why there are so many different twists and turns of the same tunes. And Miles would get rid of you after six months if he heard you playing the same notes every time," notes Foley.

The band was now made up of Miles, Foley, Jones, Irving, Holzman, Garrett, Wellman and Cinelu. "The band I had in 1987 was a motherfucker, man;

I loved the way they were playing," said Miles.[36] Foley seconds that view. "I agree with Miles completely. That band was like a mini Parliament/Funkadelic. There was [so much] energy and it sounded so much like a band even though it couldn't have been more different off-stage with all the personalities. On-stage, it sounded like we had been playing together for years. That band could play anything."

But not everybody was impressed. "The band sounded like a funky, rock garage band," says Branford Marsalis. "It was the shit he originally appropriated from Tony Williams in the '60s and Lifetime [band], so it never really got far away from the whole *Bitches Brew* vibe. That's because Miles would not have been able to put together the right kind of band because it's not the music he grew up listening to – it was not the music that made sense to him. I used to go and hear the band because it was Miles, but if Miles wasn't in that band none of those bands were ones I would particularly want to jump over a fence and hear."

Others were also critical about Miles's funk/rock repertoire. When interviewed for the *Miles Davis Radio Project*, Keith Jarrett declared: "I love the way Miles sounds now … but when he isn't playing … it's worse than ever."[37] In the same programme, critic Martin Williams said: "The last time I heard him, it was a nightmare to me. He was standing up on-stage in what looked like a whole Halloween fright suit. He was stalking around playing one or two plaintive notes, with these speakers on either side that were bigger than this room. But the thing that bothered me the most was this deafening sound and I felt about that the way I feel about so much rock music now. It gets louder and louder and louder because it's not saying anything   it doesn't have any story. And the musicians are so frustrated that they just keep turning it up … it gave me physical pains across my chest, just the booming of those speakers. I had to get up and leave."[38]

The arrival of Foley would also see Miles add two of his compositions to the band's set, "The Senate/Me And You." Foley had written "The Senate" as a tribute to Miles, never dreaming that Miles would actually play it one day. It was one of the tunes on the demo tape that Miles heard. "They were two different songs that Miles put together. He broke the melody up and totally rearranged it. I loved it. We played those songs every night whatever the set list, which is why I couldn't believe it didn't make any of those compilations until ten years later," says Foley.[39] "The Senate" is based around a driving funk-rock riff and is a showcase for a solo by Foley. The tune segues into "Me And You," with Miles blowing some phrases on open horn. The bassist would copy Miles's phrases before taking an extended solo that built up to a storming climax.

In June 1987, Miles added yet another tune to the set – "Movie Star," by Prince. Although Miles toured Europe that summer, he didn't play at the Montreux Jazz Festival. In the autumn, Mino Cinelu left the band to join Sting. Although Cinelu had enjoyed being reunited with Miles and Jones, he found the music was radically different to that played in his early days with Miles. "The first time I played with Miles I was learning a lot about how to play percussion or keep a groove. I was learning about space. The first band was an incredible band, capable of playing together and grooving together and sounding like a band. When I came back it was not a band of virtuosos. The music was much more disciplined and more rooted and that was a shock," he said. His replacement was a young percussionist, Rudy Bird.

The band was now composed of Miles, Garrett, Foley, Irving, Holzman, Jones, Wellman and Bird and the set list was now "One Phone Call/Street Scenes," "Star People/New Blues," "Perfect Way," "The Senate/Me And You," "Human Nature," "Wrinkle," "Tutu," "Movie Star," "Splatch," "Time After Time," "Full Nelson," "Don't Stop Me Now," "Carnival Time" and "Tomaas." The encore usually comprised three tunes – "Jean-Pierre," "Burn" and "Portia."

In late October 1987, the band toured Scandinavia, covering Norway, Finland, Sweden and Denmark. Sayydah Garrett flew over to join her husband for the tour, which later went on to cover continental Europe. "A lot of travelling was on a tour bus. It was really comfortable with bunk beds, seating areas and media area with TV and video. We spent many hours on the bus and we always stayed in the best hotels," she says. But despite the hours spent with Miles, Sayydah Garrett never had a prolonged conversation with him. "Miles didn't talk a lot. I can't say we ever had a rambling type of conversation. He was very respectful. But we never really sat down to chat, and I regret the fact that I wasn't a little bit more aggressive. I could have just walked to the front of the bus and sat down and talked to him, but I was in such awe of his musicianship and his coolness."

A large portion of a concert the band played in Hamburg on November 24, 1987 was broadcast on German radio and the difference Wellman, Garrett and Foley made to the sound can be readily discerned. Wellman added a variety of patterns and accents to the beat on snare and kick drum, while Foley's guitar sound gave a more rock-like feeling to the overall sound. There was also a high degree of interaction between Miles and Garrett, with the latter copying many of Miles's phrases.

This was particularly noticeable on two tracks where Garrett got to play extended solos, "Tomaas" and "Human Nature." By now, the latter had developed into a *tour de force* performance by Garrett, whose solo would often make up almost half of the tune's entire length (this performance lasts thirteen minutes and Garret starts soloing at the seven-minute mark). As usual, Garrett would start off slowly and gradually build up to a soaring climax. "It wasn't like Miles said 'Go play for ten minutes.' It just happened that way. People would say 'This is the Kenny Garrett Show,' and I'd say 'No – this is the Miles Davis Show – I'm just here to learn!"[40] "I could tell more by Miles's actions how much he admired Kenny's playing. He gave Kenny a lot of freedom and I think Kenny just grew in those five years," says Sayydah Garrett. "I remember one concert in Finland, where they played for three hours. Miles didn't play a lot – I think his health was failing a bit – so he gave the guys lots of space. But when he did play with them, it was just awesome." Unusually, on this gig, Miles starts "Human Nature" by playing open horn, but, after blowing just a few phrases, he inserts the Harmon mute.

In early 1988, Ron Lorman left to become vice-president of Hartke Systems, a company that makes speakers for the music business, and so Murray took over the role of concert sound engineer. In February 1988, Miles was in New York, rehearsing a new tune with the band and the event was recorded and later transmitted on the *Miles Davis Radio Project*.[41]

The tune, commonly known as "Wayne's Tune," is actually called "Bookends," says its composer Wayne Linsey. "Bookends" was written in 6/8 time and Miles can be heard teaching the band how to play it. First he shows percussionist Rudy Bird how to groove over the beat and then he coaches Irving and Wellman. Irving, in particular, is given a hard time by Miles, who tells him to stop playing in a way that sounds "sissified." Irving explains what he meant. "Remember during the post-bop period when Miles would ask Herbie to lay out completely and/or to play very minimalistic? Similarly there were times when he would tell me not to play any diminished 7th chords, because they sounded sissified. This chord didn't have many functions except in 'New Blues.' I eventually replaced it with a 6/9 chord with a flatted 5th, but then I would add some gospel-influenced nuances that would then be classified as sissified. I think it became somewhat of a game for him." Commenting on Miles's method of instruction, Bird says: "I think he's one of the greatest teachers we have in our time."[42]

"Bookends" was first played in a concert at Miramas, France on February 16, 1988. By then the arrangement had been tightened up and Garrett plays a fine solo. But Linsey was not totally happy with the finished article. "I wish Miles had let me come in and teach the band because they never played it right. If you listen to them rehearsing it, you can see the trouble they were having pulling the parts off it," he says. This concert also saw Miles introduce a new concert opener, "In A Silent Way," from the 1969 album of the same name. The tune was revamped with Miles blowing over swirling, dream-like synthesizer sounds before it segued into another new uptempo tune, "Intruder." The previous concert opener, "One Phone Call/Street Scenes," dropped down to third place on the set list and would soon be discarded.

This concert has been widely available on CD in Europe,[43] and while it has some interesting performances it is spoilt by an uneven mix, which has the keyboard sound pushed to the fore. A good example of this occurs on Darryl Jones's long solo on "Me And You," which is drowned out by a wash of synthesized sound.

Jones was sacked soon after this concert. Miles says it was because: "He started getting dramatic, too showbiz for my band."[44] Miles blamed Jones's tenure with Sting for this rock-style behaviour. But Jones believes that the real reason was that Miles felt it was time for the bassist to leave the band again. "I started playing around with people and I think he got the idea I was going to take off again, which I wasn't. I was pretty shocked. I got home after doing a gig with Wendy and Lisa at a festival in Italy and, when I got back to New York, Bobby told me that Miles was auditioning bass players."

Jones called Miles, who said he didn't like the way the bassist was playing with pedals and other effects. "I told him, 'I love you and whatever you decide is what's happening.' I said I really wasn't planning on leaving. I didn't want to go through any trip [argument] with him. I'd seen other musicians go through it and I just thought I didn't want to go out that way. So I thought 'When he asks me to leave, I'm just gonna leave.'" Even so, Jones and Miles remained close and would often talk on the phone or meet after gigs. And Jones would be invited to play at the reunion concert in Paris in 1991.

Jones's replacement was Benny Rietveld, who was born in The Netherlands but grew up in Hawaii. As a child, he learned to play piano, guitar, drums and bass, finally focusing on the latter instrument. His musical influences included Jaco Pastorius, Charles Mingus, Chuck Rainey, Paul McCartney, James Jamerson and Marcus Miller. Rietveld moved to San Francisco in 1983 and played with artists such as Roy Obledo and Pete Escovedo, before joining the Sheila E Band the following year. The band was the opening act for Prince and it was the Prince connection that resulted in Rietveld getting a call from Miles.

"I don't know who actually recommended me, but [Prince's road manager] Alan Leeds called me. I remember him saying that Miles wanted someone from the Prince 'camp.'" At the time, Miles and Prince were close both personally and musically. Rietveld was asked to send a tape of him playing, plus a photograph.

Rietveld met Miles at his home in Malibu, the evening before the first rehearsal. "It was so unreal for me to conceive of actually being there in the first place. I walked in the door and the other band members were there; I think Gordon Meltzer actually introduced me to Miles. Miles just said 'Hey, glad you could make it' and embraced me. There was no sizing me up or anything like that – it was just instant acceptance. It felt like he was a musician and I was a musician and we were just there to make music. That was when I started to realize that here was someone who wasn't into the idolatry and worship aspect of his position, at least from his band. He seemed to just want things to be straight musically."

Rietveld says he got confirmation of this later that evening when Miles had the band listen to some demo recording of music he wanted to play in the forthcoming tour. "They were pretty rough and crazy sounding and one band member commented 'Damn, Chief, that shit sounds good!' and Miles immediately shot back 'Fuck you!' It was nasty, but still done in a loving way. It was his way of reminding us, 'Hey, come on, it's just me.'"

At the same time that Rietveld joined Miles's band, Marilyn Mazur returned as percussionist, the fourth member of Miles's post-1980 bands to return for a second stint. In early 1988, Mazur had just completed a nine-month tour with Wayne Shorter. "I was actually a bit tired of being far from home so much, when Miles called and wanted me back. How could I do anything but jump back to the U.S. again!" The 1988 band was smaller than the nonet Mazur had played in 1985. "It made a difference being the only percussionist, giving me even more space and solos. The music wasn't that different, I think, although Miles always was on top of the new influences of the time. The group as a whole was more playful and social," she says.

Rietveld says his role was to provide the foundation, help propel the music forward, act as a bridge between the harmonic and rhythmic elements, and to make people move. He also knew that Jones was a hard act to follow. "It was easy to find my own voice in the band because I knew I couldn't play like him, no matter how hard I tried. So I thought 'Sod this. I should just do what I think I can do.' It was quite uncomfortable for most of the band for a while, but eventually they just put up with me and all was fine," says Rietveld.

Rietveld is being modest here because, although his playing style is different from Jones, he proved to be a strong player who could hold down a groove and play melodically when the material demanded it. Rietveld says Miles didn't give him too much direction, although one comment did make an impression on his playing. "He would say 'Don't get cute.' I think he was meaning not to be too clever or intellectual about what one would play. He really wanted music to be from the heart and soul and nowhere else; he was very adamant about that," he says.

Rietveld describes how Miles directed the band on-stage. "He would insist that we get really soft and if we weren't soft enough, he would give a loud 'Shhh!' with his finger in front of his lips and we would come down to where we were barely touching our instruments. He loved dynamics. He also really valued the downbeat of a bar and where it was placed. To indicate to me or to the band that we were rushing too much to the next bar, he would sometimes point downwards rhythmically on every one beat or sometimes on every one and three beat and tap his foot at the same time on the same beats. That would tell us to take our time and not to hurry to the next measure," says Rietveld.

Sometimes Miles would ask Rietveld or Wellman to give the music a lift. "That would be a kind of way of saying that he wanted some upbeat accents on some line or section; usually he seemed to like accent on the last sixteenth note. He would also hoarsely whisper or sing the figure so we could hear the swing of it as well as the accent. The funny thing was because of the way his voice was working and maybe because of his age, the figure sometimes sounded unsteady and me and Ricky would be scratching our heads and wouldn't know what we were supposed to play," says Rietveld.

Finally, Miles used a variety of musical cues, such as on the vamp at the end of "Human Nature." "We would be in [the] BbMaj7b5 [B-flat major 7th chord] for a certain time while Miles played and no matter what we played, we stayed right there, even when he didn't play anything. Then there was a certain descending series of notes – E, D, C, B, A, G, F, E – that would indicate for us to go into the A minor section, where Kenny [Garrett] would start his solo. It really forced one to be right there on the moment on every note, because you never knew when he was going to play that series. Sometimes he would almost play it and you'd have to stay in B-flat and sometimes it would be played fast, slow or some other way, and you had to catch it each time. It was really cool and fun and a great exercise in focus," recalls Rietveld.

The band now comprised of Miles, Garrett, Irving, Holzman, Foley, Rietveld, Wellman and Mazur. The set now consisted of "In A Silent Way/ Intruder," "Star People," "Perfect Way," "The Senate/Me And You," "Human Nature," "Wrinkle," "Tutu," "Movie Star," "Splatch," "Time After Time," "Heavy Metal," "Don't Stop Me Now," "Carnival Time" and "Portia."

The origins of the new song, "Heavy Metal," are unclear. According to Holzman, Miles was given an S900 sampler by Akai and some sound disks, including one labelled "heavy metal guitar." Inspired by MTV, Miles began playing with the distorted guitar sound from the sampler and recorded a four-track demo. Holzman and Irving then took the demo, divided it into different sections and structured an arrangement for the band.[45] The credits for "Heavy Metal" on *The Complete Miles Davis At Montreux* boxed set state that the song was "written by Miles Davis and arranged by Adam Holzman,"[46] but Jason Miles claims that he co-wrote the tune with Miles.[47] Whatever the origins, this is a song title that neatly describes the sound, with the tune being a showcase for Foley to play an extended rock guitar solo, with lots of distortion.

On April 22, 1988, the band played at the Coach House in San Juan Capistrano, California. Critic Don Heckman noted that the current band was "as close as he has come to building an ensemble with both the vigorous panache and easy accessibility of a major rock band." The repertoire was "bristling with the kind of sharp, chunky, funk-based rhythms that can energize improvisational soaring."[48]

In spring, the band's touring schedule included shows in Australia, New Zealand and Hawaii. In June, the band was in the U.S., where a new song was added to the set. Originally known as "Funk Suite," it is now more widely known as "Heavy Metal Prelude." The tune was an extended percussion jam featuring Mazur and Wellman, both of whom played over a bass/keyboard vamp. Mazur cannot recall how this number got introduced into the set. In the summer, Miles was back in Europe and he played at the Montreux Jazz Festival on July 7, 1988.

The band played a full set, which included a greatly extended version of "Carnival Time." When Miles last played this number at Montreux in 1986, it lasted less than five minutes, but now it was extended to over thirteen minutes, with almost half of the number taken up by a drum solo by Wellman. Miles also resurrected "Jean-Pierre," which had last been played in February that year. After this performance, "Jean-Pierre" would be dropped from the set and only played again at a special concert in Paris in July 1991. This 1988 Montreux gig is featured in *The Complete Miles Davis At Montreux* boxed set.

Three days later, the band played at the Philharmonica in Munich and almost all this concert has been released on a DVD, *Live in Munich*. The video reveals a tight band with Miles in good form and playing a lot. He solos movingly and exquisitely on "New Blues" and "Time After Time," and plays a lot of the time with an open horn. But he also gives all the band members plenty of space to stretch out and solo.

Foley plays fast and furious on tunes such as "Tutu" and "Heavy Metal," but also gets a chance to show another side to his playing on "Don't Stop Me Now," where he sits on the edge of the stage and plays a reflective solo. On "New Blues," he plays a long, blues-drenched solo. Kenny Garrett plays explosively on "Human Nature," and such is his physical exertion that Garrett has to literally stop and catch his breath as the tune segues into "Wrinkle." Miles watches on as Garrett gasps for air, rolling his eyes at one stage.

On "Tomaas," Garrett advances into the middle of the audience, plays a blistering solo and then returns to duel with Foley on-stage, who wildly strums his lead bass. "Me And You" is a fine showcase for Rietveld, while Irving and Holzman each sling a portable keyboard around their shoulders and play solos on a rocking version of "Splatch." As each keyboardist solos, Garrett supports them on a honking baritone saxophone. Wellman and Mazur play extended and highly energetic percussion duets on "Heavy Metal Prelude" and "Carnival Time," and the latter ends with a long solo from Wellman. On "Tutu," Mazur, wearing bells around her ankles, moves forward on to the stage to perform a talking drum solo, accompanied by some dancing. The encore "Portia" ends with Miles leaving the stage before the rest of the band, as Garrett continues to solo.

Miles spent part of September 1988 in the recording studio laying down tracks for his next album, *Amandla*. Miles also got sick around this time, which further delayed any touring. When Miles resumed touring in October 1988, there was yet another personnel change, with the departure of his long-time musical director Robert Irving III.

During the break in touring, Irving had been working on some other projects, and his first solo album, *Midnight Dream*, had just been released. When Miles asked Irving to continue touring with him, Irving decided to decline the offer. During his tenure as Miles's musical director, Irving had seen many musicians come and go, so which ones especially impressed him? "Bob Berg was one of the most impressive players that I played with. Everything he played on his horn, he could play on piano. He had attitude yet he was a very funny guy. Gary Thomas was another sax player who stood out in terms of innovation and energy. I must say that I was quite impressed by Robben Ford's ability to walk into the group with no rehearsal and take care of business with a natural sense of the right things to play."

When it came to bass players, Darryl Jones and Felton Crews topped Irving's list. "They were the most impressive to me. Darryl had the charisma and that foundational 'groovism' that made your head jerk to the rhythm. Felton was under-rated and even under-appreciated by Miles, because the board tapes that Miles listened to at that time didn't convey the truth of Crews' sound. His fluidity was unmatched by any player that preceded or succeeded him. As for drummers, Vince Wilburn played with big spirit and he was dedicated to making the music better. Vince has now evolved into an even more phenomenal musician that the music world is going to hear from in the coming years."

Not surprisingly, Irving learned a lot by playing with Miles for so long. "The education I received from Miles was immense. I learned to follow my intuition and to utilize spontaneity when initiating ideas for new compositions. He inspired me to go beyond the mundane as an arranger. He required me, as musical director of his groups, to listen to recordings of each concert with him (each night immediately after the performance). He would have ordered food prior to the concerts – he never ate before a performance. He encouraged all of the musicians not to eat as well. So we would sit and eat as we listened to the performances late into the night. At times, various band members would attend. We would critique the performances; particularly the new arrangements we had tried. I learned that this process was essential to the development of the music, which would evolve significantly from the beginning of a tour 'til the end."

Irving's role as musical director also taught him a lot about leadership and working with other musicians, he says. "I developed a strong work ethic due to the demands Miles placed on me as an arranger. There was a period when he was listening to a lot of pop music like the music of Nik Kershaw and Chaka Khan as well as the music of John McLaughlin and Maurice Ravel. He would often ask me to transcribe and arrange various tunes. We would rehearse the arrangements during sound checks, which Miles almost never attended. He would ask me if the band was comfortable with the arrangement(s). If so, we might play it live without him ever having rehearsed it with us. I spoke to Wayne Shorter about this and he said that Miles gave him specific writing and arranging assignments and then never even rehearsed the music. Nevertheless, as an arranger, I derived the additional benefit of practising my craft and accumulating a catalogue of works."

Miles also taught Irving a lot about cooking and painting, and their relationship to music. "He said that music, art and cooking were different aspects of the same thing in that they each mix colours, textures and flavours for presentation." Irving, who also paints, says this integrated approach to the arts was one of the greatest lessons he learned from Miles. "In terms of his approach to cooking, we once spent several hours preparing a meal; marinating fish in lime, sesame seed oil, white wine or Jack Daniel's whiskey, fennel seed, garlic and spices. We made what Miles liked to call 'dirty rice,' which was, essentially, brown rice with a colourful array of vegetables. The mixture of the colours was as important to him as the combinations of cayenne, fresh ginger, garlic and just the right amount of soy sauce. While something was marinating, Miles might add touches to a painting while talking about music – he was a master of multi-tasking."

Irving's departure saw Holzman promoted to the band's musical director. "Of course I enjoyed my new role, but it was a real challenge! My main responsibility was to rehearse new music with the band – before Miles came in and changed everything around!" says Holzman. The band also acquired a new keyboardist, the teenager Joey DeFrancesco. DeFrancesco was born in Philadelphia in 1971 and was a keyboard protégé (he also plays trumpet). His main instrument was the Hammond B3 organ and by the time he was ten he was already making his mark around Philadelphia.

In 1987, when DeFrancesco was sixteen, he was asked to play organ in a house band at a school talent show where Miles was the guest of honour. Miles had come to see four young trumpet players perform and then discuss their playing, but Miles was more interested in the young organist. "Miles came up to me and punched me in the chest and said 'You can play, motherfucker,'" recalls DeFrancesco. Miles took his number. "A year later I came home from school and my grandmother told me 'David Miles or somebody called.' I was knocked out, excited and scared, Miles was as influential as anything I was listening to at that point: Jimmy Smith, Trane [Coltrane], Larry Young, Dizz [Dizzy Gillespie] and Bird [Charlie Parker]."

DeFrancesco became one of a select group of teenagers who played with Miles, which included Tony Williams, Michael Henderson, Steve Grossman and Ndugu Chancler. Miles was protective of his young player. "Miles looked after me like a dad when we were in Europe. We were always together and I was always looking at him, I mean just staring. He would catch me occasionally and say 'What are you lookin' at, you young motherfucker?'" When it came to playing the music "Miles had specific ideas and sometimes that was challenging, but he allowed us to put our stamp on things; even though some of the tunes were considered more commercial at that time. I played lots of parts and pads and we all had the opportunity to solo."

The band, now comprised of Miles, Garrett, Foley, Holzman, DeFrancesco, Rietveld, Mazur and Wellman, toured Europe in the autumn, with no changes to the set list. The band finished off the tour with four concerts (two in each day) at Indigo Blues on December 17 and 18, 1988. A large portion of the second concert on December 17 was broadcast over two programmes on the *Miles Davis Radio Project*.[49]

The tunes played were "In A Silent Way/Intruder," "Star People/New Blues," "Perfect Way," "The Senate/Me And You," "Hannibal," "Wrinkle," "Time After Time," "Movie Star" and "Don't Stop Me Now." The recordings were made by Miles's concert sound engineer, Patrick Murray, who recorded them from the soundboard onto DAT digital tape. The programme's narrator, the actor Danny Glover, highlights a solo by DeFrancesco during "Don't Stop Me Now."

Miles spent the latter part of December 1988 and January 1989 recording the album *Amandla*, using Wellman, Foley, Garrett and DeFrancesco in the sessions. "The one thing I remember about those sessions was Miles tripping over some cables and cursing that someone was trying to kill him!" says DeFrancesco.

In March 1989, Holzman, DeFrancesco and Mazur departed. Holzman, who had been on the road with Miles for more than three years, needed a break. "At the end of 1988 I was getting burned out from the constant touring, I had an opportunity to start on my own album, plus I had offers to work with other people. Miles was the only real gig I had done for the previous three and a half years," says Holzman. "I needed a change, so I took a brief 'leave of absence.' Basically, I only missed one three-week tour (which was in the spring of '89). While the band was out on that tour my home phone rang one day. It was Miles asking 'When are you coming back?'"

DeFrancesco left to pursue a solo career. "Columbia had put out my first solo release. Miles understood and pushed me out the door to pursue that opportunity. In hindsight, I wish I had stayed a bit longer," says DeFrancesco. The keyboardist has fond memories of his time with Miles. "Miles was a ball buster [joker] and that was misunderstood; especially by the media, who seem to literally hang on his every word, especially when he was breaking balls. I found him to be warm, caring and giving."

Mazur also felt it was time to move on. "In 1989 I simply decided that it was time for me to go back home, I didn't have the desire to move to the U.S. I felt at home in Denmark and had received a grant for starting my band Future Song here. Of course I have since wondered why I didn't stick around to the end! But I think I just needed to be at home. However, I was invited to play a couple of concerts in Italy with the band, where Miles couldn't make it (I think he was ill). One was where Chick Corea was his substitute and the second was with Herbie Hancock playing sampled Miles on his keyboard! And the year after leaving Miles I had my son Fabian, so it again all seems to have its own logic," she says. Reflecting on her time with Miles, Mazur says "When I think about him, I can feel his strength and the glow in his eyes. I feel like Miles taught me more patience, and a lot about grooving and musical flow and gathering a band's energy."

Miles recruited two new keyboardists, Kei Akagi and John Beasley, and the percussionist Munyungo Jackson. Akagi was born in Sendai, Japan in 1953 and moved to Cleveland, Ohio when he was four. He returned to Japan in 1965 in his teens and studied classical and jazz composition in the U.S. and Japan, moving back to the States in 1975. Akagi played with a number of artists including Art Pepper, Blue Mitchell, Eddie Harris, and The Flora Purim and Airto Moreira Band. "I was touring with The Al DiMiola Group and his road manager David Lang was friends with Miles's road manager Gordon Meltzer. When Miles lost both of his keyboard players, my name came up," says Akagi. "I was contacted by Gordon, who told me to send an audition tape to Miles if I was interested in the gig. I sent Miles a collection of predominantly straight-ahead acoustic work, plus a sprinkling of synthesized recordings and I got the call to join the band a few days later."

Akagi once said: "I'd been studying [Miles's] music for so long, I felt like I had a musical relationship with him. I had been thoroughly influenced by him. Consequently, I already knew what to do in his band."[50] He elaborates on this comment: "I had gravitated towards the sound of Miles's pianists in my late teens and early twenties; my own bands reflected this compositionally as well. This is not to say I understood what Miles's music was about. [But] I was familiar with Miles's sound and the keyboard requirements of his music well enough so that when I joined the band at thirty-six I had at the very least a background of sonorities to go by, including chordal and solo styles. However, even though I knew the 'how' and the 'what' of Miles's music, I didn't know the 'why' and this was the single greatest thing I learned from Miles." Akagi met Miles at the initial rehearsal in New York. "What I remember most is the incredible amount of material I had to assimilate quickly without the benefit of written music," he says.

John Beasley was born in Louisana and moved to Los Angeles. A self-taught musician, Beasley had played with Hubert Laws, Freddie Hubbard and John Pattituchi before joining Miles. "I had a band in L.A. called Out of your Mind and I met Vince Wilburn Jr. at a gig. We became friends. At one point he said, 'Man, you should just give me a tape.' I didn't think Miles was even looking at that time. So I went into a studio and improvised over a drum machine and made a tape. When I gave it to Vince I thought 'I'm just going to forget about this now, it will never happen.'" Almost a year later, Miles made the call. "He said 'Man, you're a bad motherfucker. I want you to come and join the band.' I was excited and honoured and all of that." Beasley's wife was pregnant at the time, but she encouraged him to join the band.

"My first meeting with Miles was at the rehearsal in New York. He walked up to me and shook hands. I had thought 'What am I gonna do when I meet this guy?' and I decided I'm just going to look right into his eyes," recalls Beasley. "We shook hands and had a long look. I'd heard the stories and I didn't want him to walk over me or think I was some wimp and I wanted him to see that I was sincere. From that point we were cool and everything he said to me was constructive."

Munyungo Jackson was born Darryl Jackson and acquired his new first name when he was playing with a group of African and Caribbean musicians (in Zulu it means 'door'). Jackson learned classical piano as a child but became interested in percussion when he was in his late teens. Jackson was playing with Joe Zawinul, when Wilburn referred him to Miles. Jackson was asked to send an audition tape and he used a video tape of him playing with Zawinul. "Vince called me back and said 'Miles says you're a bad motherfucker. He wants to know if you would like to do the gig for an "x" amount of money.' It wasn't a lot. Playing with Miles is a good experience. It's like a school, so you don't get paid a lot of money. Miles was like 'When you play with me, you're going to get famous. Do I have to pay you too?'" says Jackson.

The band rehearsed together for around two weeks and, although no longer in the band, Adam Holzman was involved in some of the preparation. "Adam was there rehearsing us and he'd help us out and say things like 'Bobby [Irving] was playing this and this is the part I was playing,'" recalls Beasley. "At the time, the keyboardists had separate roles," says Akagi. "One would adhere strictly to the parts that were integral to the arrangement and the other would be freer and improvisational, providing accompaniment and backgrounds, much of a manner of a jazz pianist. John Beasley and I were together for about a month and did not get to the point of consolidating roles."

The octet featuring Miles, Garrett, Beasley, Akagi, Rietveld, Foley, Wellman and Jackson toured Europe in April 1989. "At this time his band was coming from an R&B angle rather than a jazz angle, so there were a lot of parts," says Beasley. "The band was mostly R&B players except for me, Kenny and Kei and Miles. I learned how to comp on that tour. How to stay out of the way and not feed the soloist, but let him decide the direction and react off of that. Miles liked me to play up in the range above middle C and lock into the same range as the trumpet – he liked that for some reason. Solo-wise, he'd say 'Don't use your left hand,' and he would come up to me sometimes and grab my left hand if I was using it too much. A couple of times before the show he'd say 'If you can't comp like Ahmad Jamal don't play,'" says Beasley.

The band set list now included several tunes from the forthcoming *Amandla* album, "Jilli," "Hannibal," "Amandla" and "Mr. Pastorius." A performance on Italian television saw the band playing "Cobra," but this was a one-off. "Movie Star" was dropped from the set. "I liked 'Movie Star,' even though the rest of the band thought it was kinda silly, which was strange since they played the shit out of it!" says Rietveld. "I liked playing the stuff from *Amandla*, 'Mr. Pastorius,' 'Amandla,' stuff that was more jazzy and open and you had room to grow during the solo section. The denser harmony stuff," says Beasley.

In late April 1989, the band played three gigs in the UK, and the opening night in Manchester saw the band performing below par; as Meltzer (who is Jewish) recalls, it was "a disastrous first show of a tour. It was in an old theatre in Manchester, with a long narrow stairway to an upstairs dressing room. There were the two new keyboard players, Kei Akagi (who played nothing at all that first night) and John Beasley (who wouldn't stop playing). So Miles leaves the stage early and he trudges slowly up the stairs, deep in thought. Then he turns around and says, 'You know, Hitler should have left the Jews alone and killed all the piano players.'"

The performance was reviewed in the *London Sunday Times* by critic Richard Cook, who described it as a "ragged and inauspicious affair, lacking any focus or inner life. Festooned in shapeless, glittering clothes, his face masked as ever by huge glasses, Davis seemed reliably bad-tempered, prowling the stage with his customary off-hand menace." The problem, said Cook, was that apart from Garrett none of the other musicians were good enough. "Foley McCreary and the keyboard player Kei Akagi held little interest; McCreary, especially, was insufferably fussy and mannered in the way he dealt out mundane rock licks. Worst of all, the rhythm section filled in space the way concrete pours into foundations." Cook concluded that Miles's live performances had become a "tiresome spectacle."[51]

But while some critics may have been less than impressed with Akagi's playing, Miles had no doubts about his abilities. "He's a hell of a musician. He's so funny. He never did say anything. I just told him to learn the parts. I walked up to him one night and said: 'Kei, is there anything we play that you'd really like to play on?' He's quiet you know. The next day he came to rehearsal and said 'I'd like to play "Tutu."'" He is so good; he just set a whole new groove. The groove is him. So I ask him again 'Is there anything else you want to do?' He says 'Wrinkles' [*sic*]. I know that still waters run deep because I was quiet like that. He's going to be something. He's already something."[52]

All three new band members talk about how Miles made them see music in a new way and how to listen. "His keyboardists share a similarity, I believe, because Miles himself had a unique way of hearing notes and their inner relationship that is very removed from the norm," says Akagi. "When he performs with his band, he is not only aware of the music being played at the moment, but also of everything that is not being played, but nonetheless would be an integral part of the music if it was played. In effect, the parameters of a musical event are much wider for Miles than they would be for most people."

Akagi says this unique approach to music affected how he played. "You gradually start veering away from the ordinary or expected and you become more comfortable with silence, because you realize that the music does not stop with silence; you learn to deliberately play silence instead of treating it as a mere absence of sound. Ultimately what I learned from Miles is that music is much wider than that which is being performed at the moment. Everything one plays hints at a multitude of other possibilities and one must be aware of them at all times." Beasley says: "On-stage, I heard every note he played – I was listening so hard. So when I finally got off the band, I could just concentrate. He taught me to listen and not feel that I have to react to everything I hear, but to leave space."

Jackson discovered Miles's ability to seemingly hear everything after a rehearsal in which Miles was not present. "I was rehearsing 'Tutu,' and it's a tune where the percussionist plays behind Foley. So I'm trying all these things and they were taping the rehearsal. Anyway, we went to Miles's place and Miles was in his foyer painting on a big canvas on the floor." Miles sent the band into his living room. "One of the guys puts the rehearsal tape on. There are a couple of other people in the house, the phone's ringing and Miles is in his foyer doing his painting. Then we go to Miles's bedroom, which has a TV and a couch. Miles turns on the TV and it's real loud and I'm trying to listen to the rehearsal tape playing down the hall. Miles keeps going back and forth, painting in his foyer and then coming in to change channels on the TV. I'm too busy trying to listen to my solo on 'Tutu.' Then, as we're leaving, he says 'Jackson' – he couldn't say my first name – 'Keep it in six [6/8 time].' That amazed me, because with all that going on – the phone ringing, TV blaring, everybody talking – he heard it."

Jackson learned another lesson at a rehearsal. "Miles and Kenny were working on something and Miles says to Ricky 'You like what we're playing?' and Ricky says 'I didn't hear what you played.' Miles says 'What! Motherfucker, you didn't hear what we play?' Then he turns to me, 'Jackson, did you hear what we play?' I couldn't lie and say yes so he wouldn't cuss me out so I said no and he said to me 'Fuck you!' and then we took a break." Wellman tried to reassure Jackson that he shouldn't take anything personally. "Funnily enough I hadn't and then Miles came back and completed the whole sentence. He told me that if somebody is playing and you don't hear what they're playing, you play louder."

Miles continued the conversation and said: "Another reason is that if you don't like how somebody is playing, you play louder and are in effect saying 'Fuck you.' So if he's playing and we're not listening, it's like we don't like the way he's playing." When Miles's band was off the road, Jackson would sit in on gigs around Los Angeles. "I thought everyone was playing too loud because Miles's thing was that it's not about playing loud, but bringing it down and making it more intense. There's more groove if you can hear everybody. And that's what I really dug about him – it's about playing and listening and not just playing."

Beasley left the band in June 1989. "My wife had our baby and Miles was cool about me leaving. He said the invitation was still open and that I could come back. I talked to him a lot on the phone afterwards. I feel that I grew up as a man when I was with Miles." Holzman, refreshed from his break, returned to the band. "Adam assumed more of a free role and I for the most part played rather strictly defined ensemble passages, with the exception of solos," says Akagi. "After Adam left, I assumed both roles."

The band, now comprising Miles, Garrett, Foley, Holzman, Akagi, Rietveld, Wellman and Jackson, toured the U.S. in June. The band played at the Coach House, in San Juan Capistrano on June 15, and two performances from this gig, "Tutu" and "Mr. Pastorius," were broadcast on the *Miles Davis Radio Project*. In July, "In A Silent Way" was dropped and the set list was now "Intruder," "Star People," "Perfect Way," "Hannibal," "Human Nature," "Mr. Pastorius," "Tutu," "Jilli," "Time After Time," "Jo-Jo," "Amandla," "The Senate/Me And You," "Wrinkle" and "Portia."

Another change was the arrival of Rick Margitza on tenor saxophone, a stand-in for Garrett, who was unavailable for a European tour. Margizta was introduced to Miles by Tommy LiPuma and had played on "Jo-Jo" on the *Amandla* sessions. When Margitza heard he had got the gig: "I thought it was a friend playing a practical joke. After that, I felt disbelief, fear and finally acceptance."

On July 14, 1989, the band played in Peruga, Italy, which was recorded by Italian television. By a quirk of European copyright law, a CD from this gig was released in Europe. The album, *Live Tutu*, contains four tracks, "Human Nature," "The Senate/Me And You,"[53] "Jo-Jo" and "Tutu." On "Human Nature" Margitza plays a long, excellent solo on tenor saxophone. Although Margizta's style and sound were markedly different from Garrett's, Miles liked his playing. "The first thing he said to me was 'How the fuck did you learn to play that way?' I also had a problem with one of the tunes in our show and when I went up to him to say that I felt corny over this slow blues he said, 'Don't worry, corny isn't you,'" remembers Margitza.

Margitza also recalled some amazing playing from Miles. "One night...he played something that was so incredible that I got the gig tape and transcribed it. The next night, I tried to play it during one of my solos. After the concert, I went up to him and said, 'Miles, I tried to play some of your shit and it didn't come out right.' He laughed. Two nights later, he walked up to me during the concert, stood about two feet away and played it right back to me, as if to say 'Here it is for you again.' "[54]

On July 21, the band was back at the Montreux Jazz Festival and when they performed "Human Nature," Chaka Khan sat in on vocals. Khan explains the background. "It was just a spur of the moment thing. He just said 'Come up on the stage with me.'[55] We were talking and having fun backstage and we were talking about what song I could possibly do in his set on-stage together."

The crowd erupts when Khan makes her entrance at just after the second minute. Khan sings explosively, sounds shrill in places and forgets some of the lyrics, but she and Miles are clearly having fun. Khan copies Miles's phrases when he plays "A-Tisket, A-Tisket," and the crowd hollers. She sings a couple more verses, copies Miles's phrases again and then leaves the stage to a cheering audience. Reflecting on her performance, Khan says: "I think I botched it. I didn't plan, we were having fun and I would have done a much better job if I had done it on a different day. But it is what it is. I was thrilled. I felt like 'I could die now.'" But Miles was more than happy with her performance, though, telling promoter Claude Nobs "I tried to outwit her and changed the key five times! But she always followed me!"[56]

Writer Roy Carr reviewed the concert and was very impressed with Foley's performance. "In lead-bassist Joseph Foley McCreary, Miles Davis has discovered a truly formidable team player," he said. Carr also quoted Foley, who had clearly gained confidence in the two years playing with Miles. "The difference between me and the other guys he's worked with," said Foley, "is sure, I respect Miles, but I sure as hell ain't frightened of him. He kicks my ass, I kick his!"

Carr continued: "And that's where the chemistry works. The pair have raised their performance level to a contact sport; eye-eye contact, locking foreheads with Miles pushing Foley away with a grin. Miles might choose the route, but often it's Foley and drummer Ricky Wellman who let the boss know if they're heading in the right direction. One moment they're out-funkin' even Prince; then, in the space of a single drum beat, the entire band executes a full 360-degree turn to lunge dramatically into a spinechilling blues walk."[57] The entire Montreux concert was widely available in Europe on a double CD years before it appeared as part of *The Complete Miles Davis At Montreux* boxed set.

Margitza's stint with the band ended in July. "It had been really challenging and really great fun at the same time. Playing with the band was an honour and a rite of passage," says Margitza, who also has fond memories of Miles. "He was very observant and liked to sit in his hotel room window and look at people with binoculars. He would sometimes make comments about people while he watched their behaviour at an airport such as 'That couple won't stay together,' or 'He used to be a junkie.' So I learned to be aware of my surroundings. This translated on-stage. I learned the importance and power of space in music. He was powerful in what he didn't play. This ties back to being aware. You can't leave space if you aren't listening to what's around you."

Around August 1989, "Intruder" was dropped as the concert opener and was replaced by "Perfect Way." "In A Silent Way" would now appear intermittently and often as the concert closer. At almost every concert, band members would learn new lessons from Miles. Jackson recalls a time when Miles's instincts came to the fore. "I really enjoyed playing 'Jilli' and I had worked out a really good melodic groove for it. One day, Miles called me to his room before one of the concerts and said 'On "Jilli" I want you to play a reggae.' We played 'Jilli' and so I go into this reggae thing that Miles wants and it felt like crap – it just didn't feel right. So I went back into what I did before. The next day, he calls me in again and says 'I want you to play reggae on "Jilli"' and before I could tell him that it didn't work, he said 'I don't care how fucked up it feels, play reggae.' So I go out and 'Jilli' comes up and I played what he told me to play and it felt wonderful."

But with material from *Tutu* and *Amandla* now dominating the set, the song arrangements were becoming increasingly inflexible and highly organized, with the music sounding more like the album recordings. There seemed less space for experimentation or improvisation. "It would depend on that person's role in the band at the time," says Holzman. "The concept and musical structure was, of course, not like the total group improvisations of the second quintet [of the 1960s]. This was a more arranged sound, with the improvisation coming from the soloists reacting to the solid structure of the rhythm section. Within that structure, however, we would find ways to add little parts, change things around, etcetera." Patrick Murray recalls that: "The show was constantly changing and we never had a set list. Even if we did, you might not recognize a tune from night to night because Miles was always experimenting with the arrangements."

"It was arranged and very organized," says Rietveld, "but there was definitely 'breathing room.' The challenging thing was to find a way to express your individuality while working within the confines of what Miles's vision was. As long as some of the key requirements are met, you can do what you want. And ultimately, if you understand what the overall vision is, the choice you make becomes quite obvious and to some [it] may seem quite narrow. I can draw the parallel to an actor in a well-written and well-directed movie. The overall vision is strong and the actor will instinctively know what is called for in a given scene."

There was another change in the band's line-up in the autumn, when Jackson left the band. "The music was changing and he wanted to hear even less. Gordon called and said 'Miles wants to try something different,'" says Jackson. Looking back on his time with Miles, Jackson notes: "When Miles said things or played, he didn't have to say the whole phrase. He would just play a few notes or say the important words and you'd know what the whole sentence was about. A lot of people thought he was mean, but he was funny and he was real. Everybody has an up and a bad side. I never looked at him as intimidating. He let people be who they are. I really dug being there and learned so much from being with him."

Jackson's replacement was John Bigham. Miles encouraged Bigham to write songs for him, and every so often Bigham would go to Miles's home with demos of songs played on a drum machine. Bigham, who had originally been a drummer, joined the band by accident. "He needed a percussionist and he called me up because I was doing all these tunes which were kinda like a street style, a cross between go-go and hip-hop rhythms. He asked me if I knew anybody who could play like that. I had a friend who I called to do the gig, but he didn't call me back. I wasn't doing very much other than writing songs and I just said 'Man, I'll do it.'" Bigham put together an electronic percussion kit, using a sampler and octopads, electronic drum pads that could be programmed to make different sounds. "I went out to Miles's house and showed him how I was going to do it and he was like okay," says Bigham.

It was around this time that Holzman left the band for a second and final time. "After I had been in the band for four years it seemed like the right time for a change. I had an offer to do a record and tour with Michel Petrucciani, a kind of keyboard collaboration. It was a chance to play with other great musicians and do something completely different. Also, I was a big fan of Michel. For me, it was the right time to play some different music," says Holzman.

Reflecting on his time with Miles, Holzman says: "Of course I learned a lot musically, but I also learned how to run a band and to be more patient. For example, if a new piece of music didn't sound that great initially, Miles wouldn't panic. He would keep performing it and it would eventually develop into something really hip. Personally, Miles had a great sense of humour. He joked around more than most people might think. He also had this incredible presence. When he walked into a room, everybody knew it."

The band, now a septet, consisted of Miles, Garrett, Akagi, Foley, Rietveld, Wellman and Bigham. In October 1989, Miles toured Europe again and part of a performance at Le Zenith in Paris on November 3, 1989 was released on video. "That was like my second or third show. I hadn't really refined my technique yet! It got better!" said Bigham. The stage set-up consisted of two ramps, which led up to a second circular stage. Behind this was a platform on which Wellman, Bigham and Rietveld were positioned. Akagi's keyboards were set to the side of the stage while Miles, Foley and Garrett spend most of their time at the front. Multi-coloured lights bathe the stage.

Sadly, the video's director decided to inter-cut the performances with short interviews of Miles, which ruins the continuity. The only tune not to suffer from this treatment is the opening number on the video, "Human Nature." Once again, Garrett gets to solo but he seems oddly reluctant to begin. Miles coaxes him by talking into his trumpet microphone, "Go ahead, this is your night, go ahead." But Garrett still seems less than enthusiastic. The reason is because Garrett was having problems with his wireless microphone (at one point he can be seen discussing the problem with Miles). That is why, when Garrett finally solos, Miles stays close to him, holding his trumpet microphone next to Garrett's instrument. The arrangement for the coda is interesting. Miles normally signalled the end of Garrett's solo (and the tune) with a sharp blast on the trumpet but, on this occasion, Garrett pulls away from Miles's horn, effectively fading out his saxophone. The band continues playing on for a little longer and then Miles blows his horn.

At the end of Garrett's solo, Miles holds up a board with the name "Kenny" written on it; it's a far cry from the days when Miles would not even acknowledge the audience. "The signs were made because, prior to that, Miles would speak the names of the guys into the microphone at the end of his horn and nobody could understand him," says Murray, "so our stage manager Rodney Lucas made the signs at Miles's request. There was even a sign for Miles himself that said 'Me!' However, I've no doubt that Miles told the guys the signs were for when they messed up."

But the use of such stage props has led writer Paul Tingen to suggest that Miles's shows were "on a slide towards toothless, middle-of-the-road entertainment," while the highly arranged music was "in danger of toppling over into kitsch."[58] But Rietveld disagrees. "The quality of the music has nothing to do with people holding up signs. 'Accessibility' is not the same as 'kitsch' or 'MOR [middle-of-the-road].' Coltrane's ballads are highly accessible but also about as far from 'kitsch' or 'MOR' as you can get. The signs were just a fun thing to do because (and this will be a shock to many) Miles was a fun-loving guy with a wicked sense of humour."

Miles and Foley both give tender performances on "Don't Stop Me Now," while, frustratingly, Akagi's solo on "Amandla" is faded out just as he starts to play. Incidentally, this performance must have come from a different set as both Miles and Garrett are both wearing different clothes (Garrett has swapped his black suit for a casual shirt and baggy pair of trousers). On "Tutu," Miles, Foley and Bigham all play solos and on "Wrinkle," Wellman puts on a display of hyperactive drumming. "New Blues" features some strong and inventive playing from both Miles and Foley.

Miles ended 1989 playing at the Beacon Theatre in New York and there would be a two-month break before the band was back in action again. In February 1990, the band toured Canada and it was on this tour that two new songs were introduced to the set. "Little Davis," a slow-groove number with a creeping, menacing bass line, was written by Foley and saw Miles playing both open and muted horn.

But "Little Davis" proved to be less enduring than Foley's other tune, "The Senate/Me And You" and was soon dropped from the set. "We played 'Little Davis' like two times and he hated the way we played it so we stopped playing it. I couldn't believe there was a bootleg of it because we only did it twice," said Foley.[59] The other tune was Cameo's "In The Night," a funky number which Miles had recorded with Cameo in 1988. On this number Foley sang lead vocals and explains how he got to sing on-stage with Miles. "I was an R&B guy, I was basically a garage band, rock 'n' roll, funk guy and we used to have to play and sing at the same time, so I was used to it. I was the only guy in the band that could sing, so he said, 'You sing the part.'"

In March 1990, the band took part in recording sessions for the soundtrack to the film *Dingo*, which took place in Los Angeles. April saw the departure of Benny Rietveld, who left to join Carlos Santana's band. "I felt it was the right time to move on and I also felt that Miles liked it if you didn't stay too long in his band," says Rietveld.

Rietveld had enjoyed his tenure with the band. "I liked playing a lot of the tunes we did. 'Wrinkle' was always really fun and 'Perfect Way' was such a romp. I also loved 'Intruder,' especially coming out of 'In A Silent Way.' 'Human Nature' was always fantastic, especially Kenny at the end – I could never believe how almost every night he could play such an intense solo on a one-chord vamp. 'Time After Time' was also a favourite." Looking back on Miles, Reitveld notes: "I hardly ever got to hang with Miles for the simple reason that he lived in New York or Malibu and I lived in San Francisco. But he was pretty open with the band and I have no doubt that almost anytime I had knocked on the door he would have said 'Hey, come on in.'"

His replacement was yet another bassist from the network of Chicagoan musicians who had played together in the 1970s. Richard Patterson had played in Data along with Vince Wilburn Jr., Bobby Irving and Randy Hall, and had played bass jam sessions with Darryl Jones and Angus Thomas. "I played with a high-powered fusion/funk band called Insight and we became real popular in Chicago. As a result we got a gig in New Orleans and it was here where I met Ron Lorman and Larry Hartke [vice-president and founder of Hartke Systems respectively]. At the time, Ron was also doing the monitors for Miles. He really liked my bass playing and he wanted me to endorse their speakers. The bass chair opened up and Ron Lorman recommended me." Patterson was called by Miles's road manager Gordon Meltzer and offered the post. "I was excited and also fearful, because at this time I was well aware who Miles was and I was just in awe of the whole mystique around Miles. It was a little scary."

Patterson was asked to send a demo tape of his playing. "The only things I had recorded were jingles and some local record projects and I just put them all together," he says. Miles also wanted a photograph of Patterson.

Around a week after sending the package to Miles, Patterson received a second call from Meltzer, who formally offered him the gig. "Gordon also gave me Miles's number to call and I think I looked at that number for a week and a half before I called – I just couldn't call it. Eventually I called and I remember thinking 'What do I call him, "Mr Miles?" ' In the end I called him Miles."

Patterson was given concert tapes to learn the music and he spent almost all his waking hours listening to Miles's music. "I was just inhaling it, anything with his name on." Patterson had two days' rehearsal and Miles was not present at them. "The music was challenging because they were sending me a lot of different live tapes and on certain songs every live tape was different!" The first time Patterson met Miles was just five minutes before the band was due on-stage. Patterson met Miles in his dressing room. "He asked me how I felt and I said 'A little nervous,' and he put his hand on my back and said 'It's going to be cool.'"

The band's set now contained around a dozen songs, "Perfect Way," "Star People/New Blues," "Hannibal," "The Senate/Me And You," "Human Nature," "In The Night," "Tutu," "Amandla," "Jilli," "Jo-Jo," "Don't Stop Me Now" and "Carnival Time." "During the opening number, 'Perfect Way,' Miles pulled me to the front of the stage and we did a back and forth response thing," recalls Patterson. "To this day I think he did this because after that song was over all the nervousness went away. It was like Miles was thinking 'Let me just throw you all the way into the fire and so that everything else just feels warm.' That was one of my favourite Miles moments."

Patterson soon learned how Miles would move the band on to the next tune. "Miles would do trumpet cues. Like if someone was soloing, he would play a little motif of the next section and we all knew it was time to move to the next section. A couple of times we were vamping on a major chord and he's soloing over and you had to constantly listen to him because he would play one little minor riff and from that we would know to go to the next section. You had to have your ears and eyes open. Miles had some of the hugest ears on-stage – there was nothing that he didn't hear. If something was the slightest bit out of tune and you thought you were the only one that noticed it, Miles would hear it as well."

John Bigham left the band in the summer of 1990. "I did it until I got tired. My buddies in the [L.A. band] Fishbone asked me to play with them and I said 'Yes.' I was a little bit bored because percussion wasn't my instrument and I wasn't trying to pursue that. I did it to have some fun though, and Miles was very cool about my leaving the band." Bigham adds that Miles "let you do what you do. I was free to do what I wanted. He'd only cut you off if he thought you were heading in the wrong direction. He'd say something short and sweet like 'Do something else.' Or 'Why you wanna do that?' Through Miles, I learned how to run a band and how to let people be free to do what they do, but keep order in the midst of chaos. He was an amazing band leader because you always knew who was boss, but you could also go for it. It was very cool."

Bigham was replaced by Miles's youngest son, Erin, who, up until then, had been working as a roadie for Miles. Erin Davis's main instrument was the drums and he was not comfortable playing percussion. "I did a summer tour that was about two and a half months and I did a fall tour that was about a month and a half and that was enough for me!" he said.[60] The band, now composed of Miles, Garrett, Foley, Akagi, Patterson, Wellman and Erin Davis, toured the U.S. and Europe in the summer.

Part of a performance at Singen in Germany on July 14, 1990 was broadcast on German radio. The recording showed what a formidable rhythm section the Patterson/Wellman combination was. Like the other Chicagoan bassists that had played with Miles – Crews, Jones and Thomas – Patterson's playing had a hard edge to it, a characteristic that was amply demonstrated on a storming bass solo on "Me And You," accompanied by some frenetic drumming by Wellman. Patterson plays another ferocious solo on "Wrinkle." "He used always tell me about the one. He'd tell me 'The funk is on the one' whatever groove we were in. He said 'When you get to four, have four set up one.' It just added a whole other hump to the music," says Patterson.

In the summer of 1990, Grace Jones's "Don't Cry, It's Only Rhythm" was played over the PA system before the start of the concert and Miles would sometimes come on-stage before the rest of the band. Miles also played at the Montreux Jazz Festival on July 20 – the last time he would appear at the festival with his own band.

"The gigs were so much fun but Miles would force you to focus so much that you would forget that the audience were there, and to me that makes it more musical because it's not about being distracted by what's going on outside of the stage," says Patterson. "That was a big learning thing for me because sometimes you can go on-stage and get out of the musical part and go to some other vibe. But with Miles it was so intense that you had to remain inside the music." The 1990 autumn tour covered Germany, France and The Netherlands, and both Akagi and Erin Davis would leave the band after it.

Akagi revealed the reasons for leaving the band to Bill Kohlhaase, who reported that "There wasn't enough moving ahead for Akagi in Miles's band, which was flourishing on funk riffs and covers of Michael Jackson's 'Human Nature.' So Akagi split." Akagi told him that: "I got tired of playing those songs so much, I was ready to get back to my roots as a jazz pianist."[61] Akagi elaborates: "I was hearing things in my mind that could not be expressed in Miles's repertoire at the time and I was gradually getting frustrated. I needed to branch out on my own as a performer and composer. When a musician can no longer contribute to the music in a meaningfully creative way and the music no longer contributes to the musician's growth, then it is time to leave. Out of respect for Miles's music, I chose to leave."

Akagi adds: "The tunes I enjoyed the most were 'Mr. Pastorius,' 'Hannibal' and 'Tutu.' I was probably closest to Ricky Wellman and Richard Patterson. I had immense respect for them as musicians and they were both extremely decent human beings. I will never forget the cryptic jewels of wisdom Miles would say to me. He was tough and selfish, but he had a heart of gold."

The departure of Erin Davis saw Miles dispense with a percussionist and pare his band down to a sextet. His new keyboardist was Deron Johnson. Johnson was born in Los Angeles and was twenty-six when he joined Miles's band in early 1991. His first instrument was the bass guitar, but, after a football injury when he was sixteen, he took up the piano. His early influences were Herbie Hancock, Keith Jarrett and Donny Hathaway. Johnson was playing in bands around L.A. before he joined Miles's band. He also toured with singer Paula Abdul in 1989.

Johnson was playing in a club in L.A. called Le Café and Vince Wilburn Jr. walked in. "At that point, he was the guy who would report back to Miles about any new guys, because Miles was always into fresh young players. Vince came up to me and said 'I'm going to tell Miles about you.'" Wilburn called Johnson and asked him to put together a tape. Johnson gave Wilburn a tape and, a week later, Wilburn called him again. "He said 'Hold on for a second' and then, lo and behold, Miles gets on the phone and tells me to come up to the house. It was a whirlwind – it was all happening so fast," said Johnson.

Wilburn took Johnson to Miles's house. "I thought there might be some form of audition, but we just hung and we talked about everything but music. He had a baby grand piano and I'm thinking 'Oh shit, one thing I don't want to do is to play solo piano for Miles Davis.' But I didn't have to do that." Miles gave Johnson tapes of Prince's music and told him the band was going to Europe soon. "The next thing I know I'm on a plane to New York to rehearse," says Johnson.

Johnson was the last new recruit to a Miles Davis band and the final line-up was a sextet comprised of Miles, Garrett, Foley, Johnson, Patterson and Wellman. Johnson's first show was at Milan in March 1991. The band then performed at a number of gigs in Germany where it played four Prince tunes Miles planned to include on his next album, "Penetration," "Jailbait," "R U Legal Yet?" and "A Girl And Her Puppy." (A discussion of these tunes can be found in the chapter on *Doo-Bop*.) The band Miles now had was very different from the ones spanning 1985–88, when there were two keyboardists and often two percussionists too.

The massive keyboards rigs used by Irving and Holzman were now replaced by a more basic set-up. "I didn't have a big rig. I just had the basic materials needed. I tried to put more stuff into my playing than trying to just get every sound. The set-up was definitely basic. I had a sampler, which was cool, but basically it was one electric piano vibe, one synth, one organ. That was the great thing, though, because with that band there was just so much space," says Johnson.

Miles was back in Europe in the summer, with a set that retained Prince's "Penetration." On July 8, 1991, Miles played his last concert at the Montreux Jazz Festival, but it was not to play with his band. Instead, Miles played old Gil Evans arrangements with an orchestra and big band conducted by Quincy Jones.

Two days later, Miles was playing an extraordinary concert at La Grande Halle, La Villette, Paris, which was simply billed as "Miles and Friends." The event would see Miles's current band playing alongside musicians from his 50s, 60s, 70s and 80s periods– Jackie McLean, Dave Holland, Chick Corea, Wayne Shorter, Herbie Hancock, Joe Zawinul, John McLaughlin, John Scofield, Steve Grossman, Bill Evans, Darryl Jones and Al Foster. The sheer scope of Miles's musical career made it almost inevitable that many major figures in his musical past would be missing, including Tony Williams, Jack DeJohnette, Marcus Miller and Keith Jarrett.[62]

Few people had any inkling of the size of the event, including Miles's own band members. "We did like a week in Paris at that point," says Johnson. "Miles gave us all a tape and said we had to learn these songs and there were ones like 'In A Silent Way.' I knew it was called 'Miles and Friends,' and I'm thinking 'maybe there's a couple of guys.' Then you looked around and saw all these guys, Zawinul, Shorter, Herbie, Chick – it was crazy."

Dave Holland explains how he got involved. "I got a call from somebody who was organizing it and they said it was going to be a retrospective of Miles's music. My first question was 'Is Miles going to be there?' because I was quite surprised to hear that was happening, as Miles never, ever seemed to want to look back or recreate things from the past – he was always looking forward and trying to do new things. I was a little suspicious, to be honest, because I get a lot of calls from people wanting to do Miles Davis tributes and I've always turned them down because I feel that those things belong to the time when they happened. I was assured that he was and then I was told the names of some other people who were going to do it."

The concept was that some of the former sidemen of Miles – such as Dave Holland and John McLaughlin – would bring their own groups and perform at the Paris Festival before the concert with Miles. "It was almost like a fes-tival based around both the Miles concert and the people who had worked with him," says Holland, adding that: "We were told to turn up at 11 am on the morning of the concert to start working out the details of the concert. I don't think anybody knew what was going to go down. I was quite surprised that Miles was there and was talking to everybody and telling us what tunes he wanted to play and getting the whole programme together – he was very active in the whole process."

Miles arrived at the concert wearing a bright, multi-coloured jacket and black and white polka-dot trousers. Zawinul says Miles was very nervous before the start of the concert. "When he went up on-stage, you had to almost lift him up because he was so scared. But then the moment he was up there, man, he looked like a young guy, with all the force and all the vitality. He was a great artist and a great human bring."[63] The stage backdrop was decorated with giant paintings that had been created by Miles and Jo Gelbard.

Miles played several numbers with his current band – Prince's "Penetration," "Human Nature," "Star People/New Blues" and "Perfect Way." On "Human Nature," Garrett played an incredible solo, even by his standards. At one stage, it looks as if Garrett has finished his long solo, but he is simply pausing to walk to the other side of the stage to continue playing. Miles also wanted to play in line-ups that mixed current band members with those from other periods. "Miles asked me to play on tunes like 'Footprints,' and I said 'No.' He wanted his newest band to be featured and that's why we opened the show," recalls Johnson. But Johnson played with Miles, McLaughlin, Scofield, Jones and Wellman on a rocking version of "Katia." "I had to try and play it down, because if it got too big, I wouldn't be able to play with all these guys," he adds.

Patterson also found the experience almost surreal. "That was just unbelievable," he says. "I was like a kid in a candy store. All these great musicians that I grew up listening to [were] all on the same stage. I remember one moment when I was on-stage and it was Joe Zawinul, Wayne Shorter, Al Foster, Herbie, Miles and Kenny and we're playing. All of a sudden, I just looked around and I almost freaked out. It was like 'What the heck am I doing with all these cats!'"

But the older musicians were also deeply touched by the occasion. "There was a wonderful feeling about being there and about having a chance to be with the man," says McLaughlin.[64] John Scofield says: "It was amazing to see Miles with all those guys and to be part of it. I think I said three sentences to Miles because he was so busy, but just to be included as part of that was a great honour."

The audience was also unprepared for the event. One fan reported: "It was just billed as 'Miles and Friends,' so I had absolutely no idea about what was going to happen. Then, one after the other, all those cats coming on-stage, all those wonderful musicians that once started as young newcomers with Miles and now were big headliners, gathering around their old boss just for a song or two – that was really moving. The output wasn't so great from a strictly musical standpoint and I remember [thinking] that most of the tunes and line-ups were probably completely unrehearsed but, believe me, that was largely compensated by the sheer emotion of the event."[65]

The concert ended with a rousing version of "Jean-Pierre" featuring an all-star line-up – Miles, Evans, McLean, Grossman, Corea, Johnson, Scofield, McLaughlin, Foley, Holland, Jones, Patterson, Garrett, Foster and Wellman. "I was so excited to be there. I think I just looked at him the whole time! I don't know that I heard what was really going on. I was just standing there in front of him thinking just how much I wanted to be doing that all the time," says Jones. Yet, despite the significance of the event, at the time of writing very little of this concert has been officially released.[66]

Few people saw Miles after the concert, but Katia Labèque was invited to Miles's dressing room. "I think he was very tired. He was very moved and happy about the concert. He asked me 'Did you hear? That was my band before and they were the people I could play with before. And you know what's amazing? Those people could do everything and they can do every-thing. But today, the young people can do one thing really great, but only one.' He wasn't criticizing his own musicians, but he was saying that, with his older musicians, he could explore all sorts of things and do different things with them. They loved him, they were all his children. I think John [McLaugh-lin] used to see Miles as his adopted father. He had arrived in New York with five pounds in his pocket and the day after he was in the studio with Miles. Miles also said to me 'The musician's power is given to him by the musicians he shares the stage with,' and that is so right. When he told me this I had this funny feeling that it might be the last time I saw him."

The fact that Miles did two retrospective concerts within the space of two days begs the question as to whether Miles did them because he knew he was dying. "I remember that tour and some of the band conversations like 'Miles knows something,' because he was doing these tribute things and playing all the old music. He was always about the future. In the back of minds it was like 'Where is all of this going?'" says Johnson. Miles's partner Jo Gelbard, who was with Miles in his final days, says that Miles had been aware that he was dying for some time.[67] Dave Holland suspects that Miles knew he was dying. "I didn't question him about it because I had too much respect for him. But I think he must have had some kind of feeling about that, because [the con-cert] was [a] party for Miles to be with people who loved him."

But Gordon Meltzer says Miles was not aware of his impending death when the concerts were organized. But Miles had been unwell that year. Tommy LiPuma recalls seeing Miles's at the trumpeter's 65th birthday party. "He had so much make-up on and I remember he walked up to me and some-times he had a way of greeting me where he would put his forehead against mine. And I remember he was sweating a little and when I wiped my fore-head I had make-up on it. He had so much make-up on because at that point he had been so sick that he was apparently very pale and they were trying to make him look good."

But the Paris concert was not the final event for Miles. A week later, the band was at Nice Jazz Festival. The band played a short set featuring "Perfect Way," "New Blues," "Hannibal," "Human Nature," "Time After Time" and "Wrinkle." The concert was featured on the 20th disc of the Montreux boxed set and the recordings reveal a band in fine form, with a leaner sound, more space and a fluent and fluid rhythm section.

On July 19, 1991, Miles played in London and the British photographer Allan Titmuss became probably the only photographer ever to be on-stage with Miles during a performance. Titmuss had been photographing Miles since a performance at the Royal Festival Hall in London in 1984. "The first time I photographed Miles, I managed to wangle my way into the wings and started taking pictures from there. The significance of what happened didn't occur to me until much later, but Miles spent a lot of time on the other side of the stage, starting straight at my lens. At one point, Miles played a long solo, direct to me, about five metres away from my camera. He stopped at one point, just lifted his glasses and nodded to me."

It was several years later that Titmuss learned from Miles's associates that Miles had been testing him. "I was always then able to work more closely with him than was generally allowed. We didn't hang out together, but I was always able to do a complete show if it was only supposed to be part of a show, for example. It was a nice, distant relationship."

Some years later, Titmuss was backstage in the green room with Miles, who had his bare feet up on a table as he leafed through Titmuss's portfolio, stretched out over his legs. At one point, he said to Titmuss "I don't look at pictures at myself any more. Every time I do, another piece has dropped off." In July 1991, Titmuss bumped into Miles backstage at the Royal Festival Hall in London and, on impulse, asked Miles if he could work with him on stage. Miles agreed. Titmuss then had words with road manager Gordon Meltzer and the concert promoter. "Gordon raised an eyebrow when I told him this and then he said 'Miles's stage manager is called Rodney. If Miles isn't happy about anything, he'll let Rodney know and Rodney's shadow weighs more than you and I put together!'"

Titmuss took his shots of the entire concert from the back of the stage. Titmuss recalls that "Miles had looked very frail to me that night, but it hadn't crossed my mind that it was going to be the last time I worked with him." Two months later, Titmuss heard that Miles had died. He developed the film from the last concert. "I had been avoiding looking at the contact sheets for days, because I knew if it wasn't good stuff there wasn't going to be a re-shoot. And looking at it, I don't think I've ever done another shoot remotely like it. It's hard to choose what not to print; pretty much everything was useable and strong, when normally on a good night you might find maybe three or four. It felt like a parting gift."

Miles spent part of July 1991 in New York recording music for his next album, *Doo-Bop*, and then flew to the West Coast. His last gig was on August 25, 1991 at the Hollywood Bowl. "I had no inkling that this would be the final gig, because Miles would get sick and recover, get sick and recover. But this time, he got sick and did not recover," says Foley. "I remember trying to get Joni Mitchell backstage and idiots were talking about backstage passes and all that shit. It was a crazy-assed night. And that was the last time I saw him."

Ironically Miles died at the time when Foley was beginning to feel happy about his playing in Miles's band. "I didn't enjoy any performance with Miles for the most part until the last seven gigs before it was over – I started playing that gig," he says. "We were at Venice airport one night and he told me to play half of what I normally played. It really fucked me up the whole day and then I went on-stage and tried it and I began to realize that's what would make me phrase. That was the night I started to learn how to play."

"It was a good show," says Patterson, recalling the last concert. "I used to go into Miles's dressing room after the gig and that night, when I went into the green room, there were a lot of celebrities. I walked in and Miles was there surrounded by all these people. I was just about to leave when Miles said to me 'Where are you going?' It was like 'Later to these people, it's about the band,' and that made me feel good. I looked into Miles's eyes and to me the whites of his eyes were always really white. We'd be getting a 6 am flight and we'd all have the red-eye, but Miles's eyes would be white. But this time they were reddish and I asked him if he was alright, and he just said he was tired. And that was the last time I saw him."

Patterson returned to Chicago. "We didn't have cellphones then, but my pager just kept going off. I remember when I heard the news I had a gig in Chicago that night and I was debating whether to do it, but I could hear Miles saying 'Man, what do you mean? You better go out there and make that money. Boy, get out there and play.' And I did and I felt better."

Patterson adds that: "Once you've been in Miles's band it's like a badge of honour and I'm working with people today as a result of playing with Miles. When I watched Miles and saw how comfortable he was with the music he was playing on-stage – it was like he was performing in his basement. It used to amaze me. He would find this comfort zone on-stage and that was a big lesson to me." Patterson also recalls Miles's dry sense of humour. "I remember reading a critical review and Miles walked over and said 'Did they spell your name right?'"

"I definitely didn't think it was going to be the last gig. Foley was staying at my house and we were talking to Miles on the phone or his girl Jo [Gelbard]. He was running back and forth to the hospital and then I started to get a little worried," says Johnson. "I thought I was going to be in that group at least three to five years, because it just felt right. What I'm still learning from Miles is leadership. I'll never forget one time when he asked me to 'stop playing all the tonics, don't hit C, because Kenny's playing that, he's doing that all night.' Then he showed me another chord that just opened my whole scheme up."

"He loved musicians to improvise on the spot to change the music to new peaks of excitement," recalls Wellman. "He was a man with few words but when he spoke, you listened. He was a powerful man in the fact that his insight of creativity was unbelievable. If you really tuned in and listened, you could really learn and exploit your creativity to what he wanted – to make you an overall better musician. Playing with Miles allowed me to perform around the world and people knew that Ricky Wellman was Miles Davis's drummer. I miss and enjoyed playing with all the different musicians in the band. I loved Miles Davis as a musician and as a person and he will truly be missed in my heart and the hearts of people all around the world."

Miles died on September 28, 1991 in Santa Monica, California. He was just sixty-five years old. On October 5, around 500 friends, family and musical associates attended a memorial service for Miles at St. Peter's Church in New York. The attendees included Miles's brother Vernon and his sister Dorothy, his ex-wife Cicely Tyson, childhood sweetheart Irene Cawthon and Miles's second child, Gregory. Also present were Bill Cosby, Quincy Jones, Dizzy Gillespie, Max Roach, Herbie Hancock, Dave Liebman, Jack DeJohnette, Valerie Simpson, Claude Nobs, New York mayor David Dinkins and the Reverend Jessie Jackson. Many fans stood outside in the pouring rain.

The eulogies were delivered in front of pictures of Miles, spanning his five decades of music making. Amongst them were two giant photos of Miles; one of them, taken by Annie Liebovitz, was a powerful close-up portrait shot of Miles with his hands covering his cheeks (it's on the cover of the book *The Art of Miles Davis*). Another was Gordon Meltzer's striking image of Miles on-stage looking down at his trumpet (the cover shot of the *Live Around The World* album). Throughout the service, Miles's music played softly in the background. Meltzer had asked Prince to deliver a eulogy at Miles's funeral, but Prince sent a letter and got his saxophonist Eric Leeds to deliver the eulogy. "I asked Prince, but he felt he couldn't do it," says Meltzer.

Quincy Jones described Miles's death as probably leaving the biggest hole in music in the twentieth century. Miles's dark sense of humour was remembered when the drummer Max Roach recalled the generosity of Miles, whom he discovered from a friend was paying for Roach's treatment for alcohol abuse. "Tell Max he's gotta get himself together," said Miles, "'cause he's costing me too much money." And Herbie Hancock spoke for many when he said that contrary to Miles's angry reputation: "If you listen to the music, there's no rage. There's love, there's vulnerability."[68] Miles was buried at the Woodlawn Cemetery in the Bronx, along with one of his trumpets, and close to the Duke Ellington family site.

20 *live around the world* (70:47)

Warner Bros 9 46032-2

Recorded	1988–91
Released	Summer 1996
Producer	Miles Davis live on-stage
Executive producer	Gordon Meltzer
Compilation	Gordon Meltzer, Adam Holzman
Engineers	Patrick Murray, Don Kurek ("Hannibal"), Scott Hull (digital editing), Dan Gellert (digital editing)
Mixed by	Patrick Murray, Don Kurek ("Hannibal")
Tracks	"In A Silent Way," "Intruder," "New Blues," "Human Nature," "Mr. Pastorius," "Amandla," "Wrinkle," "Tutu," "Full Nelson," "Time After Time," "Hannibal"

"I love the band better live than I like the records." *Ndugu Chancler, drummer*

One of the biggest mysteries of the last phase of Miles's recording career was the reluctance of his record label Warner Bros to release a live album while Miles was still active. It wasn't as if Warner Bros lacked sufficient material because, over the years, the company had dispatched mobile recording units to a number of Miles's concerts. When Miles performed in Nice on July 13, 15 and 16, 1986, Warner Bros recorded all the concerts. It also recorded Miles's superb performance at the Montreux Jazz Festival on July 17, 1986, which saw George Duke and David Sanborn appear as guest performers. Warner Bros recorded a fourth concert at Nice, held on July 20, 1986. There was talk of Tommy LiPuma producing a live album from the Nice recordings, but nothing came to fruition. Miles had hoped the July 17 concert would become the follow-up to *Tutu*, but it would remain in the can for the next sixteen years, finally appearing on a Montreux boxed set released in 2002 – although bootleg versions had appeared long before this.

A performance in Melbourne, Australia on May 2, 1988 was also recorded by Warner Bros, as was the 1989 Montreux Jazz Festival performance of July 1989, which saw Chaka Khan sing on-stage with Miles (this concert also turned up on the 2002 Montreux boxed set). However, Warner Bros did release a video of part of a performance at the 10th Paris Jazz Festival on November 3, 1989. But there was no corresponding CD release. Two concerts performed in the summer of 1991 were also recorded – one played at the Montreux Jazz Festival on July 8, which saw Miles working with Quincy Jones and playing an assortment of Gil Evans's arrangements, and a reunion concert at La Grande Halle, La Villette in Paris, on July 10. The Montreux concert has been released on video and CD, but, at the time of writing, only one hour of the La Villette concert has been released on video.

However, Warner Bros eventually decided to release a live album and *Live Around The World* was the result. But instead of using its stock of concert recordings, Warner Bros decided to use the concert tapes recorded by Miles's front-of-house (FOH) sound engineer Patrick Murray. Murray had begun working with Miles in March 1986. "A friend of mine, Nick Joyce, who had been working with Miles for several years, asked me if I would be interested in the keyboard gig. My original job responsibilities were as keyboard technician and lighting director. I was responsible for setting up and maintaining the three keyboard rigs for Miles, Bobby Irving and Adam Holzman. Then I would go out and run lights," explains Murray.

Later in the year, Ves Weaver was hired as lighting director as it proved necessary for Murray to be on-stage to monitor Miles at his keyboard rig. "He had the habit of playing with the pitch knob on his OBX so I had to retune it a lot during the show," recalls Murray. At the beginning of 1987, Murray's tasks included mixing the monitors and other stage management duties. "[This] eventually rolled into the production manager job – I always wore a few different hats while working with Miles," notes Murray.

Ron Lorman, who was Miles's concert sound mixer, was replaced by Brian Rinser, but in early 1988 Murray took over the house mixing position when Rinser departed. "I was responsible for troubleshooting, tuning and aligning the locally provided PA system as well as coordinating all aspects of the day-to-day show production activities," recalls Murray. One of his jobs was to make soundboard recordings for Miles, which involved plugging a tape recorder into the sound mixing desk.

"I recorded a cassette of every show for Miles so that he could critique the band and get ideas for new arrangements. He would occasionally make comments like 'The horn sounds tinny!' 'Put more bass on the horn.' He wanted his horn to be dark and warm sounding," says Murray. "I actually learned more about how he wanted his horn to sound when I was doing monitors. Miles never came to soundcheck, so we had one of his old horns and I used to walk around playing it during soundcheck with the band in order to get the sound right for him. I guess those second-grade band trumpet lessons finally paid off."

In 1987, a new audio format was launched on the market, Digital Audio Tape or DAT. DAT used cassettes the size of a large matchbox and, like the compact disc, stored sound as a computer code. DAT offered many benefits over analogue tape systems such as the audio compact cassette, including a higher frequency response, wider dynamic range, no tape hiss and almost no measurable wow and flutter (pitch variations). Digital tape can also be copied or cloned so there is no loss of sound quality when copying and editing. What is more, DAT could record sound at a quality that was even higher than that offered by the CD.

Murray recalls the first time he saw a DAT recorder. "We were on tour in Japan in August 1988 and the portable DAT machine had just come out there. I knew I had been making pretty good soundboard tapes for Miles and I had the idea that perhaps we could get a live album out of it. I began recording all of the shows to DAT from that point on." Murray purchased a Sony D-10 DAT recorder. "It was the original one without the pro inputs or digital output," notes Murray. For the technically-minded, the recorder's sampling rate was fixed at 16-bit, 48Khz with pre-emphasis, and the mix was taken directly from the soundboard left/right outputs. "The mixes on *Live Around The World* were culminated from three years of shows. They picked the best performances that had the most balanced mixes," adds Murray.

Getting the right mix could be a challenge, not least because a mix that is right for a venue may not be ideal for a record release. "There were many variables to deal with on a daily basis. Not only did I have to deal with different room acoustics, but also varying quality issues of the locally supplied sound equipment," says Murray. "I would often have to keep things low in the mix on the board for the balance to be right for the venue. But most of the time if I got the system EQ [equalization – sound balance] set up correctly and had a reasonably good sound system, the board mixes would come out sounding pretty good." Perhaps not surprisingly, Murray was given the nickname of "Pat the DAT."

In 1989, Miles's management pitched Warner Bros with the idea of making a live album from Murray's DAT recordings, but the label's then head of jazz, Tommy LiPuma, was not interested at the time. "I guess they felt that as it was not multi-tracked in a professional remote truck the quality would be inferior. So up on the shelf they went," notes Murray. But Murray had always felt that one day the tapes would be used and, in fact, some of them had been broadcast in 1990 on the American public radio series *The Miles Davis Radio Project*.

The final programmes included live recordings taken from two of Miles's gigs, a show at New York's Indigo Blues on December 18, 1988 and a second concert recorded on June 15, 1989 at the Coach House, Capistrano, California. In late 1994, Warner Bros had a change of heart and gave the go-ahead for a live album project. Peter Shukat, Miles's ex-manager and now part of the Miles Davis Estate, gave Gordon Meltzer (Miles's last road manager) responsibility for the project. "I think it was in early 1995 that I was contacted by Gordon Meltzer. He told me about the project and asked me what shows I thought were the best. He did a tremendous job of listening and sorting through all of those hours of tape," says Murray.

Meltzer spent nine months sifting through 160 DAT cassettes of Miles's performances and whittling down the choices to the best performances. Meltzer also had a cassette from Miles's last performance at the Hollywood Bowl on August 25, 1991, which had been recorded by Don Kurek, who replaced Murray in late 1990. It was decided to use a performance from this concert too.

Meltzer had hoped that Warner Bros would make the live album a double one, but the company wanted a single-disc release. The original plan was to take the best twelve performances of different tunes from twelve different concerts to create a single "virtual concert," but in the end this concept was adapted – the final mix had eleven tracks, and gigs at the Indigo Blues Club in New York in 1988 and 1990 Montreux Jazz Festival in Switzerland yielded two tunes apiece.

After Meltzer had made his selections, Miles's ex-musical director Adam Holzman was brought in to help with the editing. "Adam had a brilliant sense of where to cut and where to edit," says Meltzer. Holzman basically agreed with Meltzer's track selection. "We didn't argue. We just figured out a way to cram as much music on there as possible. Gordon picked out most of the tunes and I added a few things like 'Intruder' and 'Wrinkle,'" says Holzman.

The four-year period that *Live Around The World* covers (1988–91) saw many changes in Miles's band personnel. Only Miles, lead bassist Foley and drummer Ricky Wellman were constant elements within the band in this period. Kenny Garrett played on almost every gig, although Rick Margitza substituted for him on some European gigs in 1989. Bassist Benny Rietveld played in the band until 1990, when he was replaced by Richard Patterson. Miles used a phalanx of keyboardists during this period: Robert Irving III, Adam Holzman, John Beasley, Kei Akagi, Deron Johnson and Joey DeFrancesco. Many of these played in bands with two specialist keyboard players and Miles would often make up the third player. Several percussionists were also used: Marilyn Mazur, Erin Davis and Munyungo Jackson.

The recordings cover a period when Miles's live repertoire was dominated by tunes from the *Tutu* and *Amandla* albums, supplemented with concert favourites such as "Human Nature" and "Time After Time." When a multi-track recorder is used for recording a performance, each instrument can be allocated its own audio track(s), giving much scope for editing and mixing.

But soundboard tapes, which put everything on to two stereo tracks, don't offer this convenience, as Meltzer notes: "You can't 'fix in the mix' because the mix is done in real time as the band plays."[1]

After editing the soundboard tracks, much time was spent on adjusting the equalization to get the horn sounding just right. "I was driving the studio people crazy," recalls Meltzer. The digital editing was carried out by Scott Hull and Dan Gellert at the Masterdisk and Power Station studios in New York respectively. "There was no remixing or overdubs. Only editing for time and overall EQ and compression. And I believe some audience ambience was added for continuity. Gordon, Adam Holzman, Dan Gellert and Scott Hull really did an incredible job of putting it all together and making my mixes come to life," says Murray.

Incidentally, rumours suggested that the Japanese release of *Live Around The World* would have twelve tracks. In fact, Meltzer and Holzman had toyed with the idea of putting an additional track on the Japanese release and the extra tune would have been a four-and-a-half-minute version of "Perfect Way." In order to squeeze it on an already-crowded CD, two tracks, "Wrinkle" and "Hannibal," would have been trimmed back to produce a 12-track CD with a running time of just under 76 minutes.

Meltzer and Holzman went as far as to produce a pre-master tape containing "Perfect Way," but Warner Bros's Artist and Repertoire department in New York vetoed the idea, so the final master tape had just eleven tracks. This version was released worldwide, the only difference being that on continental Europe, *Live Around The World* was also released as a double LP. The rest of the world only had CD and cassette versions of the album.

The tracks

"Full Nelson" (2:48) (composed by Marcus Miller)

Recorded	Osaka Expo Park, *Live Under The Sky* Festival, August 7, 1988
Musicians	Miles, trumpet; Kenny Garrett, alto saxophone; Foley, lead bass; Adam Holzman, keyboards; Robert Irving III, keyboards; Benny Rietveld, bass; Marilyn Mazur, percussion; Ricky Wellman, drums

"Full Nelson" is the first of five Marcus Miller penned tracks and the shortest piece on the album. In fact, Meltzer and Holzman only removed around 45 seconds from the original version. Taken at a faster tempo than the album version, "Full Nelson" is dominated by Foley's jangling rhythm guitar lick, Wellman's driving beat and the catchy theme, which is played by both keyboardists and by Miles and Garrett in unison. The band set up a strong groove but the track comes to an abrupt end much too soon.

"New Blues" (5:35) (composed by Miles Davis)

Recorded   Greek Theater, Los Angeles, August 14, 1988
Musicians   Miles, trumpet and keyboards; Kenny Garrett, alto sax-
            ophone; Foley, lead bass; Adam Holzman, keyboards;
            Robert Irving III, keyboards; Benny Rietveld, bass;
            Marilyn Mazur, percussion; Ricky Wellman, drums

From August 1982 until his final concert in August 1991, Miles included this blues number in his live set, with the tune always following an uptempo opener. "New Blues" began life as "Star People" but Miles's discographer Enrico Merlin has noted that, over the years, it slowly transformed into a new form, although the chord sequence and feel remained the same.[2] The highlight of this performance is a stirring solo from Foley, who plays the blues elegantly and with much feeling. Anyone who thinks that Foley's guitar playing was just about loud rock chords and distortion should listen to this. Little wonder, then, that at the end of the tune Miles exclaims "Foley!"

"Human Nature" (12:48) (composed by Steve Porcaro and John Bettis)

Recorded   Liebenauer Eishalle, Graz, Austria, November 1, 1988
Musicians   Miles, trumpet and keyboards; Kenny Garrett, alto sax-
            ophone; Foley, lead bass; Adam Holzman, keyboards;
            Benny Rietveld, bass; Marilyn Mazur, percussion; Ricky
            Wellman, drums

By this time, "Human Nature" had long become a *tour de force* performance and a showcase for Kenny Garrett. Indeed, Garrett's solo would often make up almost half of the tune. This performance boasts one of the best mixes on the album, with each instrument clearly defined, coupled with a well-balanced sound. At around the five-and-a-half-minute mark, Garrett begins copying Miles's phrases, before commencing his solo just after the six-minute point.

As usual, Garrett begins his solo tentatively, gradually increasing the tension (notice how the rhythm section tightens considerably at around the 10:45 point) before reaching a blistering climax. Miles's trumpet blast marks the conclusion of the tune. When Miles was especially pleased with a musician's performance, he would hold the trumpet microphone to his mouth and say their name to the audience. In this instance, Miles seems to speak for Garrett, telling the audience that the saxophonist was capable of performing to this level at every concert. Miles says: "Kenny, Kenny, Kenny, Kenny, Kenny, Kenny, [laughs] aw man, that were nothin'. That were nothin', man   I do that every night."

"In A Silent Way" (1:49) (composed by Joe Zawinul)

> *Recorded*   Indigo Blues Club, New York, December 17, 1988
> 2nd show
> *Musicians*   Miles, trumpet; Kenny Garrett, alto saxophone; Foley,
> lead bass; Adam Holzman, keyboards; Joey DeFrancesco,
> keyboards; Benny Rietveld, bass; Marilyn Mazur,
> percussion; Ricky Wellman, drums

In February 1988, Miles dispensed with the long-standing opener, "One Phone Call/Street Scenes" and introduced an old tune as the opening number. "In A Silent Way" was the title track of the classic 1969 album that saw Miles playing with a trio of keyboardists (Joe Zawinul, Chick Corea and Herbie Hancock). Miles blows on muted horn over swirling keyboards that play the theme. A funky bass line augments the sound and the tune segues into another new tune, "Intruder."

"Intruder" (4:52) (composed by Erin Davis)

> *Recorded*   Indigo Blues Club, New York, December 17, 1988
> 2nd show
> *Musicians*   Miles, trumpet; Kenny Garrett, alto saxophone; Foley, lead
> bass; Adam Holzman, keyboards; Joey DeFrancesco, key-
> boards; Benny Rietveld, bass; Marilyn Mazur, percussion;
> Ricky Wellman, drums

"Intruder" was written by Miles with his youngest son Erin and Miles assigned full credit and copyright to Erin, probably to avoid giving Warner Bros' publishing arm Warner Chappell Music any stake in the tune. "Intruder" is an uptempo number, propelled by Wellman's driving drum beat (his bass drum remains prominent throughout the track), busy syncopated percussion support and a funk bass riff. Miles plays open horn and the tune is interspersed with keyboard stabs. Garrett solos energetically and the track then ends abruptly.

"Mr. Pastorius" (3:32) (composed by Marcus Miller)

> *Recorded*   Le Zenith, Montpelier, France, April 12, 1989
> *Musicians*   Miles, trumpet; Kenny Garrett, alto saxophone; Foley,
> lead bass; Kei Akagi, keyboards; John Beasley, keyboards;
> Benny Rietveld, bass; Munyungo Jackson, percussion;
> Ricky Wellman, drums

"Mr. Pastorius" was a highlight on *Amandla* and it is a standout track on this compilation. Miles's fragile horn sound is haunting and is well supported by

Rietveld's jazzy lines on fretless bass and Wellman's sensitive drumming. At this point in his career, Miles's music was often dominated by an orchestral wash from the keyboards section, but on this number the keyboards are for the most part under-stated. But just as the tune gets into its stride, it ends far too soon. The original version was around nine minutes in length and "Mr. Pastorius" suffers as a result of this drastic – but given the limitations of space, necessary – cutting.

"Time After Time" (9:56) (composed by Cyndi Lauper and Rob Hyman)

Recorded   Chicago Theater, JVC Jazz Festival, June 5, 1989
Musicians   Miles, trumpet; Kenny Garrett, alto saxophone; Foley, lead bass; Adam Holzman, keyboards; Kei Akagi, keyboards; Benny Rietveld, bass; Munyungo Jackson, percussion; Ricky Wellman, drums

No Miles concert since the mid-1980s was complete without this tune, which, when played live, extended and expanded upon the rather tame album version. The tune opens with a plaintive cry from Miles's trumpet. Miles sounds in fine lip and, just before the two-minute point, he switches to the Harmon mute before playing the theme. Miles plays tenderly, his trumpet sound floating on top of the band's sound, whose playing barely rises above a whisper. But around the midway point, the music increases in both intensity and volume before a blast from Miles's open horn takes the energy back down.

It is at this point that Miles calls Foley over to him and Miles plays a series of phrases on muted trumpet which Foley copies. Then the volume and intensity of the music rises again, Miles reverts back to open horn before pounding drums and a trumpet blast bring the song to a satisfying conclusion.

"Amandla" (5:52) (composed by Marcus Miller)

Recorded   Pallazo Della Civita, "The Steps," Rome, Italy, July 26, 1989
Musicians   Miles, trumpet; Rick Margitza, tenor saxophone; Foley, lead bass; Adam Holzman, keyboards; Kei Akagi, keyboards; Benny Rietveld, bass; Munyungo Jackson, percussion; Ricky Wellman, drums

"Amandla" sticks closely to the album arrangement and there are few surprises. Rietveld's fine under-stated bass lines provide good support to Miles's muted horn. Rick Margitza gets to show his prowess on tenor sax, with a blistering solo, and Foley's guitar is briefly brought to the front. The finale reaches a pitch before ending with a cymbal smash. Miles says: "Foley, Adam, Rick, Benny," ending a rousing performance of a fine song.

"Wrinkle" (7:17) (composed by Erin Davis, Randy Hall, Zane Giles and Wayne Linsey)

Recorded	Casino De Montreux, Switzerland, Montreux International Jazz Festival, July 20, 1990
Musicians	Miles, trumpet and keyboards; Kenny Garrett, alto saxophone; Foley, lead bass; Kei Akagi, keyboards; Richard Patterson, bass; Erin Davis, percussion; Ricky Wellman, drums

Don't let this song's album credits fool you (which simply credit the composer to "Davis") – "Wrinkle" was composed in 1985 during the *Rubberband* sessions by four musicians, including Miles. However, it seems that Miles may have done some further work on the tune with his son Erin and then assigned his copyright to him. "Wrinkle" is an energetic funk workout that highlights the superbly tight rhythm section of drummer Ricky Wellman and bassist Richard Patterson. Keyboardist Kei Akagi plays some busy lines on the synthesizer and the whole track crackles and fizzles.

The sound is dominated by Wellman's hyperactive cymbal work and Patterson's hard funk bass lines. Miles blows his horn over the boiling rhythm section and at around three-and-a-half minutes in, the tempo rises as Patterson plays a superb (and slightly edited) bass solo. The tension is then suddenly released by a blast of horn. The tempo slows and Patterson reverts to popping and plucking his strings in the process. Miles and Garrett play the theme together; there is a slight pause followed by a frenetic finale, complete with Wellman's furious drumming and cymbal smashes, and Foley's frantic guitar riffs. A final blast from Miles and Garrett bring this super-charged performance to an end.

"Tutu" (8:53) (composed by Marcus Miller)

Recorded	Casino De Montreux, Switzerland, Montreux International Jazz Festival, July 20, 1990
Musicians	Miles, trumpet and keyboards; Kenny Garrett, flute, alto saxophone; Foley, lead bass; Kei Akagi, keyboards; Richard Patterson, bass; Erin Davis, percussion; Ricky Wellman, drums

This is edited from a 13-minute performance (the full-length version can be found on the Montreux boxed set). The main highlights are solos from Foley and Akagi – the former plays some scorching lines, while Akagi really gets to display his virtuosity on keyboards. Towards the end there's some playful audience participation as the crowd attempts to copy Miles's phrases vocally – and laughs when Miles fires off a flurry of notes that simply cannot be copied.

"Hannibal" (7:22) (composed by Marcus Miller)

Recorded   Hollywood Bowl, August 25, 1991
Musicians   Miles, trumpet; Kenny Garrett, saxophone; Foley,
lead bass; Richard Patterson, bass; Deron Johnson,
keyboards; Ricky Wellman, drums

Hindsight is a wonderful thing and you can be sure that if anyone had known that Miles's performance at the Hollywood Bowl on August 25, 1991 would be his last, a video crew would have been dispatched to the stadium and probably a remote recording facility too. As it happened, this final performance was not even recorded professionally. Indeed, Miles's concert sound mixer, Don Kurek, didn't even use a DAT recorder. Instead, he plugged an analogue Sony Walkman Pro deck into the mixing desk and in the words of Gordon Meltzer: "Recorded on the cheapest, one-dollar non-metal tape audio cassette you could get." The resulting recording was dogged by tape hiss, pops and drop-outs (where the sound disappears because of blemishes on the tape's oxide coating).

Yet the producers of *Live Around The World* were able to salvage a recording that was good enough to include on a CD, and that was largely thanks to modern studio technology. The first step involved transferring the analogue recording on to digital tape. Once a recording is in the digital domain, it is possible to use a battery of techniques and technologies to clean up the sound, such as filters to remove the hiss and software programs to remove pops and clicks. Equalization can be applied to correct the sound balance. After the recording was cleaned up, it was edited down from its original 18-minute version to seven minutes.

The band plays sensitively behind Miles and for the most part his horn dominates proceedings. Three minutes into the tune and the energy rises a little as Garrett copies Miles's phrases before playing a superb solo that has been severely edited (on the unedited version Garrett plays for almost six minutes) – the edit point can be discerned at around 5:48. The other major casualty of the editing suite was Deron Johnson, whose long keyboard solo is left on the cutting-room floor. The track ends with a blast from Miles's horn and Garrett's saxophone – and then there is silence.

For some reason, the venue of this last performance is not listed on the CD cover, but Meltzer's sleeve notes do reveal the location. Miles's fans will be pleased to have some form of record of his last performance, but it would be nice to see the complete concert released one day. The excellent clean-up job done on the analogue recording suggests that it would be possible to do the same trick with the rest of the concert tape, but will it happen? "I think there are some technicalities regarding the Hollywood Bowl and live recordings. DATs are a better-sounding medium, but if there is a good performance on a cassette, and the sound isn't absolutely awful then – who knows? – maybe it could be issued at some point," says Adam Holzman. Gordon Meltzer adds: "Assuming the tape can still be found and there's enough oxide on it, it might conceivably happen, but whether Warner Bros would want to do it is another question."

Live Around The World – the verdict

One of the biggest ironies of Miles's final decade is how little of his live music was available on official releases and how much was being circulated on bootleg recordings. Only one full album of live material was ever released in this period (*We Want Miles*) and *Live Around The World* was the first to feature Miles's bands from his Warner Bros period.

On the positive side, *Live Around The World* gives listeners an opportunity to hear many band members who have never appeared on any official studio albums (soundtracks such as *Dingo* and DVDs such as *Miles In Paris* are discounted in this context). It's a chance therefore to hear band members such as Marilyn Mazur, Benny Rietveld, Kei Akagi, Richard Patterson, John Beasley, Erin Davis and Munyungo Jackson. The recordings by Murray are excellent and the process of editing and sweetening the sound has produced a high-quality product that belies its relative low-tech origins. Miles plays superbly on most tracks and the other star is Garrett, who really shines on this album. The album also includes several tracks not available on Miles's studio albums.

The album was also tastefully packaged, featuring a powerful cover portrait of Miles, taken by Gordon Meltzer, showing Miles on-stage, looking down at his trumpet. The booklet contained two more photographs of Miles and the CD inlay tray was transparent and covered a photograph of Miles's ghostly shadow cast over the front of a drum kit. The back of the CD case showed a ticket for Miles's evening performance at the Avery Fisher Hall in New York on June 25, 1988. The CD booklet included notes from Meltzer, Holzman, Foley, Rietveld and Erin Davis (who comments that he has waited years for these tapes to be officially released).

But *Live Around The World* is disappointing on several fronts. First, the restriction of a single CD means that many of the tunes are severely edited. One of the highlights of Miles's live performances was that the tunes were greatly expanded from their studio versions and the music developed organically on-stage. But the need to restrict the playing time to around 70 minutes meant that it was not possible to allow the music to fully speak for itself. While on the subject of album length, a CD can officially hold up to 74 minutes of music, although many exceed this by several minutes (*We Want Miles*, for example, lasts 76 minutes and has been squeezed on to a single disc).

And while it's good to see the inclusion of tunes such as "Intruder" and "Wrinkle," many other tunes including "Heavy Metal," "Carnival Time," "Don't

Stop Me Now," and the Foley-penned funk-rock *tour de force* "The Senate/Me And You" are omitted. Miles played "The Senate/Me And You" at almost every concert between 1987–91 and its exclusion is likely to have been because of its length. It's understandable that *Live Around The World* contains no performances from Miles's pre-Warner Bros days (and thus omitting the superb Scofield/Evans/Jones/Foster/Irving/Cinelu power house), but in restricting the recordings to Murray's DAT recordings many performances between April 1986 and August 1988 are omitted, when the band featured Robben Ford on guitar.

We Want Miles was a pick-and-mix affair that compiled performances from different dates, but the crucial difference is that it was the same band throughout, and thus it maintained a level of continuity that is absent from *Live Around The World*. But any disappointments are down to Warner Bros and not those who recorded, compiled, edited and sweetened the music. As a taster to Miles's live music in the latter years of his life, *Live Around The World* has much to commend. But for a more substantial offering, fans will have to pay for the (expensive) Miles's Montreux boxed set or hope that, at some time in the future, Warner Bros releases a more affordable live album comprising two or three discs.

21 miles's other recordings

'Prisoners' from *Alfred Hitchcock Presents* (1985)

In late 1985, Miles recorded the music for an episode from the NBC TV series *Alfred Hitchcock Presents*. The recording was made at Fidelity Sound Studio in Los Angeles and involved Miles, percussionist Steve Reid and Miles's musical director Robert Irving III, who also wrote the music.

"Miles's agent, Christie Barnes, was pitching Miles as a film scorer. When Drew Merish was producing new versions of old Alfred Hitchcock stories with new actors and updated scores for Universal Studios, Miles was contracted to do the music for an episode called 'Prisoners,'" explains Irving. The episode starred Yaphet Koto, who played an escape convict who breaks into the home of a deaf woman, who can lip-read and speak. Koto never knew she was deaf, so when the phone rang he told her what to "say" and thus the caller knew she was in trouble. The episode was broadcast on December 8, 1985.

"Miles called me to work on the score with him," recalls Irving. "They put me in a hotel in Malibu near Miles, which was inconvenient because the studios where we would work were in L.A. Miles picked me up in his yellow Ferrari. He drove very fast through the canyons and that was scary for me." Miles and Irving attended a spotting session together in the screening room at Universal, where they watched the episode and determined what type of music should accompany the images and where it should be placed. "Miles asked me to bring a small cassette recorder. The opening of the episode showed Koto's character escaping from prison and searching for a place to hide. Miles motioned for me to turn on the tape recorder and he hummed a bass-line motif. This was the only thing that I had to work with in terms of Miles's input," says Irving.

Irving returned to his hotel room, armed with a videotape, keyboard, drum machine and a sequencer. "That night, I created the entire score synchronized with the video and notated a few melodies and chord symbols for Miles. The next day I transferred the sequenced parts and Miles came in to overdub," says Irving. "When the show aired, I naïvely waited to see my name in the credits, but it said: 'Music by Miles Davis.'"

Street Smart (1987)

Miles and Irving also worked together on another project, the film *Street Smart*, starring Christopher Reeve and Morgan Freeman and directed by director, Jerry Schatzberg, whose other films include *Panic in Needle Park* and *Scarecrow*. "The film is a thriller based around the streets of New York. After what happened with the Alfred Hitchcock score, I called Miles's agent and told her 'If you get any more score projects for Miles that I'm involved in as composer, you hire me and I'll hire Miles.' And that's what happened with *Street Smart*," says Irving. Irving attended a spotting session with Schatzberg. "Jerry had a very good concept about what he wanted musically. He mostly wanted a New York urban jazz treatment. We just went [through] scene by scene, discussing where music was needed or not. Conceptually most of the cues were composed and performed with the idea that Miles would improvise on the top without a lot of melodies for him to sight-read."

The musicians involved in the sessions were: Miles on trumpet, Irving on synthesizers, Mike Stern and Andre Lassalle on guitar, Adam Holzman on synthesizer, Darryl Jones and Felton Crews on electric bass, Alex Blake on acoustic bass, Bob Berg and Bob Mintzer on saxophone, Steve Turre on trumpet, Vince Wilburn Jr. and Adam Nussbaum on drums and Steve Thornton on percussion. "Darryl Jones played bass on most of the cues. Miles came in after all the tracks were laid and did first-take performances on everything without having heard any music prior to the session. It was like a private two-hour Miles Davis concert," says Irving.

Whereas all the other films Miles was involved in musically over this period were released as soundtrack albums (*Siesta*, *The Hot Spot*, *Dingo* and *Scrooged*), there was never a soundtrack album for *Street Smart*. Irving explains why: "First of all the mix of music was very eclectic with everything from a short classical interlude and a period ballroom jazz piece (both in the party scene), some smooth jazz, fusion rock, an acoustic groove ballad (the title track that runs on the closing credits). There were also a couple of pop vocal tunes sung by Michael Irving (my younger brother). There was not enough music in a single genre to sustain an entire album." There were plans to put several cues from *Street Smart* on the abandoned retrospective release, *The Last Word* from Warner Bros.

Dingo (Warner Bros 7599-26438-2) (1990)

In 1986, Miles had played the part of a pimp in an episode of the U.S. cop TV series *Miami Vice*. *Dingo* saw him playing his only film role (discounting a cameo appearance in *Scrooged*). Gordon Meltzer, who was Miles's road manager at the time (and one of the soundtrack's executive producers), explained on the *Miles Davis Discussion Forum* on June 29, 1996, how the project came about.

"Miles had been approached all through the '80s to do film and TV projects. The director of *Dingo*, Rolf de Heer, showed up in New York wearing one of those funny *Crocodile Dundee* hats, real rough around the edges kinda guy, way out of place in Manhattan. He carried this goofy romantic movie script about an expatriate American jazz legend, Billy Cross, whose plane makes an unexpected fuel stop in the Outback at a tiny unused airport. The band gets out to stretch, and blows a tune next to the plane while the fuel goes in. A young boy watches and is obsessed with the sound from the horn for twenty years. The kid learns to play, runs away from wife/kids /job as a dingo hunter, goes to Paris to find the legend. Finds him, much closeness develops, sits in with his hero at a Paris jazz club." Meltzer adds that the timing was just right for Miles and involved two weeks' filming in the Australian Outback and two weeks in Paris. "He had fun, too, and amazingly they were able to mike him so his dialogue was all real intelligible, real clear."

The soundtrack album was recorded before filming started and was arranged, orchestrated and conducted by Michel Legrand, who Miles had recorded with in 1958, on the album *Legrand Jazz* (the album also featured John Coltrane, Bill Evans and Paul Chambers). "Michel Legrand came over and worked at Miles's Malibu house, writing the music. Then we put together a band consisting of Miles's regular band plus a lot of good L.A. studio types. [Trumpeter] Chuck Findley on the Australian kid's trumpet parts was great," adds Meltzer.

Miles's group at the time consisted of Kenny Garrett, Foley, Kei Akagi, Benny Rietveld, Ricky Wellman and John Bigham, and they were joined by a host of seasoned session players including drummers Harvey Mason and Alphonse Mouzon, bassist Abraham Laboriel and trombonist George Bohanan. "That was a great experience. It was a totally orchestrated thing with maybe twenty to thirty people. I had my little set-up right in front of all these people – it was crazy!" says Bigham.

Miles plays "The Arrival," "Concert On The Runway," "The Departure," "Trumpet Cleaning," "The Dream," "Paris Walking II," "The Jam Session" and "Going Home." The tracks "Departure," "The Dream" and "Going Home" are essentially different arrangements of "The Arrival." The soundtrack album also features some of Miles's dialogue. The film finds Miles playing more like his style of the 1950s and early 1960s, which no doubt pleased many fans of his older music. "The Jam Session" is a funk workout featuring Miles and Findley.

Sadly, *Dingo* remained an obscure film that is hard to find even on DVD or video. "I think that a roll of film from the early Australian shoot was destroyed in the processing lab. This wiped ten minutes off the plot, and they couldn't afford to reshoot it," recalls Meltzer. "It would have meant bringing Miles over again which might have been okay, but they would have had to rent the DC-8 jet again which was just too expensive. I think this messed up some of the plot so people were confused when they saw the film. Maybe that's why *Dingo* never got widespread commercial release."

The Hot Spot (Antilles 422 816 813-2) (1990)

The Hot Spot was directed by an old friend of Miles's, Dennis Hopper – on the album credits, Hopper explains how he had known Miles since he was seventeen, adding that Miles once punched out a heroin dealer and threatened to kill Hopper if he ever used the drug again. The soundtrack saw Miles teaming up with blues legend John Lee Hooker, who plays on a series of numbers, along with drummer Earl Palmer, bassist Tim Drummond, keyboardist Bradford Ellis and guitarists Taj Mahal and Roy Rogers. Miles plays on "Coming To Town," "Empty Bank," "Sawmill," "Harry And Dolly," "Bank Robbery," "Gloria's Story," "Murder" and "End Credits." The soundtrack album lists Miles on "Harry Sets Up Sutton," but he is not heard. Most of the music is standard blues fare, although "Bank Robbery" is a rocking number that sees Miles stretching out a little.

Miles Davis and Quincy Jones Live At Montreux (Warner Bros 9632 45221-2) (1991)

We are told that Miles never looked back, but in July 1991 he shocked (and delighted) many of his fans by performing two concerts within the space of a couple of days which saw him playing music, much of which was more than thirty years old. This album documents the performance on July 8, 1991 at the 25th Montreux Jazz Festival, which saw Miles playing the classic Gil Evans arrangements from *Birth Of The Cool* to *Sketches Of Spain*. Miles is accompanied by The Gil Evans Orchestra and The George Gruntz Concert Jazz Band, with soloists Kenny Garrett and trumpeter Wallace Roney onstage with Miles.

Wallace Roney had known Miles since 1983, when he had played at a celebratory event for Miles in 1983. When Roney joined Art Blakey's band and later played with drummer Tony Williams, his relationship with Miles grew even closer. "We'd see a lot of each other and I remember about a year or two before Miles played at Montreux, he said 'If I play the old stuff again, I want you to play with me 'cos you play it perfect,' but I just thought he was messing around," says Roney.

But later on, Roney heard that Miles was going to play the old music. "It was in 1991 and I heard Miles was going to do this special concert at Montreux. I was playing with George Gruntz's Concert Jazz Band and I heard we were playing in Montreux, so I thought 'Great, I'll be able to catch Miles at the concert.' But when we get to Montreux, George informs us that we're playing at the concert!" recalls Roney.

Roney remembers waiting for Miles to turn up at the rehearsals. "Miles didn't show up, so they asked me to fill in for him. I must have been playing for about six hours, when Miles shows up and says 'Keep playin' Wally' and, for the first time ever, we lock horns and play together. He starts teaching me things like the phrases he used on 'Boplicity.' The next day at the rehearsals he starts giving me more stuff and he's splitting the solos. He said, 'Wallace, you sure know how to play that shit' and now I'm on the gig right next to him!"

Miles and Roney spent a lot of time together over the next three days. "He talked more in those three days than he had in the time since I had known him, back in 1983. He was a different Miles. A similar thing happened with my grandfather before he died. Miles talked about Trane, and Tony [Williams] and Bird. He said 'I loved Bird and he knew I loved him and he took advantage of my love. That's the worst thing you can do to anybody. Why did he do that?'"

Roney says he had no idea that Miles was so close to death. "He was making plans for us to play this music together on tour. He told me to tell Quincy and, when I did, Quincy said that he already knew." Miles's partner, Jo Gelbard, told writer Paul Tingen: "Miles didn't like doing Montreux, he was very unhappy there" (see *Miles Beyond*, p. 26), but Roney disputes this. "I don't know what Miles told his partner but I'm telling you that Miles told me he did the concert because he had looked in the mirror and saw Gil [Evans] and Gil had told him that he got to do it. He also said, 'Wallace, this music is so hard to play. It's not like the music I'm playing now, which is just grooves.'"

The tunes played at the concert were "Boplicity," a *Miles Ahead* medley composed of "Springsville," "Maids Of Cadiz," "The Duke," "My Ship" and "Blues For Pablo;" a *Porgy and Bess* medley comprising "Orgone," "Gone, Gone, Gone," "Summertime," "Here Come De Honey Man" and "The Pan Piper;" and "Solea" from *Sketches Of Spain*. Leonard Feather wrote the CD liner notes (as he did on *Star People*). "At the end of 'Blues For Pablo,' when he let me take over, it was like the passing of the guard. Man, it was incredible," says Roney. After the concert, Miles also gave Roney one of his trumpets. Two days later, Miles performed in Paris at a concert which saw him reunited with many old band members. And a little over two months later, Miles was dead.

22 miles's guest recordings

The 1980s were a highly productive decade for Miles and, in addition to touring and recording a string of albums under his name, Miles guested on a number of albums. Miles's openness to all types of music is reflected in the range of artists he recorded with in this period, which spanned the pop, rock, soul and jazz genres.

Artists United Against Apartheid (Sun City EMI/Manhattan 2404672) (1985)

The white South African government did all it could to prolong its apartheid regime and that included the establishment of so-called "independent homelands" for the black South African tribes. Of course, there was a catch to this strategy, namely that people living in a so-called homeland would lose their South African citizenship and the homelands were still economically dependent on South Africa. One of these homelands, Bophuthatswana, was designed for the Tswana people and located in the northern part of South Africa. Like all homelands, Bophuthatswana was not recognized by the international community.

One of the ways Bophuthatswana sought to improve its economy was to establish Sun City, an entertainment resort that offered its patrons golf, gambling and live music acts. Despite the UN declaring a cultural boycott on Sun City, a number of big-name artists took the money and played there. Artists United Against Apartheid was the inspiration of Little Steven (real name Steve Van Zandt), the guitarist in Bruce Springsteen's E Street Band. Little Steven had been interested in South Africa and visited the country on a fact-finding mission. When he encountered Sun City, an oasis of luxury surrounded by a desert of poverty, he was distressed. When he discovered that some of his fellow musicians had played there, he was outraged. Encouraged by television producer Danny Schechter, Little Steven began writing a protest song about Sun City, which mushroomed into a major album project.

Little Steven and Schechter then started asking other musicians to participate and it was Schechter who called Miles. "To my delight, Miles took the call personally, responding with one question, 'When do you want me over there?'" recalls Schechter.[1]

By the time the *Sun City* album came to be recorded, fifty-four artists were involved, including Miles, Bob Dylan, Bono, George Clinton, Bruce Springsteen, Nona Hendryx, Peter Gabriel, Grandmaster Melle Mel, Duke Bootee, Keith Richards, Gil Scott-Heron, Afrika Bambaataa, Bonnie Raitt, Ringo Starr and the poet Linton Kwesi Johnson. Producer Arthur Baker volunteered his services for the project. Much of the album is a mix of rock, rap and jazz.

Schechter also organized a video crew to record the sessions and interview various musicians for a music video and a "making-of" documentary. He planned to include an interview with Miles. "When Miles started improvising in the studio that day, Steven and Arthur insisted I not approach him with a camera," recalls Schechter. "'It's Miles, man,' Baker said. 'He's erratic, idiosyncratic, explosive. Wild. Don't mess with him when he's playing.' I realized that they were intimidated by his presence and his genius. They were afraid he would walk out. 'You do your thing,' I told him. 'I'll do mine.' I barged into the booth while Davis was setting up, introduced myself and asked if we could videotape him. Through the glass I could see Steve and Arthur, heads in hands, convinced that I had blown it. Miles smiled. 'Bring it on,' he ordered. 'Bring it on.' And we did, getting priceless footage in the bargain."

During the interview, Miles exclaimed that "South Africa makes me ill, sick. All over. Everything. When I think about it I can't do nothin', can't even play." In another section, Miles was introduced to Bonnie Raitt, who informed him that he sounded great. Miles responded: "Thanks, that's my thing." In another shot, Miles is seen recording his rap: "You're the wrong colour, you don't belong here." Miles appears on four tracks on the album including the title track, a rousing number that includes the hook "I ain't gonna play Sun City." Miles also appears on "Let Me See Your ID" (which also includes Gil Scott-Heron, Grandmaster Melle Mel and Duke Bootee), "Revolutionary Situation," which features the voices of Nelson Mandela and Bishop Desmond Tutu, and "The Struggle Continues," which saw Miles teaming up again with Herbie Hancock, Ron Carter and Tony Williams.

Like many of the songs designed to raise public awareness over a social issue and which were recorded during this era ("Do They Know It's Christmas?" "We Are The World"), the message is stronger than the music, but, as Miles might have said, "So what?" The Sun City project covered an issue that was close to his heart, raised money for South African political prisoners and continued to put the spotlight on the hated apartheid regime.

Toto "Don't Stop Me Now" (*Farenheit*, Columbia CK 40273) (probably recorded late 1985)

When Miles left Columbia for Warner Bros Records in 1985, he went looking for material from a long list of potential candidates (see the *Rubberband* chapter). One of these was Steve Porcaro, keyboardist with the rock band

Toto and co-writer of "Human Nature," which Miles played right up to his last concerts. Miles travelled with producer Tommy LiPuma and keyboardist Adam Holzman to Jeff Porcaro's studio in California to consider a couple of songs written by Steve Porcaro. Sadly, the sessions were not productive, but while Miles was there he also met Toto's keyboardist David Paich and guitarist Steve Lukather, drummer Jeff Porcaro and the Porcaros' father, the percussionist Joe Porcaro. "We were all beside ourselves. This guy was the hippest and the coolest of the cool," recalls Steve Porcaro. Paich and Lukather told Miles they had written this tune and asked him if he would like to play on it. Miles agreed.

"He was amazing," says Steve Porcaro. "He did all that in, like, one pass or maybe two passes [takes]. That's how you should work with Miles Davis. He was saying 'That's like my old stuff,' which was exactly what we wanted him to do. We were just thrilled. I don't know how thrilled the record company was or our managers were, but for us it was a major feather in our cap. That was something we were really proud of as a band."

Porcaro also has warm memories of Miles as a person. "I heard comments about Miles not liking white people, but he was just the sweetest guy. He couldn't have been nicer to all of us. He was humble and mellow. He was sweet to my Dad, who was beside himself at meeting Miles Davis. You know how meeting your heroes can go? In this business I've met some of my heroes and been very disappointed. Sometimes you have to remind yourself to judge the music and not the person. But that wasn't the case with Miles. It couldn't have been a better experience."

"Don't Stop Me Now" is an instrumental with a jazzy feel, with Lukather playing the melody on guitar, with support from Miles on muted horn, who plays with great sensitivity and occasionally doubles up on the melody. A mention should be made of Jeff Porcaro's fine cymbal work too. David Sanborn overdubs some alto saxophone. At the end of the tune, Miles's horn is left isolated, as he finishes with some playful phrases that go into the fadeout. Not surprisingly, the album ends on that note. Miles intermittently included "Don't Stop Me Now" in his live set between the end of 1996 and November 1990.

Scritti Politti "Oh Patti (Don't Feel Sorry For Loverboy)" (*Provision*, Virgin Records CDV 2515) (probably recorded December 1987)

Miles had recorded Scritti Politti's "Perfect Way" on *Tutu* and had even considered making it the title track. As a result of this, Miles became friendly with the group's lead singer Green Gartside. The result of this friendship was Miles agreeing to play on this track (and feature in the accompanying video), a mid-tempo pop tune with lyrics that look back on a failed relationship. The tune opens with a syrupy, sugary synthesizer sound, before Gartside enters with breathless-sounding vocals. Miles plays over a wash of vocals on muted horn with a touch of echo effect, but not even his contribution can lift a rather lifeless song. The album also included an extended version on which Miles got to blow a little more.

"We Three Kings Of Orient Are" (*Scrooged* soundtrack, A&M 393921-2) (probably recorded December 1987)

Miles Davis records a Christmas carol? David Sanborn explains how it happened. "A very strange situation came up; we got called by the director of the movie *Scrooged* to be street musicians in one scene and it was Miles, Larry Carlton, [keyboardist] Paul Schaffer and me – what an unlikely group of musicians. We showed at Park Avenue around eleven o'clock at night and were there for five hours filming what amounted to a thirty-second scene with Bill Murray. Somebody then got the idea to do a recording of it and Marcus [Miller] did an arrangement. We [the four original musicians plus Miller] recorded it live in the studio. We also did it on *The Letterman Show*." As is fitting with the comedic nature of the movie, "We Three Kings" has an understated humorous quality to it, with Miles playing on top of a shuffling beat and bouncing bass line. The tune appears on the film soundtrack, which also includes contributions from Al Green, Natalie Cole and The Eurythmics.

Cameo "In The Night" (*Machismo*, Phonogram 836 002-2) (c. early 1988)

Cameo, the soul/funk combo headed by Larry Blackmon (the man with the giant codpiece and Sly Stone-type snarling vocals), had a number of hits in the 1980s, including "She's Strange," "Candy," "Single Life" and "Word Up." In 1987, Miles was into the music of Cameo and the group attended Miles's 62nd birthday party. Miles also said that Cameo had influenced his live act. "I learn things from Prince and Cameo," said Miles. "I like the way Cameo does [*sic*] their live shows... Seeing the way Cameo featured the other musicians first helped me do the same thing in my shows."[2]

There was also a strong Miles connection because his nephew Vince Wilburn Jr. had played drums with the band for a while. "In The Night" is a funk tune with a heavy backbeat, which is enhanced by some fine playing by Miles on both open and muted horn. Joining him on the track is Kenny Garrett, who gets to stretch out and play some powerful lines. Miles added this tune to his live repertoire during the first half of 1990, with vocals by Foley.

Zucchero "Dune Mosse" (*Zu & Co*, Polydor 9819980) (possibly April 1988)

In February and July 1988, Miles toured Italy, and on some of the summer shows he shared the bill with Italian superstar singer Zucchero ("Sugar"), whose real name is Adelmo Fornaciari (one bill featured Miles, Zucchero and Joe Cocker). Miles liked Zucchero's voice and the two of them performed this song live together on at least two occasions. Miles also recorded a studio version of "Dune Mosse" (roughly translated: shifting dunes), according to the CD sleeve notes, laying down his horn part at the Hit Factory in New York on April 1, 1988, although Miles's discographer Jan Lohmann believes that it may have been a later date, as Miles was hospitalized until late March. The tune was not officially released until spring 2004 on the album *Zu & Co*, which also includes guest artists such as Sting, Eric Clapton, BB King, John Lee Hooker and Pavarotti.

"Dune Mosse" is a pop ballad that begins with Miles counting off the introduction ("four, three, two, one"). Miles's voice is also sampled and appears in several places throughout the tune. "Dune Mosse" has a creeping rhythm section mainly played by synthesizers, and Zucchero sings with great drama and passion. Miles supports him strongly on muted horn, playing sweet melodic lines and ending with a gentle flurry of notes. A video was also made of the tune (featuring a clip of Miles) and was released on a limited-edition DVD.

Chaka Khan "Sticky Wicked," "I'll Be Around" (*CK*, Warner Bros 925707-2) (June 29, 1988)

Chaka Khan was a good friend of Miles's and he admired her singing (so much so, that at the following year's Montreux Jazz Festival Khan would sing on-stage with Miles). Miles also admired Prince, so when the latter wrote a tune for Khan's next album, *CK*, Miles was more than ready to play on it too. Prince and Khan had known each other since the late 1970s, when they met in a studio in San Francisco. "Prince wrote the song and I liked it and decided to cover it. Miles happened to be around – it was fairly impromptu. Actually Miles wanted to play on every song and I had to tell him 'No, we love you but we can't have you on every track!' It's a shame that we left it so late – we could have done more great things together. In fact, he, Prince and I were planning to get together and do a project. That was our next step after he played on my album," explains Khan. Sadly, this plan would not progress beyond the drawing board and it's not entirely certain whether Miles and Prince were ever in the studio together, although Prince claims to have jammed with Miles and recorded the results (see chapter The Road to *Tutu* – Miles and Prince).

"Sticky Wicked" is a song about urban poverty life, although this is not immediately obvious from Prince's enigmatic lyrics. "Most of his songs you have to get the meaning from the context – a lot of it is parabilistic," says Khan. Prince played almost all the instruments on this track, except for the horn section, which is provided by Miles, Atlanta Bliss (trumpet) and Eric Leeds (saxophone). The tune is instantly recognizable as a Prince tune, with funky jangling guitar, a drum machine providing a strong backbeat and stabbing horn lines – and Prince's left-field lyrics.

Miles's muted horn is mainly used in a supportive mode, although he gets to play a short solo and raps the title a few times. The humorous ending has Miles wondering if the sound of his horn sounds like a crow. This track, along with the hitherto unreleased "Can I Play With U," may well be the closest we ever get to knowing how Prince and Miles would have sounded had they ever worked in the studio on a real recording project.

By contrast, the second tune to feature Miles, "I'll Be Around," is a mellow jazzy number, complete with swirling strings and cocktail-bar piano. It features some fine bass playing by Marcus Miller and piano from Dave Grusin (who also arranged the song). Miles provides textures to the overall sound on muted horn, finally soloing at the coda and into the fadeout.

Marcus Miller "Rampage" (*The Sun Don't Lie*, Dreyfus FDM 36560-2) (probably early 1989)

When Marcus Miller released his third solo album, *The Sun Don't Lie*, he had finally found his own voice as a musician. And by then, he had also produced a string of albums for Miles. Miller's new album featured many guest musicians including Miles on the storming number "Rampage," which features some heavy slap bass playing from Miller, pounding drums from Will Calhoun and rock-guitar licks by Vernon Reid (both from Living Color).

Unlike other tracks that Miles guested on, this one started life as a recorded sample of Miles's horn. Miller described how he put the track together when writer Chris Jisi asked whether "Rampage" had been written for Miles. "Only the little section where he played," explained Miller. "I built the track around that and later brought in Sal Marquez to play some additional trumpet. I thought Vernon Reid and Will Calhoun would be perfect for the tune, and fortunately they were able to come in and do it."[3] The album also includes Miller's tribute to Miles, "The King Is Gone."

Kenny Garrett "Big Ol' Head," "Free Mandela" (*Prisoner of Love*, Atlantic Jazz 82046-1) (probably early 1989)

When Kenny Garrett recorded his first solo album, he not only included many past and current members of Miles's 1980s bands, but the man himself. Miles is featured on two tracks, "Big Ol' Head" and "Free Mandela." The former features musicians who had all played with Miles – bassist Darryl Jones, Foley on lead bass, drummer Ricky Wellman and percussionists Rudy Bird and Mino Cinelu. Miles played muted trumpet. Yet despite the all-star line-up, "Big Ol' Head" is little more than a pleasant funk tune, with Garrett and Miles copying each other's phrases. "Free Mandela" is a stronger track and its syncopated rhythm and large voice choir give it a suitably African feel. But best of all, both Miles and Garret play more convincingly and Miles plays for longer stretches on this tune.

Quincy Jones "Jazz Corner Of The World," "Birdland" (*Back On The Block*, Qwest/Warner Bros 926 020-2) (probably early 1989)

Quincy Jones's albums are stunning examples of his ability to pull together a vast ensemble of musicians – many of them major players in their own right – mix them up and get them to play on an eclectic range of music. Jones's 1989 album, *Back On The Block*, took this to new heights, mixing classic jazzers such as Miles, Dizzy Gillespie, Sarah Vaughan and Ella Fitzgerald, with established jazzers such as George Benson, James Moody, Herbie Hancock and Joe Zawinul, and rappers such as Ice-T, Melle Mel and Kool Moe Dee. "Jazz Corner Of The World" features Miles, James Moody, George Benson, Sarah Vaughan, Dizzy Gillespie, Ella Fitzgerald and Joe Zawinul, who are joined by rappers Big Daddy Kane and Kool Moe Dee.

But despite the stellar line-up, the track consists of little more than the young rappers introducing the old jazzers, who play or sing a few phrases, before making way for the next introduction. The tune segues into "Birdland," the modern classic composed by Zawinul. This is more satisfying in that Miles, Gillespie, Moody and Benson do at least get a chance to solo, if not exactly shine.

Paolo Rustichelli "Capri," "Capri (reprise)," "Wild Tribes," "Kyrie," "Get On," "Rastafario," "Love Divine," "Wild Tribes (Hi Tech Mix)" (*Mystic Jazz*, Polydor 513 415-2/*Mystic Man*, Guts & Grace 524 301-2) (July 26, 1989 and 1991)

Paolo who? is probably the reaction of many people, but this Italian keyboardist/composer has worked with many big names in the fields of jazz, rock and classical music, from Miles Davis to Carlos Santana to Placido Domingo. He was born in Rome in 1968 to soprano opera singer Eva Levi and the soundtrack composer Carlo Rustichelli. Like his father, Rustichelli also composes soundtracks. His meeting with Miles and subsequent collaboration has all the hallmarks of a fairy story. "I'm not really a jazz fan, but I like jazz. I remember listening to Miles when I was younger, *Filles De Kilimanjaro* and all the electric albums," explains Rustichelli. "The music was good, although also strange and eclectic."

But what really appealed to Rustichelli was Miles's attitude. "The way that Miles was always challenging himself and changing styles and reaching for something new, is something that people usually hate. But it's a challenge for the artist, because when you have followers who like one type of music and you do something different it can be dangerous. I also like Miles's dress style," he adds.

Rustichelli describes how he got to record with Miles. "In 1989 I had recorded a tune for Miles, 'Capri.' I went to the Umbria Jazz Festival and after the concert I spoke to Miles's road manager Gordon Meltzer. I gave him a cassette with 'Capri' on it and he told me 'Miles never generally listens to tapes.' I said 'Okay, I just did it because Miles is one of my icons.'" Days later, Rustichelli was at another Miles's concert in Italy and was called backstage after the gig to meet Miles. "I was told Miles wanted to speak to me – I was really shocked. When I met him at his dressing room, he was almost naked. He said 'Hello,' and invited me in. He said he liked the song very much and invited me to eat something with him, but I was too shy. But I immediately felt there was a feeling between us. All the stories I heard that he was a kind of racist – I didn't feel anything like this. He was a strange man, a little harsh, [and] he had a kind of wildness that I liked."

Miles told Rustichelli that they would record "Capri" one day – without giving a definite date. But some days later when Miles was playing in Rome, Rustichelli received a call from Meltzer telling him that Miles was ready to record "Capri." "It happened on the morning of July 26, 1989, the day after Miles's concert," recalls Rustichelli. "I had prepared the song on a special computer called a Waveframe Audioframe. The tracks were mixed on to two stereo tracks and Miles got other tracks for overdubs. I played the whole song myself – the drums, the bass and everything is played on a synthesizer. He did just the overdubs."

The session was productive. "He did two versions of 'Capri.' One with the normal [open] trumpet and one with the Harmon [mute]. I remember, when he had played with the Harmon I said 'Miles, why don't you play a version without?' He gave me a mean look and then said 'Yeah, yeah.' So he did two versions plus a lot of variations." It was these variations that Rustichelli used to create the "Capri Reprise." They also recorded another as yet unreleased tune, which Rustichelli thinks was called "Artemisia." "At the time of this session, my English was really limited. I remember he told me he felt really relaxed and he told me about Charlie Mingus. He asked me to do a soundtrack for a movie he was making [*Dingo*], but I didn't have the time," recalls Rustichelli.

"Capri" and its reprise appeared on the album *Mystic Jazz*. Also playing on the album were several members of Miles's current band – bassist Benny Rietveld, lead bassist Foley, percussionist Munyungo Jackson and drummer Ricky Wellman, as well as Carlos Santana, Wayne Shorter, Herbie Hancock, and Andy Summers, guitarist from the rock/pop band The Police. "I am good friends with Carlos and Wayne," says Rustichelli, "and Wayne's late wife, Ana Maria Shorter, put me in touch with so many musicians."

"Capri" is one of the most successful guest recordings Miles made, and he plays some of his best trumpet. Despite almost all the instruments being played on a synthesizer, the music doesn't sound artificial (check out the acoustic piano effect) and there is a strong sense of space about the music. Miles plays mainly with a mute, but in the final minute switches to open horn, again playing with great feeling and sensitivity. The Reprise has a dream-like quality and Miles plays exclusively on open horn. "Miles told me 'Capri' could be used in a movie," says Rustichelli and there is indeed a cinematic quality to the sound.

Rustichelli used samples from the July 26 session to produce five tunes featuring Miles's horn on the follow-up album, *Mystic Man* – these tracks were produced after Miles's death. This was the same process used for two tracks on *Doo-Bop*. "I don't know if it's ethical to do it, but I like the final results," says Rustichelli. "Kyrie" (dedicated to the memory of Miles) features samples of Miles's voice, his open horn and an operatic vocal from Mario Leonard. "I have done a version of this with Placido Domingo and I wanted to do one with Placido, Miles and Carlos [Santana] but the music business is impossible," says Rustichelli with some regret. "Get On" sounds like a Santana track, not least because Santana plays guitar and it features his trademark chugging percussive sound and Latin feel. Miles's muted horn integrates well with the music.

"Wild Tribes" features just Rustichelli and Miles, who plays muted horn over an extended vamp on piano and electronic percussion. Rustichelli and an unnamed female vocalist also sing on this track. "Rastafario" features Miles (playing with and without a mute), Rustichelli and Santana together on a rolling, mid-tempo number that seems to drift along. "Love Divine" includes some soulful singing by Brenda Lee Eager, with Rustichelli sounding more like a baritone singer (his vocals have undergone some form of electronic processing), accompanied by Miles's horn. But the soulful vocals aside, there is little of interest to grip the listener. The Hi-Tech re-mix of "Wild Tribes" is a spirited version taken at a faster tempo than the original.

"After *Mystic Jazz*, I went to the U.S. and Miles and I became more like friends," recalls Rustichelli. "I would sometimes go to his home in Malibu and he would be watching boxing on the television. I have a studio in Beverley Hills and he came two or three times and we did some sessions. We played together and recorded about six or seven songs, which have no titles. I have not even tried to get permission to release them because it's tough trying to negotiate between lawyers, managers and record labels," says Rustichelli.

Rustichelli knows he was very fortunate to record with Miles. "I once met Joni Mitchell at a party and she said 'Didn't you know how many times I have tried to record with Miles and then you come from Italy and boom! You record with him!'" Reflecting on Miles, Rustichelli says: "He was a really unique person. There's nobody like him in the jazz world today as a guide and mentor. Many of the descriptions of Miles that I've read in books were not exactly true. Miles and I spoke music and with music you don't have problems; it's a universal language."

Shirley Horn "You Won't Forget Me" (*You Won't Forget Me*, Verve 847 482-2) (August 13, 1990)

One day, in the early 1960s, the singer/pianist Shirley Horn was sitting in her mother-in-law's kitchen, when the phone rang. The caller was Miles Davis. Miles had heard Horn's first album, *Embers And Ashes*, and was so taken by her performance that he wanted to meet her in person. Horn went to Miles's home with her husband, where they also met Gil Evans and Teo Macero. Davis wanted her to be the opening act for him at the Village Vanguard, but owner Max Gordon wasn't keen on doing this, so Miles told him "If you don't take her, you don't get me."[4] So began a friendship that would last for almost thirty years. Horn says she saw a different side to Miles. "He was loving. People said he was rude, turning his back on the audience. It was just that he didn't like those flickering candles."[5]

So it was more than appropriate that Miles should give his final guest performance on the title track of Horn's 1991 album, *You Won't Forget Me*. Incidentally, the album also features Wynton and Branford Marsalis. The title tune features Shirley Horn on vocals and piano, Charles Ables on bass, Steve Williams on drums and Miles on muted horn. The song opens with the sound of Miles's horn playing over swirling cymbals before Horn sings lyrics full of both defiance and pain. Miles plays beautifully and with great tenderness over Horn's whispered vocals, some gentle piano chords and Williams's metronome-like rimshot drumming. The arrangement is sparse, the execution is superb, and the performance fittingly ends Miles's career as a sideman on a high.

23 the verdict on the music of the 1980s

"What Miles did was to move forward. He was the type of person who had to move forward." *Pete Cosey, guitarist*

History had long decided that Miles Davis was one of the giants of jazz, but how will the music of his final decade be judged? To some, Miles had stopped innovating in this period and was following rather than creating trends. Writer Paul Tingen says: "While the process of rediscovering and re-evaluating Miles's electric experiments of the '60s and '70s is ongoing, no similar interest is discernible regarding his music from 1981 to 1991. The simplest explanation is that the music of 1981 to 1991 did not announce a new musical paradigm and hence does not invite belated re-evaluation." Tingen concludes that the music of Miles's last decade was a translation rather than a transcendence.[1]

The notion that Miles had little new to say in this period has gained wider currency, including amongst some of Miles's former sidemen. "I obviously have a certain attitude based on my time with him and you can't help but compare the musical level," says Dave Liebman. "I just felt that in the '80s there were some great things and on occasions he could open up and play great, but it was his time to bask in the sun and be the personality that he had become. He was a completely different personality in the '80s, walking around, smiling, talking, giving interviews. My basic opinion is that the music that he did in the '80s was more about the personality than the music. He relinquished control. It was like easy listening when compared with what we did with him. I think he wanted to make things easy for himself, because there was no reason to fight any more, to push the envelope or prove anything. In my time, he was very competitive – he always wanted to be the first to do anything."

For Liebman, the root of the problem was Miles's long absence from the music scene and the fact that he often learned about musicians through personal recommendation. This, says Liebman, meant that he was less attuned to the contemporary music scene. "I always thought that if he wanted to come back in the '80s and be the same as he had been before, he should have chosen guys like [guitarist James] Blood Ulmer or [drummer] Shannon Jackson or [guitarist] Vernon Reid, the hot guys around New York into the new rock stuff. They were pushing the envelope in a different way to his groups. I don't think he even knew the guys. Miles found people by word-of-mouth; it wasn't like he was aware of the latest record. If he had been in a different state of mind, he probably would have had more adventurous music for at least a certain part of that period."

Liebman also feels that Miles "couldn't go back, and he didn't know how to go forward; and eventually what happened in my opinion is that he went sideways." He also wonders whether the music Miles made in this period would have got much consideration if it didn't have Miles's name on it. "If it wasn't Miles Davis who had come out with that music – *Decoy* and all those records – we would have said 'Sure, it's okay,' but it wouldn't have been the special-ness that we know. But when you went to listen to those records you were ready, because here he was, Miles Davis, back from the dead. He was the living elder statesman of fusion and could have got away with anything. But if he had been an ordinary guy, a lot of that music in the '80s would have been forgotten. Marcus [Miller] did a great production job but I don't see any art there – I see it as just music. It's okay but not on the artistic level that Miles was capable of. But then he chose to communicate and enjoy himself, which is great."

For Liebman, the last decade gave Miles an opportunity to enjoy himself. "I always felt that he deserved to have those good ten years and be in the limelight and have all that fame and notoriety, as he had deserved it. You couldn't expect things to be as they had been before. I enjoyed the music; he had some good musicians, but not great musicians. I felt it was a little bit of a step backward musically for him and for what was going on in the musical world. But of course it was Miles Davis and you went to see him and it didn't matter what he played – you were glad to see that he was alive. I felt that the criticism that a lot of people gave was a little mean-spirited because it was great to have Miles Davis on the scene as a whole generation got to see him who never would have."

Others who worked with Miles in the '60s and '70s also believe that Miles's musical achievements peaked during that period. Paul Buckmaster says: "*Bitches Brew* was the masterpiece. Nothing had ever been recorded before or since in any genre of music. *Bitches Brew* is the unique one-album. No one has ever tried to imitate it, copy it or even come up with something similar. And the great quintet of Wayne Shorter, Herbie Hancock, Ron Carter and Tony Williams is, for me, the zenith and the apotheosis of a sublime jazz ensemble." When looking at Miles's music of 1980–91, Buckmaster says: "It's very difficult to compare, but I would say it's very nice with some darkly dramatic themes. It's very well-arranged, it's like an advanced form of instrumental pop, with advanced chords and harmonies that groove – there's a pop sensibility. But what's lacking is the improvisational interplay between the musicians. Even with *On The Corner*, there's more interplay."

Mark Rothbaum, who had known Miles since the early '70s and managed him from 1978 to 1983, says of the 1980s period: "I felt there was a definite attempt for commerciality and that he wasn't the scientist any more; he wasn't in that laboratory. I don't know whether it was Miles, or Teo or the musicians, but those ['70s] sessions were like science experiments and what it accomplished was the evolution of music. I liked any collaboration with Marcus, who was probably the best musician who worked with Miles in those Warner Bros years. [But] there isn't a single Miles Davis record that I wish didn't come out and there's not a single note he ever played that I'm not happy that it was recorded. But I have some that I savour over others."

Miles's long-time producer Teo Macero is unimpressed with Miles's latter output. "I didn't like those things. That wasn't Miles. [*You're*] *Under Arrest*, *Tutu*, if you like those things fine, but that's not really Miles. You had to invigorate Miles, you had to make him work. And when these guys were doing it they were probably so intimidated by him that they laid back – I wouldn't lay back at all. You listen to those records and you listen to the ones that we made together and there's a difference of integrity, sound, feeling, emotion – everything. It just doesn't sound like Miles at all from an emotional point of view. He always used to say the best things he ever did were live. I said 'Right, but now you're so boxed in you're lucky if you ever get out of it.'"

But not all of Miles's former sidemen agree with these points of view. Mike Zwerin, who played trombone with Miles in the late 1940s, says: "Except for the final *Doo-Bop* period, I like them all. That's why he's so special. He had like four totally different styles – bebop, cool, modal and rock. The people who play the best today have all four influences. Miles is impossible to escape today. His music – all of it – was and is the most intensely pertinent music of the last fifty years. I can't really separate the '70s and '80s – it's all his 'rock' or 'binary' period. Miles played well in an entirely different way. He didn't make the groove, he fed on it. The groove got heavier. It was a very 'cool' way to conserve energy. He could be 'modern' and at the same time use his head more than his body, which increasingly failed him."

Miles's music from this period also faced criticism from critics such as Stanley Crouch and younger musicians such as Wynton and Branford Marsalis. The latter says that while Miles's sidemen such as Marcus Miller, Foley, Vince Wilburn Jr. and Kenny Garrett impressed him: "None of the keyboard players knocked me out – they were just parts players. I think that period with Scofield – that shit had a kind of edge to it and the songs had some bite to them. It had more a jazz sensibility than anything he did after. By the time he got to 'Human Nature,' it was like ear candy for middle-of-the-road jazz fans in Europe, where he mostly played. It was like a bad rock band; long extended jazz grooves, Kenny playing solos. It had more of a rock flair to it."

For Marsalis, it is the way the 1980s audiences reacted to Miles's music that is one of the most telling aspects of his decline as an innovator and a musician who could shock his audiences into silence. "Audiences would scream and holler in the middle of solos. When I listen to those records like *Miles In Berlin*, you don't hear people screaming in the middle of solos because they don't know what hit them. Coltrane is up there live in Stockholm and just slaying everybody – 'What the fuck is this?' And that's the Miles that I identify with. Not the 'Yeah, he plays shit we like, we know what he's playing now.' Jazz is supposed to be hard, it's supposed to be difficult, it's supposed to be unpopular; that's why I play jazz."

Marsalis also has a problem with Miles's 1980s recordings. "The only album that stands out for me is *Decoy* and not because I'm on it. Scofield played his ass off. It was just the record where it came together. Some people would tend to describe it as the decline of Miles Davis, but I think having records with Miles Davis on them is better than not having him. But then I think that the records towards the end were masterful jobs of production done by Marcus [Miller]. They're great records, but there's also the irony that Miles Davis had essentially become a sideman on his own records. Because for Miles to be in that forward-thinking mode, he had to relegate himself to a sideman, because he didn't know how the machines worked."

But Miller has spoken of how much he was inspired by Miles to create the harmonies and melodies on albums such as *Tutu* and *Amandla* and that Miles had a creative input (see the chapter on *Tutu*). And as Dave Holland points out: "If you take Miles out of the equation, you have a completely different album, so that's the answer to that. Miles looked to Gil Evans to create settings for him when they did *Sketches Of Spain*, but they were collaborations too. Gil was the source of the written material but Miles had a hand in assembling it. Having being on sessions with Miles, I know what a strong hand he took on reworking people's music. Joe Zawinul would bring a piece of music into the recording session and Miles would immediately start editing it, eliminating certain sections, extending others. I saw Miles personalize the compositional settings that were being given to him to work with. I don't doubt that Miles had a hand in making suggestions on how the material should be used. He had a magic touch in understanding what the essentials were of a composition or an arrangement and how to strip it down and make something that was appropriate for him to work with. I can't say that Miles was a sideman on those sessions."

And many others also feel that there is a lot of value in Miles's latter music. "I was just thrilled that Miles came back and in such a modern way," says Bobby Broom. "The average person doesn't have everything in their house from one period – clothes, furniture, artwork – we kinda move along with the times. So I don't know why people expect that from musicians. I suppose it's to do with nostalgia or they hear something at a particular time in their lives and they get hung up on the artist recreating that thing for them. But that's just not how it works. So it was exciting for me for Miles to come back and playing some funk. The music was so great. His music was developing. It started out as a live, funk thing and later in the studio with *Decoy* and *You're Under Arrest* they were developing a whole different sound. And then *Tutu* was another kind of vibe. All of it was very interesting. How do you compare? You don't compare apples and oranges. When I'm listening to music I try and hear the total picture and if that's beautiful and bad [i.e. good], then that's what it is. I bought three copies of *Doo-Bop* because I kept losing them."

Alan Burroughs says: "My own view is that Miles was always doing what he was always doing – changing the face of music without even trying. All Miles did was keep living his vision. He kept changing with the times and kept changing with the music that was around him. But he was playing the same way all through the years, but he'd always be open to what was going on. He probably would have changed two or three times more in the ten years since he died."

For Tom Barney: "Miles didn't want to go back. He'd played with everyone and played all kinds of music. He'd been there and done that. He was always looking ahead and refused to be put in a box. The critics want you to be in a box and play the same thing for the rest of your life. But Miles wouldn't do that. That part of Miles I really loved."

Miles had always faced criticism whenever he moved from one musical phase to another and especially when he moved from acoustic to electric instruments. For Stanley Crouch, the decline started with the 1969 album *In A Silent Way* when: "Davis's sound, mostly lost among electronic instruments, was no more than droning wallpaper music."[2] For Wynton Marsalis, Miles was "a genius who decided to go into rock, and was on the bandstand looking like, basically, a buffoon."[3]

"I love and respect Stanley Crouch and Wynton Marsalis," says Deron Johnson, "but my take on the music I'm creating is about always stretching, always juxtaposing, always moving things all over the place. Not sticking to one kind of sound. So that period to me was just as valid as anything he ever did from *Birth Of The Cool* on. If a guy is following his own path and his own heart and his own soul, he can't be doing anything wrong. The '80s come around, Reagan comes in, and that's another set of circumstances. Drum machines come in – why would you deny that sound? I go to jazz clubs and see these old cats playing the old sounds and that's cool, but it's just time to move on, not forgetting, but moving on. *The Man With The Horn*, *You're Under Arrest* – all that stuff is just amazing."

"I think that Miles was always searching and looking for ways to keep himself engaged in what was going on," says David Sanborn. "He wanted to engage with the world. You can see where the music would have evolved with elements of trip-hop now. The overriding truth was that he was continuing to challenge. Miles was always talking about 'the good old days that never were.' There were times when people brought the old music up he'd say 'I can't play that music.' Everybody was always after Gil to write another *Sketches Of Spain* or *Porgy And Bess* – he'd already done it." Darryl Jones recalls a conversation with Miles: "I said to him that I had to go back and listen to his previous music and he said 'Fuck that shit. That shit is old.' I think that he appreciated it, but he was just ready to go on to something else."

It would be wrong to say Miles never looked back, but his eye was always on the now and the future and this attitude remained unchanged right up until his death. Many admired Miles for his constant quest for new musical challenges and his openness to all forms of music. Munyungo Jackson says: "He put his trumpet on the things he liked. Miles wouldn't stay in just one place. He didn't go backward."

Richard Patterson adds: "Miles was always trying to do something different. It reflects his courage to step out and do something different and not be influenced by what everybody thinks he should do. That's why I dug him." Michael Henderson notes: "He believed that there's no such thing as a wrong note. He listened to all kinds of music. Marcus Miller and those guys took him into some great things."

Although Miles would often deride critics and insist that he paid little attention to them, he would have been less than human if he wasn't occasionally stung by their comments. "The thing that impressed me about Miles above everything else is that [criticism] never stopped him from doing what he felt he had to do," says Marcus Miller. "I think he was probably hurt by some of the things that were said about him throughout his career, but he just lived with the hurt. It's like somebody saying something about your face. It may hurt but you don't run to a plastic surgeon necessarily. The reason we have all this beautiful jazz that people have created over the past fifty years is because of mentalities like Miles. If Louis Armstrong had thought like some of these jazz critics, he would never taken a step to create what he did. Dizzy wouldn't have done it, Bird wouldn't have done it and we wouldn't have gone beyond King Oliver."[4] Rothbaum agrees: "For a guy of that age, in his mid-fifties, to be able to force himself to do something new, nobody ever did that."

Dave Holland says: "As far as I was concerned, any time Miles played one note on the trumpet, it was worth checking out. The context in which he worked changed radically over the fifty years of musical activity, but the essence of what he did as a trumpet player and the continual reworking of his music and reassessing the direction just continued and it was fascinating to watch. For most of our lives we had been looking forward to the next Miles Davis project and eagerly waiting to see what he would do. I just think that when you have a great master like Miles, there's not much they can do wrong as long as the integrity is there – which I felt it was all the way through his work. There was this integrity and honesty."

Looking at Miles's output for the 1980s, it's clear to see a development in his music, from the early funk-rock phrase to the funk-pop of *You're Under Arrest* and the electronic orchestrations of *Amandla* and *Tutu*. Added to this are the big-band arrangements of *Aura*, the Spanish-tinged *Siesta* and the first steps towards fusing jazz and hip-hop, which were sadly cut short.

But perhaps the best record of Miles's music during this period lies with his live performances. "I loved the band better live than I like the records. During the last five years, the records were layered [overdubbed], but live, everybody put their own thing in it. When he got Ricky Wellman, the band took on a whole different personality and I liked that. I liked the energy. When Kenny Garrett soloed, the band would build the whole thing up behind him and they painted a big picture," says Ndugu Chancler.

Looking back at Miles in the 1980s, Liebman noted that: "He had been the black renegade, mister well-dressed, the hip, cool. But now he was almost establishment black and things had changed around him and he was still the same. I think he thought he'd just be cool and enjoy himself. I think he had a good time in the last ten years."

Miles certainly received many awards and plaudits during his final decade: in 1984, he won the Sonning Music Award, in 1988 became a knight of the Order of St. John, in 1990 was awarded Lifetime Achievement award at the Grammys, and in 1991 he was awarded the Chevalier of the Legion of Honour by the French government. Miles also won most of his Grammys during this period.

For Zwerin: "Miles was the ultimate 'winner.' I hate that word, but he won on all levels – business, artistic, lifestyle. He was one of the very few to do that. Listening to Miles live in Montreux in the '80s with Robben Ford and David Sanborn or Bob Berg and Sco[field] is as much fun to listen to as Miles with Tranc [John Coltrane]. It's not the same, but it's not worse. I don't see how an intelligent ear like Crouch's could hear anything different. Listen to the *Live At Montreux* series from the '70s and '80s. There's good and bad but more good than you'd feared."

But more importantly, the qualities that made Miles were unchanged during this period, and that included his openness and his quest to reach as many people as possible through his music. "He respected and listened to and enjoyed all the other forms of music, which opened me up. Miles opened me up to really embracing some of the forms that I took lightly," says Chancler.

So what is the verdict on Miles's final decade? The answer is that we are still too close to the music to make a definitive assessment. It was more than thirty years after Miles recorded albums such as *Jack Johnson*, *Bitches Brew* and *On The Corner* before many fans, critics and musicians appreciated the true brilliance of Miles's music during this period.

Now, we have albums such as Bill Laswell's *Panthalassa* and Henry Kaiser and Wadada Leo Smith's *Yo Miles!* and the Orchestre National De Jazz's *Yester-now* albums celebrating Miles's 1970s music. Pete Cosey and Michael Henderson have even formed bands that play the music from this era (called Children of Agharta and Children on the Corner respectively). As Tingen notes, critical reaction to Miles's music has evolved: "As the years pass, criticism of his electric music is dying down and gradually being replaced by praise. Perhaps someday we'll discover that his Warner years pointed the way to the future after all."[5]

But what can be said with any certainty is that the music Miles made in the 1980s was a part of his vast musical output and cannot simply be ignored, dismissed, air-brushed or considered "sub-standard" when compared with Miles's other periods. In any case, it is meaningless to compare, say, *Tutu* with *Jack Johnson* as it is to compare *Bitches Brew* with *Kind Of Blue*. They are different albums out of different times.

But it is fair to say that Miles's creative output between 1970 and 1975 was greater than that between 1980 and 1991. There are many reasons for this. Miles was younger, healthier and his energy levels were higher. The musical climate was also different. In the 1970s, rock and jazz came together, like two tectonic plates colliding with each other. The energy released from the resulting collision would take creativity and experimentation to new heights.

But in the 1980s, the music industry became more cautious, less adventurous, less innovative – and the accountants moved in. There was also a drive towards a clean, clinical sound, where experimentation and exploration were discouraged rather than encouraged. This clashed with Miles's "If it sounds right, it is right" attitude. That is why Miles's live music is so important when it comes to viewing his music during this period, because it was often on-stage where the true genius of Miles as a band leader and a musician most manifested itself.

The fact that the musical output in Miles's final decade is being so hotly debated shows that, right up to the end, he continued to generate much feeling amongst fans and critics – and that is what Miles would have liked. One thing is certain, Miles and his music will continue to fascinate future generations and it is hard to believe that the period between 1980 and 1991 will simply become a footnote in his musical history. Long after the pages in this book have turned to dust, people will still be playing and loving the music of Miles Davis, and that will include the music he made in his final decade.

24 notes

Introduction

1. Jack Chambers, *Milestones: The Music and Times of Miles Davis*, with a new introduction (New York: Da Capo Press, 1998), Introduction, *Freaky Deaky 1981–91*, p. xiii.
2. Ibid., p. xiv.
3. Ibid., p. vii.
4. Paul Tingen, *Miles Beyond: The Electric Explorations of Miles Davis 1967–91* (New York: Billboard Books, 2001), p. 8.

Miles the man

1. Kenneth Tynan, originally in *Holiday*, February 1963. Reprinted in *Profiles* (London: Nick Hern Books, 1990), paperback edition, p. 167.
2. Paul Tingen, *Miles Beyond: The Electric Explorations of Miles Davis 1967–91* (New York: Billboard Books, 2001), p. 185.
3. See, for example, Pearl Cleage, "Mad at Miles," reprinted in Gary Carner (ed.), *The Miles Davis Companion* (New York: Schirmer Books, 1996), p. 210.

Miles – his life and music before 1975

1. Miles Davis and Quincy Troupe, *Miles: The Autobiography* (London: Macmillan, 1990), Prologue, p. v.
2. Ibid., p. 395.
3. Ibid., p. 113.
4. Ibid., p. 376.
5. Ibid., p. 264.
6. Ian Carr, *Miles Davis: The Definitive Biography* (London: Harper Collins, 1998), p. 151.
7. Bill Milkowski Rockers, *Jazzbos & Visionaries* (New York: Billboard Books, 1998), p. 177.
8. Bill Cole, *Miles Davis: The Early Years* (New York: Da Capo Press, 1995), paperback edition, p. 165.
9. Davis and Troupe, *Miles*, p. 319.

10. Carr, *Miles Davis*, p. 326.
11. Davis and Troupe, *Miles*, p. 322.
12. *The Miles Davis Story*, directed by Mike Dibb and first broadcast on the UK's Channel 4, April 14 and 15, 2001.

Into the shadows

1. Miles Davis and Quincy Troupe, *Miles: The Autobiography* (London: Macmillan, 1990), p. 325.
2. Ibid.
3. Ibid., p. 326.
4. Ibid., p. 328.
5. Cheryl McCall, "Miles Davis," *Musician, Player & Listener* 41 (March 1982), p. 40.
6. Davis and Troupe, *Miles*, p. 323.
7. *Jazz File*, presented by Ian Carr, BBC Radio 3, October 13, 2001.
8. Eric Nisenson, *'Round About Midnight: A Portrait of Miles* (New York: Da Capo Press, updated edn, 1996), p. xiii.
9. Ibid., p. xv.
10. *Miles Davis Ten Years After*, presented by Ravi Coltrane, BBC Radio 2, programme 6, November 20, 2001.
11. *Jazz File*, presented by Ian Carr, BBC Radio 3, October 13, 2001.
12. Ibid.
13. The list of visitors is taken from Davis and Troupe, *Miles*, p. 325, and musician Randy Hall, who saw Miles during this period. Nisenson (*'Round About Midnight*, p. 230) said Miles refused to let Jagger in his home.
14. Davis and Troupe, *Miles*, p. 326.
15. Ibid., p. 329.
16. Ian Carr, *Miles Davis: The Definitive Biography* (London: Harper Collins, 1998), p. 340.
17. Davis and Troupe, *Miles*, p. 324.
18. *Miles Davis Ten Years After*, presented by Ravi Coltrane, BBC Radio 2, programme 6, November 20, 2001.
19. Nisenson (1996) said that Lundvall was thrown out of Miles's house after Miles had played the album *Jack Johnson* and Lundvall had failed to recognize it (*'Round About Midnight*, p. 229).
20. This is not the same as the tune on *The Man With The Horn*; see "Back Seat Betty" entry in that chapter for more details.
21. Peter Losin's *Miles Ahead* website says the same trumpet solo is used on "Calypso Frelimo" recorded September 17, 1973 and that the rhythm track is an excerpt of a take from November 6, 1974. See entry for December 27, 1976 on the sessionography on Losin's *Miles Ahead* website, www.plosin.com/milesahead/sessions.aspx.

22. Stephanie Stein Crease, *Gil Evans Out of the Cool: His Life and Music* (Chicago: Acapella Books, 2002), p. 293.
23. Carr, *Miles Davis*, p. 337.
24. A photograph taken at the session is in John Szwed's *So What: The Life of Miles Davis* (London: William Heinemann, 2002) opposite p. 233.
25. "The Doctor Talks About Miles," sleeve notes to album *1969 Miles Festiva de Juan Pins* (Sony Music Japan SRC 6843).
26. Ian Carr says Buckmaster received a call from Miles and that Buckmaster spent June, July and August 1979 with Miles. See Carr, *Miles Davis*, p. 340. However, Paul Tingen says George Butler called Buckmaster, who then arrived in August 1979 – see Paul Tingen, *Miles Beyond: The Electric Explorations of Miles Davis 1967–91* (New York: Billboard Books, 2001), p. 180. But later on, Tingen says Buckmaster arrived in early July – see p. 192. Buckmaster cannot recall the exact date, but confirms that it was Butler who called him and that he worked with Miles "sometime between June and August 1979."
27. Carr says Evans left in disgust after not being paid – see Carr, *Miles Davis*, p. 341.
28. Davis and Troupe, *Miles*, p. 330.

The Man With The Horn

1. Miles Davis and Quincy Troupe, *Miles: The Autobiography* (London: Macmillan, 1990), p. 19.
2. Tom Tom 84's real name is Tom Washington, but Randy Hall says he gave himself the moniker Tom Tom 84 because 1984 represented the future. When 1984 arrived, he changed his name to Tom Tom 2000. It's unclear what name he goes by today.
3. Carina Prange, "Darryl Jones – Leaving The Stones Unturned," *Jazz Dimensions* 21 (March 2002). www.jazzdimensions.de/interviews/portraits/darryljones.html
4. Coincidentally or not, Earth, Wind & Fire's next album was called *I Am*.
5. Davis and Troupe, *Miles*, p. 332.
6. Ibid.
7. *The Miles Davis Story Part Two*, broadcast on UK Channel 4, April 15, 2001.
8. Ibid.
9. Ian Carr, *Miles Davis: The Definitive Biography* (London: Harper Collins, 1998), p. 348.
10. *The Miles Davis Story Part Two*.
11. Howard Mandel, "Miles Davis' New Direction is a Family Affair," *Down Beat* (September 1980), p. 17.
12. Ibid.
13. Davis and Troupe, *Miles*, p. 333.

14. Mandel, "Miles Davis' New Direction", p. 17.

15. Mark Dery and Bob Doerschuk, "Miles Davis: His Keyboardists Present," *Keyboard* (October 1987), pp. 82-88.

16. Paul Tingen, *Miles Beyond: The Electric Explorations of Miles Davis 1967–91* (New York: Billboard Books, 2001), p. 194.

17. Quoted in John Szwed, *So What: The Life of Miles Davis* (London: William Heineman, 2002), p. 355.

18. Mandel, "Miles Davis' New Direction," p. 17.

19. Davis and Troupe, *Miles*, p. 334.

20. *The Miles Davis Radio Project*, Programme 5, American Public Radio.

21. Ibid.

22. Mandel, "Miles Davis' New Direction," p. 17.

23. *Jazz File*, presented by Ian Carr and produced by Derek Dresher, BBC Radio 3, programme 5, broadcast October 6, 2001.

24. *The Miles Davis Story Part Two*. This section was seen on the rough-cut and not all of it appeared in the broadcast version.

25. *Jazz File*, programme 5.

26. Davis and Troupe, *Miles*, p. 335.

27. Ibid.

28. Davis and Troupe, *Miles*, p. 333.

29. Foster, a long-standing member of the Saturday Night Live Band, has played with many artists including Paul Simon, Jaco Pastorius and Jack DeJohnette. Foster would eventually get to play with Miles as a member of the Gil Evans Orchestra. The orchestra played at Miles's last Montreux concert in July 1991, just a couple of months before Miles died.

30. Davis and Troupe, *Miles*, p. 333.

31. Ibid., p. 334.

32. Carr, *Miles Davis*, p. 350.

33. Tingen, *Miles Beyond*, p. 194.

34. Taken from FAQ section on Marcus Miller's official website at www.marcusmiller.com. Edi Weitz manages the website.

35. *The Miles Davis Story Part Two*.

36. Marcus Miller's official website.

37. Tingen, *Miles Beyond*, p. 196.

38. Davis and Troupe, *Miles*, p. 334.

39. Cheryl McCall, "Miles Davis," *Musician, Player & Listener* 41 (March 1982), p. 43.

40. Davis and Troupe, *Miles*, p. 195.

41. Jan Lohmann, *The Sound of Miles Davis: The Discography. A Listing of Records and Tapes 1945–1991* (Copenhagen: JazzMedia, 1992), p. 167.

42. Enrico Merlin in Tingen, *Miles Beyond*, p. 329.

43. Swzed, *So What*, p. 355.

44. Liner notes by Ben Edmonds for "What's Going On?" by Marvin Gaye, deluxe edition Motown Records 440 013 405.

45. Tingen, *Miles Beyond*, p. 194.

46. Carr, *Miles Davis*, p. 351.

47. W. A. Bower, "*The Man With The Horn* Review," *Down Beat* (November 1981), p. 33.

48. *ESP2 A Tribute to Miles*, TDK Jazz Club DV-JESP2.

49. Sam Freedman, "Marcus Miller the Thumbslinger: Bassist for Hire," *Down Beat* (April 1983), p. 19.

50. Ibid.

51. *The Miles Davis Story Part Two*.

52. Ibid.

53. Ibid.

54. *Jazz File*, programme 5.

55. Davis and Troupe, *Miles*, p. 294.

56. Davis and Troupe, *Miles*, p. 280.

57. Ibid.

58. Lohmann, *The Sound of Miles Davis*, p. 158.

59. The track has long intrigued Miles's aficionados because, at the beginning of one take, Teo Macero mentions a mystery keyboardist Mark, who is about to play a solo. But no one in Miles's band has had that name. In fact, it was Mark Johnson, a friend of Michael Henderson's. "Mark is a great player but he was too bashful when he met Miles. He clammed up and couldn't play," recalls Henderson. Johnson later joined Henderson's band and played on his first two solo albums. He then joined The Brothers Johnson playing on the hit record *Stomp*.

60. Carr, *Miles Davis*, p. 359.

61. The album, on Sony Records (SSRCS6813-4), was released in November 1992.

62. The track was recorded in CBS's Studio B on 49 E. 52nd Street – the original album gives no recording date details. Discographers Jan Lohmann and Enrico Merlin put the recording around this date. The Sony Japan Original Masters and SACD releases give the date as March 1981. However Don Puluse's diary notes even suggest that the recording date could have been around mid-April.

63. Davis and Troupe, *Miles*, p. 334.

64. Ibid.

65. Ibid.

66. Barry Finnerty's website www.barryfinnerty.com.

67. Howard Mandel, "Profile: Bill Evans, Mike Stern and Mino Cinelu," *Down Beat* (November 1981), p. 52.

68. Jeff Richman, "Mike Stern's Solo on Fat Time: A Guitar Transcription," *Down Beat* (November 1981), p. 58.

69. Mandel, "Profile," p. 53.

70. Various authors, "Sketches of Miles," *Musician* (December 1991), p. 47.

71. Bower, "Review," p. 33.

72. Ibid.

73. Davis and Troupe, *Miles*, p. 337.

74. See, for example, Bower, "Review," p. 33; Tingen, *Miles Beyond*, p. 195.

We Want Miles

1. Miles says he did eight concerts (Miles Davis and Quincy Troupe, *Miles: The Autobiography* [London: Macmillan, 1990], p. 337). But the tour itinerary listed in the Japanese CD *Miles! Miles! Miles!* (Sony Records SRCS 6613-4) only shows seven.

2. Davis and Troupe, *Miles*, p. 337. George Wein says he paid Miles $70,000. See John Szwed, *So What: The Life of Miles Davis* (London: William Heineman, 2002), p. 356.

3. Davis and Troupe, *Miles*, p. 335.

4. Davis and Troupe, *Miles*, p. 336.

5. Chris Murphy, *Miles to Go* (New York: Thunder's Mouth Press, 2002), p. 132.

6. Ian Carr, *Miles Davis: The Definitive Biography* (London: Harper Collins, 1998), p. 361.

7. Murphy, *Miles to Go*, p. 137.

8. George Wein with Nate Chinen, *Myself Among Others: A Life of Music* (Cambridge, MA: Da Capo Press, 2003), p. 450.

9. Davis and Troupe, *Miles*, p. 336.

10. Murphy, *Miles to Go*, p. 139.

12. Bob Blumenthal, "Miles Glorious," *Boston Phoenix* (July 7, 1982) reports that three sets were played on Sunday June 28, and Monday June 29. A Japanese bootleg *Welcome to the Kix* Vol. 3 reportedly contains the third set from June 28, a medley comprising "My Man's Gone Now," "Kix" and "Aida" lasting around thirty minutes.

12. Carr, *Miles Davis*, p. 368.

13. Davis and Troupe, *Miles*, p. 337.

14. Murphy, *Miles to Go*, p. 140.

15. Davis and Troupe, *Miles*, p. 337.

16. Ibid.

17. Murphy, *Miles to Go*, p. 139.

18. Blumenthal, "Miles Glorious."

19. Quincy Troupe, *Miles and Me* (California: University of California Press, 2000), p. 150.

20. Quoted in Jack Chambers, *Milestones: The Music and Times of Miles Davis* (New York: De Capo Press, 1998), p. 313.

21. Robert Palmer, "Jazz Scene: Miles Davis Comeback," *The New York Times*, July 7, 1981.
22. Murphy, *Miles to Go*, p. 148.
23. Ibid., p. 149.
24. Sam Freedman, "Marcus Miller the Thumbslinger: Bassist for Hire," *Down Beat* (April 1983), p. 19.
25. Cheryl McCall, "Miles Davis," *Musician, Player & Listener* 41 (March 1982), p. 40.
26. Davis and Troupe, *Miles*, p. 259.
27. Published by Shogakukan.
28. Carr, *Miles Davis*, p. 365.
29. Liner notes to Horn's album *I Remember Miles*.
30. Paul Tingen, *Miles Beyond: The Electric Explorations of Miles Davis 1967–91* (New York: Billboard Books, 2001), p. 330.
31. See Murphy, *Miles to Go*, p. 166; Swzed, *So What*, p. 357.
32. Chambers, *Milestones*, p. 333.
33. Gene Kalbacher, "Miles Davis: I think the greatest sound in the world is the human voice," *JAZZ* (April 1984).
34. Carr, *Miles Davis*, p. 376.
35. Tingen, *Miles Beyond*, p. 202.
36. Carr, *Miles Davis*, p. 379.
37. *Miles! Miles! Miles!* has only been released in Japan.

Star People

1. Jack Chambers, *Milestones: The Music and Times of Miles Davis*, 2nd ed. (New York: De Capo Press, 1998), p. xiii.
2. Paul Tingen, *Miles Beyond: The Electric Explorations of Miles Davis 1967–91* (New York: Billboard Books, 2001), pp. 206–207.
3. Bob Doerschuk, "The Picasso of Invisible Art," *Keyboard* (October 1987), p. 70.
4. Richard Williams, "On Top Of All That Beat," *The Times*, April 28, 1983.
5. Doerschuk, "Miles Davis: The Picasso of Invisible Art," p. 69.
6. Miles Davis and Quincy Troupe, *Miles: The Autobiography* (London: Macmillan, 1990), p. 340.
7. However, the Japanese Master Sound version of *Star People* lists Evans as an arranger.
8. Larry Hicock, *Castles Made of Sound: The Story of Gil Evans* (New York: Da Capo Press, 2002), p. 223.
9. *Star People* liner notes.
10. Davis and Troupe, *Miles*, p. 344.
11. Ibid.
12. Tingen, *Miles Beyond*, p. 330.

13. Jan Lohmann, *The Sound of Miles Davis: The Discography. A Listing of Records and Tapes 1945–1991* (Copenhagen: JazzMedia, 1992), p. 180.
14. Davis and Troupe, *Miles*, p. 344.
15. *Star People* liner notes.
16. Ibid.
17. Ibid.
18. Ibid.
19. Davis and Troupe, *Miles*, p. 344.
20. *Star People* liner notes.
21. Tingen, *Miles Beyond*, p. 209.
22. Hicock, *Castles Made of Sound*, p. 224.
23. *Star People* liner notes.
24. Davis and Troupe, *Miles*, p. 344.
25. Lohmann and the Master Sound CD version give this date and venue but, according to Merlin, it does not appear on a bootleg supposedly recorded at the concert. See Tingen, *Miles Beyond*, p. 331.
26. Gibson Keddie, "Tales of the Unexpected," *Bassist* Vol. 1 No. 7 (1995), p. 15.
27. Ibid.
28. *Jazzmatazz*, presented by Alyn Shipton, BBC World Service, Programme 4, broadcast on September 28, 2001.
29. Davis and Troupe, *Miles*, p. 344.
30. Enrico Merlin first pointed this out in a discussion dated June 11, 1996 on the Miles Davis discussion forum.
31. Miles Davis and Scott Gutterman, *The Art of Miles Davis* (New York: Prentice Hall, 1991), *Miles Davis: Apart from Jazz. A Second Miles Davis Legacy* (Tokyo: Vive, 1998), *Improvisations: The Drawings of Miles Davis*, conceived and edited by Oz Karas (Lincolnwood, IL: Publication International, 2001).
32. Davis and Gutterman, *The Art of Miles Davis*, p. 5.
33. Davis and Troupe, *Miles*, p. 353.

Decoy

1 Miles Davis and Quincy Troupe, *Miles: The Autobigraphy* (London: Macmillan, 1990), p. 341.
2. Ibid., p. 355.
3. Ibid., p. 345.
4. Ian Carr, *Miles Davis: The Definitive Biography* (London: Harper Collins, 1998), p. 401.
5. Gene Kalbacher, "Miles Davis: I think the greatest sound in the world is the human voice," *JAZZ* (April 1984).
6. In his autobiography, Miles says Jones was nineteen when he joined the band. Davis and Troupe, *Miles*, p. 344. "I said to Miles, 'why did you say I

was 19 when you knew I was 21?' and Miles said: 'I was giving you a couple of extra years!' "

7. Davis and Troupe, *Miles*, p. 359.

8. Ibid., p. 349.

9. www.grammy.com shows that several albums Miles made during the last ten years of his life won awards – *We Want Miles*, *Tutu*, *Aura* and *Doo-Bop* (posthumously). The album Miles recorded with Quincy Jones at Montreux in July 1991 (*Miles Davis and Quincy Jones Live At Montreux*) also won a Grammy.

10. Paul Tingen, *Miles Beyond: The Electric Explorations of Miles Davis 1967–91* (New York: Billboard Books, 2001), p. 213.

11. John Szwed, *So What: The Life of Miles Davis* (London: William Heinemann, 2002), p. 362. Weill was born in Germany in 1900 and worked with Bertolt Brecht. He died in New York in 1950.

12. Bob Doerschuk, "Miles Davis: The Picasso of Invisible Art," *Keyboard* (October 1987), p. 69.

13. Quincy Troupe, *Miles and Me* (California: University of California Press, 2000), p. 152.

14. The original album release gives no recording dates. The original Japanese Master Sound CD version, released in September 1996, puts the date as September 10 and 11, 1983. Miles's discographers Jan Lohmann and Enrico Merlin think it was probably recorded around these dates too. However, Miles's discographer Peter Losin puts the date as September 5, 1983 and so does the re-release of the Master Sound album, released in July 2001.

15. Barry McRae, *Miles Davis* (London: Apollo Press, 1988), p. 68.

16. Philips 464184-2.

17. Doerschuk, "Miles Davis: The Picasso of Invisible Art," p. 74.

18. In 1976 Miles and his band appeared in a 20-minute commercial film for TDK, the recording media company.

19. Doerschuk, "Miles Davis: The Picasso of Invisible Art," p. 72.

20. OWL 079 830485 2. The album was released in 1995.

21. Verve 837 034-2.

22. Tingen, *Miles Beyond*, p. 216.

23. Ian Carr, "Miles Further Ahead," *Jazz* (Swiss) July 1984.

24. Davis and Troupe, *Miles*, p. 347.

25. Early versions of *Decoy* on the Master of CD Sound series, released by Sony Music Japan in the late 1990s, had a miniature cardboard version of the original gatefold sleeve. The series was reissued in 2001 with early versions having the cardboard sleeve and later releases reverting to a CD jewel case but with the CD paper sleeve folding out to reveal the full-length photograph.

You're Under Arrest

1. Nick Kent, "Lightening Up with the Prince of Darkness," *The Face* (October 1986). Reprinted in *The Dark Stuff* (London: Penguin, 1994).
2. Paul Tingen reports the latter as being recorded (Paul Tingen, *Miles Beyond: The Electric Explorations of Miles Davis 1967–91* [New York: Billboard Books, 2001], p. 217).
3. According to Columbia Record's files, one tune recorded at this session was a track called "Something Going On." Jan Lohmann thinks this probably meant to be D-Train's "Something on Your Mind," which, of course, appeared on *You're Under Arrest*. However, Anni-Frid Lyngstad of Abba (better known as Frida) had released an album in 1982 called *Something's Going On* and the title track (called "I Know There's Something Going On") was a hit single. See Jan Lohmann, *The Sound of Miles Davis: The Discography. A Listing of Records and Tapes 1945–1991* (Copenhagen: JazzMedia, 1992), p. 201.
4. Gene Kalbacher, "Miles Davis: I think the greatest sound in the world is the human voice," *JAZZ* (April 1984).
5. Miles Davis and Quincy Troupe, *Miles: The Autobiography* (London: Macmillan, 1990), p. 351.
6. Kalbacher, "Miles Davis."
7. The dates given by Jan Lohmann and Enrico Merlin are January, February or April 1984. Steve Thornton says this was the first tune he worked on and he was doing other sessions in January or February. The Japanese SACD and Sony Master Sound version put the date as January 26, 1984.
8. From the song "Cash In Your Face," on *Hotter Than July* (Motown Records 530 044-2).
9. Davis and Troupe, *Miles*, p. 396.
10. Kalbacher, "Miles Davis."
11. Davis and Troupe, *Miles*, p. 352.
12. Kalbacher, "Miles Davis." The Celeste also features on the track "The Man With The Horn."
13. Davis and Troupe, *Miles*, p. 352.
14. Kalbacher, "Miles Davis."
15. Davis and Troupe, *Miles*, p. 349.
16. Kalbacher, "Miles Davis."
17. Released in 2004 on Unspeakable Records UNSP 0001.
18. Kalbacher, "Miles Davis."
19. Ibid.
20. Miles named tracks after both women. "Mayisha" is on the 1974 album *Get Up With It*. "Mademoiselle Mabry" on the 1968 album *Filles De Kilimanjaro* and "Back Seat Betty" were named after Betty Mabry who became the second Mrs Miles Davis.

21. Ian Carr, *Miles Davis: The Definitive Biography* (London: Harper Collins, 1998), p. 440.
22. Kalbacher, "Miles Davis."
23. Richard Cook and Brian Morton, *The Penguin Guide to Jazz on CD, LP and Cassette* (Harmondsworth: Penguin, 1996), p. 336.
24. Stuart Nicholson, *Jazz–Rock: A History* (Edinburgh: Canongate, 1998), p. 228.
25. Miles took his several members of his band in June and September 1987 and from September 1988 to January 1989 to record tracks that appeared on *Amandla*. He also took bands into the studio in September 1985 and March 1991 to record tracks, but none of these appeared on an album. In March 1990 his band was involved in the recording of the soundtrack *Dingo*.

Aura

1. Miles Davis and Quincy Troupe, *Miles: The Autobigraphy* (London: Macmillan, 1990), p. 379.
2. Keith Jarrett won the award in 2004.
3. Davis and Troupe, *Miles*, p. 249.
4. Richard Cook, "Miles Runs The Voodoo Down," *New Musical Express*, July 13, 1985, p. 20.
5. *Aura* liner notes.
6. Stanley Crouch, "Play The Right Thing," *The New Republic*, February 12, 1990.
7. Angus McKinnon, "Davis Fulfils His Prophesy," *The Sunday Correspondent*, September 17, 1989.
8. Recommended Miles Davis recordings on www.miles-beyond.com.
9. Originally in Weather Bird column in the *Village Voice* (November 14, 1989) reprinted in *The Miles Davis Companion* (ed. Gary Carner; New York: Schirmer Books, 1996), p. 199.
10. Francis Davis, "Miles Agonistes" reprinted in Carner, *The Miles Davis Companion*, p. 206.
11. Troupe, *Miles and Me*, p. 155.
12. Richard Cook and Brian Morton, *The Penguin Guide to Jazz on CD, LP and Cassette* (Harmondsworth: Penguin, 1996), p. 337.

The road to *Tutu* – the background

1. Miles Davis and Quincy Troupe, *Miles: The Autobigraphy* (London: Macmillan, 1990), p. 349.
2. Kevin Rowland, "Miles Davis is a Living Legend and You're Not," *Musician* (March 1987), p. 92.

3. Quoted by Ian Carr in *Miles Davis: The Definitive Biography* (London: Harper Collins, 1998), p. 436, from Gene Lees, "Jazz Black and White Part II," *Jazzletter* Vol. 12, No. 11 (November 1993).

4. Davis and Troupe, *Miles*, p. 350.

5. Ibid.

6. Quincy Troupe, *Miles and Me* (California: University of California Press, 2000), p. 31.

7. Gene Kalbacher, "Miles Davis: I think the greatest sound in the world is the human voice," *JAZZ* (April 1984).

8. Ken Franckling, "Shining Light on the Prince of Darkness," *JazzTimes* (August 1986), pp. 14-16.

9. Ibid.

10. Troupe, *Miles and Me*, p. 32.

11. Davis and Troupe, *Miles*, p. 352. Miles says Franklin gave up all his rights, but author Paul Tingen discovered the figure was 50 per cent, still a huge amount. See Paul Tingen, *Miles Beyond: The Electric Explorations of Miles Davis 1967–91* (New York: Billboard Books, 2001), p. 229.

12. Nick Kent, "Lightening Up with the Prince of Darkness," *The Face* (October 1986), p. 276.

13. On *The Complete Miles Davis At Montreux*, the writing credits for Maze are given to (Miles's youngest son) Erin Davis, Randy Hall and Zane Giles, but this seems to be the result of Miles assigning his copyright to Erin in order to stop Warner Chappell Music (which owned half of Miles's publishing rights) having a claim on any royalties. Another mystery is that Miles was apparently performing the tune some six months before he started working with Hall and Giles.

The road to *Tutu*: the *Rubberband* album

1. The interview was broadcast as part of a radio transmission of Miles's concert in Uema, Sweden on October 26, 1985 by SR (Swedish Radio).

2. Miles Davis and Quincy Troupe, *Miles: The Autobigraphy* (London: Macmillan, 1990), p. 224.

3. Ibid., p. 289.

4. Paul Tingen, *Miles Beyond: The Electric Explorations of Miles Davis 1967–91* (New York: Billboard Books, 2001), p. 65.

5. It remained in Miles's live set from October 1985 to October 1988.

6. Musicians such as Stockhausen and John Cage often used short-wave radio sound effects in their music. See, for example, Stockhausen's *Telemusik*, *Hymnen* and *Spiral* works.

7. After the *Rubberband* sessions, Linsey composed other tunes for Miles including one entitled "Bookends," often called "Wayne's Tune." The tune was played at some of Miles's concerts in 1988. The tune, a funky groove

in 6/8 time, is on the live album *The Last Concert In Avignon* (Delta Music). In programme five of the *Miles Davis Radio Project*, Miles can be heard rehearsing the tune with his band in March 1988. Miles tells his band "Wayne writes in six. It's church. Sanctified music." Incidentally, the tune's original title was "The Tale Of The Blue Stationery" [blue writing paper] ("the tune had a kind of a literary quality to me," says Linsey), but Miles asked Linsey to change it to "Bookends," because when Miles first heard the tune the same synthesizer patch was used at the beginning and end of the track – like bookends holding the tune in place.

8. The theme to "Wrinkle" is so catchy that trumpeter Wallace Roney even used it on his album, *No Room For Argument* (Stretch Records SCD-9003-2). On the track "Virtual Chocolate Cherry," the "Wrinkle" theme is played briefly by Roney and then by saxophonist Steve Hall. Adam Holzman plays keyboards on the track – the theme can be heard at 3:11. Miles often played the theme during his solos; see for example "Human Nature" at Nice on July 17, 1991. Miles plays the theme at 4:36. The concert is on disc 20 of *The Complete Miles Davis At Montreux* boxed set.

9. See Tingen, *Miles Beyond*, p. 330. Merlin discussed this alleged link extensively on the Miles Davis discussion forum on June 13, 1996 – see the archives at http://listserv.surfnet.nl/archives/miles.html.

10. Adam Holzman's liner notes for the Miles DVD *Live In Munich* (Pioneer PA-11853).

11. See Paul Tingen, "Miles on Target: The Making of *Tutu*," *JazzTimes* (March 2002), p. 44.

12. Chaka Khan may have missed the Rubberband gig, but she would later sing with Miles at the 1989 Montreux Jazz Festival on the song "Human Nature" (the performance is on *The Complete Miles Davis At Montreux*), and Miles played on two tracks on her 1988 album *CK*. However, not everyone it seems appreciates Khan's style of singing. Commenting on Khan's appearance at the 1989 Montreux concert, British author Stuart Nicholson said her performance was "to be avoided at all costs." See *Jazz-Rock: A History* (Edinburgh: Canongate, 1998), p. 251.

13. In fact, only Hall was involved with this album.

14. Davis and Troupe, *Miles*, p. 361.

15. The interview took place in Germany and appears on the DVD *Live In Munich* (Pioneer PA-11853).

16. Miles Davis and Scott Gutterman, *The Art of Miles Davis* (New York: Prentice Hall, 1991).

17. *Live In Munich* DVD.

18. Two tracks from the sessions, "Rubberband" and "See I See" were due to be included on a Warner Bros boxed set *The Last Word*, an anthology of Miles's music made during 1985–91. It was set for release in summer 2002,

but was pulled at the last moment. See George Cole, "Miles Davis Box Set Mystery," *Jazzwise* (November 2002), p. 6.

The road to *Tutu*: Miles and Prince

1. Miles Davis and Quincy Troupe, *Miles: The Autobiography* (London: Macmillan, 1990), p. 375.
2. Davis and Troupe, *Miles*, quotes taken from pp. 374 and 375.
3. Davis and Troupe, *Miles*, p. 374.
4. Davis and Troupe, *Miles*, p. 375.
5. Quincy Troupe, *Miles and Me* (California: University of California Press, 2000), p. 104.
6. Nick Kent, "Lightening Up with the Prince of Darkness," *The Face* (October 1986), p. 276.
7. Ibid. Note, the booklet of the bootleg *Miles In The Park* has a photograph of a cassette tape labelled *Can I Play With U*, but it's a safe bet that this is not the original tape Prince sent to Miles!
8. Ken Franckling, "Shining a Light on the Prince of Darkness," *JazzTimes* (August 1986), pp. 14-16.
9. Per Nilsen with help from Duane Tudachi, "Y'all Want Some More?" *Uptown* 45 (Winter 2000/2001), pp. 16-21.
10. Ibid.
11. Davis and Troupe, *Miles*, p. 362.
12. Nilsen, "Y'all Want Some More?," p. 17.
13. Alex Hahn, *Possessed: The Rise and Fall of Prince* (New York: Billboard Books, 2003), p. 100.
14. An excellent source of information on Crucial and the various Prince/ Miles connections can be found at: DMSR an online Prince history at http://users.ids.net/~dmsr/dmsr.html. The last time the author looked at the site it hadn't been updated since 1996(!), but it obviously covers the period when Miles was alive. A good source of information on Prince bootlegs was found at www.guide2prince.org. Much of the information in this latter section is from these two sites plus *Turn It Up 2.0: The Complete Guide to Prince Recordings and Performances*, written and published by the staff of Prince fanzine *Uptown*, 2001, Linchem, Sweden.
15. Serge Simonart, "The Artist," *Guitar World*, October 1998.
16. Prince attended Miles's 62nd birthday party, which also included Nick Ashford and Valerie Simpson, Marcus Miller, and promoter George Wein (see *Miles: The Autobiography*, p. 376). Engineer Susan Rogers recalls going to Prince's home and finding Miles there with Prince's father. The meeting had some hilarious moments, including Miles and Prince's father discussing whether Miles owned a pair of striped pants! See "Y'all Want Some More?," p. 18.

17. "Movie Star" has been released on the double album *His Last Concert In Avignon* (Delta Music) and on *Time After Time* (several Miles Davis records, including some bootlegs, have this title). The *Time After Time* album featuring "Movie Star" is in fact part two of a two-CD set of *The Last Concert In Avignon* (also on Delta Music). "Movie Star" appears on disc 14 of *The Complete Miles Davis At Montreux* boxed set. Warner Bros had hoped to include several of Prince's songs on *The Last Word* boxed set, but Prince refused permission. Warner Bros gave this refusal as one of its reasons for withdrawing the boxed set from its release schedule. For more details see the section "Miles's other recordings."

Tutu

1. Bill Milkowski, "Marcus Miller: Miles's Man in the Studio," *Down Beat* (February 1987), p. 21.
2. Miles Davis and Quincy Troupe, *Miles: The Autobigraphy* (London: Macmillan, 1990), p. 360.
3. Ibid.
4. This date is provided by Miles's discographers Jan Lohmann and Enrico Merlin, and refers to the overdubbing session at Capitol Records studio in Los Angeles and not Duke's original recording at Le Gonks studio.
5. Miles's saxophonist at the time was Bob Berg. Kenny Garrett joined Miles's band in February 1987.
6. In a report by Paul Tingen, Duke is reported as saying the title: "Has to do with Miles being kind of on the other side." "Miles on Target: The Making of *Tutu*," *JazzTimes* (March 2002), p. 46. When the present author asked Duke about this, he replied: "The other side of what?"
7. When Miller played in Miles's band during 1981–83, he only played bass, but on David Sanborn's 1983 album *Backstreet*, Miller played Fender, fretless and moog bass, Fender Rhodes, acoustic piano, OBX-a, Yamaha GS-2, Prophet-5 and Jupiter-8 synthesizers, solo and rhythm electric and acoustic guitars, steel drums, tympani, chair, percussion and vocoder. He also sang background vocals on a couple of tracks.
8. *Jazz File*, interview with Ian Carr, BBC Radio 3, programme 6, October 13, 2001.
9. The albums were *Double Vision* and *Collaboration* respectively.
10. *Jazz File*, BBC Radio 3.
11. Interview with Richard Steele of WBEZ Chicago public radio on the show *Eight Forty Eight*, May 2001.
12. Paul Tingen, "The Miller's Tale," *Sound on Sound* (July 1999), p. 40.
13. Davis and Troupe, *Miles*, p. 360.
14. Ibid., p. 361.
15. *Jazz File*, BBC Radio 3.

16. Paul Tingen, *Miles Beyond: The Electric Explorations of Miles Davis 1967–91* (New York: Billboard Books, 2001), p. 252.

17. Gene Santoro, "Miles Davis: The Enabler Part II," *Down Beat* (November 1988), p. 19.

18. Ibid.

19. Tingen, *Miles Beyond*, p. 232.

20. *Jazz File*, BBC Radio 3.

21. Ibid.

22. *Miles Ten Years After*, presented by Ravi Coltrane, BBC Radio 2, programme 6, October 13, 2001.

23. Don Heckman, "Marcus Miller: All Things in Good Time," *JazzTimes* (April 1994), p. 30.

24. *Jazz File*, Radio 3.

25. Tingen, "Miles on Target: The Making of *Tutu*."

26. The programme, on the New York station One Network, was broadcast in October 1986.

27. Miles's autobiography has more than twenty page references to it in the index section; see p. 418.

28. Ian Carr, *Miles Davis: The Definitive Biography* (London: Harper Collins, 1998), p. 2.

29. Davis and Troupe, *Miles*, p. 395.

30. The project was organized by Steve Van Zandt aka Little Steven, a member of Bruce Springsteen's E-Street band, and featured many artists including Herbie Hancock, Tony Williams, Ron Carter, Peter Gabriel, Bono, Gil Scott-Heron and members of The Rolling Stones.

31. Interview with Patrice Blanc-Francard on the video *Miles In Paris* (Warner Music Vision, 1990).

32. Transcript from "Cassandra Wilson: Traveling Miles," *Jazz at the Lincoln Center*, January 5, 1998, final draft by Joseph Hooper. Yoruba-speaking people are found in the south-western region of Nigeria.

33. Much of the following description is based on Miller's explanation of how he composed "Tutu". *The Miles Davis Radio Project*, American Public Radio, programme 5.

34. Ibid.

35. Ibid.

36. Ibid.

37. Cover versions of "Tutu" have appeared on several albums: *Traveling Miles* by Cassandra Wilson (Blue Note 7243 8 5412325), *Endless Miles*, various artists (Encoded Music N2K-10027) and *Selim Sivad: A Tribute to Miles Davis*, World Saxophone Quartet featuring Jack DeJohnette (Justin Time Just 119-2).

38. Milkowski, "Miles's Man in the Studio," p. 21.

39. Ibid., p. 22.

40. The bootleg *The Kings Of Priests* has a 20-minute recording of Miles and his band rehearsing the tune in a Los Angeles studio. The arrangement is almost identical to the album version.

41. There is some mystery surrounding these comments as both Marcus Miller and Jason Miles confirm that no extra tracks were left over from the *Tutu* sessions. Urbaniak cannot recall the names of any of the additional track titles he says he played on. Furthermore, he says his performance on *Don't Lose Your Mind* was done in a single take. "I either need one take or eleven," he quips. On another related matter, Lohmann reports Urbaniak saying that Lenny White, Bernard Wright, Chaka Khan and Prince took part in the *Tutu* sessions (Jan Lohmann, *The Sound of Miles Davis: The Discography. A Listing of Records and Tapes 1945–1991* [Copenhagen: JazzMedia, 1992], p. 243) but Urbaniak says he only saw Miles and Miller at the sessions. He adds that he heard that other people were at the sessions. Bernard Wright certainly played on two tracks and Prince also wrote and performed a song slated to appear on the album. Chaka Khan was supposed to sing on one of the tunes in the Rubberband sessions, which had taken place just before the first *Tutu* tracks were being put down. Lenny White is an old friend of Miller's and two of them have played with Urbaniak. It could be that Urbaniak misheard some gossip during the sessions.

42. Miles resumed touring almost three weeks later.

43. Bob Doerschuk, "Jason Miles: Programming and Sessions with Miles Davis," *Keyboard* (October 1987), p. 84.

44. The recording appears on the bootleg *The King Of Priests*.

45. Charles Shaar Murray was first to point this out in "*Tutu* review" in *Q*, October 1986.

46. Milkowski, "Miles's Man in the Studio," p. 22.

47. A short version (2:48) of "Full Nelson" was released on the album *Live Around The World* and on a 12-inch promotional single (Warner Bros PRO-A-2684). The 12-inch remixes contain yet more samples and with an even heavier backbeat than the album version. Jason Miles, who was involved in the remixing, says the experience was: "A totally long-assed night. The night that wouldn't end. We used all kinds of samples." One effect used a sample of a metal pip being hit, to which Jason Miles added some low-frequency oscillator, producing something that sounded like underwater clanks. The next day Miles called Miller, who informed Jason Miles that "Miles likes the underwater sonar shit."

48. An example of Miles's eclectic taste can be found in *Miles Smiles*, a book featuring the work of Japanese photographer Shigeru Uchiyama that catalogues Miles's Japan tours during the 1980s, including shots of Miles in

his hotel rooms. One of them shows Miles leaning over his bed and next to it are piles of albums and CDs by artists such as Randy Crawford and Julio Inglesias. The book was published in Japan in 1993 by Shogakukan.

49. Milkowski, "Miles's Man in the Studio," p. 22.

50. Arnold Meyer, "Poet-Thinker-Dandy," *Network Press* (July 1988).

51. Ibid.

52. The bootleg *The King Of Priests* has a 25-minute recording of Miles's band at the time rehearsing the tune two days before its first performance at the Concord Pavilion, California. The band members were Bob Berg on sax, Robben Ford on guitar, Robert Irving III and Adam Holzman on keyboards, Felton Crews on bass, Vince Wilburn Jr. on drums and Steve Thornton on percussion.

53. In the film *The Miles Davis Story* (directed by Mike Dibb and broadcast on UK's Channel 4 on April 14 and 15, 2001) Miles can be seen going on the set to record the "Portia" segment of the video. Miles arrives in long flowing clothes accompanied by a young woman who smiles mischievously at the camera. Miles is filmed on a rooftop with his silhouette projected on to a wall.

54. The programme, on the New York station One Network, was broadcast in October 1986.

55. *The Miles Davis Story Part Two*.

56. Bill Milkowski, "*Tutu* review," *Down Beat* (October 1986).

57. Richard Cook and Brian Morton, *The Penguin Guide to Jazz on CD, LP and Cassette* (Harmondsworth: Penguin, 1996), p. 336. Oddly, the critics award *Tutu* three stars ("good, if middleweight") and *Amandla*, the third album which Miles and Miller collaborated on, three/four stars ("a fine record with some exceptional music").

58. Jack Chambers, *Milestones: The Music and Times of Miles Davis*, with a new introduction (New York: Da Capo Press, 1998), p. xiv.

59. Stanley Crouch, "Play the Right Thing," *The New Republic*, February 12, 1990.

60. Barry McRae, *Miles Davis* (London: Apollo Press, 1988), p. 70.

61. Two of London's most cherished landmarks, St Paul's Cathedral and the Houses of Parliament, were lambasted by critics when they were first built. Information courtesy of the Royal Institute of British Architects.

62. "*Tutu* review," *Q* magazine (October 1986).

63. *Down Beat* (October 1986).

64. *International Herald Tribune*, November 14, 1989.

65. Richard Williams, "Present Continuous," *The Guardian*, October 27, 1985, p. 13.

66. Richard Williams, *The Man in the Green Shirt* (London: Bloomsbury, 1993), p. 169.

Siesta

1. Barkin and Byrne, who met each other for the first time on the set, also became off-screen lovers and later married.
2. Hal Hinson, *Washington Post*, December 28, 1987.
3. This stands for the Society of Motion Picture and Television Engineers, which, in 1967, developed the standard for a timecode track for film and video that is based on the 24-hour clock.
4. Bob Doerschuk, "Jason Miles: Programming and Sessions with Miles Davis," *Keyboard* (October 1987), p. 84.
5. A good example occurs at around thirty-nine minutes into the movie, where Kit is sitting on a statue. Miller plays some gorgeous phrases on bass clarinet, which, alas, are not included on the soundtrack album. Warner had planned to put around ten minutes of unused cues on its abandoned boxed set *The Last Word*.

Amandla

1. Liner notes to Warner Bros Masters version of *Amandla* (81227 3611-2).
2. Andy Robson, "Speaking Your Language," *Jazzwise* (April 2003), p. 42.
3. Miles Davis and Quincy Troupe, *Miles: The Autobiography* (London: Macmillan, 1990), p. 365.
4. Peter Watrous, "Miles Davis: Rebel without a Pause," *Musician* 127 (May 1989).
5. Davis and Troupe, *Miles*, p. 373.
6. Richard Cook, "Miles Runs the Voodoo Down," *New Musical Express*, July 13, 1985, p. 20.
7. Gene Kalbacher, "Miles Davis: I think the greatest sound in the world is the human voice," *JAZZ* (April 1984).
8. Slap bass was a technique long used on the acoustic bass, with musicians such as Wellman Braud employing it in the Duke Ellington band in the 1930s.
9. Davis and Troupe, *Miles*, p. 374.
10. Quincy Troupe, *Miles and Me* (California: University of California Press, 2000), p. 57.
11. *Amandla* liner notes.
12. Ibid.
13. Ibid.
14. Bruce Miller talks about *Amandla* in the producers' video interviews section at http://recordproduction.com.
15. EQ or equalization is the process by which the levels of different frequencies are controlled, such as adjusting the bass or treble control on a hi-fi system. Studios, of course, use far more sophisticated controls than the average home stereo system. Compression is used to control the dynamic

range of a sound, usually to ensure that the audio level doesn't saturate the tape, causing distortion.

16. Gelbard speaks at some length about her life with Miles in Paul Tingen, *Miles Beyond* (New York: Billboard Books, 2001).
17. Davis and Troupe, *Miles*, p. 356.
18. Ibid., p. 381.
19. Ibid., p. 403.
20. Miles Davis and Scott Gutterman, *The Art of Miles Davis* (New York: Prentice Hall, 1991), p. 6.
21. Ibid., p. 14.
22. *Amandla!* Title given to a documentary film about the role music played in the struggle in the battle against apartheid, featuring contributions by artists such as Hugh Masekela and Miram Makeba. Directed by Lee Hirsch, it was released in 2002.
23. Liner notes of 2000 re-issue of album *Jaco Pastorius*.
24. www.jacopastorius.com (interview December 2002).
25. Carr, *Miles Davis*, p. 505.
26. Davis and Troupe, *Miles Davis*, p. 379.
27. *Miles In Paris* video (Warner Bros 9031-71550-2).
28. Miles did not perform "Cobra" live on-stage, but he did play it live in RAI television studios in Rome on July 21, 1989.
29. Ian MacDonald, *Revolution in the Head: The Beatles' Records and the Sixties*, 2nd ed. (London: Fourth Estate, 1997), p. 338.
30. Ibid.
31. *Amandla* liner notes.
32. Stuart Nicholson, *Jazz-Rock: A History* (Edinburgh: Canongate, 1998), p. 230.
33. Tingen, *Miles Beyond*, p. 242.

Doo-Bop

1. Miles Davis and Quincy Troupe, *Miles: The Autobigraphy* (London: Macmillan, 1990), caption to photograph 107 between pp. 280-81.
2. Ibid., p. 380. Max Roach has performed with the rap act Fab 5 Freddy.
3. For a thorough examination of the cultural impact of hip-hop, see Nelson George, *Hip Hop America* (New York: Penguin, 1999).
4. Alex Ogg, *The Men Behind Def Jam* (London: Omnibus Press, 2002), provides a good account of the rise of Def Jam.
5. Per Nilsen with help from Duane Tudachi, "Y'all Want Some More?," *Uptown* 45 (Winter 2000/2001), pp. 16-21.
6. The concert took place on July 8, 1991 and was subsequently released on CD and video.
7. For a full background to the Madhouse project see "Y'all Want Some More."

8. *Turn It Up 2.0: The Complete Guide to Prince Recordings and Performances*, written and published by the staff of Prince fanzine *Uptown* (Sweden: Linchem, 2001), p. 47.

9. See Alex Hahn, *Possessed: The Rise and Fall of Prince* (New York: Billboard Books, 2003) for a full description on how Prince's relationship with Warner Bros broke down.

10. Davis and Troupe, *Miles*, p. 310.

11. Ibid., p. 312.

12. Ibid., p. 374.

13. Mike Street, "James Brown: The Fifth Element of Hip Hop," posted on Bet. com, June 3, 2003.

14. Davis and Troupe, *Miles*, p. 314.

15. Paul Tingen, *Miles Beyond: The Electric Explorations of Miles Davis 1967–91* (New York: Billboard Books, 2001), p. 246.

16. Stuart Nicholson, *Jazz-Rock: A History* (Edinburgh: Canongate, 1998), p. 231.

17. Buckshot LeFonque was based on the pseudonym 'Buckshot La Funke' used by Cannonball Adderley in the 1950s when he was moonlighting on other records, such as Louis Smith's *Here Comes Louis Smith* (Blue Note, 1584).

18. The pseudonym of British musician Richard James renowned for his imaginative work with keyboards, drum machines and studio technology. In 2002, Tim Hagans with the Norrbotten Big Band (featuring Scott Kinsey) released an album, *Future Miles* (ACT 9235-2). "Sitting around the band room thirty years ago, we all wondered what Miles would do next," writes Hagans in the liner notes, "... now we sit around the band room and wonder what Miles would be up to if he was still alive. The answer is anybody's guess. This recording is ours." The album contains several tracks that combine trumpet with a drum and bass backing track.

19. Ron Frankl, *Miles Davis*, "Black Americans of Achievement" series (New York: Chelsea House Publishers, 1996), p. 117.

Miles alive

1. Priestley's comment was paraphrased in Richard Cook and Brian Morton, *The Penguin Guide to Jazz on CD, LP and Cassette* (Harmondsworth: Penguin, 1996), p. 338 and has been slightly adapted here for greater clarity.

2. Ian Carr, "Miles Davis" obituary, *The Independent*, September 30, 1991.

3. Josef Woodard, "Miles Smiles," *Jazziz* (September 1989), p. 46.

4. Chris Murphy, *Miles to Go* (New York: Thunder's Mouth Press), p. 181.

5. Lee Jeske, "Miles Davis Felt Forum Review," *Down Beat* (April 1983), p. 46.

6. Bob Doerschuk, "Miles Davis: The Picasso of Invisible Art," *Keyboard* (October 1997), p. 71.

7. Miles Davis and Quincy Troupe, *Miles: The Autobigraphy* (London: Macmillan, 1990), p. 347.
8. Ken Micaleff, "Al Foster, Drummer, Gentleman, Scholar," *Modern Drummer* (April 2003), p. 75.
9. Ibid.
10. John Ephland, "Miles to Go," *Down Beat* (October 1988), p. 19.
11. John Fordham, "Horn of Plenty," *The Guardian*, July 27, 1985.
12. Ian Carr, *Miles Davis: The Definitive Biography* (London: Harper Collins, 1998), p. 442.
13. Doerschuk, "Miles Davis: The Picasso of Invisible Art," p. 72.
14. Radio interview, part of Uema concert broadcast, Sweden on October 26, 1985 by SR (Swedish Radio).
15. Davis and Troupe, *Miles*, p. 363.
16. Davis and Troupe, *Miles*, p. 359.
17. Ibid.
18. Nick Kent, "Lightening Up with the Prince of Darkness," *The Face* (October 1986), p. 278.
19. Davis and Troupe, *Miles*, p. 359.
20. Mark Rowland, "Miles Davis is a Living Legend and You're Not," *Musician* (March 1987), p. 92.
21. *Upside Downside* on Atlantic Records (7 81656-2). It featured Jaco Pastorius and was produced by guitarist Hiram Bullock.
22. Roy Carr, "Man of Many Colours," *New Musical Express*, September 20, 1986, p. 56.
23. See Merlin's discussion of this on April 11, 2003 at http://listserv.surfnet.nl/archives/miles.html.
24. Liner notes to *The Complete Miles Davis At Montreux* boxed set by Nick Liebmann.
25. Troupe and Davis, *Miles*, p. 366.
26. Dave Gelly, "The Eloquent Poser," *The Sunday Times*, November 23, 1986.
27. Mike Guilano, "Gary Thomas Directs Jazz Program at Peabody," *Peabody News Online*, undated.
28. Rowland, "Miles Davis is a Living Legend," p. 86.
29. Ibid.
30. Kenny Burrell and The Jazz Guitar Band on Bluenote Records BN BT 85137.
31. Fred Jung, "The Kenny Garrett Interview: My Conversation with Kenny Garrett," July 1999. All About Jazz.com.
32. Ibid.
33. Ibid.
34. Davis and Troupe, *Miles*, p. 365.
35. Ibid., p. 374.
36. Ibid.

37. *Miles Davis Radio Project*, programme 5, *Retirement and Rebirth – the 1970s and 1980s*.

38. Williams died in 1992.

39. It finally appeared on *The Complete Miles At Montreux* boxed set in 2002.

40. Andy Robson, "Speaking Your Language," *Jazzwise* (April 2003), p. 41.

41. Programme 6, *Behind the Scenes with Miles Davis*. The date for the rehearsal is given as March 1988, but Miles was performing the tune in his February concerts.

42. Ibid.

43. The various titles include *From His Last Concert in Avignon* [*sic*] on Laser-Light Records (24 327/1 and 24 327/2), *Perfect Way/Time After Time* on Delta Records (47 023 and 47003), *Miles Davis Live* volumes 1 & 2 also on Delta (46 007), and *Live in Europe 88* on Jazz Records (MDCD101). All albums contain the same music and mixes.

44. Davis and Troupe, *Miles*, p. 380.

45. Adam Holzman's liner notes for *Live In Munich* DVD (Pioneer PA-11853).

46. See page 37 of the Montreux boxed set liner notes.

47. See Paul Tingen, *Miles Beyond: The Electric Explorations of Miles Davis 1967–91* (New York: Billboard Books, 2001), p. 256. When the present author queried Jason Miles about the origins of the tune, he said: "I wrote this with Miles. Period."

48. Don Heckman, "Concert Review," *Jazz Times* (September 1988), p. 26.

49. Programme seven, *Miles Davis Live*, was in two parts.

50. Liner notes, *New Smiles and Traveled Miles* (Groove Note GRV1004-2).

51. Richard Cook, "The Perils of Being a Living Legend," *The Sunday Times*, April 23, 1989.

52. Josef Woodard, "Miles Smiles," *Jazziz* (September 1989), p. 46.

53. *Live Tutu* (The Golden Age of Jazz JZCD 375). "The Senate/Me And You" is incorrectly identified as "That's What Happened" on the sleeve.

54. Bret Primack, "Remembering Miles," *Jazz Times* (January/February 1992), p. 40.

55. Promoter Claude Nobs says he asked Miles if Khan could join him on-stage – see *The Complete Miles Davis At Montreux* booklet notes, p. 10.

56. Ibid.

57. Roy Carr, "Tales of The Unexpected Monteux Jazz Festival Review," *New Musical Express*, August 19, 1989, p. 42.

58. Tingen, *Miles Beyond*, p. 260.

59. It appears on the bootleg *King Of Trumpets*.

60. *The Miles Davis Story*, Part 2, Channel 4, April 14 and 15, 2001.

61. Bill Kohlhaase liner notes on Kei Akagi's *Mirror Puzzle* (AudioQuest Music AQ-CD1028).

62. Apparently Keith Jarrett and Tony Williams were both invited but declined. Information given to author by Katia Labèque and Wallace Roney.

63. *The Miles Davis Story*, Part 2, Channel 4.

64. Ibid.

65. Edited from a report by Riccardo Capobianchi on the Miles Davis discussion forum, January 31, 2001.

66. There are persistent rumours of recordings of the concert being officially released. Nick Liebman's liner notes for *The Complete Miles Davis At Montreux* boxed set – released in 2002 – reported that CDs and videos of the concert "will soon be published." More than two years after these words were written, the only officially available material is a one-hour video. The bootleg CD *Black Devil* features the full concert. A full-length video is in private circulation. Apparently one of the biggest hurdles to releasing the material has been getting clearance from all the artists and copyright owners. Warner Bros was planning to put several tracks from the concert on the original six-disc version of the abandoned boxed set *The Last Word*. It seems they were removed in later versions because the company wants to release the La Villette concert at some time.

67. Tingen, *Miles Beyond*, p. 263.

68. Some of this section is taken from a report in *Jet* magazine, October 21, 1991, "500 Honor Miles Davis at N.Y. Memorial Service," pp. 12, 14 and 57; the report's author is uncredited.

Live Around The World

1. *Live Around The World* liner notes.

2. See Enrico Merlin's notes in Paul Tingen, *Miles Beyond: The Electric Explorations of Miles Davis 1967–91* (New York: Billboard Books, 2001), p. 337.

Miles's guest recordings

1. Schechter's comments are taken from an excerpt of his book *The More You Watch, The Less You Know*, which appears on Little Steven's website www.littlesteven.com.

2. Miles Davis and Quincy Troupe, *Miles: The Autobigraphy* (London: Macmillan, 1990), p. 381.

3. Chris Jisi, "Marcus Miller," *Bass Player* (October 1992), p. 46.

4. Taken from the liner notes to Horn's tribute album *I Remember Miles*.

5. Ibid.

The verdict on the music of the 1980s

1. Paul Tingen, *Miles Beyond: The Electric Explorations of Miles Davis 1967–91* (New York: Billboard Books, 2001), p. 266.

2. Crouch in Gary Carner (ed.), *The Miles Davis Companion* (New York: Schirmer Books, 1996), p. 34.

3. Sholto Byrne, "Wynton Marsalis: Miles Davis? He was a rock star," *The Independent*, January 12, 2003.

4. Cornet player Joe "King" Oliver (1885–1938) was Louis Armstrong's mentor and teacher.

5. Paul Tingen, "The Last Unspoken Word on Miles," *Jazziz* (February 2004), p. 45.

25 references

Books

See also Chapter 33 *Books and Websites.*

Carner, Gary, ed. (1996). *The Miles Davis Companion.* New York: Schirmer Books.

Carr, Ian (1998). *Miles Davis: The Definitive Biography.* London: Harper Collins.

Carr, Ian, Digby Fairweather and Brian Priestley (2000). *Jazz: The Rough Guide,* 2nd ed. London: The Rough Guides.

Chambers, Jack (1998). *Milestones: The Music and Times of Miles Davis,* with a new introduction. New York: Da Capo Press.

Cole, Bill (1995). *Miles Davis: The Early Years.* New York: Da Capo Press.

Cook, Richard, and Brian Morton (1996). *The Penguin Guide to Jazz on CD, LP and Cassette.* Harmondsworth: Penguin.

Crease, Stephanie Stein (2002). *Gil Evans Out of the Cool: His Life and Music.* Chicago: Acapella Books.

Davis, Miles (1998). *Apart from Jazz: A Second Miles Davis Legacy.* Tokyo: Vive.

Davis, Miles, and Scott Gutterman (1991). *The Art of Miles Davis.* New York: Prentice Hall Editions.

Davis, Miles, and Quincy Troupe (1989). *Miles: The Autobiography.* London: Macmillan.

Fordham, John (1993). *Jazz.* London: Dorling Kindersley.

Frankl, Ron (1996). *Miles Davis: Black Americans of Achievement.* New York: Chelsea House Publishers.

Hahn, Alex (2003). *Possessed: The Rise and Fall of Prince.* New York: Billboard Books.

Hicock, Larry (2002). *Castles Made of Sound: The Story of Gil Evans.* New York: Da Capo Press.

Karas, Oz, ed. (2001). *Improvisations: The Drawings of Miles Davis.* Lincolnwood, IL: Publication International.

Kent, Nick (1994). *The Dark Stuff.* London: Penguin.

Kirchner, Bill (1997). *A Miles Davis Reader* (Washington, D.C.: Smithsonian Institution Press.

Lohmann, Jan (1992). *The Sound of Miles Davis: The Discography. A Listing of Records and Tapes 1945–1991.* Copenhagen: JazzMedia.

MacDonald, Ian (1997). *Revolution in the Head: The Beatles' Records and the Sixties*, 2nd ed. London: Fourth Estate.

McRae, Barry (1988). *Miles Davis*. London: Apollo Press.

Milkowski, Bill (1998). *Rockers, Jazzbos & Visionaries*. New York: Billboard Books.

Murphy, Chris (2002). *Miles to Go*. New York: Thunder's Mouth Press.

Nelson, George (1999). *Hip Hop America*. New York: Penguin.

Nicholson, Stuart (1998). *Jazz-Rock: A History*. Edinburgh: Canongate.

Nisenson, Eric (1996). *'Round About Midnight: A Portrait of Miles*, updated edition. New York: Da Capo Press.

Ogg, Alex (2002). *The Men Behind Def Jam*. London: Omnibus Press.

Szwed, John (2002). *So What: The Life of Miles Davis*. London: William Heinemann.

Tingen, Paul (2001). *Miles Beyond: The Electric Explorations of Miles Davis 1967–91*. New York: Billboard Books.

Troupe, Quincy (2000). *Miles and Me*. California: University of California Press.

Tynan, Kenneth (1990). *Profiles*. London: Nick Hern Books.

Uchiyama, Shigeru (1993). *Miles Smiles*. Tokyo: Shogakukan.

Various (2001). *Turn It Up 2.0: The Complete Guide to Prince Recordings and Performances*, written and published by the staff of Prince fanzine *Uptown*. Sweden: Linchem.

Wein, George, with Nate Chinen (2003). *Myself Among Others: A Life of Music*. Cambridge, MA: Da Capo Press.

Williams, Richard (1993). *The Man in the Green Shirt*. London: Bloomsbury.

Articles

Anonymous (1991). "500 Honor Miles Davis at N.Y. Memorial Service." *Jet Magazine*. October 21.

Blumenthal, Bob (1982). "Miles Glorious." *Boston Phoenix*, July 7.

Bower, W.A. (1981). "The Man With The Horn Review." *Down Beat* (November).

Byrne, Sholto (2003). "Wynton Marsalis: Miles Davis? He Was a Rock Star." *The Independent*, January 12.

Carr, Ian (1984). "Miles Further Ahead." *Jazz* (Swiss) (July).

—(1991). "Miles Davis" obituary. *The Independent*, September 30.

Carr, Roy (1986). "Man of Many Colours." *New Musical Express*, September 20.

—(1989). "Tales of the Unexpected: Monteux Jazz Festival Review." *New Musical Express*, August 19.

Cleage, Pearl. "Mad at Miles." Reprinted in Carner, ed., *The Miles Davis Companion*.

Cole, George (2002). "Miles Davis Box Set Mystery." *Jazzwise* (November).

Cook, Richard (1985). "Miles Runs the Voodoo Down." *New Musical Express*, July 13.

—(1989). "The Perils of Being a Living Legend." *The Sunday Times*, April 23.

Crouch, Stanley (1990). "Play The Right Thing." *The New Republic*, February 12.

Davis, Francis. "Miles Agonistes." Reprinted in Carner (ed.), *The Miles Davis Companion.*

Dery, Mark, and Bob Doerschuk (1987). "Miles Davis: His Keyboardists Present." *Keyboard* (October).

Doerschuk, Bob (1987). "Jason Miles: Programming and Sessions with Miles Davis." *Keyboard* (October).

—(1987). "Miles Davis: The Picasso of Invisible Art." *Keyboard* (October).

Ephland, John (1988). "Miles to Go." *Down Beat* (October).

Fine, Eric (2003). "Diverse Diva Chaka Khan to Headline." *Out and About Magazine* 16, no. 10 (December).

Fordham, John (1985). "Horn of Plenty." *The Guardian*, July 27.

Franckling, Ken (1986). "Shining a Light on the Prince of Darkness." *JazzTimes* (August).

Freedman, Sam (1983). "Marcus Miller the Thumbslinger: Bassist for Hire." *Down Beat* (April).

Gelly, Dave (1986). "The Eloquent Poser." *The Sunday Times*, November 23.

Guiliano, Mike (undated). "Gary Thomas Directs Jazz Program at Peabody." *Peabody News Online.*

Heckman, Don (1988). "Concert Review." *Jazz Times* (September).

—(1994). "Marcus Miller: All Things in Good Time." *JazzTimes* (April).

Hinson, Hal (1987). "Siesta Review." *Washington Post*, December 28.

Jeske, Lee (1983). "Miles Davis Felt Forum Review." *Down Beat* (April).

Jisi, Chris (1992). "Marcus Miller." *Bass Player* (October).

Jung, Fred (1999). "The Kenny Garrett Interview: My Conversation with Kenny Garrett." All About Jazz.com (July).

Kalbacher, Gene (1984). "Miles Davis: I think that the greatest sound in the world is the human voice." *JAZZ* (April).

Keddie, Gibson (1995). "Tales of the Unexpected." *Bassist* 1, no. 7.

Kent, Nick (1986). "Lightening Up with the Prince of Darkness." *The Face* (October).

Mandel, Howard (1980). "Miles Davis' New Direction is a Family Affair." *Down Beat* (September).

—(1981). "Profile: Bill Evans, Mike Stern and Mino Cinelu." *Down Beat* (November).

McCall, Cheryl (1982). "Miles Davis." *Musician, Player & Listener* 41 (March).

McKinnon, Angus (1989). "Davis Fulfils His Prophesy." *The Sunday Correspondent* (September).

Meyer, Arnold (1988). "Poet-Thinker-Dandy." *Network Press* (July).

Micaleff, Ken (2003). "Al Foster, Drummer, Gentleman, Scholar." *Modern Drummer* (April).

Milkowski, Bill (1987). "Marcus Miller: Miles' Man in the Studio." *Down Beat* (February).

Murray, Charles Shaar (1986). "Tutu review." *Q* (October).

Nilsen, Per, with help from Duane Tudachi (2000/2001). "Y'All Want Some More?" *Uptown* 45 (Winter).

Palmer, Robert (1981). "Jazz Scene: Miles Davis Comeback." *The New York Times,* July 7.

Prange, Carina (2002). "Darryl Jones: Leaving The Stones Unturned." *Jazz Dimensions*, March 21.

Primarck, Ben (1992). "Remembering Miles." *Jazz Times* (January/February).

Richman, Jeff (1981). "Mike Stern's Solo on Fat Time: A Guitar Transcription." *Down Beat* (November).

Robson, Andy (2003). "Speaking Your Language." *Jazzwise* (April).

Rowland, Mark (1987). "Miles Davis is a Living Legend and You're Not." *Musician* (March).

Santaro, Gene Santoro (1988). "Miles Davis: The Enabler Part II." *Down Beat* (November).

Simonart, Serge (1998). "The Artist." *Guitar World* (October).

Street, Mike (2003). "James Brown: The Fifth Element of Hip Hop." Posted June 3 on Bet.com.

Tingen, Paul (1999). "The Miller's Tale." *Sound on Sound* (July).

—(2002). "Miles on Target: The Making of *Tutu*." *JazzTimes* (March).

—(2004). "The Last Unspoken Word on Miles." *Jazziz* (February).

Various (1991). "Sketches of Miles." *Musician* (December).

Watrous, Peter (1989). "Miles Davis: Rebel without a Pause." *Musician*, May 27.

Williams, Richard (1983). "On Top of All That Beat." *The Times*, April 28.

—(1985). "Present Continuous." *The Guardian*, October 27.

Woodard, Josef (1989). "Miles Smiles." *Jazziz* (September).

Zwerin, Mike (1989). "Top Records of the Decade." *International Herald Tribune* (November).

Liner notes

D'Alessio, Joseph (2000). *New Smiles and Traveled Miles* (Groove Note).

Edmonds, Ben (2001). *What's Going On* (Deluxe Edition) (Motown).

Feather, Leonard (1983). *Star People* (CBS).

Gitler, Ira (1998). *I Remember Miles* (Verve).

Holzman, Adam (2002). *Live In Munich* DVD (Pioneer).

Kohlhaase, Bill (1994). *Mirror Puzzle* (AudioQuest).

Liebmann, Nick (2002). *The Complete Miles Davis At Montreux* (Warner Bros: Switzerland).

Meltzer, Gordon (1992). *Doo-Bop* (Warner Bros).

—et al. (1996). *Live Around The World* (Warner Bros).

Metheney, Pat (2000). *Jaco Pastrorius* (Columbia/Legacy).
Nicholson, Stuart (1989). *Amandla* (Warner Bros).
Ogawa, Tokao (1993). *1969: Miles Festiva de Juan Pins* (Sony).

Radio programmes

Carr, Ian, *Tribute to Miles Davis*, BBC Radio 3, 1991.
—*Jazz File*, BBC Radio 3, 2001.
Coltrane, Ravi, *Miles Ten Years After*, BBC Radio 2, 2001.
Sanborn, David, *One Network* (NY), 1986.
Shipton, Alyn, *Jazzmatazz*, BBC World Service, 2001.
Steele, Richard, *Eight Forty Eight*, WBEZ Chicago, 2001.
Troupe, Quincy, and Steve Rowland, *et al.*, *The Miles Davis Radio Project Programme*, American Public Radio, 1990.
Unknown, Uema concert broadcast, SR (Swedish Radio), 1985.

Television and video

Dingo, directed by Rolf De Heer (video).
ESP2: A Tribute To Miles, directed by Christian Wagner (DVD).
Miles Ahead: The Music Of Miles Davis, directed by Mark Obenhaus (TV).
Miles and Friends, directed by Renaud le van Kim (TV).
Miles and Quincy, directed by Gavin Taylor (video).
Miles Davis and His Group, produced by John Abaran (DVD).
Miles Davis: Live In Montreux, directed by Tom O'Neill (DVD).
Miles Davis: Live In Munich, producer John Abaran (DVD).
Miles In Paris, directed by Frank Cassenti (video and DVD).
Scrooged, directed by Richard Donner (DVD).
Siesta, directed by Mary Lambert (video).
Street Smart, directed by Jerry Schatzburg (DVD).
The Hot Spot, directed by Dennis Hopper (DVD).
The Miles Davis Story, directed by Mike Dibb (TV and DVD).

26 compilations
(albums, boxed sets, dvds and videos featuring miles's 1980–1991 music)

This section examines the variety of audio and video releases that contain the music Miles created or performed in his final decade. It does not cover releases such as *Panthallassa* or *Panthallassa The Remixes*, which were released in the 1990s, but which cover the music Miles recorded in 1969–74. However, the video of Miles's last concert at Montreux is included. Although it covers the arrangements of Gil Evans, it is a record of one of Miles's final performances and for this reason alone is of much interest to anyone looking at the performances he gave in his last decade. A separate chapter is devoted to the *Live Around The World* album.

Compilation albums

There have been numerous compilation albums released around the world which include Miles's music of 1980–91. Below is a selection of them. Only the tracks from the final decade are listed. Unless stated, all tracks are album versions.

Blue Moods: Music For You (Columbia/Legacy 1320069)
A compliation of mellow tunes that includes "Time After Time."

Electric Shout (Columbia COL 481063 2)
An Italian release that includes "Back Seat Betty," "Shout," "Star On Cicely," "What It Is," "The Man With The Horn" and "Jean-Pierre" (edit).

Highlights From The Complete Miles Davis At Montreux (Warner Music Switzerland 8573-89895-2)
Released as a taster for *The Complete Miles Davis At Montreux* boxed set (see below) it features "Speak," from July 8, 1984; "Code MD," from July 14, 1985; "Pacific Express," from July 14, 1985; "Jean-Pierre," from July 17, 1986; "Heavy Metal Prelude," from July 7, 1988; "Jilli," from July 21, 1989; and "Hannibal," from July 20, 1990.

Ken Burns Jazz Collection: The Definitive Miles Davis (Sony Jazz 5010332)
A tie-in with the major jazz TV series that includes "Tutu."

Le Meilleur De Miles Davis [*The Best of Miles Davis*] (Columbia COL 478237 2)
A French release that includes "Jean-Pierre" (edit), "What It Is," "Time After Time" and "Human Nature."

Le Meilleur De Miles Davis [*The Best of Miles Davis*] (Columbia COL 493127 2)
Another French release, although this time a double CD release and featuring "Time After Time," "Tutu," "What It Is," "Shout," "MD1/Something's On Your Mind/MD2," "Decoy," "Jean-Pierre" (edit) and "Mr. Pastorius."

Live In Montreux (Act 9001-2)
This double-CD set includes a disc entitled "A Tribute to Neshui Ertegun" (the acclaimed producer). Miles is on one track only, "Portia," taken from the 1989 Montreux Jazz Festival.

Mellow Miles (Columbia 469440 2)
"Time After Time" and "Human Nature."

Miles Davis 1981–89 (Dizionaro enciclopedico del Jazz)
A special Italian release that appeared in 1991 and was licensed by Sony Music Italy. Uniquely amongst all compilation albums, it focuses solely on the music of Miles's final decade. "The Man With The Horn," "Jean-Pierre," "Star People," "Decoy," "Human Nature," "Ms. Morrisine," "Time After Time," "Intro" (from *Aura*), "White" (from *Aura*).

Miles Davis Love Songs (Columbia/Legacy 493389 2)
"Time After Time" (extended 5:34 version) and "Human Nature."

Miles Davis Love Songs 2 (Columbia/Legacy 512886 2)
"Time After Time" and "U 'n' I."

Miles Davis Plays The Ballads (Columbia/Legacy CK 65038)
"Time After Time" (extended 5:34 version).

Miles Davis Story (Columbia COL 467959 2)
A double-CD French compilation featuring "Tutu," "Time After Time," "What It Is," "Jean-Pierre," "Shout," "Mr. Pastorius," "Human Nature," "Come Get It," "Decoy," "MD1/Something's On Your Mind/MD2."

Miles Davis Super Hits (Columbia/Legacy 504731 2)
"Time After Time" and "Human Nature."

Miles Davis: The Best Live (Columbia 469365 2)
"Jean-Pierre."

Miles Davis: The Collection (Castle Communications CCSCD 243)
"What It Is" and "Time After Time."

Mojo Presents... An Introduction To Miles Davis (Columbia 516058 2)
A taster album of Miles's Columbia/Sony Music period from the UK music magazine *Mojo*. Includes "Time After Time" and "Blue."

Portrait: Miles Davis (Jazz Zounds 27200262 G)
A double CD released in Germany that features "Fat Time," "U 'n' I," "What It Is," "You're Under Arrest" and "Orange" (from *Aura*).

Portrait: Miles Davis Electric (Columbia 4978822000)
A French release that includes "Aida," "U 'n' I" and "Human Nature."

The Best of Miles Davis (Columbia/Legacy 1348156)
Includes "Time After Time."

The Essential Miles Davis (Columbia/Legacy STVCD 119)
Released as a companion to *The Miles Davis Story* DVD (see below), it contains "Jean-Pierre" (edit), "Time After Time" and "Portia."

The Essential Miles Davis: Jean Pierre (Columbia 474558 2)
A French release that includes "What It Is," "Jean-Pierre," "Star On Cicely," "Decoy," "Time After Time" and "Come Get It." Oddly, the only other track included is "Pharaoh's Dance" from *Bitches Brew*.

The Very Best Of Miles Davis (Sony Music Entertainment SonyTV 17CD)
"Jean-Pierre," "Human Nature" and "Shout."

This Is Jazz: Electric Miles Davis (Columbia/Legacy CK 65449)
"Aida," "U 'n' I" and "Human Nature." This contains the same music as *Portrait: Miles Davis Electric*.

This Is Miles! Vol. 2 Electric Side (Sony Records SRCS 6842)
A Japanese release that contains "Fat Time," "Back Seat Betty," "Code MD," "One Phone Call/Street Scenes," "Time After Time" (5:34 version) and "The Man With The Horn."

Time After Time (Sony Germany 511398 2)
A double CD set released in Germany that includes "Time After Time" and "Human Nature."

Boxed sets

Miles Davis: The Columbia Years 1955–1985 (CBS CK4 4500)
This four-CD set celebrating Miles's thirty-year association with Columbia Records was originally released in two different CD boxed sets. One version was the same size as an LP record boxed set and contained a large information booklet. The other version was a little larger than a CD case and included a small booklet (with the same content). Both sets contained the same music. The fourth CD, "Electric," contains "What It Is," "Ms. Morrisine," "Shout" and "Star On Cicely." This set has since been re-released with the box packaging replaced by a multi-disc CD case.

The Complete Miles Davis At Montreux 1973–1991 (Warner Music Switzerland 0927-41836-2)
Claude Nobs, the founder and promoter of the Montreux Jazz Festival, had a rule that no artist could appear at the festival for two consecutive years, but when it came to Miles he tore up the rule book. Not only did Miles visit the Montreux Jazz Festival for seven of the last ten years of his life, but he sometimes played two concerts on the same day.

This twenty-disc set is a treasure trove for anyone with an interest in the music Miles played in the final decade. The only downsides are the inevitable high price of the set and the fact that Miles did not visit Montreux in 1981 when he had the Stern/Evans/Miller/Cinelu/Foster combo. However, this omission may be a blessing in disguise, because at that stage of his career Miles was far from his best, both health-wise and in terms of technique. Nor did Miles visit in 1987, when he had what he described as a "motherfucker of a band," featuring Garrett, Foley, Jones, Irving, Holzman, Wellman and Cinelu.

But there is much to enjoy on this set and it provides a fascinating record of how Miles changed both the music and his bands during the 1980s. Two of the CDs cover Miles's 1973 visit when the band featured Pete Cosey, Reggie Lucas, Dave Liebman, Michael Henderson, Al Foster and Mtume. A third disc covers the 1991 concert with Quincy Jones when Miles played with two orchestras to re-create Gil Evans's arrangements. The 20th disc features Miles's last band in concert in Nice in July 1991 and, apart from "Hannibal" on *Live Around The World*, is the only official recording of Miles's last band. Until the release of this boxed set, many of the recordings were only available on bootlegs, so it is good to see this music reach a wider audience, albeit one with deep pockets.

None of the music has been edited or remixed and, generally, the mixes are good and capture the energy and excitement of a Miles live performance. The Montreux performances covered are July 8, 1984 (afternoon and evening); July 14, 1985 (afternoon and evening); July 17, 1986; July 7, 1988; July 21, 1989; and July 20, 1990. The Nice performance was on July 8, 1991. The 1984 and 1985 discs show how the same song could be developed within the same day. It was during these years that Miles's energy levels were approaching their peak and he plays strongly and often without a mute.

The 1986 concert gives Miles fans a chance to hear Robben Ford in the band, as well as hear guest performances from George Duke and David Sanborn. The 1988 and 1989 performances have their moments of interest (such as the performance of "Heavy Metal" in 1988 and Chaka Khan sitting in on "Human Nature" in the 1989 concert). But, at this stage, Miles's music was more highly arranged and many performances were sounding more like re-creations of the album versions. The 1990 concert shows a return to form with the powerful rhythm section of Patterson and Wellman. The 1991 Nice appearance, which saw Miles performing with a pared-down sextet, is excellent, although the set is shorter than normal. Highly recommended – if you can afford the high price.

Miles on video

Miles Davis Live In Montreal DVD (Pioneer PA105220)
This DVD contains most of a concert Miles performed at the Theatre St. Denis, Montreal on June 28, 1985 and features Miles, John Scofield, Robert Irving III, Bob Berg, Darryl Jones, Vince Wilburn Jr. and Steve Thornton. The tunes played are "One Phone Call/Street Scenes," "Speak," "Human Nature," "Something's On Your Mind," "Time After Time," "Code MD" and "Jean-Pierre/You're Under Arrest/Jean-Pierre." The tunes omitted are "Maze," "Hopscotch" and "Star People."

There is a lot of energy in many of the performances, although "Human Nature" sticks to the arrangement on You're Under Arrest. Miles sounds in good lip and Scofield and Berg get plenty of space to solo. Also worth looking out for is the powerful groove laid down by Jones's bass. The DVD extras consist of a short timeline of Miles's life and liner notes describing each song performance. A shame that the DVD didn't include the missing tunes as well.

Miles Davis Live In Munich DVD (Pioneer PA-11853)
A double-CD set that contains almost the entire performance at the Philharmonie in Gasteig in Munich on July 10, 1988 and originally recorded for German television. The band consists of Miles, Garrett, Foley, Irving, Holzman, Rietveld, Wellman and Mazur. The tunes featured are "Perfect Way," "The Senate/Me And You," "Human Nature," "Wrinkle," "Tutu," "Time After Time," "Splatch," "Heavy Metal Prelude," "Heavy Metal," "Don't Stop Me Now," "Carnival Time," "Tomaas," "New Blues" and "Portia."

The sound and picture quality are excellent and so is the performance of the band, which sounds tight. Miles plays a lot and everyone gets a solo spot. The performance also seems looser than others around this period, and there is more scope for improvisation. There are also plenty of extras, including examples of Miles's artwork (which also graces the cover), a biographical timeline of Miles's life and very informative liner notes by keyboardist Adam Holzman, who explains the background and performance of each tune.

The only downsides are that the concert opener "In A Silent Way/Intruder" is omitted and, for some reason, "New Blues," which normally came after the concert opener, is placed almost at the end. The second disc contains a half-hour interview with Miles, but is disappointing, considering the opportunity the interviewer had to ask Miles some really penetrating questions. But, these factors aside, this is an excellent DVD release and of much interest to anyone into Miles's 1980s music.

Miles Davis And His Group DVD (Toshiba EMI TOBW-3012)

A Japanese release featuring excerpts of the above 1988 Munich concert. The tunes included are "Perfect Way," "Hannibal," "Me And You," "Human Nature," "Wrinkle," "Time After Time," "New Blues" and "Portia." Leaving aside the abridged contents of this disc, there are no extras and the picture quality is poor. Avoid this and opt for the double DVD set of the same concert described above.

Miles In Paris DVD (Warner Music Vision 9031-71550-2)

Recorded at the 10th Paris Jazz Festival at Le Zenith in Paris in 1989, the band consists of Miles, Garrett, Foley, Akagi, Rietveld, Wellman and Bigham. Miles's artwork is used on the cover. Although most of the concert is featured – the tunes included are "Human Nature," "Jilli," "Hannibal," "Don't Stop Me Now," "Amandla," "Tutu," "Wrinkle," "New Blues" and "Mr. Pastorius," only "Human Nature" appears in its entirety. The rest of the tunes are interspersed with short interviews of Miles (who talks about politics, music, art and fame) or severely edited.

This title was originally released as a VHS video and the DVD version offers much sharper pictures and sound, but it is a pity that the producers didn't take the opportunity to re-edit the contents and offer full performances. All of Miles's comments could have been put into a separate section, too, so that the continuity of the music and the interview would not have been affected. It would also have been nice to have seen the tunes that had been omitted on the VHS version ("Perfect Way," "The Senate/Me And You," "Carnival Time" and "Full Nelson") included on this DVD. There are no extras, apart from multi-lingual subtitles. Miles's fans will enjoy the opportunity to see him play and talk, but it is a pity that a little more respect wasn't given to his music.

The Miles Davis Story DVD (Legacy CVD 54040)

This two-hour DVD contains the programme that was originally broadcast on the UK's Channel 4 and directed by Mike Dibb. It includes many interviews with Miles's relatives, friends, lovers and musicians through the decades. The first section focuses on Miles's early life and career, with the 1980s and onwards featured in the last 25 minutes. Those interviewed from Miles's later bands include Vince Wilburn Jr., Erin Davis, Marcus Miller, John Scofield and Bill Evans.

There are also short sections showing Miles and his band playing in London in 1982, Miles in the studio during the making of *Aura*, Miles at the *Sun City* sessions, Spike Lee directing the video of "Portia," "The Doo-Bop Song" video and Miles at the La Villette concert in Paris in July 1991. While some might grumble about certain aspects (such as the absence of Teo Macero and a too-short section on Miles's 1970s music), this is a superb documentary of Miles's life.

The DVD extras include a biography of Miles's life and album profiles, which cover the important albums from each era. Sadly, because this DVD was produced by Sony Music, there is no mention of any of Miles's latter albums on Warner Bros, including *Tutu*.

Dingo VHS (Greycat Home Video GC801)

A unique video release in that Miles not only performs much of the soundtrack, but he's also one of the lead actors. *Dingo* was made in Australia and Paris and is the story of a trumpeter, John "Dingo" Anderson (Colin Friels), whose life is transformed when, as a small boy, he sees American trumpeter Billy Cross (Miles) give an impromptu performance at an airstrip at Poona Flat in Australia. Billy Cross's last words to Anderson are that, if he is ever in Paris, he should look him up. The film then fast-forwards to the present where Anderson is a married man who hunts for Dingo (wild dogs) by day and plays trumpet by night. His dream is to go to Paris, find Billy Cross and play with him. But the complication in the story is that, if Anderson goes to Paris, he could lose his wife to an old friend who is back on the scene.

Needless to say, Anderson goes to Paris to pursue his dream. Miles simply plays himself and dispenses some mystical advice to Anderson about "the grass always being greener on the other side." Some of the dialogue has echoes of Miles's own philosophy and life. At one point, Anderson asks Miles why he doesn't play anymore and Miles responds, "I was becoming a jazz museum piece," and we also hear that Cross had had a stroke (Miles had suffered a stroke in early 1982). Miles drives Anderson around Paris, crashes his car and they end up in a jazz club, where Miles jams over a funk number with Anderson and trumpeter Chuck Findley. *Dingo*'s plot is hardly original and, despite his star billing, Miles is absent for large sections of the film. But the film provides an interesting view of another side to Miles's artistic talents.

Miles Davis And Quincy Jones Live At Montreux VHS (Warner Music Video 7599 38342-3)

This concert was recorded at the 25th Anniversary of the Montreux Jazz Festival and saw Miles playing many of Gil Evans's arrangements with The Gil Evans Orchestra and George Gruntz Concert Jazz Band. Quincy Jones conducted proceedings. Also on-stage with Miles is Kenny Garrett and trumpeter Wallace Roney. The video contains additional footage such as Miles arriving by private jet, taking pictures and rehearsing for the concert. Miles looks weak, but he shows immense courage and plays for longer than many of those present had dared hoped. The original performances with Gil Evans are better, but when you consider that Miles would be dead almost two months after this performance it is hard not to be moved by the occasion.

Scrooged DVD (Paramount Home Entertainment PHE8034)
Miles plays a musician in a street band that plays "We Three Kings" in this modern remake of the classic Dickens tale, which stars Bill Murray. Blink and you may miss Miles.

Videos featuring Miles's performances

Siesta VHS (4 Front Video 083 904 3)
This mysterious film directed by Mary Lambert is discussed in a separate chapter. Marcus Miller wrote almost all the music, but Miles adds the magic sound of his trumpet to many of the pieces. The soundtrack features some of Miles's finest playing in his final decade, but if it's just Miles's trumpet sound that you're after give the movie a miss and opt for the soundtrack CD.

Street Smart DVD (MGM 1055341)
Christopher Reeve stars as a journalist who concocts a story about a New York pimp. The problem is that it bears uncanny parallels to real-life pimp, Fast Black (played by Morgan Freeman), and he's soon in trouble with both the police and Black. Robert Irving III wrote the music to the movie and Miles played on many of the cues. One of the best, a driving funk number, "Times Square," has Miles playing some fine horn on both open and muted trumpet. It appears in the movie as Fast Black and his sidekick are being driven through New York's streets. Unfortunately, soon after the tune starts, Black's companion dons a pair of headphones and the music is faded down. The DVD is the only way of hearing the music from this film, as no soundtrack was ever released. Several cues from the movie (including a four-minute version of "Times Square") were to have been included on the abandoned Warner Bros *The Last Word* boxed set.

The Hot Spot DVD (MGM Video 908170)
A film noir set in America's deep south, *The Hot Spot* is directed by Dennis Hopper and stars Don Johnson, who plays a drifter, Harry Madox. Madox sets up a bank robbery and has a woman friend provide an alibi. But the situation becomes more complicated by the arrival of a second woman on the scene. Miles plays on many of the tunes, a number of them with John Lee Hooker.

27 tribute albums

Note that only tunes from the 1980s are listed.

Kei Akagi, *New Smiles And Traveled Miles* (Groove Me GRV1004-2) (includes "Mr. Pastorius").

Children on the Corner, *Rebirth* (Sonance 8236787100820).

George Coleman, Mike Stern, Ron Carter and Jimmy Cobb, *4 Generations Of Miles* (Chesky JD238).

Miles Davis, *Memorial Album* (Blue Note TOCJ-5657).

Dream Session '96: Miles Favorite Songs (Meldac Jazz MECJ-30015).

Endless Miles: A Tribute To Miles (Encoded Music N2K-10027) (includes "Tutu").

Benny Golson, *I Remember Miles* (Evidence 22141).

Gooey Dewey, *Bitches Brew* (Flatbed Lamborgini Records FLR 007).

Tim Hagans and Norrbotten Band, *Future Miles* (Act 9235-2).

Herbie Hancock, Wayne Shorter, Ron Carter, Wallace Roney and Tony Williams, *A Tribute To Miles* (Qwest/Reprise 9362-45059-2).

Eddie Henderson, *So What* (Columbia 510887 2).

Joe Henderson, *So Near, So Far* (Verve 517 674-2).

Shirley Horn, *I Remember Miles* (Verve 557 199-2) (includes the '80s-arranged version of "My Man's Gone Now").

Freddie Hubbard, *Blues For Miles* (Evidence 22139).

Mark Isham, *Miles Remembered: The Silent Way Project* (Columbia CK 69901).

Keith Jarrett Trio, *Bye Bye Blackbird* (ECM 513 074-2).

Henry Kaiser and Wadada Leo Smith, *Yo Miles!* (Shanchie 5046).

—*Yo Miles! Sky Garden* (Cuniform Records RUNE 191/192).

Bill Laswell, *Panthalassa* (Columbia CK 67909).

Mark Ledford, *Miles 2 Go* (Verve Forecast 537 319-2).

Dave Liebman, *Miles Away* (Owl 078 830485 2) (includes "Code MD").

Teo Macero, *Impressions Of Miles Davis* (Teo Records MD0001).

Sal Marquez, *One For Dewey* (GRP 96782).

Orchestre National De Jazz, *Yesternow* (Verve 522 511-2).

Enrico Rava Quintet Plays Miles Davis (Label Bleu LBLC 6639/HM 83).

Humberto Ramirez, *Miles Latino* (AJ records 1310) (includes "Tutu").

Various, *Kind Of Blue: Blue Note Celebrates The Music Of Miles Davis* (Blue Note 7423 5 34255 2 4).

Various, *Panthalassa: The Remixes* (Columbia CK 69897).

Jan Vervey, *The Miles Davis Project* (Willibord Jazz WJ 2076-1).

Cassandra Wilson, *Traveling Miles* (Blue Note 7243 5412325) (includes "Time After Time" and "Resurrection Blues" ["Tutu"]).

World Saxophone Quartet, *Selim Sivad* (Justin Time Just 119-2) (includes "Tutu").

DVD

ESP 2 (Robert Irving III, Adam Holzman, Randy Hall, Ricky Wellman, Mino Cinelu, David McMurray, Victor Bailey, Carla Cook).

A Tribute To Miles (TDK Jazz Club DV-JESP2) (includes "The Man With The Horn").

28 the eighties music – cover versions

Albums containing Miles's 1980s music.

Kei Akagi, *New Smiles And Traveled Miles* (Groove Me GRV1004-2) (includes "Mr. Pastorius").

Chuck Brown and The Soul Searchers, *This Is A Journey… Into Time* (Liaison Records 4) (includes "Tutu").

Dreyfus, *Night In Paris* (Marcus Miller, Kenny Garrett, Michel Petrucciani, Biréli Lagréne, Lenny White) (Dreyfus Jazz FDM 36652-2) (includes "Tutu").

Endless Miles: A Tribute To Miles (Encoded Music N2K-10027) (includes "Tutu").

Foley, *7 Years Ago… Directions In Smart-Alec Music* (MoJaz 374367001-2) (includes "The Senate" and "Little Davis").

Adam Holzman, *Overdrive* (Lipstick Records LIP 89025-2) (includes "Maze").

Shirley Horn, *I Remember Miles* (Verve 557 199-2) (includes the '80s-arranged version of "My Man's Gone Now").

Hotel X, *A Random History Of The Avant-Groove* (SST CD 298) (includes "Tutu").

George Howard, *Do I Ever Cross Your Mind?* (GRP 9669) (includes "Jo-Jo").

The Katia Labèque Band, *Unspoken* (Unspeakable Records UNSP 0001) (includes "Katia").

Dave Liebman, *Miles Away* (Owl 078 830485 2) (includes "Code MD").

Marcus Miller, *Live And More* (Dreyfus Jazz FDM 36585-2) (includes "Tutu").

—*The Ozell Tapes* (Dreyfus Jazz FDM 36640-2) (includes Miles medley ["Hannibal"/"Amandla"/"Tutu"]).

George Mraz, *Bottom Lines* (Milestone MCD-9272-2) (includes "Mr. Pastorius").

Viktoria Mullova, *Through The Looking Glass* (Philips 464 184-2) (includes "Robot 415" – original, duo, waltz, psycho and solo versions).

Humberto Ramirez, *Miles Latino* (AJ records 1310) (includes "Tutu").

Gary Thomas, *By Any Means Necessary* (JMT 919 031-2) (includes "You're Under Arrest").

Cassandra Wilson, *Traveling Miles* (Blue Note 7243 8 54123 2 5) (includes "Time After Time" and "Resurrection Blues" ["Tutu"]).

World Saxophone Quartet, *Selim Sivad* (Justin Time Just 119 2) (includes "Tutu").

29 unreleased miles – the music in the vaults

Whenever any major artist dies, there is always much interest and speculation over any unreleased works. The hope is that there are unseen gems waiting to be uncovered. So it was no surprise that, when Miles died, both his fans and his record company's executives were keen to know what was left in the tape vaults. In the case of Miles, the answer was: rather a lot. For almost all his entire career, Miles spent a vast amount of time in the recording studio, a fact readily evidenced by his enormous back catalogue.

The number of recording sessions he attended increased at an exponential rate in the 1970s, as his electric music and studio technology became intertwined. Between 1970 and his retirement in 1975, Miles released a dozen albums (almost all of them doubles). And when he was out of action in the mid-1970s, Columbia raided its vaults and released two more double albums, *Directions* and *Circle In The Round*. What is more, the tapes were invariably rolling all the time whenever Miles worked in the recording studio and nothing was ever thrown away. It was by using this material that producer Bill Laswell was able to create *Panthalassa*, a remix album of Miles's 1970s recordings.

Although Miles set a less hectic work pace in the final decade of his life, he was still in and out of the studio a lot, especially between late 1983 and 1987. Miles's death in 1991 has spawned a veritable industry based around his unreleased music. The Miles Davis Estate – which includes Miles's daughter Cheryl, nephew Vince Wilburn Jr., his youngest son Erin and his legal representatives – has worked with Columbia Records to produce a series of multi-disc sets covering various periods of his musical career. The sets, issued under the Columbia/Legacy banner, have included Miles's work with Gil Evans and John Coltrane, as well as releases covering albums such as *Jack Johnson*, *Bitches Brew* and *In A Silent Way*. Each set has been sumptuously packaged, with extensive session information and liner notes, and the music has also been remastered and remixed. In many cases, multiple takes of the same song are included in the package, allowing listeners to hear how a tune developed into its final form. The reissue sets have been generally well received by both fans and critics alike, and have won numerous Grammy awards.

But their release has also caused discomfort – even anger – in some quarters, not least because Miles has of course had no say over whether the music should ever have been released. Teo Macero, who produced much of the original material that has since been released under the Columbia/Legacy series, was originally asked to participate in the reissue project, but says he pulled out after he became unhappy with the direction the record company wanted to take. "They told me they wanted to do it their way. I said 'I'm not going to demean the importance of Miles Davis as an artist and put out a bunch of crap that I think is inferior and what we agreed was inferior,'" he explains. "They were making enough money and are still making enough money, and to make a few more thousands of dollars it's ridiculous. Instead of leaving a Picasso painting the way it is, why throw up all the outtakes, the out-paintings and say this is a reissue of all his paintings? Why do that? In the meantime, they've lost my opinion of them and it's degraded Miles in such a way that it shouldn't have been done. To put all the shit back in that we took out, even in the *Plugged Nickel* and the other things, and to say 'Later on, we discovered this, we discovered that.' Bullshit. I never erased anything we did with Miles. That was my first mistake. I should have destroyed it all. This doesn't add to history." But those behind the reissue project insist that their motives are pure. "I know people like Teo think it's about the bread, but it's about Miles," says Wilburn.

Dave Holland has mixed feelings about the reissue project. "We're now faced with all the endless issues of every outtake he ever did. As a study of a [recording] process, it's interesting, but then one has to ask 'Is this what Miles would have wanted?' We'll never know, but I somehow think not. Knowing his work and how seriously he took what he put out, I can't help but think that six versions of a piece that show the process of how he got there are not necessarily what he would have wanted. One's tempted to think of this as a commercial venture on the part of the people associated with the project, in order to capitalize on Miles's music. Personally, I find it a little bit over the top. On the other hand, one of the CDs I've bought in recent years is the Miles Davis/Gil Evans collection and I find that fascinating to hear Miles trying things out in the rehearsals and seeing how that evolved into the final take."

What is clear is that there is an immense appetite amongst sections of Miles's fans for hearing everything he recorded – good or bad. But there is a balance to be struck between feeding this demand by issuing outtakes, mistakes, alternate takes and half-abandoned musical explorations, and demeaning Miles's name and reputation in the process. Miles himself appeared quite relaxed about the notion of reissuing his work. He told writer Nick Kent in an interview that took place after he had left Columbia Records for Warner Bros, "Did I relinquish my rights to my unreleased stuff on CBS? Well, yeah, but it don't scare me, hell no! Hell, they put that shit out, it won't sell. There's enough old shit of mine bein' released as it is. I never see any of it toppin' the charts. No one wants to buy it. Why should they?" (from Nick Kent, "Lightening Up with the Prince of Darkness"). At the time of writing, Columbia has announced no plans to reissue any material from Miles's 1980s period, while Warner Bros abandoned one retrospective project – see below.

The Last Word project

Around May 2001, it was announced that Warner Bros was preparing a retrospective based around the recordings Miles did with the company – that is, from September 1985 to July 1991. The project was handled by Matt Pierson, then head of Warner Bros jazz division and Adam Holzman, Miles's former musical director. The release, known as *The Last Word: The Warner Bros Years*, was to be a six-CD set that included a mix of Miles's studio albums (*Tutu*, *Siesta*, *Amandla* and *Doo-Bop*), plus soundtrack recordings, guest recordings, live recordings and unreleased studio material. The release date was set for September 2001 and writer Paul Tingen was commissioned to write the liner notes.

The six-CD set's tracks included:
"Maze" (one of the first recordings Miles did for Warner Bros)
"Rubberband" and "See I See" (from the 1985/86 *Rubberband* sessions)
"Can I Play With U?" (performed with Prince)
"Digg That" (with John Bigham and Jeff Lorber)
"Jailbait" (a studio recording of a Prince song)
"Big Ol' Head" (with Kenny Garrett)
"Sticky Wicked" (with Chaka Khan)
"In The Night" (with Cameo)
"Don't Stop Me Now" (with Toto)
"You Won't Forget Me" (with Shirley Horn)
"Capri" (with Paolo Rustichelli)
"The Struggle Continues" (Artists United Against Apartheid)
"Prisoners" (from the *Alfred Hitchcock Presents* TV series)
"Street Smart" (several cues from the soundtrack)
"Siesta Cues" (music not used on the soundtrack CD)
"We Three Kings" (from the film *Scrooged*)
"Penetration" (a live version of a Prince tune played at the reunion concert at La Villette, Paris, in July 1991)
"In A Silent Way/It's About That Time" (from La Villette)
"Tutu" (from the NBC TV programme, *Night Music*)
"Time After Time" (from Nice 1986)
"Opening Medley" (from Nice 1986)
"Portia" (from Montreux 1986)

Nine tracks from *The Hot Spot* soundtrack – "Coming To Town," "Empty Bank," "Harry And Dolly," "Sawmill," "Bank Robbery," "Harry Sets Up Sutton," "Murder," "Blackmail" and "End Credits."

Seven tracks from the *Dingo* soundtrack – "The Arrival," "Concert On The Runway," "The Departure," "Trumpet Cleaning," "The Dream," "Paris Walking II" and "Going Home."

But *The Last Word*'s release date came and went and, in late 2001, the concept was changed to a five-disc release, with the first four discs featuring *Tutu*, *Siesta*, *Amandla* and *Doo-Bop* and the fifth disc containing live recordings, guest appearances and unreleased material. As far as is known, the five-disc set was never produced. In February 2002, it was revealed that *The Last Word* would now be a four-disc set and released in June on Rhino Records, Warner Bros' reissue label. Paul Tingen was replaced by Bill Milkowski as the liner notes writer.

In May, Rhino Records announced that *The Last Word* would be released in August 2002. More information was given about the boxed set on the company's website. "The Last Word boxed set cover is a striking image of Davis shot by photographer Anton Corbijn. With an opaque frosted-plastic O-card and four individual CD wallets, the brick-sized packaging is 5 1/4" wide x 5 3/8" high x 1 1/2" deep. The 80-page silver metallic-covered book includes an introduction by Matt Pierson and an extensive essay by jazz writer Bill Milkowski. Additionally, the liner notes feature tributes to Davis' career by an all-star cast of his colleagues, including Chick Corea, George Duke, Jack DeJohnette, Easy Mo Bee, Herbie Hancock, Dave Holland, Quincy Jones, Tommy LiPuma, Joseph 'Foley' McCreary, John McLaughlin, Marcus Miller, Wallace Roney, David Sanborn, John Scofield, Mike Stern, Vince Wilburn Jr., and the late Tony Williams."

Review copies were sent out to the press in the form of four CD-R (white label) discs with no artwork. The contents revealed that *The Last Word*'s track listing had changed radically from its original inception.

Disc One consisted of the *Tutu* album with "Rubberband," "See I See," "Digg That" and *Street Smart* cues.

Disc Two consisted of the *Siesta* album and three tracks from *The Hot Spot* ("Murder," "Coming to Town" and "Bank Robbery"). And seven tracks from the *Dingo* soundtrack ("The Arrival," "Concert On The Runway," "The Departure," "Trumpet Cleaning," "The Dream," "Paris Walking II" and "Going Home").

Disc Three consisted of the *Amandla* album with "The Struggle Continues," "Don't Stop Me Now," "In The Night," "Big Ol' Head," "Capri" and "You Won't Forget Me."

Disc Four consisted of the album *Doo-Bop* plus "Opening Medley" and "Time After Time," from Nice 1986; "Portia," from Montreux 1986; and "Tutu," "Mr. Pastorius" and "Hannibal," from the TV series *Night Music*.

In July, full-page adverts for *The Last Word* appeared in the specialist music press and reviews appear online and in print: for example, in *Jazziz*, August

2002, and on All About Jazz.com, August 2002. But just before *The Last Word* reached the stores, it was pulled. David Dorn, VP of Media Relations for Warner Strategic Marketing, told the online magazine *ICE* on July 30, 2002: "We deeply regret the fact that we will not be releasing [*The Last Word*] on August 20. Our commitment has always been to offer consumers the best possible audio and video products for the best possible value. Due to developing circumstances beyond our control, we felt that this box set would not, in its finished form, meet our standards, or the standards our customers expect from our products." Matt Pierson blamed the refusal of Prince to allow several of his tunes ("Jail-bait," "Penetration" and "Can I Play With U?") to be included in the boxed set.

At least one copy of *The Last Word* appeared on the online auction site eBay, and bids topped the $1,000 mark. In Japan, a double-CD bootleg album, *The Black Album*, features all the unreleased material from *The Last Word* four-disc set, plus several other unreleased tracks from Miles's 1980s recordings on Columbia Records. At the time of writing, there are no plans to reissue *The Last Word*.

What lies in the vaults – unreleased music 1980–1991

The following section focuses on the unreleased material from 1980–1991 that lies in the tape vaults of Columbia and Warner Bros Records. The listing does not include the numerous radio and TV recordings that were made during this period, with just a few exceptions, nor does it include sound board tapes. All of Miles's concerts were recorded by his concert sound engineers, many of them onto DAT digital tape. Miles's method of working in the studio (with the tapes rolling) means that almost all of his music has been edited, in some cases radically. Percussionist Steve Thornton says that Miles often recorded several takes of the same song.

Summer 1980: The Man With The Horn *sessions*
The group of young Chicagoan musicians that included Vince Wilburn Jr. recorded more than a dozen tracks, although most of them contain no trumpet. Miles definitely overdubbed on two tracks ("Shout" and "The Man With The Horn") and Glenn Burris, who was present at some of the sessions, says Miles played a solo on a third track, "I'm Blue," which at one stage was being considered for the title track.

In his book *Milestones*, writer Jack Chambers has suggested that, during this period, Miles went into the studio with Karlheinz Stockhausen, Paul Buckmaster and others (see Chambers, *Milestones*, p. 301). Yet Chambers provides no reference for this momentous event and, what is more, Stockhausen's son Markus says his father never met Miles (see Carr, *Miles Davis*, p. 350).

Buckmaster says he wasn't there. "I don't know where Jack Chambers got the story of Miles, Wayne Shorter, Karlheinz Stockhausen and me being present together for recording sessions around 1980, or at any other time. I can aver that if there were any such sessions I certainly was not present. I heard a rumour somewhere that there had been sessions with Miles and Karlheinz Stockhausen, but although the idea is very exciting to me I don't believe that this ever happened. I'm sure that this would have been widely known and, even if there were no official releases, I'm sure something would have got out, maybe one of the engineers or the musicians would have leaked something – hell, Miles would have talked about it! In this case Columbia [Records] too – what about the PR value of such an event!"

Early 1981: "Back Seat Betty." The track that appears on *The Man With The Horn* is an edited version of a 14-minute master that includes a longer soprano saxophone solo by Bill Evans. The band also recorded an alternative 17:36 take, which has a different groove and feel to the one that appears on the album.

June 26–29, 1981. All of Miles's Kix concerts (Miles played at least eight concerts) were recorded by Columbia Records, as well as rehearsals. At least one of them was also videoed. So far, only several tracks – "Fast Track," "Kix" and "My Man's Gone Now" – from the first concert on the 27 June, have appeared on the *We Want Miles* album.

July 5, 1981. Avery Fisher Hall concert. The full concert was recorded, but only an edited version of "Back Seat Betty" has been released.

October 2–11, 1981: Japan Tour. Ron Lorman, who was Miles's concert sound engineer at the time, says Teo Macero recorded most if not all of the seven concerts on the Japanese tour. "Jean-Pierre," from the 4 October concert, appears on *We Want Miles* and the 4 October concert was released in Japan as a double CD under the title *Miles! Miles! Miles!*

August 28, 1982: "Come Get It." This was taken from a performance from the Jones Beach Theatre and three minutes were edited from the version on *Star People*. The missing section is largely from Bill Evan's soprano saxophone solo.

January 5, 1983. A 19-minute version of "It Gets Better" is in existence.

June 30, 1983: "Freaky Deaky." An alternative version of this, featuring Miles playing trumpet, is known to exist.

July 7, 1983. "That's What Happened" is an edit from the final section of a 12-minute version of "Speak," recorded live in Montreal.

July 7, 1983. The 4:32 version of "What It Is" on *Decoy* has been edited from a 7:17 version, also recorded live in Montreal.

June 30 – September 11, 1983. Miles was in and out of the studios during these days, recording tracks for the *Decoy* album. John Scofield says a track featuring Branford Marsalis was left off the album on executive producer George Butler's advice. The most likely dates for this recording session are July 2 or August 29. Robert Irving III says a jam session was also recorded at the sessions.

November 17, 1983 – April 14, 1984. Miles attended at least eleven recording sessions between these periods and many of them were used for a planned album of pop ballads arranged by Gil Evans, but the project was abandoned. According to John Scofield, some forty tracks were recorded, including several Toto compositions, Tina Turner's "What's Love Got to Do With It?" Dionne Warwick's "Déjà Vu," as well as Lionel Richie songs and Kenny Loggins's "This Is It." (see Kent's "Lightening Up," p. 273). On January 26, 1984, "Time After Time" was recorded and at least three versions are known to be existence. A 3:37 version appears on *You're Under Arrest* and a 5:32 version appears on a 12-inch single and on several compilation albums. An 8:25 version is also known to exist.

1983–85. John Scofield says he recorded some material with Miles, with Scofield playing acoustic guitar.

Early May 1984. Bob Berg's first sessions involved recording some funk-oriented music that was never released.

September 22, 1984. A version of "Ms. Morrisine" featuring John Scofield on guitar was recorded at this session.

December 26–27, 1984. At the very last moment, Miles scrapped much of the music that had been destined for his next album and started afresh. The result was the *You're Under Arrest* album. In the process, Miles threw out several ballads and he scrapped plans to use a ballad version of "Something's On Your Mind," opting to re-record it as an uptempo tune.

January 1985. "Katia" was edited from a longer take.

September 23 and 24, 1985. Miles recorded at least two tracks: "Maze" and "Broken Wings."

October 1985. Miles, Robert Irving III and percussionist Steve Reid recorded music for the episode "Prisoners" for the NBC TV series *Alfred Hitchcock Presents*.

October 1985 – January 1986. Miles spent several months in and out of the studios with producers Randy Hall and Zane Giles in what became known as "The *Rubberband* sessions." Around a dozen tracks were recorded, including "Rubberband," "Wrinkle," "Give It Up," "It's Not A Waste of Time," "See I See," "This Is It," "Carnival Time," "Let's Fly Away," "I Love What We Make Together" and "No Time For Showtime." On all but the last track, Miles plays horn and he may also have played keyboards on "No Time For Showtime." There are at least three different mixes of "Rubberband," and two mixes of "See I See" in circulation. Miles has played some of these tunes live ("Rubberband," "Wrinkle," "Carnival Time" and "I Love What We Make Together" as "Al Jarreau"). His horn parts on "Give It Up" and (probably) "Let's Fly Away" were used on "High Speed Chase" and "Fantasy" respectively on the *Doo-Bop* album.

October 28, 1985. Miles had expected a concert recorded in Copenhagen, Denmark, would be released by Columbia Records, suggesting that the music company had recorded this event on a remote recording unit. It was recorded by Danish radio and broadcast in its entirety.

February 6, 1986: "Can I Play With U?" Miles and keyboardist Adam Holzman (and possibly percussionist Steve Reid) overdubbed their parts on a tune written and performed by Prince. At least two versions are known to exist, one lasts for 3:53 and the other is 6:35 in length. *The Last Word* was to have used the longer version.

February 10 – March 25, 1986. *Tutu* sessions violinist Michal Urbaniak claims to have recorded on some unreleased tracks from these sessions, but both Marcus Miller and Jason Miles confirm that there is no unused music. For more discussion on this, see the chapter on *Tutu*.

June 13, 1986: Nice, France. Warner Bros recorded this concert.

July 15, 1986. A second concert at Nice was recorded by Warner Bros.

July 16, 1986. A third concert at Nice was recorded by Warner Bros.

July 20, 1986. A fourth concert was recorded by Warner Bros at Nice.

October 1986: *Street Smart* soundtrack. Miles overdubbed a number of trumpet parts on many (but not all) of the cues used in this movie. The cue lengths vary from less than one minute to almost four minutes.

March 1987: *Siesta.* A number of cues (not all of them featuring Miles) were not used in the soundtrack. The six-disc version of *The Last Word* was to have been included ten minutes of unused cues.

December 31, 1987. Miles joined Prince and his band on-stage for the tune "It's Gonna Be A Beautiful Night," although Miles plays only for around four minutes. Prince claims to have recorded long improvisational pieces with Miles, which he says he will release at some point (see the chapter on Prince and Miles).

Unknown date, 1987. Guitarist John Bigham says he went into the studio and recorded "four or five" tunes with Miles, including a track called "Naked."

December 21, 1987. Miles, John Bigham and Jeff Lorber recorded "Digg That."

May 2, 1988. A concert in Melbourne, Australia, was recorded by Warner Bros.

June 29, 1988: *CK* sessions. Chaka Khan says about Miles: "He did, like, four cuts with me. We were friends for many years, and it was wonderful to work with him" (from "Diverse Diva Chaka Khan to Headline" by Eric Fine in *Out and About Magazine* Vol. 16 No. 10, December 2003). Only two cuts, "Sticky Wicked" and "I'll Be Around," were issued on Khan's *CK* album.

September 1988 – January 1989: *Amandla* sessions. Marcus Miller says he is certain that there are some unused tracks left over from these sessions; however, Miles may not have played on any of them.

July 21, 1989. Miles recorded an alternate version of "Capri" with Paolo Rustichelli. They also recorded another track, possibly called "Artemisia."

December 21, 1990: "Strawberry Fields Forever." Miles and Kenny Garrett travelled to Japan to perform in a John Lennon tribute concert in Tokyo. They performed this song to a taped backing track. John Bigham also wrote some music for this event and recorded it onto tape for Miles, although it is not known whether Miles performed it at the concert.

Unknown date, 1991. Paolo Rustichelli says he and Miles went into the studio in Los Angeles two or three times in this period and recorded six or seven untitled tunes together.

March 27, 1991. Miles took his band into a studio in Germany to record several tunes written by Prince. One of them was "Jailbait," and the others were probably "Penetration" and "A Girl And Her Puppy." According to Gordon Meltzer, Miles's tour manager at the time, Miles recorded "guide tracks" and planned to re-record his horn parts back in the U.S. He never did, but Warner Bros remixed at least one track ("Jailbait"), which was deemed good enough for inclusion on the six-disc version of *The Last Word*.

July 10, 1991. Miles performed at a giant reunion concert at La Grande Halle, La Villete in Paris, which saw him playing with many old band members. The tunes performed were:

"Penetration," "Perfect Way," "Star People/New Blues" and "Human Nature" with Miles's current band comprised of Miles, Kenny Garrett (saxophone), Foley (lead bass), Deron Johnson (keyboards), Richard Patterson (bass) and Ricky Wellman (drums).

"All Blues" with Miles, Steve Grossman (saxophone), Bill Evans (saxophone), Chick Corea (electric piano), Dave Holland (bass) and Al Foster (drums).

"In A Silent Way/It's About That Time" with Miles, Wayne Shorter (saxophone), Joe Zawinul (keyboards), Richard Patterson (bass) and Al Foster (drums)

"Katia," with Miles, John McLaughlin (guitar), John Scofield (guitar), Deron Johnson (keyboards), Darryl Jones (bass) and Ricky Wellman (drums).

"Dig" with Miles, Jackie McLean (saxophone), Steve Grossman (saxophone), Chick Corea (electric piano), Dave Holland (bass) and Al Foster (drums).

"Watermelon Man" with Miles, Herbie Hancock and Deron Johnson (keyboards), Kenny Garrett, Bill Evans (saxophones), Foley (lead bass), Richard Patterson (bass) and Al Foster (drums).

"Wrinkle" with Miles, Kenny Garrett (saxophone), Deron Johnson (keyboards), Foley (lead bass), Darryl Jones (bass) and Ricky Wellman (drums).

"Footprints" featuring Miles, Wayne Shorter (saxophone), Chick Corea (electric piano), Dave Holland (bass) and Al Foster (drums).

"Jean-Pierre" with Miles (trumpet and keyboards), Deron Johnson, Chick Corea (keyboards), Bill Evans, Kenny Garrett, Jackie McLean, Steve Grossman (saxophones), John McLaughlin, John Scofield (guitar), Foley (lead bass), Dave Holland, Darryl Jones, Richard Patterson (bass) and Al Foster, Ricky Wellman (drums).

August 25, 1991. Miles's final concert at The Hollywood Bowl in California was recorded onto low-fi audio concert by his concert sound engineer.
At least one recording from this tape, "Hannibal," was digitally cleaned and
processed and an edited version appears on the *Live Around The World* album.
The album contains a 7:20 edited version.

30 miles's live repertoire 1981–1991

This list contains the tunes Miles and his bands played on-stage during the last decade. Not included are Miles's July 1991 Montreux appearance (where he played the arrangements of Gil Evans), TV appearances or his reunion concert at La Villette in 1991, where he performed a mix of old and new tunes. Miles also played some songs which remain unidentified.

Song titles in square brackets [ ] are the correct name, although they are more commonly known by the alternative and incorrect name. Some songs have more than one title and the alternative is placed inside round brackets (). "Star People" and "New Blues" are listed twice because the latter evolved out of the former. Songs marked with an asterix* have, at the time of writing, not appeared on any official Miles Davis album release. "Wayne's Tune/Bookends" is marked with a double asterix because the tune is included on albums that are available in high-street stores in Europe. "Ife" can be found on Miles's albums released in the 1970s, but the alternative 1980s arrangement has not been released, which is why it is marked as an unreleased title.

A Girl And Her Puppy*	Come Get It
A Go-Go Beat[1]*	Decoy
A Love Bizarre/Hopscotch*	Don't Lose Your Mind
Al Jarreau [I Love What We Make Together]	Don't Stop Me Now
Amandla	Fast Track (Aida)
Back Seat Betty	Fat Time
Broken Wings*	Freaky Deaky
Burn	Full Nelson
Carnival Time	Hannibal
Code MD	Heavy Metal

---

1. This title has been given by Miles's discographer Jan Lohmann to an instrumental that showcased the drumming of Ricky Wellman, and during which Miles remarked, "Now that's what I call a go-go beat!"

Heavy Metal Prelude (Funk Suite)

Hopscotch

Human Nature

Ife*

In A Silent Way

In The Night*

Intruder

It Gets Better

Jailbait*

Jean-Pierre

Jean-Pierre/You're Under Arrest/Then
There Were None medley

Jilli

Jo-Jo

Katia

Kix

La Marseillaise*

Lake Geneva

Little Davis*

Maze

Movie Star

Mr. Pastorius

Ms. Morrisine

My Man's Gone Now

New Blues (Star People)

One Phone Call/Street Scenes

Pacific Express

Penetration*

Perfect Way

Portia

R U Legal Yet?*

Rubberband*

Something's On Your Mind

Speak (That's What Happened)

Splatch

Star On Cicely

Star People (New Blues)

Stronger Than Before*

That's Right

The Senate/Me And You

Time After Time

Tomaas

Tutu

U 'n' I

Wayne's Tune [Bookends]**

What It Is

What's Love Got To Do With It?*

Wrinkle

You're Under Arrest

31 miles's band line-ups 1981–1991

Note: Miles had a long lay-off from touring between November 1983 and June 1984, and between November 1990 and March 1991.

Key

b, bass; dr, drums; elp, electric piano; g, guitar; keyb, keyboard; lb, lead bass; per, percussion; s, saxophone; tp, trumpet

June 26, 1981 – November 1982
Miles (tp, elp), Mike Stern (g), Bill Evans (s), Marcus Miller (b), Al Foster (dr), Mino Cinelu (per)

November 7, 1982 – February 1983
Miles (tp, keyb), Mike Stern (g), John Scofield (g), Bill Evans (s), Marcus Miller (b), Al Foster (dr), Mino Cinelu (per)

February 3, 1983 – June 1983
Miles (tp, keyb), Mike Stern (g), John Scofield (g), Bill Evans (s), Tom Barney (b), Al Foster (dr), Mino Cinelu (per)

June 7–28, 1983
Miles (tp, keyb), Mike Stern (g), John Scofield (g), Bill Evans (s), Darryl Jones (b), Al Foster (dr), Mino Cinelu (per)

June 29, 1983 – August 1983
Miles (tp, keyb), John Scofield (g), Bill Evans (b), Darryl Jones (b), Al Foster (dr), Mino Cinelu (per)

August 15, 1983 – November 1983
Miles (tp, keyb), John Scofield (g), Robert Irving III (keyb), Bill Evans (s), Darryl Jones (b), Al Foster (dr), Mino Cinelu (per)

June 1, 1984 – March 1985
Miles (tp, keyb), John Scofield (g), Robert Irving III (keyb), Bob Berg (s), Darryl Jones (b), Al Foster (dr), Steve Thornton (per)

March 1985 – August 1985
Miles (tp, keyb), John Scofield (g), Robert Irving III (keyb), Bob Berg (s), Darryl Jones (b), Vince Wilburn Jr. (dr), Steve Thornton (per)

August 17, 1985 – October 1985
Miles (tp, keyb), Mike Stern (g), Robert Irving III (keyb), Bob Berg (s), Angus Thomas (b), Vince Wilburn Jr. (dr), Steve Thornton (per), Marilyn Mazur (per)

October 24, 1985 – March 1986
Miles (tp, keyb), Mike Stern (g), Robert Irving III (keyb), Adam Holzman (keyb), Bob Berg (s), Angus Thomas (b), Vince Wilburn Jr. (dr), Steve Thornton (per), Marilyn Mazur (per)

March 1986 – April 1986
Miles (tp, keyb), Mike Stern (g), Robert Irving III (keyb), Adam Holzman (keyb), Bob Berg (s), Felton Crews (b), Vince Wilburn Jr. (dr), Steve Thornton (per), Marilyn Mazur (per)

April 4, 1986 – June 1986
Miles (tp, keyb), Robben Ford (g), Robert Irving III (keyb), Adam Holzman (keyb), Bob Berg (s), Felton Crews (b), Vince Wilburn Jr. (dr), Steve Thornton (per), Marilyn Mazur (per)

June 1986 – September 1986
Miles (tp, keyb), Robben Ford (g), Robert Irving III (keyb), Adam Holzman (keyb), Bob Berg (s), Felton Crews (b), Vince Wilburn Jr. (dr), Steve Thornton (per)

September 8, 1986 – October 1986
Miles (tp, keyb), Garth Webber (g), Robert Irving III (keyb), Adam Holzman (keyb), Bob Berg (s), Felton Crews (b), Vince Wilburn Jr. (dr), Steve Thornton (per)

October 21, 1986 – December 1986
Miles (tp, keyb), Garth Webber (g), Robert Irving III (keyb), Adam Holzman (keyb), Bob Berg (s), Darryl Jones (b), Vince Wilburn Jr. (dr), Steve Thornton (per)

December 28–31, 1986
Miles (tp, keyb), DeWayne "Blackbyrd" McKnight (g), Robert Irving III (keyb),
Adam Holzman (keyb), Bob Berg (s), Gary Thomas (s), Darryl Jones (b), Vince
Wilburn Jr. (dr), Steve Thornton (per)

January 24 – February 1987
Miles (tp, keyb), Hiram Bullock (g), Robert Irving III (keyb), Adam Holzman
(keyb), Bob Berg (s), Gary Thomas (s), Darryl Jones (b), Vince Wilburn Jr. (dr),
Mino Cinelu (per)

February 26 – March 1987
Miles (tp, keyb), Bobby Broom (g), Robert Irving III (keyb), Adam Holzman
(keyb), Kenny Garrett (s), Gary Thomas (s), Darryl Jones (b), Vince Wilburn
Jr. (dr), Mino Cinelu (per)

March 25, 1987 – end March 1987 (except March 27)
Miles (tp, keyb), Bobby Broom (g), Robert Irving III (keyb), Adam Holzman
(keyb), Kenny Garrett (s), Gary Thomas (s), Darryl Jones (b), Ricky Wellman
(dr), Mino Cinelu (per)

March 27, 1987 only
Miles (tp, keyb), Alan Burroughs (g), Robert Irving III (keyb), Adam Holzman
(keyb), Kenny Garrett (s), Gary Thomas (s), Darryl Jones (b), Ricky Wellman
(dr), Mino Cinelu (per)

May 15, 1987 – October 1987
Miles (tp, keyb), Foley (lb), Robert Irving III (keyb), Adam Holzman (keyb),
Kenny Garrett (s), Darryl Jones (b), Ricky Wellman (dr), Mino Cinelu (per)

October 19, 1987 – April 1988
Miles (tp, keyb), Foley (lb), Robert Irving III (keyb), Adam Holzman (keyb),
Kenny Garrett (s), Darryl Jones (b), Ricky Wellman (dr), Rudy Bird (per)

April 9, 1988 – October 1988
Miles (tp, keyb), Foley (lb), Robert Irving III (keyb), Adam Holzman (keyb),
Kenny Garrett (s), Benny Rietveld (b), Ricky Wellman (dr), Marilyn Mazur
(per)

October 7, 1988 – March 1989
Miles (tp, keyb), Foley (lb), Joey DeFrancesco (keyb), Adam Holzman (keyb),
Kenny Garrett (s), Benny Rietveld (b), Ricky Wellman (dr), Marilyn Mazur
(per)

March 25, 1989 – June 1989
Miles (tp, keyb), Foley (lb), Kei Akagi (keyb), John Beasley (keyb), Kenny Garrett (s), Benny Rietveld (b), Ricky Wellman (dr), Munyungo Jackson (per)

June 3, 1989 – July 1989
Miles (tp, keyb), Foley (lb), Kei Akagi (keyb), Adam Holzman (keyb), Kenny Garrett (s), Benny Rietveld (b), Ricky Wellman (dr), Munyungo Jackson (per)

July 1989 – August 1989
Miles (tp, keyb), Foley (lb), Kei Akagi (keyb), Adam Holzman (keyb), Rick Margitza (s), Benny Rietveld (b), Ricky Wellman (dr), Munyungo Jackson (per)

August 24, 1989 – October 1989
Miles (tp, keyb), Foley (lb), Kei Akagi (keyb), Adam Holzman (keyb), Kenny Garrett (s), Benny Rietveld (b), Ricky Wellman (dr), Munyungo Jackson (per)

October 29, 1989 – April 1990
Miles (tp, keyb), Foley (lb), Kei Akagi (keyb), Kenny Garrett (s), Benny Rietveld (b), Ricky Wellman (dr), John Bigham (per)

April 19, 1990 – c. June 1990
Miles (tp, keyb), Foley (lb), Kei Akagi (keyb), Kenny Garrett (s), Richard Patterson (b), Ricky Wellman (dr), John Bigham (per)

c. June 1990 – November 1990
Miles (tp, keyb), Foley (lb), Kei Akagi (keyb), Kenny Garrett (s), Richard Patterson (b), Ricky Wellman (dr), Erin Davis (per)

March 13, 1991 – August 25, 1991
Miles (tp, keyb), Foley (lb), Deron Johnson (keyb), Kenny Garrett (s), Richard Patterson (b), Ricky Wellman (dr)

Artists who sat in on Miles's gigs
Mino Cinelu, George Duke, Sammy Figueroa, Chaka Khan, Dave Liebman, Marilyn Mazur, John McLaughlin, Mtume, David Sanborn, Carlos Santana, Gary Thomas, Steve Thornton and Michal Urbaniak. Marilyn Mazur recalls Chick Corea and Herbie Hancock substituting for Miles on some gigs.

32 miles's album discography 1980–1991

This discography covers the major albums Miles made under his own name and describes the various CD formats they were released in. For a comprehensive description of all of Miles's 1980s recordings, readers can do no better than to consult Jan Lohmann's *The Sound of Miles Davis* or Enrico Merlin's sessionography in Paul Tingen's *Miles Beyond* and its updates on the book's website, www.miles-beyond.com

Key

acg, acoustic guitar; arr, arranger; as, alto sax; b, bass; bcl, bass clarinet; blues g, blues guitar; cel, celeste; clg, classical guitar; dr, drums; drm, drum machine; dr prog, drum programming; el dr, electronic drums; elp, electric piano; el vio, electric violin; f, flute; flh, flugelhorn; g, guitar; lb, lead bass; keyb, keyboard; p, piano; per, percussion; ss, soprano sax; sync, synclavier; synth, synthesizer; synth b, synthesizer bass; tp, trumpet; ts, tenor sax; voc, vocals; wah-wah g, wah-wah guitar.

The Man With The Horn (Columbia CK 36790)

New York Columbia Studios May–June 1980	Robert Irving III (keyb), Randy Hall (g, cel, synth, voc-2), Vince Wilburn Jr. (dr), Felton Crews (b), Bill Evans (ss-1) "Shout" (-1) "The Man With The Horn" (-2)
New York January 1981	Miles Davis (tp), Barry Finnerty (g-1), Sammy Figueroa (per-1) "Shout" (-1) (overdub session) "The Man With The Horn" (overdub session)
	Miles Davis, Bill Evans (ss), Barry Finnerty (g), Marcus Miller (b), Al Foster (dr), Sammy Figueroa (per) "Aida" "Back Seat Betty" "Ursula"
New York March 1981 (probably)	Mike Stern (g) in, Finnerty out "Fat Time"

CD formats: In addition to a regular CD release, *The Man With The Horn* was released in Japan in September 1996 as a Sony Master Sound release (SCRS 9132). This contains identical music to the original release, but the audio has undergone a process known as Super Bit Mapping, which is designed to enhance sound quality. The early versions were limited editions with miniature versions of the original cardboard LP sleeve. Later versions reverted to the standard CD jewelbox design.

In 2000, the discs were re-released with limited-edition sleeves and then CD jewelboxes (SCRS 9722). However, these versions were also encoded with CD text, which shows the artist's name, album title and track titles on the displays of suitably-equipped CD players. *The Man With The Horn* has also been released as a Super Audio CD (SACD) album under SME Records (Sony Music Entertainment) in Japan (SRGS 4505). The SACD format has been developed by Sony and Philips and uses a different digital encoding system to standard CDs, known as Direct Stream Digital (DSD), which greatly extends the frequency response and dynamic range. The SACD version also comes in a different packaging, with a thick cardboard sleeve and thick plastic disc tray. This SACD release will not play on ordinary CD players.

We Want Miles (Columbia COL 469402-2)

Boston Kix club June 27, 1981	Miles (tp, elp-3), Mike Stern (g), Bill Evans (ss, ts), Marcus Miller (b), Al Foster (dr), Mino Cinelu (per) "Kix" "Fast Track" "My Man's Gone Now" (-3)
New York Avery Fisher Hall July 5, 1981	"Back Seat Betty"
Tokyo Shinjuku Nishi- Guchi Horoba October 3 and 4, 1981	"Jean-Pierre" (short), "Jean-Pierre"

CD formats: Although *We Want Miles* was originally released as a double LP, its 76-minutes' playing time means it can be squeezed on to a single release (Columbia COL 469402-2). This is the format used in most territories around the world. However, Japanese consumers have been offered three double-CD versions with the same track configuration of the LP release, that is, with "My Man's Gone Now" and "Kix" together on a second disc. The Japanese CBS/Sony release (CSCS 5131-2) used a double-disc CD jewelbox package. The 1996 Master Sound release (SRCS 9133-4) had a miniature version of the cardboard LP sleeve. The jewelbox version of the 2001 Master Sound release (SRCS 9763-4) placed the two discs inside a single-CD case.

Miles! Miles! Miles! (Sony Records SRCS 6513-4)

Tokyo Shinjuku Nishi- Guchi Horoba October 4, 1981	Miles (tp), Mike Stern (g), Bill Evans (ss, ts), Marcus Miller (b), Al Foster (dr), Mino Cinelu (per)

"Back Seat Betty"
"Ursula"
"My Man's Gone Now"
"Aida"
"Fat Time"
"Jean-Pierre"

CD formats: This Japan-only release of *Miles! Miles! Miles!* was issued as a double CD album, with the discs placed inside a large double-CD case. The total playing time is less than 74 minutes and a single-disc release called *Fat Time* has been widely available in Continental Europe.

Star People (Columbia CDCBS 25395)

New York Columbia Studios August 11, 1982	Miles (tp, elp), Mike Stern (g), Bill Evans (ss), Marcus Miller (b), Al Foster (dr), Mino Cinelu (per), Gil Evans (arr) "Star On Cicely"
Long Island, NY Jones Beach Theatre August 28, 1982	"Come Get It"
New York Columbia Studios September 1, 1982 (probably)	"Star People" "U 'n' I"
New York Record Plant Studios January 5, 1983	John Scofield (g) in, Mike Stern out, Gil Evans (arr) in "It Gets Better"
Houston, Texas Cullen Auditorium February 5, 1983 (possibly)	Tom Barney (b) in, Marcus Miller out. Mike Stern and John Scofield both in "Speak"

CD formats: *Star People* is available as both a standard CD release and Japan Master Sound version (SRCS 9135) and re-release (SRCS 9765).

Decoy (Columbia CK 38991)

New York
A&R Studios
June 30/July 1, 1983   Miles (synth), John Scofield (g), Darryl Jones (b), Al Foster
(dr), Mino Cinelu (per)
"Freaky Deaky"

Montreal Theatre
St Denis
July 7, 1983   Miles (tp, synth), Bill Evans (ss, ts), John Scofield (g), Darryl
Jones (b), Al Foster (dr), Mino Cinelu (per)
"What It Is"
"That's What Happened"

New York
Record Plant Studios
September 10/11, 1983
(probably)   Miles (tp, synth), Robert Irving III (synth, drm, synth b, arr)
Mino Cinelu (per)
"Robot 415"

New York
Record Plant Studios
September 10/11, 1983   Miles (tp), John Scofield (g), Branford Marsalis (ss), Robert
Irving III (keyb, arr), Darryl Jones (b), Al Foster (dr), Mino
Cinelu (per)
"Decoy"
"Code MD"
"That's Right"

CD formats: *Decoy* was released as a standard CD and in 1996 as a Master
Sound CD. The 2001 Master Sound release (SRCS 9766) included a CD jewelbox version with a paper sleeve that folded out to give the complete cover
photograph (standard CD releases only give the top-half of the picture).

You're Under Arrest (Columbia CK 40023)

New York
Record Plant Studios
January 1984 (possibly)   Miles (tp), Robert Irving III (keyb, synth, arr), John Scofield
(g), Darryl Jones (b), Al Foster (dr), Steve Thornton (per)
"Time After Time"

New York
Record Plant Studios
December 26/27, 1984   Miles (tp, voice-1), Bob Berg (ss), Robert Irving III (keyb,
synth, cel-3, arr), John Scofield (g), Darryl Jones (b), Al
Foster (dr), Steve Thornton (per, voice-1), Marek Olko
(voice-1), James Prindiville (voice-1), Sting (voice-1)
"One Phone Call"/"Street Scenes" (-1)
"You're Under Arrest"
Medley: "Jean-Pierre"/"You're Under Arrest"/"Then There
Were None" (-3)

Same date and location	Miles (tp), Robert Irving III (synth, keyb, arr), John Scofield (g), Darryl Jones (b), Vince Wilburn Jr. (dr), Steve Thornton (per)

"Human Nature"
"MD1"/"Something's On Your Mind"/"MD2"
"Something's On Your Mind"

New York Record Plant Studios early January 1985	Miles (tp), Robert Irving III (keyb, synth, arr), John McLaughlin (g), Darryl Jones (b), Vince Wilburn Jr. (dr), Steve Thornton (per)

"Ms. Morrisine"
"Katia Prelude"
"Katia"

CD formats: *You're Under Arrest* has been released as a standard CD and as a Japanese Master Sound version (SRCS 9137). There is also an SACD version, issued by SME Records (SRGS 4530).

Aura (CBS 463351 2)

Copenhagen Easy Sound Studio January 31 – February 4, 1985	Miles (tp), John McLaughlin (g), Vince Wilburn Jr. (el dr), Marilyn Mazur (per), Palle Mikkelborg (tp, flh, arr), Danish Radio Big Band (for full list see *Aura* chapter)

"Intro"
"White"
"Yellow"
"Orange"
"Red"
"Green"
"Blue"
"Electric Red"
"Indigo"
"Violet"

CD formats: *Aura*'s first CD release was marred by an mastering error, which resulted in the first half of "Green" mis-identified as the second half of "Red." This error was rectified in both the 1996 and 2001 Master Sound versions (SRCS 9327 and SRCS 9743, respectively) and in the 2000 Columbia Legacy release (CK 63962).

Tutu (Warner Bros 925 490-2)

Los Angeles Capitol Recording Studios February 6, 1986	Miles (tp), George Duke (keyb, samples, arr), Marcus Miller (b), Steve Reid, Paulinho DaCosta (per)

"Backyard Ritual"

Los Angeles
Capitol Recording Studios
February 10–13, 1986   Miles (tp), Marcus Miller (synth, keyb, b, g, drm, ss, arr),
Adam Holzman (synth-1), Paulinho DaCosta (per)
"Splatch" (-1)
"Tutu"
"Portia"

New York
Clinton Recording Studios
March 12–25, 1986   Miles (tp), Marcus Miller (synth, keyb, b, bcl, g, drm, ss,
arr), Bernard Wright (synth-1, 2), Omar Hakim (dr-1),
Michal Urbaniak (el vio-2)
"Tomaas" (-1)
"Don't Lose Your Mind" (-2)
"Full Nelson"
"Perfect Way"

CD formats: *Tutu* has been released under the Warner Bros Masters series, whereby the music has been digitally remastered from the original analogue tapes. The Master version (7599-25490-9) has a cardboard cover and includes liner notes. Marcus Miller had no involvement in this version. *Tutu* has also been released as a DVD-Audio title by Warner Bros (9362 48429-9). Like SACD, DVD-Audio offers better sound quality than CD. In this case, that means a multi-channel sound (six sound channels) mix. However, this so-called Advanced Resolution sound (which is also available as a two-channel stereo mix) can only be heard on dedicated DVD-Audio players. However, this disc will play on standard DVD-Video players, albeit in Dolby stereo sound only. The stereo channels are created by down-mixing the six channels into two. However, this new stereo mix is different from that found on the standard CD release, which has led some to speculate that different versions were recorded for the DVD-Audio release – they were not. Ordinary DVD players can also display a discography and a biography on a TV screen.

Siesta (Warner Bros 925 655-2)

New York
Sigma Sound Studios
January 7/8, 1987   Miles (tp), Marcus Miller (synth, bcl, ss, arr), John Scofield
(acg-1), Omar Hakim (dr-1)
"Siesta" (-1)
"Theme for Augustine"

Los Angeles
Amigo Studios
January 1987   Miles (tp), Marcus Miller (synth, b, ss, bcl, p, samples, arr),
Earl Klugh (clg-5), James Walker (f-6)
"Lost In Madrid Pt I"
"Kiss"
"Lost In Madrid Pt II"

"Lost In Madrid Pt IV"
"Lost In Madrid Pt V"
"Claire" (-5)
"Los Feliz" (-6)
Miller (keyb, bcl) only on "Kitt's Kiss," "Wind," "Seduction,"
"Submission," "Lost in Madrid Pt III," "Lament," "Rat Dance"
and "Afterglow"

White Plains, NY
Minot Studios
January 1987 — Marcus Miller (keyb, drm, b, samples)
"Conchita"

CD formats: There has only been a standard CD release of *Siesta*.

Amandla (Warner Bros 925873-2)

New York
Clinton Recording Studio
June 1987/September
1988 – January 1989 — Miles (tp), Marcus Miller (b, ss, bcl, g, dr, arr), Kenny
Garrett (as), Don Alias, Mino Cinelu (per)
"Catémbe"
Miles (tp), Marcus Miller (b, keyb, ss, bcl), Kenny Garrett
(as), Jean-Paul Bourelly (g), Foley (lb), Ricky Wellman (dr),
Don Alias (per)
"Big Time"
Miles (tp), Marcus Miller (b, blues g, bcl), Kenny Garrett
(as), Foley (lb), Omar Hakim (dr), Paulinho DaCosta (per)
"Hannibal"
Miles (tp), Marcus Miller (keyb, b, dr), Kenny Garrett
(as), Rick Margitza (ts), Jean-Paul Bourelly (g), Paulinho
DaCosta (per)
"Jo-Jo"
Miles (tp), Marcus Miller (keyb, b), Joe Sample (p), Kenny
Garrett (as), Omar Hakim (dr), Don Alias, Bashiri Johnson
(per)
"Amandla"

New York
Right Track Studio
January 1989
(probably) — Miles (tp), Kenny Garrett (as), Foley (lb), John Bigham (dr
prog, g, keyb), Ricky Wellman (dr), Marcus Miller (b, keyb,
g, bcl), Billy "Spaceman" Patterson (wah-wah g)
"Jilli"
Miles (tp), Marcus Miller (b, bcl, keyb), Al Foster (dr)
"Mr. Pastorius"
Miles (tp), George Duke (keyb, sync, arr), Kenny Garrett
(ss), Marcus Miller (b, keyb), Michael Landau (g), Joey
DeFrancesco (keyb)
"Cobra"

CD formats: In addition to the standard version, Warner Bros released a Masters version of *Amandla* (81227 3611-2), which includes an interview with Jason Miles by writer Stuart Nicholson in the CD booklet.

Doo-Bop (Warner Bros 9 26938-2)

New York Unique Studios July 1991 (probably)	Miles (tp), Easy Mo Bee (keyb, samples, voc-2, 3), Deron Johnson (keyb), J.R (voc-2), A. B. Money (voc-2) "Mystery" "The Doo-Bop Song" (-2) "Chocolate Chip" "Blow" "Sonya" "Duke Booty" "Mystery" (Reprise)
New York Unique Studios Late 1991/early 1992 (probably)	"High Speed Chase" "Fantasy" (-3)

CD formats: *Doo-Bop* has also been released under the Warner Bros Masters series (7599-26938-9).

Live Around The World (Warner Bros 9 46032-2)

Osaka Osaka Expo Park August 7, 1988	Miles (tp), Kenny Garrett (as), Foley (lb), Adam Holzman (keyb), Robert Irving III (keyb), Benny Rietveld (b), Marilyn Mazur (per), Ricky Wellman (dr) "Full Nelson"
Los Angeles Greek Theatre August 14, 1988	Same personnel "New Blues"
Graz, Austria Liebenauer Eishalle November 1, 1988	Irving out. Joey DeFrancesco (keyb) in "Human Nature"
New York Indigo Blues December 17, 1988 (2nd show)	Same personnel "In A Silent Way" "Intruder"

Montpelier, France Le Zenith April 12,1989	Miles (tp), Kenny Garrett (as), Kei Akagi, John Beasley (keyb), Benny Rietveld (b), Munyungo Jackson (per), Foley (lb), Ricky Wellman (dr) "Mr. Pastorius"
Chicago Theater June 5, 1989	Miles (tp), Kenny Garrett (as), Foley (lb), Adam Holzman (keyb), Kei Akagi (keyb), Benny Rietveld (lb), Munyungo Jackson (per), Ricky Wellman (dr) "Time After Time"
Rome, Italy Pallazo Della Civita July 26, 1989	Miles (tp), Rick Margitza (ts), Foley (lb), Adam Holzman (keyb), Kei Akagi (keyb), Benny Reitveld (lb), Munyungo Jackson (per), Ricky Wellman (dr) "Amandla"
Montreux, Switzerland Casino de Montreux July 20, 1990	Miles (tp), Kenny Garrett (as), Foley (lb), Kei Akagi (keyb), Richard Patterson (b), Ricky Wellman (dr), Erin Davis (per) "Wrinkle" "Tutu"
Los Angeles Hollywood Bowl August 25, 1991	Miles (tp), Kenny Garrett (as), Foley (lb), Deron Johnson (keyb), Richard Patterson (b), Ricky Wellman (dr) "Hannibal"

CD formats: *Live Around The World* has also been released under the Warner Bros Master Series (81277 3612-2).

LP release. Miles's 1980s albums were also routinely on LP (and cassette), but *Live Around The World* was the first to only be released on vinyl in limited markets. The album was available in some continental European markets as a double LP (Warner Bros Records 9362-46032-1).

33 books and websites

Books

There are many books about Miles and for anyone interested in Miles's last decade, the following are very useful. *Miles: The Autobiography* captures the voice of Miles well, although it has a few errors and most of the book focuses on Miles's earlier periods. Ian Carr's *Miles: The Definitive Biography* combines an extensive biography with an insightful analysis of Miles's music. It also devotes a lot of space to the last decade of Miles's life.

Paul Tingen's *Miles Beyond: The Electric Explorations of Miles Davis 1967–91* provides a rich analysis of Miles's electric period and contains an excellent sessionography by Enrico Merlin. Stuart Nicholson's *Jazz-Rock: A History* is a superb analysis of this genre and has many sections on the music of Miles. Jan Lohmann's *The Sound of Miles Davis* offers the most comprehensive analysis of Miles's session dates, live performances and bands.

Websites

The Internet is a mine of information for Miles Davis fans and below are a number of sites that are especially useful for anyone interested in Miles and the musicians he hired in the 1980s. Note that the Internet can be an ephemeral medium and that these web addresses were correct and the links were live as this book went to press.

The Official Miles Davis site includes news, artwork, merchandise, music downloads and a discography by Enrico Merlin.
www.milesdavis.com

Peter Losin's *Miles Ahead* website is a superb source of information for anyone with an interest in Miles and includes a detailed discography, sessionography, bibliography and much more.
www.plosin.com/milesahead

The Miles Davis Discussion Forum is a must for anyone with an interest in Miles and has archives that go back to 1995. You can also join it and contribute.
http://listserv.surfnet.nl/archives/miles.html

Jan Lohmann, author of *The Sound of Miles Davis*, has a website at:
www.jan-lohmann.com

Paul Tingen's *Miles Beyond* website focuses on Miles's electric period and is packed with useful information including images, sound files and a sessionography by Enrico Merlin.
www.miles-beyond.com

Larry Tomczyk's *Milestones* website is a multimedia-rich site with lots of artwork, graphics and memorabilia.
http://servercc.oakton.edu/~larry/miles/milestones.html

That Whole Miles Davis Thing examines the links between Miles and Prince.
http://users.ids.net/~dmsr/davisthing.html

Sony Music (which owns Columbia Records) has web pages dedicated to Miles.
www.miles-davis.com

Warner Bros Jazz has information about Miles's later albums at:
www.wbjazz.com

The website for this book is at:
www.thelastmiles.com
The author can be contacted at: george@thelastmiles.com

Miles's sidemen

John Beasley's website is at:
www.beasleymusic.com

The late Bob Berg's website is at:
www.bobberg.com

John Bigham is on the website:
www.thesoulofjohnblack.com

Bobby Broom's website is at:
www.bobbybroom.com

Hiram Bullock's website is at:
www.hirambullock.com

Mino Cinelu's website is at:
www.minocinelu.com

Felton Crew's website is at:
www.feltoncrews.com

Joey DeFrancesco's website is at:
www.joeydefrancesco.com

Bill Evans's website is at:
www.billevanssax.com

Barry Finnerty's website is at:
www.barryfinnerty.com

Foley's website (which includes some of Miles's artwork) is at:
www.smartalecmusic.com

Robben Ford's website is at:
www.robbenford.com

Kenny Garrett's website is at:
www.kennygarrett.com

Adam Holzman's website is at:
www.adamholzman.com

Robert Irving III's website is at:
www.robertirvingIII.com

Munyungo Jackson's website is at:
www.munyungo.com

Darryl Jones's website is at:
www.abasses.com/darryljones/darryl.htm

Marcus Miller's site includes an archive containing many personal references
to his time with Miles.
www.marcusmiller.com

Richard Patterson's website is at:
www.richardpatterson.com

Benny Rietveld's website is at:
www.bennyworld.com

John Scofield's website is at:
www.johnscofield.com

Mike Stern's site is at:
www.mikestern.org

Angus Thomas's website is at:
www.angusbangus.com

Garth Webber's website is at:
www.garthwebber.com

index